The Routledge Companion to Accounting, Reporting and Regulation

Financial accounting, reporting and regulation is a vast subject area of huge importance globally with interest rising significantly in the light of the ongoing global financial crisis.

In the first part, a broad overview of the subject of accounting is presented which sets the stage for some of the theoretical and practical issues and debates regarding financial reporting which follow in the second part. These issues include how to define the reporting entity, recognition and measurement of the elements of financial statements, fair values in financial reporting, and the costs and benefits of disclosure. The third part assesses the interests, needs and theories of accounting, reporting and regulation, while parts four and five look at the institutional, social and economic aspects, including issues growing in importance, such as accounting for environmental management and accounting, regulation and financial reporting in Islamic countries.

This authoritative Companion volume presents a broad overview of the state of the art of these disciplines and will provide a comprehensive reference source for students and academics involved in these areas.

Carien van Mourik is Lecturer in Accounting at the Open University Business School. Her research interests include financial accounting and reporting theory, and the public interest in international financial accounting and reporting regulation.

Peter Walton is an Emeritus Professor at the Open University Business School and IFRS Director at the ESSEC-KPMG Reporting Centre at ESSEC Business School, Paris. Peter is the Chairman of the EAA Financial Reporting Standards Committee. He is also the Editor of *World Accounting Report* and *The Routledge Companion to Fair Value and Financial Reporting* (2007).

Routledge Companions in Business, Management and Accounting

Routledge Companions in Business, Management and Accounting are similar to what some publishers call 'handbooks', i.e. prestige reference works providing an overview of a whole subject area or sub-discipline, and which survey the state of the discipline including emerging and cutting edge areas. These books provide a comprehensive, up-to-date, definitive work of reference which can be cited as an authoritative source on the subject.

One of the key aspects of the Routledge Companions in Business, Management and Accounting series is their international scope and relevance. Edited by an array of well-regarded scholars, these volumes also benefit from teams of contributors which reflect an international range of perspectives.

Individually, Routledge Companions in Business, Management and Accounting provide an impactful one-stop-shop resource for each theme covered, whilst collectively they represent a comprehensive learning and research resource for researchers and postgraduates and practitioners.

Published titles in this series include:

The Routledge Companion to Fair Value and Financial Reporting
Edited by Peter Walton

The Routledge Companion to Nonprofit Marketing
Edited by Adrian Sargeant and Walter Wymer Jr

The Routledge Companion to Accounting History
Edited by John Richard Edwards and Stephen P. Walker

The Routledge Companion to Creativity
Edited by Tudor Rickards, Mark A. Runco and Susan Moger

The Routledge Companion to Strategic Human Resource Management
Edited by John Storey, Patrick M. Wright and David Ulrich

The Routledge Companion to International Business Coaching
Edited by Michel Moral and Geoffrey Abbott

The Routledge Companion to Organizational Change
Edited by David M. Boje, Bernard Burnes and John Hassard

The Routledge Companion to Cost Management
Edited by Falconer Mitchell, Hanne Nørreklit and Morten Jakobsen

The Routledge Companion to Digital Consumption
Edited by Russell W. Belk and Rosa Llamas

The Routledge Companion to Identity and Consumption
Edited by Ayalla A. Ruvio and Russell W. Belk

The Routledge Companion to Public–Private Partnerships
Edited by Piet de Vries and Etienne B. Yehoue

The Routledge Companion to Accounting, Reporting and Regulation
Edited by Carien van Mourik and Peter Walton

The Routledge Companion to Accounting, Reporting and Regulation

Edited by Carien van Mourik and Peter Walton

LONDON AND NEW YORK

First published 2014
by Routledge
2 Park Square, Milton Park, Abingdon, Oxon OX14 4RN

Simultaneously published in the USA and Canada
by Routledge
711 Third Avenue, New York, NY 10017

Routledge is an imprint of the Taylor & Francis Group, an informa business

British Library Cataloguing in Publication Data
A catalogue record for this book is available from the British Library

Library of Congress Cataloging in Publication Data

The Routledge companion to accounting, reporting and regulation / edited by Carien van Mourik and Peter Walton.
pages cm. — (Routledge companions in business, management and accounting)
Includes bibliographical references and index.
1. Accounting. 2. Accounting—Standards. I. Van Mourik, Carien. II. Walton, Peter J.
HF5636.R68 2013
657—dc23
2012042995

ISBN: 978-0-415-62573-9 (hbk)
ISBN: 978-0-203-10320-3 (ebk)

Typeset in Bembo, ITC Stone Sans
by Apex CoVantage, LLC

Printed and bound in Great Britain by
TJ International Ltd, Padstow, Cornwall

Contents

List of Contributors

Salim Aissat is a Lecturer in finance at the Open University Business School. Previously he worked at the University of Sheffield and Durham University. He teaches across a range of finance topics and his research is in the areas of corporate governance, corporate finance and Islamic finance.

Rachel Baskerville is Professor at the School of Accounting and Commercial Law at Victoria University of Wellington. She has a long interest in both standard setting and the cultural dimensions of IFRS. Although now based in her hometown in New Zealand, she has also taught at Exeter (UK) and Auckland universities. Her current research projects include issues arising in the translation of IFRS in the EU and China.

Lisa Baudot is a PhD Candidate at ESSEC Business School in France. Her research interests lie in the political and regulatory processes around transnational standard-setting studied from a historical and institutional perspective. Before pursuing her PhD, she worked as a financial auditor for Ernst & Young LLP as well as a business process/controls auditor and a financial controller in industry. She holds certifications in public accounting (CPA) and internal auditing (CIA).

Lotfi Boulkeroua is a Lecturer in finance at the Open University Business School. His research interests are in credit risk, risk management and Islamic finance. He holds a PhD in finance from Manchester Business School, an MSc in Investment Management from Cass Business School and a BSc in Banking and Finance from Loughborough University.

Professor **Anne Britton** (retired) was the Head of the School of Accounting and Finance and Associated Dean of the Business Faculty at Leeds Metropolitan University. She is also the co-author of two textbooks, *International Financial Reporting* (Alexander, Britton and Jorrisen) and *Financial Accounting* (Britton and Waterston).

David Cairns advises companies, accounting firms and government agencies on the application of IFRS and provides extensive IFRS training. He was the secretary-general of the International Accounting Standards Committee from 1985 to 1994. He was a visiting professor at the London School of Economics and Political Science until 2012 and is now a visiting professor at the University of Edinburgh Business School.

Kees Camfferman is a Professor of Financial Accounting at VU University Amsterdam.

Marie-Andrée Caron is a full Professor in Accounting at the Business School of Université du Québec à Montréal. She is FCPA, FCMA and obtained her PhD from HEC Montreal (2003). She is an active member of the Chair of Social responsibility and sustainable development. Her special interests are accountancy profession, corporate social responsibility, environmental accounting and sustainability reporting. She has contributed to several books and written numerous articles about sustainability.

Kathryn Cearns FCA FCCA is Consultant Accountant at Herbert Smith Freehills LLP, the international law firm. She advises the firm on client-facing accounting and auditing issues. For the three years prior to joining Herbert Smith Freehills she worked for the UK ASB. Kathryn is Chairman of the ICAEW Financial Reporting Committee; Chairman, Financial Reporting Advisory Board to HM Treasury and she is a member of the FRCS UK CARP Technical Advisory Group.

Malcolm Cheetham is the Chief Accounting Officer of the Novartis Group, a major global healthcare company, responsible for all external financial reporting and accounting policies of the Group. Malcolm is an English Chartered Accountant, who prior to joining the Group, worked for Coopers & Lybrand in the UK and Switzerland, finally as a partner. He has been actively involved in the development of IFRSs in Switzerland. He was a member of the "old" IASC Board and is currently chairman of the IASB supported Global Preparers Forum.

Charles H. Cho is currently an Associate Professor at ESSEC Business School. His research interests are Social and Environmental Accounting and Corporate Social Responsibility (CSR). He has published numerous articles in this area in refereed academic journals such as *Accounting, Auditing and Accountability Journal*, *Accounting, Organizations and Society*, *Critical Perspectives on Accounting*, the *European Accounting Review*, the *Journal of Business Ethics*, and *Social and Environmental Accountability Journal*, and was an invited author of chapters in several books.

John Christensen is a Professor of accounting at the Department of Management and Economics at University of Southern Denmark. He received his PhD from Stanford University in 1979. His primary research interests are accounting theory, incentive issues related to accounting information, reporting regulation, and modern product costing. He has served as president of European Accounting Association, and as Vice-president for research and publication of American Accounting Association.

Phillipe Danjou Until his appointment he was the director of the accounting division of the Autorité des Marchés Financiers (AMF), the French securities regulator. He graduated from HEC, then qualified as a Chartered Accountant and Registered Statutory Auditor, and joined Arthur Andersen & Co. (Paris) in 1970, where he ultimately became an audit partner. He was also Executive Director of the French Ordre des Experts Comptables (OEC) from 1982 until 1986. While at the AMF he served on the IASB's Standards Advisory Council, as an observer at the Committee on Auditing of the European Commission, as a member of IOSCO's Standing Committee 1 on Multinational Accounting and Disclosure, and the Financial Reporting Committee of the Committee of European Securities Regulators (CESRFin).

Hans Frimor is a Professor at the Department of Economics and Business at Aarhus University. He received his PhD from University of Southern Denmark (Odense) in 1996. His primary research and teaching interests are in the economics of (asymmetric) information and within this topic especially the consequences of accounting choice, the role of accounting in decentralized organizations, contract theory, and discrete time finance. Recent work encompasses analysis of the effects of mandating disclosure on competition and welfare, optimal accounting-based performance measures in the presence of ordinary as well as induced moral hazard, and how option-based compensation may arise endogenously as a rational response to incentive problems.

Ann Gaeremynck is Professor at the Faculty of Business Economics at the KU Leuven. Her research focus includes: governance, institutions, IFRS and accounting quality. She has published in different accounting and governance journals: *Corporate Goverance: an International Review, Accounting and Business Research, European Accounting Review, Journal of Business Finance and Accounting, and Journal of International Accounting.*

Ahsan Habib is an Associate Professor in Accounting at Auckland University of Technology, New Zealand. His research interest spans a number of areas such as capital market-based accounting research, auditor industry specialization, and the effect of corporate governance on accounting information quality. He has published in *ABACUS, British Accounting Review, Journal of Accounting Literature, Advances in Accounting*, and *Journal of International Accounting Auditing and Taxation*, among others.

Christopher Humphrey is a Professor of Accounting at Manchester Business School (MBS), England. The Manchester Accounting and Finance Group (MAFG) at MBS is one of the leading European research units in its field. Christopher's involvement with auditing research stretches back to the mid-1980s and he has published a wide body of work on auditing and related issues, including audit expectations, audit quality, audit planning, developments in auditing methodologies, audit regulation and audit liability. He has specialized in recent years in the field of international audit regulation and the historical development of the International Federation of Accountants (IFAC).

Manfred Kaeser is Head of Accounting Principles and Special Projects in the Novartis Financial Reporting and Accounting department. He heads the team of technical accounting specialists at Novartis which gives guidance on complex accounting transactions and issues the Group's Accounting Manual. He also participates in various working groups both in Switzerland and internationally within the Pharmaceuticals industry to assess and give guidance on the impact of changes of existing or new accounting standards.

Mike Lucas is a Lecturer in Accounting at the Open University Business School. He is a Fellow of the Chartered Institute of Management Accountants and has had 12 years financial management experience in industry. He has had 17 years experience as a university teacher and researcher in accounting, specializing in management accounting

Carien van Mourik is a Lecturer in Accounting at the Open University Business School. Her research interests include financial accounting and reporting theory and the public interest in international financial accounting and reporting regulation.

Soledad Moya is an Associate Professor in the Finance and Management Control Department in Eada Business School. She earned a PhD in Business Administration at Universitat Pompeu Fabra. She has worked as a visiting professor at the Universitat Autònoma of Barcelona and is author of numerous articles on international financial reporting.

Christopher Napier is Professor of Accounting at Royal Holloway, University of London. After qualifying as a Chartered Accountant, he taught at the London School of Economics and the University of Southampton (from where he received his PhD). His research interests include the historical development of accounting and the theoretical foundations of financial reporting.

Salme Näsi is a Professor of Accounting and the Vice Dean of the School of Management at the University of Tampere, Finland, and chaired the 2009 EAA congress held there. She is a member of several academic, scientific and professional organizations. Salme has worked in various teacher and researcher positions in accounting at the University of Tampere, the University of Oulu, and the University of Jyväskylä.

Paul Pacter became a Board Member of the International Accounting Standards Board on 1 July 2010. For the ten years prior to that, he held two concurrent positions – Director in the Global IFRS Office of Deloitte Touche Tohmatsu in Hong Kong and Director of Standards for Small and Medium-Sized Entities at the IASB in London. He worked for the IASB's predecessor from 1996 to 2000, managing projects on financial instruments, interim financial reporting, segment reporting, discontinuing operations, extractive industries, agriculture, and electronic financial reporting. Previously, Paul worked for the US Financial Accounting Standards Board for 16 years, and, for seven years, was Commissioner of Finance of the City of Stamford, Connecticut. He received his PhD from Michigan State University and is a CPA. He has taught in several MBA programmes for working business managers.

Mathijs Van Peteghem is a doctoral researcher at the Accounting, Finance and Insurance Department of the Faculty of Business Economics at the KU Leuven. His research interests include accounting and corporate governance in general, board and committee structure and dynamics, and the regulatory determinants of governance effectiveness.

Bernard Raffournier is a Professor of Financial Accounting at the University of Geneva. His main research interests are international accounting standards and their application. His publications include a book on IFRS (Economica, Paris) and articles in academic journals such as *The European Accounting Review, The International Journal of Accounting* and the *Journal of International Financial Management and Accounting.*

Chiara Saccon is an Associate Professor of International Accounting at the Department of Management, Ca' Foscari University of Venice. She holds a Master of Science in International Accounting and Finance (London School of Economics and Political Sciences) and a PhD in Business Administration (Ca' Foscari University). She is director of the department of international relations and member of the PhD Faculty.

Anna Samsonova is a Lecturer in Accounting at the Manchester Business School, University of Manchester. Anna's research covers a range of topics, including audit reforms in the context of a transitional economy, various aspects of accounting and audit regulation, transnational policy processes and networks, and others. Anna is a member of the European Auditing Research Network.

Juliane Scheinert is a member of the Novartis Group Financial Reporting and Accounting department providing technical accounting guidance on a variety of subjects, such as pensions, intangible assets, revenue recognition and valuation matters. Prior to joining Novartis Juliane worked in consulting, banking and accounting.

Javed Siddiqui is Lecturer in Financial Reporting at Manchester Business School, UK.

Alfred Wagenhofer is a Professor at the University of Graz, Austria, and chairs the Institute of Accounting and Control and the Centre for Accounting Research. His research interests include financial and management accounting, international accounting, and corporate governance. He has authored and co-authored seven books and many publications in major journals. Professor Wagenhofer is also a member of the Austrian standard setter AFRAC.

Peter Walton is an Emeritus Professor at the Open University Business School, and IRFS director at the ESSEC–KPMG Financial Reporting Centre at the ESSEC Business School, Paris.

Sonja Wüstemann is Professor of Financial Accounting and Management Accounting at the European University Viadrina Frankfurt (Oder) in Germany. She is member of the editorial board of *Accounting in Europe* and has participated in working groups of EFRAG and the Accounting Standards Committee of Germany.

Preface

Try a thought experiment. For a brief moment, imagine what the world would look like without financial accounting as you know it. Would there still be any kind of accounting at all? What other system could fulfil the functions that financial accounting does? Would there still be large multinational corporations, capital markets, and investors in debt and equity securities? Would there still be markets for financial instruments, insurance, derivatives, and other instruments for large-scale risk shifting? Would there still be accounting firms and rating agencies?

It is hard to imagine what the world would look like, but it would probably be a very different place. Without some system that fulfils the functions of financial accounting economic activity would probably be organised much more locally and on a much smaller scale.

Aim of the Companion

The aim of *The Routledge Companion to Accounting, Reporting and Regulation* is to provide a review of the subject area of financial accounting, external reporting, standard setting and regulation. It is meant to be used as a comprehensive, up-to-date reference by anyone with an interest in this broad subject from theoretical as well as practical perspectives. This is a very exciting period to be interested in financial reporting standards and regulation. Since 2005, the International Accounting Standards Board (IASB)'s International Financial Reporting Standards (IFRS) have been ever more widely adopted. Nevertheless, some national governments appear to have realised that yielding the authority to set accounting standards to a private organisation amounts to giving up some of their sovereignty to the market which may be shaped by those participants with the most market power. Therefore, in some cases the necessary political will may be absent.

At the same time, capital markets and the global financial system have been shaken to the core because the 2007/2008 financial crisis and its aftermath have revealed systematic vulnerabilities that some thought had been overcome. It has also revealed the world's economy to be extremely dependent on credit, risk shifting and securitisation, and the damage that misaligned incentives in business and politics will do to society's level of trust, sense of coherence and solidarity, and its moral fabric.

It is also a challenging time to be interested in financial accounting and reporting theory. Thus far, the IASB's Conceptual Framework and most current financial accounting textbooks define the objective of financial reporting primarily in terms of the information's usefulness for making investment decisions. This perspective takes for granted an institutional environment with a high level of trust and shared norms, and strong legal enforcement of contracts. However, it is possible that in the near future we will see more emphasis placed on its role in contracting and monitoring because this role is very important across different institutional environments. Studying financial accounting theory, practice and regulation in an international context forces us to take new look at the 'facts' and perspectives we usually take for granted.

Design and structure of the Companion

The subject area of this book is accounting, financial reporting and particularly financial reporting regulation in national as well as international contexts. It is designed to present the mainstream views on accounting, reporting, regulation, international standards, the institutional aspects of standard setting, and the socio-economic consequences of international financial reporting regulation as well as to give the reader the chance to become familiar with perspectives that feature outside of the mainstream accounting literature.

The book is divided into 5 parts. Part 1 introduces financial accounting. Chapter 1 explains the functions of bookkeeping, accounting, and managerial and financial accounting. Chapter 2 outlines methodological issues in financial accounting theory and research from the perspective that it is a social science, and discusses the influence of research paradigms. Chapter 3 explains the fundamental issues in financial accounting theory. Finally, Chapters 4 and 5 contrast the evolution of financial accounting theory in the Continental European and Anglo-American traditions.

Part 2 discusses basic issues in financial accounting and reporting, from recognition and measurement in Chapter 6, fair value accounting in Chapter 7, the costs and benefits of disclosure in Chapter 8, to the statutory audit in Chapter 9.

Part 3 introduces issues in (international) accounting standard setting and regulation. Chapter 10 starts with a discussion of the public interest in accounting, reporting and regulation. Chapter 11 gives an overview of perspectives on the roles of and need for accounting regulation. Chapter 12 presents the economic theory of financial reporting regulation. Chapter 13 discusses the global convergence of accounting standards. Chapter 14 analyses the role of conceptual frameworks in standard setting, and Chapter 15 sets out the application of IFRS across different institutional environments.

Part 4 deals with institutional aspects of international financial reporting and regulation. Chapter 16 starts with the International Accounting Standards Board. Chapter 17 discusses influences on the standard-setting and regulatory process. Chapter 18 presents an analysis of the relation between stock exchanges and international financial reporting regulation. The topic of Chapter 19 is how audit firms have been impacted by international financial reporting standards, and in Chapter 20 it is how multinational corporations engage with and are impacted by IFRS. Chapter 21 discusses the IFRS for SMEs.

Part 5 provides an overview of social and economic aspects of (international) financial reporting regulation. Chapter 22 presents an outline of research on the socio-economic consequences of IFRSs. Chapter 23 discusses the influence of international organisations, particularly the IMF and the World Bank on international accounting regulation. The topic of Chapter 24 is accounting regulation in emerging markets and newly industrialising economies, and of Chapter 25 it is accounting regulation and IFRS in Islamic countries. Finally, Chapter 26 provides an analysis of the accounting tools for environmental management and communication.

We sincerely hope that readers will find the book useful and thought provoking.

Carien van Mourik and Peter Walton

Acknowledgements

This book is the result of the loving care, hard work and critical input of many people. Firstly, we would like to thank the contributing authors for enthusiastically and generously giving their time and energy to write the chapters. Furthermore, we are grateful for the cheerful and professional guidance and support from Terry Clague, Alexander Krause and Lisa Salonen at Routledge, and the copy editing from Chris Shaw. The book benefited from suggestions from three anonymous reviewers and an anonymous proofreader. Any remaining errors are, of course, our responsibility.

Personal thanks from Carien go to Peter, for giving me the chance to do this, to my colleagues at the Open University for being supportive, to Gakushuin University for their hospitality during the final six months of the process, to Yuko Katsuo, for being patient and understanding about the slow progress on our research paper, and to Debin, for being him. Peter would like to thank Carien for making the whole process easy.

List of Illustrations

Boxes

Figures

Tables

Part 1
Accounting

1

What is Accounting?

Anne Britton

1. Introduction

Accounting is a necessary requirement for any business or organization be it a large multinational business such as BP or the society or club you belong to in your local community. It is essential for a business or organization to keep track of its resources. They need to know if they have any cash available, if they have made a profit/surplus or loss/deficit, if they can meet the future needs or requirements of the business, if they can possibly remain in existence, or if they should change their operations in any way. These requirements can be divided into the need for stewardship of resources and the need for decision making. It is also necessary that owners and other interested parties have information on the stewardship of resources and decisions taken or to be taken by a business or organization. For example you might wish to know the uses your subscription money paid to the local tennis club was put to and what changes are going to be made to the club in the future so that you can decide whether you should continue with your membership or not. In the same way a shareholder in BP will also wish to know how the resource of their share capital has been used, if a dividend will be paid now and in the future and how future decisions in BP could affect that dividend. Accounting is the language of business that we use to answer these types of question and, as with all languages, in order to understand it we need to learn its rules and vocabulary.

2. Accounting definitions

The most often quoted definition of accounting is that given by the committee of the American Accounting Association (AAA), 'the process of identifying, measuring, and communicating economic information to permit informed judgements and decisions by users of the information' (AAA, 1966: 1). Another definition is that given by the American Institute of Certified Public Accountants (AICPA), 'the art of recording, classifying and summarizing, in a significant manner and in terms of money, transactions and events which are in part at least, of a financial character, and interpreting the results thereof' (AICPA, 1953: Par. 5). In 1970 the AICPA defined accounting as, 'a service activity. Its function is to provide quantitative information primarily financial in nature about economic entities that is intended to be useful in making economic decisions, in making resolved choices among alternative courses of action' (AICPA, 1970: Par. 40).

From the above we can deduce that accounting is an art form, possibly a language as we have already stated, but not necessarily a science. If it is providing a service, we therefore have to determine to whom that service is given, that is, who are the users of accounting information. Accounting is about quantitative information generally and it should enable decisions to be made about the business or organization by users. If accounting is to facilitate decision making then we can also deduce that it must be core to any successful business. Accounting therefore needs both 'an effective and efficient data handling and recording system and the ability to use that system to provide something useful to somebody' (Alexander *et al.*, 2009: 4).

3. Types of accounting compared

3.1 Accounting and book-keeping

We stated above that accounting needed an effective and efficient data handling and recording system. This is generally referred to as a book-keeping system. This system may be a manual system or it can be computerized. Book-keeping systems primarily perform the stewardship function of accounting and have been around for a number of years. Indeed, modern accounting is usually stated as commencing in 1494 when Luca Pacioli, a Franciscan friar, wrote about a system of double entry book-keeping in his book *Summa de Arithmetica Geometria, Proportioni et Proportionalita*. This text reflected the practices current at the time in Venice for recording the transactions of merchants. Book-keeping according to Pacioli was to give the trader information as to his assets and liabilities and to do this three books were required: a memorandum, a journal and a ledger. Pacioli also recorded the fact that all entries in the ledgers had to be double entries and thus for every debit there had to be a credit.

This all sounds quite simple but the book-keeping system and therefore its final output is highly dependent on what we choose to identify as our data inputs. This choice of data input is governed by what the user of such information wants to know. For example if a shareholder of a business wants to know what the business can be sold for then we need to feed into the recording system, the book-keeping system, information on the selling prices of resources held by the business not the historical price we paid for these resources. However, if a shareholder wants to know where cash raised from share issues has been spent, then we need to feed into the system historical cost of resources. Accounting therefore consists of data input decisions, a data recording system (book-keeping system) and the provision of useful information to users. Book-keeping can be seen as a subset of accounting when we identify the separate functions within the accounting process. The accounting process is shown in Figure 1.1.

3.1.1 Brief outline of the book-keeping process

The book-keeping process can be broken down into two sections: the initial recoding of transactions, and then the production of ledger accounts and a trial balance. All businesses need to record cash received and paid in some form of cash book and ensure that this is reconciled with any bank statement supplied. In addition details of sales and purchases will be made in what are generally known as day books: primarily a sales day book and a purchases day book. There may well be other day books for example to record sale returns. There is also a book of prime entry, known as the journal, where the few transactions that cannot be allocated to the cash or day books are entered. These are such items as adjustments to debtor balances or closing entries, for example inventory, so that end of period accounts can be drawn up for users. The day books and

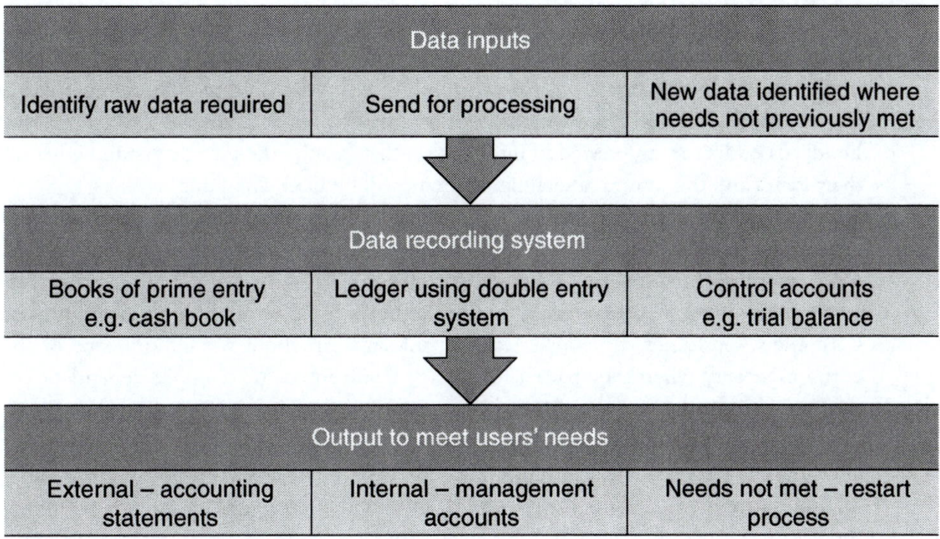

Figure 1.1 The accounting system

the cash book must be subject to controls and checks to ensure that only appropriate and correct entries are made in them as from these books the double entry ledgers will be constructed.

The double entry system codified by Pacioli is based on the accounting equation:

Assets = Capital + Liabilities

All transactions entered in the cash and day books are entered into the ledgers in accordance with this equation and to reflect that for every transaction there are two equal and opposite effects. For example the purchase of an item of equipment by cash will decrease the asset of cash and increase the asset of equipment.

A control used to check the accuracy of the double entry is the trial balance. This is a list of all the balances remaining in the ledgers at the end of a specific period and from which useful information can be summarized for users to meet their needs. At this point it is useful to identify who these users are and what their needs are.

3.1.2 Users and their needs

A comprehensive list of users of accounting information and their needs is provided by the International Accounting Standards Board in their *Framework for the Preparation and Presentation of Financial Statements* (IASB, 2001) paragraphs 9–11:

> The users of financial statements include present and potential investors. Employees, lenders, suppliers and other trade creditors, customers, governments and their agencies and the public. They use financial statements in order to satisfy some of their different needs for information. These needs include the following:
>
> a. Investors. The providers of risk capital and their advisors are concerned with the risk inherent in, and return provided by, their investments. They need information to help them determine whether they should buy, hold or sell. Shareholders are also interested in information which enables them to assess the ability of the entity to pay dividends.

b. Employees. Employees and their representative groups are interested in information about the stability and profitability of their employers. They are also interested in information which enables them to assess the ability of the entity to provide remuneration, retirement benefits and employment opportunities.
c. Lenders. Lenders are interested in information that enables them to determine whether their loans, and the interest attaching to them, will be paid when due.
d. Suppliers and other trade creditors. Suppliers and other creditors are interested in information that enables them to determine whether amounts owing to them will be paid when due. Trade creditors are likely to be interested in an entity over a shorter period than lenders unless they are dependent upon the continuation of the entity as a major customer.
e. Customers. Customers have an interest in information about the continuance of the entity, especially when they have a long-term involvement with, or are dependent on, the entity.
f. Governments and their agencies. Governments and their agencies are interested in the allocation of resources and, therefore, the activities of entities. They also require information in order to regulate the activities of entities, determine taxation policies and as the basis for national income and similar statistics.
g. Public. Entities affect members of the public in a variety of ways. For example, entities may make a substantial contribution to the local economy in many ways including the number of people they employ and their patronage of local suppliers. Financial statements may assist the public by providing information about the trends and recent developments in the prosperity of the entity and the range of its activities.

While all of the information needs of these users cannot be met by financial statements, there are needs which are common to all users. As investors are providers of risk capital to the entity, the provision of financial statements that meet their needs will also meet most of the needs of other users that financial statements can satisfy.

The management of an entity has the primary responsibility for the preparation and presentation of the financial statements of the entity. Management is also interested in the information contained in the financial statements even though it has access to additional management and financial information that helps it carry out its planning, decision making and control responsibilities. Management has the ability to determine the form and content of such additional information in order to meet its own needs. The reporting of such information, however, is beyond the scope of this framework. Nevertheless, published financial statements are based on the information used by management about the financial position, performance and changes in financial position of the entity.

The IASB has begun a programme of updating the framework and the users as specified by the framework have now changed. A primary group of users has now been defined so that financial reports can be focused on them without having to take account of the needs of other more peripheral users. The primary group is identified as existing and potential investors, lenders and other creditors. In other words those users who provide or are considering providing resources to the entity. The 2010 *Conceptual Framework for Financial Reporting* (IASB, 2010: 46–7) in its basis for conclusions states:

a. Existing and potential investors, lenders and other creditors have the most critical need for the information in financial reports and many cannot require the entity to provide the information to them directly.

b. The Board's responsibilities require them to focus on the needs of participants in capital markets, which include not only existing investors but also potential investors and existing and potential lenders and other creditors.
c. Information that meets the needs of the specified primary users is likely to meet the needs of users both in jurisdictions with a corporate governance model defined in the context of shareholders and those with a corporate governance model defined in the context of all types of stakeholders.

3.2 Financial accounting and management accounting compared

Accounting is generally divided into two areas: financial accounting, and management accounting. Financial accounting is concerned with the provision of information to external users such as shareholders, creditors and customers, whereas management accounting is concerned with the provision of information to internal users, i.e. management, to enable them to make decisions about the future operations of the business. Both types of accounting consist of the functions we described above: identification of data input, a data recording system and the provision of useful information to the external or internal user. It is essential to note that the basic information for both financial and management accounting information is the same and both can use the same recording system.

The difference between the two is the purpose of the information:

- financial accounting provides information to external users on the overall performance of the business, the financial position of the business at a point in time and how cash has been used during a period of time;
- management accounting is concerned with the costs and revenues within the overall performance, with making decisions about which products to produce or which assets to purchase to make those products. It is primarily concerned with providing information needed by internal users to manage the business.

Charles T. Horngren (1965) suggested that 'financial accounting would be better labelled as external accounting and management accounting as internal accounting'. The differences between financial accounting and management accounting are summarized in Table 1.1.

Table 1.1 Comparison of financial accounting and management accounting

Comparator	*Financial accounting*	*Management accounting*
Users	External primarily investors	Internal primarily management
Basis	Past and present information	Present and future information
Regulation	Highly regulated by company law and IASB	None
Purpose	To report on performance and position of entity	For planning, decision-making and control
Time	At a point in time for a particular period	At management request
Essential characteristics	Relevant and faithful representation plus comparability, verifiability, timeliness and understandability	Relevant, timely, useful

4. Management accounting

Let's start with a formal definition:

> The application of the principles of accounting and financial management to create, protect, preserve and increase value so as to deliver that value to the stakeholders of profit and not-for profit enterprises, both public and private. Management accounting is an integral part of management, requiring the identification, generation, presentation, interpretation and use of relevant information relevant to:
>
> - inform strategic decisions and formulate business strategy;
> - plan long, medium and short-run operations;
> - determine capital structure and fund that structure;
> - design reward strategies for executives and shareholders;
> - inform operational decisions;
> - control operations and ensure the efficient use of resources;
> - measure and report financial and non-financial performance to management and other stakeholders;
> - safeguard tangible and intangible assets; and
> - implement corporate governance procedures, risk management and internal controls (CIMA, 2005).

Within management accounting there is also something named cost accounting. CIMA defines this as 'gathering of cost information and its attachment to cost objects, the establishment of budgets, standard costs and actual costs of operations, processes, activities or products; and the analysis of variances, profitability or the social use of funds'.

4.1 Decision making

Management accounting is about making decisions which will maximize the value of the business. Value is not necessarily defined in terms of increased profit here. Value may, for example, be achieved by the business focusing on environmental issues or other social issues. This value needs to be interpreted within the objectives of a business. Management accountants will then seek to rank any choices the business has in terms of maximizing that value.

Such decisions, however, need to be made using certain principles. First, we can only take account of costs in our decisions based on the future, that is, all previous costs are assumed to be 'sunk costs'. Future decisions will not make these costs disappear or change them in any way as they have already been incurred. Second, when costing any particular course of action from all opportunities available we need to compare with the next best alternative. This introduces the idea of opportunity cost: a cost which measures the opportunity that is lost or sacrificed when the choice of one course of action requires that an alternative course of action be given up.

When costing decisions we will also enter into the realms of what is known as cost accounting. Costs can be classified in many ways but the four most common are by function, behaviour, nature and element. Function refers to whether the cost is a cost associated with production, administration, research and development, marketing, etc. Behaviour refers to whether that cost is fixed or variable. A fixed cost is one that is insensitive to activity level or, put more simply, does not change when activity levels change. In the final analysis there are no truly fixed costs as when all production ceases then all costs can be avoided. Examples of fixed costs are depreciation and executive remuneration packages. Conversely a variable cost is one that does vary with activity. Examples are production labour and materials. Variable costs are also referred to as direct costs, which brings us to our third classification of nature, that is whether costs are direct or indirect. Our fourth classification by element refers to whether the cost is material expense, labour expense, etc. To cost a particular item of production the management accountant has various methods available such as absorption costing, activity based costing and marginal costing. All three will give a different answer to the cost of production and managers need to decide which technique is appropriate for the particular circumstance under review.

The decision making we have referred to so far has been concerned with the short term but managers also need to make decisions in the long term. The techniques used here are known as capital investment appraisal techniques and involve taking account of the time value of money. For further information on all the topics identified above you should refer to a textbook on management accounting.

4.2 Planning

Business planning is vital for any business be it large or small. For the sole trader a business plan is necessary in order to raise finance from the bank. For a larger business considering an expansion it is also vital as new capital may well be required which could lead to the issue of new shares. At the heart of any new business plan is the financial plan which consists of:

- forecast cash flows;
- sales, production and capital expenditure plans;
- projected statements of income and statements of financial position; and
- performance targets.

4.3 Budgeting and control

Budgeting is part of planning and is an exercise all businesses need to buy into as it translates the long-term plans into short-term operating plans. Budgets are a method used to:

- plan the use of resources;
- identify the planned production;
- control the activities of groups or functions with the business;
- motivate individuals to achieve certain agreed performance levels;
- communicate managers' plans; and
- resolve conflict within the business.

There are various methods for the creation of budgets from planned budgeting, through incremental budgeting to zero-based budgeting. Whatever the method used once budgets are in place they can then be used to control the business. However, budgets must be used with care as, for example, if the targets contained within them are too high this could demotivate staff. There is also the phenomenon of 'spend to budget', where managers who have a budget to spend on a particular item will make that expenditure whether or not it is, at the time of spend, actually needed. Therefore budgets must be reviewed and kept up to date and reasonable; they must be flexed. Budgeting is also costly in terms of time to prepare, monitor and control and that it can lead to unethical behaviour by both managers and employees. Indeed, some managers believe it is not worth the effort and are moving 'beyond budgeting'. 'Beyond budgeting' according to official terminology issues by CIMA in 2005 is:

> An idea that companies need to move beyond budgeting because of the inherent flaws in budgeting especially when used to set contracts. It is argued that a range of techniques, such as rolling forecasts and market related budgets, can take the place of traditional budgeting.

Hope and Fraser (2003: 7) define it as:

> A set of guiding principles that, if followed, will enable an organization to manage its performance and decentralize its decision making process without the need for traditional budgets. Its purpose is to enable the organization to meet the success factors of the information economy (e.g. being adaptive in unpredictable conditions).

Beyond budgeting aims to address the many flaws in traditional budgeting identified as:

- rarely focusing on strategy and often contradictory;
- time consuming and costly to put together;
- constraining responsiveness and flexibility;
- deterring change;
- adding little value, especially given the time taken to prepare them;
- focusing on cost reduction rather than value creation; and
- strengthening vertical command and control.

5. Financial accounting

Financial accounting is concerned with the recording, processing and presentation of economic information after the event to those people outside the organization who are interested in it. But what economic information do users require? The IASB assumes that the information needs of investors mostly encompass the information needs of other financial statement users, and hence considers investors, lenders and other creditors the primary users of financial statements (IASB, 2010: OB5). This assumption can be queried, but, if it is accepted, measuring income, identified as the difference between revenues and expenses (i.e. profit or performance) and measuring wealth (identified as 'what you have got at a point in time') in some manner would meet the primary users' needs. Wealth also changes over time and in a business sense this is represented by the accounting equation:

Wealth at the beginning + profit for the period – drawings = wealth at the end of the period

$$W1 + P - D = W2$$

The recognition and measurement of assets, liabilities, income and wealth is perhaps the central problem in financial accounting. This is the topic of Chapter 6. Below is an outline of the essential issues.

5.1 Measuring income/performance

Income and performance in the traditional accounting sense, as can be seen from the equation above, are synonymous with profit. They are one and the same. Profit represents an increase in capital, again shown in the above equation. The accountant uses a Statement of Income, to show the calculation of this income. This view of income/profit is derived to some extent from that of Sir John Hicks, who stated that 'income is the maximum value which a man can consume during a week and still expect to be as well off at the end of the week as he was at the beginning' (Hicks, 1948: 172). This definition was made more specific to business by the Sandilands Committee (IAC, 1975), which adapted Hicks's statement to 'the maximum value which the company can distribute during the year and still expect to be as well off at the end of the year as it was at the beginning'. However, this is not the only view of income possible and it does cause the accountant some problems.

Adam Smith (1890) defined income as 'an increase in wealth'. Fisher (1912: 38) defined income in three parts:

- Psychic income – the actual personal consumption of goods and services that produces a psychic enjoyment and satisfaction of wants.
- Real income – an expression of the events that give rise to psychic enjoyments.
- Money income – all the money received and intended to be used for consumption to meet the cost of living.

5.1.1 The problem of capital maintenance

The problem with the traditional accountant's view of income can be best described by using as an example a very simple business. Let's suppose Richard is in business buying and selling laptop computers. We will presume for simplicity that he has no expenses within the business except the cost of the laptops to sell. Richard commences his business with £1,000 on 1 April and spends £250 on a laptop. At this stage he therefore has, according to our accounting equations given earlier, inventory of £250 and cash of £750 and therefore a capital of £1,000. On 5 April he sells the laptop for £300 and buys another for £280. His balance sheet is now as follows:

Cash	770	Original capital	1000
Inventory	280	Profit/income	50
	1050	Closing capital	1050

This would imply that Richard could withdraw £50 from the business and remain as well off as he was on 1 April. If he did this, his balance sheet would be:

Cash	720	Capital	1000
Inventory	280		
	1000		

But is he as well off? If we compare his physical position on 1 April with that on 5 April we can see that on 1 April he had one laptop and £750, whereas on 5 April he has one laptop and only £720; he has 'lost' £30. This would lead us to state that his profit/income was only £20, not £50, and if he only withdrew £20 then on 5 April he would have one laptop plus £750 as he did on 1 April. This implies that he should only declare profit/income of £20, i.e. sale £300 minus the cost of replacing the lap top sold £280. By declaring his income as only £20 Richard has evaluated his position in terms of his capacity to carry on his business, that of buying and selling laptops. This view of profit/income given here (operating capital maintenance) is different from the one the accountant currently uses that of money financial capital maintenance where the profit/income would be declared as £50.

Another possible method of valuing income/profit is real financial capital maintenance. This method is based on the purchasing power of the owner's interest in the business. Returning to our example of Richard, if the general price level increased by 5 per cent during the period 1 April to 5 April, then profit will only be made after capital of £1,050 has been maintained. Thus, under real financial capital maintenance Richard would not declare a profit.

5.2 Measuring wealth

Wealth we defined earlier as 'what you have got at a point in time'. Thus we need to be able to value our assets and liabilities. This gives rise to two questions:

- What are our assets and liabilities at a point in time?
- How do we value them?

5.2.1 What are our assets and liabilities?

We could group all the assets and liabilities of a business together and state that our wealth is the present value of the expected future net cash flows. This would lead to problems in estimating future cash flows and which discount rate to use, which in turn could lead to problems with the need to give a faithful representation. We could also take the view that the business is more than just the sum of its tangible assets minus its liabilities. For example, if you were evaluating your own personal wealth you may take the view that your wealth was more than just the sum of the assets you owned, e.g. your house, car, household articles and cash, less any loans you had. You could view your health or family as part of your wealth. For a business the intangible asset that exists is goodwill and is usually the difference between evaluating the business as a whole, which occurs generally when a sale value is placed on a whole business, and the sum of its individual assets and liabilities.

5.2.2 How do we measure the assets and liabilities?

According to the IASB:

> Measurement is the process of determining the monetary amounts at which the elements of the financial statements are to be recognized and carried in the balance sheet and income statement. This involves the selection of the particular basis of measurement (IASB, 2010: Chapter 4, Par. 4.54).

Measurement bases discussed in the 2010 IASB Conceptual Framework include the following four valuation methods, which all have one thing in common: our measuring unit is money and we assume that this is a stable measuring stick.

Historical cost

We could value at the amount we originally paid for the asset, historical cost. We could also reduce this figure according to the life of the asset as when we use an asset we are consuming part of its wealth. This is the idea of depreciation. Liabilities are recorded at the amounts of proceeds received in exchange for the obligation, or at the amount of cash the entity is expected to pay to satisfy its liability.

Current cost

We could value the asset at the amount we would have to pay to buy a new asset, i.e., replacement cost. We could extend this and reduce the value of the new asset by an amount of depreciation to match the life used up of our existing asset. We could also take the cost of buying the same asset in actually the same condition as the asset we are trying to value. Another variant here would be to identify the cost of an asset that replaces the function of the asset we wish to value. In the case of liabilities, current cost means the undiscounted amount required to settle the liability at the time of preparation of the balance sheet.

Net realizable value

We could value the asset at the amount of money less any expenses of sale we would incur if we sold it. In the case of liabilities, settlement value or realizable value means the undiscounted amount of cash expected to be paid to satisfy the liability in the normal course of business.

Net present value or economic value

We could value the asset at the present value of its current usefulness to us. This requires us to estimate the future useful values and then to discount them back to current day prices at an appropriate discount rate. Similarly, liabilities are carried at the present discount value of the cash expected to be paid to settle the liability in the normal course of business.

5.3 The different systems

In theory, if we combine the three methods of income measurement with the four methods of valuation of assets, we would have 12 versions of profit. All these profit figures would be correct in some defined way, but should the accountant show all these figures to users or just choose one to declare? In practice, the accountant's scope for choosing an accounting policy is limited by accounting principles and standards. Nevertheless, if there is a choice, the decision perhaps hinges on the objective of the information the accountant is trying to provide. We present below the objective of financial statements as given in the 2010 IASB Conceptual Framework.

> The objective of general purpose financial statements is to provide financial information about the reporting entity that is useful to existing and potential investors, lenders and other creditors in making decisions about providing resources to the entity. These decisions involve buying, selling or holding equity and debt instruments, and providing or settling loans and other forms of credit (OB2).
>
> Existing and potential investors, lenders and creditors need information to help them assess the prospects for future net cash flows to an entity (OB3).

This objective would not lead to the view that the only profit declared should be that based on historical cost valuation of assets and monetary financial capital maintenance but that is the traditional system used in financial statements currently. Note that the above objective statement from the IASB focuses on general purpose financial statements, which are not able to provide all information users need as non-financial information is absent. We will address this issue later.

A simple example is given below to demonstrate the profit and capital figures that the combination of asset valuation and capital maintenance systems could provide.

Table 1.2 Asset valuation per laptop

Asset valuation per laptop	*Start of year £*	*End of year £*
Historical cost	250	310
Replacement cost	280	340
Net realizable value	300	360

Example: Suppose Richard has an inventory of five laptops at the start of a year, which are all sold during the year, and seven laptops at the end of the year and no other assets or liabilities. Table 1.2 shows the asset valuation per laptop.

Under monetary financial capital maintenance and historical cost:

	£	
Opening value of assets	1,250	(5 × 250)
Closing value of assets	2,170	(7 × 310)
Therefore profit	920	

Under operating capital value maintenance and historical cost:

Operating capital has increased by two laptops and therefore profit is £620.

Under monetary financial capital maintenance and net realizable value:

Opening value of assets	1,500	(5 × 300)
Closing value of assets	2,520	(7 × 360)
Therefore profit	1,020	

Under operating capital maintenance and net realizable value:

Operating capital has increased by two laptops and therefore profit is £720.

Just using four of the possible combinations of capital maintenance and asset valuation gives us four profit figures in our simple example, £620, £720, £920 and £1,020. Which is the correct profit figure? All are correct but which figure do users require? Users may well require all the figures depending upon the decisions they need to take but such a plethora of profit figures can lead to confusion in the information system and therefore mislead users. Traditionally financial accounting has reported profit using monetary financial capital maintenance and historical cost valuation of assets.

5.4 Deprival value

One method of valuing assets that we did not consider in 5.2 above was deprival value which is a mixed valuation method. The asset worth to the business under this method is based on what a rational businessperson would do. The deprival value is the loss the businessperson would suffer if he/she was deprived of the asset.

Example: A business has three assets, A, B and C with valuations as in Table 1.3.

Table 1.3 Three assets with valuations

Asset	*Historical cost HC£*	*Replacement cost RC£*	*Net realisable value NRV£*	*Economic value EV£*
A	100	200	300	400
B	900	1200	1000	1100
C	1700	1600	1500	1800

All three assets are destroyed in a fire. What loss would a rational owner of the business consider he/she has suffered?

- For A more value can be obtained by replacing the asset as both NRV and EV are higher than replacement cost. Therefore the asset will be replaced and the loss is clearly RC of £200.
- For B the asset will cost more to replace than can be derived by either selling (NRV) or continuing to use (EV) therefore the asset will not be replaced and the loss will be the EV foregone, £1,100.
- For C EV is higher than RC so the asset will be replaced and the loss is clearly RC of £1,600.

In each case above the loss is termed deprival value and we can define deprival value as the lower of replacement cost and recoverable amount, which in turn is the higher of economic value and net realizable value (see Figure 1.2). It is interesting to note here that historical cost, which is traditionally used in financial accounting, is totally irrelevant when calculating deprival values.

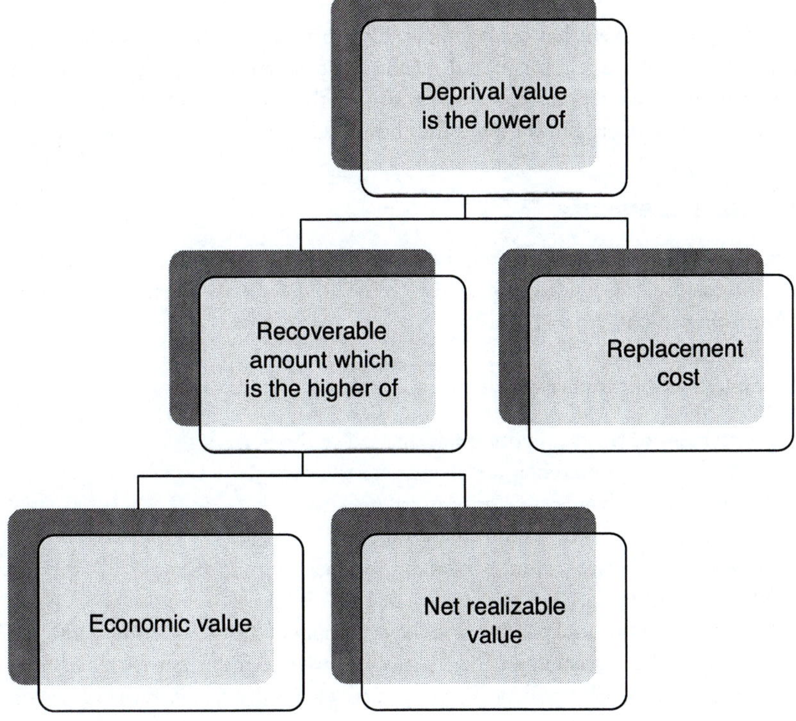

Figure 1.2 Deprival value

Deprival value is not a panacea to the problems of valuing assets as it also has some disadvantages. It leads, for example, to mixed values on a balance sheet and it fails to take account of changes in the value of the monetary measuring stick.

We end here with quotes from the preface of the IASB's 2001 *Framework for the Preparation and Presentation of Financial Statements and the Conceptual Framework for Financial Reporting*:

> Financial statements are most commonly prepared in accordance with an accounting model based on recoverable historical cost and the nominal financial capital maintenance concept. Other models and concepts may be more appropriate in order to meet the objective of providing information that is useful for making economic decisions although there is presently no consensus for change. This framework has been developed so that it is applicable to a range of accounting models and concepts of capital and capital maintenance (preface FPPFS).

The *Conceptual Framework for Financial Reporting* 2010 from the IASB para 4.65 states:

> The selection of the measurement bases and concept of capital maintenance will determine the accounting model used in the preparation of the financial statements. Different accounting models exhibit different degrees of relevance and reliability and, as in other areas, management must seek a balance between relevance and reliability. This conceptual framework is applicable to a range of accounting models and provides guidance on preparing and presenting the financial statements constructed under the chosen model. At the present time, it is not the intention of the Board to prescribe a particular model other that in exceptional circumstances, such as for those entities reporting in the currency of a hyperinflationary economy. This intention will, however, be reviewed in the light of world developments.

It is to be hoped, given that management/directors have to choose the concept of capital maintenance they believe is relevant and reliable, that we are told somewhere in the financial reports of a business which concept they are using otherwise any comparisons we make with other businesses may be invalid if those other businesses are using a different concept.

6. Financial statements

The traditional financial statements required to be prepared by a business are identified by the IASB in International accounting Standard 1 (IAS 1, 1975): Presentation of Financial Statements. According to IAS 1 paragraph 10:

> A complete set of financial statements comprises:
>
> a. A statement of financial position at the end of the period;
> b. A statement of comprehensive income for the period;
> c. A statement of changes in equity for the period;
> d. A statement of cash flows for the period;
> e. Notes, comprising a summary of significant accounting policies and other explanatory information; and
> f. A statement of financial position as at the beginning of the earliest comparative period when an entity applies an accounting policy retrospectively or makes a retrospective restatement of items in its financial statements, or when it reclassifies items in its financial statements.
>
> An entity may use titles for the statements other than those used in this standard.

In this extract, (a) was traditionally known as the balance sheet and (b) as the profit and loss account. The statement of financial position is a listing of the assets, liabilities and capital of a business and represents the accounting equation:

Assets = capital + liabilities.

In principle the statement of financial position tells us what the business is worth but whether this is useful to users is questionable given we have already questioned the capital maintenance issue, the valuation of assets and the fact that it only shows those assets and liabilities that can be measured using a monetary measuring stick. It does not necessarily show the goodwill of the business or the effect the business has on the environment. One question we haven't considered so far is: when does an entity recognize an asset and a liability? For example, is a leased asset an asset of the entity? Does this statement of financial position provide relevant information to users and faithfully represent the worth? The IASB, as you will discover later, provides copious requirements on how to prepare these financial statements in an attempt to give useful information to users.

6.1 Goodwill

The accounting treatment of goodwill and other associated intangible assets in financial statements has caused great problems for accountants over a number of years. When one entity acquires another then the price it is willing to pay is generally computed with reference to the underlying value of the assets of the entity and not the book value of those assets as shown in the statement of financial position. For example, in Tesco's group balance sheet (see Table 1.4) the net assets are shown as worth £16,623m but the actual price to purchase Tesco would be a great deal higher than this. If you look up the market capitalization of Tesco on the internet the figure will be somewhere in the region of £25bn. Some of this difference will be represented by goodwill. The problem is how to recognize and measure goodwill objectively. Goodwill is generally items of benefit to an entity, such as a highly skilled and experienced workforce, regular customers, a well-known brand name, a good reputation. Placing a value on this goodwill can only be objectively measured when it is actually purchased, that is, when an entity is bought and goodwill is regarded as the difference between the cost of an acquired entity and the aggregate of the fair values of that entity's identifiable assets and liabilities. This would then become the historical cost of goodwill. However, this value is only true at a particular point in time and will constantly change as goodwill constantly changes. Goodwill is in fact inherent in all entities, and it may even be a negative value. Accountants tend to differentiate between purchased goodwill, which we can place an objective measure on at a point in time, and inherent goodwill, which is always there in a business. But goodwill is incapable of realization separately from the business as a whole and this differentiates it from other assets of a business such as property. The value of goodwill in a business is very useful information to a provider of capital and is therefore relevant but we also need to faithfully represent its value: this proves very difficult for accountants.

6.2 Exemplar financial statements

Annual reports, which include the financial statements required by the IASB, are readily available for a wide range of entities on the world-wide-web. We have here an example taken from Tesco's 2011 annual report which includes the group balance sheet (Table 1.4), the group

Table 1.4 Group balance sheet

	Notes	***26 February 2011 £m***	*27 February 2010 £m*
Non-current assets			
Goodwill and other intangible assets	10	**4,338**	4,177
Property, plant and equipment	11	**24,398**	24,203
Investment property	12	**1,863**	1,731
Investments in joint ventures and associates	13	**316**	152
Other investments	14	**1,108**	863
Loans and advances to customers	17	**2,127**	1,844
Derivative financial instruments	22	**1,139**	1,250
Deferred tax assets	6	**48**	38
		35,337	34,258
Current assets			
Inventories	15	**3,162**	2,729
Trade and other receivables	16	**2,314**	1,888
Loans and advances to customers	17	**2,514**	2,268
Loans and advances to banks and other financial assets	18	**404**	144
Derivative financial instruments	22	**148**	224
Current tax assets		**4**	6
Short-term investments		**1,022**	1,314
Cash and cash equivalents	19	**1,870**	2,819
		11,438	11,392
Non-current assets classified as held for sale	7	**431**	373
		11,869	11,765
Current liabilities			
Trade and other payables	20	**(10,484)**	(9,442)
Financial liabilities:			
Borrowings	21	**(1,386)**	(1,529)
Derivative financial instruments and other liabilities	22	**(255)**	(146)
Customer deposits	24	**(5,074)**	(4,357)
Deposits by banks	25	**(36)**	(30)
Current tax liabilities		**(432)**	(472)
Provisions	26	**(64)**	(39)
		(17,731)	(16,015)
Net current liabilities		**(5,862)**	**(4,250)**
Non-current liabilities			
Financial liabilities:			
Borrowings	21	**(9,689)**	(11,744)
Derivative financial instruments and other liabilities	22	**(600)**	(776)

(Continued)

Table 1.4 Continued

	Notes	***26 February 2011 £m***	*27 February 2010 £m*
Post-employment benefit obligations	28	**(1,356)**	(1,840)
Deferred tax liabilities	6	**(1,094)**	(795)
Provisions	26	**(113)**	(172)
		(12,852)	(15,327)
Net assets		**16,623**	**14,681**
Equity			
Share capital	29	**402**	399
Share premium account		**4,896**	4,801
Other reserves		**40**	40
Retained earnings		**11,197**	9,356
Equity attributable to owners of the parent		**16,535**	14,596
Non-controlling interests		**88**	85
Total equity		**16,623**	14,681

income statement (Table 1.5) and the group statement of comprehensive income (Table 1.6), the group statement of changes in equity (Table 1.7), the group cash flow statement (Table 1.8) and the note pertaining to the reconciliation of net cash flow to movement in net debt (Table 1.9)

Table 1.5 Group income statement

Year ended 26 February 2011	*Notes*	***52 weeks 2011 £m***	*52 weeks 2010 £m*
Continuing operations			
Revenue (sales excluding VAT)	2	**60,931**	56,910
Cost of sales		**(55,871)**	(52,303)
Gross profit		**5,060**	4,607
Administrative expenses		**(1,676)**	(1,527)
Profit arising on property-related items	3	**427**	377
Operating profit		**3,811**	3,457
Share of post-tax profits of joint ventures and associates	13	**57**	33
Finance income	5	**150**	265
Finance costs	5	**(483)**	(579)
Profit before tax	3	**3,535**	3,176
Taxation	6	**(864)**	(840)
Profit for the year		**2,671**	2,336
Attributable to:			
Owners of the parent		**2,655**	2,327

(Continued)

Table 1.5 Continued

Year ended 26 February 2011	*Notes*	***52 weeks 2011 £m***	*52 weeks 2010 £m*
Non-controlling interests		**16**	9
		2,671	2,336
Earnings per share			
Basic	9	**33.10p**	29.33p
Diluted	9	**32.94p**	29.19p
Non-GAAP measure: underlying profit before tax		**3,535**	3,176
Profit before tax			
Adjustments for			
IAS 32 and IAS 39 'Financial Instruments'— fair value remeasurements	1/5	**(19)**	(151)
IAS 19 'Employee Benefits'— non-cash Group Income Statement charge for pensions	1/28	**113**	24
IAS 17 'Leases' — impact of annual uplifts in rent and rent-free periods	1	**50**	41
IFRS 3 'Business Combinations'— intangible asset amortisation charges and costs arising from acquisitions	1	**42**	127
IFRIC13 'Customer Loyalty Programmes'— fair value of awards	1	**8**	14
IAS 36 'Impairment of Assets'— impairment of goodwill arising on acquisitions	1	**55**	131
Restructuring costs	1	**29**	33
Underlying profit before tax	1	**3,813**	3,395

Table 1.6 Group statement of comprehensive income

Year ended 26 February 2011	*Notes*	***52 weeks 2011 £m***	*52 weeks 2010 £m*
Change in fair value of available-for-sale financial assets and investments		**2**	1
Currency translation differences		**(344)**	343
Actuarial gains/(losses) on defined benefit pension schemes	28	**595**	(322)
(Losses)/gains on cash flow hedges:			
Net fair value losses		**(22)**	(168)
Reclassified and reported in the Group Income Statement		**8**	5
Tax relating to components of other comprehensive income for the year	6	**(153)**	54
Total other comprehensive income for the year		**86**	(87)
Profit for the year		**2,671**	2,336
Total comprehensive income for the year		**2,757**	2,249
Attributable to:			
Owners of the parent		**2,746**	2,222
Non-controlling interests		**11**	27
		2,757	2,249

Table 1.7 Group statement of changes in equity

	Attributable to owners of the parent										
	Issued share capital £m	*Share premium £m*	*Other reserves £m*	*Capital redemption reserve £m*	*Hedging reserve £m*	*Translation reserve £m*	*Treasury shares £m*	*Retained earnings £m*	*Total £m*	*Non-controlling interests £m*	*Total equity £m*
At 27 February 2010	399	4,801	40	13	12	463	(180)	9,048	14,596	85	14,681
Profit for the year	–	–	–	–	–	–	–	2,655	2,655	16	2,671
Other comprehensive income											
Change in fair value of available-for-sale financial assets	–							2	2		2
Currency translation differences	–	–	–	–	–	(339)	–	–	(339)	(5)	(344)
Actuarial gains on defined benefit pension schemes	–							595	595		595
Losses on cash flow hedges	–	–	–	–	(14)	–	–	–	(14)	–	(14)
Tax relating to components of other comprehensive income					1	31		(185)	(153)		(153)
Total other comprehensive income	–	–	–	–	(13)	(308)	–	412	91	(5)	86
Total comprehensive income	–	–	–	–	(13)	(308)	–	3,067	2,746	11	2,757

(*Continued*)

Table 1.7 Continued

	Issued share capital £m	*Share premium £m*	*Other reserves £m*	*Capital redemption reserve £m*	*Hedging reserve £m*	*Translation reserve £m*	*Treasury shares £m*	*Retained earnings £m*	*Total £m*	*Non-controlling interests £m*	*Total equity £m*
Transactions with owners											
Purchase of treasury shares	–	–	–	–	–	–	(50)	–	(50)	–	(50)
Share-based payments	–	–	–	–	–	–	89	131	220	–	220
Issue of shares	3	95	–	–	–	–	–	–	98	–	98
Purchase of non-controlling interests	–	–	–	–	–	–	–	6	6	(6)	–
Dividends paid to non-controlling interests	–									(2)	(2)
Dividends authorised in the year	–	–	–	–	–	–	–	(1,081)	(1,081)	–	(1,081)
Total transactions with owners	3	95	–	–	–	–	39	(944)	(807)	(8)	(815)
At 26 February 2011	402	4,896	40	13	(1)	155	(141)	11,171	16,535	88	16,623
					Attributable to owners of the parent						
At 28 February 2009	395	4,638	40	13	175	173	(229)	7,644	12,849	57	12,906
Profit for the year	–	–	–	–	–	–	–	2,327	2,327	9	2,336
Other comprehensive income											
Change in fair value of available-for-sale financial assets	–	–	–	–	–			1	1		1

Currency translation differences	–	–	–	–	–	325	–	–	325	18	343
Actuarial losses on defined benefit pension schemes	–	–			–	(2)		(320)	(322)		(322)
Losses on cash flow hedges	–	–	–	–	(163)	–	–	–	(163)	–	(163)
Tax relating to components of other comprehensive income	–	–	–			(33)		87	54		54
Total other comprehensive income	–	–	–	–	(163)	290	–	(232)	(105)	18	(87)
Total comprehensive income	–	–	–	–	(163)	290	–	2,095	2,222	27	2,249
Transactions with owners											
Purchase of treasury shares	–	–	–	–	–	–	(24)	–	(24)	–	(24)
Share-based payments	–	–	–	–	–	–	73	168	241	–	241
Issue of shares	4	163	–	–	–	–	–	–	167	–	167
Purchase of non-controlling interests	–	–	–	–	–	–	–	91	91	3	94
Dividends paid to non-controlling interests	–	–	–		–					(2)	(2)

(Continued)

Table 1.7 Continued

	Issued share capital £m	*Share premium £m*	*Other reserves £m*	*Capital redemption reserve £m*	*Hedging reserve £m*	*Translation reserve £m*	*Treasury shares £m*	*Retained earnings £m*	*Total £m*	*Non-controlling interests £m*	*Total equity £m*
Dividends authorised in the year	–	–	–	–	–	–	–	(968)	(968)	–	(968)
Tax on items charged to equity	–	–	–	–	–	–	–	18	18	–	18
Total transactions with owners	4	163	–	–	–	–	49	(691)	(475)	1	(474)
At 27 February 2010	399	4,801	40	13	12	463	(180)	9,048	14,596	85	14,681

Table 1.8 Group cash flow statement

Year ended 26 February 2011	*Notes*	*52 weeks 2011 £m*	*52 weeks 2010 £m*
Cash flows from operating activities			
Cash generated from operations	31	5,366	5,947
Interest paid		(614)	(690)
Corporation tax paid		(760)	(512)
Net cash from operating activities		3,992	4,745
Cash flows from investing activities			
Acquisition of subsidiaries, net of cash acquired		(89)	(65)
Proceeds from sale of property, plant and equipment		1,906	1,820
Purchase of property, plant and equipment and investment property		(3,178)	(2,855)
Proceeds from sale of intangible assets		3	4
Purchase of intangible assets		(373)	(163)
Increase in loans to joint ventures		(219)	(45)
Decrease in loans to joint ventures		25	-
Investments in joint ventures and associates		(174)	(4)
Investments in short-term and other investments		(1,264)	(1,918)
Proceeds from sale of short-term investments Dividends received		1,314 62	1,233 35
Interest received		128	81
Net cash used in investing activities		(1,859)	(1,877)
Cash flows from financing activities			
Proceeds from issue of ordinary share capital		98	167
Increase in borrowings		2,175	862
Repayment of borrowings		(4,153)	(3,601)
Repayment of obligations under finance leases		(42)	(41)
Dividends paid to equity owners		(1,081)	(968)
Dividends paid to non-controlling interests		(2)	(2)
Own shares purchased		(31)	(24)
Net cash from refinancing activities		(3,036)	(3,607)
Net decrease in cash and cash equivalents		(903)	(739)
Cash and cash equivalents at beginning of year		2,819	3,509
Effect of foreign exchange rate changes		(46)	49
Cash and cash equivalents at end of year	19	1,870	2,819

Table 1.9 Note pertaining to the reconciliation of net cash flow to movement in net debt

Year ended 26 February 2011	*Note*	*52 weeks 2011 £m*	*52 weeks 2010 £m*
Net decrease in cash and cash equivalents		(903)	(739)
Investment in Tesco Bank		(446)	(230)
Elimination of net increase in Tesco Bank cash and cash equivalents		56	(167)
Debt acquired on acquisition		(17)	–
Net cash outflow to repay debt and lease financing		2,870	2,780
Dividend received from Tesco Bank		150	150
(Decrease)/increase in short-term investments		(292)	81
Increase in joint venture loan receivables		159	45
Other non-cash movements		(438)	(249)
Decrease in net debt in the year		1,139	1,671
Opening net debt	32	(7,929)	(9,600)
Closing net debt	32	(6,790)	(7,929)

7. Financial reporting

The *Conceptual Framework for Financial Reporting* was first published by the IASC in July 1989 and has since been the subject of much discussion to update it and ensure relevance in financial reports for users. The IASB completed the first phase of a joint project with the FASB in September 2010 to develop a converged and improved conceptual framework. The IASB does acknowledge that the full review of the framework will take years to complete given the inherent problems within financial reporting several of which we have already identified.

In the September 2010 update one of the first changes we note is the change of name of the framework from 'Preparation and Presentation of Financial Statements' to 'Conceptual Framework for Financial Reporting', but it as yet has not given us a definition of financial reporting nor stated its boundaries. The second change is the updating of the objectives of financial reporting:

> The objective of general purpose financial reporting is to provide financial information about the reporting entity that is useful to existing and potential investors, lenders and other creditors in making decisions about providing resources to the entity.

This is much more specific than the previous objective statement and does not include all users as it did before. It now identifies 'primary users' as investors, lenders and other creditors and quite clearly directs financial reporting at them. The 2010 document also changes the fundamental characteristics of useful information from relevance, reliability, understandability and comparability to just two characteristics: relevance and faithful representation. Also identified are enhancing qualities: comparability, verifiability, timeliness and understandability.

Financial reporting appears to be more than just financial accounting and perhaps when it is defined it will include information about such items as goodwill, environmental and social effects of the entity and even forecast information. Even though forecast information might be difficult to faithfully represent, it would prove useful to those providers of capital who are now the prime users according to the IASB.

7.1 Possible extensions to the traditional financial accounting statements

Statement of future prospects

Providers of capital to an entity would welcome information on future prospects of an entity, such as future profit levels, future employment levels and prospects, future investment levels, but such information would be highly subjective and could mislead users. Presentation of such information also carries other dangers such as:

- management may be judged on how well it meets these forecasts and therefore they may lower these forecasts to ensure they are attained; and
- for those entities suffering difficulties the provision of forecast information may lead to a collapse that could have been avoided.

Social accounting

This was proposed in 1975 in the UK by the Corporate Report published by the UK Accounting Standards Committee and is generally taken to be the:

> Process of communicating the social and environmental effects of organizations' economic activities to particular groups within society at large. As such, it involves extending the accountability of organizations, beyond the traditional role of providing a financial account to the owners of capital, in particular, shareholders. Such an extension is predicted upon the assumption that companies do have wider responsibilities than simply to make money for their shareholders.

Information in this area is important to users as society is imposing duties on entities to comply with antipollution measures, safety and health and other socially beneficial requirements. Figure 1.3 provides an extract from Tesco's corporate responsibility report 2011.

Integrated reporting

This is an attempt to bring together information about an organization's strategy, governance, performance and prospects in a way that reflects the commercial, social and environmental context within which it operates. It is being driven by the International Integrated Reporting Committee, which was in part established by the International Federation of Accountants. In its discussion paper 'Towards Integrated Reporting: Communicating Value in the 21st Century', published in September 2011, it states:

> Since the current business reporting model was designed, there have been major changes in the way business is conducted, how business creates value and the context in which business operates. These changes are interdependent and reflect trends such as:
>
> - globalization;
> - growing policy activity around the world in response to financial, governance and other crises;
> - heightened expectations of corporate transparency and accountability;
> - population growth; and
> - environmental concerns.

Community Promise	How did we do?	Performance 2008/9		Performance 2009/10	
Buying and selling our products responsibly	Supplier Viewpoint: average score (% of scores that are positive)	68%	NEW	80%	✓
	Supplier Viewpoint: response rate of suppliers	37%	NEW	51%	✓
Caring for the environment	Reduce CO_2 emissions from our 2006/7 baseline portfolio of stores and distribution centres by 50% by 2020. Annual target reported as percentage reduction against previous year	7%	✓	7.8%	✓
	Reduce CO_2e emissions from new stores and distribution centres built after 2006 by 50% by 2020, compared to new stores and distribution centres built in 2006	Environmental format developed 20.5% reduction vs. 2006	✓	28.8%	✓
	Reduce the amount of CO_2 used in our distribution network to deliver a case of goods by 50% by 2012, compared to 2006. Annual target reported as percentage reduction against previous year	9.2% (UK)	✗	6.4%	✗
Providing customers with healthy choices	Staff and customers active with Tesco	4.7m people	NEW	6.2m people	✓
Actively supporting local communities	Staff and customer fundraising		✓		✓
	Donate at least 1% of pre-tax profits to charities and good causes	1.9%	✓	1.94%	✓
Creating good jobs and careers	Staff being trained for their next job	1 in 30 (UK)	NEW	6%	✗

Figure 1.3 Extract from Tesco's Corporate Responsibility Report 2011

Against this background, the type of information that is needed to assess the past and the current performance of organizations and their future resilience is much wider than is provided for by the existing business reporting model. While there has been an increase in the information provided, key disclosure gaps remain. Reports are already long and are getting longer. But, because reporting has evolved in separate, disconnected strands, critical interdependencies between strategy, governance, operations and financial and non-financial performance are not made clear. To provide for the growing demand for a broad information set from markets, regulators and civil society, a framework is needed that can support the future development of reporting, reflecting this growing complexity. Such a framework needs to bring together the diverse but currently disconnected strands of reporting into a coherent, integrated whole and demonstrate an organization's ability to create value now and in the future.

The provision of such a report would no doubt be welcomed by users, particularly those providers of capital but is it achievable?

7.2 Financial reporting and corporate governance

Corporate governance is the system by which businesses are directed and controlled. This system specifies the distribution of rights and responsibilities among different participants in the business such as the board, managers, shareholders and other stakeholders. Corporate scandals such as Enron, Worldcom, Parmalat and the 2008 world banking crisis have focused attention on governance, accountability and disclosure. Good corporate governance should provide proper incentives for the board and management to pursue objectives that are in the interests of the business and its shareholders and should facilitate effective monitoring. Good corporate governance helps to provide a degree of confidence that is necessary for the proper functioning of a market economy; as a result the cost of capital is lower and business is encouraged to use resources more efficiently. Several bodies have reported on corporate governance and given detailed codes. For example the UK Financial Reporting Council published *The UK Corporate Governance Code* in May 2010 and a revised code was due in 2012. The code states in paragraph 1 that:

> The purpose of corporate governance is to facilitate effective, entrepreneurial and prudent management that can deliver the long-term success of the company. The code is broken down into five principles as follows:
>
> - Leadership. Every company should be headed by an effective board which is collectively responsible for the long-term success of the company.
> - Effectiveness. For example the board and its committees should have the appropriate balance of skills, experience, independence and knowledge of the company to enable them to discharge their respective duties and responsibilities effectively.
> - Accountability. For example the board should present a balanced and understandable assessment of the company's prospects and position.
> - Remuneration. Levels of remuneration should be sufficient to attract, retain and motivate directors of the quality required to run the company successfully, but a company should avoid paying more than is necessary for this purpose. A significant proportion of executive directors' remuneration should be structured so as to link rewards to corporate and individual performance.
> - Relations with shareholders. There should be a dialogue with shareholders based on the mutual understanding of objectives. The board as a whole has responsibility for ensuring that a satisfactory dialogue with shareholders takes place.

7.3 Financial reporting and auditing requirements

Financial reports as we have seen are required to provide information that is relevant and is a faithful representation. Mistakes can be made in the preparation of financial reports either consciously or unconsciously. It is possible that those involved in the preparation, if their bonus is linked to the reported profit of the business, may bend the rules of preparation to present a more favourable picture. To address these issues most businesses are required to have an audit. There are two types of audit, external and internal.

7.3.1 External audit

This is carried out by persons outside the business who should be both expert and independent. They investigate the accounting systems and transactions and then ensure that the financial statements have been prepared in accordance with the underlying books and with the law and accounting standards. The purpose of an external audit is for the auditor to be in a position to express an opinion on whether the financial statements being reported on show a true and fair view or not. Box 1.1. shows an example of such a report taken from Tesco's 2011 annual report.

Box 1.1
Independent auditors' report to the members of Tesco PLC

We have audited the Group financial statements of Tesco PLC for the 52 weeks ended 26 February 2011 which comprise the Group Income Statement, the Group Statement of Comprehensive Income, the Group Balance Sheet, the Group Cash Flow Statement, the Group Statement of Changes in Equity and the related notes. The financial reporting framework that has been applied in their preparation is applicable law and International Financial Reporting Standards (IFRSs) as adopted by the European Union.

Respective responsibilities of directors and auditors

As explained more fully in the Statement of Directors' responsibilities set out on page 92, the Directors are responsible for the preparation of the Group financial statements and for being satisfied that they give a true and fair view. Our responsibility is to audit and express an opinion on the Group financial statements in accordance with applicable law and International Standards on Auditing (UK and Ireland). Those standards require us to comply with the Auditing Practices Board's Ethical Standards for Auditors.

This report, including the opinions, has been prepared for and only for the Company's members as a body in accordance with Chapter 3 of Part 16 of the Companies Act 2006 and for no other purpose. We do not, in giving these opinions, accept or assume responsibility for any other purpose or to any other person to whom this report is shown or into whose hands it may come save where expressly agreed by our prior consent in writing.

Scope of the audit of the financial statements

An audit involves obtaining evidence about the amounts and disclosures in the financial statements sufficient to give reasonable assurance that the financial statements are free from material misstatement, whether caused by fraud or error. This includes an assessment of: whether the accounting policies are appropriate to the Group's circumstances and have been consistently applied and adequately disclosed; the reasonableness of significant accounting estimates made by the Directors; and the overall presentation of the financial statements.

Box 1.1 (*Continued*)

Opinion on financial statements

In our opinion the Group financial statements:

- give a true and fair view of the state of the Group's affairs as at 26 February 2011 and of its profit and cash flows for the 52 weeks then ended;
- have been properly prepared in accordance with IFRSs as adopted by the European Union; and
- have been prepared in accordance with the requirements of the Companies Act 2006 and Article 4 of the IAS Regulation.

Opinion on other matter prescribed by the Companies Act 2006

In our opinion the information given in the Directors' Report for the 52 weeks ended 26 February 2011 for which the Group financial statements are prepared is consistent with the Group financial statements.

Matters on which we are required to report by exception

We have nothing to report in respect of the following:
Under the Companies Act 2006 we are required to report to you if, in our opinion:

- certain disclosures of Directors' remuneration specified by law are not made; or
- we have not received all the information and explanations we require for our audit.

Under the listing Rules we are required to review:

- the Directors' statement, set out on page 45, in relation to going concern;
- the part of the Corporate Governance Statement relating to the Company's compliance with the nine provisions of the June 2008 Combined Code specified for our review; and
- certain elements of the report to shareholders by the Board on Directors' remuneration.

Other matter

We have reported separately on the Parent Company financial statements of Tesco PLC for the 52 weeks ended 26 February 2011 and on the information in the Directors' Remuneration Report that is described as having been audited.

Richard Winter (Senior Statutory Auditor)
for and on behalf of PricewaterhouseCoopers LLP
Chartered Accountants and Statutory Auditors
London
6 May 2011

Audit is not, however, an attempt to find fraud, nor is it a management control. Fraud may be discovered during an audit and the auditor will be well placed to give advice to management about potential improvements in the internal control system but these benefits are incidental. External auditing is regulated by the International Auditing and Assurance Standards Board which issues international standards on auditing. ISA 200 identifies the overall objectives of the independent auditor and the conduct of an audit in accordance with international standards on auditing. The overall objectives of the auditor are given in paragraph 11 of this standard:

a. To obtain reasonable assurance about whether the financial statements as a whole are free from material misstatement, whether due to fraud or error, thereby enabling the auditor to express an opinion on whether the financial statements are prepared in all material respects in accordance with an applicable reporting framework; and
b. To report on the financial statements, and communicate as required by the ISA's in accordance with the auditor's findings.

7.3.2 Internal audit

Internal audit is a management tool and it is generally only found in larger organizations where the cost is justified by the benefits of monitoring complex accounting systems. As internal audit is a management tool, then the standards and procedures of it are determined by the management. External auditors often use the work of internal audit to inform their own audit.

7.4 Function of financial reporting in financial and capital markets

Put simply the function of financial reporting is to provide information on the performance and position of a business to users. Some of the users are investors and potential investors in businesses and these users form the financial and capital markets. What a potential investor is prepared to pay for shares in a business is influenced obviously by their view of the business and the financial reports are some of the main pieces of information that investor has for guidance. Investors trying to make a decision on which shares to buy will compare the financial reports of businesses and will need to ensure the information is comparable in terms of:

- valuation method of assets and liabilities;
- capital maintenance concept used; and
- accounting standards applied.

The investor will also need to be aware of the industry characteristics, business and corporate strategy in order to make the investment decision. However, the investor must also be aware that, as financial reports are used to communicate the underlying business realities to outsiders, managers may use those financial reports to manipulate investors' or other stakeholders' perceptions. This is one of the reasons why so much regulation is issued by the IASB, for example, and why there is a need for external audits of business. Even with all this regulation managers are still able to choose the accounting and disclosure policies that most favour the view they wish to give. There are several incentives available to management in order to manage the financial statements:

- those driven by the contract with shareholders include:
  - low earnings volatility – high volatility of results is viewed as risky and leads to low share price;
  - recurrent and increasing stream of earnings – smooth upward trend in results is viewed as low risk and therefore higher share price. This is generally attempted by managers before a new capital issue;

  - need to meet earnings targets and benchmarks – when a business does not meet its previously issued targets it generally faces a drop in share price;
  - small loss avoidance – reporting of a small loss as opposed to a small profit can lead to a drop in share price;
  - big bath accounting – if a loss is unavoidable by choosing particular accounting methods managers may go for a one-time large loss to 'get the bad news over in one year'.
- those driven by debt contracts – managers will choose accounting methods and estimates that reduce the violation of debt covenants often expressed in terms of accounting ratios such as interest cover;
- those driven by contracts with governments and other regulatory authorities – accounting data is used as a basis for taxation charges therefore managers will be careful to ascertain the effect on charges of particular accounting policies;
- those driven by contracts with managers – compensation/remuneration to managers is often based on reported profits;
- those driven by competitive pressures – information available in financial reports is also freely available to competitors thus managers will seek to minimise the information wherever possible; and
- those driven by contracts with employees – managers may seek to achieve low earnings when in a period of salary negotiation.

With all these incentives there is clearly a need to regulate financial reporting so that a true and fair view of the business is given to users.

Bibliography

AAA (1966) *A Statement of Basic Accounting Theory*, New York: American Accounting Association.

AICPA (1953) *Review and Resume*, Accounting terminology Bulletin No.1, New York: American Institute of Certified Public Accountants.

AICPA (1970) *Basic Concepts and Accounting Principles Underlying Financial Statements of Business Enterprises*, Accounting Principles Board, Statement No.4, New York: American Institute of Certified Public Accountants.

Alexander, D., Britton, A. and Jorissen, A. (2009) *International Financial Reporting and Analysis,* 4th edn, Andover, UK Cengage Learning EMEA.

CIMA (2005) *Official Terminology*, Oxford: CIMA Publishing

Fisher, I. (1912) *The Nature of Capital and Income*, New York: Macmillan.

Gray, R. H., Owen, D. and Adams, C. (1996) *Accounting and Accountability: Changes and Challenges in Corporate Social and Environmental Reporting*, London: Prentice Hall.

Hicks, J. R. (1948) *Value and Capital*, 2nd edn, Oxford: Oxford University Press.

Hope, J. and Fraser, R. (2003) *Beyond Budgeting: How Managers Can Break Free From the Annual Performance Trap*, Boston, MA: Harvard Business School.

Horngren, C.T. (1965) *Introduction to Management Accounting*, Hemel Hempstead: Prentice-Hall International.

IAC (1975) *Inflation Accounting: Report of the Inflation Accounting Committee* (Inflation Accounting Committee; The Sandilands Report), London: HMSO

IAS 1 (1975) *Report of the Inflation Accounting Committee*, cmnd.6225, London: HMSO.

IASB (2001) *Framework for the Preparation and Presentation of Financial Statements*, London: International Accounting Standards Board.

IASB (2010) *Conceptual Framework for Financial Reporting*, London: International Accounting Standards Board.

Smith, A. (1890) *An Enquiry into the Nature and Causes of the Wealth of Nations*, London: George Routledge.

2
Methodology in Financial Accounting Theory

Carien van Mourik

1. Introduction

Recently,[1] Baruch Lev outlined how accounting research has produced research findings that are relevant to society in the areas of regulations (e.g. related to the consequences of Sarbanes Oxley), investors (with respect to determining managerial quality) and managers (regarding the advantages of providing earnings guidance). He also noted that there has been a remarkable lack of progress in research, or even serious efforts, to improve the accounting model, its framework or its practices.

Similarly, Singleton-Green (2010) asked why accounting research doesn't make a greater contribution to debates on accounting policy. Singleton-Green (2010: 132–7) discusses eight causes. First, the volume and dispersion of research causes the outsider to not know where to begin. Second, non-academics often find research methodology, particularly quantitative studies using statistics and econometrics incomprehensible. This makes a large chunk of research indigestible to many with an interest in particular accounting policy issues. Third, there is much disagreement among researchers, particularly on the validity of the methodology or the relevance of evidence presented. Fourth, accounting research has become increasingly remote from practice so that policy makers and practitioners have come to regard academic research as irrelevant to their tasks. Here, Singleton-Green (2010: 134) also mentions what he calls 'the problem of ideology'. Fifth, policy makers and practitioners do not find research useful because the descriptive research has been dominant for the past four decades or so and does not and cannot present prescriptive conclusions. The last three causes can be found in the politics of accounting research and policy, the nature of the public debate and the nature of the existing academic incentives that push researchers towards attempting to publish in highly ranked journals which appear to prefer quantitative research and eschew any topic and research method deemed unscientific. As a consequence, one can have a career as an accounting academic without thorough knowledge of accounting theory or practice.

Of the eight causes described by Singleton-Green, the third, fourth and fifth relate to methodology as it is used in this chapter: 'the logic of scientific procedure' (Merton, 1967: 140). In social science, this logic takes the form of philosophical assumptions about the social phenomena we study and about the basis on which and the way in which we justify our knowledge claims. What Singleton-Green calls 'methodology' this chapter regards as 'research methods'. Many people use the terms 'methodology' and 'methods' more or less interchangeably. Accounting PhD students, depending on their specialist subject area, will often receive a thorough training in either quantitative or qualitative research methods (or both), but rarely receive even a rudimentary grounding in social science research methodology. As the emphasis is on technical skills, it is likely that few see themselves as social science researchers. An important challenge in the social sciences is how to deal with something as subjective, context-specific and generally unscientific as value judgements.

This chapter discusses positions and developments in social science methodology, and how they are relevant for financial accounting and reporting theory and research today. An understanding of social science methodology is useful for understanding the assumptions we often make without being aware that we do, or when we intend to follow other researchers' methods and wish to know on which implicit assumptions their research questions and their methods are based. Understanding methodology can help us identify which, if any, of the assumptions we hold are inconsistent with one another. As there is no absolute basis on which to judge the value of one methodological paradigm over another, methodology cannot prescribe what assumptions to make.

Section 2.2 starts with different definitions, purposes and scope of theory. It then defines methodology and discusses ontological assumptions with respect to the nature of social reality, and epistemological assumptions with respect to different types of knowledge and the criteria that beliefs and statements would need to meet to be accepted as propositional knowledge of phenomena studied in the social sciences. Section 2.3 illustrates how different ontological and epistemological assumptions form the basis for some important theories in sociology and other social sciences which have also influenced different strands of accounting theory. The different assumptions form the basis for methodological debates in the social sciences. Section 2.4 discusses different types of financial accounting theory by their objectives and introduces the literature on financial accounting theory typologies. Section 2.5 concludes.

2. Theory and methodology

2.1 What are theories?

A theory consists of a propositional claim supported by an argument, which allows the claim to be evaluated and substantiated. An argument is a presentation of one or more reasons (premises) offered in support of a claim (conclusion). An argument can be distinguished from an opinion because an opinion is not backed by evidence. An argument will first need to be evaluated with respect to the clarity, truth or falsity, and plausibility of the reasons. Then it will need to be evaluated with respect to cogency. 'A cogent argument will be either (1) a valid deductive argument with acceptable premises, or (2) an inductive argument with acceptable premises in which the reasoning from the premises to the conclusion is legitimate and sensible' (Murray and Kujundzic, 2005: 10–11). 'A deductive argument asserts that the conclusion necessarily follows from the premises. . . . An inductive argument, on the other hand, asserts that there is (merely) a good chance that the conclusion follows from the premises' (ibid.: 307). The validity of a deductive argument will need to be tested using logic, whereas an inference based on inductive generalization will need to be assessed using probabilistic reasoning and empirical data.

In their textbook on critical thinking, Hughes and Lavery (2008: 212–13) define a theory as:

> a systematically integrated set of general principles, methods of investigation, and concepts whose function is to explain a wide array of phenomena. Theories generate hypotheses about specific phenomena, but, significantly, they also provide the filter or lens through which we interpret the observations that test hypotheses. . . . The interpretive role performed by a theory in formulating a precise observation statement is the ultimate source of some of the most profound controversies in science.

At least partly, the interpretive filter of a theory in any of the social sciences, stems from the methodology, which is 'the logic of scientific procedure' (Merton, 1967: 140) embodied in philosophical assumptions with respect to social reality, 'scientific' knowledge and the role of the researcher and his or her relation to the phenomenon to which the theory pertains.

Theories will vary in nature, depending on the underlying methodology, objective and scope. Some theories are meant to describe an observed phenomenon or to classify phenomena into groups based on shared characteristics. Others are intended to explain a phenomenon and make predictions about future phenomena in the form of testable hypotheses. Yet other theories seek to understand and interpret an individual action or phenomenon. In terms of scope, theories may range from the small, specific and sharply delineated, to the generalizing and more broadly defined middle-range, all the way to ambitious grand unifying theories.

In accounting and other social sciences, theories often have a normative or even moral dimension. Strictly speaking, such theories are not scientific theories because their evaluation depends on epistemic criteria and methods of evaluation as well as moral, practical and prudential/political criteria and methods of evaluation. As a consequence, different theories, methodologies and research paradigms may be incommensurable and have to co-exist because, as of yet, 'they are not capable of being measured by a common standard' (Hughes and Lavery, 2008: 213). In this case, the dominance of one particular theoretical paradigm will in practice depend on other factors than purely epistemic criteria.

2.2 What is methodology?

The interpretative filter of a theory stems partly from the methodology or 'the logic of scientific procedure' (Merton, 1967: 140). This logic depends on the philosophical assumptions regarding the nature of social reality, knowledge and the role of the researcher in relation to the phenomenon to which the theory pertains. It is important to keep in mind that both the logic and the problems of social science methodology 'transcend those found in any one discipline' (Merton, 1967: 140).

Ontology: assumptions about the nature of reality

Ontology refers to assumptions about the nature of reality. Many researchers distinguish between the natural sciences and the social sciences because they believe that natural phenomena and social phenomena are fundamentally different. Theories in the natural sciences are generally aimed at the description, categorization, explanation and prediction of natural phenomena. They are often based on the ontological assumptions of materialism and realism:

> Materialism is the view that everything in the world is made of matter. . . . Idealism is the view that what is real depends on the mind, and in the philosophy of perception it amounts to the claim that the material world does not exist outside of the mind (Cardinal *et al.*, 2004: 106).

Table 2.1 Ontological assumptions about the nature of reality

	Natural sciences	*Social sciences*
Materialism	Reality consists of matter → Realism	Ultimately, it is material wants and needs that drive social development → Realism
Idealism	Reality does not exist outside the mind that perceives it → Relativism	Ultimately, it is values and ideas that drive social development → Relativism
Dualism	Reality consists of both matter and ideas → In between Realism and Relativism	Social development is driven by both material wants and needs and by values and ideas → In between Realism and Relativism

Dualism claims that reality consists of both matter and mind. Realism is rooted in the belief that natural phenomena exist independently of the researchers who, therefore, are able to observe them from an objective spectator's view. The above is summarized in Table 2.1.

'The natural sciences are concerned with contingent regularities between two phenomena out of which we construct universal laws of nature' (Benton and Craib, 2011: 89). For the purpose of prediction, research methods will often approximate causality with statistical regularity and will make use of inductive reasoning. That is, generalizations are made on the basis of observed regularities. Social science researchers taking a naturalistic stance believe that the logic of explanation and research methods of the natural sciences (naturalistic methods) are generally suitable for application to social science questions as well. Others simply reject the use of anti-naturalistic methods as unscientific and will limit themselves to questions that are deemed answerable using naturalistic methods, i.e. 'scientific'.

Social science researchers taking an anti-naturalistic stance believe that observing society and individuals is complicated by the fact that the observer is also an individual with beliefs and values, and is part of a society. Furthermore, the observers and the observed possess self-consciousness, creating a 'double hermeneutic' which can lead to reflexivity where the observer and the observed tend to influence each other in the process (Benton and Craib, 2011: 76). Consequently, it is important to understand the reasons behind social science phenomena as well as the meaning and purpose of actions of both the observed and the observers. Relativism as an ontology requires a logic and research methods that take into account that theories are often value-laden and that objective observation is not always possible or even desirable. According to relativism, what counts as knowledge is often dependent on cultural and historical context (Boumans and Davis, 2010: 126). The above is summarized in Table 2.2.

It is important to note that there are many positions in between naïve or direct realism as the extreme realist position and radical relativism as the extreme relativist position. Direct realism assumes that the world is as it appears, or, in other words, that we perceive things as they are, which presupposes that we already know what they are like. Indirect or representative realism distinguishes between the objects we perceive and our perception or sensation of these objects (Cardinal *et al.*, 2004: 98–104). Further forms of realism include structural realism (Worrall, 1989, in Bortolotti, 2008: 108), internal realism (Putnam, 1987, in Bortolotti, 2008: 109) and critical realism (Bhaskar, 1975, 1978, in Benton and Craib, 2011: 202–17) among others. On the other side of the continuum, Paul Feyerabend's radical relativism holds that in the absence of theory-neutral tests to choose between incommensurable research paradigms, 'there are no methodological principles which distinguish science from non-science, and so no reason for thinking science is superior to other forms of understanding the world' (Benton and Craib, 2011: 61).

Table 2.2 Naturalism and anti-naturalism in the social sciences

	Naturalism	*Anti-naturalism*
Researcher	*Realism*: Phenomena exist independently from the researcher who can and must be an objective observer (*Objectivism*).	*Relativism*: Researchers cannot perceive phenomena objectively. Researchers will to some extent construct the reality they are observing (*Constructivism*). Observations will be subject to the double hermeneutic.
Task	Researchers must seek to discover empirical regularities in order to explain and predict phenomena.	Researchers must seek to interpret actors and actions in order to understand individual actors' intentions and the meaning of individual actions.
Paradigm	Positivist paradigms.	Interpretivist paradigms.

Epistemology: assumptions about knowledge, truth and justification

In *Nicomachean Ethics*, Book Six, Aristotle defines five intellectual virtues as the 'ways in which the soul arrives at truth' (Aristotle, 1976: 206). These include *episteme* (propositional, factual or scientific knowledge), *techne* (art or technical skill), *phronesis* (prudence or practical wisdom), *nous* (intelligence or intuition) and *sophia* (wisdom) (Aristotle, 1976: 207–13). Flyvbjerg (2001: 53) sees *phronesis* as the practical knowledge of how to balance instrumental rationality with value-rationality, and advocates a phronetic social science. A phronetic social science would give due consideration to:

- values and ethics (Flyvbjerg, 2001: Chapter 5);
- balancing conflicting interests; and
- preventing the abuse of power (Flyvbjerg, 2001: Chapters 7 and 8).

Phronetic knowledge is the kind of knowledge that Aristotle saw 'as the necessary basis for political and social enquiry . . . because such balancing is crucial to the sustained happiness of the citizens in any society' (Flyvbjerg, 2001: 4).

Epistemology is the theory of propositional (scientific) knowledge and its criteria. According to what is called the traditional justified true belief (JTB) view[2] of propositional knowledge, 'knowledge requires epistemically justified true belief' (Lemos, 2007: 3). A stricter definition holds that that factual knowledge requires an 'indefeasibly justified, true belief' (Cardinal *et al.*, 2004: 141). In other words, only true beliefs which cannot be defeated by further evidence count as propositional knowledge. According to this definition, much of what we currently use as knowledge in our daily lives is not actually *episteme* although it may be very useful. A problem with the JTB view of knowledge is that some cases of epistemically justified true belief are not instances of knowledge because they are a matter of luck or sheer coincidence.[3]

Although phronetic knowledge differs from epistemic knowledge in terms of its purpose, it also depends on evidence and logic for its epistemic justification. A difference is that, in addition to epistemic justification, it also requires explicit moral and prudential (i.e. self-interested and political) justification which is necessarily context-dependent.

Agrippa's trilemma suggests three unpalatable options for the justification of beliefs (Pritchard, 2010: 33). The first is that we do not support our beliefs, in which case a sceptic might argue that we probably do not have propositional knowledge. A foundationalist, however, believes that there is knowledge in the form of beliefs that justify themselves or beliefs that need no further justification because they are axiomatic and therefore do not require proof. This type of foundational knowledge forms the bedrock for all other knowledge that is built on top of it. Foundationalists believe that knowledge ultimately comes through perception and observation (empiricism) or through logical thought (rationalism), or perhaps through both. Rationalism searches for universal laws and truths deduced from general axioms which hold with necessity (Hollis, 2002: 29). Rationalism in science assumes that logical necessity equals causal necessity, but logical necessity cannot be proved because all proof presupposes the necessary laws of thought (Hollis, 2002: 36). Rationalists will look for the equivalent of natural laws underlying either the structures of society or causing the behaviours of the individuals in it, using deductive logic. Empiricism in science starts from the experience of sense perception of particulars, and uses inductive generalization to infer relations between cause and effect based on probability. Empiricists will attempt to infer the social equivalent of natural laws on the basis of statistical regularities. When inspired by the ideas of logical positivism (see below) in the natural sciences, empiricism applied to the social sciences or humanities is often referred to as Positivism (Hollis, 2002: 41–2).

There are at least two anti-foundational views on the justification of beliefs in answer to Agrippa's trilemma. One is to assume that our beliefs are justified when they are supported by another belief, which is in turn, inferred on the basis of another belief *ad infinitum* (infinitism). The other is to assume that a coherent chain or system of beliefs (coherentism) can justify our belief in a proposition (Pritchard, 2010: 33–6). However, even if this chain of beliefs is circular instead of infinite, the infinite regress argument shows that 'if all justification is inferential, no belief is ever more than conditionally justified' (Dancy, 1985: 56). Pragmatism is another anti-foundational approach to the justification of beliefs based on the criterion of usefulness.

If propositional knowledge requires one's belief to be both justified and true, what is the nature of truth? Correspondence theory holds that the truth of a proposition depends on its correspondence with reality.[4] Coherence theory, on the other hand, claims that the truth of a proposition depends on its coherence with other beliefs we have.[5] The coherence theory of truth takes coherence to be a condition of truth as well as a source of justification. The pragmatic theory of truth holds that usefulness is a good criterion to distinguish a true belief from a false belief.[6] The above is summarized in Table 2.3.

Table 2.3 Examples of epistemological assumptions about knowledge

	Foundationalism	*Anti-foundationalism*
Knowledge	The foundations of knowledge are axiomatic beliefs and beliefs that justify themselves. Other knowledge is built on those foundations.	*Infinitism*: Beliefs are justified by other beliefs ad infinitum. *Coherentism*: A coherent system of beliefs can justify our beliefs in a proposition.
Sources of knowledge	*Rationalism*: Knowledge increases through logical deduction. *Empiricism*: Knowledge increases through inference based on perception and observation.	Beliefs can only be conditionally justified. If the premises or conditions change, beliefs may need to be discarded or adjusted.
The nature of truth	*Correspondence theory of truth*: A proposition is true if it corresponds with reality.	*Pragmatic theory of truth*: Usefulness is a good criterion for justification. *Coherence theory of truth*: Coherence with other beliefs is a condition of truth as well as a source of justification.

Demarcation attempts and research paradigms

In the late nineteenth and early twentieth centuries, logical positivists argued for a demarcation between scientific statements (which are synthetic statements that can be verified through experience), and analytic and synthetic statements of logic, philosophy, religion, literature, etc., which are not empirically verifiable (Bortolotti, 2008: 8). More recently, Karl Popper believed that 'science differs from pseudo-science in that it aims at falsifiable hypotheses' (Bortolotti, 2008: 14). Popper presented his falsification theory as a rejection of the logical positivist's belief in foundational knowledge (Hollis, 2002: 72–3). However, it was the distinction between science and pseudo-science that caused social scientists, particularly in economics and later in accounting, to go on the defensive and try to make their social sciences appear as scientific as possible.

3. Methodological debates in the social sciences

Below is a very brief discussion of some important social science research paradigms, which illustrates the importance of the ontological and epistemological assumptions for the formulation of theories in social science. The discussion starts with the Enlightenment where the groundwork for future naturalistic paradigms was laid, and Romanticism which developed in response to the Enlightenment's rationalism and empiricism and bore the seeds of anti-naturalistic paradigms. It then moves on to naturalistic paradigms characterized by methodological holism (functionalism and conflict theory) and anti-naturalistic paradigms characterized by methodological holism (critical theory and various forms of Marxism). From there it moves to naturalistic paradigms characterized by methodological individualism (rational choice and exchange theory) and anti-naturalistic paradigms characterized by methodological individualism, and ends with globalization paradigms.

3.1 Enlightenment and romantic paradigms

Enlightenment thinking came to prominence in the eighteenth century, particularly in France, and had three main themes. First, advances in the natural sciences led to an emphasis on scientific reasoning instead of reliance on the authority of the Church when trying to understand the universe and the place of individual humans in it. Second, the power of rational thought came to be used to expose the abuse of power by the aristocracy and the Church. Finally, there was a belief in progress 'from simple social orders to more complex ones, and away from more despotic and exploitative political and economic systems towards more egalitarian ones' (Inglis with Thorpe, 2012: 28–9). Romanticism arose as a critical response to Enlightenment thinking. It criticized materialist values and a social order that destroyed any sense of community, it defended traditions, cultural diversity, and it 'regarded human mental capacities as being a mixture of more rational and more imaginative and emotional characteristics' (ibid.: 30).

Positivism (which seeks to explain and predict phenomena) has its origins in Enlightenment thinking, whereas interpretivism (which seeks to interpret and understand reasons, motivations and actions) finds its origins in Romanticism. Similarly, the ontological dispute between materialism and idealism stems from Enlightenment and Romantic thought. Materialism (and Enlightenment thought) holds that social order is driven more by material, economic and technological factors, whereas idealism (and Romanticism) maintains that social order is more dependent on ideal phenomena such as culture, values and ideas (ibid.: 32).

3.2 Naturalistic paradigms characterized by methodological holism: functionalism and conflict theory

Inspired by the natural sciences, and in particular biology, sociologists such as Talcott Parsons and Robert Merton saw society as 'a kind of *system* comprised of interrelated parts' (O'Byrne, 2011: 14), and developed a theoretical approach based on ontological holism (the idea that social structures rather than individual actors and actions are the real building blocks of social reality) named structural functionalism. Functionalism derives from Herbert Spencer's ideas about evolution towards increasing structural complexity through the process of differentiation and Emile Durkheim's idea that complex social systems are held together by a common culture including shared norms and values (Inglis with Thorpe, 2012: 38–42). Research questions within this paradigm tended to centre on the problem of socialization (or social integration) and modernization from a top-down perspective. Individual agents, their motivations, choices and actions did not receive much attention.

Parson's optimism about modern societies and the USA in particular (ibid.: 53) was apparent in the presumption was that social change was necessarily progressive (O'Byrne, 2011: 40) and leading towards a better, more modern future embracing free market capitalism and political democracy. Criticism of the functionalist approach derived from its tendency to define the ideal state or ideal society based on pro-Western values, and its view of disagreement, conflict and violence as a malfunction of the system which needs to be fixed rather than accommodated (O'Byrne, 2011: 46–7).

Conflict theory developed in response to functionalism and was inspired by Weber and Marx (Inglis with Thorpe, 2012: 54). It assumed that 'conflict exists as a basic property of society, and forms the arena in which rival interest groups compete' (O'Byrne, 2011: 48). Unlike Marxism, which holds that the conflict in society is based on class relations defined in economic terms (named dialectic materialism), the conflict theorist Ralph Dahrendorf held that class relations were 'defined by an uneven distribution of *power*'[italics in original] (ibid.: 49).

3.3 Anti-naturalist paradigms characterized by methodological holism: Marxism and critical theory

Marxism is anti-naturalist because it assumes that researchers, confronted with the objective reality of class struggle and other social phenomena they associate with the ills of capitalism, will take an ideological position from which to conduct their analyses in order to either defend the status quo or to try and change it. In the twentieth century, many different types of Marxism appeared. 'Two of the most important versions of Western Marxism are the 'critical theory' associated with the Frankfurt School, and hegemony theory, first formulated by Antonio Gramsci' (Inglis with Thorpe, 2012: 63).

Central in the early Frankfurt School (about 1920–60) was Adorno and Horkheimer's critical theory, which had the intention of identifying and overcoming the ideological repression mechanisms of capitalist society (ibid.: 69). From the 1960s, the later Frankfurt School under Habermas developed ideas about 'discursive democracy' and 'communicative rationality' as means to use rationality to bring about emancipation and freedom (ibid.: 73–80). Gramsci's hegemony theory is about how, under capitalism, political and cultural processes serve to manufacture consent from those it exploits (O'Byrne, 2011: 72) and how ruling class hegemony is always potentially fragile because ideological domination is rarely complete and stable (Inglis with Thorpe, 2012: 80–84).

3.4 Naturalistic paradigms characterized by methodological individualism: rational choice theory and behavioralism

Exchange theory in sociology and rational choice theory in economics are characterized by the methodological individualism also found in utilitarianism in ethics and behaviourist psychology. These have in common that they assume that all humans are motivated by self-interest, the maximization of their happiness (or utility or wealth), and are rational in the way they pursue their self-interests. This leads to the idea that, in all aspects of our lives, we behave more or less the way we do in market situations (Hollis, 2002: 115). 'Rational action is thus instrumentally rational action' (ibid.: 118). Hence, exchange theorists believe that in order to understand how individual actions shape society (i.e. the total outcome of all individual choices), it is necessary to observe the outcomes of the choices made by individual agents.

When looking at society as a functional structure, or as dominated by class structures or interest groups, society determines the fate of the individual. Although an individual agent has the capacity to freely make choices, the scope of these choices is largely determined by the opportunities inherent in the structure of society. Somewhat surprisingly because of their focus on the individual, utilitarianism, behavioralism, rational choice theory and exchange theory treat the individual as largely predictable (O'Byrne, 2011: 138). 'By stating what conditions preferences ought to satisfy, rational choice theory prescribes how individuals ought to choose in order to be rational' (Boumans and Davis, 2010: 177). Hence, although under rational choice theory, society is not assumed to limit the scope of the choices available to the individual, the individual's actual choice is severely limited by a value-laden interpretation of rationality (ibid.: 177–80). Similarly, in behavioralism, the individual's choices are deemed predictable because of behavioural biases that are either innate or the consequence of conditioning. In sum, some level of determinism is inherent in naturalistic approaches to social science irrespective of whether they are based on ontological and methodological holism or ontological and methodological individualism.

3.5 Anti-naturalist paradigms characterized by methodological individualism: symbolic interactionism, ethnomethodology and phenomenology

Anti-naturalistic approaches to social science characterized by methodological individualism are likely to be rooted in the ontological assumptions of idealism and relativism. Relativism as an ontology presupposes that social phenomena and social actions need to be understood, interpreted and explained from the point of view of actors and participants in specific context. Truth and knowledge are seen as context-dependent rather than absolute concepts. Symbolic interactionism, associated with George Herbert Mead, is a sociological approach to understanding how an individual's concept of self is formed through social interaction. It is rooted in the pragmatist theory of knowledge, which sees truth as a convenient fiction (O'Byrne, 2011: 139–47). Symbolic interactionism often applies case studies and ethnographic research methods and uses grounded theory (theory that emerges from and is useful in a particular situation, see O'Byrne, 2011: 141). Important insights include the way social 'labels' and roles influence an individual's concept of self.

Ethnomethodology is another theoretical approach in sociology based on relativist ontology. It seeks to understand how social reality is the product of human perception instead of the other way around. Important insights include the idea that social structure is a negotiated order which is inherently unstable. Individuals develop ways of dealing with the complexity of life, for example by devising techniques of neutralization (leading to cognitive dissonance) and strategies to legitimize their actions (O'Byrne, 2011: 173–4).

3.6 Globalization and institutional paradigms

In most social science disciplines, the notion of society was and still is decidedly territorial. However, economic, political, technical, social and cultural facets of globalization manifest themselves at distinctly different paces creating the need to transform the nature of theorising (Inglis with Thorpe, 2012: 259–61).

Those working within a positive economics paradigmatic framework tend to stress the positive potential and benefits of globalization. For example, Mishkin (2006: 5) claims that economic and financial globalization leads to a reduction of poverty in developing countries that are willing and able to become export-oriented (see Chapter 10). On the other hand, Hymer (1970) predicted two consequences of the fact that political globalization is trailing behind economic globalization, which Basu (2010) in *Beyond the Invisible Hand* identifies as having materialized. One is erosion of democracy. Reich (2009), too, presents an account of the erosion of democracy in democratic capitalist countries in the current age of big business. The other is 'the tolerance of global inequalities that would not have been tolerated in any economy under any single government' (Basu, 2010: 182–3).

In business history research has been conducted from a comparative institutional perspective since the early 1980s (e.g. Chandler, 1980). In economics, new institutional economics gained traction from the early 1990s. In financial accounting, a comparative institutional perspective initially served to describe and classify accounting practices across the world (e.g. Mueller, 1967; Nobes, 1983 and Mueller *et al.*, 2004). Classification was criticized by Roberts (1995). The search went on to explain these differences, first in terms of culture (e.g. Gray, 1988) and later in terms of predominant modes of financing (e.g. Nobes, 1998).

The legal systems, financial systems, corporate governance systems and other institutional factors analyses by La Porta *et al.* (1997, 2000) inspired comparative institutional analyses, such as Ali and Hwang (2000), Ball *et al.* (2001), Bushman *et al.* (2004) and Leuz *et al.* (2003) opening the door to new institutional accounting research. However, it was the realistic chance of worldwide adoption of IFRS after 2005 that necessitated consideration of international differences in institutional environment in earnest. Examples of neo-institutional international accounting research, which is intentionally based on the ideas of new institutional economics, include Leuz (2010) and Hail *et al.* (2010). An example of the new institutional perspective that does not have either an international or a managerial/organizational focus is Bealing (1994).

'The central message of new institutional economics is that institutions matter for economic performance' (Furubotn and Richter, 2000: 1). It is about 'designing effective and efficient institutions to structure behavior in such a way that the system performs well' (Groenewegen *et al.*, 2010: 32). Recognizing that neoclassical theory neglects institutional constraints and transaction costs, new institutional economics, often associated with Williamson (1975) and North (1990), is based on similar methodological assumptions and uses similar methods of analysis to extend microeconomics. These assumptions include:

1. methodological individualism;
2. utility maximization;
3. individual rationality;
4. opportunistic behaviour;
5. a society where the transfer of property rights by physical force or other forms of compulsion does not exist;
6. the society's governance structure protects private property rights; and
7. the definition of institutions as 'a set of formal and informal rules, including their enforcement arrangements' (Schmoller, 1900, in Furubotn and Richter, 2000: 6).

For a detailed overview of these methodological assumptions, see Furubotn and Richter (2000: Chapter 1) or Groenewegen *et al.* (2010: Chapter 2) for an informative comparison of the methodological assumptions of both schools of thought.

The original or 'old' institutional economics paradigm, is often associated with Thorstein Veblen (1899) and Commons (1931). Veblen criticized orthodox theories from the classical theory of Smith to the neoclassical theory of Marshall as 'contaminated by taxonomic, hedonistic and teleological theoretical attitudes'. He regarded the orthodoxy as taxonomic because it classified economic problems without really explaining them, hedonistic because the utility maximising *homo economicus* was invented without regard for the psychological causes of human behaviour, and teleological because the use of concepts such as 'equilibrium' was normative and convenient for developing static models that detract from the evolutionary ways in which economic society develops (Screpanti and Zamagni, 2005: 302–3). Commons believed that the study of 'collective action' should be at the centre of economics because society is formed by individuals who must maintain 'strong relations of interdependence, both in conflict and in co-operation'(ibid.: 306). He assumed that power relationships among contracting parties often influence bargaining outcomes more strongly than demand and supply in competitive markets.

The original or 'old' institutional paradigm is therefore based on the following methodological assumptions:

1. methodological holism;
2. satisficing behaviour;
3. bounded or perhaps procedural rationality, such as habits and due process;
4. opportunism must be balanced by trust;
5. property rights are not distributed equally and the institutions to protect them are shaped by a political system which reflects the power structures in a society (or international society); and
6. the human environment necessitates increasingly complex institutions, which include shared mental maps and learning in order deal with both complexity and uncertainty (see Groenewegen *et al.*, 2010: 72–7).

In financial accounting research, examples of research based the on methodological assumptions of old institutional theory would be the political economy view of A. M. Tinker (1980) and Cooper and Sherer (1984), the socio-historical approach by Merino and Neimark (1982), research based on Di Maggio and Powell's (1983) idea of institutional isomorphism[7] such as Carpenter and Feroz (2001) or the socio-economic consequences view of Someya (1993). In international financial accounting standard setting research, examples of studies based on the assumptions of the original institutional economics include Mattli and Büthe (2005), Botzem and Quack (2009), Chiapello and Medjad (2009), and Arnold (2012).

3.7 What might methodological debates mean for financial accounting and reporting theory and research?

Paradigm clashes and methodological debates in financial accounting research have become rare. An example from the early 1990s is Solomons (1991a) criticising Tinker (1985), Tinker's (1991) response and Solomons' (1991b) rejoinder. This exchange clearly illustrates the incommensurability of a paradigm that sees accounting as a technical discipline where the practitioners and standard setters can and must be neutral between competing interests and a paradigm that regards accounting practice and standards as shaped by dominant vested interests. It also shows the investment of personal values in so-called intellectual positions, and illustrates the confusion that results when we lack understanding of methodological issues and assumptions.

Superficially, financial accounting (like economics) displays a misleading image of being scientific and technical and therefore neutral, objective and value-free. Yet, at the same time, there are few disciplines that share financial accounting's importance in decisions on allocating resources and distributing income and wealth. This tension between the image of objectivity and neutrality and the reality of economic and political interests manifests itself most clearly in the areas of accounting regulation, standard setting and auditing, and particularly in an international context.

A better understanding of methodology might help (international) financial accounting and reporting research move beyond the damage that was done by the demarcation attempts. Debating methodological assumptions might help mainstream financial accounting and reporting research to acknowledge its hidden value judgements. It might help interpretive research to search for general principles across multiple contexts rather than regard everything as context-dependent. It might help critical accounting research be constructive as well as critical. It is unlikely that there is one methodological paradigm that has a monopoly on epistemic knowledge that helps improve the allocation of financial, natural, human and knowledge resources and the distribution of income and wealth across the globe. However, leaving accounting policy, standard setting and regulation decisions to public choice processes without a structural and balanced input of both epistemic and phronetic knowledge appears to be asking for trouble.

4. Financial accounting theory

4.1 What is the goal of financial accounting theory?

On the mainstream, positivist view,

> [t]he goal of accounting theory is to provide a set of principles and relationships that provide an explanation for observed practices and predict unobserved practices. That is, accounting theory should be able to explain why business organizations elect certain accounting methods over other alternatives and predict the attributes of firms that elect various accounting methods. Accounting theory should also be verifiable through accounting research (Schroeder *et al.*, 2001: 1).

This view ignores the interpretive role of theory in choosing and framing a particular research problem. It is rather limited because, as in any discipline, financial accounting theories will vary in nature, depending on the underlying methodology, objective and scope. In sum, there is not one single objective of accounting theory.

4.2 Types of financial accounting theory by objective

The body of financial accounting and reporting theory incorporates many types of theories. In terms of their objectives there are, among others, descriptive theories, prescriptive theories, inductive (predictive) theories, interpretive theories, critical and institutional theories. Descriptive accounting theories will often aim to provide a precise descriptive definition of something or identify and describe phenomena or methods used in practice. An example of the former would be descriptive definitions of accounting such as those found in Sanders *et al.* (1938: 4) or the somewhat broader definition in AAA (1966: 1). An example of the latter would be *Accounting: Its Principles and Some of its Problems* by Hatfield (1909). The above three represent descriptive definitions based on observation. Sprouse and Moonitz (1962: 6–7) represent a deductive approach to the identification of the functions of accounting based on five postulates.

Prescriptive theories may come in the form of prescriptive definitions, or in the form of rules or prescriptive methods. Rationalism is the epistemological approach to gaining knowledge using deductive logic and basic propositions which are assumed to be fundamental truths. An example of a prescriptive definition is the objective of general purpose financial reporting in the IASB Conceptual Framework (IASB, 2010: OB2). This definition is not based on deductive logic or any other explicit form of epistemic justification in the Conceptual Framework. Presumably, it derives its justification from the authority of the IASB members or is assumed to be a fundamental truth as it has been adopted from the FASB Conceptual Framework (FASB, 1978). Prescriptive income and capital concepts and income determination theories are discussed in Chapters 3, 4 and 5.

Positive or inductive theories 'seek to explain and predict particular phenomena' (Deegan and Unerman, 2006: 206). In the social sciences and philosophy 'positivism' is a term used in broad and narrow meanings and everything in between. Broadly speaking, the positivist epistemological approach to gaining knowledge about human affairs is naturalistic. In other words, it is based on roughly the same metaphysical assumptions as the natural sciences and applies similar empirical scientific methods. Positivism in the narrow sense is rooted in 'Logical Positivism, the ferocious version of empiricism which emerged from the Vienna Circle in the 1930s' (Hollis, 2002: 42).

Positive theories are inferred based on empirical observations which are generalized into predictive statements in the form of testable hypotheses using an inductive method. Capital markets based on accounting research became the mainstay of mainstream accounting journals with studies predicting and testing the stock price effects (i.e. the wealth effects on investors) of changes in accounting policy. The idea was to identify accounting policies that would yield useful information for investors. Watts and Zimmerman's (1978) positive accounting theory sought to provide a theory of how interest groups are likely to try to influence accounting regulation based on empirical observation of their behaviour.

Interpretive financial accounting theories seek to understand rather than to predict particular phenomena. The 'aim would be to understand the subjective experience of individuals in the preparation, communication, verification, or use of accounting information' (Riahi-Belkaoui, 2004: 317). Instead of seeking to explain the objective causes of behaviour interpretive research seeks to understand what an action means to the agent, i.e. the subjective meaning of an action (Hollis, 2002: 17). In financial accounting research, ethnography is mostly used to understand accountants' and auditors' understanding of professionalism and ethics. See, for example, Grey (1998), Power (1991), Coffey (1994), and Gill (2009). Benton and Craib (2011) distinguish between interpretive approaches that seek to understand the subjects' instrumental rationality (e.g. rational choice theory and game theory, which often make use of laboratory studies), and interpretive approaches that seek to understand rationality as culture and context dependent (e.g. hermeneutics and other linguistic approaches as well as grounded theory based on ethnographic methods).

Critical financial accounting theories also come in different varieties. To name two, researchers influenced by Marxist sociological thought seek to demonstrate how financial accounting is instrumental in perpetuating class structures and class struggle using an espistemological approach based on a combination of empiricism and deduction. Examples include Tinker (1980), Tinker *et al.* (1982), Galhofer and Haslam (1997), Researchers influenced by Habermas and Foucault seek to demonstrate how those in power try to establish knowledge and theories as neutral and objective in order to further their own self-interests. Examples include Miller and O'Leary (1987), Dillard (1991), Roslender and Dillard (2003), Laughlin (2004). Here the epistemological approach is a mix of the former combined with hermeneutics.

Institutional and contextual perspectives in international financial accounting research are important for understanding and analysing the issues that may arise as a consequence of the adoption of IFRS across different institutional environments. See, for example, Leuz (2010) and Hail *et al.* (2010) as representative of the new institutional paradigm in international financial accounting, and Perry and Nőlke (2006) and Arnold (2012) as more representative of the old institutional perspective.

4.3 Financial accounting typologies

The positive versus normative distinction

A conveniently simplistic manner to classify financial accounting theory is into normative accounting theory and positive accounting theory. For most purposes, this dualistic classification is somewhat misleading. First, few theories will be purely prescriptive (i.e. normative) or purely descriptive (i.e. positive). As pointed out by Christenson (1983: 2), '(l)ike other normative judgements, methodological ones may be made with varying degrees of self-consciousness.' Second, positive accounting theory does not have a monopoly claim on being 'scientific'. Third, positive accounting theory has 'the major aim of *explaining* and *predicting* accounting practice, rather than *prescribing* particular approaches'[italics in original] (Deegan and Unerman, 2006: 8). Although classification of accounting theories was probably not their primary goal, Watts and Zimmerman (1978, 1979) and Jensen's (1983)' dualistic classification neatly served to make much of the accounting literature that was not positive being regarded as 'unscientific' (Watts and Zimmerman, 1979: 273 n.1).

So what role does positive accounting theory have in accounting standard setting? Watts and Zimmerman's (1979) answer is twofold. First,

> [the] predominant role of accounting theories is now to provide excuses which satisfy the demand created by the political process; (and second) … the only accounting theory that will provide a set of observations that is consistent with the observed phenomena is one based on self-interest. … While a self-interest theory can be used to explain accounting standards such a theory will not be used to justify accounting standards because self-interest theories are politically unpalatable. As a consequence, *not only is there no generally accepted accounting theory to justify accounting standards, there will never be one* [italics in original](Watts and Zimmerman, 1979: 300–301).

There are at least two problems with this argument. First, their methodological assumption that a valid theory to (epistemically?) justify accounting standards will have to be a theory based on self-interest is not self-evidently true, nor is the evidence presented convincing. Second, they do seem to commit the naturalistic fallacy by suggesting that a theory that can be used to explain a phenomenon ought to be used (epistemically, prudentially or morally) to justify that phenomenon as well. In spite of Tinker *et al.* (1982) and Christenson's (1983) important critiques of the methodology of positive accounting, positivism became hugely influential in financial accounting research and remains so in the second decade of the twenty-first century.

Hopper and powell's classification

Hopper and Powell (1985) based on Burrell and Morgan's (1979) classification of organizational research is possibly the second most influential and the first multidimensional. It classified management accounting research along the dimensions of 'the nature of the social sciences' (ranging from subjectivism to objectivism) and 'the nature of society' (ranging from orderly to characterized by fundamental conflicts) (Hopper and Powell, 1985: 431–2). It was meant to help 'researchers into the management sciences (to) consider their own values and beliefs concerning the nature of society and the social sciences' (ibid.: 429).

Chua's classification

The next year, Chua (1986) produced a three-way classification based on assumptions with respect to knowledge, beliefs about social and physical reality, and the relationship between theory and practice into interpretive, critical and mainstream accounting research. Chua (1986) described the worldview and assumptions underlying what she calls 'mainstream accounting research' and introduced the 'interpretative' and 'critical' worldviews as two alternatives to the mainstream. She briefly mentioned Hopper and Powell (1985) and in the appendix she critiqued Burrell and Morgan (1979). Both Hopper and Powell (1985) and Chua (1986) were intended to place the dominant positivist research paradigm in a broader perspective, thereby also pointing to its limitations.

Ironically, and somewhat disrespectfully, in their textbook on research method and methodology in accounting and finance, Ryan *et al.* (2002: 39–44) collapsed Hopper and Powell's (1985) model and Chua's (1986) classification into one. Here, the classification of critical accounting research ranges from radical humanism to radical structuralism, where the objective is to induce radical change to society, and whereby the research methodologies range from those agreeing with subjectivism to objectivism. It characterizes mainstream accounting research, which Chua had characterized as using the hypothetico-deductive methodology of the natural sciences, as based on a functionalist theory of society aimed at holding society together through regulation. Finally, Ryan *et al.* (2002: 40–41) characterize interpretive research based on subjectivist research methodologies that are not aimed at changing society, but rather at interpreting society from the point of view of individual participants.

Laughlin's classification

Laughlin (1995) characterizes accounting research along the three dimensions of the level of prior theorization about social reality, the level of prior theorization in the methodology and the strength of the view that society needs to be changed, all into high, medium and low.

In his Dutch PhD thesis, Knoops (2010: 42–62) uses Laughlin (1995, 2004) to develop a classification of financial accounting theory into four groups based on ontology, epistemology, research methodology[8] and philosophical assumptions with respect to society. The first group consists of the positivist and post-positivist research perspectives which include: normative approaches, economic approaches such as positive accounting theory and market-based financial accounting research. In the second group we find the interpretative perspectives which include phenomenological and hermeneutic approaches as well as constructivist approaches to financial accounting theory. A third group consists of the critical perspectives which include financial accounting research based on critical theory and the political economy of accounting. Finally, there are the postmodernist perspectives on financial accounting theory.

Typologies of financial accounting theory are useful for gaining an understanding of the philosophical assumptions that each of us must make in order to be able to decide what to accept as knowledge and how to gain knowledge about financial accounting and external reporting phenomena. Understanding the relevant methodological issues and debates in the different social sciences helps us to trace the source of conflicting ideologies and their influence on financial accounting thought today.

5. Conclusion

At the end of the chapter we may conclude that having an understanding of social science methodology will not help researchers much when trying to solve specific research problems. Furthermore, the existence of different accounting journals for different paradigms has mitigated the consequences of researchers' paradigm choice for their careers.

However, when it comes to making progress in research needed to improve the accounting model, its framework and its practices, methodology provides a framework for looking critically at our own (and others') explicit and implicit assumptions with respect to the phenomena that we study, the research questions we ask, the sources we use, the data we collect and the methods we apply. Such an understanding breeds respect for the methodological assumptions and value judgements of others. Mutual respect enables us to bridge methodological paradigms and to reappraise the things we take for granted in search of answers and solutions to the fundamental and the practical problems faced by accounting standard setters, practitioners, auditors, teachers and financial regulators.

Notes

1 On 30 August 2012 at the Japanese Accounting Association Congress in Tokyo.
2 The JTB view of propositional knowledge is not the only view on the nature of knowledge. Alternatives include coherentism, reliabilism and virtue epistemology which are also important for understanding the justification of knowledge claims.
3 This problem is called the Gettier problem and it has not yet been satisfactorily solved (Lemos, 2007: Chapter 2).
4 The correspondence theory of truth claims that a proposition is true if it corresponds to the facts, and false if it does not correspond to the facts. Furthermore, it holds that one and the same proposition cannot be both true and false, and neither is the truth relative in that it is true for you but not for me. Some object that, without a clear notion of what a fact is, it is not possible to know if a proposition corresponds with it. As such the theory may be circular (Lemos, 2007: 9–10).
5 Critics are usually willing to accept coherence as a source of justification, but they object that a coherent set of propositions is not necessarily true (Lemos, 2007: 12–13)
6 Critics object that even if true beliefs usually provide a good basis for action and false beliefs often provide a bad basis for action, it does not follow that we should identify true belief with useful belief (Lemos, 2007: 11).
7 More often used in managerial accounting from whence it derives.
8 Knoops (2010: Section 3.3) refers to methodology as the combination of the place and task of the researcher, the research methods, research style and assumptions regarding human nature. This is based on a combination of Laughlin's (1995, 2004) three-way characterization based on level of theorizing, methodology and change.

Bibliography

AAA (1966) *A Statement of Basic Accounting Theory*, Evanston, IL: American Accounting Association.

AICPA (1973) *Objectives of Financial Statements*, New York: American Institute of Certified Public Accountants.

Ali, A. and Hwang, L. (2000) 'Country-Specific Factors Related to Financial Reporting and the Value-Relevance of Accounting Data' *Journal of Accounting Research* 38 (1): 1–21.

Aristotle (1976) *Ethics*, Harmondsworth: Penguin

Arnold, P.J. (2012) 'The Political Economy of Financial Harmonization: The East Asian Financial Crisis and the Rise of International Accounting Standards', *Accounting, Organizations and Society* 37 (6): 361–81.

Ball, R., Kothari, S.P. and Robin, A. (2001) 'The Effect of International Institutional Factors on Properties of Accounting Earnings', *Journal of Accounting and Economics*, 29: 1–51.

Basu, K. (2010), *Beyond the Invisible Hand: Groundwork for a New Economics*, Princeton, NJ: Princeton University Press.

Bealing, W.E. (1994) 'Actions Speak Louder Than Words: An Institutional Perspective on the Securities and Exchange Commission', *Accounting, Organizations and Society*, 19 (7): 555–67.

Benton, T. and Craib, I. (2011) *Philosophy of Social Science: The Philosophical Foundations of Social Thought*, 2nd edn, Basingstoke: Palgrave Macmillan.

Bhaskar, R. (1975) *A Realist Theory of Science* (in Benton and Craib, 2011: 202–17), London: Verso.

Bhaskar, R. (1978) *The Possibility of Naturalism* (in Benton and Craib, 2011: 202–17), Hemel Hempstead: Harvester Wheatsheaf.

Bohman, J. (1991) *New Philosophy of Social Science*, Cambridge: Polity Press.

Bortolotti, L. (2008) *An Introduction to the Philosophy of Science*, Cambridge: Polity Press.

Botzem, S. and Quack, S. (2009) '(No) Limits to Anglo-American Accounting? Reconstructing the History of the International Accounting Standard Setting Committee: A Review Article', *Accounting, Organizations and Society* 34 (8): 988–98.

Boumans, M. and Davis, J.B. (2010), *Economic Methodology: Understanding Economics as a Science*, Basingstoke: Palgrave Macmillan.

Bunge (1967) *Scientific Research II: The Search for Truth*, (in Riahi-Belkaoui, 2004) New York: Springer Verlag.

Burchell, S., Clubb, C., Hopwood, A.G., Hughes, J. and Nahapiet, J. (1980), 'The Roles of Accounting in Organizations and Society', *Accounting, Organizations and Society* 5 (1): 5–27.

Burchell, S., Clubb, C. and Hopwood, A.G. (1985) 'Accounting in its Social Context: Towards a History of Value Added in the United Kingdom', *Accounting, Organizations and Society* 10 (4): 381–413.

Burns, J. (2000) 'The Dynamics of Accounting Change: Interplay Between New Practices, Routines, Institutions, Power and Politics', *Accounting, Auditing and Accountability Journal*, 13 (5): 566–96.

Burrell, G. and Morgan, G. (1979) *Sociological Paradigms and Organizational Analysis: Elements of the Sociology of Corporate Life*, London: Heinemann Educational Books.

Bushman, R.M., Piotroski, J.D. and Smith, A.J. (2004) 'What Determines Corporate Transparency?', *Journal of Accounting Research* 42 (2): 207–52.

Cardinal, D., Hayward, J. and Jones, G. (2004), *Epistemology: The Theory of Knowledge*, London: Hodder Education.

Carpenter, V. and Feroz, E. (2001) 'Institutional Theory and Accounting Rule Choice: An Analysis of Four US State Governments' Decisions to Adopt Generally Accepted Accounting Principles', *Accounting, Organizations and Society*, 26, 565–96.

Chandler, A.D. (1980) 'The Growth of the Transnational Industrial Firm in the United States and the United Kingdom: A Comparative Analysis 1', *The Economic History Review*, 33 (3): 396–410.

Chiapello, E. and Medjad, K. (2009) 'An Unprecedented Privatisation of Mandatory Standards Setting: The Case of European Accounting Policy', *Critical Perspectives on Accounting* 20 (4): 448–68.

Christenson, C. (1983) 'The Methodology of Positive Accounting', *The Accounting Review* 58 (1): 1–22.

Chua, W.F. (1986) 'Radical Developments in Accounting Thought', *The Accounting Review* 61 (4): 601–32.

Coffey, A.J. (1994) 'Timing is Everything: Graduate Accountants, Time and Organizational Commitment', *Sociology* 28 (4): 943–56.

Commons, J.R. (1931) 'Institutional Economics', *The American Economic Review* 21 (4): 648–52.

Cooper, D.J. and Sherer, M.J. (1984) 'The Value of Corporate Accounting Reports: Arguments for a Political Economy of Accounting', *Accounting, Organizations and Society* 9 (3/4), 207–32.

Dancy, J. (1985) *An Introduction to Contemporary Epistemology*, Oxford: Basil Blackwell.

Deegan, C. and Unerman, J. (2006) *Financial Accounting Theory*, European edn, Maidenhead: McGraw-Hill Education.

Dicksee, L.R. (1903) *Advanced Accounting*, London: Gee and Co.

Dillard, J.F. (1991) 'Accounting as a Critical Social Science', *Accounting, Auditing and Accountability Journal* 4 (1): 8–28.

Di Maggio, P.J. and Powel, W.W. (1983) '"The Iron Cage Revisited": Instituional Isomorphism and Collective Rationality in Organisational Field', *American Sociological Review* 48: 147–160.

FASB (1978) *Statement of Financial Accounting Concepts No. 1*, Norwalk, CT: Financial Accounting Standards Board

Flyvbjerg, B. (2001), *Making Social Science Matter: Why Social Inquiry Fails and How It Can Succeed Again*, Cambridge: Cambridge University Press.

Furubotn, E.G. and Richter, R. (2000) *Institutions and Economic Theory: The Contribution of the New Institutional Economics*, Ann Arbor, MI: The University of Michigan Press.

Galhofer, S. and Haslam, J. (1997) 'Beyond Accounting: The Possibilities of Accounting and "Critical" Accounting Research', *Critical Perspectives on Accounting* 8 (2): 71–95.

Gill, M. (2009) *Accountant's Truth: Knowledge and Ethics in the Financial World*, Oxford: Oxford University Press.

Graham, W.J. (1949) 'The Effect of Changing Price Levels upon the Determination, Reporting and Interpretation of Income', *The Accounting Review* 24 (1): 15–26.

Gray, S.J. (1988) 'Towards a Theory of Cultural Influence on the Development of Accounting Systems Internationally', *Abacus* 24 (1): 1–15.

Grey, C. (1998) 'On Being a Professional in a Big Six Firm', *Accounting, Organizations and Society* 23 (5/6): 569–87.

Groenewegen, J., Spithoven, A. and van den Berg, A. (2010), *Institutional Economics: An Introduction*, Basingstoke: Palgrave Macmillan.

Grossman, S.J. and Stiglitz, J.E. (1980) 'On the Impossibility of Informationally Efficient Markets', *American Economic Review* 41 (4): 549–65.

Hail, L., Leuz, C. and Wysocki, P. (2010) 'Global Convergence and the Potential Adoption of IFRS by the US (Part I): Conceptual Underpinnings and Economic Analysis', *Accounting Horizons* 24 (3), 355–94.

Hatfield, H.R. (1909) *Modern Accounting: Its Principles and Some of its Problems*, New York: D. Appleton and Company.

Hollis, M. (2002) *The Philosophy of Science: An Introduction*, rev. edn, Cambridge: Cambridge University Press.

Hopper, T. and Powell, A. (1985) 'Making Sense of Research into the Organizational and Social Aspects of Management Accounting: A Review of its Underlying Assumptions', *Journal of Management Studies* 22 (5): 429–65.

Hoque, Zahirul (2006) *Methodological Issues in Accounting Research: Theories and Methods,* London: Spiramus Press.

Hughes, W. and Lavery, J. (2008) *Critical Thinking: An Introduction to the Basic Skills*, 5th edn, Peterborough, Ontario: Broadview Press.

Hymer, S. (1970) 'The Efficiency (Contradictions) of Multinational Corporations', *American Economic Review* 60 (2): 441–8.

Inglis, D., with Thorpe, C. (2012), *An Invitation to Social Theory,* Cambridge: Polity Press.

IASB (2010) *The Conceptual Framework for Financial Reporting*, London: International Accounting Standards Board.

Jensen, M.C. (1983) 'Organization Theory and Methodology', *The Accounting Review* 58 (2): 319–39.

Knoops, C. (2010) *Verslaggevingstheorieën: Een wetenschapsfilosophische analyse* (Financial Reporting Theories: An Analysis from the Philosophy of Science), Erasmus University PhD Thesis (in Dutch), ISBN: 978-90-5335-285-4, Rotterdam: Proefschrift Erasmus Universiteit.

La Porta, R., Lopez-de-Silanes, F., Shleifer, A. and Vishny, R. (1997) 'Legal Determinants of External Finance', *Journal of Finance* 52: 1131–50.

La Porta, R., Lopez-de-Silanes, F., Shleifer, A. and Vishny, R. (2000) 'Investor Protection and Corporate Governance', *Journal of Financial Economics* 58: 3–27.

Laughlin, R. (1995) 'Empirical Research in Accounting: Alternative Approaches and a Case for "Middle Range" Thinking'. *Accounting, Auditing and Accountability Journal* 8 (1): 63–87.

Laughlin, R. (2004) 'Putting the Record Straight – Critique of "Methodology Choices and the Construction of Facts: Some Implications from the Sociology of Knowledge"', *Critical Perspectives on Accounting*, 15 (2): 261–77.

Lemos, N. (2007) *An Introduction to the Theory of Knowledge*. Cambridge: Cambridge University Press.

Leuz, C. (2010) 'Different Approaches to Corporate Reporting Regulation: How Jurisdictions Differ and Why', *Accounting and Business Research* 40 (3), 229–56.

Leuz, C., Nanda, D. and Wysocki, P.D. (2003) 'Earnings Management and Institutional Factors: An International Comparison', *Journal of Financial Economics* 69 (3): 505–27.

Mattli, W. and Büthe, T. (2005) 'Accountability in Accounting? The Politics of Private Rule Making in the Public Interest', *Governance: An International Journal of Policy, Administration and Institutions* 18 (3): 399–429.

Merino, B.D. and Neimark, M.D. (1982) 'Disclosure Regulation and Public Policy: A Sociohistorical Reappraisal', *Journal of Accounting and Public Policy* 1 (1): 33–57.

Merton, R.K. (1967) *On Theoretical Sociology: Five Essays Old and New*. New York: Free Press.

Meyer, P. E. (1973) 'The Accounting Entity' *Abacus* 9(2), 116–26.

Milanovic, B. (2011) *The Haves and the Have-Nots*, New York: Basic Books.

Miller, P. and O'Leary, T. (1987) 'Accounting and the Construction of the Governable Person', *Accounting, Organizations and Society* 12 (3): 235–65.

Mishkin, F.S. (2006) *The Next Great Globalization: How Disadvantaged Nations Can Harness Their Financial Systems to Get Rich*, Princeton, NJ: Princeton University Press.

Morley, M.F. (1979) 'The Value Added Statement in Britain', *The Accounting Review* 54 (3): 618–29.

Mueller, G.G. (1967) *International Accounting*, London: Macmillan.

Mueller, G.G., Gernon, H. and Meek, G.K. (2004) *Accounting: An International Perspective*, 3rd edn, Homewood, IL: Richard D. Irwin, Inc.

Murray, M. and Kujundzic, N. (2005), *Critical Reflection: A Textbook for Critical Thinking*, Kingston, Ontario: McGill-Queens University Press.

Niswonger, C.R. (1949) 'The Interpretation of Income in a Period of Inflated Prices', *The Accounting Review* 24 (1): 27–32.

Nobes, C.W. (1983) 'A Judgemental Classification of Financial Reporting Practices', *Journal of Business Finance and Accounting* 10 (1): 1–19.

Nobes, C.W. (1998) 'Towards a General Model of the Reasons for International Differences in Financial Reporting', *Abacus* 34 (2): 162–87.

Nobes, C. and Parker, R. (2010) *Comparative International Accounting*, 11th edn, Harlow: Pearson Education.

North, D.C. (1990) *Institutions, Institutional Change and Economic Performance*, Cambridge: Cambridge University press.

O'Byrne, D. (2011) *Introducing Sociological Theory*, Harlow: Pearson Education.

Paton, W.A. and Littleton, A.C. (1940) *An Introduction to Corporate Accounting Standards*, Sarrasota, FL: American Accounting Association.

Perry, A. and Nőlke, A. (2006) 'The Political Economy of International Accounting Standards', *Review of International Political Economy* 13 (4): 559–86.

Power, M. (1991) 'Educating Accountants: Towards a Critical Ethnography', *Accounting, Organizations and Society* 16 (4): 333–53.

Pritchard, D. (2010) *What is this Thing Called Knowledge?*, 2nd edn, London: Routledge.

Putnam, H. (1987) *The Many Faces of Realism* (in Bortolotti, 2008: 109), La Salle, IL: Open Court Publishing Company.

Reich, R. (2009) *Supercapitalism: The Battle for Democracy in an Age of Big Business*, London: Icon Books Ltd.

Riahi-Belkaoui, A. (2004) *Accounting Theory*, 5th edn, London: Thomson Learning.

Roberts, A. (1995) 'The Very Idea of Classification in International Accounting', *Accounting, Organizations and Society* 20 (7/8): 639–64.

Roslender, R. and Dillard, J.F. (2003) 'Reflections on the Interdisciplinary Perspectives on Accounting Project', *Critical Perspectives on Accounting* 14 (3): 325–51.

Ryan, B., Scapens, R.W. and Theobold, M. (2002) *Research Method and Methodology in Finance and Accounting*, 2nd edn, London: Thomson.

Sanders, T.H., Hatfield, H.R. and Moore, U. (1938) *A Statement of Accounting Principles*, New York: American Institute of Accountants.

Schroeder, R.G., Clark, M.W. and Cathey, J.M. (2001), *Financial Accounting Theory and Analysis*, 7th edn, New York: John Wiley and Sons.
Screpanti, E. and Zamagni, S. (2005) *An Outline of the History of Economic Thought*, 2nd edn, trans. David Field and Lynn Kirby, Oxford: Oxford University Press.
Singleton-Green, B. (2010) 'The Communication Gap: Why Doesn't Accounting Research Make a Greater Contribution to Debates on Accounting Policy?', *Accounting in Europe* 7(2): 129–45.
Solomons, D. (1991a) 'Accounting and Social Change: A Neutralist View', *Accounting, Organizations and Society* 16 (3): 287–95.
Solomons, D. (1991b) 'A Rejoinder', *Accounting, Organizations and Society* 16 (3): 311–12.
Someya, K. (1993) 'Accounting Standard Selection and its Socio-economic Consequences', *The International Journal of Accounting* 28: 93–103.
Sprouse, R.T. (1957) 'The Significance of the Concept of the Corporation in Accounting Analyses', *The Accounting Review*, 32 (3), 369–78.
Sprouse, R.T. and Moonitz, M. (1962) *A Tentative Set of Broad Accounting Principles*, Accounting Research Study No. 3, New York: American Institute of Certified Public Accountants.
Story, R.K. (1959) 'Revenue Realization, Going Concern and Measurement of Income', *The Accounting Review* 34 (2): 232–8.
Tinker, A.M. (1980) 'Towards a Political Economy of Accounting: An Empirical Illustration of the Cambridge Controversies', *Accounting, Organizations and Society* 5 (1): 147–60.
Tinker, A.M., Merino, B.D. and Neimark, M.D. (1982) 'The Normative Origins of Positive Theories: Ideology and Accounting Thought', *Accounting, Organizations and Society* 7 (2): 167–200.
Tinker, T. (1985) *Paper Prophets: A Social Critique of Accounting*. Eastbourne: Holt Rinehart and Winston.
Tinker, T. (1991) 'The Accountant as Partisan', *Accounting, Organizations and Society* 16(3): 297–310.
Veblen, T. (1899) *Theory of the Leisure Class: An Economic Study of Institutions*, New York: Macmillan.
Watts, R.L. and Zimmerman, J.L. (1978) 'Towards a Positive Theory of the Determination of Accounting Standards', *The Accounting Review* 53 (1), 112–34.
Watts, R.L. and Zimmerman, J.L. (1979) 'The Demand and Supply of Accounting Theories: The Market for Excuses', *The Accounting Review* 54 (2), 273–305.
Williamson, O.E. (1975) *Markets and Hierarchies*, New York: Free Press.
Worrall, J. (1989) 'Structural Realism: The Best of Both Worlds?', *Dialectica* 43 (1–2): 99–124.
Zeff, S.A. (1978) *A Critical Examination of the Orientation Postulate in Accounting With Particular Attention to its Historical Development*, New York: Arno Press.

3

Fundamental Issues in Financial Accounting and Reporting Theory

Carien van Mourik

1. Introduction

This chapter aims to outline different views on fundamental issues in financial accounting and reporting theory. Such fundamental questions include:

1. What is (or should be) the role of the reporting entity, capital markets and regulation in society?
2. What are (or should be) the objectives of financial accounting and external reporting in society?
3. How do we define and measure the reporting entity's performance so that this incentivises the managers of reporting entities and the participants in capital markets to best fulfil the roles outlined in (1) and financial reporting best meets the objectives defined in (2)?
4. What is (or should be) the role of the independent audit with respect to lending credibility to financial statements and annual reports?

Questions 1 and 2 require normative answers based on one's ideal view of society and the role of financial accounting and reporting in it. Answers to Question 3 will, therefore, depend on the normative answers to the first two questions. However, they are also determined by the a priori logic of financial accounting theory and the structure within which the concepts of performance, recognition, measurement, capital maintenance, financial statement presentation and disclosure form a coherent and internally consistent accounting and reporting model. As Gordon (1960: 606) put it: 'Given a definition of income, the next task is to derive the measurement rules in various transaction areas that follow from it.' The answers would then need to be corroborated by empirical evidence on the relation between the objectives and the outcomes produced and, if necessary, corrected. Similarly, Question 4 requires answers with partly normative, partly a priori analytical, but also partly empirically determined corroborative content.

After some forty years of dominance of empiricism and positivism in financial accounting and reporting research, questions with explicit moral, ideological, but also a priori analytical theoretical content have come to be avoided by mainstream accounting academics. These topics came to be considered 'unscientific' and, particularly junior academics might ruin their career prospects and publication chances by engaging with them. This happened first in the US (Williams, 2003) but increasingly researchers in other countries followed suit.

By the start of the new millennium, the fundamental questions in financial accounting and reporting appeared to have been settled on the basis of the technical competence and authority of members of private standard setting bodies such as the IASB and FASB, and public choice mechanisms rather than epistemic criteria. Schroeder *et al.* (2001) and Deegan and Unerman (2006) call this the conceptual framework approach and Riahi-Belkaoui (2004) calls it the regulatory approach to the formulation of an accounting theory.

However, in the increasingly internationalized environment of the second decade of the twenty-first century, the conceptual framework approach suffers from the following problems. For example, in spite of the different mandates of the FASB and the IASB, the IASB Conceptual Framework has, to a surprisingly large extent, been established by the same people. Like the FASB, the IASB is a private standard setting body of which the members must have technical competence and business experience. It is doubtful that technical competence and business experience are sufficient to settle accounting theoretical and conceptual questions of such great economic and social importance in an international context. Furthermore, the same due process applies to the conceptual framework as to IFRSs. This due process was not designed to protect the integrity of the search and justification of accounting theoretical concepts or knowledge of the impact the allocation of resources and the distribution of wealth and income. Furthermore, the answers in the FASB and IASB Conceptual Frameworks to questions regarding the role of financial accounting, reporting entities and their performance were determined based on the institutional environment of the USA in the 1970s (as described in FASB 1978: SFAC No. 1, Par. 9–16) and have not seriously been reconsidered when the IASC applied them to the world in 1989, the IASB inherited them in 2001, and again reconfirmed them in 2010.

This chapter will present an overview of different answers to the above four questions found in the financial accounting theory literature. Section 2 starts with two prior issues that pertain to the four questions, but warrant separate discussion: first, the choice for general purpose financial statements and, second, the structure and logic of financial accounting theory. Section 3 discusses different theories on the roles of the reporting entity and capital markets in society, and Section 4 outlines how different perspectives on the objectives of financial reporting translate into different concepts of performance. Section 5 contrasts different perspectives on performance measurement, and Section 6 discusses the consequences for the presentation and disclosure of income and capital in the financial statements. Section 7 briefly outlines some key issues that lead to different perspectives on the main function of the statutory audit. Section 8 concludes.

2. Prior issues

> The objective of general purpose financial reporting forms the foundation of the Conceptual Framework. Other aspects of the Conceptual Framework – a reporting entity concept, the qualitative characteristics of, and the constraint on, useful financial information, elements of financial statements, recognition, measurement, presentation and disclosure – flow logically from the objective (IASB, 2010: OB1).

Although the above statement intuitively makes sense, the IASB Conceptual Framework does not clearly spell out the logic according to which all the other elements follow from the objective of general purpose financial reporting. Furthermore, it treats the objective as a given, but in an international context building a conceptual framework on such an assumption requires conclusive evidence and careful justification. In this chapter, the role of reporting entities and capital markets in society comes prior to the objective of financial reporting, which in turn impacts the concept(s) of performance to be measured.

Historically, accounting regulators have focused on general purpose financial statements for the following reasons. First, particularly when accounting systems were still paper based, or computerized systems were clunky and inflexible, preparing different financial reports for different external users was considered too much of a burden on companies. Second, there was a fear that simultaneously preparing financial information on different accounting bases would endanger the continuity of financial reporting information and make it less comparable over time. Third, many jurisdictions used to adhere to the definite settlement of accounts principle; in other words, taxable income, distributable income and accounting income had to be the same. Even today, usually net income in the general purpose financial statements forms the basis for the calculation of income for distribution and taxable income.

The IASB, too, is concerned with general purpose financial reporting (IASB, 2010: OB2) which it interprets as information that helps the primary users, i.e. existing and potential investors, lenders and other creditors (ibid.: OB5) to assess the prospects for future net cash inflows to an entity (ibid.: OB3). For this purpose, investors need:

- information about economic resources and claims (OB13–14), in other words a balance sheet;
- information about changes in economic resources and claims which are the result of transactions and events (OB15–17) but also changes in market prices and interest rates (OB19), in other words a statement of comprehensive income that shows performance as derived from transactions as well as changes in market prices and interest rates (OB18);
- a cash flow statement showing operating, investing and financing cash flows (OB20); and
- a statement of changes in equity which gives insight into the causes of the changes in equity (OB21).

3. Functions of corporations and capital markets in society

Historically, the corporation had a social purpose so that towns, universities and guilds 'had a life beyond that of their members' (Micklethwait and Wooldridge, 2003: xvi), and early corporations had to be engaged in public works 'to be awarded the privilege of limited liability' (Micklethwait and Wooldridge, 2003: 46). Some consider the corporation a public creation to be governed by public law and regulation, which is supposed to act in the public interest. Others consider the corporation a private creation to be governed by the private law of contract (Dine, 2001: 13) with no other purpose than increasing the wealth of its owners (Post *et al.*, 2002: 8). The corporation's capacity to amass capital from multiple sources enabled sharing of risk, fixed capital formation and investment in research and development on an unprecedented scale.

3.1 Corporations, private property rights and externalities

Limited liability companies, and particularly those that are publicly held, are a double-edged sword. Demsetz (1967) argues that private property rights are one means to counter the negative externalities that are often the consequence of communal property. Like Demsetz, Hardin believed that private property rights form a solution, although this solution does not apply to public goods (Hardin, 1968: 1245). Becker (1977: 18–19) lists the following eleven elements that make up the 'full' or 'liberal' concept of ownership based on Honoré (1961: 107–47):

- the right to possess;
- the right to use;
- the right to manage;
- the right to the income;
- the right to the capital;
- the right to security from expropriation;
- the right to sell or bequeath the thing;
- the absence of term;
- the prohibition of harmful use;
- liability to execution (as repayment for debt); and
- residuary character.

However, 'people may be said to own things in various restricted senses which omit any one or more of the incidents' (Becker, 1977: 19).

In the case of the publicly held limited liability company, these private property rights have been modified in several ways. These correspond with the five core characteristics of corporations in (Armour *et al.*, 2009: Chapter 1), which include: legal personality, limited liability, transferable shares, centralized delegated management under a board structure, and absentee investor ownership. Consequences of these modifications include the agency costs resulting from the conflicting interests of and information asymmetry between:

- owners and management;
- majority shareholders and minority shareholders; and
- the firm (including its owners) and other contracting parties (Armour *et al.*, 2009: 36).

More generally, they will include the social costs resulting from misaligned private incentives and inadequate monitoring.

These modifications provide shareholders with protection against the external effects of de facto managerial ownership (Demsetz, 1967: 358). On the one hand, they are meant to serve society and induce economic growth by enabling risk sharing, fixed capital formation and technological development. On the other, these modifications to private property rights cause moral hazard potentially resulting in considerable social costs because they may reduce the shareholders' efficiency as monitors (Alchian and Demsetz, 1972: 789). Other modifications of private property rights, such as holding companies, special purpose entities and offshore entities, create endless opportunities for private gain at public expense.

3.2 Capital markets, corporations and financial reporting regulation

In essence, capital markets and corporations are meant to serve society and induce economic growth and job creation by enabling risk sharing, fixed capital formation, technological development, participation in and the development of commodities and other markets, and providing opportunities for investing savings and funds generated from other sources. Financial reporting is currently the means by which managers enable shareholders to discharge them from their stewardship obligations, provide accountability to other stakeholders and provide information to aid investors in their investment decisions. Financial accounting standards are necessary to ensure comparability across entities and over time.

Financial reporting regulation is, on the one hand, necessary to guarantee an amount of information that is enough to prevent capital markets from breaking down due to uninformed/ unsophisticated investors withdrawing as they feel that the odds are stacked against them. Such a withdrawal would 'deprive the economy of the allocational and risk sharing benefits of large and efficient capital markets' (Lev, 1988: 7). On the other hand, information must not be such that the market for information becomes efficient. Grossman and Stiglitz (1980: 404–5) showed that, in theory, informationally efficient capital markets will break down due to a lack of incentives to spend resources on gaining an information advantage and hence to trade on this advantage and to invest. Because higher efficiency implies lower equality and vice versa, accounting standard setting and regulation involves an incentives-equity trade-off, also called efficiency–equity trade-off (McAleese, 2001: 201) which can be regarded as political and moral rather than accounting technical or theoretical in nature.

One could argue, however, that solely focusing on financial information and the financial interests of investors may contribute to lower or the wrong type of economic productivity across the globe. One reason is that the financial focus encourages diverting financial, human, natural and other resources away from productive activity with higher social returns towards activities with higher private returns (Shleifer and Vishny, 1998: 56–7). Another is that the financial focus does not encourage economic decision-making with a view to economic, social and ecological sustainability.

3.3 Multinational corporations and regulatory arbitrage

In today's world where political globalization trails behind financial and economic globalization (Basu, 2011), an international accounting standard setter such as the IASB needs to investigate how the ability of multinational corporations to exploit institutional arbitrage would impact the purpose, nature and substance of international accounting standards and their application and enforcement. Leuz (2010) and Hail *et al.* (2010) point to the fact that ignoring institutional diversity and complementarities when setting international accounting standards may impose social costs upon those countries that have very different institutional environments from the one that the standards have been designed for.

Defining the boundaries of the reporting entity presents a challenge in financial accounting theory as well as national and international accounting standard setting and regulation (e.g. IASB, 2009). On the one hand, the reporting entity could be the same as the legal entity. The challenge here is to define the legal entity, particularly in the case of multinational enterprises, international organisations, holding companies, business combinations and special purpose entities. On the other, the principle of economic substance over legal form (CSRC, 1965: 363) which can apply to transactions as well as business and other entities would require a definition of the reporting entity as an economic entity. The main challenge here is twofold. First, 'substitution of the concept of the economic entity for that of the legal entity raises the problem of the scope of the consolidation' (Moonitz, 1942: 237)'. In other words, the boundaries of the reporting entity must be determined on an appropriate basis of economic substance which is either based on legal ownership or actual control. Second, it raises the issue of the treatment of minority interests (Moonitz, 1942: 241–2).

Businesses will use loopholes in the law to structure transactions and entities so as to respect the letter of the law, if not always the spirit, to produce economic and/or financial gains, avoid losses, or present a favourable image. Window dressing in the form of repurchasing agreements and structuring ownership so as to circumvent or meet the criteria for inclusion in the consolidated financial statements is not unheard of. These criteria are usually based on the concept of legal ownership of the entity or effective control over the entity's assets.

4. Objectives of external reporting

This section presents an overview of five perspectives on the objective of general purpose financial reporting and one broader external reporting perspective. The proprietary, entity and enterprise theories belong to a group called the equity theories, which can be seen as unsuccessful attempts at formulating a comprehensive theory of financial accounting and reporting. Starting from two very different perspectives on the social objective of financial accounting, proprietary and entity theory deductively come to different conclusions about how transactions would need to be recorded, summarized and disclosed in the financial statements. Enterprise theory holds that, in addition to profit and the book-value of capital, information about value added must be disclosed. Van Mourik (2010) presents an overview of the literature on and the unresolved issues in the equity theories. For other comparative overviews see Sprouse (1957), Gynther (1967), Meyer (1973) and Zeff (1978a, 1978b). The true income and informational perspectives represent attempts to avoid the normative question of from whose perspective to account. Finally, sustainability reporting represents a move away from the single focus on financial performance and instead regards performance as a multifaceted concept aimed at promoting economic, social and ecological sustainability.

4.1 Proprietary theory: stewardship and the determination of the owners' wealth

According to Merino (1993: 170), in the first half of the twentieth century proprietary theorists in the USA successfully used proprietary theory to defend shareholders against the threat 'that the corporate form could pose to private property rights'. Proprietary theorists such as Hatfield (1909), Sprague (1913), and Husband (1938, 1954), insisted that the accounting process of companies must be conducted from the shareholders' perspective. On the proprietary or agency view of the firm, the objective of financial accounting is to determine the increase in the wealth of the company's owners.

For example, Hatfield (1909: 195) describes the profit and loss account as a proprietorship account recording changes in net wealth and sees revenue and expense accounts as 'subsidiary "proprietorship" accounts'. Proprietary theory is therefore based on the idea that, in the case of corporations as in the case of sole proprietors, it is possible to make a sharp distinction between equity and liabilities. This essential distinction is made on the basis of differences in profit and loss participation between equity and liability holders, and differences in decision rights with respect to the assets of the firm (Sprague, 1907: 53). Staubus (1952, 1959) developed the residual equity theory, according to which accounting must be done from the perspective of the residual equity holders, which for a going concern coincides with that of the common shareholders. Residual equity theory is regarded by some as a more restrictive form of proprietary theory (Belkaoui, 2004: 215).

4.2 Entity theory: the determination of dividends, creditor protection and accountability to the general public

Entity theorists such as Gilman (1939), Paton and Littleton (1940), and Chow (1942) held that accounting must take the perspective of the entity because 'corporations are quasi-public institutions' (Paton and Littleton, 1940: 2) which have responsibilities to investors, wage earners, customers, the government and the general public. Later, entity theorists such as Seidman (1956), Raby (1959) and, in particular, Li (1960a, 1960b, 1961, 1963) were convinced that in practice the corporation is operated for the purpose of its own survival (Kam, 1990: 306; Meyer, 1973: 119). Either way, 'It is the imperative duty of management ... to strive for decisions based on a balanced consideration of all the rights involved' (Paton and Littleton, 1940: 3). Entity theory views the entity as having a separate existence from its shareholders with whom it has an arm's-length relationship. This relationship is regarded as not particularly different from that to the long-term creditors (Lorig, 1964: 566).

4.3 Enterprise theory: accountability for value added to society

Suojanen's (1954, 1958) enterprise theory or social theory extended Paton and Littleton's notion that companies have become institutions in their own right. Suojanen argued that companies must account from the perspective of the entity which is accountable to society at large for the value added it produces and for how this value added is distributed. Suojanen proposed that large companies prepare a value added statement in addition to the balance sheet and income statement so that its operations can be 'assessed in terms of its contribution to the *flow* of output of the community' [Italics in original] (Suojanen, 1954: 395).

4.4 The true income paradigm: true income meets the needs of all users

The above three theories have in common a normative assumption on the social objective of financial accounting and external reporting. In an attempt to avoid the normative question of whom to account for, the true income paradigm is aimed at identifying an 'ideal income' measure that would meet the needs of all users. Riahi-Belkaoui (2004: 339–41) mentions the following examples of scholars who used a deductive approach to identifying the properties that 'ideal income' should have: Paton (1922), Canning (1929), Sweeney (1936), MacNeal (1939), Moonitz (1961), Edwards and Bell (1961) and Sprouse and Moonitz (1962). Others mentioned by Beaver (1998: 2–3) include Paton and Littleton (1940), Chambers (1966) and Sterling (1970).

On the one hand, there are the scholars who see accounting income as the true income concept owing to the objectivity of measurement at historical cost. For example Paton and Littleton (1940) focused on the matching concept, the realization concept and the objectivity of measurement at historical cost as the means to determine true accounting income.

On the other, scholars advocated current value approaches. For example, Edwards and Bell (1961) advocated the concept of business income based on measurement at replacement cost, i.e. entry prices. The business income model computes:

> a segregated income measure for the period of reporting, but it also enables traditional accounting income to be derived from it by eliminating unrealized holding gains and adding realized holding gains accrued in previous periods (Lee, 1985: 77).

If a financial capital maintenance concept is adopted, realized and unrealized cost savings, inventory holdings and capital gains of the period concerned will be treated as income. However, this would change in the case of a physical capital maintenance concept where only operating profit would count as income (Lee, 1985: 86).

Chambers (1966) and Sterling (1970) developed the idea of realizable income based on 'measurement of the periodic change in the capital of an entity when this is measured in exit value terms' (Lee, 1985: 93). Realizable income consists of realized and unrealized gains whereby any increase in wealth is treated as income (Lee, 1985: 102). However, Chambers' system of continuously contemporary accounting (CoCoA) includes a capital adjustment to account for changes in general purchasing power in the form of a capital maintenance reserve which is part of shareholders' equity (Deegan and Unerman, 2006: 147).

A third current value approach is current cost accounting based on deprival value or value to the business. The deprival value of an asset is either its net replacement cost or the recoverable amount. Unrealized value to the business changes and income statement provisions are transferred to a current cost reserve and then transferred to the income statement upon realization. The use of mixed values causes some to doubt the meaningfulness of the aggregate valuation of the capital figure (Lee, 1985: 109–20).

The idea was that income based on current values would be closest to the 'ideal income' measure, which was assumed to be economic income (Beaver, 1998: 3). Economic income is the change in the present value of future cash flows from one period to the next measured under conditions of certainty (Lee, 1985: 31).

4.5 The informational perspective: helping investors assess the amounts, timing and certainty of future cash flows

The American Institute of Certified Public Accountants (AICPA)'s *Accounting Research Study No. 3* (Sprouse and Moonitz, 1962), the Accounting Principles Board's *APB Statement No. 4* (AICPA, 1970), and the American Accounting Association's *A Statement of Basic Accounting Theory* (ASOBAT) (AAA, 1966) represented major steps through which in the late 1960s the objectives of financial reporting increasingly came to be defined from the informational perspective. In 1978 it was adopted by the FASB in their *Statement of Financial Accounting Concepts No. 1* (FASB, 1978). The IASB Conceptual Framework (IASB, 2010: OB2) is a more recent and international example of defining the objective of financial reporting in terms of the informational perspective.

Beaver (1998: 4) claims that the ensuing shift away from a focus on determining earnings towards a focus on the prediction of cash flows was partly due to an inability to reach a consensus on the 'best' method of reporting income. A second factor was the 'trend in security analysis . . . away from earnings-oriented valuation approaches to discounted cash flow approaches' (Beaver, 1998: 5). As a consequence, the main type of financial statement user is assumed to be the investors who invest in securities primarily for the purpose of maximizing their investment returns rather than shareholders aiming for a stable stream of dividends. Furthermore, information that serves investors is assumed to serve other users as well.

ASOBAT, which not only focused on the usefulness of accounting information for 'making decisions concerning the use of limited resources', also introduced four what we now call 'qualitative characteristics' (relevance, verifiability, freedom from bias and quantifiability) as criteria for the evaluation of accounting information (AAA, 1966: Chapter 2). This approach is still used today by the FASB and the IASB in their respective conceptual frameworks.

According to Scott (1997: 4), whose financial accounting theory textbook is based on information economics, the fundamental problem of financial accounting theory is how to reconcile the different roles of accounting information in one income number, 'the bottom line'. This is, however, only a problem if one is committed to general purpose financial statements. Information economics sees only two primary roles of accounting information. First, financial reporting acts as a mechanism to mitigate the adverse selection problem caused by information asymmetry between managers and prospective as well as current investors. Second, accounting net income is a measure of managerial performance which acts to mitigate the moral hazard problem caused by information asymmetry between managers and current shareholders. Net income serves both as an input in executive compensation contracts and it serves to inform the securities and managerial labour markets so that these can function more efficiently (Scott, 1997: 3–4).

Other perspectives on the quality of accounting information generated by the information perspective involve the quantification of earnings quality. This can be in terms of value-relevance of earnings (assessing the statistical association of accounting earnings measures with market value, i.e. stock price), the time-series behaviour of earnings (its statistical properties such as persistence and smoothness), and its predictive value. Dechow *et al.* (2010) provides a very informative literature review on the topic of earnings quality.

4.6 Sustainability reporting

Parallel to discussions in economics about the merit of using only financial measures of economic performance such as GDP, this question has also arisen in accounting and external reporting with respect to the performance of businesses, and especially large multinational corporations. Some considered the idea of total impact accounting, that is, the idea that externalities would need to be included in the financial statements. Early attempts at accounting for externalities by Abt (1977) and Estes (1976) were heavily criticized by Benston (1982: 97), who claimed that the measurement of social costs and benefits is 'beyond the ability or province of accountants'. He believed that measuring corporate performance using both private and public costs and benefits is 'conceptually impossible' and '*cannot* be attained, now or ever' [Italics in original] (Benston, 1982: 97). Rappaport (1977) and Zeff (1978a, 1978b) brought to attention the socio-economic consequences of accounting policies.

Social responsibility reporting and environmental impact reporting also developed since the 1970s but as the ideological climate changed in the 1980s and 1990s, these ideas did not make it into the mainstream ideas about performance and importance for economic decision making. However, as serious ecological and social damage appears to be done by humans making short-term decisions either in their own or in what they perceive to be the public interest, sustainability reporting might just be what we need to create incentives for more responsible decisions and actions by managers, investors, policy makers, regulators and the general public.

5. Concepts of income and capital

Accounting entities that strictly operate on a cash basis and that have little or no capital expenditure (investments in non-current assets) will measure their performance as the net increase or decrease in cash during a period. Cash accounting will be sufficient for only the tiniest of businesses which will likely be sole traders, but is also used in clubs, some not-for-profit entities, and at the other end of the scale in national accounts (the accounts of countries). All other entities operating as going concerns will be faced with, what Thomas (1969, 1974) called 'the allocation problem in financial accounting theory'. This section first explains what the allocation problem is and how it impacts on performance measurement. It then sets out different concepts of performance and approaches to income measurement.

5.1 Performance measurement and the allocation problem in accounting

The allocation problem is really three problems instead of one. First, there is the problem of how to allocate revenues and expenses to a period in order to determine performance for the period (i.e. how to determine accounting income). Second, there is the question of whether or not to include unrealized gains and losses in the measure of performance. If not, this measure of performance would be called net profit or net income, and if unrealized gains and losses are included it would nowadays be called comprehensive income. The final question is whether or not to include changes in the value of intangible assets (or goodwill) during the period. If changes in the value of goodwill are included the measure of performance is called economic income. See Solomons' reconciliation of accounting income to economic income (Solomons, 1961: 376).

5.2 The transactions approach to income determination

What we could call 'archetypical[1] accounting income' is determined using the transactions approach. The transactions approach sees performance as income earned from the transactions and productive efforts of a reporting entity during a period where the entity is assumed to be a going concern. It is also called the income statement or revenue–expense approach to the determination of income. The archetypical accounting income concept does not include unrealized gains and losses. It defines assets as unexpired costs, values all assets and liabilities on the balance sheet at historical cost, and recognizes revenues on the basis of the realization principle and expenses on the basis of the matching principle.

The transactions approach is consistent with Schmalenbach's dynamic balance sheet where the activa (= items on the assets side of the balance sheet) include: cash, payments – not yet expenses, payments – not yet receipts, revenues – not yet expenses, and revenues – not yet receipts, and the passiva (= items on the liabilities side of the balance sheet) include: capital, expenses – not yet payments, receipts – not yet payments, expenses – not yet revenues, and receipts – not yet revenues (Flower, 1996: 178; see also Chapter 3 of this book). The transactions approach is consistent with Paton and Littleton's (1940) idea of expenses as expired and assets as unexpired costs.

Most theorists have not defined the archetypical accounting income described above because they had to make compromises in response to challenges reality throws up. Therefore, in the case of unrealized gains or losses on inventory, the lower-of-cost-or-market valuation was deemed acceptable on the basis of prudence. Others, for example Dicksee (1903: 5) in the UK and Hatfield (1909: 81) in the US, distinguished between the valuation of permanent assets at cost and circulating assets at current values (in Storey, 1959: 235–6). Unfortunately, the transactions approach had its obvious limitations for capital maintenance purposes in periods of moderate to high inflation (e.g. Graham, 1949; Niswonger, 1949). Therefore, inflation presented another challenge for the transactions approach, which required adjustments for the purpose of capital maintenance. A third problem for the transactions approach comes in the form of long-term contracts for which revenues and expenditures require matching which invites the abuse of accounting policy. A fourth problem is presented in the forms of accounting for speculative transactions, hedging, futures and other financial instruments where using historical cost is often not very meaningful (Whittington, 2005: 138–9). A similar challenge comes in the form of off balance sheet financing such as leasing, derivative transactions and financial instruments.

Hence, some theorists advocate the use of current cost, replacement cost or net present value in some cases and stick to historical cost in others. One problem for them is that income is determined and the assets and liabilities in the balance sheet shown on a mixed attributes basis, which is likely to hamper comparability and according to Chambers (1998) goes against the logic of measurement. Another problem is what to do with the unrealized gains and losses arising upon valuation. The transactions approach would show these in a revaluation reserve in the equity section of the balance sheet. In other words, the equity section will then show a dirty surplus.

As the transactions approach regards the income statement as the main financial statement and the balance sheet as a place for rest posts (see also Chapter 3) in the determination of periodic income, dirty surplus is not considered a problem. For this reason, the transactions approach to the determination of income is compatible with the objectives of financial reporting in accordance with entity theory and enterprise theory. It could fit with the stewardship objective as per proprietary theory to the extent that the relationship between the business and shareholders is a long-term one, that is, the entity must be a going concern and the shareholders' aim must be a return in the form of stable dividends. Performance measurement is expressed as earnings.

Critics pointed to the practice of using arbitrary reserves for income smoothing and earnings manipulation purposes. Sprouse (1966) criticized the existence of what-you-may-call-its in the balance sheet and, according to Basu and Waymire (2010), prodded the FASB towards the balance sheet approach. Solomons (1995) vocally proclaimed the conceptual primacy of the balance sheet and was an advocate of economic income because of the so-called objectivity of market prices. Others complained about the lack of relevance for investment decision-making of information based on historical costs (AICPA, 1973: 15–16).

5.3 The valuation approach to the determination of income

The 'archetypical valuation approach' defines performance and measures income as the increase in wealth (= net assets at current values) from one period to the next, and does include unrealized gains and losses in the determination of income for the period. It sees performance as an all inclusive income concept determined using the balance sheet approach (also called assets–liabilities or capital maintenance approach to income measurement) expressed as comprehensive income (Kieso *et al.*, 2004: 127 n.5). Consequently, it crucially depends on precise definitions and measurement (valuation) of assets and liabilities. Although, in principle, measurement of all the assets and liabilities in the balance sheet at historical cost is possible, the valuation approach would logically require valuation at the current sales price in an active market or, if that is not available, the replacement cost.

Although some appear to see the valuation approach and the economics approach to the determination as the same thing, this is not necessarily true. Economic income is a subjective income concept that includes subjective goodwill (Solomons, 1961). According to Lee (1985: 31), when measured under conditions of certainty, it is also termed 'ideal income'. Although many have argued for the inclusion of internally generated intangible assets and some for the inclusion of intangible liabilities in the balance sheet in order to reduce the difference in book and market values of net assets, subjectivity goes against objectivity and verifiability as the spirit of financial reporting.

Problems arising with the valuation approach start with the question whether to define 'fair market value' as entry value, exit value or value in use (Barth and Landsman, 1995: 101–2). They also include the difficulty of obtaining market values because markets for many assets and liabilities in the balance sheet are not equally active (and efficient) (Bromwich, 2007). As a consequence, market prices or current prices may not be established reliably, which introduces an element of arbitrariness and moral hazard into the valuation process (Ronen, 2008: 186). Similarly, there is the controversial issue of 'own credit risk' where, as the entity's financial condition worsens the fair value of an entity's liabilities declines, this decrease is accounted for as a gain in the entity's income statement. See, for example, the IASB (2009) discussion paper *Credit Risk in Liability Measurement*. Finally, the question arises whether or not valuation applies to individual assets and liabilities, or groups also called cash generating units (see also Chapter 7).

As the balance sheet is considered the main financial statement, the determination of income as a measure of performance becomes a secondary aim. The equity section of the balance sheet must obey the clean–surplus relation if the increase in net assets is the measure of performance. For this reason, the valuation approach to the determination of income is compatible with the objectives of financial reporting in accordance with proprietary theory if the entity is not a going concern because the liquidation basis of accounting requires valuation at current sales values. In the case of a going concern, the reporting objective could be in accordance with the true income paradigm and the informational perspective to the extent that the markets for all the assets and liabilities in the balance sheets are complete and efficient. Market imperfections present a problem for the valuation approach to the determination of income because this introduces scope for moral hazard (manipulating asset and liability values and using off balance sheet financing and special purpose vehicles to misrepresent financial position and risk exposure) and estimation errors.

5.4 Dual concepts of performance

Dualistic approaches to performance measurement do not place conceptual primacy on either the income statement or the balance sheet, but give equal weight to the determination of income and the correct measurement of capital. These are different from the mixed attributes approaches to measurement as a result of compromises outlined above. Examples include: in Germany, Moxter's dual approach, which will be discussed in Chapter 4; in Japan, the released-from-risk recognition concept in the 2006 Accounting Standards Board of Japan's Conceptual Framework (ASBJ, 2006); and in IFRS the 'amortized cost' and 'fair value through profit and loss' and 'fair value through equity' approaches for different classes of assets and liabilities. The released-from-risk recognition concept takes into consideration managerial intention for assets and liabilities (not unlike the three-tier system for financial instruments in IAS 39) as well as the characteristics of the market for the assets or liabilities to be valued (again, not unlike the IAS 39 three-tier system) when recognizing income and increases in the value of shareholders' capital (ASBJ, 2006).

5.5 Multidimensional concepts of performance: value added, triple bottom line, economic, social and ecological sustainability

Thus far, our discussion of periodic performance measurement has been limited to income (be it net cash inflow, accounting, comprehensive or economic income) as a measure of performance. In parallel to developments in economics where the question is raised whether gross national product (GNP) is still an appropriate measure of national economic performance, in financial accounting, too, the question is raised whether income should not be measured including externalities or should be supplemented with other measures of performance that give due recognition to economic, social and ecological sustainability.

Suojanen's (1954, 1958) enterprise theory is associated with the introduction of a value-added statement. Value added statements have been used in Britain, Germany, South Africa and other countries since the 1970s. The value added statement shows the sources of net income and how value added has been distributed to employees, lenders, the government, minority interests and shareholders (Morley, 1979). Unfortunately, value added can be defined as net value added (after deducting depreciation) and gross value added (before deducting depreciation), and discretion exists as to the treatment of taxation (Burchell *et al.*, 1985: 387–90). Although meant as a social performance measure which could help to reduce conflict between the variety of stakeholders and introduce value added-based incentive schemes, calculative diversity and confusion about the benefits created a decline in the disclosure of and interest in value added statements in Britain in the early 1980s (Burchell *et al.*, 1985: 405).

Triple bottom line reporting, environmental reporting, total reporting, and other initiatives have been developed with the idea that performance is not only economic performance. Unfortunately, this is a complicated area because concepts need to be clearly defined and measurement developed, and securities, accounting and other regulators do not seem inclined to commit themselves to broadening their idea of performance. Chapter 26 discusses some of the issues involved.

6. Presentation and disclosure in the financial statements

Researchers who believed in the efficient markets hypothesis thought that issues regarding the presentation and disclosure of information in the financial statements or in the notes or in supplementary schedules were irrelevant. If capital markets were efficient in the semi-strong form, users of financial statements would not be fooled by the form in which the information was presented or where the information appeared as long as it was disclosed in the annual reports or elsewhere. This led to the development of the full disclosure principle which requires that 'no information of substance or of interest to the average investor will be omitted or concealed' (Riahi-Belkaoui, 2004: 225). However, empirical evidence regarding the efficiency of the US capital market is inconclusive, and in the case of many other capital markets it is clear that they are not efficient. Financial statement preparers did not require empirical evidence about the average investor to know that investors and analysts can be misled by the way information is presented. Furthermore, full disclosure has led to the problem of the disclosure of too much information (i.e. information overload).

6.1 Articulation or non-articulation

Thus far, standard setters have required the preparation and disclosure of financial statements that articulate because '[f]inancial statements are fundamentally related' (AICPA, 1970: Par. 35). For example, the income statement explains the change in the retained earnings account in the statement of changes in equity. The statement of changes in equity details which changes in equity derive from transactions with shareholders, which changes derive from the entity's performance, and which changes derive from changes in market prices. The cash flow statement reconciles the balances on the cash account at the beginning and the end of a period. Finally, the income statement and the cash flow statement can be reconciled via the accruals.

'An example of the non-articulated view would be the use of LIFO in the income statement and of FIFO in the balance sheet' (Riahi-Belkaoui, 2004: 175). Although, in the past, some have criticized the articulation requirement as unduly restrictive (AICPA, 1973: 16; Black, 1993; Cearns *et al.*, 1999: 54–6), non-articulation amounts to reducing the information value of accruals because the reconciliation between cash flow statement and income statement will no longer work as intended. Articulation of the financial statements is essential in preserving the continuity and comparability of information from one period to the next.

6.2 Income statement, cash flow statement and statement of changes in equity

The current operating concept of income and the dirty surplus relation with equity have already been discussed in relation to entity theory and the transactions approach to income measurement. Similarly, the all-inclusive concept of income and the clean surplus relation with equity have been discussed in relation to proprietary theory and the valuation approach to income measurement. As we currently live with a mixed measurement and mixed recognition model, IFRS requires a comprehensive income statement where net income, other comprehensive income (OCI) and comprehensive income are disclosed separately.

For some items IFRS require recycling from OCI to net income upon realisation and for others it does not allow recycling. The principle behind this distinction is not clear. However, for those who take a valuation perspective, recycling amounts to double counting of comprehensive income. On the other hand, to those who lean towards the transactions approach, not recycling OCI to net income upon realization amounts to fudging net income, not respecting the distinction between income and capital, and adopting a non-articulation view. The reason is that in this case the cash flow statement can no longer be prepared using the indirect approach, reconciling net profit to net cash generated from operations. Although Cearns *et al.* (1999) were aware of this consequence, they believed that the necessary information was readily available from the cash flow statement and recommended using the direct approach as a conceptually superior method for preparing the cash flow statement.

6.3 Statement of comprehensive income

For the purpose of predicting future income and future cash flows it is usually better to have less variable numbers to work with. Hence, in principle, an income statement can be presented in multiple steps where gross profit and operating income are the least variable and shown separately from extraordinary gains and losses. Net income will be more variable as it includes non-recurrent or extraordinary gains and losses. With the IASB's introduction of the comprehensive income statement in 2007, profit for the year is shown after finance costs, share of profit of associates, income tax expense and profit or loss from discontinued operations. It then showed the elements of other comprehensive income (OCI) to arrive at comprehensive income at the bottom line. An amendment to IAS 1 in 2011 required a new presentation that separates the OCI items that will not be recycled from OCI items that may be recycled. The conceptual basis for this classification has still not been addressed.

Comprehensive income includes changes in market prices that have not even been realized. Empirical tests of the persistence and value relevance of OCI and comprehensive income get mixed results (e.g. Jones and Smith, 2011). However, there would be no reason not to disclose both as long as the conceptual basis and the recycling issue are clear.

6.4 Balance sheet

Balance sheets can be presented in a horizontal or a vertical format either in order of increasing or decreasing liquidity. In the UK, a specific version of the vertical format, the net assets format, has been used for many years. The horizontal format is most compatible with the entity theory because it does not give priority to any of the providers of funds on the liabilities side of the balance sheet, whereas the net assets format is most compatible with proprietary theory because it shows equity as equal to net assets. Furthermore, the horizontal balance sheet format shows working capital as current assets balanced by current liabilities, whereas the net assets format shows current assets less current liabilities, i.e. the net working capital of the business.

7. The statutory audit

Financial statements and financial reporting can be seen as mechanisms in the service of corporate governance. For this purpose, it is important that there is an audit trail and that the information in the financial statements can be verified and understood as being in accordance with the pertinent standards and regulations. The statutory audit plays a crucial role in helping financial statements fulfil their corporate governance function by giving the information credibility. Surprisingly, financial accounting standard setters do not routinely make auditability an issue of concern when setting accounting standards. Hopefully, this is something that will change in the future.

The first fundamental issue with respect to the theory and practice of auditing is the fact that it is a three party economic arrangement.

> In simple terms, management uses owners' money to hire auditors to provide a stamp of approval on management's reports on its own performance to owners. There is no basis for expecting that such an arrangement will satisfactorily serve either society in general or the investing public in particular (Staubus, 2005: 9).

The second issue, which is related to the first, is the fact that there is a discrepancy between what the public expects from the audit function and what auditors regard as their responsibility, i.e. the audit expectations gap. Chapter 9 outlines the main issues in auditing and Chapter 19 discusses auditing and international financial reporting.

8. Conclusion

At the end of this chapter, it will be clear that there may not be any definitive answers to any of the four fundamental questions. However, this must not deter accounting researchers from the wide variety of institutional environments in the world from engaging with the fundamental issues in financial accounting and reporting theory. National standard setters, but also those involved in developing international conceptual frameworks and international financial reporting standards, must deal with these issues, with or without academic research to help them.

Notes

1 Archetypical is used here as a model, not as an actual income determination approach used in practice.

Bibliography

AAA (1966) *A Statement of Basic Accounting Theory*, Evanston, IL: American Accounting Association.

AAA (2009) 'Response to the FASB's Preliminary Views on Financial Instruments with the Characteristics of Equity', *Accounting Horizons*, 23 (1), 85-100.

Abt, C.C. (1977) *The Social Audit for Management*, New York: Amacon.

AICPA (1970) *APB Statement No. 4: Basic Concepts and Accounting Principles Underlying Financial Statements of Business Enterprises*, New York: American Institute of Certified Public Accountants.

AICPA (1973) *Objectives of Financial Statements*, New York: American Institute of Certified Public Accountants.

Alchian, A.A. and Demsetz, H. (1972) 'Production, Information Costs and Economic Organization', *The American Economic Review*, 62 (5), 777–95.

Armour, J., Hansmann, H. and Kraakman, R. (2009) 'Chapter 1: What is Corporate Law?' *The Anatomy of Corporate Law: A Comparative and Functional Approach*, 2nd edn, Oxford: Oxford University Press.

ASBJ (2006) 'Conceptual Framework of Financial Accounting' (Accounting Standards Board of Japan) Discussion Paper, tentative English translation, 16 March 2007, available at www.asb.or.jp/asb/asb_e/asbj/begriff/ConceptualFramework200612.pdf (accessed 28 March 2013)

Barth, M.E. and Landsman, W.R. (1995) 'Fundamental Issues Related to Using Fair Value Accounting for Financial Reporting', *Accounting Horizons* 9 (4): 97–107.

Basu, K. (2011) *Beyond the Invisible Hand: Groundwork for a New Economics*, Princeton, NJ: Princeton University Press.

Basu, S. and Waymire, G.B. (2010) 'Sprouse's What-You-May-Call-Its: Fundamental Insight or Monumental Mistake?', available at http://ssrn.com/abstract=1583068 or http://dx.doi.org/10.2139/ssrn.1583068

Beaver, W.H. (1998) *Financial Reporting: An Accounting Revolution*, 3rd edn, Upper Saddle River, NJ: Prentice Hall.

Becker, L.C. (1977) *Property Rights: Philosophic Foundations*, London: Routledge & Kegan Paul.

Belkaoui, A.R. (2004) *Accounting Theory*, Jakarta: Salemba Empat

Benston, G.J. (1982) 'Accounting and Corporate Accountability', *Accounting, Organizations and Society*, 7 (2), 87–105.

Black, F. (1993) 'Choosing Accounting Rules', *Accounting Horizons* 7 (1): 1–17.

Bromwich, M. (2007) 'Fair Values: Imaginary prices and Mystical Markets, A Clarificatory Review', in Walton, P. (ed.) *The Routledge Companion to Fair Value and Financial Reporting*, London: Routledge, pp. 46–67.

Burchell, S., Clubb, C. and Hopwood, A.G. (1985) 'Accounting in its Social Context: Towards a History of Value Added in the United Kingdom', *Accounting, Organizations and Society*, 10 (4): 381–413.

Canning, John B. (1929) *The Economics of Accountancy*, New York: The Ronald Press Company.

Cearns, K., Australian Accounting Standards Board, Canadian Accounting Standards Board, International Accounting Standards Committee, New Zealand Financial Reporting Standards Board, United Kingdom Accounting Standard Board, United States Financial Accounting Standard Board (1999) 'Reporting Financial Performance: Proposals for Change' (G4 + 1 Position Paper) available at www.frc.org.uk/Our-Work/Publications/ASB/Reporting-Financial-Performance-Proposals-for-Chan.aspx (accessed 11 March 2013).

Chambers, R.J. (1966) *Accounting, Evaluation and Economic Behavior*, Englewood Cliffs, NJ: Prentice Hall.

Chambers, R.J. (1998) 'Wanted: Foundations of Accounting Measurement', *Abacus*, 34 (1): 36–47.

Chow, Y.C. (1942) 'The Doctrine of Proprietorship', *The Accounting Review*, 17 (2): 157–63.

CSRC (1965) 'The Entity Concept' (author is 1964 Concepts and Standards Research Committee – The Business Entity Concept, of the AAA), *The Accounting Review*, 40 (2): 358–67.

Dechow, P., Ge, W. and Schrand, C. (2010) 'Understanding Earnings Quality: A Review of the Proxies, Their Determinants and Their Proxies', *Journal of Accounting and Economics*, 50 (2/3): 344–401.

Deegan, Craig and Unerman, Jeffrey (2006) *Financial Accounting Theory*, European edn, Maidenhead: McGraw-Hill Education.

Demsetz, H. (1967) 'Toward a Theory of Property Rights', *American Economic Review*, 57 (2), 347–59.

Dicksee, L.R. (1903) *Advanced Accounting* (reference in Storey, 1959), London: Gee and Co.

Dine, J. (2001) *Company Law*, London: Sweet and Maxwell.

Edwards, E.O. and Bell, P.W. (1961) *The Theory and Measurement of Business Income*, Berkeley, CA: University of California Press.

Estes, R. (1976) *Corporate Social Accounting*, New York: John Wiley & Sons.

FASB (1978) *Statement of Financial Accounting Concepts No. 1* (FASB), Norwalk, CT: Financial Accounting Standards Board.

Flower, J. (1996) 'Schmalenbach, Zappa and Limperg: Three "Accounting Heroes" of Continental Europe', in Lapseley, I. (ed.) *Essays in Accounting Thought: A Tribute to WT Baxter*, Edinburgh: Institute of Chartered Accountants of Scotland, pp. 173–92.

Gilman, S. (1939) *Accounting Concepts of Profit*, New York: The Ronald Press Company.

Gordon, M.J. (1960) 'Scope and Method of Theory and Research in the Measurement of Income and Wealth', *The Accounting Review*, 35 (4): 603–18.

Graham, W.J. (1949) 'The Effect of Changing Price Levels Upon the Determination, Reporting and Interpretation of Income', *The Accounting Review*, 24 (1): 15–26.

Grossman, S.J. and Stiglitz, J.E. (1980) 'On the Impossibility of Informationally Efficient Markets', *American Economic Review*, 70 (3): 393–408.

Gynther, R. S. (1967) 'Accounting Concepts and Behavioral Hypotheses', *The Accounting Review*, 42 (2): 274–90.

Hail, L., Leuz, C., and Wysocki, P. (2010) 'Global Convergence and the Potential Adoption of IFRS by the US (Part I): Conceptual Underpinnings and Economic Analysis', *Accounting Horizons*, 24 (3), 355–94.

Hardin, G. (1968) 'The Tragedy of the Commons', *Science*, 162 (3859), 1243–8.

Hatfield, H.R. (1909) *Modern Accounting: Its Principles and Some of its Problems*, New York: D. Appleton and Company.

Honoré, A.M. (1961) 'Ownership', in Guest, A.G. (ed.) *Oxford Essays in Jurisprudence*, Oxford: Clarendon Press.

Husband, G.R. (1938) 'The Corporate-Entity Fiction and Accounting Theory', *The Accounting Review*, 13 (3), 241–53.

Husband, G.R. (1954) 'The Entity Concept in Accounting', *The Accounting Review*, 29 (4), 552–63.

IASB (2009) *Discussion Paper: Credit Risk in Liability Measurement*, London: International Accounting Standards Board.

IASB (2010) *The Conceptual Framework for Financial Reporting*, London: International Accounting Standards Board.

Jones, D.A. and Smith, K.A. (2011) 'Comparing the Value Relevance, Predictive Value and Persistence of Other Comprehensive Income and Special Items', *The Accounting Review*, 86 (6): 2047–73.

Kam, V. (1990) *Accounting Theory*, New York: John Wiley & Sons.

Kieso, D.E., Weygandt, J.J. and Warfield, T.D. (2004), *Intermediate Accounting*, 11th edn, New York: John Wiley & Sons.

Lee, T.A. (1985) *Income and Value Measurement: Theory and Practice*, 3rd edn, London: Chapman & Hall.

Leuz, C. (2010) 'Different Approaches to Corporate Reporting Regulation: How Jurisdictions Differ and Why', *Accounting and Business Research*, 40 (3), 229–56.

Lev, B. (1988) 'Toward a Theory of Equitable and Efficient Accounting Policy' *The Accounting Review*, 63 (1), 1–22.

Li, D. H. (1960a) 'The Nature of Corporate Residual Equity Under the Entity Concept', *The Accounting Review*, 35 (2): 258–63.

Li, D. H. (1960b) 'The Nature and Treatment of Dividends Under the Entity Concept', *The Accounting Review*, 35 (4): 674–79.

Li, D. H. (1961) 'Income Taxes and Income Tax Allocation Under the Entity Concept', *The Accounting Review*, 36 (2): 265–68.

Li, D. H. (1963) 'Alternative Accounting Procedures and the Entity Concept', *The Accounting Review*, 38 (1): 52–5.

Li, D. H. (1964) 'The Objectives of the Corporation Under the Entity Concept', *The Accounting Review*, 39 (3): 946–50.

Lorig, A. N. (1964) 'Some Basic Concepts of Accounting and Their Implications', *The Accounting Review*, 39 (3): 563–73.

McAleese, D. (2001) *Economics for Business: Competition, Macro-stability and Globalization*, 2nd edn, Harlow: Pearson Education.

MacNeal, K. (1939) *Truth in Accounting*, Philadephia, PA: University of Pennsylvania Press.

Merino, B.D. (1993) 'An Analysis of the Development of Accounting Knowledge: A Pragmatic Approach', *Accounting, Organizations and Society*, 18 (2/3): 163–85.

Meyer, P. E. (1973) 'The Accounting Entity', *Abacus*, 9(2), 116–26.

Micklethwait, J. and Wooldridge, A. (2003) *The Company: A Short History of a Revolutionary Idea*, New York: Random House, Inc.

Moonitz, M. (1942) 'The Entity Approach to Consolidated Statements', *The Accounting Review*, 17: 236–42.

Moonitz, M. (1961) *The Basic Postulates of Accounting*, Accounting Research Study No. 1, New York: American Institute of Certified Public Accountants.

Morley, M.F. (1979) 'The Value Added Statement in Britain', *The Accounting Review*, 54 (3): 618–29.
Niswonger, C.R. (1949) 'The Interpretation of Income in a Period of Inflated Prices', *The Accounting Review*, 24 (1): 27–32.
Paton, W.A. (1922) *Accounting Theory*, New York: Ronald Press.
Paton, W.A. (1965) *Corporate Profits: Measurement, Reporting, Distribution, Taxation, A Survey for Laymen and Accountants*, Homewood, IL: Richard D. Irwin, Inc.
Paton, W.A. and Littleton, A.C. (1940) *Monograph No. 3: An Introduction to Corporate Accounting Standards*, New York: American Accounting Association.
Post, J.E., Preston, L.E., and Sachs, S. (2002) *Redefining the Corporation: Stakeholder Management and Organizational Wealth*, Stanford, CA: Stanford University Press.
Raby, W.L. (1959) 'The Two Faces of Accounting', *The Accounting Review*, 34 (3): 452–61.
Rappaport, A. (1977) 'Economic Impact of Accounting Standards: Implications for the FASB' *The Journal of Accountancy*, (May): 89–99.
Riahi-Belkaoui, A. (2004) *Accounting Theory*, 5th edn, Cengage Learning EMEA.
Ronen, J. (2008) 'To Fair Value or Not to Fair Value: A Broader Perspective', *Abacus*, 44 (2): 181–208.
Schroeder, Richard G., Clark, Myrtle W. and Cathey, Jack M. (2001) *Financial Accounting Theory and Analysis*, 7th edn, New York: John Wiley & Sons.
Scott, W. R. (1997) *Financial Accounting Theory*, Ontario: Prentice Hall
Seidman, N. B. (1956) 'The Determination of Stockholder Income', *The Accounting Review*, 31 (1): 64–70.
Shleifer, A., and Vishny, R.W. (1998) *The Grabbing Hand: Government Pathologies and Their Cures*, Cambridge, MA: Harvard University Press.
Solomons, D. (1961) 'Economic and Accounting Concepts of Income', *The Accounting Review*, 36 (3): 374–83.
Solomons, D. (1995) 'Criteria For Choosing an Accounting Model', *Accounting Horizons*, 9 (1): 42–51.
Sprague, C.E. (1907) [AQ]
Sprague, C.E. (1913) *The Philosophy of Accounts*, New York: The Ronald Press Company.
Sprouse, R.T. (1957) 'The Significance of the Concept of the Corporation in Accounting Analyses', *The Accounting Review*, 32 (3): 369–78.
Sprouse, R.T. (1966) 'Accounting for What-You-May-Call-Its', *Journal of Accountancy (Pre-1986)*, 122 (4): 45.
Sprouse, R.T. and Moonitz, M. (1962) *A Tentative Set of Broad Accounting Principles*, Accounting Research Study No. 3, New York: American Institute of Certified Public Accountants.
Staubus, G.J. (1952) 'Payments for the Use of Capital and the Matching Process', *The Accounting Review*, 27 (1): 104–13.
Staubus, G.J. (1959) 'The Residual Equity Point of View in Accounting', *The Accounting Review*, 34 (1): 3–13.
Staubus, G.J. (2005) 'Ethics Failures in Corporate Financial Reporting', *Journal of Business Ethics*, 57 (1): 5–15.
Sterling, R.R. (1970) *Theory of the Measurement of Enterprise Income*, Lawrence, KS: University Press of Kansas.
Storey, R.K. (1959) 'Revenue Realisation, Going Concern and Measurement of Income', *The Accounting Review*, 34 (April): 233.
Suojanen, W.W. (1954) 'Accounting Theory and the Large Corporation', *The Accounting Review*, 29 (3): 391–98.
Suojanen, W.W. (1958) 'Enterprise Theory and Corporate Balance Sheets', *The Accounting Review*, 33 (1): 56–65.
Sweeney, H.W. (1936) *Stabilized Accounting*, New York: Harper & Row.
Thomas, A.L. (1969) *The Allocation Problem in Financial Accounting Theory*, Studies in Accounting Research No. 3, Sarasota, FL: American Accounting Association.
Thomas, A.L. (1974) *The Allocation Problem: Part Two*, Studies in Accounting Research No. 9, Sarasota, FL: American Accounting Association.
Van Mourik, C. (2010) 'Equity Theories and Financial Reporting: An Analysis', *Accounting in Europe*, 7 (2): 191–211.
Whittington, G. (2005) 'The Adoption of International Accounting Standards in the European Union', *European Accounting Review*, 14 (1): 127–53.
Williams, P.F. (2003) 'Modern Accounting Scholarship: The Imperative of Positive Economic Science', *Accounting Forum*, 27 (3): 251–69.
Zeff, S.A. (1978a) *A Critical Examination of the Orientation Postulate in Accounting With Particular Attention to its Historical Development*, New York: Arno Press.
Zeff, S.A. (1978b) 'The Rise of "Economic Consequences"', *The Journal of Accountancy*, (December): 56–63.

4

European Accounting Theory: Evolution and Evaluation

Salme Näsi, Chiara Saccon, Sonja Wüstemann and Peter Walton

1. Introduction

The origin of this chapter lies in the observation that international standard-setters never refer to any of the prominent European theorists of accounting, and that the theoretical basis of standard-setting primarily acknowledges (Anglophone) financial economics rather than anything else. This chapter therefore sets out to provide a brief introduction to the better-known theorists from mainland Europe. What emerges is that our predecessors identified fundamental issues in financial reporting that still remain unresolved, even if each generation perhaps sees them as problems of their own period.

In the twenty-first century, academic publishing requires researchers to cite authoritative literature when they write. This means that we can establish at least some kind of presumption of what their influences are. At a simplistic level, if Schmalenbach, for example, is cited we can presume that they have, on the face of it, considered his writings. The further back you explore authoritative literature, the less you are likely to find these citations, particularly in normative writing. As a consequence, although we should like to be able to assert that such and such an accounting thinker influenced future generations, there is rarely any way that can reasonably be done. The research literature would also tell you that (a) people can be influenced by ideas without being conscious of that connection, and (b) what people believe influences them may not have done so. Mostly, therefore, we cannot make connections of flows of ideas across Europe, nor show a massive current of distinctly European thought that can be contrasted with the (often American) Anglophone literature of financial economics such as agency theory, information economics, and market pricing which more obviously is cited in accounting textbooks today.

Within those confines, we should like to point out that we believe there is some tradition of exchanging accounting technology within mainland Europe, and also some appearance of a cleavage in exchanges between the Anglo-Saxon accounting tradition and the continental European stream of accounting. The literature of comparative international accounting, and in particular Nobes (1984), establishes that there are two 'families' of accounting and reporting: the Anglo-Saxon tradition (centred on the US and UK), and the continental or code law tradition (centred on France and Germany). There is some evidence of limited borrowing of company law between these two streams, but they have largely evolved independently of each other, and the theorizing within these cultural traditions also remains largely separate, one reason for dealing with it in two separate chapters in this collection.

The usual analysis of Anglo-Saxon accounting is that it evolved in the nineteenth century as a by-product of the industrial revolution, and, as the UK was narrowly the first country to experience industrialization, this stream of accounting had its origins in the UK. The industrial revolution called for much larger investments than the previous small business structure was able to provide. This in turn led to a much wider use of share-issuing companies as a vehicle for multiple investors to share the high risks and a need for structured reporting to investors. Government intervention was also needed to help the functioning of the capital markets and protect investors. We should point out that, although the concept of income tax had been developed in the UK at the end of the eighteenth century, the accounting requirements developed in company law in the nineteenth century made no attempt to bring the separate streams of law together.

This kind of economic development and its legal accompaniment transferred to the US where it was further developed and also transferred across the then British empire (see for example Walton 1995). This stream of accounting requirements was shared within the Anglophone world, which had ignored earlier developments in European accounting, and remained largely separate from the European stream until the movement towards global harmonization which first manifested itself in the 1970s, at which time regional harmonization was also pursued in Europe. Curiously the development of accounting technology in the Anglophone world in the nineteenth century did not apparently generate any significant theoretical debate as to what accounting was supposed to address, while in Germany and Italy a body of theorizing was evident.

The separate continental European stream of regulation had its origins much earlier than the industrial revolution. The first attempt by the state to regulate accounting occurred in seventeenth-century France with the publication of the Savary Ordonnance of 1673 (Bocqueraz 2010). The analysis usually provided suggests that the French government was concerned at a spate of bankruptcies amongst businesses in Paris. A small business would fail, leaving other businesses owed a great deal of money, causing them to fail in turn. The government believed that this could be contained by requiring business to draw up an annual inventory of assets and liabilities, and in particular to keep detailed records of debtors and creditors. From this came the second current of accounting development where accounting was seen at a micro level as a means of controlling and analysing business activity and at a macro level as a means of regulating the economy, and when income tax became widespread in the early twentieth century, of measuring taxable income.

Schmalenbach (cited in Walton 1995) says that the Prussian government became aware of the need to introduce accounting requirements in the eighteenth century and borrowed the French approach. The latter was expanded in the broad legal reforms introduced in France with the codification of law and the creation in particular of the 1807 Commercial Code. Napoleon's military campaigns across Europe were accompanied by the installation of French code law in a number of countries, including Spain, Italy, Belgium and the Netherlands, thus expanding this approach to regulating accounting and developing a common system. As the English Channel was an obstacle that halted Napoleon to the west, it would have helped preserve UK isolation from this school of thought.

Mikol (1995) suggests that France dropped into its Commercial Code share-issuing companies in 1862 and some notion of audit, borrowed from the UK company statutes, and, while Germany also developed share-issuing companies, it created the small company vehicle (Gesellschaft mit beschränkter Haftung – GmbH) which does not have a counterpart in the Anglo-Saxon tradition. The GmbH came into French legislation as a result of the transfer of Alsace-Lorraine from Germany to France in the early twentieth century.

Apart from such historical accidents, there is some evidence that continental European accountants did make some attempts to discuss what was happening in each other's countries (Forrester 1993). However, given the difficulties tracing the evolution of thought, the bulk of this chapter will look at accounting theory through a national framework, where action and reaction are sometimes clearly documented. It will start with developments in France, then move to Italian theorists, followed by a discussion of the German theorists, and then look at the work of Finnish Professor Martti Saario (see Table 4.1).

Table 4.1 Summary of the German theorists and Saario

	Purpose of accounting	*Recognition principles*	*Measurement principles*
Simon	- Primary objective: provide information about a firm's financial position Secondary objective: determination of income defined as increases in net assets	- Reliability restrictions for assets and liabilities: rights only qualify for recognition if costs were incurred Intangible assets need to be purchased from a third party Only legal obligations recognizable	- Core measurement attribute: individual value Current assets held for sale: individual sales price with market exit price as an upper limit Fixed assets held for use: purchase price reduced for depreciation
Schmalenbach	- Determine a periodic income number that allows management to control the business Profit as an indicator of a firm's operating efficiency	- Realization principle requires revenues (and the related expenses) to be recorded at the point of sale, even in the case of long-term construction contracts	- Strong emphasis on prudence principle in the later theory: assets are measured at historical cost and depreciated over their useful lives Depreciation charges shall rather be measured too high than too low
Schmidt	- Determine a firm's 'real' capital (reproduction value) in the balance sheet and 'real' profit in the income statement	- Full recognition of intangible values for the acquisition or development of which the firm has incurred costs	- Core measurement attribute: replacement cost gains and losses resulting from changes of replacement costs shall be directly put into equity
Moxter	- Prudently and reliably determine distributable profit Provide additional information in the appendix	- Assets and liabilities shall be reliably identifiable Profit shall be virtually certain substance-over-form-approach	- Assets: measured at acquisition or purchase price (historical cost) and depreciation over useful live impairments in case of a decline in value
Saario	- Calculate the annual income: monetary profit as the difference of revenues and expenses based on the matching principle	- Realization principle in recording and matching principle in profit calculation	- Historical cost: book-keeping understood as the description of the monetary process of the firm

One of the significant characteristics of the evolution of continental European thinking on accounting is that it has often focused on classification of accounts in the ledger, rather than on financial statements. This focus on competing ways of classifying transactions is notwithstanding a discussion both of the objectives of accounting and the objectives of the company and its role in society. From an Anglo-Saxon perspective it is easy to dismiss this theorizing as being 'just about book-keeping', a subject seen as having no intellectual content in the Anglo-Saxon literature, by contrast with the serious business of financial reporting. One could hypothesize that, because the continental European stream of thought has its origins well before the development of listed companies and capital markets as they emerged in the nineteenth century, the focus was not on reporting to the outside world, but rather on theorizing about what was the entity, which aspects of it should be highlighted in the accounting system (and as a consequence be a focus of management) and which relationships needed to be reflected.

The Anglo-Saxon stream of accounting by contrast has its origins in reporting to the capital markets, so it is not surprising that the literature focuses on reporting, even if there is also some literature on classification issues. UK company law is silent about accounting records, only requiring records to be adequate to enable true and fair financial statements to be prepared. However, the relationship between the ledger classification and the financial statements is of course direct.

Specific types of information in the financial statements cannot be provided unless the data in the ledger is held on the basis of that classification, so whether the theorist starts with the ledger or with the financial statements, the end result is the same – a classification and measurement approach. A minor irony of the twenty-first century is that Anglo-Saxon financial reporting vaunts the advantages of using eXtensible Business Reporting Language (XBRL), apparently without noting that XBRL requires the use of an accounts taxonomy, which is in effect a ledger classification system. Our analysis of European contributions to accounting thinking starts with the earliest contributions to ledger classification systems.

2. France and the development of classification

Forrester (1985) observes that 'Knowledge of double-entry bookkeeping spread north from Italy, first to the Low Countries. Pacioli's views were disseminated through varied authors, writing in Dutch or published in Antwerp or Amsterdam.' He says that works were translated into French in the seventeenth century and French authors took up the subject. All this was given a boost when France issued the 1673 Ordonnance de Savary (mentioned above) which was the first European statutory requirement to maintain accounting records. The statute appears to have stimulated publication of a number of guides to book-keeping and business administration generally. Savary went on to publish his book *Le parfait négociant* in 1697.

Forrester (1985) says:

> Another famous French text, *Le guide de negocians* was written by a Dutchman, Matthew De la Porte, and printed in Paris in 1685. It is largely a manual implementing the 1673 code. Its successor of 1704, *La Science des negocians*, contains a clear exposition and illustration of a systematic classification of accounts into three main classes, analyzed in progressive detail.

Boyns *et al.* (1997: 401) translate these as:

- chief accounts: capital, profit and loss, expenditure and commissions;
- effects in kind: liquid assets, goods and fixed assets; and
- correspondent accounts (accounts with suppliers and customers).

They say in their review of the historical French literature that prior to 1800 most texts were largely restricted to a discussion and explanation of the Italian system of double-entry book-keeping as applied to mercantile activities. They note that, as industrialization started to take place, texts started to appear that addressed 'industrial accounting':

> An increasing number of texts began to consider the technical issue of costing within the double entry system.
>
> [. . .]
>
> The main additional activity that needed to be addressed by the industrial accounting literature concerned the movement of goods through the enterprise, from one stage of economic activity to another. A particular feature of the early texts was the attempt to formulate a suitable classification of accounts and, although it is clear that production and/or cost accounts were seen to be essentially subservient to the main accounts, there was little agreement as to the number of the latter (ibid.: 400, 401).

France was, of course, the first European country to have a government-organized chart of accounts, which in its most developed form (Plan Comptable Général 1957) provided a standard codification of the ledger, together with an integrated costing system and a link through the financial statement presentation (Scheid and Walton, 1992: 114–29).

3. Italian theorists and *economia aziendale*

The significant theoretical debate in Italian accounting that arose between the eighteenth and nineteenth century was the search for an explanatory framework for double-entry book-keeping. The technique of book-keeping started to be influenced by French elaborations of the subject, especially De La Porte (Zan, 1994: 273). His 'personalization' or 'personification' of accounts influenced Italian accounting theorists' thinking about the nature of the different accounts in the double-entry book-keeping system. Degrange (father and son) developed the method called *cinquecontisti* and Vannier proposed in 1840 (ibid.: 276) the 'theory of the fictitious personification of the accounts'. All these represent attempts to classify accounts in order to provide a more rigorous logic to the structure of the double-entry book-keeping system, while at the same time being based on particular notions of value and of the objectives of the business.

Starting with the Lombard School (1840–60) followed by the Tuscan School (1860–80) and culminating in the Venetian School (1880–1960) the idea started to spread that the nature, objectives and domain of the accounting discipline must be viewed in relation to the wider administrative process in which it is included. In other words, 'there seems to be a strong interest in 'self-reflective' observations on theoretical and epistemological issues among Italian scholars and not just a focus on narrow technical ones' (ibid.: 283). This approach led, in the first half of the twentieth century, into the establishment of *economia aziendale* (science of economic administration) as the most prominent discipline in Italy (see Table 4.2).

3.1 Francesco Villa – the Lombard school

In an accounting environment dominated by French personalization theories, Francesco Villa (1801–84), the founder of the Lombard school, elaborated his significant contribution in 1841 in his essay *La contabilità applicata alle amministrazioni pubbliche e private* (Accountancy applied to private and public administrative bodies) and in 1850 *Elementi di amministrazione e contabilità* (Elements of administration and accountancy).

Table 4.2 Summary of the Italian accounting schools of thought

	Orientation	*Recognition and measurement*
Villa (Lombard School)	Accounting as part of the wider administrative process	Mixed theory of accounts (personalist and materialist approach)
Marchi, Cerboni (Tuscan School)	Economic administration creates and is informed by accounting	Theory of all personal accounts (*logismografia*)
Besta (Venetian School)	Atomistic view of the firm (*azienda*). Economic control through accounting	Value-based theory, patrimonial orientation
Zappa (Venetian School)	Holistic conceptualization of the firm *Economia aziendale* as discipline	Wealth as an abstract fund of values. Income measurement

Villa views accounting as part of a wider administrative process. In doing this he envisages accounting in relation to the basic unit of economic activity entitled *azienda* (firm), as mainly reflecting the processes dealing with the administration of wealth and the recording of economic transactions. Thus, Villa notes that book-keeping represents the mechanical part of accounting and that accountants cannot properly fulfill their tasks without an appropriate knowledge of the interactions between the accounting and administration of the *azienda* (Villa, 1841, 1850). Because of his intuition, he is considered to be the first Italian scholar to deal with *economia aziendale* (Catturi, 1989: 120), which was then developed by Zappa in the twentieth century. Villa's contribution can certainly be seen as an innovative work; even if there are some ambiguities and contradictions (Giannessi, 1980: 25), his contribution to the definition of the accounting domain is genuine.

Technically, his work presents some interesting features. For example, he proposes the *teoria mista*, a mixed theory of accounts, partly based on personalist theory and to a degree on materialistic theory (a focus on structuring the ledger around objects). Furthermore, he provides some rules to address adjustments at the end of the financial year, although he does not lay any emphasis on the continuity of the firm over time. He also established the economic concept of *wealth* as an aggregated value. The latter idea was later adopted and developed by Fabio Besta who acknowledged Villa as his main influence.

3.2 Francesco Marchi and Giuseppe Cerboni – the Tuscan school

While the Lombard school shows traces of Austrian domination, (owing to the fact that, following the Congress of Vienna in 1814–15, the 'Lombard and Venetian regions fell under the administrative regime of the Austrian-Hungarian Empire'; Zan, 1994: 278), the Tuscan school has clearly been influenced by French tradition. Francesco Marchi (1822–71) was the first Italian scholar to propose a new and rational theorization of double-entry book-keeping aiming at developing and substituting the French *cinquecontisti* theory. Marchi elaborates the 'theory of all personal accounts', which is based on a real personification of accounts in contrast to the fictitious French personification. Zan explains this as follows:

> The contribution of Francesco Marchi (1867) is strictly focused on accounting issues, and in particular represents an effort to refuse the 'five accounts' theory of Degranges by

> replacing it with an alternative theory. Marchi argues that the basic rule for debiting and crediting is incomplete and obscure and points out that the claim that the 'general accounts' represent the merchant is a mere fiction, given that two of them refer to things, two refer to persons, and just one refers to the owner as such. Marchi's counter-proposal is based on a 'legal view', given that 'associated with the right to things there is always the duty to care for them'. The charge of this duty of care might in bigger firms be passed to nominated 'consignees' or in smaller ones be consigned to the owner himself or his steward. On a basis of what is clearly a 'subject'-based view – as it emphasizes the relations between persons – a full 'personal accounts theory' emerges, wherein accounts are classified according to the persons who are the consignees for the object of the accounts (Zan, 1994: 280).

Marchi's theory represented a basis for later developments and was subsequently expanded by Giuseppe Cerboni (1827–1917). He contributed significantly to an interdisciplinary approach in explaining the foundations of accounting based on the systematization of a *logismografico* thought, an approach coming from the synthesis of three aspects of accounting: economic, administrative and computational (ibid.: 281). Cerboni defines the relation between economic administration and accounting similarly to the one between will and reason; will is concerned with action, while reason informs it (Cerboni, 1889).

The method of presenting the administrative facts is called *logismografia* meaning a reasoned description of accounts. This new and complex accounting technique consists of two book-keeping systems - one patrimonial and the other financial - and it is mainly used by public administrative bodies. The patrimonial system calls for separate accounts for owners on the one hand, and agents and all other related parties in another account. The *logismografia* elaborated by the Tuscan school was recognized by some American accounting theorists and it influenced the attempt to develop an accounting discipline called 'accountics' (Viganò, 1998: 384).

Italian scholars belonging to the Lombard and Tuscan schools initiated significant debates about the accounting domain, while maintaining the technical classification of accounts, which was the result of foreign influences. In the late nineteenth and early twentieth centuries the Venetian school, represented by the works of Besta and Zappa, abandoned personalist theories and focused on the economic entity of the *azienda*.

3.3 The Venetian school

3.3.1 Fabio Besta (1845–1923)

In 1872, Fabio Besta was appointed to the first Italian Chair of Accounting at the Royal High School of Commerce in Ca' Foscari, Venice, where he spent his entire academic life providing great contributions to the development of the accounting discipline. The contribution of Besta is fundamental to the Venetian school as it is coherent, complete, relevant and determinant to the evolution of subsequent accounting thought (Giannessi, 1980). The scientific work of Besta was carried out in the late nineteenth and the early twentieth centuries. By then interest in the *logismografia* of the Tuscan school had largely disappeared because of the difficulty of its practical use and other perceived shortcomings.

Besta was opposed to the legal approach of the Tuscan school and the theoretical viewpoint of *logismografia*. This is reflected by his central work *La Ragioneria* (Accountancy), which derives from lectures given in the 1880s at the Venice Royal High School and was first published as a book in 1910 and in a final version in 1922. His analysis focuses on the concept of *azienda*, which is described as 'the sum of phenomena, businesses and relationships concerning a given set of capital assets' (Besta, 1922: 5) belonging to a person, a family or to any other kind of owner. Economic administration is defined as 'the governance of phenomena, businesses, and relationships linked with the evolution of an *azienda*'s wealth'. (ibid.)

Economic administration is split into three elements:

- operations (*gestione*), i.e. the 'economic labour' dedicated to activities concerning the acquisition, transmission and use of wealth;
- management (*direzione*), which governs the economic labour; and
- economic control (*controllo*), which records and analyses the effects of the 'economic labour' in order to properly manage it (Zan, 1994: 286).

Due to the wide variation in the activities of *azienda*, the first two elements in Besta's opinion differ among firms so these cannot be studied conveniently as a unified discipline.

However, economic control, done through accounting, works in a comparable way in all types of firms, so its activities can be generalized (Besta, 1922: 31). The focus on economic administration consequently becomes narrower and accounting is positioned at the centre of Besta's theories. Accounting focuses on the dynamics of the entity's wealth in order to avoid its loss (ibid.). Current wealth is the element best expressing the entity's value and its control requires careful consideration of the value, composition, and changes in a firm's assets and net worth. Wealth is seen as a variable which is commensurate with, and obtained as an aggregation of, the values assigned to the goods one owns, should receive from others or owes to others (ibid.: 79).

Besta stresses the economic concept of wealth, relying on the valuation of a firm's resources, in opposition to the legal and personalist approach espoused by Cerboni and the Tuscan School. Besta's value-based theory classifies objects in order to keep track of their variations and the only common aspect that makes them measurable and comparable is their value. The accounting system derived from this approach is called wealth- or value-centered, and described as a patrimonial[1] system (*sistema patrimoniale*).

The balance sheet is the most important statement as it represents the firm's wealth (values of assets and liabilities and their composition), as the central phenomenon of the firm's economy. Income measurement is subsidiary to the balance sheet measurement of assets and liabilities. Income consists of revenues and expenses deriving from the management of the individual components of a firm's wealth. Capital is the relevant quantity to be measured, income is the accounting measurement of changes in capital over time.

The patrimonial approach adopts an atomistic-reductionist perspective: the *azienda* is a sum of many independent elements – atoms – where each element can be measured individually and the income statement is an aggregation of changes associated with specific individual assets. In this framework, margins which relate to specific areas of activity can be determined and be presented in the income statement. Consistent with the purpose of wealth measurement, the general valuation principle should be replacement cost (*costo di riproduzione*) to give the 'true and real value' of individual assets.

3.3.2 Gino Zappa (1879–1960)

Fabio Besta's approach was disseminated and developed by numerous followers, but particularly Gino Zappa. Zappa studied under Besta at Ca' Foscari at the beginning of the twentieth century. After then spending some years teaching at the Geneva School of Commerce, in 1921

Zappa was called to Venice to succeed his mentor. In the 1920s, Zappa published his own ideas, somewhat different from those of Besta, in several scientific works *Il reddito d'impresa* (Firm's income; Zappa, 1937 [1920]), *Tendenze nuove negli studi di ragioneria* (New trends in accounting studies; 1927) and *Le produzioni nell'economia delle imprese* (Production in the economy of the firm; Zappa, 1957).

Sensitive to the changing times, characterized by widespread industrialization, he moved towards an holistic conceptualization of the *azienda* and economic discipline. Zappa conceived the *azienda* as the economic unit of production or consumption, embedded in its specific context in space and time. Coordination and continuity through time were emphasized as important features of the *azienda* in its subsequent definitions. The *azienda,* the economic profile of any organized entity where economic activities take place, is seen as an economic co-ordination of process, where single operations and elements are considered as parts of a unitary whole or as a system of relationships, more than as isolated elements (Zappa, 1927). Furthermore, the *azienda* is an economic institution designed to persist, to continue its existence through time (Zappa, 1957).

The unitary and systematic concept of the *azienda* across space and time represents the most important innovation of Zappa's thought (Zan, 1994: 288) and the conceptual construction for an encompassing economic discipline is based on it. Zappa argued that *economia aziendale* is a new unitary discipline: a science studying the conditions of the existence and manifestations of a firm's life. Closely related areas of this unitary discipline are the study of *gestione* (operations), *organizzazione* (organization) and *rilevazione* (accounting).

The systemic view of *economia aziendale* sees all diverse activities within a firm as a whole and consequently all the disciplines studying them should be a whole. In the new conceptualization, Zappa reserved to accounting a mere instrumental role within the broader *economia aziendale* in contrast with the orientation of the nineteenth century's Italian scholars (Amodeo, 1983: 624) and some criticisms were expressed of this narrow view. Zappa's theoretical framework had important implications for the accounting discipline.

The idea of *azienda* as no longer a sum of the phenomena or facts administrated but as an economic coordination, which diverged from Besta's concept of firm's wealth represented by a set of goods/assets. Zappa regards wealth as an 'abstract fund of values' from which income flows and to which it is continuously added: wealth is generated by income and does not generate income. Besta's belief is rejected, income assumes the most prominent role, since it represents the result of the unitary economic coordination. In this context, the accounting system, which focuses on income determination, is labeled *sistema del reddito* (income-based accounting system) and the profit and loss account becomes the central statement.

Taking a holistic view of the firm, and seeing it as a process, income is seen as coming from the entire set of operations and not generated by specific assets or particular transactions. Because of this approach, a break-down of results or margins from different operations is not logically determinable within the income-centred system. The only format of profit and loss account consistent with this view is the horizontal statement (*a costi, ricavi e rimanenze*) where global expenses, revenues and adjustments for incomplete operations are put together in a single account.

The horizontal format of income statement therefore entered the Italian accounting tradition and from 1970s represented the usual format required from companies by the civil code. The progressive income statement, presenting intermediate results consistent with Besta's accounting system, is rejected by Zappa. As for the balance sheet, the items displayed, except for monetary items, are considered to be unexpired costs and unearned revenues. Their value is not based on replacement cost as Besta required, but on their capacity to contribute to the firm's activity (Catturi, 1989: 157).

Given the conceptual view of the firm as an indivisible system that continues through time, generating income by a continuous flow of operations, a periodic measurement of income represents merely an accounting fiction, since the only relevant measurement of income, from a theoretical point of view, would be the total-life income. The periodic income determination, in annual as well as interim reporting, is needed, and so acceptable, for practical reasons only. Because of the economic continuity of the firm's operations and of income being continuously in the process of formation, any fictitious break aiming at determining periodic results has to be undertaken cautiously by trying to minimize the loss of meaning that such a fiction inevitably causes.

4. Herman Veit Simon: early static accounting theory

4.1 Simon's background

Herman Veit Simon (1856–1914), a German lawyer, was the first one to design a comprehensive system of accounting principles and rules in Germany, based on the existing legal framework. It is referred to as static accounting theory (though not by himself) because it aims at providing information about a firm's capital (Schmalenbach, 1962: 44), or, more precisely, its financial position ('*Vermögenslage*') (Moxter, 1993a: 294). The first edition of his book '*Die Bilanzen der Aktiengesellschaften und der Kommanditgesellschaften auf Aktien*' was published in 1886, the third and (unchanged) fourth editions were published in 1899 and 1910 respectively. His work is considered as the best description of the early static accounting theory in the German literature (Moxter, 1984: 1). It exercised wide influence on both accounting theory and practice in Germany during the twentieth century (Schneider, 1974: 290). Some of his theory's elements can be found in prominent US accounting monographs, such as by Sprouse and Moonitz (1962), and the IASB's currently preferred asset and liability view. In his discussion of measurement attributes, Simon already struggles with the conflict between relevance and reliability and thereby provides interesting insights for the present measurement debate in international financial reporting.

4.2 Purpose of accounting

In Germany, the theoretical discussion on objectives of financial reporting and consequential recognition and measurement principles was initiated by a verdict of the Federal Commercial Court ('*Reichsoberhandelsgericht*') in 1873. The Court stipulated that assets shall be measured at their current (exit) market price ('*allgemeiner Verkehrswert*') – an objective value that is free from subjective judgments and mere speculations (Moxter, 1977: 672; Simon, 1899: 290). Consistent with this measurement principle, the determination of a firm's capital accessible to creditors in case of liquidation was considered as the underlying objective of financial statements (Moxter, 1993a: paras 295–6).

Simon strongly disagreed with both the objective and the measurement attribute. According to Simon, the primary purpose of financial statements is to provide information about a firm's (individual) financial position ('*Gewährung einer Übersicht über die Vermögenslage*') under the premise of going concern (Simon, 1899: 2, 303–4). The determination of a firm's profit is regarded as a secondary objective (ibid.: 5). In the static accounting theory, profit is defined as the increase in net assets during an accounting period and thus represents a mere 'by-product' of the accounting process (Moxter, 1984: 5–6).

4.3 *Recognition principles*

4.3.1 Assets

Under the static accounting theory, assets generally represent expected positive contributions to a firm's net present value (ibid.: 7–8). In order to ensure the 'correctness' of financial statements and to prevent 'fictitious' accounts Simon introduces several reliability restrictions (Simon, 1899: 158). Physical objects and receivables are generally considered as assets (ibid.: 149–68). Rights, other than receivables, only represent assets if the firm has paid something for their acquisition. Accordingly, a filed patent meets the asset definition while a concession that has been received free of charge does not (ibid.: 168–9). Other intangible objects (non-rights) that are expected to yield future economic benefits only qualify for recognition if they have been purchased from a third party (ibid.: 169, 167).

4.3.2 Liabilities

Liabilities generally represent expected negative contributions to a firm's net present value under the static accounting theory (Moxter, 1984: 11). Again, Simon imposes strong reliability restrictions: only legal obligations are allowed for recognition as liabilities (Simon, 1899: 173 ff.; see for details Moxter, 1984: 11–12).

4.4 *Measurement principles*

Simon's core measurement attribute – an asset's 'individual value' – directly follows from the objective to provide information on a firm's (individual) financial position. Current assets held for sale shall thus be measured at the individual sales price, i.e. the price that the specific firm could achieve in a sales transaction (Simon, 1899: 360). However, Simon restricts the measurement judgment by determining the (objective) market price as an upper limit (ibid.: 361). The recognition of unrealized holding gains consistently fits into Simon's theory. Only for purposes of profit distribution shall those gains be put into a reserve (ibid.: 337).

In the case of fixed assets that are held for use the individual value corresponds to the purchase price reduced for depreciation in later accounting periods (ibid.: 408). Simon explicitly rejects value in use estimations – on the one hand, due to their arbitrariness, and, on the other hand, because the resulting gains and losses will never be realized and thus do not provide meaningful information (ibid.: 409).

5. Eugen Schmalenbach: dynamic accounting theory

5.1 *Schmalenbach's background*

Eugen Schmalenbach (1873–1955) was professor of business administration at the University of Cologne. His work is referred to as dynamic accounting theory because it aims at providing information on the movements within a firm during a certain period of time, especially the development of a firm's income (Schmalenbach, 1962: 44). After several journal publications between 1908 and 1919 Schmalenbach further developed and significantly revised his theory in a monograph '*Dynamische Bilanz*',[2] which was published in 13 editions. The last edition, which was published posthumously in 1962, is intended to give a comprehensive picture of Schmalenbach's theory by reintegrating parts from previous works (Schmalenbach, 1962, foreword by R. Bauer).

Schmalenbach's work did not only have a strong influence on German accounting theory and practice, his theory was also widely recognized on an international level. It was translated into many languages, such as English,[3] Japanese, French, Spanish and Russian (Moxter, 1966: 30), and discussed in numerous international research publications (e.g. Forrester, 1993; Graves *et al.*, 1989 and Mattessich and Küpper, 2003). Schmalenbach's dynamic accounting theory can be regarded as a pioneer of US works in this field, such as Paton and Littleton (1940) and Bevis (1965), as well as the revenue and expense view that prevailed in US accounting practice until the 1970s (Storey, 2007).

5.2 Purpose of accounting

Schmalenbach developed his dynamic accounting theory in the early twentieth century as a reaction to the static accounting theory that dominated German accounting theory and practice at that time. He claims that the objective under the static accounting theory – to ascertain both the 'real' capital and the 'real' income – is not attainable and thus discards this dualistic approach as unscientific (Schmalenbach, 1962: 44–5). Moreover, Schmalenbach shows that the balance sheet is not capable of determining a firm's real capital because it necessarily leaves out values that are difficult to measure (ibid.: 45–9). As a consequence, Schmalenbach's dynamic accounting theory focuses on the income statement. It aims at determining a periodic income number that allows management to control the business (ibid.: 53–4). Profit is therefore designed as an indicator of a firm's operating efficiency; it reveals the 'up and down' of the firm's profitability (Schmalenbach, 1919: 9). Since not the absolute amount of profit, but rather its change in comparison to previous periods is important for this purpose, one of the main principles of Schmalenbach's theory is to ensure comparability of periodic income across different accounting periods (Schmalenbach, 1962: 54).

Profit is defined as the excess of the accomplishment ('*Leistung*') of an economic business (measured in terms of revenues) over its expenses (Schmalenbach, 1919: 3). According to the 'overriding' accrual principle an entity's receipts and costs shall be recognized as revenues and expenses in the periods in which they were caused by the respective business activities and other events. In the dynamic accounting theory the balance sheet has the mere (auxiliary) function to store profit and loss items in suspense, waiting to become revenues and expenses in the future (ibid.: 14–16).

5.3 Recognition principles

5.3.1 Revenues

Revenues from the sale of goods are realized at the point of sale, either when cash is received or the invoice sent to the customer (Schmalenbach, 1962: 76). In the case of long-term construction contracts, Schmalenbach's quest for comparability of periodic income across periods principally requires revenue to be recognized as construction (the business activity) progresses. However, for reasons of prudence, Schmalenbach sticks to the realization principle and argues for the recognition of revenue at contract completion. He explicitly accepts the distortion of the comparability of the profit figure in this case (ibid.: 77).

5.3.2 Expenses

Costs are generally recorded as expenses in the periods in which the related benefits (revenues) are yielded (realization principle). Accordingly, when an entity has acquired a machine or produced an inventory it has accomplished an 'advance performance' ('*schwebende Vorleistung*'). The incurred costs are initially stored in the balance sheet as assets and then matched with the related revenues when the machine is used or the inventory sold. When the revenues have been realized before the related costs are incurred, the expenses are anticipated at the point of sale in the form of a provision for outstanding performances ('*schwebene Nachleistungen*'), e.g. in the case of warranties (ibid.: 66–71).

Costs resulting from particular hazards ('*spezielle Wagnisse*'), such as losses and damages caused by natural catastrophes or clients' defaults, shall be anticipated in the form of a provision and thus allocated over several accounting periods in order to ensure comparability of periodic income across accounting periods (ibid.: 171–173).

5.4 Measurement principles

In the course of the revisions of his theory Schmalenbach increasingly put emphasis on the prudence principle. With regard to measurement, he argues that an overestimation of income is considerably more dangerous than an underestimation (ibid.: 99). According to the realization principle that directly follows the principle of prudence, assets are measured at historical cost and depreciated over their useful lives. Schmalenbach discusses the measurement of fixed assets at replacement costs and the measurement of assets held for speculation purposes at (exit) market prices, but rejects both, mainly due to reasons of uncertainty and lacking reliability (ibid.: 186–196). The emphasis on the prudence principle also shows as to depreciation: depreciation charges should rather be measured too high than too low in order to avoid asset impairments that would distort the comparability of periodic income (ibid.: 141–142). Furthermore, Schmalenbach (1919: 88) disapproved of the lower of cost or market principle in the beginning, but later included it in his theory, again for reasons of prudence (see also Moxter, 1982: 194–5).

6. Fritz Schmidt: organic accounting theory

6.1 Schmidt's background

Fritz Schmidt (1881–1950) was professor of business administration at the Johann Wolfgang Goethe University Frankfurt am Main. His work is referred to as organic accounting theory because it regards the 'integral role of the individual firm as part of the national economy' (Clarke and Dean, 1986: 65), or, in Schmidt's words, the firm as 'a cell within the organism of the overall economy' (Schmidt, 1929: 47). Schmidt published his theory as a monograph in German in 1921 ('*Die organische Bilanz im Rahmen der Wirtschaft*'), which became '*Die organische Tageswertbilanz*' in the third edition in 1929. Between 1929 and 1931, parts of his theory appeared as articles in US journals (Schmidt, 1929, 1930a, 1931).

Though Schmidt's organic accounting theory was not adopted by the German accounting practice it contributed to the advancement of business administration as a distinct academic discipline in Germany. Moreover, 'by those able to pass through the language barrier', Schmidt's work has been described as 'pioneering' with regard to inflationary (replacement cost) accounting; it was later built on and further developed in the US by Sweeney (1976); Edwards and Bell (1962); Clarke and Dean (1986) and Mattessich (1984). Beyond this, Schmidt was one of the first to propose excluding unrealized gains and losses from the income statement by putting them directly into equity – a practice that was later adopted by major accounting regimes, such as US GAAP and IFRS.

6.2 *Purpose of accounting*

The organic accounting theory follows a dualistic approach by aiming at ascertaining the 'real' capital in the balance sheet and 'real' profit in the income statement (Schmidt, 1929: 81–84). According to Schmidt (1929: 74; 1930b: 239) the sum of all assets less liabilities represents a firm's reproduction value, i.e. the amount of capital that would have to be expended in order to rebuild the firm at the balance sheet date. The profit figure measured as 'what is produced above the maintenance of business assets' shall 'enable the enterprise to function properly as an economic unit in all economic situations'; it is supposed to 'give ... a value-picture in the profit and loss statement corresponding to the current economic situation' (Schmidt, 1930b: 235).

6.3 *Recognition principles*

Schmidt does not formulate definition or recognition criteria for assets and liabilities. Explicitly, he only addresses the recognition of intangible values. In order to provide a roughly complete picture of a firm's financial position Schmidt argues for a full recognition of all intangible values for the acquisition or development of which the firm has expensed something (Schmidt, 1929: 118). The given examples – patents, advertising, customer base, secret methods and start-up expenses – evidence that Schmidt does not introduce any (further) reliability restrictions.

6.4 *Measurement principles*

Schmidt rejects the current exit price because its adoption as a measurement attribute would lead to the recognition of revenues before they have been verified in a sales act and thus infringe the realization principle. He also refuses the purchase or acquisition price since it has – after initial recognition – only historical importance. The measurement attribute that consistently fits into the organic accounting theory is replacement cost ('*Tagesbeschaffungswert*'), i.e. 'the market price for which one can obtain the economic good in question of the day of real or assumed replacement' (Schmidt, 1929: 71; 1930b: 239). Since Schmidt sticks to the realization principle (holding) gains and losses that result from changes of the replacement costs before the sales act takes place shall bypass the income statement and be directly put into equity ('*Wertänderungen am ruhenden Vermögen*') (Schmidt, 1929: 305 ff.; 1931).

7. Adolf Moxter: neo-static accounting theory

7.1 *Moxter's background*

Adolf Moxter (1929–) was professor of business administration at the Johann Wolfgang Goethe University, Frankfurt am Main in 1965–97. His work is referred to as 'neo-static accounting theory' because:

- it aims at ascertaining the 'real' capital and the 'real' income (dualistic approach); and
- it is built within the existing legal framework (Moxter, 1977: 675–6).

Since the 1960s, Moxter has continuously shaped and refined his theory by means of journal articles and the publication of monographs, most importantly '*Bilanzlehre, Band I*' (Moxter, 1984 [1974]), '*Betriebswirtschaftliche Gewinnermittlung*' (1982), '*Bilanzrechtsprechung*' (Moxter, 2007 [1982][4]) and '*Grundsätze ordnungsgemäßer Rechnungslegung*' (Moxter, 2003).

Moxter's theory had a strong impact on German accounting theory and practice (Hommel *et al.*, 2004). His work contributed to the change from the dynamic to the static accounting theory ('*statische Wende*') in the 1970s (Moxter, 1993b) and, even today, it 'dictates' the Federal Court of Justice's interpretation of the statutory accounting principles in the German Commercial Code (Schmidt, 1996). Another of Moxter's contributions to accounting theory lies in revealing the limits of financial statements, which is also interesting and relevant for the present discussion relating to international financial reporting (Moxter, 2000).

7.2 Purpose of accounting

In his early works Moxter elaborately demonstrates that the purposes of the previous accounting theories are not attainable by means of financial statements. With regard to Schmalenbach's dynamic accounting theory, he points out that periodic income cannot properly indicate a firm's operating efficiency ('*Vergleich barkeitsmythos*' – 'comparability myth') (Moxter, 2000: 2144–5). That is because of the uncertainty of future events and the incapability of financial statements to adequately include those (Moxter, 1966: 44–5). With regard to the early static and organic accounting theory, he demonstrates that a firm's 'real' capital is not ascertainable in financial statements since the balance sheet is incapable of capturing certain assets and liabilities, such as synergy effects and internal goodwill (Moxter, 1984: 25, 72–5).

Moxter argues that information about a firm's 'real' capital and income (the future net cash flows expected to flow to the firm) need to be multivalent, e.g. in the form of a finance plan (Moxter, 1966: 45). He claims that one of the few purposes that (monovalent) financial statements can – and, according to the German law, should – fulfil is the determination of distributable profit (Moxter, 1966, 1984). If the prudently and reliably determined accounting figures provide 'distorted' information, additional 'healing' information shall be given in the appendix (Moxter, 1995). Especially in his latest works, Moxter addresses the legally stipulated information requirements and makes suggestions about classifications and explanations of financial statement elements (Moxter, 2003: 223–300).

7.3 Recognition principles

Moxter adopts the superordinate principles stipulated by the law – the prudence principle, the realization principle, the imparity principle and the reliability requirements. As an advocate of the static accounting theory Moxter only allows reliably identifiable resources and obligations to be recognized as assets and liabilities. In contrast to Simon, legal concepts only represent a starting point of analysis. Moxter strongly emphasizes that the economic facts and circumstances also need to be considered in the interpretation and application of accounting principles ('*wirtschaftliche Betrachtungsweise*' – 'substance over form approach') (Moxter, 1989). Another contrast to Simon is that Moxter requires revenues and profit to be virtually certain to be recorded. The recognition of holding gains is incompatible with the realization principle and thus prohibited (Moxter, 2004).

7.4 Measurement principles

According to the prudence principle and the realization principle assets are to be measured at the acquisition or purchase price (historical cost) at initial recognition and depreciated over their useful lives. The imparity principle requires impairments in case of a decline in value.

8. Martti Saario: the Finnish expenditure–revenue theory

8.1 Saario's background

Professor Martti Saario (1906–88) took a law degree at the University of Helsinki, and a bachelor's degree, master's degree, and licentiate degree in business administration at the School of Economics in Helsinki in 1932. He started his career as a lecturer in book-keeping at the Viipuri (Vyborg) College of Commerce, where he served about ten years from 1929 until 1939. He wrote his first articles on the topic of business taxation, based on his Master's thesis. These were published in the Finnish business magazine '*Liiketaito*' under the title '*Verotuskysymys*' ('Taxation issue') (See *Liiketaito* 15, 1929; 16, 1930). (For Finnish articles on Martti Saario's biography, work and publications, see Honko, 1966; Pihlanto and Lukka, 1993; Pajunen, 2011),

During the Second World War the Finnish city of Viipuri (Vyborg) was ceded to the Soviet Union. In 1939 Saario applied and won a stipend for his doctoral studies from the School of Economics in Helsinki. During the war Saario acted as a senior controller of the war economy (*sotatalouden tarkastuksen ylireviisori*) in the period 1942–4 and wrote his doctoral thesis on the depreciation of fixed assets. Right after the end of the war Saario presented his dissertation entitled 'The realization principle and depreciation of fixed assets in profit calculation' (*Realisointiperiaate ja käyttöomaisuuden poistot tuloslaskennassa*) for public examination and he was awarded his PhD degree in 1945, as only the second doctor ever from the School of Economics in Helsinki.

Saario taught book-keeping at the School of Economics from 1943 and was appointed to a professorship in business accounting in 1948. He then served the School of Economics as a tenured professor of accounting with specialization in financial accounting, taxation and finance between 1948 and 1971. In addition he served the Turku School of Economics as an acting professor from 1964–73.

8.2 Saario's theory of book-keeping

8.2.1 Background

Martti Saario developed his expenditure–revenue theory of book-keeping as part of his doctoral dissertation. In the same year Finnish book-keeping legislation was reformed (Book-keeping Law 6.7.1945 and Statute 9.8.1945). The war had greatly increased the need for and extent of state control over the business sector. In order to compare the capacity of firms to pay income taxes, companies had now for the first time in Finland to follow, when preparing their financial statements, the form and content of a model set out in the new accounting legislation. The authorities needed, and the firms themselves also wished, to present uniform and comparable information for the purposes of governmental price control and taxation.

The new 1945 legislation standardized the terminology, the form and content of the income statement and the balance sheet, both presented in T-account (horizontal) form, with extraordinary items presented separately from the ordinary revenues and costs. The primary purpose of accounting was to calculate the annual profit of the firm, but assets valuation was the key factor in the profit calculation process. A significant feature of the new legislation was the prudence principle and the lower of cost or market rule in the valuation of the assets, e.g. inventories.

In this respect the new legislation was based on static balance sheet thinking. The legislation allowed a firm to smooth its annual result by using the fixed or normal stock method for inventories (introduced by the dynamic theorist Eugen Schmalenbach: see Section 5 above), which aimed at preserving a company's real capital and at eliminating cyclical fluctuations in profit calculations. Depreciation of fixed assets was to be made mainly according to a predetermined plan.

Martti Saario immediately criticized the 1945 legislation. He was convinced that depreciation according to plan was a wrong solution and wrote:

> The last and regrettable mistake is made in the new legislation, whereby depreciation is to be made in equally large amounts every year according to a plan prepared beforehand without any consideration of the annual result (Saario, 1945: 278–9),

He concluded that 'the appearance of such an unhappy and erroneous regulation in the law can be understood as the fruit of a lack of expertise' (ibid.).

Saario wrote later in many of his magazine articles about 'the constricted and out-of-date balance equation' or about 'the static balance concept handed down from our fathers' and offered in its place an 'easier and more open' dynamic accounting theory. As a professor of accounting he taught book-keeping using his expenditure–revenue theory and his own way of thinking.

8.2.2 The objectives of accounting

Saario's theory is called and translated as book-keeping theory because it was based on recording three kinds of business transactions – expenditures, revenues and money transactions – following constantly the realization principle. In closing the accounts at the end of the financial year two bipartite divisions were to be made:

- allocation of revenues to absorbing expenses and releasing profit; and
- allocation of expenditures between current expenses and balance sheet *aktiva*.

The aim of the first division was to match a part of expenditures as expenses against corresponding revenues. In the second division the rest of the expenditures were transferred through the balance sheet to later financial years, to be matched against later financial years' revenues. The main aim was to follow the matching principle in the annual income measurement.

In Saario's thinking money (extended cash, including money receivables and money payables) was important. Saario understood a firm as a means for its owner(s) of earning money.[5] To earn money was the factual purpose of an entrepreneur or a businessman. This way of thinking emphasized the entrepreneur's private economic benefits at the expense of more general national economic benefits.

In this Schmalenbach and Saario represented different thinking (see Pihlanto and Lukka, 1993: 256). The purpose of the profit calculation in Saario's theory was to find out how much profit (purchasing power, money) the owner(s) of the company had earned (Saario, 1945: s. 23 and Pihlanto and Lukka, 1993: 256). To Saario 'book-keeping was nothing more than money counting' (Saario, 1945: 53).[6]

Profit was calculated as the difference between the money/purchasing power obtained in sales (revenues) and lost in purchase (expenditures). The total (lifetime) profit of the firm could be calculated objectively in two congruent ways:

- as a difference of the total (lifetime) revenues and total (lifetime) expenditures; and
- by counting the money in cash at the end of the total period of the firm when all the debts and other payables had been paid.

The period (annual) profit calculation was arbitrary but recognition and income measurement problems were resolvable following the realization and matching principles.

From revenues realized during the period were subtracted the expenditures needed to create the revenues (matching). The rest of the expenditures were moved and capitalized on the balance sheet, which in Saario's thinking was a pure money balance and transfer account. *Aktiva* (the debit side amounts) of the balance sheet were interpreted to be expenditures (money or purchasing power spent) from which the revenues had not yet been received. *Passiva* (the credit side amounts) are in money terms, equity and debt, sources of finance. As to the measurement principles Saario's theory was based on historical cost, money spent and received in business transactions.

8.3 Saario's influence

A comprehensive presentation of the expenditure–revenue theory was published by Saario as the form of a textbook in 1959. This textbook was widely used in business school education in Finland, also in the newer business schools established in the middle of the 1970s.

Saario was very influential as a professor and thinker in the field of financial accounting in Finland; the expenditure–revenue theory was not the only innovation he developed. The other theory well known in Finland was the cost priority theory (Saario 1959), where income is used to first cover the running costs (wages, salaries, materials, energy, etc.), then depreciation of fixed assets and finally profit, the owners' portion. Saario could, in his position of professor at both the Finnish-speaking business schools existing at that time, spread and inculcate his theoretical ideas in business students for several decades (from the middle of the 1940s to the beginning of the 1970s). He also influenced practitioners and decision-makers with his numerous public presentations and articles. Most of the articles were written in Finnish and published in professional journals. Some were written in Swedish and a few in German. Obviously this may be one reason why Saario did not become well-known outside Finland in his lifetime.

Accounting legislation was reformed in Finland at the beginning of the 1970s. This legislation (the Accounting Act and Statute 1973) adopted both the expenditure–revenue and the cost priority order theories in book-keeping, profit calculation and the presentation of the financial statements. The expenditure–revenue theory was also adopted as the basis of the reform of company taxation in 1968. Prudence was also an essential feature of the annual income measurement both in accounting and taxation. Provisions for future costs and losses (for example bad debts, warranties and inventories) were deductible in income taxation on condition that they were made in accounting too.

The next accounting legislation reform took place at the beginning of the 1990s as a part of the preparation for Finland's membership of the European Union. The expenditure–revenue theory was still retained as the basis of accounting, but certain individual regulations undermined the theoretical foundations of Finnish book-keeping. One of these was the introduction of depreciation according to a preset plan and abolition of most provisions. In most recent accounting legislation reforms in Finland, international financial reporting standards have had a strong influence and Saario's theory can only be used as an easy way to teach double-entry book-keeping, if indeed it can be used at all. But Saario's theory influenced Finnish financial accounting and tax legislation for almost half a century.

9. Conclusions

A study of continental European accounting theorists seems to make clear that many of what are current issues in accounting doctrine are not new and indeed have been argued over for nearly two centuries. We can see the perpetual argument about whether accounting should be measuring assets and liabilities or business transactions, and the discussion about whether the business model should influence the way in which accounting should be done. The history of accounting suggests that there is no definitive answer to these questions, and what happens in practice is likely to be due to a combination of other influences. For example, Richard (2004) points to the rise of corporate income tax, and shareholders' interest in dividends as the capital markets have evolved, as causing attention to switch from the balance sheet to the profit or loss account in the twentieth century.

A significant aspect of continental European thinking about accounting is that it has often been expressed in terms of the classification and measurement of items in the ledger as opposed to the financial statements. The ledger classification system has a direct consequence for what is in the financial statements, but the arguments about the objectives of financial reporting, the nature of the firm's relationships and the comparative importance of different aspects of the firm are expressed as discussions of the ledger system, not the financial statements. The literature does show a certain exchange between European countries on classification. In more recent times we can point to the French *Plan comptable général* as having been largely imported from Germany, where the development of charts is generally credited to Schmalenbach. Ledger systems have remained an important element of European accounting but are absent from Anglo-Saxon accounting. In particular, countries such as Germany, Switzerland and Italy have standard ledger classification systems that are widely used by companies, while France, Belgium, Spain and Greece have statutory charts of accounts.

What is disappointing from a European accounting perspective is that this relevant theorizing about accounting and reporting has disappeared almost without trace, except in the countries of origin, and is not referred to in current policy debates by international standard-setters. Not only do the economics of information and markets seem to have taken over from business economics, but people seem quite unaware that what are treated as current issues, such as a transaction approach or a value approach, balance sheet versus income statement, current value or historical cost, are issues that have been debated for centuries. They are more doctrinal issues, pursued with almost religious fervour by some participants, as opposed to being 'new' technical problems that are susceptible of resolution.

Notes

1 While the term 'patrimony' is not generally used in accounting in the Anglophone world, in Italy and France it sometimes refers to equity. The notion of a patrimonial system is assimilable to a proprietary view in the Anglophone literature.
2 The first three editions were titled '*Grundlagen der dynamischen Bilanzlehre*'.
3 Schmalenbach (1959).
4 The first edition from 1982 was titled '*Bilanzierung nach der Rechtsprechung des Bundesfinanzhofs*'.
5 Besides owners, the other important stakeholder of the firm was the tax authorities who were – and still are – central partners in profit sharing. Since the first Finnish accounting legislation (the Book-keeping Obligation Act in 1925 and the Financial Statements Publication Act 1928) linkage between financial accounts and company income taxation in Finland has been strong.
6 At least partly as a consequence of Saario's book-keeping thinking, the Capital Circulation Model with the real process (or flow) of production factors and products, and a monetary process as the mirror image of the real process has been since the 1960s a common way to describe and define a business firm in Finland (see e.g. Näsi and Näsi 1997, or Näsi and Mäkelä, 2010). Purchasing power moves into the firm at the moment of selling (and billing) and equally out of the firm at the moment of purchasing (and invoicing). Using this model book-keeping has often been defined as a description of the monetary process.

Bibliography

Amodeo, D. (1983) 'La Natura della Ragioneria', *Rivista dei Dottori Commercialisti*, 4, pp. 617–32.

Besta, F. (1922) *La Ragioneria* (Milan: Vallardi).

Bevis, H.W. (1965) *Corporate Financial Reporting in a Competitive Economy* (New York: Macmillan).

Bocqueraz, C. (2010) 'France', in Previts, G., Walton, P. and Wolnizer, P. (eds) *A Global History of Accounting, Financial Reporting and Public Policy: Europe* (Bingley: Emerald Publishing).

Boyns, T., Richards, J.R. and Nikitin, M. (1997) 'The Development of Industrial Accounting in Britain and France before 1880: A Comparative Study of Accounting Literature and Practice', *European Accounting Review*, 6:3, 393–437.

Catturi, G. (1989) *Teorie contabili e scenari economico-aziendali* (Padua: Cedam).

Cerboni, G. (1889) *Elenco cronologico delle opere di Computisteria e Ragioneria venute alla luce in Italia dal 1202 al 1888* (Rome: Tipografia Nazionale Reggiani).

Clarke, F. L. and G.W. Dean (1986) 'Schmidt's *Betriebswirtschaft* Theory', *Abacus*, 22(2), 65–102.

Edwards, E. O. and P.W. Bell (1962) *The Theory and Measurement of Business Income* (Berkeley, CA: University of California Press).

Forrester, D.A.R. (1985) *Aspects of French Accounting*, Academy of Accounting Historians, Working Paper no. 64.

Forrester, D.A.R. (1993) *Eugen Schmalenbach and German Business Economics* (New York and London: Garland Publishing).

Giannessi, E. (1980) *I precursori in Economia Aziendale* (Milan: Giuffrè).

Graves, O. F., G.W. Dean and F. L. Clarke (1989) *Schmalenbach's Dynamic Accounting and Price-Level Adjustments* (New York and London: Garland Publishing).

Hommel, M., R. Schmidt and J. Wüstemann (2004) 'Adolf Moxter und die Grundsätze ordnungsgemäßer Rechnungslegung' [Adolf Moxter and the Principles of Orderly Accounting], *Die Wirtschaftsprüfung*, Special Issue 'Wirtschaftsprüfung und Zeitgeist, Prof. Dr. H. C. Mult. Adolf Moxter zum 75. Geburtstag', S84–S98.

Honko, J. (1966) *On Investment Decisions in Finnish Industry* (Helsinki: Weilin and Göős).

Mattessich, R. (1984) 'Fritz Schmidt (1882–1950) and His Pioneering Work of Current Value Accounting in Comparison to Edward's and Bell's Theory', *Proceedings of the Fourth International Congress of Accounting Historians*, Editrice, Pisa.

Mattessich, R. and H.-U. Küpper (2003) 'Accounting Research in the German Language Area: First Half of the 20th Century', *Review of Accounting and Finance*, 2(3), 106–37.

Mikol, A. (1995) 'The History of Financial Reporting in France', in Walton, P. (ed) *European Financial Reporting: A History* (Academic Press, London).

Moxter, A. (1966) 'Die Grundsätze Ordnungsmäßiger Bilanzierung und der Stand der Bilanztheorie', *Zeitschrift für Betriebswirtschaftliche Forschung*, 18, 28–59.

Moxter, A. (1977) 'Bilanztheorien' [Accounting Theories], in W. Albers *et al.* (eds), *Handwörterbuch der Wirtschaftswissenschaft (HdWW)*, Erster Band (Stuttgart and New York: Gustav Fischer)..

Moxter, A. (1982) *Betriebswirtschaftliche Gewinnermittlung* [Theory of Income Determination] (Tübingen: Mohr Siebeck).

Moxter, A. (1984) *Bilanzlehre, Band I: Einführung in die Bilanztheorie* [Accounting Doctrine, Vol. 1: Introduction to Accounting Theory], 3rd edn (Wiesbaden: Gabler).

Moxter, A. (1989) 'Zur Wirtschaftlichen Betrachtungsweise im Bilanzrecht' [Substance-over-form-approach in Accounting Law], *Steuer und Wirtschaft*, 66/19, 232–41.

Moxter, A. (1993a) 'Statische Bilanz' [Static Accounting Theory], in K. Chmielewicz and M. Schweitzer (eds) *Handwörterbuch des Rechnungswesens*, 3rd edn (Stuttgart: Schäffer Poeschel, para. 1852–60).

Moxter, A. (1993b) 'Entwicklung der Theorie der Handels- und Steuerrechtlichen Gewinnermittlung' [Development of the Theory of Commercial and Fiscal Income Determination], *Zeitschrift für Betriebswirtschaftliche Forschung*, Special Issue 32, Ökonomische Analyse des Bilanzrechts: Entwicklungslinien und Perspektiven, 61–84.

Moxter, A. (1995) 'Zum Verhältnis von Handelsrechtlichen Grundsätzen Ordnungsmäßiger Bilanzierung und True-and-fair-view-Gebot bei Kapitalgesellschaften', in G. Förschle *et al.* (eds), *Rechenschaftslegung im Wandel: Festschrift für Wolfgang Dieter Budde* (München: C.H. Beck, pp. 419–58).

Moxter, A. (2000) 'Rechnungslegungsmythen' [Accounting Myths], *Betriebs-Berater*, 55(42), 2143–9.

Moxter, A. (2003) *Grundsätze Ordnungsgemäßer Rechnungslegung* [Principles of Orderly Financial Reporting] (Düsseldorf: IDW-Verlag)..

Moxter, A. (2004) 'Gewinnrealisierung nach den IAS/IFRS: Erosion des HGB-Realisationsprinzips' [Income Recognition According to IAS/IFRS: Erosion of the German Realization Principle?], *Zeitschrift für Vergleichende Rechtswissenschaft*, 103, 268–80.

Moxter, A. (2007) *Bilanzrechtsprechung* [Accounting Law according to Jurisprudence] (Tübingen: Mohr Siebeck).

Näsi, Salme, and Mäkelä Hannele (2010) 'Incorporating Stakeholder Thinking into the Neo-Classical Capital Circulation Model of the Firm', *Journal of Business Ethics*, 96 Supplement 1.

Näsi, Salme and Juha Näsi (1997) 'Accounting and Business Economics Traditions in Finland: From a Practical Discipline into a Scientific Subject and Field of Research', *The European Accounting Review*, 1996, 6:2, 199–229.

Nobes, C.W. (1984) *International Classification of Financial Reporting* (London and New York: Croom Helm).

Pajunen, Kati (2011) 'Martti Saario: Henkilökuva', *Liiketaloudellinen Aikakauskirja*, 4/2011, 452–66.

Paton, W. A. and A. C. Littleton (1940) *An Introduction to Corporate Accounting Standards* (Ann Arbor, MI: American Accounting Association).

Pihlanto, Pekka and Lukka, Kari (1993) 'Martti Saario: suomalaisen laskenta-ajattelun kehittäjä' [Martti Saario: the Developer of Finnish Accounting Thinking], *The Finnish Journal of Business Economics*, 41:3, 251–77.

Richard, J. (2004) 'The Secret past of Fair Value: Lessons from History Applied to the French Case', *Accounting in Europe*, 1, 95–108.

Saario, Martti (1945) 'Realisointiperiaate ja käyttöomaisuuden poistot tuloslaskennassa' [Summary: Realization Principle and Depreciation], Doctoral thesis, Liiketaloustieteellisen tutkimuslaitoksen julkaisuja 6, Helsinki.

Saario, Martti (1959) 'Kirjanpidon meno-tulo-teoria' [The Expenditure–Revenue Theory of Bookkeeping], Liiketaloustieteellisen tutkimuslaitoksen julkaisuja 28, Keuruu.

Scheid, J.-C. and Walton, P. (1992) *European Financial Reporting: France* (London: Routledge) .

Schmalenbach, E. (1919) 'Grundlagen Dynamischer Bilanzlehre' [Foundations of Dynamic Accounting Theory], *Zeitschrift für Handelswissenschaftliche Forschung*, 13, 1–50.

Schmalenbach, E. (1959) *Dynamic Accounting*, trans. G.W. Murphy and K. S. Most (London: Gee and Co).

Schmalenbach, E. (1962) *Dynamische Bilanz* [Dynamic accounting theory], 13th edn, revised by R. Bauer (Cologne and Opladen: Westdeutscher Verlag).

Schmidt, F. (1929) *Die Organische Tageswertbilanz* [The Organic Accounting Theory], 3rd edn (Leipzig: Gabler).

Schmidt, F. (1930a) 'The Basis of Depreciation Charges', *The Harvard Business Review*, 8(3), 257–64.

Schmidt, F. (1930b) 'The Importance of Replacement Value', *The Accounting Review*, 5(3), 235–42.

Schmidt, F. (1931) 'Is Accretion Profit?', *The Accounting Review*, 6(3), 289–98.

Schmidt, R. H. (1996) 'Betriebswirtschaftslehre und Rechtspolitik', [Business Administrations and Legal Politics], *Die Aktiengesellschaft*, 41, 250–60.

Schneider, D. (1974) 'Die Vernachlässigten Begründer der Klassischen Bilanzdiskussion (I): Herman Veit Simon und Staubs Kommentar zum HGB' [The Neglected Founder of the Classical Accounting Discussion (I): Herman Veit Simon and Staub's Commentary to the German Commerical Code], *Wirtschaft und Steuer*, 3, 288–92.

Simon, H.V. (1899) *Die Bilanzen der Aktiengesellschaften und der Kommanditgesellschaften auf Aktien* [Financial Statements of Corporations and Associations Limited by Share], 3rd edn (Berlin: Guttentag).

Sprouse, R. T. and M. Moonitz (1962) *A Tentative Set of Broad Accounting Principles for Business Enterprises*, Accounting Research Study No. 3 (New York: AICPA).

Storey R. K. (2007) 'The Framework of Financial Accounting Concepts and Standards', in D. R. Carmichael, O. R. Whittington and L. Graham (eds) *Accountants' Handbook, Volume One: Financial Accounting and General Topics*, 11th edn (New York: John Wiley & Sons).

Sweeney, H.W. (1976 [1935]) *Stabilized Accounting* (New York: Arno Press).

Viganò, E. (1998) 'Accounting and Business Economics Traditions in Italy', *The European Accounting Review*, 7(3), 381–403.

Villa, F. (1841) *La contabilità applicata alle amministrazioni pubbliche e private*, two volumes (Milan: Angelo Monti).

Villa, F. (1850) *Elementi di amministrazione e contabilità* (Pavia: Tipografia Bizzoni).

Walton, P. (1995) 'International Accounting and History', in Walton, P. (ed) *European Financial Reporting: A History* (London: Academic Press).

Zan, L. (1994) 'Towards a History of Accounting Histories: Perspectives from the Italian Tradition', *The European Accounting Review*, 3 (2), 255–307.

Zappa, G. (1927) *Tendenze nuove negli studi di ragioneria* (Milan: Istituto Editoriale Scientifico).

Zappa, G. (1937) *Il reddito d'impresa: Scritture doppie, conti e bilanci di aziende commerciali* (Milan: Giuffrè).

Zappa, G. (1957) *Le produzioni nell'economia delle imprese* (Milan: Giuffrè).

5

English-Language Theories of Financial Reporting

Christopher Napier

1. Introduction

In Chapter 2, different notions of 'theory' were introduced and applied to financial reporting. The various theories can be divided into two broad but overlapping groups, reflecting the main purpose for which the theories have been developed. Some theories are intended to provide a structure for understanding existing accounting practice, usually with a view to its improvement. Such theories may be labelled 'prescriptive' or 'normative', and have sometimes been classified as 'theories *of* accounting' (for example, Kinney, 1989: 121). Other theories also aim for an understanding of existing accounting practice, but here the objective is to explain the behaviour of those who prepare and use financial reports of businesses and not-for-profit entities, and to predict the accounting choices that preparers and users may make. Such theories may be labelled 'descriptive' or 'positive', and come within the classification 'theories *about* accounting' (Kinney, 1989: 121). However, as is argued in Chapter 2, these classifications are not always helpful, as they often mask presuppositions as to what a theory should be. Writers of textbooks with titles such as *Accounting Theory* (for example, Hendriksen and van Breda, 1992; Riahi-Belkaoui, 2000) sometimes evade the provision of a single definition and claim that there are multiple approaches to accounting theory, perhaps appealing to the American Accounting Association's *Statement on Accounting Theory and Theory Acceptance* (AAA, 1977), which argued that a collection of theories was required to address the different contexts of accounting.

In broad terms, financial reporting theories seek to provide a framework of principles or general concepts that abstract from financial reporting practice. The purpose of such a framework may be to ensure the consistent and systematic development of practice, to improve practice, or to understand, explain and predict practice. The framework may come from within accounting, or it may draw on another field of knowledge, such as economics, information theory, psychology, political theory or law. This eclecticism may be observed in two current textbooks, both entitled *Financial Accounting Theory*. The book by Scott (2012), widely used in North America, is almost entirely grounded in economics. This book refers to 'theories *of* accounting' only in a brief historical sketch. The book by Deegan and Unerman (2011), popular in many countries within the British Commonwealth, makes use of a wider range of theories, including behavioural and critical perspectives. The authors give equal weight to 'theories *of* accounting' and 'theories *about* accounting'. So, even among leading textbooks, there is no consensus as to what constitutes financial reporting theory.

Whittington (1986) offers a study of financial accounting theory that combines a taxonomy with a historical narrative. He identifies three main 'approaches or strata', which he labels 'empirical inductive', 'deductive' and 'the new empiricism based on positivism' (Whittington, 1986: 6–7). However, his taxonomy illustrates how the boundaries between different approaches to financial accounting theory are blurred: his 'deductive' category includes what he calls 'true income', 'user needs' and 'information economics' approaches, the first two of which are often labelled as normative, while the third provides the theoretical underpinning for the 'new empiricism'. Beattie (2002) adopts a similar historical approach, seeing financial accounting theory as originally emerging from, and helping to shape, corporate financial reporting practice, then moving through a deductive or a priori period, before settling on a decision-usefulness framework to shape practice and an empirical research tradition grounded in neo-classical economics to shape academic enquiry. Unlike Whittington, however, Beattie also acknowledges the growing interdisciplinary and critical stream of financial accounting research, drawing on a wide range of social, political and economic theories. Another historical review of financial accounting theory is that of Lee (2009), who identifies an exploratory period before 1940, a period of 'classical theory' from 1940 to 1970, and finally a period of 'scientific theory' after 1970.

This chapter also adopts a historical approach, examining five main periods. The first of these covers the long period from the emergence of accounting as a practice in English-speaking countries to the early 1920s. At that point, accounting was no longer simply a practice, but rather the object of university education and academic study. The 1920s and 1930s saw some early attempts at providing both descriptive and deductive theories of accounting, but the so-called 'golden age' of a priori research in accounting (Nelson, 1973: 4) was to come later, in the 1950s and more particularly the 1960s. By the end of that decade, what was to become 'market-based accounting research' had emerged, while the 1970s and 1980s experienced a radical split in financial accounting research, with accounting standard setters attempting to develop and apply conceptual frameworks and statements of accounting principles in order to improve financial reporting, while academic researchers concentrated on social science-based empirical research. More recently, scholars and practitioners of financial reporting have continued to draw on an eclectic range of theories to guide their research and practice.

2. The emergence of financial accounting theory

2.1 Early theoretical ideas about accounting

Textbooks and treatises on accounting (specifically double-entry bookkeeping) were printed and published in the English language from the sixteenth century onwards. The writers of textbooks were often teachers of bookkeeping, and although they often speculated as to whether accounting should be regarded as an art or a science, their main goal was to educate merchants and their children into the mysteries of debit and credit. Jackson (1956) observes that many of the textbook writers attempted to develop one or more rules for determining which account would be debited and which credited, either in general or for specific transactions. Jackson (1956: 288) quotes the earliest surviving English-language textbook (the edition by John Mellis of Hugh Oldcastle's *A Briefe Instruction and Maner how to Keepe Bookes of Accompts*, published in 1588) as establishing the rule that 'all things received, or the receiver, must owe to all things delivered, or the deliverer', a rule that survived well into the twentieth century as 'debit the account that receives value and credit the account that gives value'.

Early British writers attempted to provide a general structure for double-entry through 'personification' of accounts. Although many accounts in a merchant's ledger would relate to people with whom the merchant transacted, others, such as income and expense accounts, were more abstract. Personification encouraged the merchant to think of such accounts as representing either independent living entities or aspects of the merchant's own personality. By the nineteenth century, personification had mutated (particularly in early US textbooks) to an early form of the 'proprietorship theory' of accounts, where transactions are regarded primarily as affecting the owner's interest in the business rather than as simply giving rise to debits and credits. Jackson (1956: 307) traces this approach back to Hustcraft Stephens, writing in 1735, and he notes how Stephens began his book by stating that he planned 'to offer no rules, until he has shown them to be consequences of conclusions, plainly drawn from self-evident principles'.' Here we see a forerunner of the 'deductive' approach to accounting theory. The proprietorship approach placed emphasis on what was to become known as the 'balance sheet equation', where ownership interest was equated to assets less liabilities, and this equation approach was expressed algebraically by F. W. Cronhelm, in *Double Entry by Single* (published in 1818). However, as Jackson (1956: 312) notes, the proprietary approach, with the balance sheet equation, was to disappear from British textbooks before being rediscovered in the latter part of the nineteenth century in the USA.

2.2 Professional theorizing in Britain

A demand for systematic thinking about financial accounting and reporting emerged with the growth of the corporate economy and the establishment of professional accountancy bodies, whose roles included training and examining accountants. The earliest professional body in the English-speaking world was the Society of Accountants in Edinburgh, founded in 1854, while professional bodies began to be established in England from 1870 (Poullaos, 2009: 250–51). A weekly magazine, *The Accountant*, established in London in 1876, provided an outlet for articles and lectures, often by leading accountants of the day such as Edwin Guthrie and Ernest Cooper, some of which have been collected by Brief (1976). Their articles 'show an originality and an emphasis on *principle*' (Kitchen and Parker, 1980: 22) rather than being merely ad hoc responses to issues of current interest. Moreover, textbooks oriented towards the aspiring professional accountant rather than the bookkeeper began to be published. Francis Pixley, an eminent chartered accountant, wrote the first textbook on auditing, published in 1881 (Kitchen and Parker, 1980: 23), while Lawrence Dicksee combined a professional practice with both writing and teaching, becoming the first professor of accounting at a British university in 1902 (ibid.: 60) and subsequently going on to hold the first chair in accounting at the London School of Economics (Napier, 2011: 188).

As well as writing a standard textbook on auditing, which was to inspire the leading US auditing textbook by Montgomery (Power, 1992), Dicksee was the author of *Advanced Accounting* (Dicksee, 1903), which he intended for both professional and university students. Dicksee stressed the importance of principles, but his main framework was the distinction between capital and revenue. This was important in determining when profits could be recognised in financial statements, and the amounts at which assets and liabilities should be stated in the balance sheet, but it drew mainly on legal notions, developed over decades in the British courts, but not necessarily in a systematic and rational way. Dicksee often supported his recommendations with little more than the instinct for 'good practice' that he had developed over his professional career. For example, he rejected annual revaluations to determine the expense to recognize for the use of assets (a method that he described as 'theoretically the most perfect') because it would lead to uneven amounts being charged from year to year (ibid.: 227).

Dicksee's books, together with other studies (such as Garcke and Fells' 1887 *Factory Accounts* and Ewing Matheson's 1884 *The Depreciation of Factories* – see Napier, 1996: 455), provided some systematic understanding of financial accounting and reporting, but they are only rudimentary attempts at developing an accounting *theory*. Principles were not always stated explicitly, although it is possible to discern a general belief that dividends should be paid out of income but that capital should be maintained – what 'capital maintenance' actually involved in practice, though, was debated. Moreover, the professional accountants who contributed to the early British theoretical literature were influenced by their experience of corporate failures and tended to advocate conservative accounting, with a strong realization concept and prudence in asset measurement. Prudence was, however, tempered by an acknowledgement that accounting should regard most businesses as going concerns, so assets could in most cases be measured using a cost-based approach rather than in terms of current market values.

2.3 Emergence of theory in the USA

In the USA, writers had been discussing 'the science of accounts' since the mid-nineteenth century (McMillan, 1998: 3). Early textbook writers, such as Thomas Jones and Benjamin Franklin Foster (Previts and Merino: 1998: 78–80) rejected the rote learning of rules of bookkeeping and argued that a genuine understanding of accounting could come only through a grasp of principles. Just as the establishment of *The Accountant* provided a forum for British accountants to discuss conceptual issues, so the creation of *The Book-keeper* in 1880 furnished an outlet for writers such as Charles E. Sprague, whose articles under the title 'The algebra of accounts' presented accounting as a branch of mathematics (McMillan, 1998: 9) and used the balance sheet equation to derive specific bookkeeping entries for various classes of transaction. This periodical was published by an early US professional body, the Institute of Accountants and Book-keepers of the City of New York (subsequently known simply as the Institute of Accounts), founded in 1882 with the aim of establishing the practice of accounting on a 'scientific' basis (McMillan, 1999). The Institute modelled itself on the American Society of Mechanical Engineers, and, by analogy with the science of mechanics, advocated a science of 'accountics'. Although this term did not catch on, the notion that accounting should be understood as a system grounded in logic rather than as a collection of specific and arbitrary practices stimulated a way of studying accounting that was quite alien to British accountants.

Among the important early theoretical studies was Sprague's (1908) *The Philosophy of Accounts*, which proposed a proprietary theory of accounting, with income regarded as the change in owners' capital. Of more lasting influence was the work of Henry Rand Hatfield, one of the earliest professors of accounting in the USA (Mills, 1994; Zeff, 2000; Parker, 2002). Hatfield did not come from a professional accounting background, but rather had studied economics and later worked in banking. His major theoretical work, *Modern Accounting: Its Principles and Some of its Problems* (Hatfield, 1909), emphasized the balance sheet as a statement of financial position, with income being determined as the by-product of asset and liability measurement. Asset valuation should be based on an assumption that the business was a going concern, rather than reflecting liquidation value, and accountants could disregard fluctuations in the market value of property, plant and equipment. Hatfield also stressed the need to provide for depreciation, viewing this as a measure of the cost of using an asset rather than as an optional provision for asset replacement. Although Hatfield did not disapprove of the upward revaluation of land to reflect current market values, his overall approach provides a paradigm of what was later to be called 'historical cost accounting'.

3. Applying economics to accounting

3.1 1920s and 1930s – USA

By the early 1920s, accounting in English-speaking countries was being taught and studied at universities as well as within the profession, but with an emphasis on practice rather than theory. To the extent that a coherent theoretical position was articulated, it tended to be based on making sense of existing practice rather than deduction from general principles. Perhaps reflecting the importance of stock markets in the UK and USA, businesses were viewed from the owners' perspective (proprietary theory) rather than as pools of assets against which various stakeholders had claims (entity theory). This was to change in different ways during the 1920s and 1930s, as entity theory was developed as a potential counterbalance to proprietary theory, while various scholars drew on economic theory and employed methods of logical deduction to make recommendations about improvements to accounting practice.

The scholar most associated with entity theory was William A. Paton, author of *Accounting Theory: With Special Reference to the Corporate Enterprise* (Paton, 1922; see also Previts and Robinson, 1994). Rather than seeing the role of financial reporting as showing the financial position of the business to its owners, Paton argued that managers needed information to allow them to maintain the assets of the business ('properties') and hence protect the claims of creditors as well as owners (which Paton referred to collectively as 'equities'). This led Paton to advocate replacement costs rather than historical costs, to enable managers to maintain the physical capital of the business by retaining sufficient resources to allow for replacing assets as they were used. Paton also used an approach that was to recur in the 1960s, when he attempted to identify various fundamental principles – 'postulates' – of accounting. Paton's ideas were taken further by Henry W. Sweeney, who also drew on theoretical approaches from Germany (including the work of Schmalenbach and Schmidt; see Chapter 4). Sweeney's book *Stabilized Accounting* (Sweeney, 1936; see also Tweedie and Whittington, 1984: 32–4) advocated the use of general price level adjustments to restate the amounts in financial statements in units of constant purchasing power, thus correcting for the impact of general price change (inflation and deflation) on costs and values measured at different points in time. Sweeney distinguished between general inflation and the change in prices of specific goods and services, and proposed the use of replacement costs to show how individual items in the financial statements were affected by changing prices. He also called for an income statement that separated gains and losses that were realized, through actual transactions, from gains and losses that arose through remeasurement and hence were unrealized.

Although the proprietary theorists stressed the importance of the balance sheet, the stock market boom in the 1920s saw investors increasingly looking to the income statement as a measure of business performance. Because assets and liabilities in the balance sheet were measured using different bases, with some items shown at original cost, others at cost less depreciation and still others at valuations, and because many businesses used 'income-smoothing' accounting methods such as spreading the recognition of various expenditures over several periods, the number shown as owners' equity in the balance sheet often bore no systematic relationship to the value of the business to its owners. Similarly, the net profit shown in the income statement was the outcome of applying often arbitrary accounting policies. One scholar who attempted to overcome this by going back to economic principles was John B. Canning, whose *The Economics of Accountancy* (Canning, 1929) drew on the ideas of economists such as Irving Fisher to propose a view of assets as embodying 'future services in money'. On this basis, the income of a business was, in principle, the amount by which the value of the business (conceptualized as the discounted net present value of its future cash flows) had increased during a period, with assets and liabilities being measured in terms of expected future cash flows (which would often be equivalent to current market values). Canning believed that income was a real phenomenon capable of objective measurement, and claimed of conventional accounting that:

> What is set out as a measure of net income can never be supposed to be a fact in any sense at all except that it is the figure that results when the accountant has finished applying the procedures which he adopts (Canning, 1929: 98).

3.2 1920s and 1930s – UK

Canning's study was to influence some young scholars at the London School of Economics, including Ronald Edwards and Ronald Coase. These theorists also took on board ideas of economists working in the UK in the 1930s, including Lionel Robbins, Friedrich von Hayek and John Hicks (Napier, 1996: 464). These economists emphasized the notion of economics as the science of choice among alternatives where resources are limited but wants are unlimited. Making the best possible choices requires appropriate information, and Edwards saw the object of published accounts as being 'the provision of information for a judgement of net worth [to allow] the shareholder to calculate his income' (Edwards, 1977: 139). Edwards endorsed the use of discounted cash flow for asset measurement, and was highly critical of existing accounting practices such as the use of mechanistic depreciation methods. Coase (1973) argued for the use of opportunity costs for decision-making, where the 'cost' of an action is regarded as the incremental revenues foregone by not taking the best alternative action. Both Edwards and Coase considered that information for decision-making within the enterprise should be consistent with information for decision-making by the owners of the enterprise (they took for granted the view that the duty of managers is to maximize returns to owners, although they were aware that this duty was not always put into practice). Hence, measurement methods that were rational for internal decisions should also be appropriate for external financial reporting. The opportunity cost of using an asset was often, though not always, the cost of replacing the asset, so if opportunity cost was rational for business decisions, then replacement cost would generally, but not always, be appropriate for financial reporting.

A more nuanced version of replacement cost, reflecting those situations where it would not be rational to replace a resource used by the business, was available in the form of 'value to the owner' (also referred to as 'value to the business' and 'deprival value'), a concept usually attributed to Bonbright (1937). This is equal to replacement cost when it is rational for the business to replace, which will be whenever the replacement cost is less than the amount that the business expects to earn from selling the resource (net realizable value) or from using the resource on an ongoing basis in the business ('economic value', usually measured as the present value of incremental net cash inflows from using the resource). If it is not rational to replace the resource, then the resource is valued at net realizable value or economic value, whichever is greater. This approach to valuation is equivalent to opportunity cost, but it suffers from the practical difficulty that some or all of the three measurement bases (replacement cost, net realizable value and economic value) may not be easily observable, and all of them may involve some element of estimation.

3.3 *The quest for accounting principles*

Theoretical ideas in accounting often reflect the economic background against which they are developed. In the late nineteenth century, the growth of the corporate economy in the UK and USA gave rise to a demand for external financial reporting. This came against a background of long-term deflation, where the use of current values rather than cost-based measures for assets was perceived as introducing an undesirable element of volatility into profit determination. The 1920s were a period of inflation, when historical costs were increasingly out of date as indicators of asset values. The 1930s, on the other hand, were a time of economic depression, when investors and financial regulators reacted against what was seen with hindsight as the excessively optimistic financial reporting of the 1920s. This led to both a 'mainstream' and a 'minority' reaction. In the USA, the American Accounting Association published a short document containing various 'accounting principles' (AAA, 1936). This document proposed an 'unexpired cost' approach to measuring physical assets – the amount at which such assets were to be shown in the balance sheet was that part of the original cost that had not yet been treated as an expense relating to the use of the asset. The income statement was to show the period's operating profit separately from capital gains and losses and extraordinary items, and accurate calculation of earnings per share was explicitly mentioned as a key aim of financial reporting. This was a system of strict historical cost, with profit determination being the main aim of financial accounting.

The AAA's historical cost approach was to be largely endorsed by the US accountancy profession, and it was expanded upon by two important studies. The first of these was *A Statement of Accounting Principles* (Sanders *et al.*, 1938). This was significant in introducing the notion of 'generally accepted accounting principles' (GAAP), which could be deduced from observation of accounting practice or from authoritative statements by recognized organizations or leading accountants (themselves likely to be distilling current practice). The second study, *An Introduction to Corporate Accounting Standards* (Paton and Littleton, 1940), is heavily focused on income measurement (the balance sheet is scarcely mentioned), driven by recognition of revenues, to which costs are matched ('costs attach' – Paton and Littleton, 1940: 13), while 'unexpired costs' are carried forward to later periods. Paton and Littleton propose an entity theory: 'Accounting theory ... should explain the concepts of revenue and expense in terms of enterprise asset-changes rather than as increases or decreases in proprietors' or stockholders' equities' (Paton and Littleton, 1940: 9), with a presumption that the business entity is a going concern. Accounting is not about valuation: assets are acquired and paid for as sources of potential services, which are then utilized over time, so measures of current value are normally irrelevant.

However, acceptance of this historical cost approach was not unanimous. One important exception was Kenneth MacNeal, author of *Truth in Accounting* (MacNeal, 1939; see also Zeff, 1982). MacNeal argued that the use of historical costs provided managers with wide opportunities to manipulate reported earnings, for example through the timing of transactions and consequential recognition of gains and losses. Historical cost accounting also allowed for both understatement and overstatement of assets and liabilities; the amount at which an asset was shown in the balance sheet might bear no relationship to its current value. MacNeal saw the remedy as lying in the use of market values for items in the balance sheet. Market values, which MacNeal (1939: 87) emphasized were the prices at which commodities were actually being bought and sold, had the virtues of objectivity and verifiability (virtues that were also admired by Paton and Littleton, 1940: 18, but regarded by them as attributes of historical costs), and limited scope for managerial manipulation. As Zeff (1982: 539) observes, MacNeal was not an unqualified advocate of market prices: 'MacNeal applies market prices only to marketable securities and raw materials. It was evidently his belief that other classes of assets could not normally be found to trade in acceptable markets.' In such circumstances, MacNeal tended to favour replacement cost as a surrogate for market price.

By 1940, therefore, most of the elements of accounting theory that would be debated over the next 40 years or so were already in place. In the USA, statements of accounting principles were being promulgated, based on a combination of induction from existing practice and scholarly reflection, and these tended to uphold a conservative, historical cost-based form of financial accounting. On the other hand, some theorists found within economics a body of ideas and concepts that led them to advocate alternative measurement approaches, including replacement cost, discounted cash flow, market value and combinations of these. Issues of the measurement unit (money or purchasing power) and the components of income were associated with different views as to the objectives of corporate financial reporting, the stakeholders to whom businesses were deemed accountable, and the concepts of capital to be maintained. Over the following decades, these ideas were to be mobilized in different combinations by various 'grand theorists' seeking either general theories of accounting or more specific theoretical foundations for financial reporting.

4. Grand theories of financial reporting

4.1 Induction or deduction? Littleton versus Chambers

The late 1930s and early 1940s saw the beginnings of formal involvement by professional accountancy bodies in the development of statements of accounting 'principles', although this term usually implied the provision of guidance on how to account for particular transactions and situations rather than general foundations for financial reporting. In the USA, the American Institute of Accountants started to issue accounting research bulletins in 1939 (Previts and Merino, 1998: 284). In the UK, the Institute of Chartered Accountants in England and Wales began issuing its recommendations on accounting principles in 1942 (Zeff, 2009). With a few exceptions, these pronouncements did little more than legitimize existing practice, and the recommendations and bulletins often lacked a statement establishing the reasons why the issuing bodies had reached the conclusions expressed in the documents. The dominant role played by preparers and auditors of financial statements in the development of these pronouncements meant that changes to current practice were resisted. To some extent, this resistance to change was endorsed by Littleton (1953), whose *Structure of Accounting Theory* put forward a 'survival of the fittest' view: accounting methods found in practice were likely to have survived because they were most appropriate. Hence, current practice should be the starting point for the accounting theorist, whose main role would be to extract the underlying principles and postulates that help to explain and structure observed practice. Given that existing practice in the 1950s was grounded in historical cost, matching and income measurement, which was consistent with the earlier Paton and Littleton (1940) study, Littleton's approach defended rather than challenged the status quo.

However, several academic writers developed general critiques of existing financial accounting practice and often provided alternative systems. An early contributor not only in substantive terms but also in his analysis of what a theory of accounting should be was the Australian accounting professor Raymond Chambers (Gaffikin, 1994). In an early publication, *Blueprint for a theory of accounting* (Chambers, 1955), he denounced those who described systematic descriptions of existing practice as 'theories of accounting', and suggested that a theory should involve 'building up a series of relevant propositions from a few fundamental axioms' (ibid.: 19). These propositions would enable 'the development of ideal systems of accounts' (ibid.: 24), and hence allow accountants not only to identify the flaws in current accounting practice but also to correct the flaws in a logical rather than ad hoc way. Chambers considered that the entities that carry on organized activities (including but not limited to businesses) are managed rationally, that 'statements in monetary terms of the transactions and relationships of the entity' help to achieve rational management, and that deriving such statements is a service function (ibid.: 19). To Chambers, an effective theory of accounting had to be 'scientific' in the sense that it was grounded in sound assumptions and principles from which hypotheses about the real world could be derived and tested. Although this provided a conceptual model of how Chambers saw the structure of an accounting theory, it needed to be fleshed out, and over the next ten years he drew on ideas from a wide range of disciplines, including management science, economics and psychology, to develop the system of Continuously Contemporary Accounting. His book *Accounting, Evaluation and Economic Behavior* (Chambers, 1966) represents a tour de force of eclectic scholarship, moving from multi-disciplinary theoretical foundations to practical recommendations. Chambers considered that the main requirement for financial reporting was to provide information about the ability of organizations to respond to changes in their circumstances, and this led him to favour the use of realizable values for assets (and settlement values for liabilities), with a stable purchasing power measuring unit to overcome the problem that measurements undertaken in previous periods were not directly comparable with contemporary measurements because of general price change.

4.2 The North American contribution

The 1960s saw a range of monographs and reports addressing the objectives of financial reporting and what these might imply for the detailed form and content of financial statements. Edwards and Bell (1961) attempted to develop a system for the measurement of enterprise income that would be useful for a wide range of users and that would overcome the problems of financial reporting in conditions of changing prices. Their system had similarities with that of Sweeney, with use of replacement costs for most assets (though with realizable values for short-term assets) and adjustments for general price change. Edwards and Bell focused on income rather than on the balance sheet, and critics regarded the use of a mixed measurement system as theoretically incoherent, but their income statement drew clear distinctions between profits from operations and from holding assets, 'nominal' gains (where the economic impact of general price change is disregarded) and 'real' gains (where the 'fictitious' profits generated purely by inflation are removed), and realized and unrealized gains (Tweedie and Whittington, 1984: 54). Separately measuring and reporting all these elements would make it possible for different users, with different perceptions of what constitutes income, to combine components of comprehensive income in the way they found most useful. The information perspective was taken further by Staubus, who asserted that 'The purpose of accounting is to provide information which will be of assistance in making economic decisions' (Staubus, 1961: 11). He focused on what he called the 'investment' decision, which related to granting credit to or investing in an economic unit, while sidelining other uses and users. Staubus argued that investors would be particularly interested in what he called 'residual equity': assets minus liabilities. This led him to emphasize the balance sheet over the income statement, with income being conceptualized as the change in residual equity. Staubus (1961: 51) ranked various measurement techniques in terms of their 'relevance to residual equity holders', preferring discounted future cash flows and net realizable values to replacement costs, with historical costs given the lowest ranking.

Other 'grand theories' were proposed by Mattessich (1964), who, like Chambers, drew on a wide range of disciplines, including management science, to develop an analytical framework for financial reporting, and by Ijiri (1967), who advocated the provision of 'objective' information and saw historical cost accounting as the best way of achieving this. Ijiri argued that the double-entry system, by recording transactions as they happened in a systematic way, provided the most appropriate basis for the provision of objective information. Sterling (1970), on the other hand, considered historical cost information to be effectively meaningless, and favoured current market prices as providing all of the information that would be relevant to the key economic decisions that he believed were fundamental to the use of financial statements. Moonitz (1961) and Sprouse and Moonitz (1962) used the approach of stating 'postulates' and deriving 'principles' to advocate a movement away from historical cost accounting and the then prevalent emphasis on income measurement.

4.3 Applying theories of accounting – standards and inflation

By the end of the 1960s, a wide range of theories of accounting existed. These theories almost always criticized existing accounting practice, which antagonized those practitioners who saw little if anything wrong with existing practice. However, they offered a wide range of remedies, which were often inconsistent with those of rival theories. For the remedies to be considered, the 'patient' – preparers, users and auditors of financial statements – needed to accept that accounting was 'sick', which would then provide a context for attempts to 'make accounting better' (Napier, 2006: 468). Two factors encouraged such self-awareness: financial scandals in the late 1960s in the USA, UK, Australia and other countries that exposed financial accounting as open to manipulation by unscrupulous managers, and the rapid increase in the rate of general inflation in the early 1970s, which seemed to suggest that historical cost accounting needed to be replaced by a system that dealt properly with changing prices. The solution to the first problem, improved procedures for issuing accounting standards, provided some promise to grand theorists of accounting that their ideas would be reflected in more rigorously grounded pronouncements, ultimately developed within a conceptual framework. An important catalyst for this was *A Statement of Basic Accounting Theory* (AAA, 1966), which endorsed the user needs/decision usefulness approach of Staubus and argued that this was best fulfilled through the provision of information on different bases, not just historical cost but also 'current cost' (essentially replacement cost) numbers. After the establishment of the Financial Accounting Standards Board in the USA in 1973, and other standard-setting bodies in predominantly English-speaking countries, financial accounting theory took the form of the development of a conceptual framework for financial reporting (this is considered later in this chapter).

Attempts to address the impact of inflation on accounting gained particular prominence in the UK. Academics at the London School of Economics, including William Baxter, Harold Edey and David Solomons (the so-called 'LSE triumvirate' – Whittington, 1994), had evinced a particular interest in accounting for price changes, with their ideas often communicated through teaching (many of the first generation of UK accounting professors studied at the LSE) and articles in the professional accountancy press rather than monographs. Baxter's major book, *Accounting Values and Inflation* (Baxter, 1975) summed up several decades of developing thought, and proposed a system combining the use of 'deprival value' for measurement of assets with general price level adjustment to address what Baxter called the 'time-lag error' arising from inflation. As Whittington (1994: 259) notes, Baxter's more radical proposals were combined 'with the traditional prudence of the professional accountant (in avoiding recording unrealised real holding gains in the profit and loss account).' The rapid rise in general inflation in the early 1970s in the UK led the recently established Accounting Standards Steering Committee to propose a supplementary system of financial reporting based on a current purchasing power approach (basically historical cost adjusted for inflation using a general price index). The British government, which resisted the use of widespread indexation of prices and incomes for fear that this would lead to ever-increasing rates of inflation, set up a committee of enquiry into accounting for inflation (known, after its chairman, as the Sandilands Committee). The committee recommended a system of current cost accounting, with assets measured at 'value to the business' (that is, deprival value), but without any indexation of amounts in the financial statements to reflect general price change (Inflation Accounting Committee, 1975). Attempts to implement the recommendations of the Sandilands Committee met with resistance from accountants in practice and industry. A version of the proposals that incorporated some ad hoc adjustments was eventually to become a requirement for UK listed companies, as supplementary financial statements. The requirement lasted only for a few years, until the rate of inflation fell and an interest in adjusting financial statements to reflect the impact of price changes diminished.

The Sandilands Committee's report is interesting for its attempts to base its recommendations on discerning 'the requirements of users of accounts' (Inflation Accounting Committee, 1975: para. 144), without necessarily providing specific empirical evidence of what users actually wanted. The style of reasoning, where conclusions are arrived at through the use of discursive arguments that are presented in a way that challenges readers to dare to disagree, echoes the writing style of many of the 'grand theorists' of accounting. But the debate over inflation accounting was perhaps the swansong of grand theory, at least as a central factor in accounting discourse. This is not to suggest that theories *of* accounting disappeared; rather, it is to acknowledge that such theories became increasingly marginalized in academic accounting discourse. Instead, leading academic accountants in English-speaking countries began to claim that theories *of* accounting were not really 'theories' at all, and to advocate greater use of theories *about* accounting.

5. Theorizing financial reporting within a (social) science framework

5.1 The rejection of grand theories

With few exceptions, the grand theorists believed that current financial reporting practice was deficient, and aimed for the improvement of accounting. But companies continued to use traditional accounting methods and reject what the grand theorists believed to be almost self-evidently superior approaches. Was there evidence that traditional methods actually served important functions? In other words, did traditional financial reporting meet the needs of relevant users better than alternative approaches? From the late 1960s, accounting researchers, particularly in the USA, attempted to explore these issues through research into the statistical relationship between information in financial statements and variables such as security prices and returns. A huge body of research followed the study by Ball and Brown (1968) of the extent to which variations in corporate earnings were associated with variations in stock market returns. Ball and Brown had begun their paper with a denunciation of grand theory, suggesting that theories *of* accounting could not be assessed independently of their own assumptions: 'and how does one explain the predictive power of propositions which are based on unverifiable assumptions such as the maximization of utility functions?' (ibid.: 159). They set out to demonstrate that claims of grand theorists 'that income numbers cannot be defined substantively, that they lack "meaning" and are therefore of doubtful utility' (ibid.: 159), had no empirical basis, and they were able to find a statistical association between the reporting of higher than expected earnings with supernormal share price returns, and between the reporting of lower than expected earnings with sub-normal share price returns.

The Ball and Brown study can be read as actually vindicating rather than refuting the claims of the grand theorists, as the researchers found that only a small amount of the variation in returns was explained by variation in reported earnings. They suggested that this was because most of the 'information content' of earnings announcements was already known to investors from other sources, so that annual financial statements largely functioned as confirmations of other information rather than news in their own right. However, theorists such as Chambers and Sterling were slow to respond to the new empiricism in financial accounting research. Perhaps this was because they saw this trend not as rejecting their general methodological approach but rather as putting it into practice. Chambers regarded the way he thought about accounting as 'scientific', and Sterling was subsequently to write a monograph with the title *Toward a Science of Accounting* (Sterling, 1979), so the claims of the new empirical researchers that they were 'doing science' could have been regarded as building on rather than rejecting grand theories. But, by the mid-1970s, the grand theorists were increasingly marginalized in academic research (though they continued to be influential in standard-setting contexts).

5.2 Positive accounting theory

The research of Ball and Brown and their followers used economic theory, more specifically the new theory of finance that was emerging in the 1960s, to provide a justification of how accounting disclosures could be expected to affect security prices. When the empirical evidence supported theory-based predictions and hypotheses, this was interpreted as establishing the use (and hence usefulness) of accounting information. But the rapidly expanding programme of 'market-based accounting research' was, in the opinion of some researchers, not actually 'accounting theory' at all, but rather an application of finance theory. To count as 'accounting theory', within the social science model, a theory should be explaining accounting practice, such as the choices made by firms and managers as to how to account for particular types of transaction and event, or the preferences of different individuals and groups for particular forms of accounting regulation, such as accounting standards. In short, accounting theory should explain and predict accounting choices. This implied that accounting theory should be a theory of human choice, and the dominant theory that attempted to explain human choice was neo-classical economic theory.

As this chapter has demonstrated, many of the grand theories of accounting appealed to economics, usually seeing the primary role of accounting as the provision of information useful for making economic decisions. But theorists had often characterized the information process as one of neutral and objective measurement of real-world phenomena. The new economic theory *about* accounting rejected this assumption of neutrality and objectivity, and argued that accounting numbers made a difference to the income and wealth of various individuals and groups involved in organizations. For example, managers were frequently rewarded through profit-related pay and through shares and options whose value depended on investors' perceptions of a company's financial position and future prospects. If financial statements provided information to investors in assessing these (and this was a core belief not only of grand theorists but also of accounting standard-setters), then managers would have a clear economic incentive to choose accounting practices that would be likely to lead to the reporting of higher profits. On the other hand, other stakeholders, such as lenders, might have an incentive to insist on accounting policies that led to reporting of lower profits and more conservative asset values, as this could enhance the security of their loans by restraining risky management behaviour. Ideas of how economic incentives and constraints, built into regulatory structures and contracts, could be predicted to influence accounting policy choices and preferences became formalized as positive accounting theory, associated in particular with Watts and Zimmerman (1978, 1986).

Advocates of this approach to accounting theory reject theories *of* accounting as 'normative', tainted because they lead to value judgements over which accounting methods are 'better' or 'worse' than others. A 'positive' theory, on the other hand, is seen as capable of escaping from value judgements. It 'takes the world as it is', assuming that economic actors such as managers and investors behave rationally, and that the outcome of rational economic choices is the best possible within the constraints of available knowledge, technology and institutions. The role of theory is to allow researchers to deduce hypotheses – predictions about the relationships between variables that can be tested by reference to real-world data. Positive accounting theory may provide predictions of how accounting regulators and standard-setters are likely to respond to self-interested lobbying by preparers, auditors and users of financial statements, and what may be the consequences of adopting particular accounting standards: it is not, however, the role of a positive theory of accounting to determine what those standards ought to be.

Positive accounting theory has been heavily criticized (often by grand theorists such as Chambers, 1993, and Sterling, 1990, but also by more radical scholars such as Tinker, 1988) for mistaking the important roles of theory in shaping a practical activity. To critics, accounting theory that does not help to guide accountants towards 'better' practices is of little value (although the critics do not agree on which practices are 'better'). Moreover, positive accounting theory is criticized for hypocrisy – its use of neo-classical economic theory, privileging investors and creditors over other stakeholders, is claimed to be far from value-free. Accounting research within the positive tradition has become increasingly sophisticated in terms of its use of statistical techniques and mathematical analysis, but genuinely surprising findings emerge only rarely. However, positive accounting theory is not the only theory *about* accounting. Researchers have drawn on many different intellectual traditions and academic disciplines to provide theoretical frameworks for understanding aspects of financial reporting. For example, legitimacy theory (Suchman, 1995), which suggests that companies are granted an implicit 'licence to operate' by society that will be withdrawn or curtailed if companies are viewed as behaving in ways regarded by society as 'illegitimate', has been used widely as a way of explaining corporate social and environmental disclosures (see for example Deegan, 2002). Accounting researchers have moved beyond the financial statements to investigate and analyse corporate disclosures not just in printed annual reports but also through the internet (see for example Craven and Marston, 1999). There appears to be no limit to the disciplines from which theories *about* accounting may be drawn: for example, Davison (2007) uses the ideas of the French cultural theorist Roland Barthes to 'decode' photographs appearing in the financial reports of a non-governmental organization.

There is no doubt that the wide range of theories *about* accounting, often applied in ways that their originators, in fields far from accounting, would not have predicted, has provided many insights into accounting and financial reporting practice in its widest sense. However, these theories are of little use to those who still see the main role of theory as lying in its capacity to improve accounting. Hence, theories *of* accounting, while out of favour for a long time in the academy (at least in English-speaking countries), insinuate themselves into the process of accounting regulation, through the need for accounting standards to be adequately grounded in a rational structure of principles – a conceptual framework. Hence this chapter concludes with a brief review of the tenacity of theories *of* accounting, while suggesting that the dichotomy between theories *of* and theories *about* accounting may be losing its relevance.

6. Conceptual frameworks

While much accounting research went off in an 'archival–empirical' direction from the late 1960s, accounting standard setters needed to have theoretical justifications to rationalize their pronouncements. Many of the leading theorists *of* accounting became involved as members or advisers of standard-setting bodies, while professional accounting organizations increasingly sponsored fundamental research. In the USA, the Trueblood Committee, established by the American Institute of Certified Public Accountants, reported in 1973 on the objectives of financial statements, endorsing the widely accepted theoretical position that 'The basic objective of financial statements is to provide information useful for making economic decisions' (AICPA, 1973: 61). The Financial Accounting Standards Board regarded the establishment of a 'conceptual framework for accounting and reporting' as one of its main objectives, and the influence of theorists such as Staubus, Sterling, Solomons and others may be detected in the various statements of financial accounting concepts that emerged from the Board over subsequent years (for an overall review, see Macve, 1997).

The conceptual framework embodied a range of theoretical notions, including the user needs/decision usefulness approach, a core belief that useful accounting information should be both relevant and reliable (later this was to develop into the notion of representational faithfulness), and an emphasis on the balance sheet (or statement of financial position) over the income statement. However, specifying a conceptual framework was not sufficient in itself to provide a mechanistic way of addressing financial reporting problems – the conceptual framework provided the language through which the problems could be analysed and debated, but not the 'right answers'. This suggested to some theorists, for example Edward Stamp (CICA, 1980), that the nature of a conceptual framework had been misunderstood – it was not an axiomatic system of principles from which accounting practices could be deduced, but rather it was more like a legal constitution, which needed constant interpretation and reinterpretation. Arriving at solutions to accounting issues was more like the process by which judges reached verdicts and lawyers provided advice than like the activities of a mathematician or logician. Stamp's understanding of the nature of a conceptual framework can be seen in the ways in which conceptual ideas are mobilized in accounting debates, for example the ongoing debate over fair value measurement. A distinguished example of this is provided by the analysis of fair value in the light of the current joint project to update the conceptual framework, being undertaken by the Financial Accounting Standards Board and the International Accounting Standards Board, where Whittington (2008) teases out the assumptions that he considers are implicit in the standard-setters' position and proposes alternative assumptions, that would lead to different conclusions. This study demonstrates clearly the continuing relevance of theories *of* accounting.

To those who reject such theories, however, such assumptions are, in the words of Ball and Brown already quoted, 'unverifiable'. To Watts and Zimmerman (1979), accounting theories were economic commodities that were demanded by regulators and others to provide rationalizations for their own self-interested positions on accounting practices, and supplied by professional and academic accountants seeking money and fame. To Hines (1991), accounting theories were a means by which accountants established and maintained their role in society and provided legitimacy to accounting as an occupational category. The mere existence of a conceptual framework, on this analysis, is as important as its substantive content. Theories *of* accounting tend to see the function of financial reporting as representing an economic reality that may be complex and difficult to discern but nonetheless exists independently of accounting. Hines (1988) denies this, claiming that accounting actually helps to construct the reality that it reports. This provides interesting opportunities for the future direction of financial accounting theory – the use of theories *of* accounting in addressing accounting issues can itself be an object of study that can be understood through the application of theories *about* accounting, while accounting standard-setters can use theories *about* accounting to make explicit the assumptions they make and pressures they react to when developing accounting proposals, rather than applying theories *of* accounting without being fully aware of what they are doing. To paraphrase Keynes (1936: 383), practical accountants, who believe themselves to be quite exempt from any intellectual influences, are usually the slaves of some defunct accounting theorist. The future role for theory in financial reporting may be to expose such slavery and at the same time provide the means for emancipation.

Bibliography

AAA (1936) 'A Tentative Statement of Accounting Principles Affecting Corporate Reports', *The Accounting Review* 11(2): 187–91.

AAA (1966) *A Statement of Basic Accounting Theory* (Sarasota, FL: American Accounting Association).

AAA (1977) *Statement on Accounting Theory and Theory Acceptance* (Sarasota, FL: American Accounting Association).

AICPA (1973) *Objectives of Financial Statements*, report of the study group on the objectives of financial statements, Chairman R. M. Trueblood (New York: American Institute of Certified Public Accountants).

Ball, R. and Brown, P. (1968) 'An Empirical Evaluation of Accounting Income Numbers', *Journal of Accounting Research* 6(2): 159–78.

Baxter, W. T. (1975) *Accounting Values and Inflation* (London: McGraw-Hill).

Beattie, V. (2002) 'Traditions of Research in Financial Accounting', in B. Ryan, R. W. Scapens and M. Theobald (eds) *Research Method & Methodology in Finance & Accounting*, 2nd edn (Andover: South-Western, pp. 94–113).

Bonbright, J. C. (1937) *The Valuation of Property* (New York: McGraw-Hill).

Brief, R. P. (1976) *The Late Nineteenth Century Debate over Depreciation, Capital and Income* (New York: Arno Press).

Canning, J. B. (1929) *The Economics of Accountancy: A Critical Analysis of Accounting Theory* (New York: Ronald Press).

Chambers, R. J. (1955) 'Blueprint for a Theory of Accounting', *Accounting Research* 6(1): 17–25.

Chambers, R. J. (1966) *Accounting, Evaluation and Economic Behavior* (Englewood Cliffs, NJ: Prentice-Hall).

Chambers, R. J. (1993) 'Positive Accounting Theory and the PA Cult', *Abacus* 29(1): 1–26.

CICA (1980) *Corporate Reporting: Its Future Evolution*, author E. Stamp (Toronto: Canadian Institute of Chartered Accountants).

Coase, R. H. (1973) 'Business Organization and the Accountant', in J. M. Buchanan and G. F. Thirlby (eds) *L.S.E. Essays on Cost* (London: Weidenfeld & Nicolson, pp. 97–132. Originally published in *The Accountant*, October–December 1938).

Craven, B. M. and Marston, C. L. (1999) 'Financial Reporting on the Internet by Leading UK Companies', *The European Accounting Review* 8(2): 321–33.

Davison, J. (2007) 'Photographs and Accountability: Cracking the Codes of an NGO', *Accounting, Auditing & Accountability Journal* 20(1): 133–58.

Deegan, C. (2002) 'The Legitimising Effect of Social and Environmental Disclosures: A Theoretical Foundation', *Accounting, Auditing & Accountability Journal* 15(3): 282–311.

Deegan, C. and Unerman, J. (2011) *Financial Accounting Theory*, European edn (Maidenhead: McGraw-Hill Education).

Dicksee, L. R. (1903) *Advanced Accounting* (London: Gee & Co., reprinted New York: Arno Press, 1976).

Edwards, E. O. and Bell, P. W. (1961) *The Theory and Measurement of Business Income* (Berkeley, CA: University of California Press).

Edwards, R. S. (1977) 'The Nature and Measurement of Income', in W. T. Baxter and S. Davidson (eds) *Studies in Accounting*, 3rd edn (London: Institute of Chartered Accountants in England and Wales, pp. 96–140. Originally published in *The Accountant*, July–October 1938).

Gaffikin, M. (1994) 'Raymond Chambers (b. 1917): Determined Seeker of Truth and Fairness', in J. R. Edwards (ed.) *Twentieth-Century Accounting Thinkers* (London: Routledge, pp. 1–18).

Garcke, E. and Fells, J. M. (1887) *Factory Accounts: Their Principles and Practice: A Handbook for Accountants and Manufacturers* (London: Crosby, Lockwood).

Hatfield, H. R. (1909) *Modern Accounting: Its Principles and Some of its Problems* (New York: D. Appleton).

Hendriksen, E. S. and van Breda, M. F. (1992) *Accounting Theory*, 5th edn (Chicago, IL: Irwin).

Hines, R. D. (1988) 'Financial Accounting: In Communicating Reality, We Construct Reality', *Accounting, Organizations and Society* 13(3): 251–61.

Hines, R. D. (1991) 'The FASB's Conceptual Framework, Financial Accounting and the Maintenance of the Social World', *Accounting, Organizations and Society* 16(4): 313–31.

Ijiri, Y. (1967) *The Foundations of Accounting Measurement* (Englewood Cliffs, NJ: Prentice-Hall).

Inflation Accounting Committee (1975) *Report of the Inflation Accounting Committee*, Chairman F. E. P. Sandilands, Cmnd 6225 (London: Her Majesty's Stationery Office).

Jackson, J. G. C. (1956) 'The History of Methods of Exposition of Double-entry Book-keeping in England', in A. C. Littleton and B. S. Yamey (eds) *Studies in the History of Accounting* (London: Sweet & Maxwell, pp. 288–312).

Keynes, J. M. (1936) *The General Theory of Employment, Interest and Money* (London: Macmillan).

Kinney, W. R, Jr. (1989) 'Commentary on "The Relation of Accounting Research to Teaching and Practice: A 'Positive' View"', *Accounting Horizons* 3(1): 119–24.

Kitchen, J. and Parker, R. H. (1980) *Accounting Thought and Education: Six English Pioneers* (London: Institute of Chartered Accountants in England and Wales).

Lee, T. A. (2009) 'Financial Accounting Theory', in J. R. Edwards and S. P. Walker (eds) *The Routledge Companion to Accounting History* (London: Routledge, pp. 139–61).

Littleton, A. C. (1953) *Structure of Accounting Theory* (Sarasota, FL: American Accounting Association).

McMillan, K. P. (1998) 'The Science of Accounts: Bookkeeping Rooted in the Ideal of Science', *Accounting Historians Journal* 25(2): 1–33.

McMillan, K. P. (1999) 'The Institute of Accounts: A Community of the Competent', *Accounting, Business & Financial History* 9(1): 7–28.

MacNeal, K. F. (1939) *Truth in Accounting* (Philadephia, PA: University of Pennsylvania Press).

Macve, R. H. (1997) *A Conceptual Framework for Financial Accounting and Reporting: Vision, Tool or Threat?* (New York: Garland Publishing).

Matheson, E. (1884) *The Depreciation of Factories, Mines and Industrial Undertakings and their Valuation* (London: E. & F. N. Spon).

Mattessich, R. V. (1964) *Accounting and Analytical Methods* (Homewood, IL.: Irwin).

Mills, P. A. (1994) 'Henry Rand Hatfield (1866–1945): Life and Humor in the Dust of Ledgers', in J. R. Edwards (ed.) *Twentieth-Century Accounting Thinkers* (London: Routledge, pp. 293–308).

Moonitz, M. (1961) *The Basic Postulates of Accounting*, Accounting Research Study No. 1 (New York: American Institute of Certified Public Accountants).

Napier, C. J. (1996) 'Accounting and the Absence of a Business Economics Tradition in the United Kingdom', *The European Accounting Review* 5(3): 449–81.

Napier, C. J. (2006) 'Accounts of Change: 30 years of Historical Accounting Research', *Accounting, Organizations and Society* 31(4–5): 445–507.

Napier, C. J. (2011) 'Accounting at the London School of Economics: Opportunity Lost?', *Accounting History* 16(2): 185–205.

Nelson, C. L. (1973) 'A Priori Research in Accounting', in N. Dopuch and L. Revsine (eds) *Accounting Research 1960–1970: A Critical Evaluation* (Champaign, IL: Center for International Education and Research in Accounting, University of Illinois, pp. 3–19).

Parker, R. H. (2002) 'Henry Rand Hatfield (1866–1945): The Triumphs and Travails of an Academic Accounting Pioneer', *Accounting History* NS 7(2): 125–35.

Paton, W. A. (1922) *Accounting Theory: With Special Reference to the Corporate Enterprise* (New York: Ronald Press).

Paton, W. A. and Littleton, A. C. (1940) *An Introduction to Corporate Accounting Standards* (Evanston, IL: American Accounting Association).

Poullaos, C. (2009) 'Professionalisation', in J. R. Edwards and S. P. Walker (eds) *The Routledge Companion to Accounting History* (London: Routledge, pp. 247–73).

Power, M. K. (1992) 'From Common Sense to Expertise: Reflections on the Prehistory of Audit Sampling', *Accounting, Organizations and Society* 17(1): 37–62.

Previts, G. J. and Merino, B. D. (1998) *A History of Accountancy in the United States: The Cultural Significance of Accounting* (Columbus, OH: Ohio State University Press).
Previts, G. J. and Robinson, T. R. (1994) 'William A. Paton (1889–1991): Theorist and Educator', in J. R. Edwards (ed.) *Twentieth-Century Accounting Thinkers* (London: Routledge, pp. 309–18).
Riahi-Belkaoui, A. (2000) *Accounting Theory*, 4th edn (London: Thomson Learning).
Sanders, T. H., Hatfield, H. R. and Moore, U. (1938) *A Statement of Accounting Principles* (New York: American Institute of Accountants).
Scott, W. R. (2012) *Financial Accounting Theory* 6th edn (Toronto: Pearson Canada).
Sprague, C. E. (1908) *The Philosophy of Accounts* (New York: Ronald Press).
Sprouse, R. T. and Moonitz, M. (1962) *A Tentative Set of Broad Accounting Principles for Business Enterprises*, Accounting Research Study No. 3 (New York: American Institute of Certified Public Accountants).
Staubus, G. J. (1961) *A Theory of Accounting to Investors* (Berkeley, CA: University of California Press).
Sterling, R. R. (1970) *Theory of the Measurement of Enterprise Income* (Lawrence, KS: University Press of Kansas).
Sterling, R. R. (1979) *Toward a Science of Accounting* (Houston, TX: Scholars Book Company).
Sterling, R. R. (1990) 'Positive Accounting: An Assessment', *Abacus* 26(2): 97–135.
Suchman, M. C. (1995) 'Managing Legitimacy: Strategic and Institutional Approaches', *Academy of Management Review* 20(3): 571–610.
Sweeney, H. W. (1936) *Stabilized Accounting* (New York: Harper).
Tinker, T. (1988) 'Panglossian Accounting Theories: The Science of Apologising in Style', *Accounting, Organizations and Society* 13(2): 165–89.
Tweedie, D. and Whittington, G. (1984) *The Debate on Inflation Accounting* (Cambridge: Cambridge University Press).
Watts, R. L. and Zimmerman, J. L. (1978) 'Towards a Positive Theory of the Determination of Accounting Standards', *The Accounting Review* 53(1): 112–34.
Watts, R. L. and Zimmerman, J. L. (1979) 'The Demand for and Supply of Accounting Theories: The Market for Excuses', *The Accounting Review* 54(2): 273–305.
Watts, R. L. and Zimmerman, J. L. (1986) *Positive Accounting Theory* (Englewood Cliffs, NJ: Prentice-Hall).
Whittington, G. (1986) 'Financial Accounting Theory: An Over-View', *The British Accounting Review* 18(2): 4–41.
Whittington, G. (1994) 'The LSE Triumvirate and its Contribution to Price Change Accounting', in J. R. Edwards (ed.) *Twentieth-Century Accounting Thinkers* (London: Routledge, pp. 252–73).
Whittington, G. (2008) 'Fair Value and the FASB/IASB Conceptual Framework Project: An Alternative View', *Abacus* 44(2): 139–68.
Zeff, S. A. (1982) 'Truth in Accounting: The Ordeal of Kenneth MacNeal', *The Accounting Review* 57(3): 528–53.
Zeff, S. A. (2000) *Henry Rand Hatfield: Humanist, Scholar and Accounting Educator* (Stamford, CT: JAI Press).
Zeff, S. A. (2009) *Principles Before Standards: The ICAEW's 'N Series' of Recommendations on Accounting Principles 1942–1969* (London: Institute of Chartered Accountants in England and Wales).

Part 2
Reporting

6

Recognition and Measurement

Peter Walton

1. Introduction

Decisions about recognition and measurement are fundamental to any comprehensive basis of accounting, and to how that is applied in the accounting records and the financial statements of a reporting entity. Above all, recognition and measurement are boundary decisions in financial reporting and determine what part of the economic, social and legal whole that is a business or other entity is reported in the financial statements and how it is represented. Put another way, recognition and measurement decisions have the effect of defining the reporting entity.

In this chapter, the aim is to introduce the key issues that need to be addressed in making recognition and measurement decisions. These issues are discussed in detail in related chapters, and therefore this chapter will direct you to a full discussion elsewhere in the book, if you wish to pursue the issue further. The chapter will consider defining the entity, the objectives of financial reporting, recognition issues, measurement using a monetary unit, primacy of orientation, measurement bases and inflation.

1.1 Defining the reporting entity

The first logical step in recognition is to define what is the essential nature of the reporting entity and the elements it comprises, since that fixes what you want to recognize, before considering what aspects you privilege and how you portray them. For example, one way to think about the entity is that it consists of a series of legal rights and obligations. The criterion for what would be identified would be rights and obligations which could give rise to litigation or to prosecution, in other words all legal rights and obligations, whether contractual or statutory in origin. You would need a sufficient working knowledge of the law to define this, and then you would have to say how you would convey the existence of these rights and obligations to someone else – in other words, what attribute of the legal rights and obligations would you try to measure?

Would this be an adequate way to define the entity? The disadvantage of this approach is that there will be areas of uncertainty as to whether a legal obligation exists or not. For example, if you sell a product with a warranty, until someone claims against the warranty you do not know if there is a certain claim or not. Similarly there may be things to which the entity does not have a legal claim but which potentially can be used to advantage. The entity may have given good service in the past to a client, who is, as a consequence, predisposed to do more business with the entity. The entity may benefit from this but has no legal rights. The customer relationship has economic value to the entity but not legal value. Hence, there is a tension between seeing the reporting entity as either a legal or an economic entity.

We can say that there is a spectrum of certainty which applies to this, and probably any other, approach to defining the entity, and the more the way in which we convey this information can deal with uncertainty, the fuller will be the description. An economic assessment may incorporate more uncertainty than a legal assessment, but it is not clear whether this is useful or not. However, the possibility or otherwise of measurement is part of how the recognition and measurement process limits and defines what view of the entity can be presented.

The IASB Conceptual Framework provides a basis for the international standard-setter's recognition and measurement decisions, and we will review this as we proceed in this chapter. However, Chapter 14 of this book addresses the evolution and use of the IASB's Conceptual Framework, and includes a brief discussion about the reporting entity, which is not currently defined by that framework. The framework was written in a context where recognition and measurement rules for financial reporting already existed.

Another relevant chapter is Chapter 10, which considers the public interest in financial reporting. It asks what, if the objective of a standard-setter is to write standards 'in the public interest', does that imply for the decisions to be made about the nature of the reporting entity and the elements that should be recognized and measured?

Recognition and measurement asks: what are we going to define as within the entity, and how are we going to measure or otherwise describe that so as to provide useful information? Of course financial reporting is achieved by assigning a monetary value to everything, and so the portrayal decision is narrowed to 'how to assign a monetary value?' question, or measurement. Addressing uncertainty remains a major issue in monetary measurement, because of the need to assign a value.

For an interesting analysis of the question of border decisions in financial reporting, you should read Hines (1988) who fictionalizes the subject as a monk walking round the boundaries of a monastery with an acolyte and discussing how the boundaries have been drawn. Hine makes the point that in measuring reality, we define reality. This is generally the fundamental significance of recognition and measurement: it defines what is reported, and therefore fixes how people think about the entity.

2.1 Objective of financial reporting

Once you have identified the entity, the next stage is to determine what aspects of the entity you wish to report. This is a function of what you believe to be the objective of your financial reporting. How you define what characteristics you are using to determine the view of the entity affects both what goes in the accounting database and what goes in the financial statements. For the purposes of this chapter, however, we will just talk about the latter, not least because the literature, and certainly international financial reporting standards, is mostly written that way.

In deciding what characteristic you will use to define the entity, you need to have a view, consciously or not, of what is your objective in describing the entity. It could be because you want to buy the entity, or you want to sell it, or sell insurance to it, or decide whether you want to accept a job and so on. If you were selling insurance, you would want to know what risks the entity was exposed to, and what factors mitigated those. If you were thinking of working for it, you could be interested in the future sales possibilities and competition.

In the evolution of financial reporting, the objectives assigned to it have rarely been made clear. The earliest legal requirements date back to seventeenth-century France, and were introduced to try to combat frequent bankruptcies amongst businesses. The requirements were above all to carry out an annual inventory including details of payables and receivables. Presumably the idea was that the business would take stock of its 'wealth' at least once a year and would not carry on with a business that had more debts than assets. The focus could be seen to be legal rights and obligations, emphasizing the entity's relationship with the surrounding community, rather than individual trading transactions.

Richard (2004) argues that this orientation continued through the industrial revolution and imbued the financial reporting of nineteenth-century companies. This can be seen in UK legislation which called for a balance sheet only, and in Germany with the concept of 'static' accounting (see Chapter 4). Richard argues that only around the turn of the century did the focus start to move towards performance as measured by transactions. This can be seen in the UK with a slow movement towards supplementing the balance sheet with some sort of profit or loss account, and in Germany with Schmalenbach's 'dynamic' accounting theory. Richard argues that companies in France faced pressure from shareholders to pay dividends, and from the government to pay income tax, so the focus switched gradually to the wealth generated by that year's transactions, as opposed to looking at rights and obligations at a particular time.

2.2 Consensus model

Statute law does not usually specify what is the objective of financial reporting. The only formal approach to that is the US Conceptual Framework, which was an attempt to instil some consistency into standard-setting, and the related frameworks subsequently developed by other standard-setters (Chapter 14). Lawmakers probably have some idea as to what is the objective of financial reporting when they frame laws, but this is not explicit. Indeed laws are generally made piecemeal, by addressing a particular problem that has arisen, rather than by setting out to reassess the whole set of laws addressing accounting. Theorists suggest that change in accounting typically takes place on a contingent basis, as set out in Figure 6.1.

An obvious example of this is the Enron collapse in the US that gave rise to the Sarbanes Oxley Act, which had many unintended consequences, including a rapid rise in audit fees, the Securities and Exchange Commission wanting to inspect the work of foreign auditors, etc. The contingent approach usually implies that there is no consistent underlying objective assigned to financial reporting. Indeed Hoarau (1995) discusses French standard-setting which is designed specifically to reach a social consensus between conflicting interests on an issue by issue basis.

This has not, of course, stopped people from theorizing about what the objectives should be. In the Anglophone literature this was much debated in the 1940s and 1950s. The entity school of thought is that the financial statements should focus on the entity as a whole. In such an approach, there is no particularly pressing need to distinguish between debt and equity, because both are obligations of the entity to outsiders. The competing proprietary approach suggests that the focus should be on the shareholders' interests, and there, of course, it is important to distinguish between claims from shareholders and claims from anyone else. There are many variants on these two approaches, and anyone wanting to explore this should read van Mourik (2010), who provides a definitive analysis.

2.3 Conceptual framework

Neither proprietary nor entity approaches have ever been formally adopted as an objective by a standard-setter. However, commentators such as Macve (1981: 22) have pointed out that people who are trying to reach agreement on an accounting issue must have an implicit framework on which those views are based. In the US there was a crisis in financial reporting in the late

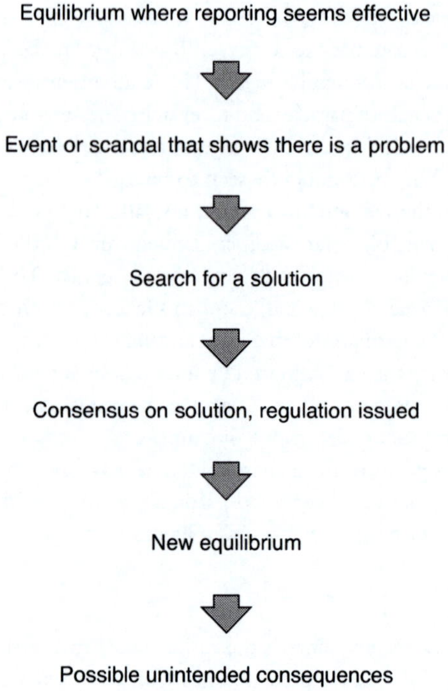

Equilibrium where reporting seems effective

Event or scandal that shows there is a problem

Search for a solution

Consensus on solution, regulation issued

New equilibrium

Possible unintended consequences

Figure 6.1 Changes in accounting on a contingent basis

1960s which drove people to review the inconsistencies inherent in the contingent approach to making accounting rules. In the US this gave rise to two sets of recommendations: the report of the Wheat committee (AICPA 1972) recommended the creation of an independent, professional standard-setter, the Financial Accounting Standards Board (FASB), and the report of the Trueblood committee (AICPA 1973) recommended that the FASB should introduce more consistency into rule-making through the use of a conceptual framework, the main lines of which were identified in the report. In the following years the FASB went on to elaborate the conceptual framework, which was later adapted by the International Accounting Standards Committee (IASC, the predecessor body to the IASB) and by many Anglophone standard-setters. (For a discussion of the role of conceptual frameworks see Chapter 14).

The US (and IASB) Conceptual Framework in its current form specifies that the objective of financial reporting is to provide information that is useful to providers of capital in making investment decisions. This is very significant because it means that when making standard-setting decisions, the FASB and IASB look to the investing community and ask them what information they need. They do not routinely take account of any other users' needs, nor do they consider the practicality of the rule from the perspective of the entity or the auditor. Those aspects are considered in the context of aiming to set rules whose benefits (better investor information) are greater than the costs (preparation and audit of the financial statements), but that is all.

The current framework takes the view that:

- financial statements alone cannot provide all the information any stakeholder needs; and
- since investors take the greatest financial risks, information that is useful to them should be useful to other stakeholders.

This approach is often contested (in Chapter 10 of this book you will find a discussion of the public interest and financial reporting). The IASC considered that stewardship, generally defined as meaning being able to review, as a provider of capital, what management has done with your money, was also an important objective in financial reporting. This notion has somewhat disappeared from the current framework, not least because FASB members did not accept that it differed in any meaningful sense from information that was useful for investment decisions.

3. Recognition

Having an objective should then lead you to recognition decisions – what kind of aspects of the entity should you recognize in the financial statements? The conceptual framework answer is simple: you recognize everything that is a right to a possible future cash inflow, and everything that is an obligation to make a future cash outflow. The conceptual framework takes the view that investment decisions are based on a comparison of future cash inflows to the investor with the cost of the investment. This is of course drawn from financial economics. It implies that the financial statements either give an economic picture or contain enough information to enable the investor to make their own picture when combined with knowledge of the economic environment. From this comes the conceptual framework definitions of assets (probable future cash inflows controlled by the entity) and liabilities (probable future cash outflows that the entity is obligated to make).

You should notice that the asset definition contains significant boundary conditions. First, the cash inflows should be *probable*, and not just possible. The conceptual framework does not say what probable means in this context, although in US GAAP it is generally taken to be more than 75 per cent likely, whereas under IFRS it is usually considered to be more than 50 per cent likely. The second boundary condition is that the future cash flow must be *controlled* by the entity. These are very important conditions because without them the entity could potentially recognize all its expected future cash flows for ever into the future. You do not control future sales, even if you do control a product that is highly likely to generate those sales, so you only recognize the rights to the product (patents, trademark, brand etc.) and the equipment to produce it. This is a critical function of recognition criteria: they determine what is included in the financial statements and what is left out.

It may be useful to consider alternative recognition criteria, such as taxation. The tax authorities in most countries are not primarily interested in an economic assessment of the entity, they are interested in either measuring assets to levy a capital tax, or measuring profit to levy a profits tax, or both. Tax authorities, and their taxpayers, tend to want certainty in the taxation process. Uncertainty is bad for the authorities (many disputes make collection slow and expensive) and bad for the entity, 'more resources have to be devoted to liaising with the tax authorities and it is not clear how much profit is available for dividends or investment in growth'.

An efficient system provides certainty in the application of the law and does not concern itself with issues such as equitable treatment or economic evaluation. As a consequence, taxation is usually based on completed transactions. It requires sales to have been made (invoices issued, cash collected) and expenses incurred in making those sales (invoices received, cash paid out). The tax system only looks at realized transactions, and takes each year on its own merits (you're making a loss in the immediately following period, you still owe tax on the previous period, you cannot look ahead) and does not recognize unrealized gains or losses. Tax recognition is therefore based more on a legal approach with visible transactions than on an economic approach. The boundary condition is that a transaction must have been carried out by the entity and have been finalized. It is a legal question as to whether a particular transaction was carried out by the entity (or for example by its management on their personal account). That transaction could be a trading transaction giving rise to profit or loss, or the purchase or sale of an asset which would affect the capital value of the entity.

4. Measurement issues

4.1 Boundary issues

Since the subject of this book is financial reporting, our measurement unit is monetary. There could be alternatives, but money is fundamental to a developed western economy. Basic economic texts describe it as a store of value, a medium of exchange, and a unit of account (Mankiw 2007) and it runs throughout economic activity. Its use for measurement enables comparisons to be made across widely different things. It plays a central role in everybody's life in the sense that we use it every day to make exchanges, and so we are also very familiar with monetary values. In theory we could perhaps derive some more meaningful approach, but in practice our familiarity with markets where money is the medium of exchange leads to the use of monetary values.

So this is another boundary condition: if you are using monetary values, you can only include in your financial reports those things to which you can attach a monetary value. Of course that leads to boundary disputes, particularly in the area of estimates and techniques that are acceptable in addressing uncertainty. For example, if you want to recognize a liability for (say) litigation, do you use a 'best estimate' (a single point figure representing management's judgement of the most likely outcome) or do you use a probability weighted expected value (a figure that takes account of a range of possibilities but will never be the exact figure)? Some people say that a large company with a number of estimations should use the expected value because it reflects all possible outcomes and the global figure is highly likely to be the real outcome, whereas the best estimates may be subject to systematic bias.

Equally there are many possible 'assets' and 'liabilities' that cannot be measured with a monetary value. Many management researchers would accept that the accumulated knowledge of your 'assembled workforce' (to use the jargon) is a valuable asset because they can and do run your business. However, there is no technique for valuing the availability of that collective knowledge, and of course you do not control it, if you are thinking of the conceptual framework. Some people suggest a usable proxy measurement is what you would have to pay to recruit and train new staff to an equivalent standard. To the extent that your business is affected by weather, the weather is an unquantifiable liability of some kind. Many potential assets and liabilities just cannot be measured in monetary terms.

Using monetary values is therefore a major constraint on both recognition and measurement, because you cannot recognize what you cannot measure. However, it does have the considerable benefit that all measurements become comparable to some degree, and everyone in the developed world at least is familiar with using money as a basis of exchange in transactions.

4.2 Qualitative characteristics

The issue of comparability is central to the idea of using a monetary measuring unit. You use a monetary unit precisely so that you can reflect items that are different in nature (for example a factory and a trade payable) using the same system. However, a problem with a monetary unit is that it is usually subject to inflation, and, depending on the degree of inflation, comparability may be substantially impaired. Another issue is that some people suggest that not all items should be measured using the same attribute, but we will come to these points later.

The US/IFRS Conceptual Framework discusses the qualitative characteristics of financial information, and does not put comparability in first place. It says the primary characteristics are relevance and faithful representation. Comparability is an 'enhancing' characteristic, along with verifiability, timeliness and understandability. We would not necessarily agree with that order of priority, but it is worth noting that when using monetary measurement you have to decide what aspect of an asset or a liability you are going to measure.

The conceptual framework aims to provide guidance, saying that the 'measurement attribute' must be relevant to the view of the entity you are trying to show, and must give a faithful representation of that aspect – it must not be misleading. Indeed the conceptual framework illustrates the measurement decision process:

- what kind of view of the entity do you want? (a view that helps making economic decisions);
- the measurement must be relevant to an economic decision (capacity to generate cash inflows and outflows);
- it must be a faithful representation (it must focus on the cash flows that will most likely affect future value); and
- it would be better, but not essential, if measurements were comparable, verifiable, understandable and delivered in a timely manner.

The original US Conceptual Framework ran into difficulties when the FASB tried to develop the recognition and measurement chapter. As a result the IASB framework is also extremely vague about measurement, just noting that there are several possible measurement approaches. The FASB/IASB have worked in the last few years to revise the conceptual framework with the aim more of filling in gaps rather than significantly changing what is the accepted substance of the original framework. Measurement is one of these. Until the sub-prime financial crisis hit the standard-setters' timetables, the FASB was working hard on producing a new measurement chapter, but this was not progressing very quickly, probably not least because different board members had quite different aspirations as to what could be achieved by such a chapter. That project has been set aside for the time being, although it will no doubt be revived in due course.

However, one idea that seemed well received at the time was the concept that there were at least two distinct types of asset that might have different measurement attributes. Staff suggested that entities owned two types of asset: one that generated cash inflows in its own right, and another that only generated cash inflows when used in conjunction with other assets, materials, staff inputs, etc.

Staff suggested that this might be the basis for using a different measurement attribute. An asset that was in itself a stand alone 'cash generating unit' (CGU) would offer more measurement alternatives because it had identifiable future cash flows. When an asset is part of a larger CGU, by definition it does not attract identifiable cash flows to itself. The identifiable cash flows are generated by the CGU as a whole and cannot be allocated on a meaningful basis to the individual parts of the unit. This might lead you to an analysis that market value gave the most relevant measure of the single asset CGU, but that measurement of an asset that was part of a bigger CGU should relate to the cost of making the asset available.

This is an example of the application of the conceptual framework where the measurement attribute is different, but is comparable in that the aim is to provide the most relevant information relating to cash flows, and also that the measurement unit is the same monetary unit (e.g. the US Dollar). Information relevance (for forecasting cash flows) gets preference over direct comparability of the measurement attribute (cost in one case, market value in another). In fact both the FASB and the IASB do use what they describe as a 'mixed attribute' model, where amortized historical cost is the basis for most measurements, but market value is used for some measurements, and also a series of alternative estimation approaches in specified other cases. Some people would argue that this is confusing, and a more helpful approach to reporting, if no single measurement basis is acceptable, would be to produce two financial reports, each consistent in itself, but using a different measurement basis.

4.3 Primacy of orientation

In discussing the historical evolution of measurement we did mention that, while in the nineteenth century the balance sheet was the focus, in the twentieth century this moved to the profit and loss account. While for most practitioners, the profit and loss account remains the prime focus, the FASB and IASB are visibly oriented more round a balance sheet approach. This comes from the conceptual framework which defines assets and liabilities while leaving equity as the residual owners' interest. Standard-setters now typically carry out an analysis of what economic rights and obligations exist as part of a transaction and how they change as the transaction proceeds.

This is easily seen in the IASB/FASB revenue recognition project. A traditional approach would say you recognize a sale when the goods or services have been passed to the customer. Prior to that you accumulate costs relevant to that sale as assets, and expense them against the revenue you recognize on completing the sale. The new standard, however, says that as soon as you have a contract with the client you have an asset (the right to receive cash inflows from the contract) and a liability (the obligation to perform services or deliver goods).

However, although in their early analysis the boards were prepared to look at the liability being less than the asset and therefore some element of profit being recognized at inception (which would be logical, as the entity has incurred selling costs which it would expect to cover), in the end they recognized this would be seen as very controversial. They decided that the 'performance obligation' (the liability) should systematically be measured at the value of the asset, unless it was an onerous contract. The net effect is therefore nil, and revenue will still be recognized as goods and services are delivered. However, it illustrates the asset and liability orientation of the boards.

People have debated for well over a hundred years whether you should start with measuring the transaction and leave the assets and liabilities to be the residuals of the transaction measurement process, or whether you should start with measuring assets and liabilities and derive the transaction values from the movements in assets and liabilities. Under a strict historical cost basis (everything measured at cost, with long-lived assets amortized) you would end up with the same figures irrespective of whether you start with the asset or the expense, because the measurement attribute is allocated cost. However, if you used a mixed attribute model, you would get different figures.

To give a concrete example, supposing a company buys a delivery truck for €30,000. It expects to use it for four years, and sell it for €2,000 at the end of that period. Under the amortized cost basis, the entity would depreciate the truck at (30,000 – 2,000)/4 = 7,000 a year, giving the following figures:

Year	*Expense*	*Carrying value*
1	7,000	23,000
2	7,000	16,000
3	7,000	9,000
4	7,000	2,000

However, if a balance sheet perspective was chosen, you would ask what would be a relevant attribute to measure – the main candidates would be either an entry value such as replacement cost (how much would it cost you to provide an asset in this condition?) or an exit value such as current sales value (how much can you sell the asset for?). Let's say we decide a selling value is not relevant because we need the van to enable the business to keep operating, and so an entry value would be better. If there is a market for used vans, it could be we could buy a similar van that was one year old for €20,000, two years' old €12,000, three years' old €6,000 and four years' old €2,000, our figures would now be:

Year	*Carrying value*	*Expense*
1	20,000	10,000
2	12,000	8,000
3	6,000	6,000
4	2,000	4,000

The carrying value is determined from the market, and the change becomes the expense for the year. We can draw a number of points from this. First, that over the life cycle of the asset, the cost to the business is exactly the same, so the measurement process is actually allocating costs to different years, but not fundamentally changing the cost of the asset to the business. Second, we should note that under amortized cost, the balance sheet value of the asset does not have any meaning beyond unexpensed future costs, whereas under the balance sheet measure the carrying value is replacement cost and the year on year change shows the consumption of value, rather than the allocation of cost. The different measurement bases give us different information. It is a matter of personal judgement whether you think one is better than the other.

The traditional argument is that the annual profit or loss is just a conventional way of measuring performance that necessarily involves lots of estimates because of the variety of life cycles of assets and liabilities. As such it is never going to be accurate and all that is required is an effective estimation system that is as easy as possible to apply and always comes back in the end to the actual cash flows. That could be summed up as profit is a rough estimate, that is all. The alternative view is that you are trying to measure each year's profit as accurately as possible and should incorporate current information.

Some members of the FASB and IASB argue that a completed transaction approach lacks a clear set of criteria for recognition, and results in deferrals of costs and revenues that do not meet the conceptual framework definition of an asset or a liability. They also argue that recognizing rights and obligations gives you a clear basis for identifying changes, and then you can classify the changes as to whether they are operations giving rise to profits and losses or other value changes (which might be reported elsewhere). In effect they think a balance sheet orientation is closer to a wider economic appreciation of the entity than a transaction-based approach. That said, in practice companies measure transactions, and then are supposed to step back at every reporting date and ask themselves questions about carrying values.

There is a considerable literature about income measurement. The classic economics text is Hicks (1939) whose basic proposition is that income is the amount a person can consume during a period and still be as well off at the end as at the beginning of that period. This leads to measurement of 'wealth' as the starting point, which Hicks develops into a series of alternative approaches to measuring wealth. Solomons (1961) contrasts Hicksian income with a tradition view of accounting income. He notes that the difficulty with Hicksian income is that it requires a measure of wealth. Accounting income is based on realization, and therefore the creation of cash asset or a near-cash financial instrument. It does not, under historical cost, consider the potential to generate future income and does not assess value changes in assets.

A detailed review of issues in income measurement is to be found in Lee (1985). Income measurement theory is discussed in Chapter 3 of this book and the historical evolution of approaches to recognition and measurement is addressed in Chapters 4 and 5.

4.4 Executory contracts

Perhaps a side issue, but related to the recognition boundary is the question of executory contracts. One of the very significant issues related to recognition is that a classical transactions-based approach measures revenues only when the transaction has been completed or realized, as Solomons (1961) notes. In entities that have a long transaction cycle, this means that significant economic information is not reflected in the financial statements. A contract that has been entered into by an entity but not yet performed is called an 'executory contract'. In a business with long transaction cycles, such as service contracts to provide computer maintenance, an executory contract represents upcoming sales.

Under a traditional transaction approach, the executory contract is not reported anywhere, and only gets recognized when the services are delivered to the client. The new IASB revenue approach in effect addresses this by recognizing an asset as soon as the contract is signed, so the point at which the contract is first recognized is earlier – the boundary has been moved.

The recognition boundary can also be moved by using market value. Using a market exit value – what you would receive if you sold an asset, or sold your contractual rights – can be taken as a simulation of realization. This tells you what you would have received had the transaction been realized at that point, and therefore brings the recognition forward through a simulated realization (Walton 2006).

5.1 Measurement bases

An exhaustive list of possible approaches to measurement will be found in Alexander (2007). It may be helpful to recognize that these approaches fall into two camps: entry values and exit values. The most widely used entry value is *historical cost*, which in its pure form retains the initial cost as the accounting value, but apportions it over periods if this is necessary because of the life cycle of the item. However, historical cost is typically modified not only for allocations but also for impairments. Historical cost fits easily into a stewardship objective for financial reporting: the manager is explaining what has happened from a historical perspective.

People dispute the usefulness of the historical cost basis for making investment decisions. The convention is that the historical record can be used to project forward when it is allied to the investor's perceptions of how the economics will evolve in the future. Financial analysts would say that their job is to take a view about the future, and blend that with the entity's factual report about the past. Research suggests that 'clean surplus' accounting (historical cost accounting with all expenses allocated against revenue) is the best predictor of future cash flows.

At the other extreme, people argue that financial economics tells us that the market price reflects the market's expectations of the discounted future cash flows for the entity. Consequently a valuation of the entity's assets and liabilities that is based on their expected future cash flows would give important information to investors. In theory you could divide the assets and liabilities into CGUs (under IFRS the smallest collection that is capable of generating cash flows independently of the rest of the entity), estimate the future cash flows of each CGU, discount them and aggregate them, and you have the value of the entity.

The discounted cash flows of each CGU represent the market price of each CGU, or in accounting, the *fair value*. IFRS 13 defines fair value as the price for which an entity could sell an asset or the price it would have to pay to transfer a liability to someone else. It is an exit value, and that value is what the market, not the entity, puts on the asset. A fair value represents the market's assessment and so its enthusiasts point out it is an objective value and gives comparability across entities. (The subject of fair value is explored in depth in Chapter 7 of this book.)

We can sum up the two extremes as being that historical cost is entity-specific (the values are not necessarily comparable across entities) and is a historical (backward-looking) entry value, but it is easily ascertained in most cases. Fair value is a market value, and as such is an objective measurement that is comparable across entities and is forward-looking (reflecting expected future cash flows). However, a major disadvantage is that in many cases observable market prices are not available, so in practice its use as an accounting measurement basis involves estimates which are not necessarily objective.

Another measurement basis recognized in the literature is *replacement cost*. This is a current value, like fair value, but it is an entry value and not an exit value. As in the example above, replacement cost is a market value and is used to show you what it would cost to replace an asset already in use. Just like fair value, it is objective, current and comparable, but replacement prices for used assets are not necessarily freely available for business-specific assets, and so it is not widely used in practice.

A variant on this is the concept of *deprival value*. Some standard-setters argue that deprival value is not itself a measurement basis but is rather an algorithm for determining which basis to use in a mixed-attribute model. The idea of deprival value is that the most relevant valuation of an asset from an investor's point of view is that which reflects the management's view of how to maximize utility of that asset. Deprival value says you should use a measurement basis that reflects the most advantageous cash flows from the asset. If the entity would get more cash from selling the asset as opposed to operating it, it should be measured at fair value. If, however, the entity would generate more net inflows by operating the asset as part of a cash generating unit, then it should be valued at replacement cost (on the basis that though it will generate more than its cost, the asset cannot be worth more than replacement cost). The approach is called deprival value because it measures what value would be lost to the entity if the asset were lost.

5.2 The effects of inflation

An obvious disadvantage of converting everything to a monetary unit is that the intrinsic value of that unit is not stable. In practice, accounting measurement can tolerate a low level of inflation (for example less than 10 per cent per annum) without being significantly damaged from an operational perspective. However even a 10 per cent annual rate does distort the relationship between long-lived (non-current in IFRS jargon) assets and current assets, and long-lived liabilities are having value transferred from the creditor to the debtor in such circumstances.

Experience would suggest that there are three rough bands within which the accounting reaction to inflation is different. We think that past behaviour suggests that where inflation is less than 10 per cent, standard-setters and investors largely ignore it. Where inflation is more than 30 per cent per annum, usually referred to as 'hyper-inflation' financial statements are routinely restated. IAS 29 *Financial Reporting in Hyperinflationary Economies* calls for the financial statements to be restated by using inflation indices so that the monetary unit is adjusted to current values.

The most problematical area is between these two, i.e. in the 10–30 per cent range. Many countries in the developed world suffered inflation of 15–25 per cent in the 1970s as a result of a severe increase in the price of oil. This gave rise to a revisiting of the literature on inflation accounting which had been developed in the 1920s, which was the last time severe inflation had occurred in Europe.

While adjusting your measuring unit for its loss of value is a simple solution, it has a number of hidden problems. In the first place, how do you measure the loss of value? This is typically done using a price index, but that is sensitive to the composition of the index: what prices do you use to monitor the general state of inflation in the economy? The second point is that reflecting the price index is believed to install inflation systematically in the economy. The anecdotal evidence is that in highly inflationary economies, people put prices up and employees seek pay increases to compensate for perceived inflation. In other words, if the government says inflation in the economy was 20 per cent last year, employees will feel they need a pay increase of at least 20 per cent and businesses will also put prices up by at least 20 per cent. Governments therefore are not enthusiastic about index-linked adjustments. In Germany the government even passed a law forbidding indexation adjustments after the 1920s bout of inflation.

In the 1970s and 1980s there was therefore renewed debate about inflation accounting. Much of this started with the notion of capital maintenance. This asks what is your objective in adjusting for inflation: are you trying to preserve the purchasing power of equity (financial capital maintenance) or your operating capacity (physical capital maintenance). The central idea is that, in inflationary times, a historical cost measurement means you are overstating profits, because you are not recognizing that replacing your assets and raw materials will cost much more than what you are charging in the profit or loss account. Broadly, if your aim was financial capital maintenance, you measured profit at historical cost and then made a charge against earnings for the loss of purchasing power of equity. If your aim was physical capital maintenance you charged depreciation based on the replacement cost of your productive capacity, and raw material costs were adjusted to their replacement cost from historical cost.

Standard-setters in both the US and the UK responded to inflation but in different ways. The US required selected supplementary disclosures on both a 'constant dollar' basis (i.e. by indexing the monetary unit) and a current cost basis. The UK required a full set of financial statements drawn up using what was called current cost accounting. These measures were highly controversial at the time, and were withdrawn as general inflation levels dropped away dramatically later in the 1980s (see for example Tweedie and Whittington 1997).

5.3 Measurement under IFRS

This final section of the chapter reviews IFRS and the different measurement bases used in its mixed attribute model. (Chapter 7 of this book is devoted to a detailed analysis of the IASB's measurement bases and the use of fair value in particular, the section in this chapter is a brief overview only.)

Even if some commentators would have one believe otherwise, the fundamental approach of IFRS is to use historical cost as the measurement basis (indexed in the special case of hyper-inflationary economies) and certainly not fair value. However, fair value is used in a number of cases. In particular IFRS use fair value for most financial instruments, even if in practice only the financial sector tends to have a significant involvement in financial instruments.

A form of fair value is a requirement for biological assets in IAS 41 *Agriculture*, and fair value is used as an allocation device when making the first consolidation of a newly-acquired subsidiary under IFRS 3 *Business Combinations*. When a significant business within an entity is to be disposed of, the fair value of its net assets is shown as a 'disposal group' in the balance sheet, after deduction of expected selling costs (IFRS 5 *Non-current Assets Held for Sale and Discontinued Items*). IAS 2 *Inventories* has the requirement that stocks should be held at the lower of cost or net realizable value. Net realizable is fair value less costs to sell.

IFRS allow optional use of fair value for investment property (IAS 40) and for property, plant and equipment (IAS 16). In practice, fair value is widely used by investment property companies, and its use is likely to increase when the FASB introduces compulsory use of fair value for that industry in the US. In some countries (such as the UK), holding property plant and equipment at current value was a widespread practice before IFRS, not least to compensate for inflation. However, where the option is used under IAS 16, the standard requires that values be regularly updated. This is quite costly because companies usually use a professional valuer whose fees are not negligible, so few companies make use of the option.

The IASB also has in development an option to report investments in subsidiaries at fair value in the consolidated accounts of investment companies. The exception will allow that where an investment is managed on a fair value basis and is held for investment purposes rather than operational ones, it need not be consolidated line by line by the investor, but can be shown at fair value.

Outside the straight use of fair value and historical cost, IFRS contain a number of measures to address special situations. A significant case is that of impairment (IAS 36) where the general rule is that an asset cannot be carried in the balance sheet at more than its 'recoverable amount'. The recoverable amount is the higher of (a) fair value less costs to sell, and (b) 'value in use' which is the discounted net cash flows expected to be gained from continuing to operate the asset. (You can see this has links to the concept of deprival value). An impaired asset will be held at something other than historical cost or fair value as such.

A controversial measurement issue arises in IAS 37 *Provisions, Contingent Liabilities and Contingent Assets*. The standard says (paragraphs 36, 37) that

> The amount recognised as a provision shall be the best estimate of the expenditure required to settle the present obligation at the end of the reporting period. The best estimate of the expenditure required to settle the present obligation is the amount that an entity would rationally pay to settle the obligation at the end of the reporting period or to transfer it to a third party at that time.

The IASB has extensively redebated this question and has a thwarted an attempt to amend the standard, which is now parked off the current agenda. The phrase referring to what the company would pay to transfer to a third party means a fair value measurement – a market price.

The IASB considers that this would obviously include compensation to the transferee for taking the risk. Preparers respond that that is unrealistic as generally liabilities of this nature are settled directly, not passed on to someone else. If you were planning to settle directly, why would you value it differently?

The second issue is whether the estimate in either case should be a single point estimate (the most likely case) or a probability weighted estimate (expected value). Constituents say that the expected value may be significant statistically over a range of transactions, but for the individual transaction it represents a hybrid number which is by definition not likely to be the settlement number. The responses to the IASB proposals suggest that current practice is to measure provisions at a number which the management think they are likely to have to pay. This will be a current exit value but specific to the entity, not a market value.

This standard addresses a range of contingencies. A provision is made if an estimate can be made that is sufficiently reliable to be used in the financial statements. There is therefore a boundary condition of being able to make a reliable estimate (and many companies use that condition not to put a number on continuing litigation provisions). If the entity cannot make a sufficiently reliable estimate, the solution is a disclosure, which the entity makes if it thinks it is more likely than not for the contingency to crystallize in the future.

In looking at how to reflect existing contingencies in an acquired company, the IASB came up with the idea that the on/off switch of the 50 per cent probability threshold was too crude, and decided that in a business combination a contingent liability or asset should be valued based on the probability of it occurring. If you thought you had a 20 per cent chance of having to pay €100,000, you showed a liability of €20,000. The analysis was that (a) you decided whether you had a liability (or an asset) – i.e. was there something to recognize? – and then (b) if so, you decided what measurement to use based on probability. This analysis fits in with how the IASB applies the asset and liability definitions as discussed above.

The IASB liked this solution to what it believed was a particularly opaque area in financial reporting. It decided that it would amend IAS 37 as well, so that this new approach would be applied generally and there would be no more discontinuities in recognition of liabilities. All non-financial liabilities would be measured at their expected value. Unfortunately constituents did not like the idea, and it remains stalled, awaiting a period when the IASB is no longer fire-fighting nor converging.

6. Conclusion

In reviewing the issues related to recognition and measurement this chapter has pointed out that no reporting system gives a complete view of the economic entity, but rather any recognition and measurement system sets boundary rules that determine what can be included in the portrait of the entity and what is left out – the recognition and measurement rules fix what is identified as the entity.

These rules must be informed by some idea, explicit or implicit of what is the objective of financial reporting, and they must fix a measurement convention, which in financial reporting involves the assignment of a monetary amount to all items reported. We noted that under the IASB/FASB Conceptual Framework the objective of financial reporting is to provide information to help providers of capital make investment decisions, and this led to reporting information that was related to expected future cash flows, encapsulated in assets and liabilities.

Having decided what is recognized, the next step is how to measure them. The chapter discussed the differences between historical cost and fair value, as well as between entry and exit values. It reviewed the effect of inflation on the measurement unit. Finally the chapter reviewed the different measurement approaches in the IASB's mixed attribute model.

Bibliography

AICPA (1972) *Establishing Financial Accounting Standards* (the Wheat Report), New York: AICPA

AICPA (1973) *Objectives of Financial Statements* (the Trueblood Report), New York: AICPA

Alexander, D. (2007) 'Recent History of Fair Value', in Walton, P. (ed) *The Routledge Companion to Fair Value and Financial Reporting* London: Routledge, pp. 71–90

Hicks, J. R. (1939) *Value and Capital*, Oxford: Clarendon Press

Hines, R. (1988) 'Financial Accounting: In Communicating Reality, We Construct Reality', *Accounting, Organizations and Society*, 13: 251–62

Hoarau, C. (1995) 'American Hegemony or Mutual Recognition with Benchmarks?', *European Accounting Review*, 4.2: 217–33

Lee, T.A. (1985) *Income and Value Measurement*, 3rd edn, Wokingham: Van Nostrand Reinhold

Macve, R. (1981) *A Conceptual Framework for Financial Accounting and Reporting: The Possibilities for an Agreed Structure*, London: ICAEW

Mankiw, N. G. (2007) *Macroeconomics*, 6th edn, New York: Worth Publishers

Richard, J. (2004) 'The Secret Past of Fair Value: Lessons from History Applied to the French Case', *Accounting in Europe*, 1.1, 95–108

Solomons, D. (1961) 'Economic and Accounting Concepts of Income', *The Accounting Review*, 36: 3, 374–83

Tweedie, D. and Whittington, G. (1997) 'The End of the Current Cost Revolution', in Cooke, T.E. and Nobes, C.N. (eds) *The Development of Accounting in an International Context*, London: Routledge

Van Mourik, C. (2010) 'Equity Theories and Financial Reporting: An Analysis', *Accounting in Europe*, 7.2, 191–212

Walton, P. (2006) 'Fair Value and Executory Contracts: Moving the Boundaries in International Financial Reporting', *Accounting & Business Research*, 36.4, 337–43

7
Fair Value and Financial Reporting

David Cairns

The chapter deals with the role of fair value measurement in the context of financial reporting under International Financial Reporting Standards (IFRS). Many commentators see IFRS as fair value-based standards and some believe that IFRS require many assets and liabilities to be measured at fair value at each reporting date. This chapter addresses these issues. In doing so, it distinguishes between the use of fair value measurement at each reporting date (the fair value model) and other uses of fair value measurement, a distinction which some commentators do not make.

Section 1 considers measurement in IFRS financial statements from the standpoint of the IASB's Conceptual Framework. It notes that the balance sheet approach that underlies the Framework is equally applicable for different measurement models and, in so doing, refutes the widespread myth that the approach requires fair value measurement for all assets and liabilities.

Section 2 describes the measurement models in IFRS, in particular the fair value model, the historical cost model and the present value model. These three models feature strongly and to varying degrees in IFRS financial statements. Other measurement models used in IFRS financial statements and discussed in professional and academic literature, including the equity method and the current or replacement cost model, are beyond the scope of the chapter.

Section 3 explains how the different measurement models affect the measurement of profit. Changes in the measurements usually meet the definition of income and expenses in the Framework but some changes are excluded from profit. In the past, these exclusions were limited mainly to capital maintenance adjustments. More recently, the exclusions have been extended to the effects of some volatility arising from the use of particular measurement models and have led to the emergence of separate notions of profit, comprehensive income and other comprehensive income.

Section 4 discusses why IFRS require or permit the use of the fair value model for some financial assets and financial liabilities, investment property and biological assets. It explains that, contrary to a widely held belief, the cost model is used for many financial assets and financial liabilities as well as many other assets and liabilities. In both IFRS and IFRS financial statements, the use of the fair value model is quite limited.

Section 5 discusses why the use of the fair value model has been contentious before, during and after the financial crisis which started in 2007. It notes that concerns focus on both the use and consequences of the fair value model and the measurement of fair value. Many of these concerns have been expressed for many years and considered by both the IASC and the IASB as part of their due process. Nevertheless, the financial crisis reinforced those concerns.

Section 6 deals with the IASB's responses to the concerns about the use and consequences of the fair value model and the measurement of fair value. IFRS 13 *Fair Value Measurement* will alleviate some of, but not all, the concerns about the measurement of fair value. It is, however, unlikely that the IASB will significantly reduce the requirements or options to use the fair value model.

1. Measurement and the IASB's framework

1.1 The elements of financial statements

Financial reports provide information about, among other things, the reporting entity's financial position and its financial performance. Financial position consists of the entity's assets, liabilities and equity. Financial performance reported in terms of accrual accounting consists of income, expenses and profit. Financial performance is also reported in terms of cash flows but cash flows are not affected by fair value measurement and, therefore, are not dealt with further in this chapter.

The Framework defines assets and liabilities and specifies when those assets and liabilities are recognised on the statement of financial position. Equity is defined as the difference between assets and liabilities recognized in the statement of financial position. Income and expenses are defined as changes in assets and liabilities that result in changes in equity other than changes resulting from contributions from or distributions to equity participants. Profit is the difference between income and expenses. However, as explained in section 3, some items of income and expense are excluded from profit under certain concepts of capital maintenance and, more recently, through the distinction between profit and other comprehensive income.

The fact that income and expenses are defined as changes in assets and liabilities is sometimes referred to as the balance sheet approach. Some argue that the primacy given to the definitions of assets and liabilities means that the IASB believes that financial position is more important than financial performance. This is not the case. The balance sheet approach is simply the only way in which the IASB (and some national standard setters) have found to define income and expenses.

Some also argue that income and expenses have traditionally been defined in their own right without first defining assets and liabilities. This is not the case. Accountants have always found it necessary to get assets and liabilities right first, however defined and measured, before determining income and expenses. For example, the need to get inventories, receivables and payables right before determining revenue, costs of sales and profit is long established. Similarly, the need to confirm the existence and recoverability of receivables has played a key part in determining both revenue and bad debt expense. The practice of looking for the existence of future economic benefits before recognizing expenditure as an asset is also well established. Of course, there have been, and are, exceptions to this approach in IFRS and national GAAPs as well as in practice but the exceptions do not hide the fact the balance sheet approach has dominated accounting practices and accounting standards for many years.

Some also believe that the balance sheet approach requires the fair value measurement of assets and liabilities at each reporting date. This is also not the case. The Framework acknowledges that the balance sheet approach is applicable to a range of accounting models and the use of different measurement bases and that financial statements are most commonly prepared in accordance with the cost model, something which is obvious to anybody who has prepared, audited or studied IFRS financial statements.

1.2 Measurement

Measurement is the process of determining the monetary amounts at which assets, liabilities, income and expenses are carried in the balance sheet and income statement (IASB, 2010: Par. 4.54). This involves the selection of the particular basis of measurement. The Framework lists and defines four measurement bases:

- historical cost;
- current cost;
- realizable or settlement value; and
- present value.

These four bases were commonly used in the late 1980s when the measurement section of the Framework was written. Fair value was not used by the IASC as a measurement basis until after the Framework was written and is, therefore, not listed as a measurement base.[1] This deficiency will undoubtedly be addressed in the IASB's Conceptual Framework project.

While the Framework does not define or explain what it means by measurement basis, it clearly intends the measurement bases to be used in measurement models which are specified at standards level (see Section 2). The Framework acknowledges that the balance sheet approach is applicable to a range of accounting models and the use of different measurement bases (IASB, 2010: Introduction). It explains that IFRS financial statements are most commonly prepared in accordance with the cost model (IASB, 2010: Introduction and Par. 4.56). It recognizes that other measurement models may be more appropriate in order to meet the objective of providing information that is useful for making economic decisions. It does not express a preference for a particular model or for the circumstances in which particular models are appropriate. The IASB has, however, expressed preferences at standards level.

Prior to developing and issuing the Framework, the IASC gave extensive consideration to the appropriateness of a current cost (or replacement cost) model for tangible assets (property, plant and equipment and inventories). Those considerations led to the issue of IAS 6 *Accounting Responses to Changing Prices* and its replacement IAS 15 *Information Reflecting the Effects of Changing Prices* but did not result in an international consensus with the result that compliance with IAS 15 became non-mandatory in 1989 (Camfferman & Zeff, 2007: 106–10). The IASC and the IASB have subsequently given little consideration to the appropriateness of the current cost (or replacement cost) model.

Also prior to developing and issuing the Framework, the IASC decided that the present value model, in particular an actuarial model, was the most appropriate model for some post-employment benefit obligations. This decision explains why present value is listed in the Framework as one of the measurement bases. In this case, international consensus has been achieved with the result that the present value model not only continues to be used but has been refined and strengthened in successive versions of IAS 19 *Employee Benefits*.

More significantly, the IASC and then the IASB decided that the fair value model was the most appropriate model for some financial assets and financial liabilities, investment property and biological assets (see Section 4). This step began about the time that the Framework was being developed but too late and with insufficient commitment to persuade the IASC to include fair value as a measurement basis in the Framework. As with the present value model in IAS 19, so the use of the fair value model has been refined and strengthened over the ensuing 20 years.

As part of its conceptual framework project, the IASB is likely to seek to strengthen the measurement chapter by, among other things, specifying the circumstances in which different measurement models are appropriate in order to meet the objective of providing information that is useful for making economic decisions. While the outcome of those efforts is uncertain, it seems likely that the IASB will retain a mixed measurement approach under which the cost model, the fair value model and other models are appropriate in specific circumstances.

2. Measurement models in IFRS

Three measurement models are used extensively in IFRS: the fair value model; the cost model; the present value model. Each model uses one of the measurement bases as the starting point for the measurement of assets and liabilities but may adjust the resulting amount to reflect events since the measurement date. This is particularly the case for the cost model where the measurement date for historical cost usually precedes the reporting date (in some cases by many years) and the asset or liability may have changed between the measurement date and the reporting date (in some cases to a very significant extent). It is less the case for the fair value model and the present value model because the measurements usually reflect circumstances at the reporting date.

2.1 The fair value model

2.1.1 Fair value

In IFRS, fair value is a measure of the current value of an asset, liability or equity instrument. Fair value has no natural meaning but is, instead, defined in IFRS.[2] Immediately prior to the issuance of IFRS 13 *Fair Value Measurement*, fair value was defined as:

> The amount for which an asset could be exchanged, a liability settled or an equity instrument granted could be exchanged, between knowledgeable, willing parties in an arm's length transaction.

IFRS 13 defines fair value as:

> the price that would be received to sell an asset or paid to transfer a liability in an orderly transaction between market participants at the measurement date.

The definitions have much in common, most notably that:

- fair value is a current value of the asset, liability or equity instrument at the measurement date; and
- fair value is the market value for assets, liabilities and equity instruments traded in an active market.

The IFRS 13 definition also confirms that fair value is the exit price for the asset or liability in a transaction with market participants at the measurement date.

2.1.2 Fair value model

Under the fair value model, assets and liabilities are measured at fair value at each reporting date and changes in fair values are reported in each period as income or expenses. Section 4 deals with whether the resulting changes in fair value are included in the measurement of profit or other comprehensive income.

In IFRS financial statements for 2013, the use of the fair value model is:

- required for held-for-trading financial assets and financial liabilities and available-for-sale financial assets;
- permitted, but rarely used, for other financial assets and financial liabilities;
- required for most biological assets;
- permitted and frequently used for investment property; and
- permitted in certain circumstances, but rarely used, for most other assets and liabilities (see for example Cairns *et al*, 2011).

2.1.3 Other uses of fair value measurement

In IFRS, fair value measurement is also used as part of both the fair value model and the cost model[3] for:

- the measurement of assets, liabilities and equity instruments on their initial recognition in the financial statements;
- the measurement of the consideration given or received for assets, liabilities and equity instruments; and
- the allocation of the initial amount at which a transaction or other event is recognized among its constituent parts.

The use of fair value measurement in these ways does not imply, let alone require, the subsequent use of the fair value model. In fact, the fair value measurements in each case are most frequently used as the historical costs of the relevant assets, liabilities or equity instruments in the application of the cost model.

Fair value measurement is also used as an essential part of the cost model for the measurement of the recoverable amount of assets. Under the cost model, the carrying amount of an asset must not exceed the amount that the entity expects to obtain from the sale, use or other means of recovery of the asset.[4] Fair value measurement is used to determine any impairment losses for some assets which the entity can recover through sale, for example property, plant and equipment and intangible assets.

The separate measurement of recoverable amount is largely irrelevant to the fair value model as fair value reflects the condition of the asset at reporting date and there is rarely, if ever, any justification for reducing the carrying amount of an asset below its fair value.

2.2 The cost model

2.2.1 Historical cost

The historical cost of an asset is defined in the Framework as the amount of cash or cash equivalents paid or the fair value of the consideration given to acquire the asset at the time of its acquisition. The historical cost of a liability is defined as the amount of proceeds received in exchange for the obligation or the amounts of cash or cash equivalents expected to be paid to satisfy the liability in the normal course of business.

Historical cost is, therefore, the entry price for the asset or liability. Historical cost often coincides with fair value of the asset or liability at the date that the asset or liability is acquired or assumed. It rarely coincides with fair value at any other date.

2.2.2 The cost model

Under the cost model, assets and liabilities are measured at each reporting date by reference to their historical costs. The historical cost is adjusted for some changes in the asset or liability since the measurement date. For example, the historical costs of assets are adjusted by means of depreciation, amortization and impairment write-downs to reflect the consumption or loss of economic benefits embodied in the asset. The historical costs of liabilities are adjusted for changes in the estimates of the amounts of cash or cash equivalents expected to be paid to satisfy them. The historical costs of financial assets and financial liabilities are also adjusted for the amortization of premiums and discounts.

Under the cost model, adjustments are not made for changes in the fair values of the assets or liabilities. In fact, the adjusted amounts rarely, if ever, coincide with fair values of the assets or liabilities. However, the carrying amount of an impaired asset will coincide with the asset's fair value at the date at which the impairment loss is recognized and if fair value measurement is used to determine the impairment loss.

The adjustments made to the historical costs of assets and liabilities under the cost model give rise to income or expenses which are included in the measurement of profit.

2.3 The present value model

2.3.1 Present value

The present value of an asset is defined in the Framework as the present discounted value of the future net cash inflows that the asset is expected to generate in the normal course of business. The present value of a liability is the present discounted value of the future net cash outflows that are expected to be required to settle the liability in the normal course of business. Present value is, therefore, an exit price for the asset or liability.

As the assumptions required by IFRS to measure present value differ from the assumptions used to measure fair value, present value rarely coincides with fair value. In particular, present value is usually measured using entity-specific assumptions while fair value should be measured using market participant assumptions.

Present value is included among the measurement bases in the Framework and is used as a measurement basis in IAS 19 *Employee Benefits* and IAS 37 *Provisions, Contingent Liabilities and Contingent Assets*.

2.3.2 Present value model

Under the present value model, assets and liabilities are measured at present value at each reporting date and changes in present values are reported in each period as income or expenses which are usually included in the determination of profit. However, under IAS 19, some changes in present values of defined benefit obligations are included in other comprehensive income.

2.3.3 Other uses of present value

Present value is also used as an essential part of the cost model for the measurement of the recoverable amount of assets which the entity can recover through use, for example property, plant and equipment and intangible assets.

3. Fair value measurement and the measurement of profit

The Framework defines profit as the difference between income and expenses. As income and expenses are defined as changes in assets and liabilities, the measurement of assets and liabilities affects income and expenses and, therefore profit. If the fair value model is used for assets and liabilities, changes in fair values meet the definitions of income and expenses and, therefore affect the measurement of profit. However, both the Framework and current IFRS exclude some items of income and expenses from the measurement of profit, in particular some income and expenses arising from the remeasurement of some assets and liabilities.

3.1 Capital maintenance adjustments

The Framework reflects its 1980s origins by taking a capital maintenance approach. It excludes from profit those items of income and expenses arising from the remeasurement of assets and liabilities that are capital maintenance adjustments (IASB, 2010: Par. 4.36). Capital maintenance considerations are among the reasons why changes in the fair values of property, plant and equipment accounted for under the fair value model in IAS 16 *Property, Plant and Equipment* are excluded from profit. However, little or no consideration has subsequently been given to concepts of capital and capital maintenance by the IASC or the IASB. In particular, the consideration of capital maintenance issues has played no part in IASC or IASB decisions about whether other changes in fair values arising from the use of the fair value model should, or should not, be included in profit.

3.2 Other remeasurements

In IFRS effective from 2013, the following remeasurements are excluded from IFRS profit:

- changes in the fair values of property, plant and equipment accounted for using the fair value model (see Section 3.1);
- exchange differences arising on the translation of an entity's net assets from functional currency to presentation currency;
- changes in the fair values of available-for-sale financial assets; and
- remeasurements arising on the net liability for post-employment benefits.

In addition, from 2015, IFRS 9 *Financial Instruments* will replace the requirements for available-for-sale financial assets and introduce a new requirement to exclude from profit the effects of own credit risk on financial liabilities accounted for using the fair value model.

One of the current driving forces for the exclusion of some remeasurements from the measurement of profit is the desire to remove some volatility from the measurement of profit. While there is widespread agreement that volatility arising from the underlying business operations of an entity, for example in the levels of its sales or operating costs, must be included in the measurement of profit, there is much less agreement about volatility arising from the remeasurement of assets and liabilities, in particular those remeasurements arising from changes in fair values.

This concern about volatility arising from remeasurements first arose in the early 1980s with the end of fixed currency exchange rates. Some national standard setters, together with the IASC, concluded that foreign exchange differences arising on the translation of a foreign entity's net assets from functional currency to presentation currency should be excluded from profit. The original version of IAS 21 *The Effects of Changes in Foreign Exchange Rates* issued in 1983 explained that such differences are excluded from profit because, among other things, the 'inclusion of such differences would distort the income statement'.[5]

The emergence of the fair value model for financial assets and financial liabilities (see Section 4) had added considerable impetus to the exclusion of the effects of some remeasurements from profit. Under IAS 25 *Accounting for Investments* (issued before the Framework was developed), changes in the measurement of long-term investments were excluded from profit; there was also an option to exclude changes in the measurement of current investments from profit. Possible volatility in profit was one reason for the exclusions. Others were the fact that changes in fair values might be unrealized or not distributable as dividends to shareholders.

IAS 39 *Financial Instruments: Recognition and Measurement* was based on US GAAP and, therefore, imported the notion of available-for-sale financial assets which are measured at fair value at each reporting date but with most changes in fair values excluded from profit. The incorporation of this approach into US GAAP was clearly influenced by the desire of US entities, in particular US banks, to keep the volatility arising from changes in fair values of such investments out of profit. Its inclusion in IAS 39 was driven solely by the need to use US GAAP as the basis for the new standard.[6]

IFRS 9 *Financial Instruments* retains the IAS 39 approach but restricts its use to investments in equity instruments that are not held for trading. The IASB justifies the approach on the basis that the inclusion of changes in fair values in profit 'may not be indicative of the performance of the entity' (IFRS 9.BC5.22) and that users of financial statements differentiate between fair value changes arising from 'equity investments held for purposes other than generating investment returns' and 'equity investments held for trading'(IFRS 9.BC5.23). While there is no mention of seeking to exclude some volatility from profit, it is hard to find a more substantive principle supporting the exclusions from profit.

IFRS 9 also introduces a further exclusion from profit: the effects of own credit risk on the changes in the fair values of some financial liabilities. In this case, volatility in profit is not the major concern. Commentators are far more concerned that the use of the fair value model for financial liabilities will allow an entity to report lower liabilities and income as a result of deteriorating credit risk, something which commentators find not useful and difficult to explain (IFRS 9.BCZ5.30). Many commentators suggested that the effect of the entity's own credit risk should be excluded from the fair value measurement or, if it is included, any resulting gains should be excluded from profit. The IASB has rejected the first suggestion but acceded to the second (IFRS 9.5.5.1c and BC5.31 to BC5.64).

The revised IAS 19 *Employee Benefits* issued in 2011 requires that the effects of remeasuring defined benefit obligations and plan assets should be excluded from profit. While the potential volatility arising from the inclusion of such remeasurements in profit was a concern of many preparers of IFRS financial statements, the IASB justifies its approach by the need to distinguish remeasurements from service cost and net interest in the most informative way given their different predictive values (IAS 19.BC88 and 90). In reaching this decision, the IASB acknowledged that the Framework does not describe a principle that would identify the items that would be treated in such a way.

3.3 Comprehensive income, other comprehensive income and profit

Until 2006, the income and expenses excluded from profit were included in equity and disclosed in the statement of changes in equity. The IASB subsequently decided that greater prominence should be given to these items and that a total should be presented for all income and expenses irrespective of whether or not they are included in profit. The outcome was the reporting of total comprehensive income, other comprehensive income and profit:

- total comprehensive income is the difference between all income and all expenses;
- other comprehensive income consists of income and expenses that are excluded from profit in accordance with specific requirements of IFRS; and
- profit is the difference between total comprehensive income and other comprehensive income.

As there is no concept or principle underpinning what is included or excluded from profit, there is no concept or principle underpinning other comprehensive income. For the most part the items are the result of compromises made by national standard setters, primarily in the UK or the USA, to win support for some current measurements in the statement of financial position.[7] The IASC, IASB and some other national standard setters have accepted the same compromises. More recently, the IASB has made its own decisions about what should be included or excluded from profit.

Many of the items included in other comprehensive income result from the remeasurements of assets and liabilities. However, not all remeasurements are included in other comprehensive income. In particular, the dividing line between those changes in fair values that are included in profit and those which are excluded from profit is based on compromises on individual IFRS. However, the introduction of total comprehensive income and the statement of comprehensive income has, perhaps, made the IASB's job a little easier. Before 2006, exclusions from profit were hidden in equity or the statement of change in equity. Now they are given greater prominence so they are more visible.

4. Measurement in IFRS

This section discusses why the IASB has required or permitted the use of the fair value model in the IFRS on financial assets and financial liabilities, investment property and biological assets. It also discusses briefly the options to use the fair value model for other assets and liabilities.

4.1 Financial assets and financial liabilities

The fair value model has emerged in the past 30 years as the appropriate way of accounting for financial assets and financial liabilities. The evolution of the model and the need for its use were accelerated by the explosion of new financial instruments in the late 1980s and were made possible by changes in attitudes of securities and prudential regulators.

IAS 25 and IAS 26 were small, but important, steps in the emergence of the fair value model in IFRS. IAS 25 *Accounting for Investments* permitted the use of market value for current investments that were readily realizable and could be sold without effort. It also allowed the use of the cost model, because it avoided recognizing unrealized gains and the effects of fortuitous swings in stock market prices notwithstanding that it allowed management to recognize income at its discretion. The choice reflected different opinions which were prevalent at the time and are clearly still prevalent (see Section 5). IAS 25 was later replaced by IAS 39 and IAS 40.

IAS 26 *Accounting and Reporting by Retirement Benefit Plans* requires fair value measurement for the investments of retirement benefit plans. It explains that fair value is market value for marketable securities (IAS 26.35). It argues that fair value measurement is the most useful measure of the investments at the reporting date and the investment performance of the period. IAS 26 remains in effect.

Both IAS 25 and IAS 26 were relatively limited in scope and were written before the explosion of new financial instruments in the latter half of the 1980s led to calls for a much broader project. The IASC and the Canadian Accounting Standards Board responded by setting up a joint financial instruments project which, from the outset, was intended to apply to all types of financial instruments and all businesses.[8]

The use of the fair value model was a key issue throughout the project. The IASC issued two exposure drafts (E40 *Financial Instruments* and E48 *Financial Instruments*) in the early 1990s which proposed the retention of a mixed measurement model under which:

- the fair value model should be used for financial assets and financial liabilities resulting from operating activities; and
- the cost model should be used for financial assets and financial liabilities resulting from investing and financing activities.

The choice of measurement model was based on managements' intentions with respect to the financial assets and financial liabilities. Operating activities included transactions undertaken as part of an active programme of buying and selling financial instruments with a view to short term gain. Therefore E40 and E48 proposed the use of the fair value model. There was no option to use the cost model for such assets and liabilities.

Investing activities were defined as transactions that result in the acquisition of financial assets that are intended to be held for the long-term or until maturity. Financing activities were defined as transactions that result in the assumption of financial liabilities that are intended to be held for the long term or to maturity. The IASB believed that the use of the cost model would 'avoid volatility in reported earning that may be misunderstood and an undue emphasis on short-term fluctuations in value that may tend to reverse over time'. It suggested that carrying amounts under the cost model were reliable and avoided the need to estimate fair values in circumstances in which such values may not be determinable on a sufficiently precise and accurate basis. The cost model also incorporated 'a reasonable degree of prudence' by not permitting the recognition of unrealized increases in fair values unless it was probable that they will be realized (E40.135). Lastly, the IASC believed that cost model was used in many countries and was, therefore, well known and supported and relatively easy to for entities to adopt and apply and users to understand.

Notwithstanding the support for the cost model, both E40 and E48 proposed an option to use the fair value model for financial assets and financial liabilities resulting from investing and financing activities. The option acknowledged that fair value measurement was routinely used in financial markets and more closely reflected the present value of the reporting entity's expected future cash flows. The fair value model minimized the application of judgement by management in determining carrying amounts and required the same accounting for assets and liabilities having the same economic characteristics. The fair value model was also seen as the long-term goal for financial reporting.

In 1994, the IASC decided not to proceed with the measurement proposals in E40 and E48 partly because of concerns raised by some national standard setting bodies that some aspects of the proposals were a step backwards. In particular, US GAAP had started to move towards the use of the fair value model for investments in equity and debt securities and derivatives, a step which had been made possible only with a change of attitude by the Securities and Exchange Commission, a long-time supporter of the cost model.

In 1997, the IASC and the Canadian Accounting Standards Board published a discussion paper that proposed that all financial assets and financial liabilities should be accounted for using the fair value model. All changes in fair value, except some hedging gains and losses, would be included in profit. The discussion paper argued that the historical cost of financial assets and financial liabilities had little relevance to financial risk management decisions and that a mixed measurement system provided opportunities for abuse and would inevitably lead to accounting mismatches when linked transactions are measured using different models. It argued that the successful management of financial risks required information on the nature and value of financial instruments, financial risk and exposures, liquidity and the effects of changes in the value of financial instruments.

Many responses to the discussion paper argued that the IASC had gone too far, in particular by proposing the use of the fair value model for traditional banking activities. Rather than proceed with the proposals in the discussion paper, the IASC took the pragmatic decision to develop an interim standard based on US GAAP requirements for financial instruments.[9] The outcome of this decision was IAS 39 *Financial Instruments: Recognition and Measurement* which was completed within a year and with scant due process. It introduced several significant parts of US GAAP into IFRS including the use of the fair value model for all derivatives, held for trading financial assets and financial liabilities, and available-for-sale financial assets. It required that changes in the fair values of available-for-sale financial assets should be excluded from profit, a compromise made by the FASB to accommodate the wishes of US banks. It incorporated detailed requirements on hedge accounting which were significantly different from the proposals in E40 and E48. It retained the cost model for loans and receivables, held to maturity investments and non-derivative liabilities but with some new restrictions on the model's use and much more implementation guidance.

Unlike the proposals in E40 and E48, IAS 39 did not include an option to use the fair value model for assets and liabilities measured using the cost model. The IASB subsequently added a fair value option in 2004 and the FASB followed suit. However, prudential supervisors of banks, securities companies and insurers expressed concern that the fair value option might be applied to financial assets or financial liabilities whose fair values were not verifiable, lead to increased volatility in profit or loss and result in the recognition of gains or losses associated with changes in an entity's own creditworthiness (see Section 5).

Notwithstanding the issuance of a revised IAS 39 in 2004, the IASB made no secret of its disdain for IAS 39. It proposed first that the complexity of IAS 39 could be reduced by requiring that all financial assets and financial liabilities should be accounted for using the fair value model but, again, this lacked support. IFRS 9 *Financial Instruments*, the eventual replacement for IAS 39, retains the mixed measurement approach with many financial assets and financial liabilities measured using the same measurement model as under IAS 39. IFRS 9 retains the fair value option but makes some changes to that option.

4.2 Investment property

The fair value model has also emerged as an appropriate way of accounting for investment property. IAS 25 permitted the use of the fair value model for investment property[10] but with changes in fair values excluded from profit. In this case, the move was heavily influenced by requirements in the United Kingdom where property investment companies had resisted national, EU and international requirements for the depreciation of property. UK property companies believed that changes in the fair values of investment properties were more important than depreciation.

When IAS 25 was superseded by IAS 39, the IASC developed a separate standard for investment property. The exposure draft proposed that all investment property should be accounted for using the fair value model with changes in fair value included in profit. The IASC argued (IAS 40.B44 and 45):

- fair value measurement give users of financial statements more useful information than other measures, such as depreciated cost;
- rental income and changes in fair value are inextricably linked as integral components of the financial performance of an investment property; and
- an investment property generates cash flows largely independently of the other assets held by an entity which makes a fair value model more appropriate for investment property than for owner-occupied property.

The responses to the exposure draft identified significant conceptual and practical reasons that precluded the mandatory use of the fair value model (IAS 40.B47). Therefore, the IASC decided that it was impracticable to require the use of the fair value model. It believed that it was desirable to permit the use of the fair value model in order to allow preparers and users to gain greater experience working with the model and allow time for certain property markets to achieve greater maturity (IAS 40.48). Therefore IAS 40 allows a free choice between the fair value model and the cost model.

4.3 Biological assets

The IASC also concluded that the fair value model is the appropriate way of accounting for biological assets and harvested agricultural produce. As a result, IAS 41 *Agriculture* requires that the fair value model should be used for all biological assets (with limited exceptions) and all harvested agricultural produce (with no exceptions). Changes in fair values are included in profit.

The IASB concluded that the fair value model should be used 'because of the unique nature and characteristics of agricultural activity' (IAS 41.B19). It rejected an option to use the cost model 'because of the greater comparability and understandability achieved by a mandatory fair value approach in the presence of active markets' (IAS 41.B21). In reaching these conclusions, the IASC rejected counter-arguments that market prices are often volatile and cyclical, active markets may not exist for harvested agricultural produce in some countries and fair value measurement results in the recognition of unrealized gains and contradicts the principles on revenue recognition.

4.4 Other assets

IAS 16 *Property, Plant and Equipment* allows a choice between the cost model and the fair value model for property, plant and equipment but, in practice the fair value model is rarely used.[11] The choice reflects the practices in the United Kingdom, the Netherlands, Australia, New Zealand, South Africa and some other British Commonwealth countries. The same choice is included as a member state option in the EC Fourth Directive, again as a result of the influence of the United Kingdom, Ireland and the Netherlands.

With effect from 1995, IAS 16 has required those entities using the fair value model to revalue the assets to fair value; and keep the revaluations up to date. The practical effect of these restrictions was a reduction in the number of companies using the fair value model. The UK incorporated the same restriction in its national standard with the same effect. Therefore, very few companies now use the revaluation model.

IAS 38 *Intangible Assets* allows a choice between the cost model and the fair value model for intangible assets but the fair value model may be used only when there is an active market for relevant assets. Therefore, in practice, the fair value model is never used.

5. Why is the fair value model contentious?

The choice of an appropriate measurement model that is appropriate in order to meet the objective of providing information that is useful for making economic decisions requires judgment. There is no single right answer shared by preparers and users of financial statements, standard setters and regulators. This lack of agreement is clearly evident whether seeking the appropriate model for the whole financial statements of a reporting entity or for part of those financial statements. The experiences of the IASC and the IASB on investments and financial assets show that there is even not agreement for a portfolio of marketable equity securities which are held with the express purpose earning income and capital appreciation.

Some, but far from all, of the objections to the use of the fair value model result from using a different objective for financial statements, for example providing information that can be used to monitor the adequacy of capital or the solvency of a bank or determining taxable or distributable profits. While there is no right answer to the choice of measurement model to be used to meet such objectives, there may be a greater consensus that the cost model is appropriate. However, these objectives are not those that the IASC had, or the IASB has, in mind when developing accounting standards.

So what are the objections to the use of the fair value model in financial statements that are intended to provide financial information about the reporting entity that is useful to existing and potential investors, lenders and other creditors in making decisions about providing resources to the entity? At its simplest level, there is a strong body of opinion that believes that the use of the cost model can provide such information for all assets and liabilities including those that are held for investment purposes. Some base their support for this model on its reliance on information derived from transactions undertaken by the reporting entity. Others use arguments based on notions of prudence under which the carrying amounts of assets should never exceed the amounts measured under the cost model.

A similar objection to the use of the fair value model focuses on the role of management in measuring fair values. These objectors believe that the financial statements should report what management has done using objective evidence derived from the transactions management has carried out. Beyond this, management should not be able to influence, let alone determine, the monetary amounts that are reported in the financial statements.

Many objectors to the use of the fair value model question the measurements of fair values, in particular when those fair values are not measured from transactions or quotations in active markets. They question the reliability of purported fair values obtained from inactive markets and the use of models to measure such fair values.

The financial crisis which started in 2007 has also brought to light concerns that the ability to use the fair value model may influence the behaviour of management. In particular, some have asserted that managements may take more risks by buying assets if they can use the fair value model when accounting for those assets.This argument leads to the suggestion that the use of the fair value model is pro-cyclical – in a rising market, entities buy more assets so pushing the values of those assets even higher – in a falling market, entities are forced to sell so pushing the values even lower.

Some objectors to the use of the fair value model focus on its use for particular types of assets and liabilities. Many would probably object to the use of the fair value model for operating assets (property, plant and equipment, and inventories). Many in the banking industry and many banking regulators oppose strongly the use of the fair value model for banking book assets and liabilities, in other words the customer loans, advances and deposits of banks. However, many bankers also object to the use of the fair value model for investment securities, hence the notion of available-for-sale financial assets in IAS 39 and US GAAP under which changes in fair values are excluded from profit.

There is extensive literature setting out the arguments against the use of the fair value model. Some of this literature is summarised in IASB discussion papers and the bases for conclusions in IFRS. One of the best and most balanced summaries of the arguments for and against the use of the fair value model was published by the European Central Bank (2004) (*Fair Value Accounting and Financial Stability*) at the time the Bank and bankers were objecting to the introduction of a fair value option in IAS 39.

6. The IASB'S responses to concerns about the use of the fair value model

As Section 5 explains, two major concerns have been raised about the use of the fair value model: the requirement or permission to use the fair value model; the measurement of fair value.The IASB has dealt with the former concerns during the development of new and revised IFRS, in particular IFRS 9 *Financial Instruments*. It has dealt with the latter concerns in IFRS 13 *Fair Value Measurement*.

6.1 The use of the fair value model

Requirements about the use of the fair value model are included in IFRS dealing with specific assets and liabilities. As explained in Section 4, the standards on financial assets and financial liabilities (financial instruments) require the use of the fair value model for some financial assets and financial liabilities and allow its use for many other financial assets and financial liabilities. The IASB has remained committed to this approach and there are no signs that it will reduce, to any measurable extent, the use of the fair value model. It may, in fact, wish to extend its use but has, so far, found strong opposition to any significant extension.

The retention in IFRS 9 of the fair value model for some financial assets and financial liabilities seeks to help users to understand the financial reporting of financial assets by aligning their measurement with the way that the entity manages its financial assets (business model) and their contractual cash flow characteristics, thus providing relevant and useful information to users for their assessment of the amounts, timing and certainty of the entity's future cash flows. However, the discussion in the basis for conclusions focuses entirely on the circumstances in which financial assets should be measured at amortised cost rather than on the need for any financial assets to be measured at fair value. In other words, the basis for conclusions in IFRS 9 reflects the IASB's preference for measuring financial assets at fair value.

IFRS 9 reduces the measurement categories in IAS 39 from four to two but the practical effect of these changes is likely to be that those financial assets that were measured at fair value under IAS 39 will also be measured at fair value under IFRS 9. In other words, IFRS 9 does not reduce the requirements to use the fair value model. In contrast, IFRS 9 increases the use of the fair value model in certain limited circumstances, in particular for investments in unquoted equity securities and for financial assets which include embedded derivatives.

The IASB's support for the use of the fair value model for financial assets and financial liabilities was clear in its 2008 discussion paper *Reducing Complexity in Reporting Financial Instruments*. This discussion paper responded to concerns that the then requirements for reporting financial instruments were complex and that one of the main causes of complexity was the many ways of measuring financial instruments and the associated rules with those measurements. The discussion paper suggested that a long term solution was to measure in the same way all types of financial instruments within the scope of a standard for financial instruments. It observed: 'fair value seems to be the only measure that is appropriate for all types of financial instruments'. It noted that many documents previously published by the IASB expressed this view. The paper argued that the use of the cost model for all types of financial instruments was not a feasible alternative and that, for example, the use of the cost model for derivative financial instruments did not provide users of financial statements with information about future cash flow prospects for the instruments.

Against this background, it is not surprising that the IASB has continued to favour the fair value model as the appropriate measurement model for some financial assets and financial liabilities.

6.2 Fair value measurement

IFRS 13 *Fair Value Measurement* deals only with how fair value should be measured when other IFRS require or allow the use of fair value measurement. It does not change when fair value measurement is required. Instead IFRS 13 seeks to ensure that fair value is measured consistently for any asset, liability or equity instrument irrespective of whether they have market values or are quoted or traded in an active market.[12]

IFRS 13 will not satisfy those who object to the use of the fair value model or to the use of fair values that are not derived from active markets. It may satisfy some, including some regulators, who have been concerned about the way some entities have measured fair values.

Notes

1 The IASC had required or proposed the use of other current value measurements, in particular current cost and market value, as alternatives to the use of historical cost based amounts.

2 The evolution of the definition of fair value and definitions in different IFRS are dealt with in Cairns (2006).

3 Some national accounting requirements may permit or require the use of some amount other than fair value to deal with such issues. For example, they may permit the use of the carrying amounts in the acquiree's financial statements when accounting for business combinations. They may also permit or require the use of the carrying amount of the non-cash asset given up as the initial amount for the non-cash asset received.

4 Impairment requirements are generally unnecessary under the fair value model because there is no need to reduce the carrying amount of an asset below its fair value. However, it is sometimes necessary to consider whether negative changes in the fair value of an asset accounted for under the fair value model are impairment losses.

5 The text referring to the distortion of the income statement was included in paragraph 17 of the original version of IAS 21 issued in 1983. The text was removed in the 1993 version of IAS 21. The current version of IAS 21 retains only the notion that the changes in exchange rates have little or no effect on the present or future cash flows from operations (see IAS 21.41).

6 However, IAS 25 had permitted a similar treatment.

7 There is one important difference between the UK and US compromises which has found its way into IFRS. Those items of other comprehensive income that originated in UK GAAP, principally revaluation surpluses on property, plant and equipment and actuarial gains and losses on defined benefit plans, are not recycled out of other comprehensive income into profit at some later date. Those items that originated in the USA, principally gains and losses on the translation of foreign operations from functional currency to presentation currency, gains or losses on available-for-sale financial assets and gains or losses on hedging instruments in a cash flow hedge, are recycled out of other comprehensive income into profit at some later date.

8 For more details of the project, see Cairns (2002), pp. 364–7.

9 This decision was influenced by the IASC's commitment to the International Organisation of Securities Commissions (IOSCO) to develop, by 1999, a set of core standards for the purpose of cross-border capital raising and listing in all global markets. That set of standards had to include a standard on the recognition and measurement of financial instruments.

10 IAS 25.24, 25 and 45. The standard referred to 'revalued amount' but the explanation referred to 'fair value which is usually market value'. The treatment was consistent with the treatment for other long-term investments. IAS 25 also allowed investment property to be accounted for as property in accordance with IAS 16 *Property, Plant and Equipment* which allowed measurement under either the cost model or the fair value model.

11 See, for example, Cairns *et al.* (2011) and Christensen and Nikolaev (2008).

12 The evolution of the term fair value and its definition in IFRS are dealt with in Cairns (2007).

Bibliography

Cairns, D. (2002) *Applying International Accounting Standards*, London: Tolley LexisNexis.

Cairns, D. (2006) 'The Use and Evolution of Fair Value in IFRS', *Accounting in Europe* 3: 5–22.

Cairns, D. (2007) 'The Use of Fair Value in IFRS', in Walton, P. (ed.) *The Routledge Companion to Fair Value and Financial Reporting*, London: Routledge, pp. 9–23.

Cairns, D., Massoudi, D., Taplin, R. and Tarca, A. (2011) 'IFRS Fair Value Measurement and Accounting Policy Choice in the United Kingdom and Australia', *The British Accounting Review*, 43(1): 1–21.

Camfferman, K. and Zeff, S.A. (2007) *Financial Reporting and Global Capital Markets: A History of the International Accounting Standards Committee 1973–2001*, Oxford: Oxford University Press.

Christensen, H.B. and Nikolaev, V. (2008) 'Who Uses Fair Value Accounting for Non-financial Assets after IFRS Adoption?', University of Chicago Booth School of Business Working paper, No 09–12.

European Central Bank (2004) *Fair Value Accounting and Financial Stability*, Occasional Paper Series No. 13, April (available at www.ecb.de/pub/pdf/scpops/ecbocp13.pdf, accessed 29 September 2012)

IASB (2010) *The Conceptual Framework for Financial Reporting*. London: International Accounting Standards Board.

8

Costs and Benefits of Disclosure

Ann Gaeremynck and Mathijs Van Peteghem

1. The relevance of disclosure

When judging the financial statements quality attention is usually paid to the two most relevant issues: measurement and disclosure. Over the years, questions related to disclosures have arisen. The fact that disclosures in the notes have significantly expanded has on the one hand led to questions regarding how meaningful such disclosures are, and has on the other hand raised serious concerns about the overall quality of the disclosures. Furthermore, the global financial crisis and the introduction of IFRS have contributed to the renewed interest in disclosure issues.

IFRS being a principles-based accounting framework has caused the emergence of additional disclosures in the financial statements. Some examples underline the relevance of those disclosures in this context. A first example, the impairment standard (IAS 36) stipulates that the circumstances under which an impairment is booked should be motivated in the notes of the financial statements (key assumptions used in the identification process, discount and growth rate of cash generating units, sensitivity analysis, etc.). This information is highly relevant to investors and allows a better judgment of how the value of the goodwill has been derived; the true and fair value of goodwill. A second example, IAS 40 *Investment property*, demands that the investment property valuation method (historical cost, market fair value, comparables or model fair value) is disclosed in the notes, but IAS 40 does not demand that the underlying parameters of the valuation process are specified, though they are highly relevant for decision making. A third example, transparency, requires recognized fair value estimates be supplemented with disclosures about reliability (Ryan, 2002; Barth, 2006; Bies 2005; Landsman, 2006; Blacconiere *et al.*, 2011). Disclosures about the reliability can be very diverse: disavowals of fair value disclosures in the notes (Blacconiere *et al.*, 2011) as well as disclosures on the underlying parameters used to value investment property to overcome problems with the estimation accuracy of the fair value measurements (Vergauwe *et al.*, 2012). Overall, disclosure has become more and more important in a US GAAP and IFRS context as measurement methods such as fair value demand more and more judgment from the preparer's side. The user's side should be informed about the judgments made to assess the reliability of the measurement choices made, which is a key characteristic in the decision process of different users. There is also a renewed interest in disclosure because of the financial crisis, especially in the banking sector (Goldstein and Sapra, 2012). Different national banks undertake annual stress tests to know whether banks have enough capital to absorb adverse economic conditions. The purpose of these stress tests is to discipline the market. However, the question has been raised whether the outcome of these stress tests should be disclosed as they may have adverse economic effects, such as sub-optimal economic decisions and excessive reactions of the public to bad news. As such disclosure can result in bank behavior which does not maximize firm value but maximizes the likelihood of passing the stress tests.

This short introduction illustrates the relevance of disclosures. The purpose of this study is not to give an overview of all disclosure studies published, which is a rather impossible task. Moreover, there are some very good reviews already published in the literature (Healy and Palepu, 2001; Core 2001; Leuz and Wysocki, 2008; Beyer *et al.*, 2010). This chapter discusses some issues which are relevant in all disclosure decisions:

- What is the role of disclosure?
- What are the costs of disclosure?
- How to disclose the information (form of disclosure)?
- When to disclose the information (timing of disclosure)?

2. The role of disclosure

It has been long recognized in the literature that disclosure fulfills a double role. First, disclosure fulfills an *ex ante* role to capital investors for informing them about firm value because of problems of asymmetry in information and of uncertainty. Second, disclosure also fulfills a stewardship role *ex post* in limiting agency problems between company insiders and outsiders.

Ex ante disclosure fulfills a role of solving asymmetries in information and uncertainty. A well-accepted rationale for disclosing information is that disclosures result in a decrease of the information asymmetries between company insiders and outsiders with positive effects on firm value. Asymmetries in information occur because management have privately held information about the profitability and the risk of future projects. Enhanced disclosure not only results in a decrease of the asymmetries in information but also helps firms to make better decisions. Disclosure serves as a monitoring mechanism (Lambert *et al.*, 2007). Therefore, more disclosure reduces uncertainty about the 'real' value of the firm. Disclosures which reveal private information to the market are typically labeled as efficient disclosures (Holthausen *et al.*, 1983; Holthausen, 1990; Healy and Palepu, 1993). If market participants do not receive any information, they will undervalue firms with good projects and overvalue firms with bad projects. Disclosing information can solve this potential market failure.

The positive market reactions to more disclosure have been extensively illustrated in the literature (Welker, 1995; Healy *et al.*, 1999; Leuz and Verrecchia, 2000; Verrecchia, 2001). Providing value relevant information to otherwise uninformed investors enhances firm visibility and investors' willingness to invest in the firm (Diamond and Verrecchia, 1991; Chang *et al.*, 2008), facilitates the placement and trading of shares at fair prices, improves the market liquidity and lowers the cost of capital (Diamond and Verrecchia, 1991; Kim and Verrecchia, 1994; Botosan 1997; Piotroski 1999; Botosan and Plumlee 2002). Furthermore, evidence also exists that investors punish firms for insufficient disclosure (Welker, 1995; Leuz and Verrecchia, 2000; Lambert *et al.*, 2007) as they want to "price protect" themselves against potential losses from trading with better informed market participants. Along the same lines, Gelb and Zarowin (2002) document a positive relation between voluntary disclosure and stock price informativeness, indicating the importance of providing sufficient information to investors. Francis *et al.* (2007) focus on the complementary role of disclosure and earnings quality and attribute the reduction in a firm's capital cost more to improved earnings quality than to increased disclosure. Firms with high earnings quality typically also have more expansive voluntary disclosures (Francis *et al.*, 2007).

The rationale to disclose information because of possible asymmetries in information does not only apply to shareholders but also to debtholders. Debtholders lend money to a firm to give that firm the possibility to invest in new projects. The interest rate charged will reflect general market uncertainty as well as firm-specific risks. Enhanced disclosure allows lenders to gain increased insight in a borrowing company, thereby reducing uncertainty and asymmetries in information. Consequently, if a firm discloses more, debt holders will charge a lower interest rate to the firm with also a direct positive effect on firm value (Sengupta 1998; Chen *et al.*, 2002). A remark which especially concerns debtholders is that incentives to publicly disclose information typically apply to public debt and not to private debt (such as loans granted by banks). All the necessary information to supply a loan can be provided in private meetings without the risk of having specific costs linked to the disclosure, such as proprietary costs (see Section 3.1 below).

However, *ex post* disclosure also fulfills a stewardship role with the purpose of decreasing agency costs. Agency costs arise for different reasons. First, agency costs arise because the suppliers of capital are not the same persons as the ones responsible for managing the funds provided (Shleifer and Vishny, 1997). Management has the ability to make decisions that are in their own interests, possibly expropriating investors' funds and harming shareholders (Jensen and Meckling, 1976). Furthermore, management can withhold bad news for the owners because of opportunistic reasons (e.g. management compensation or career concerns). In an environment with separation of management and ownership, disclosure fulfills a monitoring role in evaluating management performance and strategy (Lambert *et al.*, 2007). If the information is truthfully disclosed, the likelihood that company insiders realize private benefits of control is smaller, which will positively impact firm value. Investors anticipate the existence of these possible agency problems by demanding a premium which increases the firm's cost of capital (Lang and Lundholm 1996) and which has a negative effect on the market liquidity (Verrecchia, 2001).

A typical example of a setting where disclosure can fulfill a stewardship function is the disclosure of executive compensation. Performance-based compensation schemes are a central part of corporate governance practices and allow for a strong link between executive remuneration and performance. This offers incentives to the management to maximize firm value. However, since performance is mostly defined using accounting numbers, managers are tempted to manipulate earnings in order to inflate remuneration. Shareholder monitoring is particularly relevant in this setting, but outside monitoring may also prove useful. Consequently, more recently regulators have started requiring firms to disclose executive remuneration as firms do not disclose them on a voluntary basis (Liu and Taylor, 2008; Hitz and Werner, 2012).

However, the specific characteristics of the environment will also influence the type of stewardship role disclosure fulfills. In a European setting, where the majority of the shares are typically held by a single shareholder, the agency problem is of a fundamentally different nature. The principal-agent problem of dispersed ownership is no longer a concern due to the increased monitoring of majority shareholders (Shleifer and Vishny, 1986) while a new agency problem is introduced: a principal-principal problem. This encompasses conflicts between majority and minority shareholders, where the former abuse their power at the expense of the latter (Young *et al.*, 2008). With a controlling shareholder, the fundamental governance problem is not opportunism by executives and directors at the expense of public shareholders at large but rather opportunism by the controlling shareholder at the expense of the minority shareholders (Bebchuk and Weisbach, 2010). Majority ownership most likely implies too much shareholder involvement, where the controlling shareholder enjoys private benefits of control and uses its voting power and influence on management to extract even more benefits (Claessens *et al.*, 2002; Renders and Gaeremynck, 2011). These benefits include the appropriation of corporate resources by the majority shareholder or related-party transactions at unconventional transfer prices. The value generated by these transactions is not shared among all the shareholders in proportion of the shares owned, but is enjoyed exclusively by the party in control (Dyck and Zingales, 2004). In this setting, disclosure is even more important when a controlling shareholder is present. Minority shareholders have no influence on firm policies or practices and are largely dependent on the information made available by the management. Enhanced disclosure, whether disclosed on a voluntary or regulatory basis, provides them with the means on which to base their judgment. This allows them to signal shareholder expropriation or other power abuse by the majority shareholder.

In an environment where disclosure fulfills a stewardship role, different mechanisms can help to encourage disclosure such as the institutional setting as well as the quality of firm governance. Of particular importance is the board of directors (Adams *et al.*, 2010) and especially the audit committee in disclosure settings. Better-governed firms are found to make more informative disclosures (Beekes and Brown, 2006). In the literature extensive evidence is found that well-functioning boards and especially audit committees can encourage disclosures (Ho and Wong, 2001; Cheng and Courtenay, 2006). In a context of IFRS adoption, Verriest *et al.* (2013) find that firms with stronger governance have a higher degree of voluntary disclosure, comply more fully with the minimum disclosure requirements set in the IFRS standards, and use IAS 39's carve-out provision less opportunistically. Finally, when studying the relationship between disclosure and governance, it may not be ignored that both can be substitutes. As an illustration, disclosure as well as a well-functioning remuneration committee can both avoid excessive compensation being paid to management.

3. Costs of disclosures

Even if everyone is convinced that more disclosure creates benefits, increased transparency by disclosing more information leads to more indirect as well as direct costs for the company. Because of the existence of costs, independent of whether disclosure fulfills a stewardship or signaling role, full disclosure of all the private information will not occur in practice. In the case of voluntary disclosure, the assumption is that managers will disclose information if they expect that the benefits from doing so outweigh the costs. In the case of mandatory disclosure, while firms have less discretion over the decision itself, they determine the quantity (e.g. the number of lines), the nature (e.g. good or bad news or neutral) of the information or more qualitative characteristics disclosed. In this decision, costs as well as benefits will determine those characteristics of the information disclosed.

When investigating the costs of disclosure, there are different types of disclosure costs. First, there are the direct costs of collecting, processing and publishing the information (e.g. organizing a conference call or organizing the internal reporting system in such a way that the information is available, for example segmental reporting). Direct costs of preparing disclosures are related to firm size as well as to the characteristics of the reporting environment (e.g. listed or not). It is well accepted that in some institutional settings, where the difference between local

GAAP and IFRS is big, the introduction of IFRS standards resulted in a substantial increase of the direct reporting costs. If a firm is cross-listed in the US, firms have to disclose a Form 20-F, which demands additional costs.

Second, there are also indirect costs such as proprietary, verification and litigation costs. Indirect costs explain disclosure practices although the specific setting and the accounting issue studied will determine the relative importance of each category. While proprietary costs can be highly important for issues such as segmental reporting, litigation costs can influence risk reporting strategies and verification costs can impact the level of detail as well as frequency of voluntary earnings' forecasts releases.

3.1 Proprietary costs

Proprietary costs arise when information disclosure results into competitively sensitive information to the market (Verrecchia, 1983; Wagenhofer, 1990; Feltham and Xie, 1992; Depoers and Jeanjean 2010). Competitors may use this information to obtain a competitive advantage towards the disclosing company. IFRS 8 is a typical example of competitive sensitive information. If segments are identified on a very disaggregated level, the disclosure of the profits by segment can attract entry in the market and it can harm the competitive position of the firm. However, in a situation of losses and bad market prospects it can also deter entry in that market segment. Using confidential plant-level data Bens *et al.* (2011) show that proprietary costs of separately reporting segment information influence the level of aggregation in external reporting. The higher the level of proprietary costs, the higher the level of aggregation. Likewise, Botosan and Stanford (2005) find evidence that managers conceal profitable segments which operate in industries with a low degree of competition as compared to their primary operations. However, Berger and Hann (2007) test the proprietary costs hypothesis for withholding information relating to segmental reporting and find only mixed empirical evidence. The proprietary cost rationale is only significant in a minority of models and is non-robust to other specifications.

Notice that proprietary costs are not only applicable to the competitive market position but also to other markets such as the labor market. Scott (1994) provides evidence that the propensity to disclose pension plan related information was negatively associated with measures capturing labor market power. Disclosing the wages of top managers results in a higher employee turnover of a firm's top management as they more often get good job offers by headhunters.

3.2 Verification costs

Disclosure of information can only fulfill its role of decreasing asymmetries in information when it is reliable, truthful and free from manipulation (Ball *et al.*, 2011; Crawford and Sobel, 1982). Consequently, if a firm wants to disclose additional information truthfully to the market, the firm has to spend additional resources to verify this information. Therefore, another important, albeit indirect, cost factor of disclosing information identified is the verification cost. This is the cost of establishing credibility by enhanced financial statement verification (Ball *et al.*, 2011). In this context, the most important verification mechanism is provided by the internal and external audit function. Firms have incentives to invest substantially in their auditor as larger and more qualified audit firms will in general be more expensive but the market values high quality audits (Francis and Wang, 2008). This results in accurate and reliable disclosure. The external auditor is complemented by the internal audit function. Accordingly, Prawitt *et al.* (2009) find evidence of a positive relation between internal audit quality and earnings informativeness as proxied by the level of earnings management. Firms have an incentive to invest in the audit as it contributes to the credibility of the information provided, which has a positive effect on the stock price (Lundholm and Myers, 2002). Finally, empirical evidence shows that verification costs will also be smaller in circumstances where disclosure does not relate to measurement issues (Ball *et al.*, 2011).

Firms can also employ other verification mechanisms than the audit function to provide credibility to the information provided. An external appraiser report for the measurement of the investment property provides credibility to the measurement of the investment property (Vergauwe *et al.*, 2012). Another example is an evaluation of corporate environmental practices by experts. This will signal an open information policy to investors and enhance disclosure credibility (Darnall *et al.*, 2009).

3.3 Litigation costs

Associated with the verification costs is another category of indirect disclosure costs, being the litigation costs. A firm incurs litigation costs when third parties file complaint and sue for damages on the basis of insufficient or misleading disclosure. The legal proceedings entail real expenses on representation and damages, as well as a loss of reputation. Karpoff *et al.* (1998) document these effects relating to environmental violations and find a loss in market value of equity almost equal to the legal penalties following the violation. In this setting, reputational concerns are of secondary importance. Conversely, a law suit encourages firms to decrease the provision of disclosures for which they may later be held accountable (Rogers and Van Buskirk, 2009). Finally, in studying the relationship between litigation costs and disclosure, it is important to notice that an endogenous relationship exists between disclosure and litigation as is also the case for proprietary costs.

4. Types and timing of disclosures

Next to the disclosure decision itself, costs and benefits also influence the types of disclosures made. Characteristics of the information studied in previous literature are the quantitative versus the qualitative as well as the nature of the information provided.

4.1 Types of disclosure

Qualitative versus quantitative information

Whether disclosure is of a quantitative or qualitative nature, depends to a large extent on the event to which the disclosures relate. If disclosures relate to foreign currency risk, it is obvious that quantitative information about the risk can be provided. The exposure to credit risks also allows quantitative disclosures. Notice that quantitative disclosures can always be supplemented with qualitative information but the opposite is often more difficult. Furthermore, although one would expect investors to attach more value to quantitative aspects, qualitative disclosures as well can have a non-negligible impact. Another class of highly relevant non-quantitative disclosures made are environmental, by which the firm aims to promote its environmental awareness. Aerts and Cormier (2009) state that environmental legitimacy is mainly about perception, and this perception is significantly and positively affected by the extent and quality of environmental disclosures in the annual report and press releases. Relating to environmental disclosures, Cho and

Patten (2007) acknowledge firms' use of disclosure as a legitimizing tool towards society. Aerts and Cormier (2009) apply the same reasoning to media legitimacy. Media legitimacy is found to strongly influence the public opinion on a company (Carroll and McCombs, 2003). Accordingly, Botan and Taylor (2004) emphasize the importance of information issues for corporate reputation. Another example where qualitative information is highly relevant is corporate social responsibility (CSR), which has recently emerged as a topic of increased interest to practitioners and academics (Lindgreen and Swaen, 2010). CSR is a way to introduce ethics into the organizational structure, whereby companies integrate social and environmental concerns in their business operations and in their interaction with their stakeholders on a voluntary basis (European Commission, 2011). In practice, CSR disclosure appears limited. Holder-Webb *et al.* (2009) find that firms tend to keep most of the CSR information private. As a possible explanation, the authors suggest investors do not take this information seriously without assurance as to its quality. The importance of verification and reliable data is stressed. The disclosure on CSR is also related to the strength of corporate governance settings (Aguilera *et al.*, 2006). Firms with higher CSR are associated with higher disclosure (Gelb and Strawser, 2001), as well as less risky stocks (Becchetti and Ciciretti, 2009).

While the costs of qualitative information (e.g. verification costs, proprietary costs) are lower, the benefits will also be smaller as the information is less precise (Danckaert *et al.*, 2008). Furthermore, where quantitative information is less subject to discretion and often verified by an independent auditor, qualitative disclosure is largely at the discretion of management and not verified by an independent external party. Finally, disclosure can result in increased litigation, where not only the disclosure itself but also the nature as well as the quantitative character of the news is relevant (Beyer *et al.*, 2010).

Nature of the news

The reaction of investors to news will depend not only on the precision but also on the type of information being released, i.e. whether disclosures made contain good or bad news for the company. Previous studies that have examined the relation between disclosure and stock price reactions conclude that good news disclosures are associated with positive stock price responses (Lang and Lundholm, 2000; Henry, 2008; Demers and Vega, 2008; Davis *et al.*, 2008). Moreover, Skinner (1994) finds that stock price reactions to bad news disclosures are larger in absolute value than stock price reactions to good news events.

4.2 The timing and the way to disclose the information

Next to the disclosure decision itself as well as the type of disclosures made, costs and benefits also influence the timing (early or late) and where to disclose the information (in the annual report, the MD&A (Management Discussion and Analysis) analysis or by using another means).

The timing of disclosure

Sengupta (2004) shows that the reporting lag is shorter for firms with larger benefits (i.e. a greater investor demand for information) and larger costs (i.e. greater litigation costs). To avoid litigation costs, firms make not only high quality but also timely disclosures (Lang and Lundholm, 1993; Sengupta, 2004; Kothari *et al.*, 2009b). Furthermore, the nature of the news also influences the timing although the evidence is mixed. Skinner (1994, 1997) documents that firms with bad news are more likely to pre-disclose compared to those with good news. On the contrary, empirical evidence (Givoly and Palmon, 1982; Chambers and Penman, 1984; Kross and Schroeder, 1984; Begley and Fischer, 1998; Kothari *et al.*, 2009b) also shows that managers are successful in withholding much of the bad news from investors until it becomes inevitable that the bad news will be released. Managers' tendency to withhold bad news is lower for firms with high litigation risk, but higher for managers with greater career concerns (Kothari *et al.*, 2009b). While litigation costs are highly relevant for the timing of the disclosures made, proprietary costs do not influence the timing of disclosures. The frequency of the segment disclosures made does not depend on the level of proprietary costs (Botosan and Harris, 2000).

The form of disclosure

a) The annual report

Disclosures can be done in different ways: in the annual report, in the MD&A analysis or by using another means (such as conference calls). The annual report of a company is the primary instrument to disclose information to shareholders. Firms are required by law to provide an overview of the annual accounts as well as several other disclosures related to environmental issues, firm risks, corporate governance in the notes, etc. The importance of a firm's annual report cannot be exaggerated. The annual reports have therefore been extensively regulated to force firms to disclose a number of items which they would not have disclosed on a voluntary basis. The quality of disclosure matters as well as the quantity (Beretta and Bozzolan, 2012). Furthermore, evidence also shows that despite regulation, firms still aim to obscure negative news to investors. S. Li (2010) finds firms with lower earnings to have more complicated annual reports which are less accessible to the reader. Firms with persistent positive earnings have easier to read annual reports. They therefore appear to misuse discretion allowed for by the legislation to mitigate the adverse consequences of bad news. While everyone is convinced about the value of regulated information (e.g. earnings, disclosures about the valuation methods), not everyone is convinced about the value of voluntary disclosures in the financial statements. Although Banghøj and Plenborg (2008) acknowledge the use of voluntary disclosure in reducing information asymmetries, they do not find that voluntary information in the annual accounts is relevant to investors. This could mean that investors are not capable of incorporating this voluntary information in the firm value estimates.

The impact of information can also differ depending on the form in which it is disclosed. The primary difference between these forms is the verification and reliability of information. Among the various forms, the balance sheet and profit and loss accounts have the most authority, since these have been thoroughly inspected by an external auditor. This involves an objective expert opinion on the reliability and truthfulness of the firm's financial situation. Hence, investors largely base their judgment on the information found in the audited financial statements. Balance sheet and profit and loss account are intertwined: value relevance of one aspect is complemented by the other (Black and White, 2003). A correctly valued balance sheet offers a constraint to managerial discretion in manipulating the financial data (Barton and Simko, 2002). Recognizing the importance of the balance sheet, managers voluntarily include these data in quarterly earnings announcements to inform investors when current earnings are less informative or future earnings are more uncertain (Chen *et al.*, 2002). Therefore, balance sheet disclosures are more prevalent among younger firms and those operating in high tech industries, since these firms face increased uncertainties. They are also more likely for firms reporting losses, with larger forecast errors, engaging in merger and acquisitions and with more volatile stock returns (Chen *et al.*, 2002).

Another important aspect of firm disclosure are the notes found in the annual report. In the notes, a company provides clarification on several items in the financial statements as well as explains the firm's financial and operational performance. Issues treated are various and contain information on debt, corporate governance, risks and uncertainties facing the firm, environmental disclosures, etc. The notes offer management an opportunity to decrease information asymmetries and inform stakeholders on matters which it finds relevant. However, lack of verification may threaten the perceived reliability of these disclosures. Next to the notes where those disclosures about the valuation choices are made, the most well-known element added to the balance sheet and the profit and loss account is the Management Discussion and Analysis (MD&A). In the MD&A, management has to state its view on the company's operations as well as future prospects. This is a source of useful information and is part of a firm's overall disclosure quality (Clarkson *et al.*, 1999; Cole and Jones, 2004). In a recent study, Brown and Tucker (2011) find the primary users of the MD&A-schedules to be investors rather than analysts and also document stagnation in MD&A content. This suggests firms tend to 'copy and paste' the schedule with only minor changes between years, which results in only a limited usefulness towards investors. However, the tone changes between subsequent MD&A filings do have an impact. Management's tone change adds to portfolio drift after taking into account accruals and earnings surprises (Feldman *et al.*, 2010). The incremental value of the information conveyed by the tone change is stated to depend on the strength of the firm's information and disclosure environment. F. Li (2010) confirms the importance of tone in the MD&A, as well as the limited use analysts make of these schedules. MD&As are also evidenced to have an impact on a firm's cost of capital, stock return volatility and analyst forecast dispersion (Kothari *et al.*, 2009a).

The reason why the relevance of the annual report is often questioned is its timeliness. Annual reports are only issued within some months after the year-end. This means some (possibly outdated) information is aggregated and jointly disclosed towards investors. New bad news disclosures made at the time of the annual report issue can result in a sudden shock in stock prices. The gap between the financial year end and the issue of financial statements is influenced by proprietary costs, information cost savings and relative good or bad news (Leventos and Weetman, 2004). The timeliness of information also has an impact on litigation costs: less timely disclosure of negative earnings news increases firms' litigation consequences (Billings, 2008). When restatements are involved, the gap considerably widens (Badertscher and Burks, 2011). Gigler and Hemmer (2001) relate the timeliness of disclosure to a firm's accounting policy in a theoretical framework. Overall, annual reports may provide insufficient or untimely disclosure to investors. This explains why large firms opt for quarterly reports as well. However, the issue or verification arises in this setting, since these statements are not subject to a statutory audit in most countries.

b) Conference calls

A common practice used in larger firms to overcome the problems of the timeliness with the annual report is the use of conference calls. The role of these conference calls is to communicate important information to investors and stakeholders by the use of digital meetings. Information is then disseminated on a more frequent basis, resulting in reduced information asymmetries. The information disclosed by conference calls is also evidenced to contain new and material information for market participants (Frankel *et al.*, 1999). Consequently, firms regularly holding conference calls are found to display low information asymmetries and have a lower cost of capital as compared to firms with a less open disclosure policy (Brown *et al.*, 2004). Furthermore, conference calls result in a significant reduction of analyst forecast error (Kimbrough, 2005) and more informative earnings (Kohlbeck and Magilke, 2002).

There are different types of conference calls. Bushee *et al.* (2003) distinguish between 'open' and 'closed' conference calls. Whereas closed conference calls contain only a limited number of participants (major investors, important stakeholders, invited professionals, etc.), open conference calls allow all parties, including analysts, unlimited access to the call. The authors find open conference calls to be associated with a large number of shareholders, lower institutional ownership, lower analyst following and higher average share turnover. Open conference calls result in fast and wide information disclosure and are upcoming standard practices, matching advances in technology, regulatory and market pressures (Skinner, 2003). Closed conference calls on the other hand are found to be subject to managerial opportunism in respect to the analysts involved: favorable and prestigious analysts have higher participation probabilities than unfavorable and less prestigious analysts (Mayew, 2008). This managerial opportunism can also manifest itself in deception and manipulation at the conference call (Larcker and Zakolyukina, 2010).

Conference calls are an important means of increasing disclosure frequency towards investors and allow firms flexibility and discretion in determining the content of new information. However, discretion also offers scope for opportunism. In order to minimize credibility issues, firms may incur verification costs to enhance disclosure reliability in conference calls.

5. Regulation and its impact on disclosure

Given the possible benefits of disclosure the question can be raised whether disclosure should be regulated or mainly remain voluntary. An extensive overview of the pros and cons of disclosure regulation can be found in Leuz and Wysocki (2008), who make the interesting statement that disclosure regulation is demanded when non-disclosures create externalities that make disclosures in fact socially desirable. If we look to the recent financial crisis, one could argue that regulation of risk disclosures in the financial statements of banks are socially desirable as non-disclosure has resulted in serious financial distress and the need of financial aid by the government.

While it has been shown theoretically that firms are motivated to provide voluntary disclosure if the benefits outweigh the costs (Healy and Palepu, 2001), the benefits and costs of mandatory disclosures are far from clear (Bushee and Leuz, 2005) and have been heavily debated in the past (e.g. Coffee, 1984; Easterbrook and Fischel, 1984). In an environment with low costs of disclosure and few benefits to retaining private information, disclosure should not be extensively regulated. An equilibrium is likely to occur where all firms except the worst one will disclose the relevant information (Milgrom, 1981). However, the costs of mandatory disclosures are not always low and therefore regulation is sometimes needed to force firms to reveal the private information. Regulatory pressures may also have an impact on voluntary disclosure (Baginski *et al.*, 2002). Fernandes *et al.* (2010) provide an illustration on the market impact of loosening disclosure requirements.

An example that regulation is not without cost but has significant capital market effects is the introduction of IFRS. Given the globalization of the capital markets, the introduction of IFRS is likely to lead to more transparent and more comparable financial statements between firms of different countries. S. Li (2010) shows that the extent to which IFRS adoption increases financial disclosure, using the number of additional disclosures required by IFRS (GAAP in 2001) compared to local GAAP, influences the capital market benefits of the IFRS introduction. The reduction in the cost of equity is significantly greater among mandatory adopters in countries with a large increase in disclosures than in countries with a small increase in disclosures. This result is consistent with increased disclosure being one of the possible mechanisms behind the cost of equity effect of IFRS adoption (S. Li, 2010).

The introduction of IFRS in the EU and many other jurisdictions is also a clear example that regulation shifted from a local to a more international level. The institutions of accounting regulation have changed with the increasing worldwide adoption of International Financial Reporting Standards (IFRS). For many jurisdictions this event replaced government regulation with that of the IASB as a private standard setter (Wagenhofer, 2011). However, in the US next to the accounting standards, there is also substantial federal regulation (e.g. SOX) and stock market regulation (SEC regulation). That stock market regulation can be effective in enhancing disclosures is exemplified by Form 20-F. Cross-listed firms on NYSE are subject to specific disclosure requirements (Adhikari and Tondkar 1992; Salter 1998), which exceed mandatory reporting requirements demanded by the accounting standards, such as the business and industry risk disclosures. These requirements not only affect the disclosure quality of cross-listed firms in the US market with an improved market liquidity but also create spillovers to the annual report of the cross-listed firm in the home market (e.g. Danckaert, 2012).

Whether additional disclosures demanded by accounting standards or by other regulatory bodies result in increased disclosure, depends to a large extent on the enforcement regime. Empirical evidence shows that not all countries implement the standards equally rigorously (Leuz and Wysocki, 2008). Leuz *et al.* (2008) point out that a country's legal and institutional environment affects firms' financial reporting incentives and hence influences financial statement quality. Most prior literature finds that firms operating in countries with strong legal enforcement disclose more information than firms operating in a weak legal environment (Vanstraelen *et al.* 2003; Brown and Tucker 2011; Hope 2003; Fogarty *et al.* 2006). S. Li (2010) also finds that mandatory adopters in countries with weak enforcement mechanisms and a small increase in disclosures from mandatory IFRS adoption actually experience an increase in their cost of equity, consistent with more discretion afforded under IFRS having a detrimental effect to shareholders when the standards are not properly enforced. Furthermore, in a US context, the SEC views enforcement of financial disclosure requirements as an essential element in a reliable financial accounting regime and a central part of the SEC mission (e.g. Levitt 1998; Paredes 2009). That SEC enforcement activities are effective is shown in a study on executive compensation regulation (Cassell *et al.*, 2011). While firms reviewed by the SEC corrected all the identified disclosure defects, firms not reviewed by the SEC exhibited little change in their compliance levels. This finding is consistent with the SEC's conclusion (Parratt, 2009) that non-compliance with the new regulations persists until defective disclosures are publicly identified in SEC reviews. Although SEC enforcement can improve quality of executive disclosure compensation, neither negative media attention nor a focused SEC enforcement action seems to be effective in disciplining CEO compensation (Cassell *et al.*, 2011).

In the debate on whether disclosure should be regulated or not, it is important to highlight that, whatever disclosure issue is considered, it can never be fully regulated. A certain part always remains voluntary. An accounting standard or a stock exchange can demand that certain information is disclosed but can never fully regulate the tone of the news, the precision of disclosures given or the extent (the number of lines) designated to the news. Those issues are especially relevant for qualitative more than quantitative disclosures. However, the tone of the news also reveals private information. Firms with bad environmental performance are more likely to use optimistic language in their environmental disclosures (Cho *et al.*, 2010). Furthermore, these qualitative characteristics of information are useful for the capital market.

Even for a regulated item such as credit risk, Danckaert *et al.* (2008) find that the stock market reaction, the decrease in the market spread, is larger when the credit risk information is more precise, i.e. whether the firm elaborates the actions that have been taken to limit the risk, the risk is expressed in monetary items or information is given how the risk is expected to evolve in the future. Taken together, even in a setting of regulated information, the whole picture can never be fully regulated.

6. Conclusion

The preceding sections have offered an initial understanding of the value of disclosure in the current economic environment. Firms face a trade-off between costs and benefits when deciding upon the level of disclosure. When the costs exceed the gains, this will lead to a suboptimal amount of information disclosed to investors and stakeholders. The resulting information asymmetries produce agency costs and inefficiencies, since lack of information impedes investors' decisions and transparent markets. Towards investors, firm disclosure is the primary source of information. Hence, they predominantly rely on firms' self-reported data. Since firms are themselves responsible for the content and extent of disclosure, reliability issues may arise. Investors will not find all information equally credible. Verification costs may then be incurred to enhance disclosure credibility and stimulate investors' knowledge of the organization.

In deciding upon the optimal disclosure level, firms have a choice between a wide range of options in tailoring disclosure to their specific needs. Annual reports are compulsory and extensively regulated, but a variety of additional schedules and mediums allow more flexibility. The core source of information remains the quantitative data found in the financial statements and the notes, since these are verified by an external auditor and are considered reliable and less prone to manipulation. However, additional qualitative oriented disclosures constitute an almost equally important source, albeit managerial discretion is high in respect to environmental disclosures, conference calls, press releases, etc. These disclosures are made on a more voluntary basis and allow firms to increase disclosure frequency, thus being more informative to investors. Interim reports, earnings announcements and conference calls serve the same purpose.

Despite a positive appreciation of disclosure by investors, the stock market exhibits a strong negative reaction when the voluntary disclosure contains bad news – measured by adverse earnings announcements – as opposed to a positive reaction for good news disclosures (Skinner, 1994). Comparable results are obtained concerning unexpected bond downgrades by Goh and Ederington (1993). The nature of the news may therefore influence corporate disclosure decisions. Important information may be withheld when disclosing the information would entail adverse consequences for the firm. Regulation can constrain this risk of managerial opportunism by imposing legal requirements, but this is at the expense of flexibility. However, complete regulation is impossible. Companies will always have some leeway in applying the rules and complementing regulatory disclosure with voluntary information. Regulation should therefore focus on key data aspects and verification costs, as to stimulate firms to provide a minimum of objective disclosure to investors.

Lastly, when studying disclosure issues, the economic and regulatory situation will highly determine which disclosure issues are the most in the picture. A regulatory topic related to disclosures is the convergence issues related to IFRS 8. Although FASB and the IASB spend a lot of time on the convergence project between IFRS and US GAAP standards, whether convergence has been successful or not is an open question. However, if we want to realize a global framework for financial reporting, this is a highly relevant topic. An example of how the current financial crisis determines relevant disclosures is the disclosure of stress tests done on financial institutions (Bischof and Daske, 2012). Disclosure of the stress tests will encourage appropriate behavior by the financial institutions as well as by the regulatory agencies, which have to disclose the tool used to apply the stress tests. However, in the studies investigating the stress disclosure test, next to the direct costs of disclosures some 'new' endogenous costs are identified. Banks could probably take the short profit maximizing investment decisions to pass the stress test instead of maximizing the long-term value, which illustrates that more disclosure is not always a good thing. Furthermore, those disclosures could also lead to instability of the financial market (Goldstein and Sapra, 2012). Allowing for flexibility may mediate these problems.

This chapter has made clear that disclosure practices cannot be considered in isolation. One has to link the form, time and content of disclosure to firm-level determinants and market reactions, taking into account the costs and benefits as perceived by the firm for each of these decisions. Disclosure practices therefore largely differ between firms and will continue to do so despite regulation. However, a minimum level of disclosure towards investors is warranted to establish an environment characterized by low information asymmetries.

Bibliography

Adams, R. B., B. E. Hermalin and M. S. Weisbach (2010) 'The Role of Boards of Directors in Corporate Governance: A Conceptual Framework and Survey.' *Journal of Economic Literature, American Economic Association* 48 (1): 58–107

Adhikari, A. and R. Tondkar (1992) 'Environmental Factors Influencing Accounting Disclosure Requirements of Global Stock Exchanges.' *Journal of International Financial Management and Accounting* 4 (2): 75–105

Aerts, W. and D. Cormier (2009) 'Media Legitimacy and Corporate Environmental Communication.' *Accounting, Organizations and Society* 34 (1): 1–27

Aguilera, R. V., C. A. Williams, J. M. Conley and D.E. Rupp (2006) 'Corporate Governance and Social Responsibility: A Comparative Analysis of the UK and the US.' *Corporate Governance: An International Review* 14: 147–58

Badertscher, B. and J. J. Burks (2011) 'Accounting Restatements and the Timeliness of Disclosures.' *Accounting Horizons* 25 (4): 609–29

Baginski, S. P., J. M. Hassell and M. D. Kimbrough (2002) 'The Effect of Legal Environment on Voluntary Disclosure: Evidence from Management Earnings Forecasts Issued in U.S. and Canadian Markets.' *The Accounting Review* 77 (1): 25–50

Ball, R., S. Jayaraman and L. Shivakumar (2011) 'Audited Financial Reporting and Voluntary Disclosure as Complements: A Test of the Confirmation Hypothesis.' *Journal of Accounting and Economics* 53 (1–2): 136–66

Banghøj, J. and T. Plenborg (2008) 'Value Relevance of Voluntary Disclosure in the Annual Report.' *Accounting & Finance* 48: 159–80

Barth, M. (2006) 'Including Estimates of the Future in Today's Financial Statements.' BIS Working Paper No. 208, available at http://ssrn.com/abstract=947525 or http://dx.doi.org/10.2139/ssrn.947525, accessed 2 July 2012

Barton, J. and P. J. Simko (2002) 'The Balance Sheet as an Earnings Management Constraint.' *The Accounting Review* 77 (Supplement): 1–27

Bebchuck, L. and M. Weisbach (2010) 'The State of Corporate Governance Research.' *Review of Financial Studies* 23: 939–61

Becchetti, L. and R. Ciciretti (2009) 'Corporate Social Responsibility and Stock Market Performance.' *Applied Financial Economics* 19 (16): 1283–93

Beekes, W. and P. Brown (2006) 'Do Better-Governed Australian Firms Make More Informative Disclosures?' *Journal of Business Finance & Accounting* 33: 422–50

Begley, J. and P. Fischer (1998) 'Is There Information in an Earnings Announcement Delay?' *Review of Accounting Studies* 3 (4): 347–63

Bens, D. and S. Monahan (2004) 'Disclosure Quality and the Excess Value of Diversification.' *Journal of Accounting Research* 42: 691–730

Bens, D. A., P. G. Berger and S. J. Monahan (2011) 'Discretionary Disclosure in Financial Reporting: An Examination Comparing Internal Firm Data to Externally Reported Segment Data.' *The Accounting Review* 86: 417–49

Beretta, S. E. and S. Bozzolan (2012) 'Quality Versus Quantity: The Case of Forward-Looking Disclosure.' *Journal of Accounting, Auditing & Finance* 23(3): 333–76

Berger, P. and R. Hann (2007) 'Segment Profitability and the Proprietary and Agency Costs of Disclosure.' *The Accounting Review* 82 (4): 869–906

Beyer, A., D. Cohen, T. Lys and B. Walther (2010) 'The Financial Reporting Environment: Review of the Recent Literature.' *Journal of Accounting and Economics* 50: 296–343

Bies, S. (2005) 'Fair Value Accounting.' *Federal Reserve Bulletin* 91: 26–9

Billings, M. B. (2008) 'Disclosure Timeliness, Insider Trading Opportunities and Litigation Consequences.' Working paper, available at http://ssrn.com/abstract=1011759 or http://dx.doi.org/10.2139/ssrn.1011759, accessed 2 July 2012

Bischof, J. and H. Daske (2012) 'Can Supervisory Disclosure Mitigate Bank Opaqueness and Reduce Uncertainties during a Financial Crisis? Evidence from EU-wide Stress-testing Exercises.' Working paper, available at http://research.chicagobooth.edu//arc/journal/docs/bischof_daske_20120229_stress_test.pdf, accessed 18 February 2013

Blacconiere, W., J. Frederickson, M. Johnson and M. Lewis (2011) 'Are Voluntary Disclosures that Disavow the Reliability of Mandated Fair Value Information Informative or Opportunistic?' *Journal of Accounting and Economics* 52: 235–51

Black, E. L. and J. J. White (2003) 'An International Comparison of Income Statement and Balance Sheet Information: Germany, Japan and the US.' *European Accounting Review* 12 (1): 29–46

Botan, C. H. and M. Taylor (2004) 'Public Relations: State of the Field.' *Journal of Communication* 54: 645–61

Botosan, C. (1997) 'Disclosure Level and the Cost of Equity Capital.' *The Accounting Review* 72 (3): 323–49

Botosan, C. A. and M. S. Harris (2000) 'Motivations for a Change in Disclosure Frequency and Its Consequences: An Examination of Voluntary Quarterly Segment Disclosures.' *Journal of Accounting Research* 38 (2): 329–53

Botosan, C. and M. Plumlee (2002) 'A Re-examination of Disclosure Level and the Expected Cost of Equity Capital.' *Journal of Accounting Research* 40: 21–40

Botosan, C. and M. Stanford (2005) 'Managers' Motives to Withhold Segment Disclosures and the Effect of SFAS no. 131 on Analysts' Information Environment.' *The Accounting Review* 80 (3): 751–71

Brammer, S. and S. Pavelin (2006) 'Voluntary Environmental Disclosures by Large UK Companies.' *Journal of Business Finance & Accounting* 33: 1168–88

Broberg, P., T. Tagesson and S.-O. Collin (2010) 'What Explains Variation in Voluntary Disclosure? A Study of the Annual Reports of Corporations Listed on the Stockholm Stock Exchange.' *Journal of Management and Governance* 14 (4): 351–77

Brown, S. and J. Tucker (2011) 'Large-Sample Evidence on Firms' Year-over-Year MD&A Modifications.' *Journal of Accounting Research* 49: 309–46

Brown, S., S. A. Hillegeist and K. Lo (2004) 'Conference Calls and Information Asymmetry.' *Journal of Accounting and Economics* 37 (3): 343–66

Bushee, B. and C. Leuz (2005) 'Economic Consequences of SEC Disclosure Regulation: Evidence from the OTC Bulletin Board.' *Journal of Accounting and Economics* 39: 233–64

Bushee, B. J., D. A. Matsumoto and G. S. Miller (2003) 'Open versus Closed Conference Calls: The Determinants and Effects of Broadening Access to Disclosure.' *Journal of Accounting and Economics* 34 (1–3): 149–80

Butler, M., A. Kraft and I. S. Weiss (2007) 'The Effect of Reporting Frequency on the Timeliness of Earnings: The Cases of Voluntary and Mandatory Interim Reports.' *Journal of Accounting and Economics* 43 (2–3): 181–217

Campbell, J., H. Chen, D. Dhaliwal, H.-M. Lu and L. Steele (2010) 'The Information Content of Mandatory Risk Factor Disclosures in Corporate Filings,' available at http://ssrn.com/abstract=1694279 or http://dx.doi.org/10.2139/ssrn.1694279, accessed 2 July 2012

Carroll, C. E. and M. McCombs (2003) 'Agenda-setting Effects of Business News on the Public's Images and Opinions about Major Corporations.' *Corporate Reputation Review* 6 (1): 36–46

Cassell, C. A., L. M. Dreher and L.A. Myers (2011) 'The Determinants and Costs of Non-Compliance with SEC Reporting Requirements: Evidence from SEC 10-K Comment Letters.' Working paper, available at http://ssrn.com/abstract=1951445 or http://dx.doi.org/10.2139/ssrn.1951445, accessed 2 July 2012

Chambers, A. and S. Penman (1984) 'Timeliness of Reporting and the Stock Price Reaction to Earnings Announcements.' *Journal of Accounting Research* 22 (1):21–47

Chang, M., G. d'Anna, I. Watson and M. Wee (2008) 'Does Disclosure Quality via Investor Relations Affect Information Asymmetry?' *Australian Journal of Management* 33 (2): 375–90

Chen, S., M. L. DeFond and C. W. Park (2002) 'Voluntary Disclosure of Balance Sheet Information in Quarterly Earnings Announcements.' *Journal of Accounting and Economics* Volume 33 (2): 229–51

Cheng, E. and S. Courtenay (2006) 'Board Composition, Regulatory Regime and Voluntary Disclosure.' *The International Journal of Accounting* 41(3): 262–89

Cho, C.H. and D. M. Patten (2007) 'The Role of Environmental Disclosures as Tools of Legitimacy: A Research Note.' *Accounting, Organizations and Society* 32 (7–8): 639–47

Cho, C., R. Roberts and D. Patten (2010) 'The Language of US Corporate Environmental Disclosure.' *Accounting. Organizations and Society* 35 (4): 431–43

Claessens, S., S. Djankov, J. Fan and L. Lang (2002) 'Disentangling the Incentive and Entrenchment Effects of Large Shareholdings.' *The Journal of Finance* 57: 2741–71

Clarkson, P. M., J. L. Kao and G. D. Richardson (1999) 'Evidence That Management Discussion and Analysis (MD&A) is a Part of a Firm's Overall Disclosure Package.' *Contemporary Accounting Research* 16: 111–34

Coffee, J. (1984) 'Market Failure and the Economic Case for a Mandatory Disclosure System.' *Virginia Law Review* 70 (4): 717–53

Cole, C. J. and C. L. Jones (2004) 'The Usefulness of MD&A Disclosures in the Retail Industry.' *Journal of Accounting, Auditing and Finance* 19 (4): 361–88

Conrad, J., B. Cornell and W.R. Landsman (2002) 'When Is Bad News Really Bad News?' *The Journal of Finance* 57: 2507–32

Core, J. (2001) 'A Review of the Empirical Disclosure Literature: Discussion.' *Journal of Accounting and Economics* 31 (1–3): 441–56

Crawford, V. and J. Sobel, (1982) 'Strategic Information Transformation.' *Econometrica* 50, 1431–51

Danckaert, I. (2012) 'Spillovers of Stock Market Regulation to the Home-Country Annual Report of Cross-Listed Firms: A Comparison of Disclosure Practices between US and UK Cross-Listed Firms.' PhD Dissertation, KU Leuven

Danckaert, I., A. Gaeremynck and N. Huyghebaert (2008) 'Do Incremental Form 20-F risk Disclosures Affect Market Liquidity? Evidence from Firms Cross-listed on NYSE.' Working paper, KU Leuven

Darnall, N., I. Seol and J. Sarkis (2009) 'Perceived Stakeholder Influences and Organizations' Use of Environmental Audits.' *Accounting, Organizations and Society* 34 (2): 170–87

Davis, A. K., J. Piger, and L. M. Sedor. (2008) 'Beyond the Numbers: Managers' Use of Optimistic and Pessimistic Tone in Earnings Press Releases.' Working paper, available at http://papers.ssrn.com/sol3/papers.cfm?abstract_id=875399, accessed 2 July 2012

Demers, E. A. and C. Vega. (2008) 'Soft Information in Earnings Announcements: News or Noise?' Working paper, available at http://papers.ssrn.com/sol3/papers.cfm?abstract_id=1152326, accessed 2 July 2012

Depoers, F. and T. Jeanjean (2010) 'Determinants of Quantitative Information Withholding in Annual Reports.' *European Accounting Review* 21 (1): 115–51

Diamond, D. and R. Verrecchia (1991) 'Disclosure, Liquidity and the Cost of Capital.' *The Journal of Finance* 46 (4): 1325–55

Donnelly, R. and M. Mulcahy (2008) 'Board Structure, Ownership, and Voluntary Disclosure in Ireland.' *Corporate Governance: An International Review* 16: 416–29

Dyck, A. and L. Zingales (2004) 'Control Premiums and the Effectiveness of Corporate Governance Systems.' *Journal of Applied Corporate Finance* 16: 51–72

Easterbrook, F. and D. Fischel (1984) 'Mandatory Disclosure and the Protection of Investors.' *Virginia Law Review* 70 (4): 669–715

European Commission (2011) 'Communication from the Commission to the European Parliament, the Council, the European Economic and Social Committee and the Committee of the Regions,' available at http://ec.europa.eu/enterprise/newsroom/cf/_getdocument.cfm?doc_id=7010, accessed 2 July 2012

Feldman, R., S. Govindaraj, J. Livnat, and B. Segal (2010) 'Management's Tone Change, Post Earnings Announcement Drift and Accruals.' *Review of Accounting Studies* 15 (4): 915–53

Feltham, G. and J. Xie (1992) 'Voluntary Financial Disclosure in an Entry Game with Continua of Types.' *Contemporary Accounting Research* 9: 46–80

Fernandes, N., U. Lel and D. P. Miller (2010) 'Escape from New York: The Market Impact of Loosening Disclosure Requirements.' *Journal of Financial Economics* 95 (2): 129–47

Fogarty, T., Markarian, G. and Parbonetti, A. (2006) 'It's a Small World After All: The Convergence of Disclosure Practices Across Legal Regimes over Time'. Working paper No. 14, Dipartimento di Scienze Economiche, University of Padua, available at www.decon.unipd.it/assets/pdf/wp/20060014.pdf (accessed 3 April 2013)

Francis, J. R. and D. Wang (2008) 'The Joint Effect of Investor Protection and Big 4 Audits on Earnings Quality around the World.' *Contemporary Accounting Research* 25: 157–91

Francis, J., D. Philbrick and K. Schipper (1994) 'Shareholder Litigation and Corporate Disclosures.' *Journal of Accounting Research* 32 (2): 137–64

Francis, J., D. Nanda and P. Olsson (2007) 'Voluntary Disclosure, Earnings Quality and Cost of Capital.' *Journal of Accounting Research* 46 (1): 53–99

Frankel, R., M. Johnson and D.J. Skinner (1999) 'An Empirical Examination of Conference Calls as a Voluntary Disclosure Medium.' *Journal of Accounting Research* 37 (1): 133–50

Gelb, D. S. and J. A. Strawser (2001) 'Corporate Social Responsibility and Financial Disclosures: An Alternative Explanation for Increased Disclosure.' *Journal of Business Ethics* 33 (1): 1–13

Gelb, S. and P. Zarowin (2002) 'Corporate Disclosure Policy and the Informativeness of Stock Prices.' *Review of Accounting Studies* 7 (1): 33–52

Gigler, F. and T. Hemmer (2001) 'Conservatism, Optimal Disclosure Policy, and the Timeliness of Financial Reports.' *The Accounting Review* 76 (4): 471–93

Givoly, D. and D. Palmon (1982) 'Timeliness of Annual Earnings Announcements: Some Empirical Evidence?' *The Accounting Review* 57 (3):486–508

Goh, J.C. and L. H. Ederington (1993) 'Is a Bond Rating Downgrade Bad News, Good News, or No News for Stockholders?' *The Journal of Finance* 48 (5): 2001–8

Goldstein, I. and H. Sapra (2012) 'Should Banks Stress Test Results be Disclosed? An Analysis of the Costs and Benefits,' Working paper, University of Chicago Booth School of Business, available at http://finance.wharton.upenn.edu/~itayg/Files/stresstests.pdf

Healy, P. and K. Palepu (1993) 'The Effect of Firms' Financial Disclosure Strategies on Stock Prices.' *Accounting Horizons* 7 (1): 1–11

Healy, P. and K. Palepu (2001) 'Information asymmetry, corporate disclosure, and the Capital Markets: A Review of the Empirical Disclosure Literature.' *Journal of Accounting and Economics* 31 (1–3): 405–40

Healy, P., A. Hutton and K. Palepu (1999) 'Stock Performance and Intermediation Changes Surrounding Sustained Increases in Disclosure.' *Contemporary Accounting Research* 16 (3): 485–520

Henry, E. (2008) 'Are Investors Influenced by How Earnings Press Releases Are Written?' *Journal of Business Communication* 45 (4): 363–407

Hitz, J.-M. and J. R. Werner (2012) 'Why do Firms Resist Individualized Disclosure of Management Remuneration?' Working paper, available at http://ssrn.com/abstract=1588186 or http://dx.doi.org/10.2139/ssrn.1588186, accessed 2 July 2012

Ho, S. and K. Wong (2001) 'A Study of the Relationship between Corporate Governance Structures and the Extent of Voluntary Disclosure.' *Journal of Internation Accounting, Auditing and Taxation* 10(2): 139–56

Holder-Webb, L., J. R. Cohen, L. Nath and D. Wood (2009) 'The Supply of Corporate Social Responsibility Disclosures among US Firms.' *Journal of Business Ethics* 84: 497–527

Holthausen, R. (1990) 'Accounting Method Choice: Opportunistic Behavior, Efficient Contracting, and Information Perspectives.' *Journal of Accounting and Economics* 12 (1–3): 207–18

Holthausen, R., R. Leftwich and D. Mayers (1983) 'Large-block Transactions, the Speed of Response, and Temporary and Permanent Stock-price Effects.' *Journal of Financial Economics* 26 (1): 71–95

Hope, O. (2003) 'Firm-level Disclosures and the Relative Roles of Culture and Legal Origin.' *Journal of International Financial Management and Accounting* 14 (3): 218–48

Hutton, A., G. Miller and D. Skinner (2003) 'The Role of Supplementary Statements with Management Earnings Forecasts.' *Journal of Accounting Research* 41: 867–90

Jensen, M. and W. Meckling (1976) 'Theory of the Firm: Managerial Behavior, Agency Costs and Ownership Structure'. *Journal of Financial Economics* 3: 305–60

Karpoff, J. M., J. R. Lott and G. Rankine (1998) 'Environmental Violations, Legal Penalties, and Reputation Costs.' Working paper Chicago Law School, available at www.law.uchicago.edu/files/files/71.Lott_.Environment.pdf, accessed 2 July 2012

Kim, O. and R. Verrecchia (1994) 'Market Liquidity and Volume around Earnings Announcements.' *Journal of Accounting and Economics* 17 (1–2): 41–67

Kimbrough, M. D. (2005) 'The Effect of Conference Calls on Analyst and Market Underreaction to Earnings Announcements.' *The Accounting Review* 80 (1): 189–219

Kohlbeck, M. J. and M. J. Magilke (2002) 'The Impact of Concurrent Conference Calls on the Information Content of Earnings Announcements.' Working paper, available at http://ssrn.com/abstract=302230 or http://dx.doi.org/10.2139/ssrn.302230, accessed 2 July 2012

Kothari, S. P., S. Shu and P. D. Wysocki (2009a) 'Do Managers Withhold Bad News?' *Journal of Accounting Research* 47: 241–76

Kothari, S. P., X. Li and J. E. Short (2009b) 'The Effect of Disclosures by Management, Analysts, and Business Press on Cost of Capital, Return Volatility, and Analyst Forecasts: A Study using Content Analysis.' *The Accounting Review* 84 (5): 1639–70

Krishnaswami, S. and V. Subramaniam (1999) 'Information Asymmetry, Valuation, and the Corporate Spin-off Decision.' *Journal of Financial Economics* 53 (1): 73–112

Kross, W. and D. Schroeder (1984) 'An Empirical Investigation of the Effect of Quarterly Earnings Announcement Timing on Stock Returns.' *Journal of Accounting Research* 22: 153–76

Lambert, R., C. Leuz and R. Verrecchia (2007) 'Accounting Information, Disclosure, and the Cost of Capital.' *Journal of Accounting Research* 45: 385–420

Landsman, W. (2006) 'Fair Value Accounting for Financial Instruments: Some Implications for Bank Regulation.' BIS Working paper No. 209, available at http://ssrn.com/abstract=947569 or http://dx.doi.org/10.2139/ssrn.947569, accessed 2 July 2012

Lang, M. and R. Lundholm (1993) 'Cross-Sectional Determinants of Analyst Ratings of Corporate Disclosures.' *Journal of Accounting Research* 31 (2): 246–71

Lang, M. and R. Lundholm (1996) 'Corporate Disclosure Policy and Analyst Behavior.' *The Accounting Review* 71 (4): 467–92

Larcker, D. F. and A. A. Zakolyukina (2010) 'Detecting Deceptive Discussions in Conference Calls.' *Journal of Accounting Research* 50: 495–540

Leuz, C., and R. Verrecchia (2000) 'The Economic Consequences of Increased Disclosure.' *Journal of Accounting Research* 38 (Supplement): 91–124

Leuz, C. and P. Wysocki (2008) 'Economic Consequences of Financial Reporting and Disclosure Regulation: A Review and Suggestions for Future Research', available at http://dx.doi.org/10.2139/ssrn.1105398, accessed 2 July 2012

Leuz, C., H. Daske, L. Hail and R. Verdi (2008) 'Mandatory IFRS Reporting around the World: Early Evidence on the Economic Consequences.' *Journal of Accounting Research* 46 (5): 1085–142

Leventos, S. and P. Weetman (2004) 'Timeliness of Financial Reporting: Applicability of Disclosure Theories in an Emerging Capital Market.' *Accounting and Business Research* 34 (1): 43–56

Levitt, A. (1998) 'The "Numbers Game",' available at www.sec.gov/news/speech/speecharchive/1998/spch220.txt, accessed 2 July 2012

Li, F. (2010) 'The Determinants and Information Content of the Forward-looking Statements in Corporate Filings: A Naive Bayesian Machine Learning Approach.' AAA 2009 Financial Accounting and Reporting Section (FARS) Paper, available at http://dx.doi.org/10.2139/ssrn.1267235, accessed 2 July 2012

Li, K. and G. Meeks (2006) 'The Impairment of Purchased Goodwill: Effects on Market Value.' Working paper, available at http://dx.doi.org/10.2139/ssrn.930979, accessed 2 July 2012

Li, S. (2010) 'Does Mandatory Adoption of International Financial Reporting Standards in the European Union Reduce the Cost of Equity Capital?' *Accounting Review* 85 (2): 607–36, available at http://dx.doi.org/10.2139/ssrn.1113353, accessed 2 July 2012

Lindgreen, A. and V. Swaen (2010) 'Corporate Social Responsibility.' *International Journal of Management Reviews* 12: 1–7

Liu, J. and D. Taylor (2008) 'Legitimacy and Corporate Governance Determinants Of Executives' Remuneration Disclosures.' *Corporate Governance* 8 (1): 59–72

Lundholm, R. and L. A. Myers (2002) 'Bringing the Future Forward: The Effect of Disclosure on the Returns–Earnings Relation.' *Journal of Accounting Research* 40: 809–39

Mayew, W. J. (2008) 'Evidence of Management Discrimination Among Analysts during Earnings Conference Calls.' *Journal of Accounting Research* 46: 627–59

Milgrom, P. (1981) 'Good News and Bad News: Representation Theorems and Applications.' *The Bell Journal of Economics* 12 (2): 380–91

Nagar, V., D. Nanda and P. Wysocki (2003) 'Discretionary Disclosure and Stock-Based Incentives.' *Journal of Accounting and Economics* 34: 283–309

Paredes, T. (2009) 'Remarks Before the Symposium on "The Past, Present, and Future of the SEC,"' available at www.sec.gov/news/speech/2009/spch101609tap.htm, accessed 2 July 2012

Parratt, S. (2009) 'Executive Compensation Disclosure: Observations on the 2009 Proxy Season and Expectations for 2010,' available at www.sec.gov/news/speech/2009/spch110909sp.htm, accessed 2 July 2012

Piotroski, J. (1999) 'The Impact of Newly Reported Segment Inforrnation on Market Expectations and Stock Prices.' Working paper, University of Michigan

Prawitt, D. F., J. L. Smith and D. A. Wood (2009) 'Internal Audit Quality and Earnings Management.' *The Accounting Review*, Vol. 84 (4): 1255–80

Renders, A. and A. Gaeremynck (2012) 'Corporate Governance, Principal–Principal Agency Conflicts, and Firm Value in European Listed Companies.' *Corporate Governance: An International Review* 20 (2): 125–43.

Rogers, L. and A. Van Buskirk (2009) 'Shareholder Litigation and Changes in Disclosure Behavior.' *Journal of Accounting and Economics* 47 (1–2): 136–56

Ryan, S. (2002) *Financial Instruments and Institutions: Accounting and Disclosure Rules*. Hoboken, NJ: John Wiley & Sons, Inc

Salter, S. (1998) 'Corporate Financial Disclosure in Emerging Markets: Does Economic Development Matter?' *International Journal of Accounting* 33 (2): 211–34

Scott, T. (1994) 'Incentives and Disincentives for Financial Disclosure: Voluntary Disclosure of Defined Benefit Pension Plan Information by Canadian Firms.' *The Accounting Review* 69 (1): 26–43

Sengupta, P. (1998) 'Corporate Disclosure Quality and the Cost of Debt.' *The Accounting Review* 73 (4): 459–74

Sengupta, P. (2004) 'Disclosure Timing: Determinants of Quarterly Earnings Release Dates.' *Journal of Accounting and Public Policy* 23 (6): 457–82

Shleifer, A. and R. Vishny (1986) 'Large Shareholders and Corporate Control.' *Journal of Political Economy* 3: 461–88

Shleifer, A. and R. Vishny (1997) 'A Survey of Corporate Governance.' *Journal of Finance* 52: 737–83

Skinner, D. J. (1994) 'Why Firms Voluntarily Disclose Bad News.' *Journal of Accounting Research* 32 (1): 38–60

Skinner, D. J. (1997) 'Earnings Disclosures and Stockholder Lawsuits.' *Journal of Accounting and Economics* 23 (3): 249–82

Skinner, D. J. (2003) 'Should Firms Disclose Everything to Everybody? A Discussion of "Open vs. Closed Conference Calls: The Determinants and Effects of Broadening Access to Disclosure."' *Journal of Accounting and Economics* 34 (1–3): 181–7

Vanstraelen, A., M. Zarzeski and S. Robb (2003) 'Corporate Nonfinancial Disclosure Practices and Financial Analyst Forecast Ability Across Three European Countries.' *Journal of International Financial Management & Accounting* 14: 249–78

Vanza, S., P. Wells and A. Wright (2011) 'Asset Impairment and the Disclosure of Private Information.' Working paper University of Technology, Sydney, available at http://sssrn.com.abstract=1798168, accessed 2 July 2012

Vergauwe, S., A. Gaeremynck and D. Stokes (2012) 'The Impact of Auditing and Disclosure on the Reliability of Fair Value Estimates in the Real Estate Industry,' available at https://lirias.kuleuven.be/handle/123456789/334082, accessed 2 July 2012

Veronesi, P. (1999) 'Stock Market Overreactions to Bad News in Good Times: A Rational Expectations Equilibrium Model.' *Review of Financial Studies* 12 (5): 975–1007

Verrecchia, R. (1983) 'Discretionary Disclosure.' *Journal of Accounting and Economics* 5 (1): 179–94

Verrecchia, R. (2001) 'Essays on Disclosure.' *Journal of Accounting and Economics* 32 (1–3): 91–180

Verriest, A., A. Gaeremynck and D. Thornton (2013) 'The Impact of Corporate Governance on IFRS Adoption Choices.' *European Accounting Review* 22(1): 39–77

Wagenhofer, A. (1990) 'Voluntary Disclosure with a Strategic Opponent', *Journal of Accounting and Economics* 12 (4): 341–63

Wagenhofer, A. (2011) 'Towards a Theory of Accounting Regulation: A Discussion of the Politics of Disclosure Regulation along the Economic Cycle.' *Journal of Accounting and Economics* 52 (2–3): 228–34

Webb, K., F. Cahan and J. Sun (2008) 'The Effect of Globalization and Legal Environment on Voluntary Disclosure.' *The International Journal of Accounting* 43 (3): 219–45

Welker, M. (1995) 'Disclosure Policy, Information Asymmetry, and Liquidity in Equity Markets.' *Contemporary Accounting Research* 11 (2): 801–27

Young, M., M. Peng, D. Ahlstrom, G. Bruton and Y. Jiang (2008) 'Corporate Governance in Emerging Economies: A Review of the Principal–Principal Perspective.' *Journal of Management Studies* 45: 196–220

9

Auditing, Regulation and the Persistence of the Expectations Gap

Christopher Humphrey, Anna Samsonova and Javed Siddiqui

1. Introduction

The statutory financial audit for a limited company is essentially a process through which the credibility of the financial statements produced by the company's management are independently assessed by an external auditor, who then reports his/her opinion to the company's members (i.e. its shareholders). However, as Humphrey (1997) points out, the auditing assessment or examination should not regarded as an exact science, ensuring 100 per cent accuracy of the information contained in the financial statements. Rather, the assumed purpose of an audit is to ensure that the financial statements are reasonably free from material misstatements and errors, with auditors having a formal responsibility to express their opinion regarding the 'truth and fairness' of the financial statements prepared by the entity.[1]

It is often said in relation to audit practice that a fundamental obligation on the part of any auditor or audit team is to maintain an audit trail – a level of documentary detail that would enable another auditor or member of the audit team to follow and appreciate the audit work undertaken. The importance of an audit trail is usually raised or highlighted in the context of auditors needing to protect themselves from any potential legal liability claim by being able to demonstrate at the time that the audit work was performed that it represented a reasonable set of tests and judgements – and avoids the audit process being judged inappropriately with the benefit of a level of hindsight that, by definition, was not available to the auditor.

1.1 Developing a perspective on the audit function

Intriguingly, when the role and efficacy of auditing is discussed in public policy circles and reforming initiatives or strategic imperatives are proposed as ways of delivering a better or more comprehensive form of auditing, the contextual emphasis that is so critical to the practice of individual audits is usually lacking. Debates are often extracted or isolated from their historical context, such that reform proposals can be represented as distinctive, new initiatives and options, even though they may have been considered (or even tried) a number of times in the past. They are given a contemporary feel and status that belies their past, their historical trail.

Such a state of affairs has three important implications for any study or analysis of the audit function. First, it is crucial to appreciate that while standard setters and regulators may be keen to use terms and phrases that claim that 'an audit is an audit', the subject of auditing is neither something that is, nor should be studied from a perspective that takes it as, fixed and absolute. Indeed, rather than being clear cut and with a definite pattern of development and advancement, the history of auditing is, and continues to be characterized by (or at least associated with), the notion of an auditing expectations gap – that auditors are not performing to the levels expected of them and/or that there is an educational mismatch between what auditors say they are supposed to do and what the investing public and others to whom the auditor is responsible thinks they should be doing.

Second, this standing and status of auditing means that, conceptually, it is important to recognize that there are a multiplicity of theories and perspectives that can be applied to the role of auditing and the study of its practice. As earlier analyses of the subject of auditing have illustrated (see Humphrey, 1997), it is evident that auditing can be studied from several broadly defined perspectives, including:

- a *normative* approach (stating what auditing and auditors 'should' do);
- an *economic* approach (which seeks to understand the individual and corporate incentives and motivations that influence the demand for and supply of audits); or
- a *critical* approach (which seeks to understand the social and political influences on the provision of audit services and which challenges, rather than takes as given, appeals to notions of professionalism and the claimed pursuit of the 'public interest').

In essence, such approaches can be represented on a contextual continuum, wherein auditing is capable of being studied in quite acontextual terms or in very tightly specified conditions and contextual constraints. Audit can be examined through approaches which drop the assumptions of political neutrality typical in traditional perspectives on professionalism and root themselves in the political forces that help to shape audit practice and govern the environments within which audit work is undertaken. Additionally, it is possible to classify studies of auditing in terms of those that seek to evaluate the performance of auditors and measure what audit practice has or has not achieved – as compared to those that seek to understand the reasons, factors and influences that have served to shape, refine and develop such practice. The analysis of auditing can also be at a micro- or macro-level, obtaining specific insights of the audit approaches applied on individual audits and within individual firms or seeking to draw general conclusions about the broad nature and impact of the audit function.

Third, there is a strong imperative not to seek to study auditing in absolute terms but to focus on understanding key thematic movements, disruptions and shifts in emphasis over time. For instance: to recognize emergent tendencies and patterns of change (and resistance to change); to be sensitive both to linear development and to evident circularity in attempts to reform practice; to understand and question the degree to which there is consistent and effective process of learning from experience and the events of the past; to review the status and influence of claims to expertise and associated shifts in ruling forms of expertise and the reliance place on any such expertise/assumed forms of authority, and to appreciate the significance of changes in the scope of audit practice and its relative societal reach and influence.

1.2 Auditing as an object of inquiry and a brief summary of this chapter's objectives

It is always important to keep a clear sense of perspective and focus with respect to the precise subject for study regarding the development of audit practice. It is also essential that the value and interest in what is being studied is both well understood and made clear to the reader. In the field of auditing practice, this very often leaves the role of the researcher as being one that seeks to put such practice more visibly under the public microscope; to make sure that claims made for audit practice are adequately supported by and assessed through a sound knowledge of what is being done in the name of practice.

This role is reinforced by the substantial invisibility of audit practice, or at least the quality attained by such practice. The formal, published audit report has been said in the past to be one of the most expensive professional reports when measured in terms of the word length of the audit report divided by the audit fee. However, relative to other professional services offered by accounting firms, it is not one of the most visible and easily appreciated. You may well hear a client saying how well their accountant had performed in reducing their tax liability or providing sound business planning advice, but you are unlikely to hear them praising the quality of the audit that they had just received. Further, what auditors can and cannot say in public with respect to their audit work seems to be very tightly governed, whether formally or through established custom and myth, by notions of client confidentiality and professional ethics. If the deterrent effect of the audit is sufficiently strong, in terms of providing some form of external check on corporate management and discouraging errant behaviour, the audit report is only likely to have a significant information value in the rare (or surprise) cases when something is wrong. The norm being that the audit opinion is an expected affirmation of an assumed state of affairs and of normally low surprise value. Finally, as with many functions which are rooted in verification and proof-testing, as second-order control functions rather than first-order production functions, they are commonly associated with notions of the routine and images of being boring and tedious to all but those with an attraction to checklists and a strict adherence to rules and procedures.

The consequences of such a state of affairs for the development of auditing knowledge are multifaceted. At one level, it very often means that developments in auditing are not deemed to be 'newsworthy', while at another level the relative invisibility of audit can mean that we hear more about general claims as to what auditing can do as against definitive evidence as to what it does achieve in practice. Further, the difficulty in getting close to practice can also mean that researchers are required to rely extensively on proxy variables when seeking to measure audit quality or key dimensions of audit work; such that the significance of research findings is invariably disputed depending on how credible and plausible one finds the chosen proxies – and leaving some authors to conclude that we know a great deal about audit quality while others argue that we know a lot about proxies for audit quality but not very much about the intricacies and complexities of real life, day-to-day audit practice. It can also mean that the social significance of auditing is underestimated or misrepresented, and that key changes and developments in the world of auditing are missed or underappreciated because auditing is seen as a 'boring' and tedious practice. Alternatively, the profession (with its massively successful multinational accountancy firms) can be seen more as a commercialized business venture (as against a public-spirited mission or calling), leading to criticisms made by the profession as to perceived threats to audit quality being regarded as special-pleading, rather than fair and appropriate comment.

Taking the above factors into account, this chapter addresses one specific but very important dimension of the auditing arena – namely, contemporary developments in auditing regulation and their implications for auditing practice and the auditing profession more generally. Earlier studies of auditing expectations (e.g. Humphrey, 1997) have highlighted the frequent degree of contrasts over time between assessments of auditing at a particular point in time (as being a dull and tedious function) with much more positive future projections (in which auditing is set to be much more socially significant and even exciting) or between the claimed rise of an all powerful

Audit Society (see Power, 1994, 1997) and a growing scepticism and doubt over the capacity of the traditional financial audit to meet basic expectations of primary stakeholders. Such questioning brought with it over the past fifteen years a growing commitment to, and belief in, systems of independent regulation, public oversight and international audit standard setting. Yet the establishment of such systems were not sufficient to prevent the recent global financial crisis, which raises the question as to what has been achieved by such alternative regulatory systems and what has been their impact on the development of a professionalized audit function.

An intriguing but very simple way of capturing the issue is to consider how attitudes towards auditing standards have changed over the years. When the first formal set of auditing standards and guidelines were being developed (e.g. in the UK in the mid-1970s), it was commonplace to see such standards referred to as setting a basic minimum, with the assumption that the larger and more outward looking audit firms were performing to levels well above minimum standard. A sentiment well captured in the Foreword to Stoy Hayward & Co.'s *Audit Guide* (1983), which emphasized that 'although our audits must be up to standard, they must not be standard' (p. iv). Nowadays, when asked to describe their audit methodology or approach, most firms will characterize it as being fully compliant with International Standards on Auditing (ISAs) but say very little, if anything, as to whether (and how) it delivers a level of quality that exceeds that specified by ISAs. We no longer talk of standards of audit quality but the quality of audit standards. The issue we pose here is the extent to which such a change is practically significant and what the implications are for a profession that seems to have become more content with, or at least resigned to, fairly intrusive and exacting systems of regulation and oversight.

The chosen topic for analysis is interesting on a number of fronts. It has a very evident international dimension and appeal in that independent oversight and inspection processes in auditing now dominate globally and have largely replaced systems of professional self-regulation. Such internationalism is also appealing in that it introduces a new dimension to the analysis, inviting discussion that is not the standard one of pro- or anti-regulation but one interested in understanding the implications of changing regulatory structures and affiliations for the practical context within which auditing assignments and associated learning and professional processes are undertaken. Finally, with the observed persistence of the auditing expectations gap and the questions that this persistence directs at the auditing profession, both in terms of public communication and underlying rationales of audit practice, it is important to ask where processes of innovation and professional and technological development stand in relation to international auditing.

2. Regulating auditor independence

The demand for independent audits is frequently represented as deriving from a typical agency dilemma – a separation of control and ownership – resulting in information asymmetries (Watts and Zimmerman, 1983). Managers are perceived, particularly by shareholders, as being potentially able to maximize their benefits at the expense of the company's owners' 'self-serving behaviour'. Auditing, accordingly, is said to serve as a tool to help company investors in terms of forming an opinion on the trustworthiness of information presented by the management, which is especially useful if shareholder structure is diversified and ownership widespread. Such verification of the company's financial reports by an external auditor effectively provides an instrument with which company investors (agents) can monitor, control, and discipline their stewards (managers). Hence, auditing is often seen as a facilitator of corporate governance. In addition, Wallace (1985) argues that audited financial statements present an essential source of information that investors and third parties may use to minimize their risks (both systematic and business-related) when making decisions (*information hypothesis*). Furthermore, management, investors, and various third parties may view auditors as a sort of insurers to whom to shift their financial liabilities to lower the possible losses or to direct financial claims in the event of litigation.

It is also important to view accountancy, and auditing in particular, beyond organisational boundaries as an element of the society's social fabric (Hopwood and Miller, 1994). Indeed, auditing, as well as accounting, has an important social meaning in terms of promoting general economic stability and public welfare. Historically, however, there have been significant differences in the perceptions of auditors' responsibilities among the public and auditors themselves, or what has been otherwise referred to as an *audit expectations gap*. Humphrey (1997) defines such a gap as 'a representation of a feeling that auditors are performing in a manner at variance with the beliefs and desires of those for whose benefit the audit is being carried out'. Since the term 'audit expectation gap' first appeared in late 1970s in the terms of reference of the Cohen Commission set out by the American Institute of Certified Public Accountants in the US, the reasoning attached to it and the associated concerns have not changed much. Characteristically, the existence of the gap has been assigned to both lack of education on the part of the users and the failure of auditors themselves to dynamically interpret and respond to the changing public demands. The resilient nature of the gap has been documented and empirically illustrated in a variety of national context (see, for example, Porter *et al.*, 2009, for some recent reference), suggesting that the problem should not be viewed in isolation but rather as a continuation of the debate on some more fundamental issues relating to the nature of auditors' responsibilities.

In recent years, financial auditing has seen a significant growth in the scope of regulatory and standardization activities, driven, to a great extent, by the 'pressures for rationalization, formalization and transparency of the audit process' (Power, 2003, p. 392) stemming from the very nature of audit and specifically the fact that it is difficult for an outside party to observe what it is that auditors do or evaluate audit quality. Historically, bodies concerned with regulation of the audit professional have been concerned with the ability of the auditors to perform their responsibilities in an independent and objective manner. A few illustrations serve to make this point.

2.1 Promoting auditor independence

In the United Kingdom, the Cadbury Committee (1992) produced a highly influential study of various aspects of corporate governance. With regards to the state of audit practice, the Committee identified an audit expectations gap as an area of concern, arguing it was a result of unrealistic expectations toward the auditors. The Committee's report also discussed the consequences of the provision of non-audit services (NAS) by the incumbent auditor and, after a lengthy discussion, concluded that imposing a ban on the provision for NAS would unduly limit the freedom of companies to select their sources of advice and consultancy. At the same time, the Cadbury Committee strongly advocated for full disclosure of audit and non-audit services provided by auditors and recommended that the 1991 regulations under the Companies Act on the disclosure of remuneration for NAS should be reviewed and amended as necessary in order to apply this principle.

In 1995, the UK's Financial Reporting Council (a body responsible for regulating the accountancy profession) set up the Hampel Committee, *inter alia*, to implement the recommendations in the Cadbury Committee's report. The Hampel Committee (1998) subsequently argued in favour of a stronger role for internal audit committees in monitoring the independence of the external auditor, especially in the case of the joint provision of audit and non-audit services.

Some of these suggestions were later incorporated into the UK's Combined Code of Corporate Governance(FRC, 2003).

At the turn of the century, a series of accounting scandals involving large US corporates, such as Enron, WorldCom, Waste Management, and Sunbeam, attracted significant public attention to the role of an auditor in safeguarding corporate accountability and transparency. The scandals created a major credibility crisis for the auditing profession, and exposed the problematic nature of the relationship between auditors and their clients (Copeland, 2003). This was acknowledged by a number of regulators around the world:

> 'Confidence in global financial markets was seriously shaken a little over a year ago by the high profile failure of Enron. As the scale of the accounting irregularities and the role of the auditors, Andersen, became clear, the credibility and reputation both of company directors and of the accountancy profession – and of auditors in particular – were called into question in a fundamental way' (CGAA, 2003, p. 4).

In an attempt to restore the credibility of the auditing profession, policy makers and professional accountancy bodies in various countries concentrated their efforts on developing regulatory strategies that would be able to address public concerns over the issues of auditors' independence and professional scepticism. This led most notably to the Sarbanes-Oxley Act 2002 in the US (SOX, 2002). In particular, this Act introduced a complete ban on the provision of some NAS and required the audit committee's approval for the provision of others. Following these provisions, the US Securities and Exchange Commission (SEC) (2003) required extended disclosures in listed companies' annual reports of the remuneration paid for a range of audit and non-audit services. The SOX Act (2002) also required mandatory partner rotation on the audit engagement team. Such measures were also mirrored in related regulation introduced by the European Commission (the executive body of the European Union) which prohibited the provision of a number of NAS while suggesting effective safeguards for others, and also, proposed for key audit partners to be rotated every seven years. Further important changes with regards to the regulation of auditing in Europe occurred as a result of the issuance in May 2006 of the revized Eighth Company Law Directive (2006/43/EC) on auditing, which among other things, provided for a stronger role for independent regulatory oversight of the audit profession (a subject that will be addressed in more detail later in the chapter).

2.2 A new crisis and European action

The 2008/9 financial crisis raised further questions about the state of corporate governance, particularly in the financial services sector. Although auditors were not initially blamed for the crisis, the efficacy of auditing as a control function gradually came under increased scrutiny. In the UK, the Treasury Select Committee of the House of Commons, published a series of reports into the governance practices of financial sector institutions (Treasury Select Committee, 2009). Although the reports found little evidence to suggest that the auditors had failed to perform their duties, important questions were raised about the general usefulness of the audit function and suggested the need for a major overhaul of the role of the auditor. Furthermore, the Treasury Select Committee raised continuing concerns with auditor independence, and specifically, the risks associated with the joint provision of audit and NAS, and asked the Financial Reporting Council (FRC), the UK's regulator for the accountancy profession, to consider introducing a complete ban on the joint provision of audit and NAS. In response to such a call, the FRC's

Auditing Practices Board launched, in October 2009, a consultation on the proposed revision of the Ethical Standards for auditors. Although the new version of the standards issued in 2010 (APB, 2010) did not impose any blanket prohibitions on the provision of NAS, it proposed a range of safeguards to protect auditor independence.

At the European level, against the backdrop of the financial crisis, the European Commission issued a Green Paper outlining its plans for future audit reform (EC, 2010). The Green Paper acknowledged that the financial crisis had exposed some inherent weaknesses in the audit function, as a large number of companies, despite being in poor financial condition, had managed to receive unqualified audit reports. According to the Green Paper, this raised serious concerns regarding the role of audit and highlighted again the significant presence of an audit expectations gap. The Green Paper sought consultation on a wide range of audit-related issues, clearly privileging reform of independence rules and regulations and the development of enhanced levels of competition in the audit market. Major reforms proposed by the Green Paper included extending the role of the audit, improving communications between the auditors and the shareholders, addressing problems associated with conflicts of interest, reducing audit market concentration, and improving independent oversight. Humphrey *et al.* (2011) analysed the underlying assumptions of the EC (2010) reform proposals. They pointed out that although the Green Paper proposed a number of reforms designed to influence the nature and scope of the market for audit services, there was a paucity of evidence that such measures would have the desired effect on audit quality. Similarly, a number of proposals were based on the premise that audit quality suffers due to lack of auditor independence. However, prior research investigating the effect of measures such as mandatory auditor rotation, provision of NAS, and audit firm governance on audit quality has been largely inconclusive. However, despite this, after some intense negotiations, the final reform proposals were published in November 2011 (EC, 2011), with provisions for mandatory rotation of audit partners, a complete prohibition on the provision for NAS, and extended supervision of the audit sector in the EU.

2.3 The developing role of audit committees

A final illustration regarding the regulatory focus with respect to auditing relates to the developing role of the audit committee. In addition to limiting the provision of NAS and introducing audit partner rotation, tendering etc., the role of the audit committee (AC) in mitigating threats to audit independence has been a significant continuing item on the regulatory agenda for more than a decade. ACs are expected to lead to higher transparency and reliability of financial statements as well as reduce the risk of the auditor providing an incorrect audit opinion (McElveen, 2002; Turley and Zaman, 2004). Moreover, they are expected to protect auditor independence by assuming responsibility for the appointment and remuneration of auditors, and providing an independent platform for auditors to express their opinions on management policies. In the UK, although the Cadbury Committee (1992) first proposed enhanced role of ACs in ensuring auditor independence, a more detailed guideline regarding the actual role of the AC was provided in the post-Enron era by the Smith committee. ACs were required to play a more pro-active role in decisions relating to auditor selection and remuneration. Also, the ACs were asked to produce a NAS policy for the company that would detail and justify the types of NAS the company would purchase from the auditors without posing a threat to auditor independence. Similar roles for the AC were also proposed by the EC (2002), which went on to suggest AC involvement in auditor selection, remuneration, and NAS selection process. The recently published EC Green Paper on audit policy (EC, 2011) also suggested strengthening the role of the AC in order to ensure audit quality, including playing an active role in the mandatory tendering process.

Prior research provides mixed evidence regarding the role of AC in ensuring audit quality. Although there is an abundance of studies on corporate governance and auditor remuneration in the highly regulated environment of the US (see for example, Ashbaugh *et al.*, 2003; Carcello and Neal, 2000; Krishnan and Visvanathan, 2009; Larcker and Richardson, 2004; and Zhang *et al.*, 2007), in less regulated environments, including the UK and Australia, there is less evidence on the relationship between corporate governance quality and auditor remuneration, and the evidence that does exist is largely inconclusive. Whereas Peel and Clatworthy (2001), examining audit fees in the pre-Cadbury (1992) period, find no significant evidence that board structure variables significantly affect audit fees, more recent studies (such as Zaman *et al.*, 2011), find that effective ACs play an active role in ensuring audit independence.

3. Promoting (international) auditing standards

The transformation in processes of audit regulation, especially in terms of the growing importance of international influences and market-based solutions, is well evidenced by the growing influence of International Standards on Auditing (ISAs). The capacity to set auditing standards, traditionally associated with national professional bodies and nation states, has been gradually shifting towards the realms of global governance, with a key role played by the International Auditing and Assurance Standards Board[2], the body that develops International Standards on Auditing (ISAs) (Tamm Hallström, 2004; Loft *et al.*, 2006; Humphrey and Loft, 2010b). The IAASB states that its mission is to become a global audit standard setter and make ISAs the world's preferred standardization framework for the delivery of high-quality audit services designed to appeal to adopters from a variety of national contexts. Therefore, ISAs have been envisaged as a type of global standard of audit best practice and a vehicle for international audit harmonization (IAASB, 2007).

As with many other voluntary standards, ISAs are principles-based in the sense that they prescribe how to do things by defining 'the types of administrative processes that are supposed to lead to high quality' (Brunsson and Jacobsson, 2000, p. 4–5). First called International Auditing Guidelines, they started to appear in 1979, and now the total number of ISAs has reached thirty-six (at the time of writing). ISAs have been adopted in over 120 countries worldwide. The standards are presented in groups governing various aspects of an audit. ISAs 200–299, for example, outline the auditors' responsibilities as well as the nature and general organization of an audit, including audit documentation and internal quality control. Other groupings of ISAs provide technical guidance on specific stages of the audit process from audit planning (ISAs 300–499) to evidence gathering (ISAs 500–599), using the work of others during the audit (ISAs 600–699), and the preparation of an auditor's report (ISAs 700–799). In 2004–2009, the IAASB undertook the so called 'Clarity Project' with a key objective to make ISAs more understandable in terms of the clarity of definitions and prescriptions used in order to stimulate further uniformity in audit practice (IAASB, 2004). The IAASB's recent pronouncements (IAASB, 2008) characterized 'clarified ISAs' as a comprehensive and adequate response to recent changes in accounting practice, such as a growing acceptance of fair value accounting.

The global travel of ISAs has been underpinned by their appeal as credible methodological guidelines as well as by their perceived ability to serve as a means of improving the public image of audit practice and its quality. In the wake of the 1997/98 Asian financial crisis, for example, the Financial Stability Board (then Forum) recommended 12 international standards of best practice, including ISAs and International Financial Reporting Standards (IFRS), to be adopted by national governments as a way to boost their levels of corporate governance, increase financial transparency, and restore investor confidence (Kristof and Wudunn, 2000). This event was significant in terms of helping to build a global image of ISAs as it effectively meant that 'public authority was accordingly being placed behind private standards, giving them a more important status not just in terms of processes of corporate reporting but also to the larger project of insuring financial stability' (Humphrey *et al.*, 2009, p. 811).

3.1 From standards' adoption to compliance with standards

While the emphasis on the importance of adopting ISAs remains, one can observe some major concerns growing in professional and regulatory circles over the workability of the standards, the actual degree of 'compliance with standards', and perceived deficiencies in the strategies of enforcement (see, for instance, IAASB, 2011). Some individual country experiences illustrate what Power argued over a decade ago (Power, 1997, p. 8) that audit routines can be 'loosely coupled to the purposes which they are intended to serve and rarely function according to the official blueprint'. In this regard, the IAASB Chairman Arnold Schilder noted in a recent public speech:

> the standards themselves are only one part of the equation: there is also the essential matter of implementation. Plans need to be made for adoption, yes, but planning must also consider training and support. We should not, and do not, underestimate the practical challenges of implementation (Schilder, 2011, p. 3).

The existing academic and professional literature has provided ample evidence of the challenges of international audit harmonization and the complexities of achieving global compliance with one set of international auditing standards (Wong, 2004; Hegarty *et al.*, 2004; Walter, 2008). Wong (2004), for example, notes significant inconsistencies in localized understandings of the notion of standards adoption across countries and, specifically, what full convergence with ISA should entail – which, he argues, makes it difficult to assess progress toward international harmonization. Furthermore, Wong points to the complex and changing structure of the standards themselves as well as significant institutional constraints (such as those relating to the market infrastructure, legal systems, education level, and others) as key factors contributing to the inconsistent application of ISAs. Furthermore, a fundamental challenge with regard to assessing the actual level of compliance with ISAs has been to break through the layers of auditors' declarative statements in order to understand what working with the standards actually involves in every-day practice. Despite a few attempts to unveil the audit firms' internal dynamics and work processes (see, for example, Mennicken, 2008, and Samsonova, 2011, focusing on the Russian context), the true limits of what ISAs can (and cannot) achieve remain insufficiently understood.

Additionally, the value of auditing standards in terms of setting the boundaries for the kind of assurance that auditors can reasonably be expected to provide cannot be viewed independently of the actual quality of financial reporting rules and practices. In particular, it has been argued that the growing acceptance of fair value accounting, promulgated in the standards issued by major accounting standard setting bodies such as the International Accounting Standards Board (IASB) and the Financial Accounting Standards Board (FASB) in the US could have had an adverse effect on the auditability of accounts based on such standards (Power, 2010). As the recent global financial crisis demonstrated, times of extreme volatility in financial markets do not only lead to uncertainty in the application of fair value measurements and arguably reduce the information value of such valuations but also significantly challenge audit systems and techniques in terms of their capacity to determine and assess the relative reliability of such valuations, the risks facing companies and the stability of their reported financial positions.

But even more challenging than determining the precise level or degree of standards compliance has been the task of understanding the underlying reasons for any such compliance/non-compliance. From an individual country perspective, a greater level of compliance with international standards such as ISAs has been traditionally associated with a high degree of internationalization of the general business and audit professional environment, evident from the presence and influence of foreign capital, international audit firm networks, and a greater orientation of local companies towards the demands of the global capital market (Hegarty *et al.,* 2004). However, there have been those arguing that, even in countries with sufficient institutional capabilities, international pressures alone are often not enough to trigger substantive changes in the actual practice of financial reporting and auditing (and a degree of movement that goes substantially beyond declarative statements of intent). Walter (2008), for example, in his analysis of standardization projects in the countries of East Asia points to the economics of standards compliance (i.e. a correlation between costs and benefits of compliance) and the effectiveness of monitoring and external oversight arrangements as having a stronger influence (compared to international pressure) on how global standards, such as ISAs, are followed and the likelihood of what he terms 'mock', i.e. disguised, non-compliance.

On the international stage, a significant project directly concerned with issues of substantive compliance is the ROSC (Reports on Standards and Codes) initiative, introduced by the World Bank and the IMF (International Monetary Fund) in 1999. The ROSC initiative has examined the degree to which developing and emerging nations observe the aforementioned 12 international standards of best practice, including ISAs, which were endorsed by the Financial Stability Board. ROSC country reports are designed to 'assist the country in developing and implementing a country action plan for improving institutional capacity' and 'raise awareness of good corporate governance practices among the country's public and private sector stakeholders'.[3] A like-minded initiative, launched in 2004 by the International Federation of Accountants (IFAC), namely its Compliance Program, seeks to ensure that 'international audit standard-setting processes are seen to be globally credible and sufficiently responsive to public interest demands' (Humphrey and Loft, 2010b). As part of the Program, IFAC member bodies (i.e. national professional accounting institutes) are required to make their best efforts to comply with the provisions of the Statements of Membership Obligations (SMOs), and specifically, provide regular updates as to the state of progress with regards to accounting and audit reforms.

4. The rise of regulatory oversight

With this growing emphasis on compliance with, and enforcement of, (international) standards has come a greater concern with the development of systems of external oversight over the auditing profession – and especially in relation to the auditing of 'public interest entities'. The rise of independent and quasi-governmental audit oversight at a national level is evident from the growing number of regulatory oversight agencies established in various countries – and through which a body of inspectors carries out control checks of the quality of public company audits. Among prominent examples of this trend is the formation of the PCAOB (Public Company Accounting Oversight Board) in the United States, following the publication of the Sarbanes–Oxley Act 2002 (SOX) in the wake of the Enron scandal and the subsequent demise of the company's auditor Arthur Andersen (see Shapiro and Matson, 2008; Canning and O'Dwyer, 2011;

Malsch and Gendron, 2011). SOX entrusted the PCAOB with the responsibility of undertaking quality control inspections of audit firms with public company clients. The expectation was that PCAOB inspections would be more impartial than the former 'peer reviews' that were being undertaken by the larger auditing firms; the PCAOB was considered as a body independent of the audit profession and the inspectors would be selected on the premise that they could not be current employees of audit firms. However, recent studies have expressed doubts as to the effectiveness of such inspections. Lennox and Pittman (2010), for example, demonstrate that PCAOB inspection reports are perceived as less informative (compared to peer reviews) by auditors' clients and have not affected the clients' audit firm choices, raising questions, in turn, regarding the PCAOB's failure to disclose certain information, such as the detected weaknesses in the audit firms' quality control systems and firms' overall quality ratings.

This rise of independent public oversight has developed in parallel with the establishment of umbrella transnational institutions to provide support to the activities of national audit regulators – two notable examples being the European Group of Auditors' Oversight Bodies (EGAOB) and International Forum of Independent Audit Regulators (IFIAR). IFIAR was set up in 2006 with the aim of fostering knowledge sharing and collaboration between national audit regulators and achieving consistency in their approaches to monitoring and promoting audit quality. IFIAR now has a membership of 41 independent national regulators, including the PCAOB (US), FRC (UK), H3C (France), and *Abschlussprueferaufsichtskommission* (Germany). IFIAR's meetings are formally observed by such influential transnational bodies in the field of financial market regulation and stability as the Financial Stability Board (FSB), IFAC's Public Interest Oversight Board (PIOB), the International Organization of Securities Commissions (IOSCO) – a development which further highlights the growing significance of global regulatory arrangements for public audit oversight.

4.1 The influence of oversight on the audit profession

The regulatory arrangements and developments described above have been said to represent one of the most potentially substantive and fundamental changes in the history of contemporary public accounting (for further discussion, see Malsch and Gendron, 2011, p. 456). They have been heralded, for instance, as marking the end of the audit profession's self-determination to define and defend the boundaries of auditing as a professional practice and auditors' specified social roles. That said, it has also been claimed that, despite such changes, there remains a major regulatory gap. According to Malsch and Gendron (ibid., p. 473), even with the rising importance and international coordination of the national approaches to audit regulatory oversight, there are insufficiently strong oversight arrangements at the global level to respond adequately to the truly international nature of the largest audit firms. IFIAR, for example, provides a platform for communication among the national oversight bodies but does not possess the authority to determine the direction of their monitoring activities, nor does it have the capacity to act independently as a global audit oversight body itself. An additional interpretation of the regulatory environment at the global level is that it is taking on the form of a 'shared (public–private) system'. In analysing the development of governance arrangements associated with international auditing standard setting, most notably the establishment of the IFAC's Public Interest Oversight Board (PIOB), and exploring the relationship between IFAC and international bodies such as IOSCO, the Basel Committee and the EU, Loft *et al.* (2006) classified the PIOB as a form of 'embedded oversight'. In reviewing subsequent global regulatory developments in the aftermath of the recent global financial crisis, Humphrey *et al.* (2009, p. 814) extended this form of argument to suggest that 'there is a form of allegiance' (ibid. p. 817) developing between private professional interests, namely large international audit firm networks, and national and international audit public oversight bodies, where the firms are deemed successful in achieving (informal means of) influence – and essentially regaining a degree of authority to determine the boundaries of audit practice and the public accountability of auditors.

Such patterns of development are also a reminder that in an era where talk of globalization is so prominent, it is important to keep such notions in context – and to recognize that there are potential limits to the spread and influence of globalization, given the scale of differences in the legal, political and social cultures that still exist across countries. For instance, it is intriguing that, despite the evident emphasis on public interest standard setting and oversight, there does not seem to be a universally accepted understanding across different national audit communities as to whose 'interests' exactly the category of 'public interest' represents. In the specific context of auditing, what the most appropriate forms and ways by which such interests serve to define (and change) existing conceptions of the nature and scope of auditors' responsibilities are left open to debate. Country regimes of auditor civil liability serve as a pertinent illustration here.

4.2 Auditor liability as a disciplining tool

Auditor liability can be regarded as implicit form of enforcement of certain standards of auditing practice, with legal claims and resulting court cases yielding an opportunity for 'public' interests (be they corporate shareholders owners and/or various third parties) to test ruling conceptions of the scope of the auditors' duty of care and the requisite quality of audit work. The existence, therefore, of any significant differences in national auditor liability regimes can be taken as indicative or reflective of cross-country variation in the treatment of issues pertaining to auditors' public accountability. With regard to the scope of auditor liability, for example, some countries (e.g. the UK), rely on the principle of *joint-and-several* liability which implies that any auditor can be required to pay for the whole amount of damages, regardless of the degree of his/her involvement in the audit engagement in question or the responsibility of other parties. In other countries (e.g. Austria and Germany), auditor liability is limited to a certain level (capped liability) or (e.g. Spain) is determined in proportion to the auditor's actual degree of responsibility (proportionate liability). Significantly, cross-country variation also relates to the parties to whom an auditor is believed to owe a duty of care. In the UK, for instance, the notable legal decision in *Caparo Industries v Dickman* (1990) established that the auditor's duty of care should be owed to the client only (i.e. a company as a collective body) as opposed to individual shareholders or other third parties. In contrast, in France, where there is an especially strong emphasis on the auditor's social role and public duty, liability to third parties is defined in tort law and states that an auditor may be held liable not just towards an audited company but also to its shareholders and third parties reasonably expected to have been affected by the auditor's unprofessional conduct (Chung *et al.*, 2010). The European Commission has sought to act in this area in the face, it should be noted, of considerable pressure from the accounting profession in a number of member states. It duly issued a recommendation in 2008 aimed at harmonizing the national legislative approaches to auditor liability across EU member states (EC, 2008). However, the impact of the document looks to be modest, which further highlights the weight of context-related complexities attached to the issue of auditors' public accountability and, ultimately, to the very meaning of the standards and quality of auditing practice and its overall value to society (Humphrey and Samsonova, 2011). In particular, it does suggest that the essential 'meaning' of audit is never likely to be fixed or absolutely defined, despite the globalizing tendencies and the rise of international regulatory oversight regimes. This has important consequences and implications for the way in which auditing as a subject should be regarded and studied. The closing two sections of the chapter will address such issues.

5. The persistence of the expectations gap

When the Cadbury Committee published its report in 1992, it identified the *audit expectations gap* as one of the major problems facing the auditing profession. It pointed out that public expectations of auditors were unrealistic and therefore damaging, and also supported the establishment of a 'new system' that would set out tighter specifications of what is to be expected from auditing and associated audit work. The sections above have outlined a range of regulatory interventions undertaken by governments and regulatory agencies around the world aimed at improving public perceptions of audit quality and auditor independence, such as placing restrictions on the provision of NAS, reducing mandatory rotation of audit firms and partners, introducing measures to reduce audit market concentration. Such efforts have certainly increased substantially in scope and intensity in the aftermath of Enron and a number of other major corporate scandals of a decade or so ago, with Porter and Gowthorpe (2004) vividly capturing the fragility of the auditing profession's public image and the challenges facing it:

> The most damaging criticisms are those that suggest that an auditing firm has failed the society in which it works. So it is vital to understand what society expects of auditors. Of course it may be that society's expectations of auditors are unreasonable, or fall outside the framework to which auditors must work, but if so auditors need to explain why it is impossible to meet them (Porter and Gowthorpe, 2004, p. 1).

However, even with the passing of the SOX Act in the US, copy-cat legislation in a number of other countries, a revized Eighth Company Law Directive on auditing and, more recently, the Green Paper on audit in Europe, the global financial crisis of the past few years has served to expose, yet again, the resilience of the audit expectations gap. As the Select Committee of the House of Lords in the UK recently demonstrated, there remain significant official concerns that the auditing profession has failed to respond adequately to public demands:

> Investors and others demand that audit should provide broader, more up-to-date, assurance on such matters as risk management, the firm's business model and the business review. This additional assurance would help the audit to meet the current expectations of investors and the wider public (House of Lords, 2011, p. 24).

The auditing profession in the UK has disputed a number of the conclusions of the House of Lords report and there have also been some robust challenges to the premises on which the recommendations of policy documents such as the EU Green Paper are based (for a discussion, see Humphrey *et al.*, 2011). It is also worth acknowledging though that there is some evident national variation in terms of the scale and significance of the auditing expectations gap – with Porter *et al.* (2009) reporting the establishment, over the past decade, of more favourable societal perceptions of auditors' performance in New Zealand.

In remaining consistent with the themes and perspectives outlined at the beginning of this chapter, it is not our intention to close our analysis by trying to provide an absolute measure of the current scale of the auditing expectations gap – not least, because the nature, scale and causes of the gap are likely to vary significantly depending on the perspective and position from which it is being viewed. That said, it is probably fair and sufficient to say that the auditing profession continues to be under significant pressure to respond to the claimed significance and persistence of the auditing expectations gap. What is potentially more interesting than the pursuit of any definitive measure of the expectations gap is to recognize and seek to understand key patterns and transformations in the way in which the expectations gap is operationalized, referenced and acted upon. For example, it is fascinating to see the differing or alternative rationales that are put forward as potential reasons for the persistence of the gap. In prior regulatory discourse, the ambiguity of auditing standards was identified as an important reason for 'unreasonable' social expectations of auditors. However, some recent studies and policy reports (e.g. Sikka, 2009; House of Lords, 2011) have argued that the gap represents a much more fundamental failing on the part of the auditing profession in terms of providing an audit function that adequately cater for the needs of society. In this respect, Malsch and Gendron (2009), for example, report that the trustworthiness of audited financial statements and the claimed public belief in the quality of auditing are both mythical representations whose function essentially serves to maintain the current status quo within the financial system. They argue that company investors are, in practice, far more reliant on the perceived quality of management rather than the content of audit reports in their decision-making. Such 'reality' highlights the need for further research into the nature and sources of the changing social expectations towards auditors as well as the existing capability within the audit profession to respond appropriately and adequately.

Furthermore, the aforementioned changes in the audit regulatory arena and, particularly, the rise of independent regulation and external audit oversight, are argued to have had a profound influence on the nature of auditing as a professional practice and the internal dynamics underlying audit firms' governance (Cooper and Robson, 2006; Robson *et al.*, 2007; Knechel, 2007; Gendron, 2009). Such literature provides evidence suggesting that among the major consequences of these contextual pressures has been an effective rise in a controlling, disciplining, self-protective and compliance-driven mentality towards auditing and a more restricted frame of reference for, if not fear towards, the making and exercising of professional judgement. Gendron (2009, p. 1021), for example, reports in this regard that 'bureaucratic control is increasingly privileged to the detriment of clan control [or peer pressure] – in managing large accounting firms'. Furthermore, he argues, audit partners rarely 'show enthusiasm about his or her career' and 'are increasingly considered as controllable cogs and disposable bodies'.

In the light of such observations, it is well worth asking, with respect to audit development, where the creative, free thinkers are now, the outspoken voices in the auditing profession. Are they being constrained and controlled by a compliance mindset which increasingly drives professional and regulatory circles? Leading members of the profession, especially those charged with senior management responsibilities in the large international audit firms, may criticise the profession's representative bodies for allowing regulators to get as far as they have in imposing their restrictive agendas. But to what extent do the profession and its leading professional firms find themselves on the back foot, struggling to regain the initiative in terms of the pursuit of reform? Who now is able to express radical, 'off the wall' views about auditing, the sort of views that may be something of an abstraction from the daily routines and restrictions of practice but whose effect and influence could be both stimulating and liberalizing? If auditors themselves are increasingly apprehensive about exercising professional judgement and/or perceive themselves as having little incentive to stand apart (even if the circumstances provide justification) from what accepted (international) auditing standards stipulate, this, arguably, represents a significant source of conceptual weakness in relation to the determination of the underlying rationales and nature of the contemporary audit function and its value to society.

Such tendencies can also invoke and legitimate a sense of defensiveness on the part of the profession in responding to corporate collapses and financial crises, and the questions for auditors that often result. On this issue, comparisons between the auditing profession's response to the 1997/8 Asian financial crisis, the 2001/2 Enron scandal and the 2007/8 global financial crisis reveal some interesting differences and consequences. For instance, the public questioning of the role of the auditors post-Enron contrasts quite significantly with the relative lack of discussion of the role of auditors in the immediate aftermath of the global financial crisis, suggesting that the profession drew some lessons from past experience and managed to mitigate to some degree the potential adverse effects of the crisis on the profession's public image and the attribution of blame. Humphrey *et al.* (2009, p. 816) demonstrate, in this respect, how the large audit firms actively shaped international regulators' sentiment behind the scenes in order to create 'a sense of preparedness for events and consequences that might follow from the crisis' – they did this, among other things, by 'relying on official assurances by independent oversight bodies as to the general quality of audit work' (ibid., pp. 810–11) and partaking in the IAASB's work on the development of fair value audit guidelines (arguably the most challenging and controversial area of auditing at present), which subsequently resulted in a revized ISA 540 'Auditing Accounting Estimates, Including Fair Value Accounting Estimates, and Related Disclosures'. Humphrey *et al.* concluded that the resulting outcomes of these activities were such that the profession had, so far, 'largely escaped critical comment and the apportionment of blame' (ibid., p. 810) to which other market agents (such as banks, rating agencies, and others) had been subjected. Indeed, the audit profession was quick to use the infamous statement of Paul Boyle, the chief executive of the UK's Financial Reporting Council, back in 2008 that the audit profession had had a 'good crisis'. Nevertheless, such conclusions proved to be something of an intermediate period of satisfaction and tranquillity – and have come back to bite the profession hard, with several subsequent inquiries (as mentioned above) raising critical questions as to what external auditors were doing in giving clean opinions to major banks that collapsed or went into serious financial trouble shortly after. Further, there remains a significant constant between the current and past periods of turmoil and questioning. While there has been a considerable amount of recent activity in developing new governance codes for audit firms and enhancing communications between auditors, audit committees and prudential regulators, four to five years after the start of the global financial crisis, it is still pertinent to ask just how much more have we gleaned and now know of the practical quality and value of the work of auditors? The auditing expectations gap continues to be characterized and fuelled by both knowledge and performance gaps.

6. Implications for the future of audit practice, research and regulation

A persistent expectations gap, in some ways, can be a comforting thing, in that it is clearly capable of being regarded, if not dismissed, as something that the profession just has to live with. If past efforts, whether genuine, half-hearted or self-serving, have failed to substantially close or eliminate the gap, why worry so much about it now? Indeed, a gap can be a positive feature as it implies that there is always something to improve, to develop and innovate. Better to have aspirationally high standards of expectation than standards so low that they are not only easily reached but also reflect a lack of social esteem on the part of the profession providing the requisite service or function.

There is also an inherent danger when formulating or recommending strategic action and different forms of public policy engagement that the familiarity and immediacies of the present are allowed to dominate over a sound knowledge of historical trends, patterns and intransigencies – with the result that contemplated and recommended action can subsequently prove to be either ineffectual, misplaced and/or counterproductive. That said, it is possible to see some potentially distinctive features in the present regulatory environment within which the profession is operating which collectively help to build a constructive and persuasive case for action on the part of the profession.

At one level, there has to be some doubt, especially in the EU context with the current insistence of reform under Commissioner Barnier, as to who is listening to the profession in its comments on audit reform proposals. Criticisms of reforms can run the risk of being rooted in a desire to retain the status quo when the status quo has been deemed by the profession's regulators as no longer acceptable. Alternatively, convincing arguments built up by one or a group of audit firms or professional institutes are likely to be undermined by the fact that the audit profession has not, on significant occasions, responded in a uniform way. For example, when reforms offer market opportunities to smaller firms, it has to be acknowledged that some such firms will choose to break away from the rest and promote themselves as offering a more viable and constructive option to the current status quo. A divided profession is most likely in a weaker position in terms of its negotiations with regulators and lawmakers.

Audit research explicitly focused on practice and the daily realities experienced by auditors and audit firms is starting to highlight the problematic nature of the topic of 'audit innovation'. In the pre-Enron days of business risk-based auditing approaches, there was a real buzz associated with the subject of innovation in auditing – new approaches were being trialled and even implemented (in some cases on a big scale). The motives for such innovation were varied, ranging from a desire to do better audits or more interesting audits to a more commercial orientation for more profitable audits. But whatever the motives, arguably the subject of innovation was alive. Firms talked of their own audit methodologies, of the special developments they were undertaking, of their distinctiveness and special advantages over other firms. There was a fresh and positive atmosphere associated with audit and the scope for innovation.

A decade or so on and the audit world appears to be very different. A critical question is the extent to which the technology and practice of auditing has developed in recent years and to what degree, and in what ways, it is comparable to technological advancements in areas such as mobile telecommunications, medicine, computing and motor manufacturing. What is the equivalent advancement in the field of auditing to the smart phone, laser surgery or the hybrid/electric car? A common form of response to this question is for audit practitioners to point to information technology developments that have taken place in the audit arena: how audit files are now electronically set up, developed and maintained; how it is now so much easier for files to be updated by individual audit team members; and how any member of the team can immediately access the up-to-date version of the file. But what do all of these changes say about the level of innovation in audit as a professional knowledge base?

One example of the impact that technological development can have on the nature of financial reporting and audit practice, and the objectives served by business accountants and audit practitioners, is the implementation of the eXtensible Business Reporting Language (XBRL) since the late 1990s. A growing use of XBRL by companies worldwide has been encouraged by professional bodies, e.g. the American Institute of Certified Public Accountants (AICPA) and the Canadian Institute of Chartered Accountants, and by institutions such as the Securities and Exchange Commission (SEC) in the US and Her Majesty's Revenue and

Customs (HMRC) in the UK – who, respectively, mandated this new technology for the filing of company accounts in 2008 and 2010. XBRL has been designed to make it easier for companies to gather information about their financial performance in an electronic format, so that such information can then be posted on the Internet and shared instantaneously with various users, such as investors, members of the financial community and regulators. Such a system is said to have minimized the need for human intervention in the financial reporting process by providing a web-based platform where company financial information is stored and, when needed, retrieved by an interested user directly from XBRL 'instance documents' consisting of a collection of data points classified ('tagged') based on their common descriptive qualities (e.g. areas of financial reporting). Hence, the system allows for a tailored approach to how company financial statements are generated in a way which meets the demands of specific users. From the audit perspective, the spread of XBRL effectively promotes a continuous interactive process of internal audit and control where auditors gain an ability to notify company management of financial reporting issues as they arise. Whilst one can clearly imagine a variety of practical difficulties with providing an external audit assurance on the financial reports prepared using XBRL (such as the problem of applying substantive testing techniques in the electronic data environment or ensuring that all financial information is included in the tagging process and properly classified – see, for example, a report on the implementation challenges by the Canadian Institute of Chartered Accountants, 2005), the potential influence of XBRL arguably goes beyond the issue of technical implementation and relates to the very nature of audit work. Specifically, with such a technology, the content of company reports as well as the notion of a user of such reports becomes a flexible category as traditional general purpose financial reporting shifts more toward financial reporting for specific interests and objectives, which is bound to have some influence on public expectations as to the nature of the auditor's role. For example, with regard not just to what auditors are assuring with respect to the quality of the view provided by any one particular set of financial statements but the quality of the underlying systems producing the many varied sets of financial information demanded and extracted by users.

In terms of audit innovation, the initiative and power to drive through changes in practice arguably seems to have been passed to independent regulators and oversight bodies. Regulators increasingly determine what needs to happen in terms of audit development, they look more and more like the truth-sayers in terms of operational levels of audit quality and the font of knowledge in terms of what needs to happen or change. In a European context, there is certainly a very expansionary set of noises emerging from bodies such as the European Securities and Markets Authority (ESMA) as it looks to bolster its regulatory oversight role and capacity (for a discussion, see EU, 2012, p. 4). However, even the most cursory of glances at regulatory reports quickly suggest that this position is not one beyond question and challenge. Regulatory reports, for example, seldom give much indication as to where audit has worked well (and how, why and to what effect), tending to prefer to list series of failings. It is also routinely difficult to judge whether the fundamental failing was one of the quality of audit output and outcomes or a problem of process recording and documentation. What can be said with some certainty though is that the current so-called failings of audit in relation to the global financial crisis have happened under the very explicit and detailed watch of independent audit regulators. So if, for example, auditor scepticism or communication with banking supervisors has declined, it is something that regulators have either served to stimulate or proved incapable of stopping.

Whenever we contemplate new regulatory reform proposals, it is important to remember that regulatory reform does not start, and has never started, from a clean sheet. It is tainted by past experience, and both successes and failures – we should not assume that we are somehow living in a 'regulatory heaven', where regulatory failure is essentially beyond challenge and inevitably followed by yet more 'much needed' (but untested and untried) new regulations. That said, given the reported, or at least claimed, closeness (as noted earlier in this chapter) between the profession and its 'independent' regulators, it is also risky to assume that the profession has been a passive and uninfluential bystander in terms of the regulatory systems within which it is has to work. Indeed, it could be asked whether the profession and its response to criticism and crisis has ended up with the regulatory regime it deserves or what it needs given the business interests it pursues and the organisational structures it operates. This is an interesting issue as, ultimately, it goes to the heart of what professionalism means or comes to represent in the context of auditing.

When we talk of professionalism in auditing, we routinely evoke images of independence and freedom of thought, of individuals committed to truth and justice, of reasonableness and a rationality of evidence-based judgement and an overriding commitment to and belief in transparency. However, it may be that the auditing profession, at least in recent years but arguably for many years, has adopted a very much more pragmatic and business-oriented perspective on 'professionalism', one that prioritises commercial survival over a strong and undying adherence to a 'professional' code of practice. This is not an easy point to establish given that notions of professionalism and audit quality have a considerable degree of subjectivity and social construction. However, the profession has not been without opportunities to make the quality of its audit work more visible and better appreciated – and there is an important trade-off to consider with respect to whether a function is more valued when it is transparently performing to a certain level or when it retains a mystical quality wherein actual performance levels could well be lower than those perceived and/or anticipated. The idea of a ruling sense of commercial pragmatism is also suggested by an evident trend which sees proposed audit regulations very often being resisted strongly by the profession but once put into practice quickly becoming accepted ways of behaving.

Whether this is a commercially opportune decision or an inevitable and natural response (e.g. why continue to fight losing battles?) is an open question. But, significantly, it should also serve as a substantial reminder that there is much that the audit profession (and future entrants to the profession) can and should learn about the importance of remembering and not losing a sense of history. We need to ensure that professional qualified auditors, both in their initial and continuing professional education, have a far better appreciation of the history of auditing and the economic, political, social and cultural contexts in which the practice has developed and been shaped. We also need to think much more seriously about the intellectual (and not just ethical or commercial) values that govern the auditing profession. Ultimately, this is the audit trail that the profession really does need to maintain and promote.

Notes

1 For detailed textbooks analysing the audit process and the legal framework within which auditing is practised, see Gray and Manson (2011); Porter *et al.* (2008).

2 IAASB sits within the International Federation of Accountants (IFAC), a private organization for the global accountancy profession that brings together 159 national professional accountancy bodies from around the world.

3 See a statement on the World Bank's web-site: http://www.worldbank.org/ifa/rosc_cg.html.

Bibliography

APB, *The Provision of Non-Audit Services by Auditors*, London: Auditing Practices Board, 2010.

Ashbaugh, H., LaFond, R. and Mayhew, B.W. 'Do Non-Audit Services Compromise Auditor Independence?', *The Accounting Review*, 78 (3), 611–39, 2003.

Brunsson, N., and Jacobsson, B. 'Following Standards', in Brunsson N. and Jacobsson B. (eds), *A World of Standards*, Oxford: Oxford University Press, 2000.

Cadbury Committee, *Report of the Committee on the Financial Aspects on Corporate Governance*, London: Gee Publishing Limited, 1992.

Canadian Institute of Chartered Accountants, 'Audit and Control Implications of XBRL'. Report. December, pp. 1–9, 2005.

Canning, M., and O'Dwyer, B. 'The Dynamics of a Regulatory Space Realignment: Strategic Responses in a National Context'. Working paper, Dublin City University Business School/University of Amsterdam Business School, 2011.

Carcello, J. and Neal, T. 'Audit Committee Composition and Auditor Reporting', *The Accounting Review*, 75 (4) (October), 453–67, 2000.

CGAA, 'Final Report to the Secretary of State and Chancellor of Exchequer'. Co-ordinating Group on Auditing and Accounting issues, Department of Business and Innovation Skills, URN 03/567, 2003.

Chung, J., Farrar, J., Puri, P., and Thorne, L. 'Auditor Liability to Third Parties after Sarbanes–Oxley: An International Comparison of Regulatory and Legal Reforms', *Journal of International Accounting, Auditing and Taxation*, 19, 66–78, 2010.

Cooper, D., and Robson, K. 'Accounting, Professions and Regulation: Locating the Sites of Professionalisation', *Accounting, Organizations and Society*, 31, 415–44, 2006.

Copeland, J.E., 'The Future of Corporate Reporting: From the Top', *Financial Executive*, 2003. Available at www.feiorg/mag/articles/3–2003.

EC, *Recommendation on 'Statutory Auditors' Independence in the EU*, Brussels: European Commission, 2002.

EC, *Commission Recommendation of 5/VI/2008 Concerning the Limitation of the Civil Liability of Statutory Auditors and Audit Firms*, 2008/473/EC Brussels: European Commission, 2008.

EC, *Audit Policy: Lessons from the Crisis*, Green Paper, Brussels: European Commission, 2010.

EC, *Reform of the Audit Market*, Brussels: European Commission, 2011.

EU, 'Library Briefing: Audit Reform in the EU', Library of the European Parliament, 8 February, available at www.blog-audit.com/wp-content/uploads/2012/03/Library-of-the-european-parliament-briefing-feb-20122.pdf, 2012 (accessed 2 April 2013).

FRC, *The Combined Code: Principles of Good Governance and Code of Best Practice*, Committee on corporate governance, London: Financial Reporting Council, 2003.

Gendron, Y. 'What Went Wrong? The Downfall of Arthur Andersen and the Construction of Controllability Boundaries Surrounding Financial Auditing', *Contemporary Accounting Research*, 26, 987–1027, 2009.

Gray, I. and Manson, S., *The Audit Process: Principles, Practice and Cases*. 5th rev. edn, Andover: Cengage Learning, 2011.

Hampel Committee, *Report on Corporate Governance*, London: Gee Publishing Limited, 1998.

Healey, T. and Kim, Y., 'The Benefits of Mandatory Auditor Rotation', *Regulation*, 26 (3), 10–11, 2003.

Hegarty, J., Gielen, F., and Hirata Barros, A. *Implementation of International Accounting and Auditing Standards: Lessons Learned from the World Bank's Accounting and Auditing ROSC Program*, Washington, DC: World Bank, 2004.

Hopwood, A.G. and P. Miller (eds) *Accounting as Social and Institutional Practice*, Cambridge: Cambridge University Press, 1994.

House of Lords, *Auditors: Market Concentration and their Role*, Select Committee on Economic Affairs, London: TSO, 2011.

Humphrey, C. 'Debating Audit Expectations Gap', in Sherer, M. and Turley, S. (eds), *Current Issues in Auditing*, London: Paul Chapman Publishing Limited, 1997.

Humphrey, C. and Loft, A. 'Regulating Audit through Standards in a Globalising World', Paper presented at the Department of Accounting seminar, London School of Economics, 17 March, 2010a.

Humphrey, C. and Loft, A. 'The Complex World of International Auditing Regulation', *QFinance: The Ultimate Financial Resource*, Bloomsbury Information Ltd./Qatar Financial Centre Authority, 2010b.

Humphrey, C. and Samsonova, A. 'Transnational Governance in Action: The Pursuit of Auditor Liability Reform in the EU'. Paper presented in the Interdisciplinary Perspectives on Accounting conference, Cardiff, 2011.

Humphrey, C., Moizer, P. and Turley, S. 'The Audit Expectations Gap: Plus Ca Change, Plus C'est La Meme Chose?' *Critical Perspectives on Accounting*, 3, 137–61, 1992.

Humphrey, C., Loft, A. and Woods, M. 'The Global Audit Profession and the International Financial Architecture: Understanding Regulatory Relationships at a Time of Financial Crisis', *Accounting, Organizations and Society*, 34, 810–25, 2009.

Humphrey, C., Kausar, A., Loft, A. and Woods, M. 'Regulating Audit Beyond the Crisis: A Critical Discussion of the EU Green Paper', *European Accounting Review*, 20 (3): 431–57, 2011.

IAASB, *The Clarity Standards: A Foundation for Global Audit Quality*, Annual Report, New York: International Auditing and Assurance Standards Board, 2004.

IAASB, *International Auditing and Assurance Standards Board: A Brief History of its Development and Progress*, New York: International Auditing and Assurance Standards Board, 2007.

IAASB, *Implementation of the Clarified International Standards on Auditing*, New York: International Auditing and Assurance Standards Board, 2011.

Knechel, R. 'The Business Risk Audit: Origins, Obstacles and Opportunities', *Accounting Organisations and Society*, 32, 101–29, 2007.

Krishnan, G.V. and Visvanathan, G., 'Do Auditors Price Audit Committee's Expertise? The Case of Accounting versus Non-accounting Financial Experts', *Journal of Accounting, Auditing & Finance*, 24 (1), 115–44, 2009.

Kristof, N., and Wudunn, S. *Thunder from the East: Portrait of Rising Asia*, New York: Vintage, 2000.

Larcker, D. F. and S.A. Richardson, 'Fees Paid to Audit Firms, Accrual Choices, and Corporate Governance,' *Journal of Accounting Research*, 42 (3), 625–58, 2004.

Lennox, C., and Pittman, J, 'Auditing the Auditors: Evidence on the Recent Reforms to the External Monitoring of Audit Firms', *Journal of Accounting and Economies*, 49, 84–103, 2010.

Loft, A., Humphrey, C., and Turley, S., 'In Pursuit of Global Regulation: Changing Governance Structures at the International Federation of Accountants (IFAC)', *Accounting, Auditing and Accountability Journal*, 19, 428–51, 2006.

McElveen, M. 'New Rules, New Challenges', *Internal Auditor*, (December), 40–47, 2002.

Malsch, B. and Gendron, Y. 'Mythical Representations of Trust in Auditors and the Representation of Social Order in the Financial Community', *Critical Perspectives on Accounting*, 20, 735–50, 2009.

Malsch, B. and Gendron, Y. 'Reining in Auditors: On the Dynamics of Power Surrounding an "Innovation" in the Regulatory Space' *Accounting, Organizations and Society*, 36, 135–55, 2011.

Mennicken, A. 'Connecting Worlds: The Translation of International Auditing Standards into Post-Soviet Audit Practice', *Accounting, Organizations and Society*, 33, 384–414, 2008.

Peel, M.J. and M.A. Clatworthy, 'The Relationship Between Governance Structure and Audit Fees Pre-Cadbury: Some Empirical Findings', *Corporate Governance: An International Review*, 9 (4), 286–98, 2001.

Porter, B. and Gowthorpe, C., 'Audit Expectations Gap in the UK in 1999 and Comparison with the Gap in New Zealand in 1989 and 1999', Edinburgh: Institute of Chartered Accountants of Scotland, 2004.

Porter, B., Hatherly, D. and Simon, J. *Principles of External Auditing*, 3rd edn, Chichester: John Wiley & Sons, 2008.

Porter, B., O'Hogartaigh, C. and Baskerville, R. 'Report on Research Conducted in the United Kingdom and New Zealand in 2008 Investigating the Audit Expectation–Performance Gap and Users' Understanding of, and Desired Improvements to, the Auditor's Report'. Report prepared for IFAC, September, 2009.

Power, M. 'The Audit Society', in Hopwood, A.G. and Miller, P. (eds) *Accounting as Social and Institutional Practice*, Cambridge: Cambridge University Press, pp. 299–316, 1994.

Power, M. *The Audit Society: Rituals of Verification*, Oxford: Oxford University Press, 1997.

Power, M. 'Auditing and the Production of Legitimacy', *Accounting, Organizations and Society*, 28, 379–94, 2003.

Power, M. 'Fair Value Accounting, Financial Economics and the Transformation of Reliability', *Accounting and Business Research*, 40, 197–211, 2010.

Robson, K., Humphrey, C., Khalifa, R., and Julian, J., 'Transforming Audit Technologies: Business Risk Audit Methodologies and the Audit Field', *Accounting Organisations and Society*, 32, 409–38, 2007.

Samsonova, A. 'Local Sources of a Differential Impact of Global Standards: The Case of International Standards on Auditing in Russia'. Working paper, Manchester Business School, 2011.

Schilder, A. 'International Auditing and Assurance Standards: Implementation Challenges and Success Factors'. Public speech, Buenos Aires, Argentina, 30 June 2011, available at www.ifac.org.

SEC, *Commission Adopts Rules Strengthening Auditor Independence*, Washington, DC: SEC, 2003, available at www.sec.gov/news/press/2003-9.htm

Shapiro, B., and Matson, D. 'Strategies of Resistance to Internal Control Regulation', *Accounting, Organizations and Society*, 33, 199–228, 2008.

Sikka, P, 'Financial Crisis and the Silence of the Auditors'. *Accounting, Organizations, and Society*, 34 (6), 868–73, 2009.

SOX 'The Sarbanes–Oxley Act, 2002'. Available at www.sarbanes-oxley.com (accessed 21 February 2013), 2002.

Stoy Hayward & Co, *Audit Guide*, London: Lexis Law Publishing, 1983.

Tamm Hallström, K. *Organizing International Standardization,* Cheltenham: Edward Elgar, 2004.

Treasury Select Committee, *Banking Crisis: Reforming Corporate Governance and Pay in the City*, House of Commons Treasury Committee, London: TSO, 2009.

Turley, S. and Zaman, M, 'The Corporate Governance Effect of Audit Committees', *Journal of Management and Governance*, 8, 305–32, 2004.

Wallace, W. A. 'The Economic Role of the Audit in Free and Regulated Markets', in Wallace, W. A. *Auditing Monographs*, New York: Macmillan Publishing Company, 1985.

Walter, A. *Governing Finance: East Asia's Adoption of International Standards*, New York: Cornell University Press, 2008.

Watts, R. L., and Zimmerman, J. 'Agency Problems, Auditing, and the Theory of the Firm: Some Evidence', *Journal of Law and Economics*, 26, 1983.

Wong, P. *Challenges and Successes in Implementing International Standards: Achieving Convergence to IFRSs and ISAs*, New York: International Federation of Accountants, 2004.

Zaman, M., Hudaib, M., and Haniffa, R., 'Corporate Governance Quality, Audit Fees, and Non-audit Service Fees', *Journal of Business, Finance, and Accounting,* 38(1–2), 165–97, 2011.

Zhang, Y., J. Zhou and N. Zhou, 'Audit Committee Quality, Auditor Independence and Internal Control Weaknesses', *Journal of Accounting and Public Policy*, 26, 300–327, 2007.

Part 3

(International) Accounting Standard Setting and Regulation

10

The Public Interest in International Financial Accounting, Reporting and Regulation

Carien van Mourik

1. Introduction

Professional accountants in public practice (i.e. auditors) and both public and private accounting standard setters and regulators including the IASB (see IFRS Foundation, 2010: par. 2), claim to be serving the public interest. While some are sceptical about how seriously such claims should be taken, there is a growing literature that analyses what is implied by 'the public interest' and what implications different interpretations of the public interest might have for accounting, auditing, reporting and regulation. This chapter aims to provide an analysis of the growing literature on the subject.

A recent ICAEW report *Acting in the Public Interest: A Framework for Analysis* characterizes 'the public interest' as an abstract notion (ICAEW, 2012: 4, 12). It sets out a framework for evaluating proposals that are made with a claim to being in the public interest in general, but also talks about the accounting profession's public interest responsibilities.

Dellaportas and Davenport (2008) represent a systematic attempt to understand the public interest in accounting as viewed by the accounting profession. They attempt to answer the questions: Who exactly is the public, what are the interests of the public, and what does it mean to serve the public interest? Like Sikka *et al.* (1989), Lee (1995) and Canning and O'Dwyer (2001) before them, Dellaportas and Davenport (2008: 1095) conclude that '(t)he concept of the public interest in accounting appears to be disjointed and without clear or precise meaning and understanding.' Because of the ambiguity of the concept, it has no operational definition and will be interpreted differently by members of the profession and members of the public (Dellaportas and Davenport, 2008: 1089). Hence there exists an expectations gap with respect to the function of the statutory audit (see Chapter 9). In the same way, this ambiguity may cause a discrepancy between the expectations of the general public and accounting standard setters regarding the public interest function of accounting standards and regulation.

The journal entitled *Accounting and the Public Interest* and a special issue of the *Accounting, Auditing and Accountability Journal* in 2005 are entirely devoted to the public interest in accounting and discuss different issues that have a bearing on the public interest. Literature that directly and systematically deals with the public interest in financial accounting and reporting in an international context appears to be scarce or even non-existent.

The public interest in accounting standard setting and regulation is often approached from perspectives focusing on the objectives of regulation or the costs and benefits of regulation. See for example Chapter 11 which considers the literature on arguments for and against accounting regulation and Chapter 12 which sets out the economic theory of accounting regulation. However, the concept of 'the public interest in international financial accounting, reporting and regulation' (PI) appears underdeveloped and has received rather less attention. A possible explanation is that, until relatively recently, financial accounting standards, economic policies and ethics were of a distinctly national nature.

This chapter is meant to present an overview of issues that have shaped thinking about the public interest in financial accounting, reporting and regulation, as well as perspectives on how to determine and pursue it. It also considers the question of how to extend these issues to an international context. The chapter proceeds as follows. In Section 2 it will first identify perspectives on what is the public interest and how to determine and pursue it. Then, in Section 3, it discusses how the relation between private standard setters and the public interest may have caused the search for accounting principles. Section 4 describes Demski's Impossibility Theorem and four responses in the literature which were adopted by the FASB and the IASB. Section 5 discusses how three academic 'revolutions' in accounting shape made it possible to regard the public interest in standard setting as a matter of technical competence and due process. Section 6 shows how the international public interest in financial accounting, external reporting and regulation creates social responsibilities on the part of the international accounting academy and the IASB, which both appear reluctant to accept. Section 7 concludes.

2. Perspectives on the public interest

This section discusses the difference between the common good and the public interest, and different perspectives on the public interest and how it should be determined.

2.1 The common good and the public interest

In everyday use, the 'public interest' often indicates the common good, which implies both the existence of something or things that are good for society at large, that is, all of us, as well as a shared understanding of what these things are. Douglass (1980: 104), however, draws a distinction between the 'common good' and the 'public interest':

> [t]he common good consisted in a number of specific objectives designed to promote general human well-being – such as peace, order, prosperity, justice and community. Government served the common good effectively, therefore, when it promoted not simply its own well-being but that of the larger society as well.

The common good has the following three characteristics:

- it includes everyone;
- the benefits are objectively beneficial; and
- the benefits are shared.

Douglass (ibid.: 107) claims that under the influence of Hobbes and the democratization of politics, the public interest increasingly came to be characterized as the aggregate of the private interests (often the material interests of individuals who defended their private property rights) of individuals. 'By making all valuation, including morality, a function of appetite Hobbes radically undercut the bases of the traditional common good doctrine' (ibid.)' As a consequence, according to this perspective, the public interest does not necessarily include everyone, the benefits might be perceived by the individual rather than be objectively determinable, and they need not be shared.

Cochran (1974) employed four categories of public interest concepts which include:

- normative theories of the public interest based on rationalist ethics close to the common good idea which apply to the members of a group or community;
- abolitionist theories which deny the validity of the public interest concept;
- process theories such as public choice theory (which sees the public interest as the outcome of a public choice process), conflicting interests theory (which sees the public interest as the outcome of a clash of conflicting interests), and due process theory (which sees the fairness of the procedure as the main issue in determining the public interest); and
- 'consensualist' theories which see the public interest as the outcome of public debate (Cochran, 1974: 329–31).

Below follows a discussion of four perspectives along the lines of the above categories, however, owing to the more technical nature of accounting, the last category does not really apply and in its place there is a technical view of the public interest based on the idea of objectivity and neutrality.

2.2 Rationalist ethics-based public interest theories

Rationalist ethics-based theories, such as deontological, utilitarian and contractualist theories assume that there are moral principles that provide administrators with guidance in balancing the needs and interests of different individuals, groups and the general public. Lipman described the public interest as 'something that is obtainable when men think rationally and logically, while acting in a disinterested and benevolent way' (reference in King *et al.*, 2010: 956).

'Deontological moral theories argue for a rule-based approach to ethics in which moral principles have an absolute and categorical prescriptive status' (Hutchings, 2010: 38).' Consequentialist or teleological ethical theories argue that the value of moral principles depends on the outcomes of adopting them (Hutchings, 2010: 29). Utilitarianism sees the common good as 'maximising the greatest benefit to the greatest number of people' (Dellaportas and Davenport, 2008: 1084), which assumes that this can be rationally calculated by individuals and groups. Under utilitarianism, for accountants and accounting standard setters to act morally is for them to act impartially. Contractualist ethics assumes that accountants and accounting standard setters would do so voluntarily in order to uphold the social contract which necessitates rational individuals to sometimes act in the public interest rather than in their private self-interest (Hutchings, 2010: 33–5).

Examples of rationalist ethical thinking include self-regulation by the accounting profession stressing its technical competence, and its search for principles such as independence, neutrality and objectivity after the Great Depression. Today's examples can be found in the codes of ethics and professional behaviour of professional accounting organizations, and the focus on technical competence of members of delegated regulatory bodies such as the IASB.

2.3 Pluralism and abolitionist theories

By the 1950s, many political scientists dismissed the idea of the public interest altogether as 'too normative and theoretical because the public interest had no empirical referent' (King *et al.*, 2010: 957) and regarded the public interest as a rhetorical and symbolic device aimed at legitimizing public institutions, or judging public decisions. According to Dellaportas and Davenport (2008: 1085), abolitionist theorists deny that there is a public interest and 'see only potential groups that compete to advance their own interests'. Pluralism

> opposes the Hegelian veneration of the nation state, on the one hand, but fears the anarchistic and laissez-faire individualistic extremes, on the other, and ends up seeking safety in a society in which a number of important private associations provide a cushion between the individual and the state (Olson, 1971: 111–12).

It advocates protecting the public interest by having private associations of all kinds taking a larger constitutional role in society in order to balance state control by means of pressure groups. As will be shown below, an example of this kind of thinking can be found in the due process of the IASB. Its predecessor, the IASC, did not have a formal due process, but the IASB gave different interest groups the opportunity to influence the IASB's decisions on the principles and substance of accounting standards at the discussion paper and exposure draft stages (see also Chapter 16).

2.4 Public choice, process theories and Olson's logic of collective action

Under the influence of neoclassical economics and its methodological individualism, many came to regard the public interest as the aggregate of the preferences of rational and self-interested individuals. Rational Choice Theory paved the way for regarding the public interest as an empirical concept embodied in revealed preferences via social choice (in politics) or public choice (in economics) mechanisms. Arrow's (1950) Impossibility Theorem showed that the conditions necessary for public choice mechanisms to lead to Pareto-optimal (i.e. efficient) choices are unlikely to be met by any social choice mechanism. In addition, as will be discussed below, in the case of accounting standards, the outcome of public choice processes does not necessarily produce internally consistent standards.

Hence, the legitimacy of accounting policy makers and policies became even more strongly associated with due process and technical competence. Process theories assume that '(t)he process of interest group conflict resolution serves the public interest as long as standards of due process are observed' (Dellaportas and Davenport, 2008: 1085). Unfortunately, due process as a mechanism to improve public choice mechanisms has its limits as Olson (1971) makes clear in his theory based on self-interest and free riding which will be discussed in detail in Section 5.

2.5 The technical view of the public interest

Another approach, which is perhaps more particular to accounting standard setting and other more technical problems, is a theoretical framework. In addition to the public choice mechanism and due process, the intellectual authority of a consistent and theoretically sound conceptual framework would help to defend politically contentious decisions. In order to be able to substantiate their claim to professionalism, neutrality and objectivity, professional accountants and private standard setters, particularly in the USA and the UK, embarked on a search for the scientific and technical principles of financial accounting. The current IASB Conceptual Framework can be seen as an ongoing attempt to keep 'political interference' at bay.

3. Private standard setting and the public interest in financial accounting, reporting and regulation

A claim on the public interest implies a social responsibility. The social responsibilities of professional accountants, particularly those in public practice, accounting standard setters, accounting and financial regulators derive from the functions of financial reporting in capital markets and economies more generally. Financial reporting information prepared in accordance with the accounting standards of a jurisdiction and independently verified serves the public interest by promoting the efficient allocation of scarce resources in a society and economy through enabling capital and other markets to function efficiently (Duska *et al.*, 2011: 11). Interpretations of what these social responsibilities entail are many and varied, and appear to change over time.

3.1 Professional accountants in public practice

Carrying out professional responsibilities as an external auditor with integrity, competence, due care and objectivity whilst maintaining independence from the client should serve the public interest, which the *AICPA Professional Code of Conduct*, Section 53 defines as 'the collective well-being of the community of people and institutions the profession serves' (Duska *et al.*, 2011: 83). Note that 'the collective well-being' could be understood as the common good, whereas the 'community of people and institutions the profession serves' does not necessarily include the general public and probably indicates some notion of the public interest.

Usually, professional accounting organizations will each have their own code of ethics and standards of professional behaviour. In addition, there is the Code of Ethics issued in 2009 by the International Ethics Standards Board for Accountants (IESBA Code) and revised with effect from 1 January 2011.[1] Unfortunately, the IESBA Code is not freely available to the public. It describes the fundamental principles of integrity, objectivity, professional competence and due care, confidentiality and professional behaviour, and lays out a framework for dealing with ethical issues that may confront auditors and accountants employed by businesses.

3.2 Self-regulation and the search for accounting principles

According to Schroeder *et al.* (2001: 527), society has granted many of the professions autonomy, including self-regulation as a privilege. For the accounting profession, this may have been the case in countries such as the UK and the USA. In most European and other developed countries, public sector financial accounting regulation preceded the establishment of an organized accounting profession. This can in part be explained by the fact that in later industralized countries the state adopted a more interventionist role in order 'to encourage industrial catching up' (Foreman-Peck, 1995: 19). Gerschenkron's (1962) thesis of relative economic backwardness sets out institutional differences between early industrializing countries and laggards. The latter countries had financial systems where firms rely more on indirect financing through banks and other intermediaries rather than direct financing through capital markets. There, the accounting profession had neither the opportunity for self-regulation nor did it have the incentive to search for accounting principles that would legitimize self-regulation.

Following the Great Depression, the US Securities and Exchange Acts of 1933 and 1934 established the Securities and Exchange Commission (SEC) as the authority in charge of developing accounting principles and standards. Under the influence of the accounting profession (particularly George O. May of the AIA), the SEC decided to delegate this responsibility to the accounting profession. The profession was then faced with the task of protecting its own and its customers' interests whilst meeting the requirements of the SEC (Merino, 2003).

Under the pressure of losing this opportunity for self-regulation, the American Accounting Association scrambled to come up with *A Tentative Statement of Accounting Principles Underlying Corporate Financial Statements* (AAA, 1936). Its fundamental axiom was that accounting is the 'allocation of historical costs and revenues to the current and succeeding fiscal periods' (ibid.: 188). A revised statement was issued in 1941 followed by another revision entitled *Accounting Concepts and Standards Underlying Corporate Financial Statements* (AAA, 1948). These statements merely surveyed contemporary practices. *A Statement of Accounting Principles* by Sanders *et al.* (1938) warned against the abuse of conservatism but also advocated the use of adequate reserves.

The American Institute of Certified Public Accountants (AICPA)'s *Accounting Research Study No. 3* by Sprouse and Moonitz (1962) represented a systematic attempt at a coherent set of principles. Most of these were not adopted for some time, but its influence on the FASB and IASB Conceptual Frameworks is clearly recognizable. It advocated decoupling of accounting and taxable income, abandoning the realization concept and promoted the idea of conceptual primacy of the balance sheet, which translates into a balance sheet approach to the periodic determination of income. According to Sprouse and Moonitz (1962: 55), '(a)ccounting draws its real strength from its neutrality as among the demands of competing special interests'.

In *A Statement of Basic Accounting Theory* (ASOBAT) (AAA, 1966: 3), usefulness of accounting information was established as the all-inclusive criterion for its inclusion in financial statements. Its influence on the FASB and IASB Conceptual Frameworks can be found in this objective as well as in the use of qualitative criteria of useful accounting information. ASOBAT listed relevance, verifiability, freedom from bias and quantifiability (ibid.: 8). The AICPA adopted the decision-usefulness objective and qualitative characteristics of useful information in its APB Statement No. 4, *Basic Concepts and Accounting Principles Underlying Financial Statements of Business Enterprises* (AICPA, 1970: pars 21–4). It extended the qualitative characteristics to include: relevance, understandability, verifiability, neutrality, timeliness, comparability and completeness.

ABP Statement No. 4 (AICPA, 1970: pars 6, 24) and *Statement on Accounting Theory and Theory Acceptance* (AAA, 1977: Preface) indicate the profession's frustration with the gradual realization 'that there are no easy theoretical answers to many of the urgent problems faced by the profession'.

4. Four consequences of Demski's impossibility theorem

Demski, using Arrow's Impossibility Theorem, proved that

> [n]o set of standards exists that will always rank alternatives in accordance with preferences and beliefs – no matter what these preferences and beliefs are, as long as they are consistent in admitting to the expected utility characterisation. . . . Further observe that the basic difficulty does not rest with a multiperson orientation (Demski, 1973: 721).

The conditions that a social choice mechanism must fulfil are unlikely to be met in practice. See also Bromwich (1992: 258). Ultimately, this means that financial accounting standard setting involves trading off one stakeholder's gain against another's loss.

For public regulators in democratic jurisdictions, the main implication is that there may have to be complementary institutional responses to this trade-off, i.e. the government is likely to have in place redistributional mechanisms in order to compensate the losers. For private regulators, the main concern is their legitimacy to make these trade-offs. Private regulators will usually be more responsive to their constituents and less responsive to stakeholders outside the constituency. On top of that, they will often be less independent from their constituents and less sensitive to the general public interest. For an overview of advantages and disadvantages of public and private regulation, see Riahi-Belkaoui (2004: 138–41) and Dellaportas and Davenport (2008).

There were basically four responses to Demski's theorem. The first, by Chambers (1976), argued that current value accounting does not suffer from this problem. He claimed that information on 'the current money and money's worth of assets and the amounts currently owing to others at any time' is superior to any alternative class of accounting information (ibid.: 651)'. His argument rests on the idea that current value accounting is invariant with respect to choice because it does not need to take into account stakeholders' specifications of future states, beliefs or preferences. In other words, Chambers assumed that current value accounting serves all users' information needs equally well.

The second response, by Cushing (1977), explored the consequences of relaxing the assumption that users of financial statements have heterogeneous information needs based on Arrow's idea of 'Similarity as the Basis of Social Welfare Judgements'. He developed the idea of decomposing total expected utility differentials for all users, assuming that when a new standard increases the fineness of information this will increase all users' utilities (ibid.: 316). Gambling (1977: 142), on the other hand, held that with regard to conflict resolution, 'information can be counterproductive in certain situations where the dispute is not strictly "resolvable" – other than by the use of "authority", "arbitration", or outright "confrontation"'.

The third response indicated the need for a generally accepted conceptual framework which would make accounting regulation a technical rather than a public choice problem. Bromwich (1980: 289), like Demski (1973: 721), stressed that 'not all the obstacles to progress with the partial standards approach arise from the different preferences, beliefs and decision settings of individuals in a multi-person setting. Accounting standards that are determined by public choice mechanisms do not necessarily result in a system in which all standards are internally consistent. In addition, Bromwich (1992: 261–2) discusses problems with the true revelation of preferences: 'Therefore, ... the assumption of homogeneity between individuals suggested by Cushing [1977: 311–13] may not open up wide avenues for progress in solving the problems of standard setting.'

The fourth response, by Johnson and Solomons (1984), is a pragmatic argument for both substantial and procedural legitimacy in the form of the FASB's ability to defend the rules it promulgates and the process by which it decides the rules based on technical competence and due process. According to Johnson and Solomons (1984: 165), Demski suggests that an accounting standard setting process must satisfy Arrow's conditions in order to be legitimate. Johnson and Solomons dismiss Demski's Impossibility Theorem as irrelevant to 'assessment of the legitimacy of a real world institutional process like the FASB ... due to the inability of any real world accounting standard-setting process to meet Arrow's conditions' (ibid.: 165–6). Although the issue of legitimacy of standard setters is very important in itself, it is used by Johnson and Solomons to stand the issue on its head. In other words, they turn the problem, that setting financial accounting standards involves intentionally or unintentionally trading off one stakeholder's gain against another's loss, into a matter of assessing the legitimacy of the FASB to make this trade-off.

Johnson and Solomons viewed the legitimacy of the FASB as a matter of a balance between procedural and outcome controls. They acknowledge potential difficulties in assessing process legitimacy on the basis of this approach.

> First, in order to be feasible, such a process must be compatible with the economic and political environment in which it operates. ... Second, due to political and other costs involved, a private sector regulatory process like the FASB cannot adopt different decision-making procedures for each possible subset of issues that may come before it. ... Finally, as a practical matter, the political viability of a private sector regulatory process like the FASB depends on its ability to sustain itself against criticism of both its rule-making procedures and the rules it promulgates (ibid.: 17).

The FASB developed a conceptual framework that, to some extent, combined all four approaches in one. Although the IASC Conceptual Framework was closely modelled on the FASB Conceptual Framework, the IASC did not adopt due process. Its successor, the IASB did.

5. Three academic accounting revolutions and the public interest in financial accounting, reporting and regulation

Three academic accounting 'revolutions' that would have an enormous impact on conceptions of the public interest were starting to gain momentum around the time that the FASB and the IASC were established in 1973. The efficient market hypothesis, the economic income ideal and the informational paradigm influenced the concept of the public interest in the conceptual frameworks of the FASB (1978) and the IASC (1989) and much of the mainstream financial accounting research in the past four decades or so. The FASB, given its mandate, had the American public interest in mind, whereas the IASC aimed for harmonization in the interests of its constituents, i.e. accounting firms, multinational corporations and investors in multinational corporations. In spite of its changed mandate, the concept of the public interest in the 2010 IASB Conceptual Framework and the IFRS Foundation's Constitution (IFRS Foundation, 2013) has not changed, nor have any challenges been taken seriously.

The three 'revolutions' do not stand on their own. They have their origins in classical and neoclassical economic thought and are interconnected because they share many of the core methodological assumptions regarding individuals, society and factual knowledge as well as the justification of epistemic knowledge and the role of researchers in this process. For these methodological assumptions see Chapter 2. They are also interconnected because they build on each other and, in this way, they continue to influence accounting practitioners, standard setters and regulators, mainstream academic accounting research and teaching. This section discusses the impact of these three 'revolutions' on conceptions of the public interest in financial accounting and reporting.

5.1 The efficient markets hypothesis

The first revolution in accounting to affect the concept of the public interest is the Efficient Markets Hypothesis (EMH) and the random-walk stock market model first formulated by Fama (1965). In a situation 'where stock prices follow random-walks and at every point in time actual prices represent good estimates of intrinsic values ... the primary concern for the average investor should be portfolio analysis' (Fama, 1965: 40):

> Portfolios which by diversification minimise the risk attached to obtaining a given level of expected or average return are called efficient portfolios. They allow all the risk attaching to each security to be diversified away. Rational investors will only hold portfolios that belong to this efficient set. . . . An individual's choice among efficient portfolios will depend on the amount of risk the individual is willing to bear (Bromwich, 1992: 206).

From an information economics perspective, the idea is that strong-form efficient markets fully and quickly impound all publicly available and private information in the stock price. Hence, the average investor does not need protection because he/she is protected by the information contained in the stock price and is, in effect, facing a fair gamble (Grossman and Stiglitz, 1980: 404–5). Accounting standard setting and regulation would not be necessary (Wyatt, 1983: 61). However, in the case of fully efficient capital markets, there would be little incentive for private searches for information as the benefit of obtaining this information would be offset by the cost. In other words, perfectly efficient stock markets would break down due to insufficient incentive to invest (Grossman and Stiglitz, 1980: 404–5).

Semi-strong form efficiency implies that all public information is quickly absorbed by the stock price, but it is possible to profit from private information. Investors need to protect themselves by holding a well-diversified portfolio. Investors need to be protected by full disclosure of accounting information, but what matters is the substance of the information rather than the form in which it is presented and the way it is disclosed (Bromwich, 1992: 215). Markets are said to be weak-form efficient when the stock prices reflect all the information contained in historical security prices. Weak-form market efficiency suggests that technical analysis on the basis of past stock prices alone would not be sufficient to beat the market in the long run. Accounting standard setters generally assume that capital markets are semi-strong form efficient.[2]

Market imperfections are often used as economic rationales for regulation. Lev (1988: 2–3) asked 'what public interest criterion *does* and/or *should* determine the choices made by accounting regulators? [Italics in original]' and defined inequity in capital markets as 'the existence of systematic and significant information asymmetries across investors' (ibid.: 1). He warned against its 'social consequences in the form of high transaction costs, thin markets, low liquidity and, in general – decreased gains from trade' (ibid.: 3) and argues for the regulation of disclosure because capital markets could break down when, 'suspecting gross information asymmetries, uninformed investors may quite rationally withdraw from trading in specific securities or from the stock market altogether' (ibid.: 7). He goes on to advocate an operational public interest criterion for disclosure choices in the form of a systematic decrease of information asymmetries and suggests *ex post* evaluation of accounting standards with respect to the realization of this objective.

So, financial accounting standard setters serve the public interest by establishing standards that prevent capital markets from breaking down either due to 'uninformed' investors' withdrawing from capital markets (Lev, 1988) or due to 'informed investors' having insufficient incentives to invest because private information searches will not be worth their while (Grossman and Stiglitz, 1980). Accounting standard setters and regulators do not appear to make the equality–efficiency trade off[3] at a conscious level. On the contrary, the IASB has so far refused to take into account that IFRSs may have consequences for distributional justice other than where it concerns investors. They place the burden to address this problem squarely on the national regulators.

5.2 The economic income and wealth ideal

The economic wealth of an entity is the present value of its net assets at a point in time. In accounting it would be estimated as the difference between the discounted expected future cash inflows associated with the entity's assets and the discounted expected future cash outflows associated with the entity's liabilities. Economic income is the change in the present value of net assets between two points in time which does not arise from capital contributions or withdrawals plus the net cash inflow for the period (or less the net cash outflow for the period) (Bromwich, 1992: 37). It is also called subjective income because it is based on the manager's expectations regarding the entity's future cash flows, choice of discount rate and time horizon. As such, it is an *ex ante* concept of income, which, in the same way as budgeted income, under conditions of uncertainty is likely to differ from realized income.

Corbin (1962: 626) called the adoption of 'the economists "forward-looking" approach' in managerial and financial accounting 'The Revolution in Accounting' and seemed convinced that '(w)ith the tools of economic theory and accounting history, a rational foundation of accounting theory may be constructed'. *Accounting Research Study No. 3* by Sprouse and Moonitz (1962) had been heavily influenced by Canning (1929) and the idea that accounting income did not provide very useful information for investors. Some advocates of economic income echoed this view (e.g. Solomons, 1961; Staubus, 1961; Corbin, 1962; Lemke, 1966; Revsine, 1970). Their arguments managed to convince many people that economic income was the ideal income measure and that accounting income ought to be brought closer to the ideal by using current cost accounting. For example, Philips's (1963) 'The Revolution in Accounting Theory' held high hopes for a 'pure theory of accounting'. Philips argued that, 'if we accept, as the ideal for valuation, present market values at any given point in time, there are no conceptual problems of determining an appropriate discount rate or establishing degree of certainty or time of flow' (ibid.: 706).

In Statement of Financial Accounting Concepts No. 3 (SFAC No. 3) *Elements of Financial Statements of Business Enterprises*, the FASB (1980) defined comprehensive income resulting from 'a desire to incorporate in one final figure all non-owner changes in equity for a period' (Robinson, 1991: 108). The all-inclusive concept of income demands that all revenue and expense items be reported in the income statement and that no items bypass the income statement directly into equity. Clean surplus equity shows equity as share capital and retained earnings, and without revaluation or other reserves. Robinson (1991) argued that the time had come to report comprehensive income (including earnings) on the basis that the semi-strong form of the EMH 'assures us that the user community will be able to analyze the information in a statement of comprehensive income' (Robinson, 1991: 110).

In June 1999, the G 4+1 (the accounting standard setters of Australia, Canada, New Zealand, the UK and the USA, together with the IASC) produced a position paper on reporting performance which recommended reporting comprehensive income using a 'components' approach rather than a 'holding tank' approach to recycling (Cearns *et al.*, 1999: 54–6). This proposal meant:

- abandoning the realization concept in favour of recognition on the basis of measurable changes in market prices and/or interest rates; and
- abandoning the articulation of the financial statements.

As a consequence, comprehensive income for the period would no longer be reconcilable to net cash flow for the period. In other words, comprehensive income thus disclosed would be a surrogate for economic income and would render accounting net income meaningless.

In April 2004, the IASB and the FASB agreed to carry out jointly a project on reporting comprehensive income.[4] In 2007, IAS 1 was amended to introduce comprehensive income into the income statement. Soon after, the *Exposure Draft: Presentation of Items of Other Comprehensive Income* proposed to disclose comprehensive income the main income concept and, like the G4+1 position paper, it advocated abandoning the recycling of items in OCI to net income upon realization (IASB, 2010b). This proposal did not make it because commentators demanded that the IASB clarify its income concept and conceptual approach to income determination and recycling in its conceptual framework (IASB, 2010c). In June 2011, IAS 1 was amended again to change the presentation of the comprehensive income statement so that items that may be recycled are shown separately from items that may not be recycled.

Although many deny that the IASB is moving towards a full fair value model (e.g. Cairns, 2007), the use of fair market values would accord with the idea of increasing the usefulness of accounting information by making it more forward looking (Whittington, 2005). In addition, the shift towards the balance sheet approach to the determination of comprehensive income, and the intention to do so without recycling items in OCI combined with the ideal of showing equity as a clean surplus, appears to be part of a move away from accounting income towards a surrogate economic income concept.

Three questions follow from this move towards comprehensive income:

- Is comprehensive income more useful for making decisions than accounting income?
- Would the disclosure of both accounting income and comprehensive income be more useful than disclosing one or the other?
- What is the connection between measurement at fair value raises and the characteristics of the markets for the assets and liabilities to be valued? (See also Bromwich, 2005: 64–5.)

Ideal markets are perfectly competitive, complete and well organized and will therefore enable the invisible hand to allocate resources most efficiently and fairly. What are the welfare consequences when markets are poorly organized, not perfectly competitive and incomplete?

5.3 The informational paradigm and decision-usefulness

Beaver (1998) called the shift from economic income measurement to an informational approach 'a financial reporting revolution'. The high hopes for economic income of the 1960s had been disappointed but the EMH and portfolio theory opened up a new perspective: the informational perspective. From this perspective, according to Beaver (1998: 26), the role of financial reporting information is to alter undiversified investors' beliefs about a security's unsystematic risk. The information perspective assumes that well-diversified investors have little use for financial reporting information (Beaver, 1998: 9, 26). Based on the logic of the EMH, the informational paradigm assumes that:

> for an information system to have value some of the signals must alter beliefs. If unexpected earnings can alter the beliefs of market participants in a systematic way, increases in stock prices would be associated with favourable unexpected earnings, and conversely for unfavourable expected earnings (Beaver, 1998: 89).

Scott (1997: 100) put it as follows: 'This equating usefulness to information content is called the *information perspective* on financial reporting, an approach which has dominated financial accounting theory and research since 1968 [italics in original].' Ball and Brown (1968) provided the first evidence that security market prices do respond to accounting information in predictable ways and since then this research paradigm has proved very prolific and influential.

5.4 In sum

Standard setters and regulators adopted the assumption that markets were semi-strong form efficient, which allowed them to also adopt the full disclosure principle, and which caused the number of disclosures to skyrocket. Financial statements, notes and supplementary schedules in the annual reports ballooned. However, recognition on the face of the financial statements was limited by the materiality principle.

The materiality principle is interpreted by the FASB and IASB in the tautological manner that characterizes the influence of the EMH. It holds that information is material if it has the ability to influence investors' decisions (IASB, 2010a: QC11). This definition can only be operationalized when it is known what information investors take into account when they make their decisions. Furthermore, the primacy of investors' information needs is an assumption, not an undisputed fact, but it serves the purpose of being able to assume that stock prices reveal investors' preferences for anything in between recognition and measurement methods and disclosure policies. This is the logic behind the tautological decision-usefulness argument that accounting standards should be adopted on the basis of the strength of the association between stock prices and accounting numbers (or between market values and book values).

In 1978, the FASB's SFAC No. 1 adopted the information perspective, the IASC followed in 1989 and the IASB inherited it and kept it as the basis of its 2010 Conceptual Framework. However, this does not warrant the conclusion

> that the 'best' accounting policy is the one that produces the greatest market response. . . . Accountants may be better off to the extent that they provide useful information to investors, but it does not follow that *society* will be better off [italics in original] (Scott, 1997: 118–19).

The economic income and wealth ideal, again places primacy on market values, as a consequence of which, at least at the conceptual level, a shift from the transactions approach to the valuation approach to the determination of income appears to have taken place. Whittington (2008: 156–60) contrasts what he calls the 'fair value worldview' and the 'alternative worldview'. The former roughly corresponds to what Cairns (2007, and Chapter 7) calls the 'full fair value model' and in Chapter 3 is called 'the valuation approach to the determination of income'. The latter roughly corresponds to the transactions approach to the determination of income. At the standards level this shift has not been wholesale, but has primarily affected the valuation of financial instruments as it is there that the transactions approach is most deficient.

The combination of the informational paradigm and self interest theories leads Scott (1997) to describe two primary roles of accounting information. First, it acts to mitigate the adverse selection problem caused by information asymmetry between managers and shareholders, and, second, it provides a measure of managerial performance which acts to mitigate the moral hazard problem caused by information asymmetry between managers and shareholders (Scott, 1997: 3–4). Because of the focus on the role of financial accounting information in decision-usefulness, its role in contracting and monitoring has received rather less attention from accounting standard setters and researchers.

6. The international public interest in financial accounting, external reporting and regulation

International financial reporting standards are meant to improve the functioning of international capital markets. The idea of a unified set of global accounting standards is premised on the assumption that financial and economic globalization serve the public interest. This section first briefly explores the idea that the social benefits of financial and economic globalization do not necessarily outweigh the social costs, or that the benefits and the costs are not evenly distributed. It then discusses the social responsibilities that globalization creates for the international accounting academy and for the IASB.

6.1 The two faces of globalization[5]: what does this mean for financial accounting, reporting and regulation?

Milanovic (2003) shows that the mainstream view of globalization as an automatic and benign force leading to converging world incomes and institutions is flawed. The financial deregulation and globalization of financial, capital and commodity markets that started in the 1980s have been rationalized because of the theoretical potential to reduce inequality and poverty. For example, according to Mishkin (2006: 5), economic and financial globalization leads to a reduction of poverty in developing countries that are willing and able to become export-oriented. He claims that financial globalization will lower the cost of capital, improve the allocation of capital, and help 'promote the development of better property rights and institutions, both of which make the domestic financial sector work better in putting capital to productive uses' (Mishkin, 2006: 8).

Economic globalization is supposed to be accompanied by convergence in countries' incomes for four reasons:

- low wages and a high return on capital should attract direct investment in poor countries and increase their economic growth rate;
- technological catch-up is cheaper than inventing new technologies;
- poor countries can make use of their comparative advantage when free trade allows them to specialize; and
- late developers do not need to reinvent the wheel when it comes to institutions, governance and policies that enable economic growth (Milanovic, 2011: 104–5).

In reality, capital primarily flows from rich countries to rich countries and from poor countries to rich countries (capital flight) in a phenomenon termed 'the Lucas Paradox', but less from rich to poor countries (see Milanovic, 2011: 106; Lucas, 1990; Mishkin, 2006: 7; Collier, 2008: 91). According to Milanovic (2011: 106–8, 225 n.5) the Lucas Paradox also applies to labour which migrates from rich to rich or from poor to rich countries. Technology is excludable through patents and intellectual property rights, and technological development is very much dependent on the institutional environment in a country. And, finally, the development of a country's institutions is path-dependent and therefore institutions that work well in one country cannot simply be replicated in another country. Mishkin (2006: 13) makes the point that good institutions need to be home grown.

Furthermore, the 2007/8 financial crisis and the following credit crunch and sovereign debt crises have proved that developed countries, too, can still be hit hard by financial crises. There are lessons to be learned about the limits of Adam Smith's invisible hand in economic orthodoxy (Basu,

2011), how Keynes's animal spirits govern much of economic activity (Akerlof and Shiller, 2009), and the invisible fault lines that continue to threaten the global economic system (Rajan, 2010).

Questions were raised about the role of financial accounting and particularly fair value in exacerbating the credit crunch. Some accounting researchers came to its defence (e.g. Barth and Taylor, 2010) and others tried to weigh the arguments on either side (e.g. Laux and Leuz, 2009). However, an important issue raised by Rajan (2010: 7) also impacts the role of international financial reporting standards. It is the fact that '(b)ecause different financial systems work on different principles and involve different forms of government intervention, they tend to distort each other's functioning when they come into close contact.'

Financial reporting information needs vary between market economy and financial systems because performance is conceptualized differently, and because there is a great variety in the mix of social, legal, financial and economic institutions dealing with competition, co-operation, contracting, risk, uncertainty and moral hazard. Leuz's (2010) solution of a separate global reporting segment is based on the concept of institutional complementarity between market and government arrangements. However, as Leuz's (2010) new institutional financial accounting approach is based on the methodological assumptions of new institutional economics (see Chapter 2), it does not consider how the multinational corporations that might fit such a segment are the most likely to benefit from the discrepancy between economic and political globalization.

Basu names two consequences of the fact that political globalization is trailing behind economic globalization. One is erosion of democracy. Another is 'the tolerance of global inequalities that would not have been tolerated in any economy under any single government' (Basu, 2011: 182–3). The ability of multinational corporations to exploit the differences in national regulations and the lack of global governance create huge opportunities to seek 'high private rewards disproportionate to their social productivity' (Tobin, 1984: 294 in Skott and Ryoo, 2008: 858). A third consequence is a sharp increase in the market and political power of the financial sector where some firms have now become too big to fail, creating moral hazard due to government bailouts in the process. By the way, please note that the IASB only considers institutional arbitrage to the extent that companies engage in it to avoid IFRS.

6.2 The social responsibilities of the international accounting academy

As accounting educators, the academy is responsible for teaching accounting students at any level to think critically about the public interest in financial reporting and accounting standard setting. However, because the IASB presents its conceptual framework as objective truth rather than merely one possible perspective, accounting students too often simply memorise and absorb the IASB doctrine of decision-usefulness and protecting the interests of investors. When these accounting students become PhD students, professionally qualified practitioners, standard setters or teachers themselves, they are unlikely to start questioning the doctrine that they are familiar with, even though its primary epistemic justification was the accounting–technical competence and business experience of the IASB and FASB board members.

As social science researchers, the accounting academy is responsible for understanding that financial accounting is not a natural science. This means that international accounting researchers need to be particularly aware of their own and others' value judgements and methodological assumptions and how these affect research topics, questions, methods of analysis, sample selection and outcomes. In an international context even more than in a national context, there probably is no objective basis for making value judgements, although it is still possible to judge the research on epistemic criteria.

As the fundamental issues in financial accounting, reporting and regulation theory (see Chapter 3) are even more urgent in an international context, researchers need to engage with these questions from different methodological perspectives and compare answers. They also need to engage with standard setters and regulators. So far, there have been remarkably few responses from accounting academics, even those who have made a career based on critical accounting research, to the IASB's invitations to comment on the Conceptual Framework discussion papers and exposure drafts or the public consultation on the Status of Trustees' Strategy Review.

6.3 *The social responsibilities of the IASB*

Following its public consultation on the Status of Trustees' Strategy Review of 5 November 2010, the IFRS Foundation's *Report of the Trustees' Strategy Review*[6] of April 2011 simply reasserts its definition of the public interest as that of investors in capital and financial markets. In addition, the Trustees now also acknowledge the importance of global financial stability and sound economic growth (IFRS Foundation, 2011:A1). In this report, the IFRS Foundation claims that sustainability reporting is not directly pertinent to capital allocation decisions (ibid.: 11).

This perspective allows the IASB to focus on the financial aspects of capital allocation decisions by investors and to defer issues to do with the economic, social and ecological sustainability until 'the system stabilises' and 'resources permit' (ibid.: 11, A4). It assumes that the IASB can legitimately trade off all stakeholders' interests in favour of the interests of investors in the public interest as long as it follows due process and demonstrates accounting–technical competence. Furthermore, it allows the IFRS Foundation to interpret its own responsibilities primarily in terms of benchmarking and oversight of the IASB's due process (IFRS Foundation, 2011: 15–19).

In essence, the IASB exists to develop and promote a single set of financial reporting standards in order to increase the global comparability of financial accounting information. As such, it is premised on the idea that the social benefits of financial and economic globalization outweigh the social costs. This may explain why the IASB does not explicitly define the meaning of the 'public interest in international financial accounting, reporting and regulation' (PI). The IASB does not recognize any social responsibilities beyond those associated with establishing high quality financial reporting standards in order to increase the global comparability of financial reporting information and its decision-usefulness.

However, in the interest of maintaining its institutional legitimacy, sooner or later, the IASB will need to define the PI it claims to serve. Social responsibilities following from this claim include:

- addressing the IASB's intellectual and institutional bias;
- assessing the appropriateness of the decision-usefulness objective in the variety of institutional environments where IFRS has been adopted or accepted; and
- improving due process in the particular case of the conceptual framework and more generally to mitigate public choice problems in accounting standard setting.

6.3.1 Institutional bias

The 2010 IASB Conceptual Framework was issued in September 2010. It was the result of a joint FASB/IASB project in which US accounting thought strongly dominated. For example, on 10 April 2010, in addition to the FASB members, there were seventeen IASB members, two of whom (one from Germany, one from South Africa) had not yet started. There were four members from the US, two from the UK, two from France, two from South Africa and one each from Australia, Sweden, Japan, Brazil, China and India. In the case of the IFRS Foundation, there were twenty-one trustees, among which five were from the US alone.

This American institutional bias in the IASB Conceptual Framework will not disappear simply by changing the mix of trustees and IASB members to 'reflect the world's capital markets, and diversity of geographical and professional backgrounds' (IFRS Foundation, 2010: pars 6, 26). To a certain extent, IASB membership will be self-selecting because every new board member has to subscribe to the existing conceptual framework (IFRS Foundation, 2010: par. 29) and 'be committed to serving the public interest through a private standard setting process' (IFRS Foundation, 2010: Annex, par. 8). Hence, the intellectual and institutional bias is already a firmly established part of the IASB and its conceptual framework.

6.3.2 Decision-usefulness

The decision-usefulness objective of financial reporting which forms the basis of both the IASB and FASB Conceptual Frameworks is a product of the USA's intellectual and institutional environment of the 1970s (FASB, 1978: SFAC No. 1, pars 9–16). Of course, the FASB is legally bound to serve the American public interest as defined by the American public choice process, and the IASC adopted the decision-usefulness objective in 1989 when it did not have or need due process. In addition, the 2010 IASB Conceptual Framework is the result of a convergence project between the IASB and the FASB which was never meant to question the appropriateness of the framework's intellectual foundations for other institutional environments or rebuild it from scratch.

According to the IAS Plus website, more than 80 jurisdictions require IFRS for listed and unlisted companies, and more than 100 jurisdictions require or permit the use of IFRS for domestic listed companies.[7] It is clear that all of these countries have very different institutional environments where the public interest is likely to be perceived in very different ways. It is highly questionable that the IASB's decision-usefulness objective and its shift towards the balance sheet approach to the determination of (comprehensive) income is equally suitable for the great variety of institutional environments where IFRS is currently used. Some of these countries do not even have a stock exchange. Possible reasons for accepting IFRS are discussed in Chapters 24 and 25.

6.3.3 The IASB conceptual framework and due process

Olson's (1971) *The Logic of Collective Action: Public Goods and the Theory of Groups* uses a theory based on self-interest and incentives to explain how

> unless the number of individuals in a group is quite small, or unless there is coercion or some other special device to make individuals act in their common interest, *rational, self-interested individuals will not act to achieve their common or group interests.* In other words, even if all the individuals in a large group are rational and self-interested, and would gain if, as a group, they acted to achieve their common interest or objective, they will still not act to achieve that common or group interest [italics in original] (Olson, 1971: 2).

If this theory is true, the implication is that, even if the individual members of a group as large as the international general public really do know what is in their common interest, they will not act to achieve it unless they are coerced or unless the incentive for action provides a greater benefit than the cost of not acting. As a consequence, the policy process can easily be captured by small interest groups with the means and the incentives to act in their narrow private interests. In other words, the social choice approach to discovering what the public interest is may be very costly to society at large, but nobody is keeping score.

The IASB's due process, particularly when it comes to establishing the conceptual framework, does not ensure that the framework is coherent and internally consistent. There are several reasons for this:

- First, the logic according to which the elements of the conceptual framework fit together is unclear because the due process does not require epistemic justification or clarification of logic.
- Second, the IASB does not intend to change Chapters 1 and 3 (on the objectives of general purpose financial reporting and the qualitative characteristics of useful information) even though it has not formally decided on a performance concept and its measurement yet.
- Third, even when it comes to a performance concept and its approach to income measurement, the IASB is still presenting its work in progress as different elements. It presents the definition of elements of financial statements, separate from their recognition and measurement without clarifying any theoretical and logical connections between them.

The due process would need to include rules for both the epistemic justification of the concepts and the logical structure connecting the concepts. Ideally, it would also include rules for communication (perhaps based on Habermas's ideal speech situation) and the referencing to sources so that it becomes possible to trace the development of the ideas. The process would also need to be open and freely accessible to all.

7. Conclusion

The IASB needs to provide a stipulative and operational definition of the public interest in international financial accounting, reporting and regulation in order to lend credibility to its claim of serving the public interest. Such a definition will need to refer to the relation between performance concepts and the functions of financial accounting and external reporting in different institutional environments. In today's world where economic globalization has progressed much further than political globalization, and which is creating perverse incentives and opportunities for private gain at public expense, the public interest deserves to be taken seriously.

Notes

1 www.ifac.org/publications-resources/2010-handbook-code-ethics-professional-accountants.
2 The empirical evidence for the EMH in its semi-strong form, even in the US, appears ambiguous and inconclusive. This is not surprising, because ideological bias may play a part in research design and interpretation of the results on either side (Frankfurter and McGoun, 1999). Furthermore, in some countries with very different institutional environments, for example Arab countries, there is little evidence to support even the weak form of the EMH (Abdmoullah, 2010). Selected Asian markets showed excess returns before the 1997 Asian crisis (Chancharoenchai *et al.*, 2005). Socialist China, with its segmented capital market and many state-owned companies also shows little evidence of capital market efficiency (Wang *et al.*, 2009).
3 In economics, the general idea dates at least to Kuznets (1955), but the term equality–efficiency trade off and the general argument were probably made popular by Okun (1975).
4 www.iasplus.com/agenda/perform.htm, accessed 21 October 2011.
5 Title based on Milanovic (2003).
6 www.iasb.org/NR/rdonlyres/A490566E-EFF5-4F27-8DEF-D2ECCF9C5FFF/0/Trustees_Strategy_Review_2011.pdf, accessed 28 May 2011.
7 www.iasplus.com/country/useias.htm, accessed 6 September 2012.

Bibliography

AAA (1936) *A Tentative Statement of Accounting Principles Underlying Corporate Financial Statements.* Sarasota, FL: American Accounting Association.

AAA (1948) *Accounting Concepts and Standards Underlying Corporate Financial Statements.* Sarasota, FL: American Accounting Association.

AAA (1966) *A Statement of Basic Accounting Theory*. Sarasota, FL: American Accounting Association.

AAA (1977) *Statement on Accounting Theory and Theory Acceptance.* Sarasota, FL: American Accounting Association.

Abdmoulah, W. (2010) 'Testing the Evolving Efficiency of Arab Stock Markets'. *International Review of Financial Analysis* 19: 25–34.

AICPA (1970) *Basic Concepts and Accounting Principles Underlying Financial Statements of Business Enterprises.* American Institute of Certified Public Accountants.

AICPA (1973) *Objectives of Financial Statements.* Durham, NC: American Institute of Certified Public Accountants.

Akerlof, G.A. and Shiller, R.J. (2009) *Animal Spirits: How the Human Psychology Drives the Economy and Why It Matters for Global Capitalism.* Princeton, NJ: Princeton University Press.

Alchian, A.A. and Demsetz, H. (1972) 'Production, Information Costs and Economic Organization'. *The American Economic Review* 62 (5): 777–95.

Arrow, K.J. (1950) 'A Difficulty in the Concept of Social Welfare'. *Journal of Political Economy* 58 (4): 328–46.

Ball, R.J. and Brown, P. (1968) 'An Empirical Evaluation of Accounting Income Numbers'. *Journal of Accounting Research* 6 (2):159–78.

Barth, M. and Taylor, D. (2010) 'In Defense of Fair Value: Weighing the Evidence on Earnings Management and Asses Securitizations'. *Journal of Accounting and Economics* 49: 26–33.

Barton, A.D. (1974) 'Expectations and Achievements in Income Theory'. *The Accounting Review* 49 (4): 664–81.

Basu, K. (2011) *Beyond the Invisible Hand: Groundwork for a New Economics.* Princeton, NJ: Princeton University Press.

Beaver, W.H. (1998) *Financial Reporting: An Accounting Revolution*, 3rd edn. Upper Saddle River, NJ: Prentice-Hall.

Bromwich, M. (1980) 'The Possibility of Partial Accounting Standards', *The Accounting Review* 55(2): 288–300.

Bromwich, M. (1992) *Financial Reporting, Information and Capital Markets.* London: Pitman Publishing.

Bushman, R. and Landsman, W.R. (2010) 'The Pros and Cons of Regulating Corporate Reporting: A Critical Review of the Arguments'. *Accounting and Business Research* 40 (3): 259–73.

Cairns, D. (2007) 'The Use of Fair Value in IFRS', in Walton, P. (ed.) *The Routledge Companion to Fair Value and Financial Reporting*, Chapter 2, pp. 9–23. London: Routledge.

Canning, J.B. (1929) *The Economics of Accountancy.* New York: The Ronald Press Company.

Canning, M. and O'Dwyer, B. (2001) 'Professional Accounting Bodies' Disciplinary Procedures: Accountable, Transparent and in the Public Interest?' *Accounting, Auditing and Accountability Journal* 10 (4): 725–49.

Cearns, K., Australian Accounting Standards Board, Canadian Accounting Standards Board, International Accounting Standards Committee, New Zealand Financial Reporting Standards Board, United Kingdom Accounting Standards Board, United States Financial Accounting Standards Board (1999) *Reporting Financial Performance: Proposals For Change* (G4 + 1 Position Paper). London: ASB, available at www.frc.org.uk/Our-Work/Publications/ASB/Reporting-Financial-Performance-Proposals-for-Chan.aspx, accessed 11 March 2013.

Chambers, R.J. (1976) 'The Possibility of a Normative Accounting Standard'. *The Accounting Review* 51 (3): 646–52.

Chancharoenchai, K., Dibooglu, S. and Mathur, I. (2005) 'Stock Returns and the Macroeconomic Environment Prior to the Asian Crisis in Selected Southeast Asian Countries' *Emerging Markets Finance and Trade* 41 (4): 38–56.

Cochran, C.E. (1974) 'Political Science and "The Public Interest"'. *The Journal of Politics* 36 (2): 327–55.

Collier, P. (2008) *The Bottom Billion.* Oxford: Oxford University Press.

Corbin, D.A. (1962) 'The Revolution in Accounting'. *The Accounting Review* 37 (4): 626–35.

Crane, A. and Matten, D. (2007) *Business Ethics*, 2nd edn. Oxford: Oxford University Press.

Cushing, B.E. (1977) 'On the Possibility of Optimal Accounting Principles'. *The Accounting Review* 52 (2): 308–21.

Dellaportas, S. and Davenport, L. (2008) 'Reflections of the Public Interest in Accounting'. *Critical Perspectives on Accounting* 19 (7): 1080–98.

Demsetz, H. (1967) 'Toward a Theory of Property Rights'. *American Economic Review* 57 (2): 347–59.

Demski, J.S. (1973) 'The General Impossibility of Normative Accounting Standards'. *The Accounting Review* 48 (4): 718–23.

Douglass, B. (1980) 'The Common Good and the Public Interest'. *Political Theory* 8 (1): 103–17.

Duska, R., Shay Duska, B. and Ragatz, J. (2011) *Accounting Ethics*, 2nd edn. John Wiley & Sons.

Fama, E.F. (1965) 'The Behaviour of Stock Market Prices'. *Journal of Business* 38: 34–105.

FASB (1978) *Statement of Financial Accounting Concepts No. 1: Objectives of Financial Reporting by Business Enterprises*. Norwalk, CT: Financial Accounting Standards Board.

FASB (1980) *Statement of Financial Accounting Concepts No. 3: Elements of Financial Statements of Business Enterprises*. Norwalk, CT: Financial Accounting Standards Board.

Foreman-Peck, J. (1995) 'Accounting in the Industrialization of Western Europe', in Walton, P. (ed) *European Financial Reporting: A History*. Burlington, MA: Academic Press Limited.

Frankfurter, G.M. and McGoun, E.G. (1999) 'Ideology and the Theory of Financial Economics'. *Journal of Economic Behavior and Organization*, 39: 159–77.

Gambling, T. (1977) 'Magic, Accounting and Morale'. *Accounting, Organizations and Society* 2 (2): 141–51.

Gerschenkron, A. (1962) *Economic Backwardness in Historical Perspective: A Book of Essays*. Cambridge MA: Belknap Press of Harvard University Press.

Grossman, S.J. and Stiglitz, J.E. (1980) 'On the Impossibility of Informationally Efficient Markets'. *American Economic Review* 70 (3): 393–408.

Hutchings, K. (2010) *Global Ethics: An Introduction*. Cambridge: Polity Press.

IASB (2010a) *The Conceptual Framework for Financial Reporting*. London: International Accounting Standards Board, September 2010.

IASB (2010b) *Exposure Draft: Presentation of Items of Other Comprehensive Income*. London: International Accounting Standards Board, May 2010.

IASB (2010c) *Staff Paper: Presentation of Items of Other Comprehensive Income – Comment letter analysis*. London: International Accounting Standards Board, October 2010.

IASC (1989) *Framework for the Preparation and Presentation of Financial Statements*, London: International Accounting Standards Committee.

ICAEW (2012) *Acting in the Public Interest: A Framework for Analysis*. London: Institute of Chartered Accountants in England and Wales.

IFRS Foundation (2010) *IFRS Foundation Constitution*. London: IFRS Foundation. Available at www.iasb.org/NR/rdonlyres/B611DD9A-F4FB-4A0D-AEC9-0036F6895BEF/0/Constitution2010.pdf, accessed 30 September 2012.

IFRS Foundation (2011) *Report of the Trustees' Strategy Review, IFRSs as the Global Standard: Setting a Strategy for the Foundation's Second Decade*. April, London: IFRS Foundation.

IFRS Foundation (2012) *IFRSs as Global Standards: Setting a Strategy for the Foundation's Second Decade*. Available at www.ifrs.org/NR/rdonlyres/37493F6D-3E73-4ED8-A993-23D57BC76B68/0/TrusteesStrategyReviewFeb2012.pdf, accessed 17 April 2012.

IFRS Foundation (2013) 'Constitution', available at www.ifrs.org/The-organisation/Governance-and-accountability/Constitution/Documents/IFRS-Foundation-Constitution-January-2013.pdf, accessed 11 March 2013.

Jensen, M. and Meckling, W. (1976) 'Theory of the Firm: Managerial Behaviour, Agency Costs and Ownership Structure'. *Journal of Financial Economics* October: 305–60.

Johnson, O. and Gunn, S. (1974) 'Conflict Resolution: The Market and/or Accounting?'. *The Accounting Review* (4): 649–63.

Johnson, S.B. and Solomons, D. (1984) 'Institutional Legitimacy and the FASB'. *Journal of Accounting and Public Policy* 3 (3): 165–83.

King, S.M., Chilton, B.S. and Roberts, G.E. (2010) 'Reflection of Defining the Public Interest'. *Administration and Society* 41 (8): 954–78.

Kothari, S.P., Ramanna, K. and Skinner, D.J. (2010) 'Implications for GAAP from an Analysis of Positive Research in Accounting'. *Journal of Accounting and Economics* (50): 246–86.

Kraakman, R., Armour, J., Davies, P., Enriques, L., Hansmann, H., Hertig, G., Hopt, K., Kanda, H. and Rock, E. (2009) *The Anatomy of Corporate Law: A Comparative and Functional Approach*. Oxford and New York: Oxford University Press.

Kuznets, S. (1955) 'Economic Growth and Income Inequality'. *American Economic Review* 45: 1–28.

Laux, C. and Leuz, C. (2009) 'The Crisis of Fair Value Accounting: Making Sense of the Recent Debate'. *Accounting, Organizations and Society* 34: 826–34.

Lee, T. (1995) 'The Professionalisation of Accountancy: A History of Protecting the Public Interest in a Self-Interested Way'. *Accounting, Auditing and Accountability Journal* 3 (3): 48–69.

Lemke, K.W. (1966) 'Asset Valuation and Income Theory'. *The Accounting Review* 41 (1): 32–41.

Leuz, C. (2010) 'Different Approaches to Corporate Reporting Regulation: How Jurisdictions Differ and Why'. *Accounting and Business Research* 40 (3): 229–56.

Lev, B. (1988) 'Toward a Theory of Equitable and Efficient Accounting Policy'. *The Accounting Review* 63 (1): 1–22.

Lucas, R. (1990) 'Why Doesn't Capital Flow from Rich to Poor Countries?'. *American Economic Review* 80 (2): 92–6.

Merino, B.D. (2003) 'Financial Reporting in the 1930s in the United States Preserving the Status Quo'. *Accounting Forum* 27 (3): 270–90.

Milanovic, B. (2003) 'The Two Faces of Globalization: Against Globalization as We Know It'. *World Development* 31 (4): 667–83.

Milanovic, B. (2011) *The Haves and the Have-Nots*. New York: Basic Books.

Mishkin, F.S. (2006) *The Next Great Globalization: How Disadvantaged Nations Can Harness Their Financial Systems to Get Rich*. Princeton, NJ: Princeton University Press.

Okun, A. (1975) *Equality and Efficiency: The Big Tradeoff*. Washington DC: Brookings Institution.

Olson, M. (1971) *The Logic of Collective Action: Public Goods and the Theory of Groups*. Cambridge, MA: Harvard University Press.

Philips, G.E. (1963) 'The Revolution in Accounting Theory'. *The Accounting Review* 38 (4): 696–708.

Rajan, R.G. (2010) *Fault lines: How Hidden Fractures Still Threaten the World Economy*. Princeton, NJ, and Oxford: Princeton University Press.

Revsine, L. (1970) 'On the Correspondence Between Replacement Cost Income and Economic Income'. *The Accounting Review* 45 (3): 513–23.

Riahi-Belkaoui, A. (2004) *Accounting Theory*, 5th edn. South-Western: Cengage Learning.

Robinson, L.E. (1991). 'The Time Has Come to Report Comprehensive Income'. *Accounting Horizons* June, 107–12.

Sanders, T.H., Hatfield, H.R. and Moore, U. (1938), *A Statement of Accounting Principles* New York: American Institute of Accountants.

Schroeder, Richard G., Clark, Myrtle W. and Cathey, Jack M. (2001) *Financial Accounting Theory and Analysis*, 7th edn. New York: John Wiley & Sons.

Scott, W.R. (1997) *Financial Accounting Theory*, international edn. Upper Saddle River, NJ: Prentice-Hall.

Shleifer, A. and Vishny, R.W. (1998) *The Grabbing Hand: Government Pathologies and Their Cures*. Cambridge MA: Harvard University Press.

Sikka, P., Wilmott, H. and Lowe, T. (1989) 'Guardians of Knowledge and Public Interest: Evidence and Issues of Accountability in the UK Accounting Profession'. *Accounting, Auditing and Accountability Journal* 2 (2): 47–71.

Skott, P. and Ryoo, S. (2008) 'Macroeconomic Implications of Financialization'. *Cambridge Journal of Economics*. 32, 827–62.

Solomons, D. (1961) 'Economic and Accounting Concepts of Income' *The Accounting Review* 36 (3): 374–83.

Sprouse, R.T. and Moonitz, M. (1962) *A Tentative Set of Broad Accounting Principles*, Accounting Research Study No. 3. New York: American Institute of Certified Public Accountants.

Staubus, G.J. (1961) *A Theory of Accounting to Investors*. Berkeley, CA: University of California Press.

Wang, W., Liu, L. and Gu, R. (2009) 'Analysis of Efficiency for Shenzen Stock Market Based on Multifractal Detrended Fluctuation Analysis' *International Review of Financial Analysis* 18: 271–276.

Watts, R.L. and Zimmerman, J.L. (1978) 'Towards a Positive Theory of the Determination of Accounting Standards'. *The Accounting Review*. 53 (1), 112–34.

Whittington, G. (2005) 'The Adoption of International Accounting Standards in the European Union'. *European Accounting Review* 14 (1): 127–53.

Whittington, G. (2008) 'Fair Value and the IASB/FASB Conceptual Framework Project: An Alternative View'. *ABACUS*. 44 (2), 139–68.

Wyatt, A. (1983) 'Efficient Market Theory: Its Impact on Accounting'. *Journal of Accountancy* (February): 56–65.

11

Perspectives on the Role of and Need for Accounting Regulation

Lisa Baudot

1. Introduction

This chapter examines different perspectives on the role of and need for the regulation of accounting information. Accounting information is distinguished in this chapter as information on the economic activities of the firm including information presented on the face of the financial statements as well as information disclosed in the footnotes to the financial statements or through other means of disclosure. This information can serve the role of communicating with both public and private sources, where 'public' in this sense refers to the debt and equity (capital) markets and 'private' refers to other, non-market providers of financing. The perspectives presented in this chapter focus primarily on regulation in jurisdictions in which the primary role of accounting information is its usefulness to shareholders in making investment decisions in the capital markets. However, the primary role of accounting information in many economies has been on information useful to other stakeholders and for purposes outside of capital market decision-making (i.e. stewardship, debt contracting, etc). The chapter also addresses the perspectives on such non-market roles of accounting information albeit to a lesser extent as globalization has in a large way shifted the focus of accounting information worldwide such that the capital market role of accounting information has become more and more relevant and, to a certain extent, reduced its non-market roles.

The bulk of this chapter is organized around the arguments refuting the need for accounting regulation and the arguments confirming the need for accounting regulation. Before entering into these debates, Section 2 provides the platform for these debates in presenting a historical overview of regulatory developments in a number of environments, that of the United Kingdom, the United States, France and Germany. Section 3 then looks at the theoretical arguments refuting the need for regulating accounting information, the problematics of unregulated information and the theoretical arguments promoting regulation as solutions to these problematics. Section 4 goes on to discuss different perspectives on the nature of regulation, the beneficiaries of such regulation, and the motivations of the various regulatory structures from a socio-political perspective as well as a professional-practice perspective. Section 5 concludes.

2. A brief history of the development of regulation[1]

Financial accounting as practice can be traced back to the thirteenth and fourteenth centuries; however, the regulation of accounting information in most economies has only developed during the past two hundred years. Despite its relative youth, the regulation of business enterprise, and the regulation of accounting information that accompanied it, is a phenomenon with deep roots. This section traces those roots through the eras of industrialization in the UK, the US, France and Germany, distinguishing the particularities of each setting and the influence of those particularities on the way in which accounting regulation developed.

2.1 Anglo-American development of regulation[2]

The eighteenth and nineteenth centuries in the UK were marked by transformation from an agricultural-based economy towards commercial and manufacturing activities. Business enterprises during this period were small, with owners directly involved in day-to-day control of operations, and financial information was largely outside the public domain. As such, accounting information served mainly as a stewardship function. However, growth in the size of business enterprises in the post-Industrial Revolution period brought about the separation of ownership and control, changing the role of accounting information dramatically. This change was necessitated in order to adapt the stewardship role of accounting information to the reporting of information to owners no longer directly involved in managing the day-to-day operations of the company.

Changes to the way in which business enterprises were formed in the UK further transformed the role of accounting information in the nineteenth century. For instance, the Joint Stock Companies Act of 1844 allowed business enterprises to be incorporated by registration.[3] Registration required the company to maintain 'books of account', to present a balance sheet but no profit and loss statement at shareholders meetings and to file such information with the Registrar of joint stock companies (Nobes and Parker, 2004). In addition, the Act required the appointment of auditors and the preparation of an audit report for the annual shareholders meetings; however, the auditing profession had not then been formally established.

While the 1844 Act intended to cultivate business and increase the public's confidence in economic institutions, the prevailing attitude of the state not to interfere in business matters was apparent and the new joint stock companies found the requirements of the Act simple enough to breach. The Joint Stock Companies Act of 1856 abandoned mandatory requirements in favour of a voluntary model containing clauses for both accounting information and the audit of that information. Further, where the 1844 Act had not addressed shareholder liability, it was followed in 1855 by the Limited Liability Act which restricted the liability of the individual owners of a business enterprise to their personal investment in the company. These changes appear to have been the result of the view that shareholders (and creditors) were free to enter into an agreement with management and that such agreements were matters of private contract.

Near the turn of the century the Company Law Amendment of 1895 brought accounting information back into the public domain with the mandatory filing of annual balance sheets with the Registrar; however, there was a general absence of guidance on filing requirements that went unresolved until the Companies Act of 1948. The 1948 Act not only reinstated the accounting and audit requirements of the 1844 Act but made those requirements much more explicit. For example, all companies were called on to file consolidated, audited financial information showing a 'true and fair view'[4] and providing many new disclosure requirements designed to preserve financial stability and encourage investor confidence in the market. Some tend to consider the requirements of the UK Companies Act of 1929/1948 as the basis for the requirements which would follow not long after in the US environment.

Similar to the UK, the industrialization of the US economy engendered profound changes in the nature of business enterprise. In particular, the second half of the nineteenth century saw a wealthy group of industrialists, including the Carnegie steel, Rockefeller oil, and Vanderbilt railroad trusts, come to dominate fractions of the developing economy through the consolidation of their industrial holdings (Lamoreaux, 1985). The wealth of these trusts, and the economic and political power they demonstrated, prefigured even more profound trends. Those trends came in the development of a new form of economic organization – the corporation – which captured markets across sectors and regions, and the emergence of new centres of financial power to accommodate the capital requirements of these corporations (Lamoreaux, 1985).

The rise of these corporations and financial centres may be seen as inadvertently fashioning the US regulatory state because it was in response to the rise of business power that the appeal for regulation originated (Djankov *et al.*, 2003). For example, debates over the potentially abusive power of trusts and corporations are largely considered to have prompted the passage of the Sherman Act in 1890 which aimed to restrict the capacity of the new corporations to manipulate market competition (Moran, 2010). However, events of the early twentieth century reignited the tradition of suspicion of big business, and especially of big business identified with the money trusts of Wall Street. These events include the collapse of production, mass unemployment, and revelations of fraud, culminating in financial catastrophe with the stock market crash of 1929 and the subsequent economic depression (Moran, 2010). Out of this came the 'New Deal', a series of social and economic reforms which created some of the key institutions of the US regulatory state and instilled a distinctly US way of structuring the relations between business and the state (Moran, 1991). The new regulatory institutions were structured to restore public confidence in the capital market through a kind of cooperation between business and the state represented by a series of securities legislations.

First, the Securities Act of 1933 required any offer or sale of securities to be registered as opposed to governed by state laws as they had been previously. While the 1933 Act applies to the original issue of securities, the secondary trading of those securities falls under the purview of the Securities Exchange Act of 1934. The 1934 Act established the requirement for companies seeking to trade their securities to provide periodic reporting of accounting information and independent verification of that information, and also formally established the Securities and Exchange Commission (SEC) as the federal agency responsible for regulating the securities markets. The primary function of the SEC is to ensure that issuers fully disclose all accounting information that a reasonable shareholder would require in making investment decisions. As such, the Acts aim to protect capital market investors not only by ensuring the availability of accurate and complete accounting information but also through establishing penalties for non-compliance with the Acts.

In contrast to the focus on the control of private business enterprises in the UK and the protection of capital market investors in the US, creditor protection has been at the crux of French and German financial regulation for several centuries. Zysman (1983) distinguished the French system as credit-based governmental compared to the German system of credit-based financial institutions. The historical development of the role of accounting information in these two systems is highlighted within this section.

2.2 Continental European development of regulation[5]

From the eighteenth-century French Revolution, business tradition recognized private property as the key organizing principle of economic activity. Therefore, the establishment of property rights laws that supported the existence of small agricultural holdings, small family-owned businesses and the defence of private wealth represents an early influence on the role of accounting information in France. In this environment, a form of accounting emerged which placed primary emphasis on the balance sheet as opposed to income or cash flows with a focus on debt, solvency, liquidity and capital maintenance (Nioche and Pesqueux, 1997). The primacy of this role of accounting information was also reflected in how French public companies took shape during the Industrial Revolution in the early nineteenth century.

The Industrial Revolution in France was spearheaded by a small number of entrepreneurs who addressed the considerable financial and management resources necessitated by the growing industrial environment through partnership formation (Nioche and Pesqueux, 1997). Partnerships therefore became the dominant business structure with a smaller number of business enterprises, which were either directly or indirectly state run, seeking financing through incorporation as joint-stock companies. The right to incorporation was consolidated within Napoleon's 'Code de Commerce' ('Commercial Code') of 1807. While French companies were previously created by a special act of the French state, the 'Code' allowed joint-stock companies to be formed according to general company laws though the state's permission was still required. In addition, the 'Code' recognized limited liability for members of the joint stock company. Ultimately, the 'Code' came to serve as a model for later European statutes, including the one in Germany discussed in this section.

Through the Companies Act of 1856, financial accounting requirements in France, as elsewhere, grew out of the desire for limited liability companies to publish their accounts. However, these requirements were created in consideration of the particularities of the structure of business as largely controlled by the state. Other influences on the role of accounting information in the French credit-based governmental system included the introduction of income taxes in 1920 and a doctrine of fiscal administration. Finally, the role of accounting information in the French system is influenced by the French 'Plan Comptable Général' ('PCG' - General Chart of Accounts) of 1947. The objective of the 'PCG' was to facilitate better government decision making and therefore maintained the focus on debt and solvency issues as opposed to profitability (Nioche and Pesqueux, 1997). However, all business forms are covered by the 'PCG' and follow the same accounting procedures and formats despite having objectives which may vary from national fiscal and economic policy.

Corporate ownership remained in the hands of the state and families through the late 1980s and early 1990s when a significant number of corporations owned by the state went public lessening the direct influence of the government on the economy. Up until this period of deregulation, nationalized financial institutions had been an important tool in providing financing for firms and supporting critical industries. The relationship between the banks and the public companies were regulated by contracts designed to ensure that the future actions of the firm comply with solvency and liquidity covenants thereby limiting dividends to shareholders and highlighting the role of accounting information in this environment in private contracting.

Similarly, the German business environment is characterized by large holdings by financial institutions that not only provide loans to companies but also control major proportions of firms' equity capital (Leuz and Wustemann, 2004). Here, the creditor protection principle emphasizing the need to protect creditors against losses is so fundamental to German accounting that dividend restriction is built directly into accounting rules. The German focus on creditor protection was established with the introduction of early German law such as the 'Preußisches Allgemeines Landrecht' ('ALR' – Prussian Civil Code) of 1794. The 'ALR' required business enterprises to maintain orderly records of their transactions and was intended to reinforce growing creditor involvement in trade activities and serve as evidence which could be used in the protection of creditors in court proceedings (Eierle, 2005).

Creditor protection gained additional importance in the German financial reporting model through nineteenth-century enactments such as the 'Allgemeines Deutsches Handelsgesetzbuch' ('ADHGB'– General German Commercial Code) of 1861. This was superseded by the 'Handelsgesetzbuch' ('HGB' - German Commercial Code) of 1897 which remains the basis for accounting in Germany today. The 'ADHGB' was strongly influenced by the French Code whose measures had emerged within an environment of state control over business (Eierle, 2005). As such, debates arose about the appropriateness of the 'ADHGB' when applied within the German economy and in 1897 the legislators enacted the 'HGB'. The 'HGB' further adapted the 'ADHGB' towards the principle of prudence (i.e. historical cost approach and conservatism) in acknowledging the extensive participation of government and banks in business transactions (Eierle, 2005).

The importance of creditor protection is also revealed through a number of other enactments. For example, the role of accounting information in Germany is also influenced by income tax law which dictates that the (prudence) principles of the 'HGB' shall be applied in determining the tax accounts. Further, the enactment of Public Company Law of 1884, which occurred in reaction to a significant loss of investor funds after the collapse of a number of important corporations during the late 1800s, led to rules for restricting excessive capital distribution (Eierle, 2005). Likewise, economic crisis in Germany during the early 1900s led to the enactment of the Stock Corporation Emergency Decree of 1931 and to the Stock Corporation Law of 1937. These enactments specified extensive modifications with regard to financial reporting in annual financial statements, yet maintained the traditional principles of creditor protection given the continued financing role of financial institutions and the state.

3. Accounting regulatory debates: economic burden or necessary evil?

As indicated in the previous section, the regulation of accounting information is a fairly recent phenomenon which developed with the role of accounting information in different environments. In the Anglo-environment, the regulation of accounting information developed alongside the role of accounting information in the public debt and equity (capital) markets. On the other hand, while the capital markets have played a more recent role in the regulation of accounting information in the EU, the early primacy of other sources of financing, i.e. government and financial institutions, translated to a greater role for accounting information provided to non-market actors. This section presents the competing schools of thought on the need for regulation in consideration of these varied roles for accounting information.

3.1 Considerations refuting the need for regulation

> There is one and only one social responsibility of business – to use its resources and engage in activities designed to increase its profits so long as it stays within the rules of the game, which is to say, engages in open and free competition without deception or fraud.
>
> *Milton Friedman, Economist*

The fundamental argument against regulation (i.e. for reducing or eliminating regulation) proposes that accounting information should be treated like any other economic good and that forces of demand and supply, as opposed to regulatory forces, should be allowed to determine the optimal amount of information to be produced (Buchanan, 1968). In the 'market' for accounting information, financial statement users represent the demanders of information while managers/firms act as the suppliers. The quantity of accounting information produced will then be a function of the amount of information that financial statement users demand and managers/firms supply (Sunder, 2002). As the primary users are linked to the role of accounting information in a given economy, users of information in environments where financing is raised in the public markets will demand different types of information and in different ways than users of information in environments where financing is obtained through non-market sources.

For example, in a system based on sources of capital obtained from the public debt or equity markets, users of accounting information who are ultimately potential investor-owners will reside largely outside of the firm where they do not have access to the same level of information as managers of the firm (Ball *et al.*, 2000). This raises the possibility of what is referred to as 'information asymmetry' in that the managers, as firm insiders, know more than the investors, as firm outsiders, about the true state of a firm's performance (Stigler, 1961). Argumentation, based on the work of Arrow (1963), Akerlof (1970), Jensen and Meckling (1976) and Watts and Zimmerman (1978), shows how private incentives encourage a firm and its management to voluntarily provide full and credible information to outsiders, reducing the information asymmetry issue, and negating the need for regulatory action.

The capital market-based system can be contrasted with the system in which a firm relies more on financing from non-market sources. In the second type of system, firm insiders establish close relationships through contracts with banks and other financial intermediaries (Leuz, 2010) and the focus of accounting information facilitates the protection of these contractual arrangements by limiting the claims of firm outsiders to dividends and external payments (Leuz and Wustemann, 2004). Here, the need for regulation is refuted in that private channels of communication keep key contracting parties reasonably well informed. However, the traditionally low focus on public dissemination of information in this system means that, as capital markets grow, investors face a potential lack of transparency in not having access to these private communications, bringing us back to the problem of information asymmetry (Ball *et al.*, 2000). The information asymmetry-based arguments refuting the need for regulation involves a presentation of the notions of adverse selection and moral hazard as well as a consideration of the role of governance factors. These notions are introduced in the following sections.

3.1.1 Adverse selection

Adverse selection refers to a situation of asymmetric information presented by firms which results in the highest quality firms being squeezed out because they are unable to distinguish themselves as high-quality to potential investors. The theory, developed in the 1970s by George Akerlof, was based on a study of the used car market (i.e. the market for 'lemons'[6]). Akerlof's study determined that buyers might be willing to pay for high-quality used cars; however, it is difficult for them to distinguish high-quality cars from low-quality cars given that the sellers of the cars do not have an incentive to be completely honest. Thus, asymmetric information between buyers and sellers regarding true quality causes the buyers, fearing to get a 'lemon', to offer only a lemon price. On the other hand, the sellers offer only lemons for sale, so the high-quality used cars are 'driven' out of the market.

Adverse selection translates to the accounting environment in terms of the information exchange between market participants where buyers (i.e. outsiders = investors/creditors) have access to less information than sellers (i.e. insiders = firms/managers). As the outsiders do not have the same level of information as the insiders, they are hesitant to invest, doubting that they can make good investment decisions on the basis of limited or potentially biased information (Kothari *et al.*, 2010). Firms will be encouraged to provide sufficient and credible information to the market, even if that information represents 'bad news', in order to avoid being punished for the absence of information (Grossman, 1981; Kothari *et al.*, 2010).

Punishment can potentially affect the liquidity of the firms' stocks and occurs through shareholders reducing the amount they will pay for shares and securities analysts or investment managers penalizing firms through negative reputational information (Bushman and Landsman, 2010). Therefore, firms and managers have an incentive to voluntarily supply accounting information in order to reduce information asymmetry and avoid punishment. Firms can reduce information asymmetry even further by ensuring the accounting information that they supply to the market is credible and are presumed to do so by subjecting such information to voluntary certifications by independent auditors (Fama and Jensen, 1983). Finally, as discussed in the section on pro-regulatory arguments, financial reporting and disclosure regulation itself is another possible factor reducing adverse selection issues.

3.1.2 Moral hazard

Moral hazard involves information asymmetry in a contracting situation in which one party has more information than the other. The party that has more information, feeling protected from risk or at least from the consequences of their actions, has the tendency to perform at a less than desirable level, leaving the second party to hold the risk/responsibility for the first party's actions. The party with more information has no incentive to consider the full costs of their behaviour to the other party due to the protection they perceive under the contract and the fact that their behaviour cannot be fully observed by the other party.

Moral hazard translates to the accounting environment through the information exchange between contracting parties who maintain ownership (or accept financing risk) of firms versus parties who maintain management control. The relationship between such parties has been characterized in the literature by Jensen and Meckling (1976) as a principal–agent relation (i.e. agency theory[7]). Under this theory, conflict between ownership (financing risk) and management control functions results because the agents (managers) who control the firm's operating activities clearly have more information about their own actions and intentions than the principals (shareholders or creditors). In the absence of information, the shareholders or creditors of the firm will assume that managers may be operating the business with the goal of maximizing their personal wealth rather than with the aim of maximizing firm value or meeting the requirements of contractual debt covenants (Kothari *et al.*, 2010).

The focus is then on designing manager incentives in such a way that, even under conditions of asymmetric information, the manager's goals of wealth maximization can be more closely aligned with shareholders' (creditors) presumed goals (Watts and Zimmerman, 1986). Addressing the moral hazard problem involves measuring and presenting financial information in a way that accomplishes contracting goals through management performance. This implies constraining managers through contractual commitments so that certain strategies against the interests of shareholders and creditors will not be undertaken. For example, management contracts with shareholders may require the managers' performance to be tied to profits; contracts with bond holders may require profits to cover interest expense by a number of times; and contracts with financial institutions may require adhering to certain solvency and liquidity ratios.

What is clear is that contract terms are often tied to accounting information and here the perspective refuting the need for regulation deems the contracting parties to be in the best position to determine both the terms and the information that should be produced (Leuz, 2010) to satisfy and resolve potential moral hazard issues. Under this view, regulation is seen as restricting the set of accounting methods available for producing information and implies that some managers will be prohibited from using the accounting methods which they believe best reflect their particular performance and position relative to their contractual obligations (Leuz and Wustermann, 2004). However, the methods which managers believe best reflect their particular performance and position may also be the most opportunistic methods; those bringing the most personal wealth to the manager and potentially shifting wealth from the shareholders.

3.1.3 Governance factors

Where contracting may not provide absolute control over managerial opportunism, monitoring through governance by internal and/or external actors plays a role to further constrain such opportunism. Fama and Jensen (1983) identified several governance solutions to resolve contracting issues, including:

- accounting information being subject to verification by independent auditors;
- the market for corporate control; and
- the related market for the hiring/firing of managers.

Relative to the first governance solution, verification of financial information by an independent party is deemed to increase the reliability of accounting information and decrease the information asymmetry perceived by outsiders (Watts and Zimmerman, 1983). Those who favour unregulated accounting environments expect management to issue credible information for outsiders to monitor their behaviour in the market, which implies that financial statement audits could be expected to be undertaken even in the absence of regulation and some research provides evidence of this (e.g. Watts and Zimmerman, 1983).

The second set of governance solutions mentioned, the market for corporate control (hostile takeovers, mergers and acquisitions, etc.) and the market for management resources, assume that accounting information will be voluntarily produced due to perceived threats. In the first instance, the market for corporate control argument predicts that an underperforming firm will be taken over by another entity and the existing management team will be subsequently replaced. Under such threat, managers would be motivated to maximize firm value in order to minimize the likelihood that another entity could seize control of the firm. On the other hand, the market for management resources argument (Fama, 1980) assumes an efficient labour market in which managers' prior performance will impact their level of remuneration in future periods. Under the threat of not maximizing their future wealth, managers adopt strategies to provide a favourable view of their current performance by maximizing the value of the firm. However, both arguments assume that in maximizing firm value managers are able to determine the 'optimal' level of accounting information to provide.

Finally, the governance factors discussed previously apply more to environments in which the role of accounting information is to serve the needs of the capital market. In environments in which the role of accounting information is to (primarily) serve the needs of non-capital market sources of finance, such as governments and financial institutions, a different set of governance factors apply. For example, considering that financial institutions may not only play a major role in financing but also may control substantial equity stakes in a firm, these institutions are typically represented on the supervisory board of the firms they finance (Ball *et al.*, 2000).

The supervisory board is the main instrument of governance in the German environment, for instance, and the financial institution's role on the board and stake in the firm indicates that both governance and control are in the hands of insiders (Leuz and Wustermann, 2004). In this particular setting, the regulation of accounting information is argued to be unnecessary since the primary users of information represent parties to a contract who agree contractually to the accounting information to be privately communicated by the firm (Ball *et al.*, 2000).

3.2 Considerations supporting the need for regulation

> Regulations may, no doubt, be considered in some respect a violation of natural liberty. But exertions of the natural liberty of a few individuals, which might endanger the security of the whole society, are, and ought to be, restrained by the laws of all governments; the most free as well as the most tyrannical.
>
> *Adam Smith, Political Economist*

The previous section highlighted a number of reasons refuting the need for accounting regulation. The primary reasoning given was that accounting information is similar to any other economic good and, as such, financial statement users will demand information to the extent it is useful and firms will supply the desired information. Here, it was argued that firms will voluntarily produce accounting information without regulation mandating that they do so in order to avoid any potentially negative consequences of uncertainty about the firm. The consequences of uncertainty were presented as potentially increased costs of capital to the firm or increased reputational and labour market risks to the manager.

Again, these arguments relied on the view that accounting information is an economic good, analogous to a product or service produced and consumed in a market that operates efficiently (Fama, 1970). Fama's 'efficient market hypothesis' states that markets fully reflect at all times the collective knowledge and information that is publicly available. As such, wealth maximizing investors will take new information into consideration in their investing decisions immediately upon the release of that information (Fama, 1970). Yet markets have been shown to not always operate efficiently so that the other side of the argument is that intervention in the form of regulation is necessary in order to compensate for inefficiency in the supply and demand of information (Taylor and Turley, 1986). In addition, the true nature of accounting information is such that consumers do not pay for the information being produced as they do for economic goods. Therefore, a consideration must be made for the need for regulation from the perspective that accounting information is a not an economic good but a social good and, as such, must be regulated so as to protect society from its potentially negative consequences.

3.2.1 Inefficient markets

The efficient market hypothesis has been challenged as inconsistent with the 'real world' behaviour of the market. For example, at the market level, observations of excess stock market volatility and stock market bubbles – and at the extreme financial crises and stock market crashes – all indicate that the market does not operate efficiently. At the investor level, investors may not incorporate all available information contemporaneously and investor reactions may be biased, constrained or overconfident. Finally, additional evidence of market inefficiency has been noted at the firm level based on firms that produce fraudulent or misleading information which investors are generally unable to evaluate as to its faithful representation (or reliability), due to a situation of information asymmetry.

This situation brings us back to the arguments from Section 3.1, which assumed that firms and management are incentivized to voluntarily provide sufficient and credible information to the market. Critics of the unregulated view propose that, in the absence of regulation, firms may not voluntarily provide the information that users desire to make informed assessments about the firm. In addition, critics consider the ability to secure sufficient information about a firm as being based on power and resources and assume that parties with limited power and limited resources will be ill-informed, worse informed or not informed in a timely manner (Sutton, 1984). Similarly, in an environment in which the role of accounting information is to serve the needs of non-market actors, where firms are more likely to provide accounting information only to private contracting parties, regulation can serve to ensure that outside parties also have access to private information (Leuz, 2010).

Such imbalances are considered to affect the overall social welfare, in that redistributions of wealth will occur on the basis of unequal access to information linked to uneven power and resources. Therefore, regulation protects investors from the information asymmetry resulting from unequal access to information (adverse selection) and uneven distributions of power (moral hazard) given the modern-day configuration of the firm. This argument for regulation can be thought of as a 'level playing field' argument that promotes equal access to the same information by all parties. On a level playing field, parties are presumed to have greater confidence that transfers of wealth are not occurring unfairly due to one party having access to more or different information which others do not have access to.

In addition to the question of equal access, there is the question of whether users of accounting information are capable of evaluating the credibility of the information they are presented with and the role that external audit plays in helping them to do so. The role of external audit, as indicated by Jensen and Meckling (1976), is one of reducing information asymmetry and increasing reliability through the monitoring and verification of a firm's financial reporting. In an unregulated environment, firms are presumed to not only present the desired level of accounting information but also to voluntarily submit that information to external verification. One only needs to consider the accounting scandals of the 1990s and early 2000s (i.e. Parmalat, Enron, Worldcom, etc.) and the ambiguous role that external audit and verification played in those scandals to question the validity of this argument.

Even with a high quality of external verification, the regulatory view sees regulation as necessary to manage the complexity of the market by setting the minimum requirements of reporting as well as the bounds within which that reporting must be prepared and presented, thereby minimizing the number of methods used, reducing the risk of 'creative' accounting, improving the level of transparency in reporting information, and increasing the amount of uniformity in accounting treatment. A similar argument may be made for regulation of accounting information which serves the needs of non-market actors in that regulation may help reduce transaction costs through a common set of rules for all or many contracts, rather than negotiating a particular set of rules on a contract-by-contract basis (Ball *et al.*, 2000). At the same time, Bromwich (1985) noted that, despite regulatory controls, firms continued to hold considerable discretion as to accounting practices and choices were often permitted in the method of dealing with given accounting items, which serves to refute the view that imposing regulation impacts firms' reporting efficiency. In summary, under the regulatory view, financial reporting and disclosure regulation is well thought to aid in ensuring that information asymmetry is reduced and to act as a mechanism by which misleading information is minimized.

3.2.2 Public goods

Under the regulatory view, accounting information is argued to have the characteristics of a social (or public) good (Olson, 1965).[8] This means that once accounting information is available, consumers (i.e. prospective shareholders) can use and share the information freely without incurring any associated costs of production for their use (Barth, 2006; Kothari *et al.*, 2010). As such, few users will have incentive to pay for accounting information as they know they themselves can act as 'free-riders' (Olson, 1965). The effect is that, in the presence of free-riders, demand is understated because users obtain accounting information at no cost. In turn, firms will under-produce information, given their own lack of incentive to produce above what users demand. In this sense the market mechanism fails due to the inability of market forces to produce the socially acceptable amount of information. Here, regulation is argued as necessary to reduce the impacts of market failure, in other words regulation is put forth as a mechanism for alleviating the underproduction of information by mandating the minimum requirements for information that firms might not otherwise provide (Barth, 2006; Kothari *et al.*, 2010).

As a public good, both the economic and social impacts of accounting information must be taken into consideration in the regulatory process. Such a view requires an extension from the view of investors and creditors as the primary users of accounting information to a view that encompasses other users. For example, other users can refer to a company's suppliers who seek information on whether amounts owed will be repaid when due, customers seeking information on probability of continued supply of products, parts and after sales service, or union and employee groups who desire information on the stability and distribution of wealth by the company. Users can also refer to the company's competitors interested in information on the relative strengths and weaknesses of the company for comparative and benchmarking purposes as well as social responsibility groups who monitor information on the use of the environment and natural resources, safety, protection and respect for human resources. Finally, users can refer to government agencies themselves interested in information on company profitability and operations for income tax purposes or information on payroll and benefits which affect state retirement/pension and medical systems. Such a complex societal web of users with their own demands for and uses of accounting information is indicative of the challenge regulatory bodies would seem to have in establishing accounting regulations socially acceptable to all users.

4. Considering the nature of accounting regulation: theory and practice

Once regulation is introduced there are various considerations to be made in terms of the nature of regulation, those responsible for developing regulation and their motivations, and the ultimate beneficiaries of such regulation. These considerations can be categorized as theoretical considerations and practical considerations. Each will be discussed in the following sections in terms of the relevant theories and practical matters put forth to explain accounting regulation.

4.1 Theoretical considerations

> We cannot expect that any public authority will attain, or will even whole-heartedly seek, the ideal. Such authorities are liable alike to ignorance, to sectional pressure and to personal corruption by private interest. A loud-voiced part of their constituents, if organized for votes, may easily outweigh the whole.
>
> *A.C. Pigou, Welfare Economist*

In this section, the theoretical perspectives shaping the nature of, motivation for and beneficiaries to regulation are presented and contrasted. These perspectives include both public interest theories and private interest theories. Public interest theory and its counterpart regulatory capture theory promote regulation as being (at least initially) designed to protect the public interest and are presented first. Later, the economic theory of regulation is discussed which explains how the design of regulation can be affected by, and come to serve, private interests.

4.1.1 Public interest theory

Advocates of the public interest theory (Pigou, 1932) of regulation see its purpose as achieving certain publicly desired results which, if left to the market, would not be obtained. The public interest theory of regulation proposes that regulation, supplied in response to public demand for the correction of inefficient or inequitable market practices, is designed to protect and benefit society as a whole rather than certain vested interests (Posner, 1974). As an example, new regulation is often established in response to high profile accounting failures where it is argued that such regulation will help prevent a repeat of the accounting failure and protect members of the public who have suffered a financial loss as a result of such failure. This can be seen with the enactment of the Securities Acts of 1933 and 1934 as well as with the enactment of stricter corporate governance regulations being imposed in many countries following the accounting failure at Enron, Worldcom, Parmalat and others in the early 2000s.

Under this theory, the regulatory body is presumed a neutral intermediary representing the public interest, one which allows neither its own self-interest to impact on the rule-making processes nor the self-interest of particular individuals/groups subject to regulation. As put by Scott (2003), the public interest regulator 'does its best to regulate so as to maximize social welfare. Consequently, regulation is thought of as a trade-off between the costs of regulation and its social benefits in the form of improved market efficiency'. As such, regulation represents the mechanism by which the public obtains confidence that capital markets efficiently allocate resources towards productive use. Public interest theory was the dominant view of regulation into the 1960s and still retains many adherents. However, determining what is 'in the public interest' is a normative question and the basis for objectively answering this question and then executing their objective function is often at issue (Kothari *et al.*, 2010). As such, additional questions surrounding the public interest approach include those directed at the regulators themselves. These questions include whether it is reasonable to assume that regulators fulfil their responsibilities in a disinterested manner and whether it is realistic to expect that the interests of various affected parties will not impact regulatory outcomes. In considering these questions, the public interest approach is revealed to underestimate the effects of economic and political influences on regulation. Such effects are highlighted by two alternative theories in the following sections.

4.1.2 Regulatory capture theory

Similar to the public interest theory of regulation, regulatory capture theory (Bernstein, 1955) argues that regulatory bodies and the regulations they enact are initially established to protect the public interest, often in response to systemic failures. However, in distinguishing itself from public interest theory, regulatory capture theory relaxes the assumption that regulators are neutral and predicts that regulatory mechanisms are ultimately controlled by the regulated parties (Bernstein, 1955).

Bernstein (1955) presented regulatory capture as the natural consequence of the regulatory 'life cycle'. His life-cycle-based theory denotes the regulatory process as commencing in response to a call to protect the public from some undesirable activity. The regulatory life-cycle then takes the regulatory body from a high-profile, but inexperienced, position where regulators zealously install regulation in the public interest to a lower-profile, but more experienced position (Bernstein, 1955). During the transition from one position to another, the public is deemed to become apathetic to the initial objectives of the regulation while the private interests remain. As a result, the regulatory body becomes more inclined to defer its attention from public to private interests. Thus, the regulated parties tend to 'capture' the regulators such that the original purposes of the regulatory programme are displaced by the efforts of the regulated parties (Kothari *et al.*, 2010). A third view extends from regulatory capture theory to presume that the 'captures' will ultimately seek to ensure regulation is advantageous to themselves.

4.1.3 Economics of regulation theory

In contrast to Bernstein, Stigler (1971) posited that regulators are made up of individuals who are self-interested and those individuals will introduce regulations which are more likely to securing their continuity as individual regulators and legitimacy as a regulatory body through political support (Kothari *et al.*, 2010). Stigler's argument identifies the tendency for regulators to acknowledge their continuity and legitimacy as dependent on satisfying the expectations of those being regulated which ultimately means taking those actions in the interest of the individuals who have enough voting and monetary power to influence regulatory decisions. Further, his overall assertion was that regulation is supplied by politicians and regulators in response to the demand for regulation by various interest groups. These various interest groups compete against each other in the regulatory arena to achieve objectives that increase their income and wealth. That is, interest groups vie to shape regulatory initiatives in a way that serves their own interests. The tendency is then a shift in protection from society as a whole to the interest of particular self-interested groups within society.

As a student of Stigler, Peltzman's (1976) refined the supply- side of Stigler's demand-side analysis. Peltzman (1976) put forth that those interest groups concerned for a particular regulation are considered more likely to influence the regulators towards implementing their preferred outcome by forming into large, organized groups with strong cohesive power (i.e. lobbying). Here, regulation is viewed as the product of relationships between different groups and the regulator as well as relationships between different groups of individuals. Therefore, advocates for the economic theory of regulation believe regulation is less about the public interest than about competition for power between different interest groups, who in turn have the power to influence outcomes (Bushman and Landsman, 2010). Consequently, private interests are served.

The theories in this section highlight the political aspect of accounting regulation and this aspect is expanded upon in the next section. The history of accounting regulatory activity contains many examples of lobbying by interested parties and such behaviour has come to be recognized as inevitable in the regulatory process, despite the seemingly technical nature of accounting (Solomons, 1978). The lobbying behaviour of powerful interest groups may significantly influence accounting regulation with undue emphasis placed on the preferences of certain powerful groups to the detriment of others. In particular, the preferences of two powerful groups, governmental actors and professional accountants, have been denoted as potentially influencing accounting regulation. Considerations relative to the role of these two groups in the development of accounting regulation are highlighted in the last section of this chapter.

4.2 Practical considerations

As a general phenomenon, the regulation of accounting information refers to the hierarchy of rules (or standards) mandated by regulatory bodies guiding the preparation, content and form of accounting information communicated either to public or private users. The regulation of accounting information can be the product of either public or private undertakings set by a public entity, such as a government or administrative body, or by private body in the form of an association of organizations, a panel of expert individuals, etc. Regardless of the nature of the regulatory entity, its primary activities involve the development, coordination, promulgation, interpretation, and revision of accounting standards which establish a uniform approach to some potential or actual problematic of accounting information. The following section provides some historical perspective on different models of accounting standard-setting, the trend towards private standard-setting models and related concerns with this model.

4.2.1 Public regulatory models[9]

As highlighted in Section 2, the state has played a major role in the development of both French and German accounting regulation. However, under the impact of external factors such as the harmonization programme of the European Union and the increasingly global capital markets dominated by Anglo-oriented countries, accounting regulation in France and Germany has evolved to a dual system that distinguishes between the regulation of accounting information provided by consolidated groups listed on public markets and the regulation of accounting information provided by business enterprises.

In the French system, a body of legal rules relating to accounting information has emerged from a variety of sources including: EU directives implemented by national legislation; laws, decrees and orders of the French state (such as the 'Code' and the 'PCG'); and mixed public/private sources such as the 'Conseil National de la Comptabilité' ('CNC' – national accounting council) and the 'Comité de la Réglementation Comptable' ('CRC' – accounting regulation committee). Where the Code provides a framework of general accounting rules applicable to all businesses, the PCG, or national accounting plan, is the most distinctive part of French accounting regulation which represents a very detailed manual of financial accounting. The plan, first promulgated in 1947, includes definitions of accounting terms, valuation and measurement rules and model financial statements which owe as much to German as to French ideas. The plan has been revised at several points since its initial enactment, most recently to take account of EU accounting directives of the 1980s.

The PCG is administered by the CNC, originally established in 1957 and reorganized in 1996, who develops and issues opinions on accounting regulation to the CRC (also established in 1996) who has the power to enact regulation either following proposals from the CNC or through endorsement of international standards. Where the CNC is comprised significantly of accounting experts with more private than public sector membership, the CRC membership is more heavily tilted towards public sector representatives in that it is chaired by the Minister of Economy and Finance and includes the Justice Minister, the Budget Minister and judges from public and private law, as well as representatives of the stock exchange, professional bodies, trade unions and business enterprise. However, outside of its seat on the CNC, the French financial markets authority ('AMF' – 'Autorité des Marchés Financiers') does not have a responsibility for the development of accounting regulation. Further, as professional accountancy developed much later in France than in the UK or the US, the French professional accounting bodies have never been responsible for setting accounting standards.

In the German system, similar to the French system, the sources of authoritative regulation of accounting information also include the EU directives and commercial and tax laws of the German state; however, in Germany, authorities such as the German stock exchange and trade unions are of minor importance to accounting while accounting practice and the accounting profession play important roles. The influence of the German institute is mainly through practice recommendations as well as by consultation in the law making process. As with the French Code, the German HGB consolidates all general accounting rules for all business entities into one single source. According to the HGB, every form of business must prepare annual financial statements in accordance with the 'Grundsätze ordnungsgemäßer Buchführung' (principles of orderly accounting) established by accounting practice over time. While the principles of orderly accounting are to a certain extent codified in the HGB, this is not formal and the system functions more on the interpretation of the principles set out in the HGB as well as in public and private company law, tax legislation, and statements from the German institute of accounting professionals and academics.

As a result, there is currently no exact equivalent to 'accounting standards' in Germany. In response to criticism, the Accounting Standards Committee of Germany (ASCG) was created in 1998 and recognized for the first time that a private organization was responsible for developing accounting standards for consolidated financial reporting, consulting on accounting legislation being developed by public bodies, and representing German interest in the development of international accounting standards. However, similar to the CNC/CRC relationship in the French regulatory environment, ASCG-developed standards are only opinions or recommendations which need to be enacted by the German Ministry of Justice and therefore face possible rejection by decisions of the court. Such public models of accounting regulation stand in stark contrast to Anglo-American models of regulation by professional models presented in the next section.

4.2.2 Professional regulatory models[10]

Up until the twentieth century in the Anglo-environment there was a general absence of regulation concerning how and what information companies were required to present. This meant that practitioners used those rules which they believed were most appropriate to the particular circumstances. As such, limited uniformity between the accounting information presented created problems of comparability in the public (i.e. market) domain. Around the 1920s, researchers undertook to understand practice and identify commonly employed and accepted accounting conventions. Early researchers providing detailed descriptions of accounting conventions in existence at the time include Paton (1973), Sanders *et al.* (1959), and Paton and Littleton (1940). These studies outlined concepts such as materiality and consistency as well as the doctrines of conservatism and the matching principle. However, such studies, by simply describing current practice, did little to critically examine those practices or suggest improvements/best practices which would reduce the perceived comparability gap.

According to Zeff (1972), a 1930 US publication resulting from cooperation between the accounting profession and the stock exchange produced a list of broadly used accounting conventions which set the foundation for their eventual codification and acceptance as what we know today as generally accepted accounting principles, or GAAP. In 1938, the SEC stated that it would only accept financial statements prepared in accordance with the generally accepted principles of the accounting profession, giving a great deal of power to the profession through the American Institute of Certified Public Accountants (AICPA). While the SEC allowed the accounting profession to take an authoritative lead in developing accounting standards and thereby in determining acceptable practice, the arrangement was designed to ensure the SEC maintained control over the ultimate determination of these standards (Zeff, 1972). From 1939, an AICPA committee, the Committee on Accounting Procedure (CAP), comprised of members of the accounting profession, began issuing statements on accounting principles called Accounting Research Bulletins (ARB).

Later, in 1959, the AICPA formed the Accounting Principles Board (APB), which released pronouncements referred to as APB Opinions. Neither the ARBs nor their APB Opinions were mandatory and as a result there tended to be many departures from the rules. From July 1973, the SEC deferred the establishment of accounting standards and principles to a private organization called the Financial Accounting Standards Board (FASB),[11] thereby replacing the CAP and the APB. As a private, expert-driven standard-setting organization, the FASB operates essentially under the oversight of the SEC and has as its primary purpose the development of US GAAP in the public interest through the 'establishment and improvement of standards of financial accounting and reporting for the guidance and education of the public'.

In the UK, the Institute of Chartered Accountants in England and Wales (ICAEW), a professional body of accountants established in 1880, released a series of non-binding 'Recommendations on Accounting Principles' to its members.[12] In 1970, the ICAEW formed the Accounting Standards Steering Committee (ASSC) with the objective of 'developing definitive standards for financial reporting', adding the Irish and Scottish professional institutes as members in the same year. These standards were referred to as Statements of Standard Accounting Practice (SSAPs) and maintained the same status as 'Recommendations' issued by the ICAEW. Later, in 1976, the ASSC became the Accounting Standards Committee (ASC) which continued to produce SSAPs until 1990 when the UK government announced the establishment of the Financial Reporting Council (FRC). With the FRC, came the creation of a private organization, the Accounting Standards Board (ASB), granted responsibility to issue UK standards called Financial Reporting Standards (FRS). However, the FRC's responsibility for developing FRS was dramatically changed by the European Union's decision to adopt international accounting standards as promulgated by the International Accounting Standards Board (IASB).

In fact, the IASB was preceded by the International Accounting Standards Committee (IASC),[13] a private body of professional accounting representatives[14] responsible for the development of international accounting standards. The IASC was formed in 1973 and initially produced voluntary accounting standards intended to ensure a minimum level of quality and comparability across developed countries and to offer a substitute to developing countries who did not have standards (Camfferman and Zeff, 2007). While providing an exchange of information and enabling national standard-setters a better understanding of practice elsewhere, the IASC and the international accounting standards (IAS) that it developed lacked authority to regulate the practice of reporting accounting information (Tamm-Hallstrom, 2004). Even when the IASC was reorganized as a blended geographic- and expert-driven organization and rebranded as the IASB in 2001, its lack of regulatory authority was retained; what changed not long after was European regulatory policy which mandated the application and use of the IASB's International Financial Reporting Standards (IFRS) by companies publicly listed in the European Union (Botzem and Quack, 2006), including companies listed on the UK stock exchange. Thus, since 2005, European companies have been subject to a private standard-setting model highly analogous to that of the US model.

4.2.3 Trends in regulatory models

The private standard-setting model which operates in the contemporary regulatory environment is unique. The standard-setters function with the overall aim of publishing financial accounting and reporting standards; however, in some jurisdictions, they do not have authority to mandate or enforce the use of the standards they issue. Thus the design of contemporary regulatory system often distinguishes the rule-maker from the rule-enforcer (Djelic and Sahlin-Andersson, 2006). In such systems, the various enforcement bodies – nation states, governments, and stock exchange authorities choose to support or not to support the standards promulgated, to support only certain aspects of the standards, or to contest and overrule positions issued by the private standard-setter[15] and therefore in some way hold the survival and legitimacy of the rule-makers in their hands (ibid.).

At the same time, the enforcement bodies entrust the standard-setters to set accounting standards for accounting information in the 'public interest', a notion that remains largely contested in terms of its meaning, but alludes to the standard-setters' responsibility to satisfy a variety of stakeholders. Here, economic theory of regulation, which assumes that these stakeholders form groups in order to protect their particular (private) economic interests, including those of the regulators themselves, plays a role. As discussed, these interest groups, having incompatible or mutually exclusive interests and objectives, are often viewed as being in conflict with each other and as lobbying the standard-setting body to establish standards which are beneficial to them. The lobbying of private standard-setters such as the FASB and the IASB occurs through their participation in standard-setting process.

The standard-setting process begins with the formal consideration and identification of what constitutes an accounting problematic that necessitates a standard, a stage which is referred to as agenda setting. The addition of a problematic to the standard-setting agenda is a pre-condition for the subsequent development of new (or amended) accounting standards. Once added to the agenda, the development of a standard to resolve the accounting problem identified indicates entry into the actual standard-setting stage. As mentioned, standard-setters are responsible for establishing accounting standards; however, the resolution of accounting problems requires some level of acceptance of the solution by the affected stakeholders (Sutton, 1984). This acceptance does not imply that stakeholders actually determine accounting standards, but only that they are granted the opportunity to express their views on the accounting standards they will eventually adhere to (Zeff, 2002) through the due process of standard-setting.

Due process generally refers to the means by which ethical constraints are placed on decision-making authorities, where the means are represented by a set of procedures and safeguards ensuring that authoritative bodies do not abuse their power (Richardson and Eberlein, 2011). In the accounting standard-setting environment, the particular procedures and safeguards of the standard-setting due process model include a series of activities which are open to public participation or observation, as well as established protocols for the standard-setters in conducting those activities. These protocols require the standard-setters to consider, represent and deliberate the views expressed by affected stakeholders and interest groups, balanced with their own particular views, so one can see how the influence of a particularly powerful interest group might come into play in this process. For this reason, due process procedures and safeguards are embedded in governance structures designed around the concepts of independence and accountability; even so, the independence and accountability of the private standard-setters has been questioned given the difficulties in designing structures that are completely neutral and free from stakeholder influence (Richardson and Eberlein, 2011).

5. Conclusion

The chapter opened with a historical presentation of regulatory developments in comparative economies and the role of accounting information in those economies. In response to the growth of business enterprises and the separation of ownership and management control as well as to financial abuse and shocks which arose in the form of accounting scandals and related business and market failures, the business environment has gradually incorporated regulation. However, the way in which regulation has been incorporated has varied depending on the primary users of and role for accounting information in a given environment. This discussion served as a contextual platform for meeting the primary purpose of this chapter in elaborating the arguments denying and affirming a need for the regulation of accounting information. Arguments opposing the need for regulation centre on the concept of the 'market' for accounting information as a self-regulating, efficiently operating mechanism while arguments supporting the need for regulation propose it as a tool for correcting the inefficiencies of the market for accounting information. These arguments have been presented in light of two critical problematics, adverse selection and moral hazard, and relative to other important governance and public policy-related factors. Finally, the chapter explored various theoretical and practical perspectives on the nature of regulation, the motivations of the regulator and the beneficiaries of regulation. In doing so, the economic, social and political factors were identified as associated with the development of accounting regulation and events were examined that shaped the evolution of the accounting regulatory system as we know it today.

Notes

1 This section provides a flavour of how the role of financial information developed in different economies and is not at all exhaustive or complete. For further reading on the details of the evolution of financial information in all major economies see Previts *et al.* (2011), and Nobes and Parker (2004).

2 This section is based on the work of Napier (2010) and Moehrle and Reynolds-Moehrle (2011) in their work on the history of accounting and reporting in the United Kingdom and the United States, respectively (both contained in different volumes of Previts *et al.*), as well as the contributors to the Nobes and Parker (2004) work on comparative studies of international accounting.

3 Joint stock companies refer to entities involving two or more individuals ('shareholders') having ownership through shares of stock issued by the company. Shares are issued in return for contributions of capital and the shareholders are free to transfer their ownership at their discretion by selling their shares to other individuals.

4 The true and fair concept, as referred to in this chapter, can be understood as the recognition, measurement, presentation and disclosure of financial information in a way that reflects economic reality, or in other words a full and accurate depiction of the activities of a business enterprise.

5 This section is based on the work of Ballweiser (2010) and Bocqueraz (2010) in their work on the history of accounting and reporting in Germany and France, respectively (both contained in the volumes of Previts *et al.*, 2011), as well as the contributors to the Nobes and Parker (2004) work on comparative studies of international accounting.

6 Lemon laws refer to US state laws that provide a remedy for car buyers in order to compensate for cars that fail to meet standards of quality and performance. Such vehicles are called 'lemons'.

7 Note that under agency theory, owners (shareholders), as principals of the firm, are assumed to have no management control role, and managers, as agents, are assumed to have no ownership.
8 A public good refers to a good which is not necessarily destroyed or altered by individual consumption.
9 See note 5.
10 See note 2.
11 For specifics on the relationship between the US SEC and the FASB, see Zeff (2010).
12 This paragraph is largely based on Willmott (1986) and his work studying the development of the major accounting bodies in the UK.
13 Camfferman and Zeff (2007) provide an extensive history of the IASC.
14 The constitution of the IASC was signed by representatives of national professional accounting bodies from nine countries: Australia, Canada, France, West Germany, Japan, Mexico, the Netherlands, the UK and the US.
15 Whether the enforcement body has the authority to contest and overrule, endorse fully or with carve-outs or otherwise depends on the formal relationship between the rule-maker and the enforcement body.

Bibliography

Akerlof, G. (1970) '"The Market for Lemons": Quality Uncertainty and the Market Mechanism'. *Quarterly Journal of Economics* 84, 488–500.

Arrow, K.J. (1963) 'Uncertainty and the Welfare Economics of Medical Care'. *American Economic Review* 53 (5): 941–73.

Ball, R., Kothari, S. and Robin, A. (2000) 'The Effect of International Institutional Factors on Properties of Accounting Earnings'. *Journal of Accounting & Economics* 29, 1–51.

Ballweiser, W. (2010) 'Germany', in G. Previts, P. Walton and P. Wolnizer (eds), *A Global History of Accounting, Financial Reporting and Public Policy: Europe; Studies in the Development of Accounting Thought,* Volume 14A (pp. 59–88). Bingley: Emerald Group Publishing Limited.

Barth, M. (2006) 'Research, Standard Setting, and Global Financial Reporting'. *Foundations and Trends in Accounting* 1, 71–165.

Bernstein, M. (1955) *Regulating Business by Independent Commission.* Princeton, NJ: Princeton University Press.

Bocqueraz, C. (2010) 'France', in G. Previts, P. Walton and P. Wolnizer (eds), *A Global History of Accounting, Financial Reporting and Public Policy: Europe; Studies in the Development of Accounting Thought,* Volume 14A (pp. 37–58). Bingley: Emerald Group Publishing Limited.

Botzem, S. and Quack, S. (2006) 'Contested Rules and Shifting Boundaries: International Standard Setting in Accounting'. in M.-L. Djelic and K. Sahlin-Andersson (eds), *Transnational Governance: Institutional Dynamics of Regulation* (pp. 266–86). Cambridge: Cambridge University Press.

Bromwich, M. (1985) *The Economics of Accounting Standard Setting.* Englewood Cliff, NJ: Prentice-Hall International.

Buchanan, J. (1968) *The Demand and Supply of Public Goods.* Chicago, IL: Rand McNally & Co.

Bushman, R. and Landsman, W. (2010) 'The Pros and Cons of Regulating Corporate Reporting: A Critical Review of the Arguments'. *Accounting & Business Research* 40(3), 259–73.

Camfferman, K. and Zeff, S. (2007) *Financial Reporting and Global Capital Markets: A History of the International Accounting Standards Committee, 1973–2000.* Oxford: Oxford University Press.

Djankov, S., La Porta, R., Lopez-de-Silanes, F. and Shleifer, A. (2003) 'The New Comparative Economics'. *Journal of Comparative Economics* 31 (4): 595–619.

Djelic, M.-L. and Sahlin-Andersson, K. (2006) 'Introduction: A World of Governance – The Rise of Transnational Regulation', in M.-L. Djelic and K. Sahlin-Andersson (eds) *Transnational Governance: Institutional Dynamics of Regulation* (pp. 1–30). Cambridge: Cambridge University Press.

Eierle, B. (2005) 'Differential Reporting in Germany: A Historical Analysis'. *Accounting, Business & Financial History* 15(3), 279–315.

Fama, E.F. (1970) 'Efficient Capital Markets: A Review of Theory and Empirical Work'. *Journal of Finance* 25: 383-417.

Fama, E.F. (1980) 'Agency Problems and the Theory of the Firm'. *Journal of Political Economy* 88(2).

Fama, E.F. and Jensen, M.C. (1983) 'Ownership and Control'. *Journal of Law and Economics* 26 (2): 301-325.

Grossman, S. (1981) 'An Introduction to the Theory of Rational Expectations under Asymmetric Information'. *Review of Economic Studies* 48 (4), 541–59.

Jensen, M. and Meckling, W. (1976) 'Theory of the Firm: Managerial Behaviour Agency Costs and Ownership Structure'. *Journal of Financial Economics* 3, 305–60.

Kothari, S., Ramanna, K. and Skinner, D. (2010) 'Implications for GAAP from an Analysis of Positive Research in Accounting'. *Journal of Accounting & Economics* 50, 246–86.

Lamoreaux, N. (1985) *The Great Merger Movement in American Business, 1885–1904*. New York: Cambridge University Press.

Leuz, C. (2010) 'Different Approaches to Corporate Reporting Regulation: How Jurisdictions Differ and Why'. *Accounting & Business Research* 40(3), 229–56.

Leuz, C. and Wustemann, J. (2004) 'The Role of Accounting in the German Financial System', in J. P. Krahnen and R. H. Schmidt (eds) *The German Financial System* (pp. 105–44). Oxford and New York: Oxford University Press.

Moehrle, S. and Reynolds-Moehrle, J. (2011) 'United States', in G. Previts, P. Walton and P. Wolnizer (eds), *A Global History of Accounting, Financial Reporting and Public Policy: Americas; Studies in the Development of Accounting Thought*, Volume 14B (pp. 105–44). Bingley: Emerald Group Publishing Limited.

Moran, M. (1991) *The Politics of the Financial Services Revolution: the USA, UK and Japan*. Basingstoke: Palgrave Macmillan.

Moran, M. (2010) 'The Political Economy of Regulation: Does It Have Any Lessons for Accounting Research?'. *Accounting and Business Research* 40(3), International Accounting Policy Forum, 215–25.

Napier, C. (2010) 'United Kingdom', in G. Previts, P. Walton and P. Wolnizer (eds), *A Global History of Accounting, Financial Reporting and Public Policy: Europe; Studies in the Development of Accounting Thought*, Volume 14A (pp. 243–73). Bingley: Emerald Group Publishing Limited.

Nioche, J.P. and Pesqueux, Y. (1997) 'Accounting, Economics and Management in France: The Slow Emergence of an "Accounting Science"'. *European Accounting Review* 6(2), 231–50.

Nobes, C. and Parker, R. (2004) *Comparative International Accounting*, 8th edn, Harlow: Prentice Hall.

Olson, M. (1965) *The Logic of Collective Action: Public Goods and the Theory of Groups*. New York: Schocken Books.

Paton, W. (1973 [1922]) *Accounting Theory*. Kansas, KS: Scholars Book Co.

Paton, W. and Littleton, A. (1940) *An Introduction to Corporate Accounting Standards*. Sarasota, FL: American Accounting Association.

Peltzman, S. (1976) 'Towards a More General Theory of Regulation'. *Journal of Law and Economics* (August), 211–40.

Pigou, A. (1932) *The Economics of Welfare*. London: Macmillan.

Posner, R. (1974) 'Theories of Economic Regulation'. *Bell Journal of Economics and Management Science* 5, 335–58.

Previts, G., Walton, P. and Wolnizer, P. (eds) (2011) *A Global History of Accounting, Financial Reporting and Public Policy: Studies in the Development of Accounting Thought* (4 vols). Bingley: Emerald Group Publishing Limited.

Richardson, A. and Eberlein, B. (2011) 'Legitimating Transnational Standard-Setting: The Case of the International Accounting Standards Board'. *Journal of Business Ethics* 98(2), 217–45.

Sanders, T., Hatfield, H. and Moore, U. (1959 [1938]) *A Statement of Accounting Principles*. Sarasota, FL: American Accounting Association.

Scott, W. (2003) *Financial Accounting Theory*, 3rd edn. Toronto: Pearson Education Canada.

Solomons, D. (1978) 'The Politicization of Accounting'. *Journal of Accountancy* 146 (5), 65–72.

Stigler, G. (1961) 'The Economics of Information'. *Journal of Political Economy* 69 (3), 213–25.

Stigler, G. (1971) 'The Theory of Economic Regulation', *Bell Journal of Economics and Management Science* (Spring), 2–21.

Sunder, S. (2002) 'Regulatory Competition Among Accounting Standards Within and Across International Boundaries'. *Journal of Accounting and Public Policy* 21(3), 219–34.

Sutton, T. (1984) 'Lobbying of Accounting Standard-setting Bodies in the US and the UK: A Downsian Analysis'. *Accounting, Organizations and Society* 9(1), 81–95.

Tamm-Hallstrom, K. (2004) *Organizing International Standardization: ISO and the IASC in Question of Authority*. Cheltenham: Edward Elgar.

Taylor, P. and Turley, S. (1986) *The Regulation of Accounting*. Oxford: Basil Blackwell.

Watts, R. and Zimmerman, J. (1978) 'Towards a Positive Theory of the Determination of Accounting Standards'. *Accounting Review* 53(1), 112–34.
Watts, R. and Zimmerman, J. (1983) 'Agency Problems, Auditing and the Theory of the Firm: Some Evidence'. *Journal of Law & Economics* 26 (October), 613–33.
Watts, R. and Zimmerman, J. (1986) *Positive Accounting Theory*. Englewood Cliffs, NJ: Prentice Hall.
Willmott, H. (1986) 'Organizing the Profession: A Theoretical and Historical Examination of the Development of the Major Accountancy Bodies in the UK'. *Accounting, Organizations and Society* 11, 555–80.
Zeff, S. (1972) 'Chronology of Significant Developments in the Establishment of Accounting Principles in the United States, 1926–1972', *Journal of Accounting Research* 10 (1): 217–27
Zeff, S. (1978) 'The Rise of Economic Consequences'. *Journal of Accountancy* 146 (6), 56–63.
Zeff, S. (2002) '"Political" Lobbying on Proposed Standards: A Challenge to the IASB'. *Accounting Horizons* 16(1), 43–54.
Zeff, S. (2010) 'A Comment on "Delegation"'. *Accounting in Europe* 7, 123–5.
Zysman, J. (1983) *Governments, Markets and Growth: Financial Systems and the Politics of Industrial Change*. Ithaca, NY: Cornell University Press.

12

Economic Theory of Financial Reporting Regulation

John Christensen and Hans Frimor

1. Introduction

The purpose of accounting is to provide information to decision makers engaging in all kinds of economic decisions. The regulation of accounting is associated with the use of accounting information for parties which are external to the firm. The demand from internal users requires no regulation, as the information can be tailored to the purposes of accounting information. Accounting can be viewed as an economic good and consequently, like any other good, the demand for accounting can be analyzed using the tools of economics. Accounting is not consumed directly and thus it is only a derived good. The demand for accounting is derived from its usefulness in economic decision-making. For this reason, we will use economics to analyze the demand for accounting regulation. We will consider both the decision and the control purpose of accounting.

Accounting has been part of corporate routines for a very long time (Christensen and Demski, 2003). The Italian monk and mathematician Pacioli described the double entry bookkeeping system that we know today. At that time, only positive numbers were used and double entry came in handy. The demand for a more systematic codification of accounting grew following the industrialization in the late eighteenth century. At first, the codification was taken care of through the creation of the professional societies of accountants and auditors starting with the establishment of the Scottish Society. Soon afterwards, the Institute of Chartered Accountants in England and Wales and the American Association of Public Accountants were established (Deegan, 2001). The separation of ownership and management in combination with the development of capital markets was the source of the demand for the codification of accounting standards. The codification was based upon membership of the institutes and was tied to the specific institute. At the time, there was no government intervention in the accounting regulation.

The demand for government regulation followed the crash of the capital market in the late 1920s and led to the establishment of the SEC in the USA. Most countries established accounting legislation as part of their company laws. In the EU member states, accounting regulation remained predominantly part of local legislation until the directives for capital markets were passed in 1978. This development followed the internationalization of capital markets and the demand for free flow of capital among EU member states. Simultaneously, the standard-setting bodies the IASB (at the time the IASC) and the FASB increased their activities in developing accounting standards. The predominant organization of accounting standard-setting has remained a mix of private and public regulation. Since the 1970s, the dominant standard-setting bodies have been the FASB on the US scene and the IASB on the international scene. Both standard-setting bodies are independent institutions and thus not directly under government control. The SEC and the EU regulators have seen an advantage in having these bodies as the standard issuing entities and the government agencies have taken on a supervisory role. Subsequent to their release the public authorities approve the standards. As a consequence of the trend of increasing international investment there is a demand for uniform accounting around the globe. The IASB and the FASB have initiated a joint project of harmonization in response to that demand.

There seems to be a close continual connection between accounting regulation and financial scandals (Clikeman, 2009). Financial scandals create renewed interest in regulation and often point to weak spots in the existing regulation. Even though accounting has been with us throughout history, the accounting regulation is dynamic. The conditions and the possibilities for using accounting information are constantly changing. Simultaneously, financial statement preparers are discovering new opportunities for opportunistic behavior, earnings management is evolving, and the accounting regulation must follow suit.

There are two main players in accounting regulation, both of which have produced a conceptual framework and issued specific standards. At a fundamental level, the ideology and the standards of the two institutions are quite similar. The conceptual frameworks are meant to provide guidelines for regulators, producers, and users of financial statements. The proposed joint framework of the IASB and the FASB lists the following items as the main issues to be included in the framework:

- the objective of financial reporting;
- the qualitative characteristics of useful financial information;
- the definition, recognition, and measurement of the elements from which financial statements are constructed; and
- concepts of capital and capital maintenance.

In the conceptual framework the objective of financial reporting is to provide financial information about the entity to decision makers (IASB, 2010). The common denominator of the decision makers is that they are using financial information (Beaver, 1998). It is therefore appropriate to frame the decision problem from an economic perspective. The focus on the decision problem can be narrowed down to include investment decisions where the matter of concern is the future cash flow to the firm as well as control decisions where the concern is how to use information for the purpose of providing incentives to act in the interest of the company. Note that these two types of decision problems are equivalent to the traditional emphasis of accounting theory on decision and control. The demands for information for the two purposes are not equivalent, as pointed out by Gjesdal (1981).

The decision problems of the users are central to the analysis of the demand for accounting information. Instead of setting out the demand for information from the decision makers for different purposes, the conceptual framework describes a set of qualitative characteristics to identify the types of information which are likely to be most useful to users for making decisions based upon financial information. The framework identifies two main qualitative characteristics of useful information labeled relevance and faithful representation. The claim is that information has to be relevant and provide a faithful representation of the underlying economics of the firm in order to be useful for the decision maker (IASB, 2010).

Accounting is often called the language of business. As is the case with language in general, accounting also serves the purpose of conveying information. There is a long tradition for regulation of the accounting language, both with respect to the content of the reporting and with respect to defining the language. Chapter 4 of the conceptual framework is used to define the key concepts of accounting (financial information) and the recognition criteria. As accounting is an artificial language, there is a demand for defining the language as well as defining what type of information is to be included in the accounts and what type is not to be included (Christensen and Demski, 2003).

Having established that financial reporting provides financial information used in economic decision making for decision and control purposes, the discussion of the reporting regulation in this chapter is cast in an economic setting.[1] The analysis will start with demand for information in a market setting in Section 2. This is consistent with the decision purpose of accounting information. In Section 3 the analysis will proceed to the control demand for information and use the agency model to describe the friction between the owners and the manager of a firm. The formal analysis is then taken to the next organizational level in Section 4, as the reporting regulation is scrutinized as a game between the regulators and the firms being regulated. This analysis provides insight into the effect of the regulators on the information content of the reported financial statements and the understanding of the qualitative characteristics. Reporting regulation is then put into a wider context, as the demand for regulation is viewed more broadly and the demand for a common language as a coordinating device is discussed in Section 5. Section 6 contains concluding remarks.

2. Information in markets

The FASB and the IASB cannot meaningfully regulate the dissemination of accounting information without a stated objective providing guidance. The FASB Concepts Statements are intended to serve the public interest by setting the objectives, qualitative characteristics, and other concepts that guide selection of economic phenomena to be recognized and measured for financial reporting and their display in financial statements or related means of communicating information to those who are interested. Concepts Statements guide the Board in developing sound accounting principles and provide the Board and its constituents with an understanding of the appropriate content and inherent limitations of financial reporting (FASB, 2012).

The Concepts Statements or Conceptual Framework provides a broad objective 'to serve the public interest', but subsequently operationalizes this to:

> The objective of general purpose financial reporting is to provide financial information about the reporting entity that is useful to existing and potential investors, lenders, and other creditors in making decisions about providing resources to the entity. Those decisions involve buying, selling, or holding equity and debt instruments and providing or settling loans and other forms of credit (FASB, 2010, p. 1, and IASB, 2010).

In FASB (2010, OB3) it is concluded that 'investors, lenders and other creditors need information to help them assess the prospects for future net cash inflows to an entity.' It appears that these concerns are primarily related to the functioning of capital markets. We will thus, for the moment, abstract from other information problems (within firms) and focus on the role of information in the functioning of capital markets in terms of liquidity.

A market is liquid when large transactions can take place without any significant effect on prices and without an uninformed party losing money to a privately informed party. As prices are determined by demand and supply, liquidity is affected by the number of market participants but also by information asymmetry between market participants. Akerlof (1970) demonstrated that private information can create adverse selection problems which reduce trade, perhaps such that the market disappears. The disappearance of markets is also illustrated by the no-trade theorems (see e.g. Milgrom and Stokey, 1982), which state that if information structures are common knowledge, if agents have traded to an equilibrium, and there are no noise traders to affect prices, then there will be no trade (prices will nonetheless reflect all information). Hence, information asymmetry is potentially detrimental to liquidity and it is widely agreed that symmetric information implies liquidity and that transparency leads to symmetric information. Further, a common conception is that when uninformed investors trade, they generally suffer from having to trade with better-informed counterparts. This was part of the reason why Regulation Fair Disclosure was introduced in the US.

We will use a noisy, rational expectations model as in Grossman and Stiglitz (1980) to illustrate some of the issues and to glean some 'new' insights. Consider a three-period pure exchange economy with a single firm, a riskless asset, and a set of investors. Trade takes place at price P in the second period, while consumption takes place in the third. Prior to the opening of the market at $t = 1$, each investor can purchase access to two pieces of information pertaining to the payoff, $\tilde{d}$, per share. One signal is a common public signal, $\tilde{y}_c$, concerning the future value of the risky asset and the other signal, $\tilde{y}_p$, is a private signal pertaining to the same. Assume that the public signal is available free of charge and let κ be the cost of acquiring the private signal. We will assume that

$$\tilde{d} = m + \tilde{y}_c + \tilde{y}_p + \tilde{\varepsilon}$$

where $\tilde{y}_c$, $\tilde{y}_p$, and $\tilde{\varepsilon}$ are normally distributed random variables such that $\tilde{d} \sim N(m, \sigma_c^2 + \sigma_p^2 + \sigma_\varepsilon^2)$, such that $\tilde{d}|\tilde{y}_c \sim N(m + \tilde{y}_c, \sigma_p^2 + \sigma_\varepsilon^2)$, and such that $\tilde{d}|\tilde{y}_c, \tilde{y}_p \sim N(m + \tilde{y}_c + \tilde{y}_p, \sigma_\varepsilon^2)$. We further assume that the per capita supply of the risky asset, $\tilde{z}$, is generated by noise traders and is random; more specifically we assume that $\tilde{z} \sim N(0, \sigma_z^2)$ and is independent of any other stochastic variable. The sequence of events is illustrated in Figure 12.1.

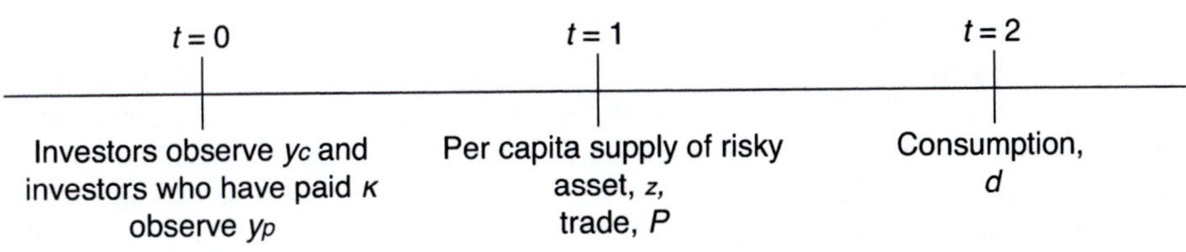

Figure 12.1 Timeline

At $t = 0$, the investors who chose to acquire the private information have an information advantage of size σ_p^2 over those who did not acquire the private information. Since we assume that $\sigma_c^2 + \sigma_p^2$ is independent of the information system, the information advantage of the privately informed investors decreases as the information content of the public source increases (σ_c^2 increases). At $t = 1$, each investor invests in the two assets so as to maximize the expected utility of consumption. At $t = 2$, the risky asset pays $\tilde{d}$ units of the single consumption good, while the riskless asset pays 1. Taking the riskless asset as a numeraire and letting P be the price of the risky asset at $t = 1$, the investor's terminal wealth, $\tilde{w}_{1i}$, is

$$\tilde{w}_{1i} = \tilde{w}_{0i} + z_i(\tilde{d} - P)$$

where $\tilde{w}_{0i}$ is an investor's initial wealth and z_i is the agent's holdings of the risky asset. We assume that agents have negative exponential utility with risk aversion r, and thus agents maximize – w.r.t. z_i – their expected utility of consumption: $\int_{-\infty}^{\infty} -\exp\{-r(w_{0i} + z_i(d - P))\} g(d|Inf_i)\, dd$, where Inf_i is the agent's information. If $\tilde{d}|Inf_i$ is normally distributed, then the expected utility of consumption is $-\exp\left\{-r\left(w_{0i} + z_i\left(E\left[d|Inf_i\right] - P\right) - \frac{1}{2}rz_i^2 Var\left[d|Inf_i\right]\right)\right\}$ Thus, demand is

$$z_i = \frac{E\left[\tilde{d}|Inf_i\right] - P}{rVar\left[\tilde{d}|Inf_i\right]}$$

If investors only pay attention to the signals $\tilde{y}_c$ and $\tilde{y}_p$, then a privately informed investor's demand is $z_p = (m + y_c + y_p - P) / r\sigma_\varepsilon^2$ and an uninformed investor's demand is $z_c = (m + y_c - P) / r(\sigma_\varepsilon^2 + \sigma_p^2)$. Letting λ denote the fraction of investors who acquired the private information, market clearing requires that $\lambda z_p + (1 - \lambda) z_c = z$, and thus, when investors only pay attention to the signals $\tilde{y}_c$ and $\tilde{y}_p$, the market clearing price is (P_u indicates investors are unsophisticated)

$$P_u = m + y_c + \frac{1}{\lambda / \sigma_\varepsilon^2 + (1 - \lambda) / (\sigma_p^2 + \sigma_\varepsilon^2)} (\lambda y_p / \sigma_\varepsilon^2 - rz) \tag{1}$$

If individual demand is affected by private information, then in general the market clearing price, P, is a function of the information available to all the agents in the economy. Sophisticated investors realize this and thus the price may provide investors with information in addition to their public and private information and P_u will no longer clear the market. At the individual level, the information available in the economy is the public information, y_c, the private information, y_p, and the market price of the risky asset, P. Rational investors form a conjecture regarding the price formation, $f(\cdot)$. This conjecture influences individual demand through their expectation, and thus the market clearing price is a function of the conjecture. If the market clearing price, $T(f(\cdot))$ is formed according to the conjecture – if $f(\cdot)$ is a fixed point in the mapping T – then the conjectured price functional is a self-fulfilling rational expectations equilibrium. In this version of the Grossman and Stiglitz model the self-fulfilling rational expectations equilibrium price at $t = 1$ is a linear function of the variables in the economy (Christensen and Feltham, 2003)

$$P = m + y_c + \pi_p y_p - \pi_z z$$

Thus, liquidity is measured by π_z – the lower π_z is, the more liquid the market will be. When $\lambda = 0$, then $P = m + y_c - r(\sigma_p^2 + \sigma_\varepsilon^2)z$ and thus the market becomes more liquid as the public signal becomes more informative (as σ_P^2 falls). When $\lambda \in (0,1)$ the price is still linear, but the expressions for π_P and π_z are more complicated, but π_z is – generally speaking – increasing in the average posterior uncertainty of the investors. Thus, holding fixed the fraction, λ, of informed investors, it still holds that liquidity is increasing in the informativeness of the public signal. In other words: as transparency increases, liquidity increases.

When λ is endogenously chosen by investors, things are less clear-cut. As the public signal is made more informative, acquiring the private information becomes less attractive and thus the equilibrium fraction of informed investors, λ, starts decreasing. At least in such a setting it is debatable whether more transparency leads to less information asymmetry; the information advantage of the informed investors is reduced, however, at the same time a larger proportion of investors are uninformed. This suggests that liquidity may not behave as expected. It turns out that liquidity may decrease as the information content of the public report increases. Since the expressions for π_P and π_z are quite complicated, we illustrate this graphically. In Figure 12.2 we graph π_z as a function of the informativeness of the public signal, σ_c^2.

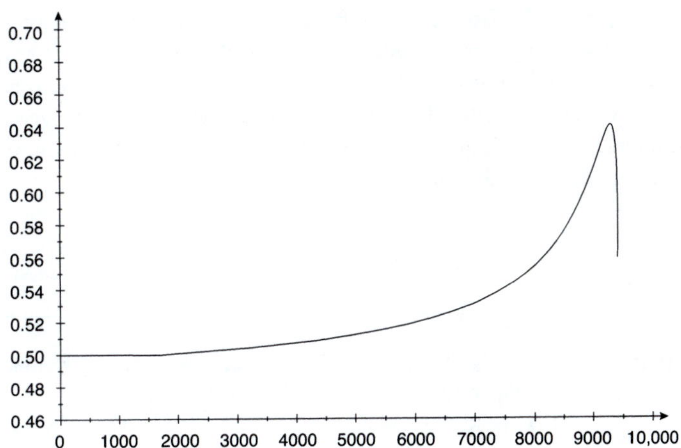

Figure 12.2 **The association between informativeness of a public signal and liquidity in the market**

As illustrated, liquidity is decreasing in σ_c^2 when $\sigma_c^2 < 9304$, after which liquidity is increasing in σ_c^2. The reason can be gleaned from (1), as it is apparent that the weight on z depends roughly on the average *ex post* variance (uncertainty) of the rational investors. As λ is decreasing, the average uncertainty is increasing and thus π_z increases – this happens even though the information content of the public information is increasing.

Further, the *ex ante* expected utility of both informed and uninformed investors, which is equal when $\lambda \in (0,1)$, is increasing in the informativeness of the public signal until the public information is precise enough such that $\lambda = 0$, after which the *ex ante* expected utility is decreasing. When the expected utility is increasing in the informativeness of the public signal it is not because information asymmetry has decreased but because average uncertainty has gone up, which enables the rational investors to better take advantage of the noise traders; i.e. the equilibrium discount or risk premium increases. Over the region where modeled investors are better off when the informativeness of the public information increases, one may expect that the unmodeled noise traders would fare worse. This is not necessarily so. It turns out that information risk (price risk) is decreasing, whereas the risk premium claimed by the rational traders is increasing, making the net effect uncertain (we are implicitly assuming that noise traders are not risk-lovers). The problem illustrated by the above example is that an immediate intuition for the consequences of altered information dissemination is often based on an all-else-equal assumption, and in the above, all-else-equal means private information acquisition is left unaffected by the information content of the public information. In a similar rational expectations model where private information acquisition is unaffected by the information system, Christensen and Frimor (2007) demonstrate that the information which can be extracted from all information sources in an economy (i.e. private information, public information, and prices) may decrease when the information content of the public source is increased. This suggests a narrow focus on accounting information, and thus disregarding other sources of information in the economy can be problematic.

FASB (2010, p. 1) lists concerns for resource allocation decisions and especially mentions investors' decisions related to the provision of equity or debt. In a pure exchange economy, information only has an influence on when uncertainty is resolved, and in a complete market resolving uncertainty early (or late) has an influence on when investors have homogeneous beliefs. In such a setting the only role for information is to dynamically complete the market (as mentioned, we are ignoring incentive problems). Christensen *et al.* (2010) demonstrate this in a setting like the one depicted in Figure 12.3, where the only added detail relative to our previous example is that trading takes place also at $t = -0$. Christensen *et al.* (2010) demonstrate that the price at $t = -0$ is unaffected by the information revealed at $t = 1$.

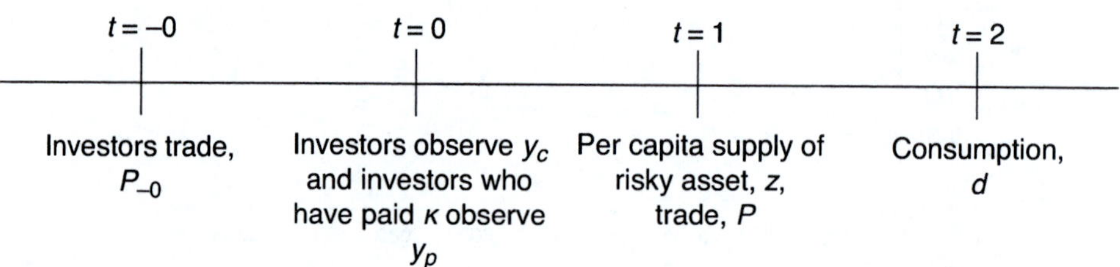

Figure 12.3 Timeline

The simplest case is if z is non-stochastic and there is only public information at $t = 0$. Then the risk premium in the second period from $t = 1$ to $t = 2$ is given by the posterior variance of the terminal dividend, while the risk premium in the first period from $t = -0$ to $t = 1$ is given by the variance (at $t = -0$) of the posterior mean of the terminal dividends at $t = 1$, i.e. the pre-posterior variance. Since the sum of the posterior and pre-posterior variances is equal to the prior variance of the terminal dividends, the total *ex ante* risk premium from $t = -0$ to $t = 2$ is independent of the informativeness of the public report at $t = 1$. The public information thus only determines when uncertainty is resolved and leaves investors' *ex ante* expected utilities independent of the public information system.

The notion of resource allocation is suggestive of real decisions, e.g. in the form of production decisions. With production, information has the ability to affect the division of resources between consumption and productive investments. In such a setting, more detailed information systems will in general improve welfare (and increase the cost of capital). However, unless there are incentive problems or accounting regulation affects what information is generated within firms, there is no role for regulation.

Regulation could be important in preventing adverse selection problems from becoming so large that markets break down causing massive illiquidity and adversely affecting production. In the above setting, more public information reduces the advantage of acquiring private information and, hence, as intuition would suggest, increased disclosure reduces the acquisition of private information. Dang *et al.* (2009) in a model of debt and illiquidity illustrate that this intuition may well be misguided and that public information may trigger harmful private information acquisition.

For regulation to be necessary it must be the case that the required information would not be revealed unless so mandated. The seminal unraveling result in the disclosure literature posits that discretion inevitably leads to full disclosure, even when such disclosure has detrimental consequences. Arya *et al.* (2010) consider *ex post* disclosure incentives of proprietary information when firms compete in multiple markets. It is demonstrated that when a firm operates in multiple segments, the unraveling result applies at the firm-wide level but not necessarily segment by segment. In fact, the *ex post* disclosure equilibrium entails aggregation of segment details and this occurs because any *ex post* temptation to disaggregate and reveal particularly favorable news in one segment entails revealing unfavorable news in another segment. A desire to balance profits across segments then leads a firm to disclose firm-wide information (a temptation that cannot be avoided), but only in the aggregate. The suppression of information (relative to full revelation) gives the firm an advantage in competition.

Regulations that mandate full disclosure of segment details are to the detriment of the informationally advantaged firm and to the benefit of its rival. However, consumers (and total welfare) may be harmed by mandated segment disclosure. The reason is that segment aggregation undercuts tacit price collusion on the part of the competing firms. This is important because if capital market concerns were the only concerns of firms, they would voluntarily disclose anyway. Hence, regulators need to consider the effects on other parties in light of the reasons firms aggregate in the first place. A full understanding of the consequences of regulation necessitates weighing the ramifications for the range of parties that will be affected.[2] Consumers in product markets may be impacted by regulation because of induced changes in firms' strategies, and this should perhaps be of greater concern than the concern for investors and competing firms.

3. The principal-agent model

Accounting data constitute an important input into the contracts used to manage the relationships between the firm and its stakeholders. One of the important relationships is between the firm and its management, where contracts regulating compensation and (implicitly) employment are often written on accounting numbers. During the preparation of the Conceptual Framework, the AAA Financial Accounting Standards Committee expressed reservations that the FASB's 'Preliminary Views on the Conceptual Framework for Financial Reporting' is too focused on an investment role of accounting, and neglects the more important stewardship role of accounting (AAA, 2007; FASB, 2008). The FASB's 'Statement of Financial Accounting Concepts No. 8' emphasizes decision usefulness and concludes that stewardship is part thereof (FASB, 2010). However, the FASB's priority remains solidly on the resource allocation/valuation role: 'in most cases, information designed for resource allocation decisions would also be useful for assessing management's performance' (FASB, 2010, p. 12).

Incentive problems are often synonymous with agency problems, and in modeling agency problems the following assumptions are typical:

- a risk neutral owner owns a production technology that
- requires an unobservable effort, a, from a
- risk-averse agent, where the action – together with some unobserved state of nature – results in an
- economic outcome or value, x, as well as an accounting report, y, which precedes outcome, x. As the action and the economics outcome are unobservable at the time the agent must be compensated, the owner writes a
- contract, $s(y)$, on the accounting report.

The contract specifies the payment the risk averse agent will receive and is meant to provide incentives for effort.

A fundamental question – of relevance also to standard setters – is what properties the accounting report, y, should have. From an agency point of view, the ideal report would reveal the agent's action; however, from a valuation point of view, the ideal report would disclose x. As the agent's effort and the state of nature combine to produce outcome x, this is not the same. It follows that there is a potential tension between the valuation and stewardship roles of accounting information, and emphasizing primarily the valuation role of accounting information risks diminishing its stewardship value (Gjesdal, 1981). Further, when remuneration depends on accounting numbers, an incentive to manage these numbers may emerge, and managed earnings may be synonymous with misleading financial information, which may adversely affect resource allocation.

The trade-offs between the valuation and the stewardship roles are illustrated by the ongoing debate on earnings quality and earnings management. Earnings quality is often perceived as synonymous with accruals quality (Schipper and Vincent, 2003), and accruals are often decomposed in a non-discretionary and a discretionary component (see, for example, Francis *et al.*, 2005). Non-discretionary accruals are driven by a firm's business model, by its operating environment, and by accounting policies that do not allow managerial discretion, whereas discretionary accruals are those controlled by managers – hence the term 'earnings management'. From a valuation perspective, higher earnings quality means that accounting reports are more informative about the size, timing, and risk of future cash flows, for example by separating transitory and persistent components of current cash flows, or by recognizing both 'bad' and 'good' news in the balance sheet. Similarly, from a stewardship perspective, higher earnings quality means that accounting reports better reflect managements' actions, for example by filtering out the effects of market movements, perhaps to the detriment of its valuation relevance. Regardless, if financial reports are to convey managers' information on firms' performance, the standards must allow managers some discretion.

The notion of earnings management indicates that earnings management is undesirable, which raises the question of whether unmanaged earnings are always better for shareholders. The answer is no if managers use judgment and discretion to manage accounting reports such that they become more informative for users. The answer is – or at least seems to be – yes if managers use judgment and discretion to manage accounting reports such that they become less informative for users. As Arya *et al.* (2003) point out, there is a difference between *ex ante* and *ex post* efficiency. The Revelation Principle posits that if contracts are unconstrained, if communication is unlimited, and if parties can commit, then the manager and the owners are as well off under truthful reporting as under any form of managed/manipulated reporting.

If the owners and management cannot abstain from altering the contract, $s(y)$, after the agent has chosen his effort, a, but before the accounting report, y, has materialized, then the owners can reap an insurance gain by offering the manager a fixed amount equal to the certainty equivalent of the contract, $s(y)$. *Ex post* this is efficient; however, *ex ante* it is highly inefficient as the manager will choose the least costly action, that is, do nothing. In such a setting, Fudenberg and Tirole (1990) demonstrate that some incentives can be preserved in equilibrium if the agent plays a mixed strategy, i.e. randomizes over effort levels. The idea is that when the owner is uncertain as to which type of agent (what effort level) he is facing, he has an incentive to screen the agent types by offering insurance only to types characterized by low effort, thus maintaining some incentives. If information is released after effort is exerted but prior to renegotiation and this information is informative about (correlated with) the final report, then this information is contractible regardless of whether the information is verifiable or not. If the information is verifiable, then it is of course possible to contract directly on the interim signal. As the interim signal will affect the expectation about the future public signal, it also affects the value the agent associates with a contract written on the public signal. It is thus possible to tailor a contract written on the public signal such that the value(s) of the contract conditional on the interim signal(s) is (are) as if the contract was written directly on the interim signal (Hermalin and Katz, 1991).

If the interim signal is unobservable to the owner, the owner does not know which type of agent (what signal the agent observed) he is facing at the renegotiation stage. As when the owner's uncertainty pertains to the agent's effort, there is an incentive to screen the agent types by offering only incomplete insurance with respect to the forthcoming public signal. This is the setting in Gigler and Hemmer (2004), where they also bring up the question of whether the interim signal should be audited, i.e. be made verifiable, or not. In the standard setup without renegotiation it is well known that it is socially optimal to make all information public; however, in the presence of renegotiation, the result is less clear. It turns out that under some conditions it is socially optimal to allow the agent to self-report and – by implication then – socially suboptimal to audit the interim report. In Gigler and Hemmer (2004) the standard result that subsequent verified information is necessary to utilize the agent's report of private information is nicely complemented by the somewhat contrary result that utilization of a subsequent public report presupposes that the prior information release is based on private information.

In Gigler and Hemmer (2004) the setting resembles a situation where a manager issues a quarterly report; however, as there is only one period, the accounting report, y, must equal outcome, x.

In Christensen *et al.* (2002) a repeated agency is analyzed. After effort is exerted in the first period, the owners can renegotiate the initial contract. In such a situation, the owners can gain by allowing the agent discretion in his reporting. By allowing the agent discretion, the manager is provided with the means to take advantage of the owners if these are tempted to offer insurance: if the owners approach the agent and offer to insure the agent against variations in compensation, the agent would gladly accept and then create a secret reserve by underreporting, i.e. taking slack into the future.[3] Christensen *et al.* (2002) show that allowing the agent to manipulate earnings can be socially optimal.

In settings where information arrives after the renegotiation encounter, it is the freedom to manipulate which is beneficial; however, in equilibrium reports are generally not manipulated. If information arrives before the renegotiation encounter the situation is different. In that case, reports must be manipulated or otherwise the same contracts would be offered at renegotiation. Demski and Frimor (1999) analyze such a situation and demonstrate that equilibrium manipulation of accounting reports can be optimal.

In a two-period setting where contracts are renegotiated after information is released in the first period, the problem is not that the owners will try to offer the agent insurance, the problem is that the owners will have an incentive to 'ratchet up' second-period incentives relative to the commitment solution. This happens because the posterior variance of second-period earnings is lower than its prior variance, and because the covariance between the first- and second-period earnings is irrelevant when the contract is renegotiated (after first-period earnings are reported). From an *ex ante* perspective, the higher second-period incentive rate makes the *ex ante* risk premium higher, which induces the shareholders to set lower first-period incentive rates to minimize the total risk premium. The losses due to renegotiation increase with the persistence of earnings, i.e. it becomes more costly to contract with the manager as the persistence of earnings increases. Christensen *et al.* (2005) show in a setting like this that changes in non-discretionary accounting policies (accrual noise), which decrease earnings persistence, increase the stewardship value of earnings. Hence, with renegotiation of contracts subsequent to earnings reports, there is a strong and direct tension between the valuation and stewardship roles of accounting. If regulators succumb to the temptation and regulate non-discretionary accruals to make earnings more persistent, then firms may counter this by inducing more earnings management through the discretionary accruals (Christensen *et al.*, 2013). Even if regulation concurrently leads to higher costs of earnings management, equilibrium earnings management may well increase.

The above discussion presents an alternative view of the common practice of earnings management. Not only can the firm tolerate some manipulation by the manager, it can actually be desired as a way of ensuring that the renegotiation encounter does not excessively derail upfront incentives. Broadly stated, an efficient firm is often portrayed as one that is quick to clamp down on employee shenanigans so as to concentrate on more pertinent tasks at hand. The view that lax oversight of self-interested employees is unhealthy has intuitive appeal. However, a word of caution is in order: providing managers with a degree of flexibility in reporting can ensure that a firm will not 'overreact' to earnings reports. In effect, by helping a firm to commit to a long-term course of action, earnings manipulation can actually improve the firm's position with its internal constituents.

4. The game of regulation

In the previous sections we have discussed the use of accounting for its two primary purposes: investment decision and control. It was noted that the two purposes are not necessarily aligned with respect to demand for financial information. The decision use of financial information centers on the predictive ability of future cash flows in accounting information, whereas control focuses on the information content in the accounting numbers about managerial decisions.

We now turn our attention to the regulation of financial information. Accounting is a source of financial information as stated by the regulatory bodies. Thus, it is an economic factor of production, like labor and materials. Financial information has no value on its own, as it is not a consumption good. However, the use of financial information (hopefully) leads to more efficient production and better allocation of capital in the society. Consequently, a cost benefit criterion should be applied to determine the amount of resources used to produce financial information. The finer details of the production function, market conditions, etc. of the firm enter this type of calculation. The conceptual frameworks of the IASB and the FASB skip these finer details and use instead the qualitative characteristics to guide both the regulators and the producers of financial statements. Indeed, many textbooks on financial accounting use the qualitative characteristics to frame the discussion of the accounting principles.

The claim from the IASB is that 'if financial information is to be useful, it must be relevant and faithfully represent what it purports to represent. The usefulness of financial information is enhanced if it is comparable, verifiable and understandable' (IASB, 2010, A33).

The economic interpretation of usefulness is that the information is capable of making a difference in the decisions made by investors (Beaver, 1998). This is almost a tautology: for information to be useful it has to be useful. The characteristic that accounting information is supposed to 'faithfully represent' is trickier and this is refined into a characterization of the ideal: complete, neutral, and free from error. The idea of the qualitative characteristics is that they should be used for choosing the information to be included in the financial statements.

Suppose we are faced with a decision problem regarding choice of accounting method. In order to assess the representation of the phenomenon the reporting question is framed in a setting in which the fundamentals of the economic situation can be assessed. This type of analysis is often cast in a market setting in which the fair value of the financial transaction can be found. The second step of the analysis is to compare the various accounting methods. The reporting issue is settled when it is determined which of the accounting methods under consideration reports the value which is closest to the fair value of the transaction in question.

When the above argument in favor of a particular accounting method relies on the qualitative characteristics, the choice does not reflect the finer details of the underlying decision problem including the economics of the reporting firm. In particular the choice of accounting method does not reflect the specific incentives that apply to the reporting (Christensen and Demski, 2007).

The question to be analyzed here is whether the qualitative characteristics form a good representation of the underlying decision problem of identifying the optimal information system for the users' decision problems. The answer to this question is no for numerous reasons. First, we will demonstrate that it is impossible to choose between two accounting alternatives without considering the finer details of the decision problem, and second we will show what happens once the actors of the accounting scene are replaced by the qualitative characteristics.

In the first example of the insufficiency of relying on the qualitative characteristics the firm is faced with two reporting alternatives. Suppose that one of the alternatives scores high on relevance, as it allows fine-tuning of the decision. On the faithful dimension the measure scores low, as the measurement error is high. The other measure scores low on relevance, as it does not allow fine-tuning of the decision but it scores high on faithful representation, as the error of the measure is low. In itself, the qualitative characteristics suggest a lexicographic ordering of the characteristics in IASB/FASB (2010), it gives priority to the relevance criterion and places the faithful representation second. In doing that, it is suggested that faithful representation is either there or not. (This is too simplistic. In our view, faithful representation is more a matter of degree.) In continuation of the example of the two competing measures, suppose that the error is invariant to scaling as in Feltham and Xie (1994). Then if the decision is low-scale (small decision) the measurement error is important for the decision and the more faithful measure is optimal. However, if the scale of the decision is large the measurement error becomes of second order concern and the optimal choice of reporting becomes the most relevant accounting method (Christensen, 2010).

The second example of the importance of the finer details of the decision problem has its roots in the fact that the decision makers are not considered in the qualitative characteristics. An example of this is found in leasing arrangements, in which the leasing agreement is constructed such that it passes as an operational lease. Apparently, it is only the qualitative characteristics of the information system that matter to the regulator. An important aspect of financial accounting is that it provides information from a reporting entity to a set of decision makers outside the entity. Not considering the setting of the decision problem also makes the choice of accounting procedure blind to the accountant's reaction to the regulation. In most cases, the decision choices faced by decision makers are continuous. This is true when the decision concerns how much to invest in a given financial instrument and equivalently when a leasing arrangement is considered. Then the decision variable is the composition of the leasing contract and this is again a continuous variable, perhaps even multi-dimensional.

Subsequently, such transactions are mapped into the accounting system. Usually, the accounting system only has a discrete number of accounting methods to choose from. This means that the representation in the accounting system is less than complete (Christensen, 2010). Part of the representation is the choice of accounting method and that choice also reveals information to the recipients. The firms produce the financial statements, and the idea is that they have superior information which is revealed to the market via the financial statements. When there is some degree of freedom in the choice of accounting method, the firms may have incentives to use this freedom to distort the financial statements or engage in earnings management (Burgstahler and Dichev, 1997; Demski, 1998; Dye, 2002). As previously discussed, the financial statements are also used to provide managerial incentives or to control management, and this leads to such incentives. If the regulation of financial statements makes earnings management of this sort impossible, then an alternative solution available to managers is to distort the decisions. The decision will be engineered such that it exactly satisfies the criterion used to define the desired accounting treatment of the transaction. In this way, the firm gets the reporting it wants and earnings management is replaced by a 'designer' transaction such that the reporting of the transaction simulates another type of transaction. The above-mentioned leasing arrangement is such a 'designer transaction.' The net result of this behavior is that the good intentions of regulation that transactions are faithfully represented fail to some degree (Christensen and Demski, 2007). Ironically, the incentives of the reporting firm result in an endogenous bias in its financial reporting as a consequence of the reaction of the regulated parties to the imposed regulation. Incentives are at work. Similar points are developed in Ewert and Wagenhofer (2005) and Dye (2002).

Financial reporting provides information and thus it is an information system. Each of the qualitative characteristics provides at most a partial ranking of the information systems and these rankings are not aligned (Demski, 1973). Consequently, the qualitative characteristics do not provide the intended guidance in the choice among accounting alternatives. As previously noted, the fundamental roles of accounting (decision and control) are fundamentally different in the demand for information. The finer details of the decision problem(s) associated with a choice of accounting method are important and cannot be replaced by a proxy called qualitative characteristics.

5. Reporting regulation

The details of the reporting firm and the relation to the decision makers are important determinants of the optimal financial reporting. If we analyze the specific relationship between one decision maker and the reporting firm, it is possible to design an optimal reporting scheme. If no incentive issues are present, the optimal communication would be simply to ask management to report the private information of the firm which is relevant to the decision under consideration.

But (un)fortunately, the world of accounting is not that simple. Incentive issues are found everywhere in relation to financial reporting (Christensen and Demski, 2003). As noted earlier, one of the primary uses of financial information is evaluation of management. The consequence is that management cannot be trusted in supplying the information without bias or omissions. Given the distance between the users and producers of financial reports, it is not possible for the users to commit not to use the information provided by management for evaluation purposes, and just producing one report for each specific decision problem is not viable. As a consequence of the incentive issues, the hard data found in the accounting library is the workhorse of financial reporting. The fundamental ingredient in the accounting report is the hard data on realized cash flows and transactions backed by hard evidence. The next level of useful information is the accounting information, which lends itself to auditing because the auditor is able to verify the information. The presence of the auditor reduces the incentive problem associated with reporting the firm's private information (Antle, 1984).

The information content of the financial report is a complex mix of hard evidence, such as cash flows, and accounting information, which is self-reported by management but which lends itself to auditing. This information system, called financial reporting, is carefully managed in consideration of the incentives of management and the incentives of the auditors. The optimal choice depends upon the decision problem at hand, the distribution (possession) of information of each actor in this game, and the prevailing incentives. In sum, the finer details are important determinants of the optimal financial reporting (Christensen and Demski, 2003).

The language of the communication from the firm is outside economic theory.[4] In our previous discussion it has been referred to as communication of the private information of the firm. This could be done in many equivalent ways: in Danish, in English, or perhaps using numbers. Now, place the firm in a market setting and suppose that many firms are included and there is no direct relation between the user and the producer of financial information. Then there is a demand for coordination of the languages. In the IASB/FASB framework this is codified in the recognition rules and the definitions of items included in and excluded from the financial statements. This is also part of the legacy in the form of textbooks and university curriculums. Traditionally, the language and algebra of valuation has been used in financial statements. This made sense historically, as the market and accounting valuation were closely connected. That is not the case anymore. For most listed firms there is a discrepancy between accounting and market value. The reason for this is that the firms are more complex today, and many assets are not traded in well-functioning markets. Furthermore, the distribution of information in the economy complicates the valuation even further. The accounting system manages this by including and excluding items from the accounts. In this way, the accounting system prescribes different accounting procedures to tangible assets (such as machines) and intangible assets (such as the output of a research activity called knowledge). The first item is accounted for using historical cost, whereas knowledge is expensed and thus not included in the balance sheet. The accounting system and the auditor have great difficulty controlling the incentive issues involved in the valuation of the research activity and it is therefore excluded from the accounts. This exclusion is public knowledge and the investors are therefore able to take that into account when the accounts are used for valuation of the firm. The accounting system is biased compared to the valuation of the firm. Nevertheless, there is certainly a demand for coordination of the language used to communicate financial information (Christensen and Demski, 2003).

In addition to the language issue, there is also a demand for regulation due to the distribution of information in society. The shares of the firm are traded in the capital markets and this creates a demand for information in order to ensure that the markets are well functioning. The key issue is that some investors, including the management of the firm, have access to more information about the future prospects of the firm than the common investor, and not regulating 'the information market' prevents the markets from being well functioning, as concluded previously. Also the separation of management and ownership creates a demand for financial information in the market such that the shareholders can control the directors, i.e. stewardship information.

6. Conclusion

Accounting serves multiple purposes and, as suggested by our analysis, there is no unique optimal set of reporting standards that simultaneously maximizes the benefit of accounting in all circumstances. The finer details of the circumstances are important to identify the optimal financial reporting in each specific decision context. At the fundamental level, the two primary purposes of accounting information are decision and control. The demand for accounting information for the two purposes is fundamentally different. Furthermore, the setting for accounting regulation is by definition a multi-person setting. Consequently, more information is not always better. The demand for accounting regulation is closely tied to the demand for coordination of the market for accounting information, as the link between the makers and users of financial reporting is indirect. There is a demand for regulating the amount of disclosure, the language, and the purpose of reporting. With this in place, the users have a chance of interpreting the published financial statements and to partially understand the underlying economics of the firm.

The response of the regulatory bodies to the complexity of the task has been to replace sensitivity to the different information demands of the users of financial statements with a strong focus on the qualitative characteristics of financial reporting information. Our analysis has found this to be a poor choice, as it blinds the view of the finer details of the economics of the reporting environment. In particular, it ignores the interaction between the preparer's incentives and the accounting standards. One of the primary qualitative characteristics is faithful representation of the underlying economics, but this view collides with the use of the accounts for control purposes.

The comparative advantage of financial reporting information is that it is audited, which increases its credibility. But this has the consequence that the accounting system is a late information source, as auditing takes time. This led Lev (1989) to conclude that the accounting system only carries 7 per cent of the total amount of information to the capital market as seen in the famous diagram by Ball and Brown (1968). This conclusion does not include the indirect use of accounting, as the accounting system might provide credibility to other, perhaps more timely, sources of information. As any regulated accounting system has a limited capacity for providing information (some accounting procedures are excluded), it might be beneficial to allow multiple competing sets of accounting standards as suggested by Dye and Sunder (2001).

In this chapter we have tried to outline the fundamental elements of economic theories which speak to regulation of financial reporting. We have only addressed a few important issues and the interrelation between some of the fundamental problems faced by regulation of this complex system. This might be far removed from the current issues faced by regulators. Research can only provide insights. The politicians are supposed to balance the different interests of users. As Schipper pointed out in her Saxe lecture in 2002:

> This example illustrates, again, an important limitation of accounting research for standard-setting: as the questions become more specific, more narrow, more implementation-oriented and, sometimes, more measurement-oriented, the ability of accounting research to provide insights disappears (Schipper, 2002).

Notes

1 Using economics to analyze accounting has a long tradition. Paton and Littleton (1940), AAA (1966), AAA (1977), Beaver (1998), Christensen and Demski (2003), and Christensen and Feltham (2003, 2005) are examples of this.

2 In his presidential address to the 2003 AAA annual meeting, Demski (2004) also stressed that the impact of changes in accounting regulation cannot be addressed without considering how firms and market participants may react to these changes.

3 This is seen most clearly if contracts are restricted to being linear and accounting reports can take values on the real axis. If an agent who can freely move income across time is offered a contract, $s(y_1, y_2) = \beta_0 + \beta_1 y_1 + \beta_2 y_2$, where $\beta_1 \neq \beta_2$, then there are no bounds to the agent's gains (the owners' losses). In such a setting the owners will always offer contracts where $\beta_1 = \beta_2$.

4 In Christensen and Demski (2003) this indeterminacy is referred to as scaling, and often the information content in accounting numbers is indifferent to the scaling of the numbers.

Bibliography

AAA (1966) *A Statement of Basic Accounting Theory.* Sarasota, FL: American Accounting Association.

AAA (1977) *Statement on Accounting Theory and Theory Acceptance.* Sarasota, FL: American Accounting Association.

AAA (2007) 'The FASB's Conceptual Framework for Financial Reporting'. *Accounting Horizons*, 21(2): 229–38.

Akerlof, G. (1970) 'The Market for "Lemons": Quality, Uncertainty, and the Market Mechanism'. *Quarterly Journal of Economics*, 84(3): 488–500.

Antle, R. (1984) 'Auditor Independence'. *Journal of Accounting Research*, 22(1): 1–20.

Arya, A., Glover, J. and Sunder, S. (2003) 'Are Unmanaged Earnings Always Better for Shareholders?'. *Accounting Horizons*, 17 (Supplement): 111–16.

Arya, A., Frimor, H. and Mittendorf, B. (2010) 'Discretionary Disclosure of Proprietary Information in a Multisegment Firm'. *Management Science*, 56(4): 645–58.

Ball, R. and Brown, P. (1968) 'An Empirical Evaluation of Accounting Income Numbers'. *Journal of Accounting Research*, 6(2): 159–78.

Beaver, W. (1998) *Financial Reporting: An Accounting Revolution*. 3rd edn. Upper Saddle River, NJ: Prentice-Hall.

Beaver, W. and Demski, J. (1979) 'The Nature of Income Measurement'. *The Accounting Review*, 54(1): 38–46.

Burgstahler, D. and Dichev, I. (1997) 'Earnings Management to Avoid Earnings Decreases and Losses'. *Journal of Accounting & Economics*, 24(1): 99–126.

Bushman, R. and Landsman, W. R. (2010) 'The Pros and Cons of Regulating Corporate Reporting: A Critical Review of the Arguments'. *Accounting and Business Research*, 40(3).

Christensen, J. (2010) 'Accounting Errors and Errors of Accounting'. *The Accounting Review*, 85(6): 1827–38.

Christensen, J. and Demski, J. (2003) *Accounting Theory: An Information Content Perspective.* New York: McGraw-Hill/Irwin.

Christensen, J. and Demski, J. (2007) 'Anticipatory Reporting Standards'. *Accounting Horizons*, 21(4): 351–70.
Christensen, J. and Frimor, H. (2007) 'Fair Value, Accounting Aggregation and Multiple Sources of Information', in R. Antle, P. J. Liang and F. Gjesdal (eds) *Essays on Accounting Theory in Honour of Joel S. Demski*. New York: Springer, pp. 35–51.
Christensen, P. O. and Feltham, G. A. (2003) *Economics of Accounting, Vol. 1: Information in Markets*. (Springer Series in Accounting Scholarship 1) New York: Springer Science+Business Media.
Christensen, P. O. and Feltham, G. A. (2005) *Economics of Accounting, Vol. 2: Performance Evaluation*. (Springer Series in Accounting Scholarship 2) New York: Springer Science+Business Media.
Christensen, P. O., Demski, J. S. and Frimor, H. (2002) 'Accounting Policies in Agencies with Moral Hazard and Renegotiation'. *Journal of Accounting Research*, 40(4): 1071–90.
Christensen, P. O., Feltham, G. A. and Sabac, F. (2005) 'A Contracting Perspective on Earnings Quality'. *Journal of Accounting and Economics*, 39(2): 265–94.
Christensen, P. O., de la Rosa, L. E. and Feltham, G. A. (2010) 'Information and the Cost of Capital: An *Ex Ante* Perspective'. *The Accounting Review*, 85(3): 817–48.
Christensen, P.O., Frimor, H. and Sabac, F. (2013) 'The Stewardship Role of Analyst Forecasts, and Discretionary Versus Non-Discretionary Accruals'. *European Accounting Review*, 22(2): 257–96.
Clikeman, P. M. (2009) *Called to Account: Fourteen Financial Frauds that Shaped the American Accounting Profession*. New York: Routledge.
Dang, T. V., Gorton, G. and Holmstrom, B. R. (2009) 'Opacity and the Optimality of Debt for Liquidity Provision'. Unpublished. Yale University.
Deegan, G. (2001) *Financial Accounting Theory*. Sydney: Irwin/McGraw-Hill.
Demski, J. (1973) 'The General Impossibility of Normative Accounting Standards'. *The Accounting Review*, 48(4): 718–23.
Demski, J. (1998) 'Performance Measure Manipulation'. *Contemporary Accounting Research*, 15(3): 261–85.
Demski, J. (2004) 'Endogenous Expectations'. *The Accounting Review*, 79(2): 519–39.
Demski, J. and Frimor, H. (1999) 'Performance Measure Garbling Under Renegotiation in Multi-Period Agencies'. *Journal of Accounting Research*, 37 (Supplement): 187–214.
Dye, R. A. (2002) 'Classifications Manipulation and Nash Accounting Standards'. *Journal of Accounting Research*, 40(4): 1125–62.
Dye, R. A. and S. Sunder (2001) 'Why Not Allow FASB and IASB Standards to Compete in the US?'. *Accounting Horizons*, 15(3): 257–71.
Ewert, R. and Wagenhofer, A. (2005) 'Economic Effects of Tightening Accounting Standards to Restrict Earnings Management'. *The Accounting Review*, 80(4): 1101–24.
FASB (2008) 'Conceptual Framework for Financial Reporting: The Objective of Financial Reporting and Qualitative Characteristics and Constraints of Decision-Useful Financial Reporting Information'. Exposure Draft, No. 1570–100, Norwalk, CT: FASB
FASB (2010) *Statement of Financial Accounting Concepts No. 8.*, Norwalk, CT: FASB.
FASB (2012) *Concepts Statements*. Available at www.fasb.org/jsp/FASB/Page/SectionPage&cid= 1176156317989.
Feltham, G. and Xie, J. (1994) 'Performance Measure Congruity and Diversity in Multi-Task Principal-Agent Relations'. *The Accounting Review*, 69(3): 429–53.
Francis, J., LaFond, R., Olsson, P. and Schipper, K. (2004) 'Cost of Equity and Earnings Attributes'. *The Accounting Review*, 79(4): 967–1010.
Francis, J., LaFond, R., Olsson, P. and Schipper, K. (2005) 'The Market Pricing of Accruals Quality'. *Journal of Accounting and Economics*, 39(2): 295–327.
Fudenberg, D. and Tirole, J. (1990) 'Moral Hazard and Renegotiation in Agency Contracts'. *Econometrica*, 58(6): 1279–319.
Gigler, F. and Hemmer, T. (2004) 'On the Value of Transparency in Agencies with Renegotiation'. *Journal of Accounting Research*, 42(5): 871–93.
Gjesdal, F. (1981) 'Accounting for Stewardship'. *Journal of Accounting Research*, 19(1): 208–31.
Grossman, S. J. and Stiglitz, J. E. (1980) 'On the Impossibility of Informationally Efficient Markets'. *American Economic Review*, 70(3): 393–408.
Hermalin, B. E. and Katz, M. L. (1991) 'Moral Hazard and Verifiability: The Effects of Renegotiation in Agency'. *Econometrica*, 59(6): 1735–53.
Holmstrom, B. (1979) 'Moral Hazard and Observability'. *Bell Journal of Economics*, 10(1): 74–91.

IASB (2010) *The Conceptual Framework for Financial Reporting*. London: International Accounting Standards Board.

Lev, B. (1989) 'On the Usefulness of Earnings and Earnings Research: Lessons and Directions from Two Decades of Empirical Research'. *Journal of Accounting Research*, 27(2): 157–78.

Milgrom, P. and Stokey, N. (1982) 'Information, trade and common knowledge'. *Journal of Economic Theory*, 26(1): 17–27.

Paton, W. and Littleton, A. (1940) *An Introduction to Corporate Accounting Standards*. Sarasota, FL: American Accounting Association.

Schipper, K. (2002) 'Implications of Accounting Research for Financial Reporting Standard-setting'. (Saxe Lectures in Accounting). Available at: http://newman.baruch.cuny.edu/digital/saxe/saxe_2002/schipper_2002.htm.

Schipper, K. and Vincent, L. (2003) 'Earnings Quality'. *Accounting Horizons*, 17 (Supplement): 97–110.

Wagenhofer, A. (2009) 'Global Accounting Standards: Reality and Ambitions'. *Accounting Research Journal*, 22(1): 68–80.

13

Global Convergence of Accounting Standards

Alfred Wagenhofer

1. The move to global convergence

Convergence of accounting standards describes the phenomenon that the accounting standards in two or more countries become more aligned or even uniform over time. It comprises harmonization of accounting standards, when standards are made broadly consistent, and standardization, which is the adoption of the same standards in several countries.

Accounting standards have usually been developed within a single country as part of its company and capital markets regulation. These legal institutions differed and continue to differ substantially across countries. The reason is that accounting is intricately embedded in the economic, financial, legal, social, and cultural environment in a country. Accounting evolved jointly with other institutions and its state is a result of the development of these institutions and the historical path they took.[1]

If there was convergence in the past, it was often caused by countries imposing their own legal systems, including the accounting regime, on their colonies and other dependent countries. With the reduction of such dependence, the systems usually began to diverge again. In other cases, there was influence through accounting theories conceived in one country, which were taken up in other countries in shaping their accounting standards. However, there was little need, and thus little effort, to formally converge accounting regimes over a number of countries for a long time. It did not make sense to strive for convergence if countries are relatively self-sustaining and there is not much interdependence among them.

One major undertaking for convergence of accounting standards was the harmonization of accounting in the EU. It began in the late 1960s with an attempt to develop a harmonized framework for financial reports of companies in the EU member states. The underlying principle was to reduce country-specific restrictions on the establishment of companies. The accounting directives were rooted in company law and should create safeguards and minimum legal requirements for financial information to protect members and third parties. The endeavour took many years before the Fourth and Seventh Directives were enacted in 1978 and 1983, respectively. The harmonization achieved by the Directives was moderate, as they include dozens of options for member states or companies directly.

At about the same time the EU started the work on harmonization, the Accountants' International Study Group (AISG) was founded. It consisted of members from the UK, Canada, and the USA and its main objective was to compare the seemingly similar accounting standards in these countries, only to find out that there were more differences than expected. Its main achievement probably was that it formed the core for the International Accounting Standards Committee (IASC), which was established in 1973 by nine countries.[2] Its original objective was to harmonize financial reporting globally, and it began developing the International Accounting Standards (IAS). The first IASs described the practice of accounting across many countries and were loaded with alternative treatments. Over time, the standards became more stringent as the IASC became more influential. In the mid-1990s some countries granted companies the option to prepare consolidated financial statements according to IAS only, and did not require consolidated statements under national GAAP. Particularly large listed companies took advantage of this option.

In 2001, the IASC was restructured into the IASB.[3] Its objectives are 'to develop, in the public interest, a single set of high quality, understandable and enforceable global accounting standards', to 'promote the use and rigorous application of those standards', and to 'bring about convergence of national accounting standards and IFRSs to high quality solutions' (Preface to IFRSs, para. 6). Since then convergence has been a major undertaking by the IASB. The focus of the IASB is the use of financial information in the capital markets, although it has more recently turned attention also to non-public, small and medium-sized companies, and emerging economies.

A landmark decision for the IASB was the adoption of IFRS by the EU with the IAS Regulation in 2002. It resulted from a number of legislative steps the EU took to foster the European capital market development. The IAS Regulation requires the consolidated financial statements of listed companies in the EU to be prepared under IFRS as of 2005, and it gives options to member states to extend the applicability of IFRS to non-listed companies and to separate accounts. This Regulation immediately made some 7,000 of the largest EU companies adopters of international accounting standards. Further, it increased the importance and the standing of the IASB as a, or rather *the*, global standard setter.

Meanwhile, IFRS has been adopted or is accepted in more than a hundred countries worldwide. This is indeed evidence of global convergence of accounting standards and an eminent success of the IASB (and its predecessor, the IASC). There are two large countries with powerful capital markets that are not (yet) on the list of countries adopting IFRS: the US and Japan. The US authorities have sent mixed signals as to acceptance of IFRS. In 2007, the SEC abolished the reconciliation requirement for foreign firms listed in the US if they prepare IFRS financial statements. It also proposed a roadmap for the acceptance or adoption of IFRS for US companies and a staff work plan. A final decision whether the US should transition to IFRS is pending. Japan has not made a decision either, but already permits some Japanese companies to prepare financial statements in accordance with IFRS. Other countries, such as China, Malaysia, and India aim to converge with IFRS. Besides the capital market pressure, the World Bank has been instrumental in pushing for convergence with or adoption of IFRS in many countries.

These major steps in the global convergence of accounting standards provide evidence of the apparently large economic benefits of converged standards. This chapter discusses the benefits and costs of convergence mainly in the context of the developments of convergence towards and adoption of IFRS. Presumably the benefits are higher than the costs since otherwise it would be difficult to rationalize the convergence that has been achieved so far. However, convergence does not occur in all accounting areas. Therefore the chapter also examines various dimensions of convergence.

The adoption of IFRS is clearly a historic event and illustrates many aspects of convergence of accounting standards. However, it should be noted that IFRS are adopted not only because they bring convergence in the sense of standardization, but they are commonly considered to be of higher quality than many local GAAP they substitute. Most of the vast literature studying economic effects of IFRS adoption does not, or cannot, distinguish between these two reasons for adoption. The focus on this chapter is on convergence and less on the quality of standards.[4]

2. Globalization as a main driver for convergence

Whereas early initiatives for harmonization in the EU were driven by minimal financial information requirements in each of the member states (so high quality of financial statements was not the objective), the main impetus for the convergence of accounting standards was the globalization of capital markets. Capital markets have grown due to increased demand of and supply for equity capital.[5] Companies began to make more use of international capital markets to raise capital, and investors began to allocate money globally to reap greater returns and to diversify risk more efficiently. The globalization of capital markets has been facilitated by technological advancements in trading and disseminating information.

Global accounting standards enhance the comparability of companies located in different countries. They reduce the costs investors incur to understand, analyse and compare financial statements and they increase the information investors are able to use to interpret companies' financial position and the risks involved to evaluate their prospects. This leads to more efficient global resource allocation and capital formation, and to increased competition among stock exchanges, which again should lower the cost of capital, increase market liquidity, and eventually boost economic growth.[6] Indeed, one of the main breakthroughs of IFRS internationally was the endorsement of the (then) IAS by the International Organization of Securities Commissions (IOSCO) in 2000 for multinational issuers of capital in cross-border offerings and listings. Cross-listing came into vogue for companies to improve raising capital, and they even prepared IFRS financial statements voluntarily, thereby incurring significant costs of preparation and auditing. The SEC also acknowledges comparability as the main driver for convergence of US GAAP with IFRS, up to adopting IFRS in the longer run.[7]

Besides the capital market effects, convergence of accounting standards facilitates transactions and relationships with other parties in global business. It improves effective communication with stakeholders regardless of where they are located, because all parties know the underlying standards according to which the financial information is prepared. So, financial statements are readily interpretable. For example, lending decisions can be based on financial information that is readily understood. Suppliers and customers can better assess the economic situation of the firm if they are familiar with the accounting standards under which the firm reports. Information that is useful for acquisitions of firms, the formation of joint ventures, and other investments becomes easier to collect and understand. These effects facilitate cooperation and trade globally.

Global standards are also useful for contracting purposes. It becomes easier to write contracts that include covenants based on accounting numbers if parties are familiar with accounting standards that are used to prepare the accounting numbers. They are in a better position to understand and forecast the numbers and, thus, the outcome of contracts will be less risky and better enforceable.

Other benefits of global standards arise on the firm level, particularly in multinational firms. If the subsidiaries report under the same accounting standards, consolidation becomes less costly, timelier, and more accurate. It also reduces the cost of preparation, communication, and analysis of management reports within the group. Internal control systems become better aligned. For example, a survey of CFOs by PricewaterhouseCoopers (2002) reveals that the adoption of IFRS benefits internal reporting systems, risk management, accounting processes, and increases trust in reported numbers.

Global standards also provide benefits from a regulatory point of view. Companies may be inclined to exploit differences in national regulation regimes and cherry-pick favourable regulatory provisions in designing its organization. Firms can structure transactions so as to target gaps in different accounting standards. This holds for industrial firms and also for banks and insurance companies, which are subject to regulatory supervision. Such actions reduce the effectiveness of supervision and oversight in capital markets and other markets and are significantly reduced if the regulatory regimes are standardized. Regulation and enforcement have become more international, and an international standard improves the coordination of such efforts.

3. Comparability of financial statements

3.1 Institutions and incentives

Accounting practice is determined not only by accounting standards, but also by institutions and incentives. Institutions include the legal systems, capital market regulation, product market competition, company law, enforcement, and firm-level incentives, such as ownership structures, financing, corporate governance, and compensation practices. Institutions, together with tradition and education, shape incentives. This has two consequences:

- convergence of accounting standards does not necessarily imply convergence of financial reporting practice;[8] and
- it is unlikely that a single set of standards works best in all institutional environments.[9]

The same standard can lead to diverse practice across countries if it allows different accounting policies, either explicitly or implicitly. For example, Kvaal and Nobes (2010, 2012) analyse accounting policy choices of companies after the adoption of IFRS in five large countries. They have found evidence that companies attempted to continue with accounting practices they complied with before adopting IFRS, thus leading to diversity in practice despite a common standard. They also found that companies in France and Spain changed their accounting policies in the years after the transition, suggesting they learnt to use options provided in IFRS that were new relative to their local GAAP.

Application of the same standards may differ even if it includes no options. For example, cultural differences across countries, such as basic risk attitude and tradition, can sustain diversity in practice. Schultz and Lopez (2001) report on an experiment with experienced auditors who work in the offices of the same global audit firm in France, Germany, and the US. They received the same information about a firm that had introduced a new product and had to estimate a provision for guarantees under IFRS. The amount of the provision differed significantly, being highest in France, then Germany, and finally the US. This finding suggests that cultural differences influence judgement in subtle ways.

Selection among options and discretionary choices are strongly affected by incentives. There are countries in which financial accounting is the basis for determining income tax payments, whereas there are other countries in which this is not the case. The direct link between financial and taxable income affects management's incentives for earnings management, and even if the same accounting standards apply, their application is likely to differ significantly. Management compensation that is heavily tied to particular earnings numbers or stock price increases incentives for earnings management, which can reduce the usefulness of financial statements. Typical management compensation packages differ across countries, and, hence, the incentives for earnings management and the comparability of financial reports differ.

A major implementation issue is the fit of new accounting standards with the legal system in a country. It has an important effect on the interpretation and application of standards. The IFRS are developed based on the legal environment of Anglo-American countries, and their form is similar to the accounting standards in these countries. The legal systems in Anglo-American countries are based on common law, whereas other countries follow very different legal traditions.[10] Applying IFRS in other countries can lead to difficulties in the application of the standards, as different legal methodologies may lead to different interpretations particularly in situations in which several views may be appropriate. IAS 8 provides guidance for the interpretation of the IFRSs, but does not describe a self-contained legal system for interpretation.[11]

Implementation of accounting concepts that are common in one country but uncommon in another may also create diversity. For example, the Fourth Directive includes a true-and-fair-view principle, which is a familiar concept in the UK, but alien to many other European countries, so it is likely that it is applied differently. Further, the Directive – and following that also IAS 1 – requires an override in the rare circumstances that a true and fair view is not achieved by following the standards, again a concept uncommon in many countries.

Translation of accounting standards into another language is another source for divergence. IFRSs are written in the original English language and then translated into many languages used around the world. Some translations are prepared by the IASB itself with the help of local institutions, and the EU endorsement process (see also below) requires translations into the EU's official languages. Translations may be of differing quality and may lead to different interpretations if there is no equivalent expression in the respective language or if the expression is associated with a term that is already used in local GAAP.[12] Curiously, Portugal and Brazil apparently use two different Portuguese translations of IFRS.

Quality assurance of financial reports varies across countries. Auditing, corporate governance, and enforcement differ significantly. In some countries, for example Japan and the Netherlands, qualified audit reports are highly uncommon, which does not mean that auditing is of low quality, but rather that there are other means for auditors to influence financial statement quality. Similarly, enforcement results differ across countries. For example, the percentage of erroneous financial statements in Denmark, Germany, and Portugal is around 25 per cent, compared with some 2 per cent in the UK and Spain.[13] It is unlikely that these large differences are attributable only to differences in the quality of financial reports in these countries; rather they suggest differences in the organization and effectiveness of enforcement. Christensen *et al.* (2013) even suggest that the enforcement is the main driver for economic effects of IFRS adoption.

Financial reports that are subject to strong quality assurance are of higher quality than financial reports prepared under the same standards but subject to lax assurance. Such differences may even affect the desirability of specific accounting measurement rules. For example, an accounting standard that requires measurement of many assets at fair value estimates may result in highly useful information if it is applied in a country with strong quality assurance in place. In another country with lax assurance the same measurement rule can result in financial numbers that are not trustworthy and therefore useless. In such a country, an accounting standard that avoids such estimates may provide a more informative and comparable view of the financial situation of companies. Another interaction between accounting standards and enforcement occurs in countries with a highly litigious environment. Preparers and auditors strongly demand rules in lieu of principles because rules reduce or eliminate judgement, which lowers the risk of being found guilty of not correctly applying the standard.

The importance of the institutional environment has been acknowledged by the IASB, but apparently it does not guide the development of its standards, which are developed with the presumption that they are enforced effectively. Rather, the IASB calls for improvements in the institutional environment to effectively enforce its standards. There are several initiatives underway to improve quality assurance which aim to increase convergence of financial reporting practices in the long run.[14] For example, the International Standards on Auditing (ISA) provide a global basis for providing assurance services, and several countries operate audit oversight bodies. Convergence of corporate governance is more difficult because company laws differ substantially across countries. Harmonization occurs on a higher level; for example, the OECD issued principles of corporate governance in 1999.

Enforcement and litigation are also difficult to harmonize as they are fundamentally embedded in national legislation. Decisions by enforcement agencies or courts affect the application of a standard in a particular country, and it is not obvious whether there is a mechanism that could be established in which decisions on global accounting standards made in one country extend to other countries. It is also likely that different enforcement agencies and courts can come to differing conclusions about similar underlying facts. Therefore, global accounting standards can lead to increasing divergence in accounting practice over time, as more conflicting legal decisions are made. In the EU, the European Enforcers Coordination Sessions (EECS) have been established under the European Securities and Markets Authority (ESMA) as a forum to exchange information regarding the enforcement of IFRS. It maintains a database of enforcement decisions to coordinate application in the member states.[15] However, it is difficult to see whether a similar mechanism to coordinate global enforcement could be established.

3.2 Comparability and IFRS adoption

The adoption of IFRS in the EU and in many other countries provides an interesting setting to study whether adopting a single set of accounting standards in fact increases comparability. Comparability requires that similar transactions and events are recorded similarly, and dissimilar transactions and events are recorded differently. This means that adopting the same accounting standards can *reduce* comparability in practice if they do not sufficiently take account of institutional differences, with the result that dissimilar events are reported similarly and users of financial statements cannot discern the different economics. Indeed, Stecher and Suijs (2012) suggest that if users across countries are heterogeneous, a single global accounting standard may become a lowest common denominator and that a reconciliation requirement may be preferable.

Recent empirical literature addresses this issue based on data around the mandatory adoption of IFRS by companies in several countries. There are several ways to measure comparability. Input-based measures are based on accounting policy choices, whereas output-based measures capture the similarity of accounting numbers resulting from similar economic events. Input-based measures indicate an increase in comparability if IFRS includes fewer options than the sum of local GAAP that were applied before the transition to IFRS. As mentioned earlier, a caveat is that discretion may still be exercised differently. In general, such analyses suggest that comparability has increased.

Output-based measures capture both the standards and the incentives effects on comparability. A common measure is based on De Franco *et al.* (2011), which essentially maps economic events into earnings. Comparability between two companies' accounting systems is considered higher if they produce more similar financial statements for a given set of economic events. They use stock returns as the proxy for similar economic events; an alternative proxy is cash flow from operations.

Empirical studies provide mixed evidence. For example, Yip and Young (2012) use a sample of companies in 17 European countries and find that the IFRS adoption increases cross-country comparability by making the mapping of similar events more similar, without making dissimilar events more similar. Lang *et al.* (2010) construct a sample from 47 countries, including IFRS adopting and non-adopting countries. They find that IFRS adoption increased earnings co-movement, which is that earnings variations are related regardless of whether the underlying economic events are similar or not. However, they also find that cross-country comparability based on the mapping of returns into earnings did not increase relative to a control sample of non-adopting firms. Barth *et al.* (2012) find that the application of IFRSs in countries previously using local GAAP enhanced financial reporting comparability with US firms, even though some differences remain. Cascino and Gassen (2011) specifically study German and Italian companies and find that the overall comparability increase is limited. However, comparability increases for firms with high compliance incentives. On the other hand, Brochet *et al.* (2012) studied companies in the UK, where the transition to IFRS did not significantly change accounting quality as UK standards were relatively close to IFRS, so any effects of IFRS adoption could be attributed to an increase in comparability. They find that IFRS adoption increases comparability and improves capital market information.

Kim, Kraft, and Ryan (2012) suggest an alternative measure of comparability, which is the variability of the adjustments that Moody's makes to better compare financial reports of companies in peer industries. They find that greater comparability is associated with lower bid-ask spreads for corporate bonds, among others. An indirect measure of comparability is the change in investment strategies. Since comparability improves the information about companies in different countries, investors are more likely to invest in foreign firms. Khurana and Michas (2011) find indeed that US investors increase the weight of stocks in countries that adopt IFRS.

The implication from these studies is that it is not necessarily the case that the adoption of the same accounting standards increases comparability. Since many countries that adopt IFRS also change their institutional environment, for example auditing, governance, and enforcement, this result is even more intriguing as one would strongly expect comparability to increase. It should be noted that the notion of comparability is different from that of quality of financial reporting, but it is difficult to separate them empirically. Thus, there may be beneficial effects of IFRS adoption that are a consequence of an increase in the quality of financial reporting rather than of higher comparability.

4. Quality of converged accounting standards

4.1 Format of the standards

Transactions and events may vary considerably across countries due to different forms of trade, different contracts, differences in legislation, and the like. Therefore, accounting standards that are globally used must encompass such differences. The IASB attempts to do this by formulating accounting principles based on the economic substance of transactions but not describing them in detail. An alternative is to add standards ('rules') for every conceivable form of transaction, something that US GAAP had followed before the convergence with the IASB. Stating principles only leaves much discretion with companies and leads to diversity in practice. Adding rules may become messy and may incorporate exceptions that contradict the main principles.

To illustrate this concern with current IFRSs, consider the situation in some countries where it is prohibited to buy land and the common way to possess land is to rent it for, say, 99 years. According to IAS 17 such a transaction is accounted for as an operating lease. IAS 40 offers a fair value model for measuring investment property, but this option does not extend to operating leases. To extend the application of the fair value model to such specific situations, IAS 40 includes an exemption for investment property that overrides the accounting principle. Another example is the classification of financial instruments as equity or liability under IAS 32. There are countries in which certain kinds of owners' equity contributions are subject to a legal redemption provision. According to the principle in IAS 32, such instruments are classified as liability, which contrasts with the view in these countries. IAS 32 has been amended to include a highly specific and detailed exemption for such capital, which contradicts the principle. Tax regulations provide another example for the need to adjust accounting standards to accommodate country-specific tax rules. For example, in some countries holding gains are taxed differently from operating gains. IAS 12 has recently been amended to include a rebuttable assumption for the applicable tax rate of the recovery of investment property.

A different kind of challenge is the inclusion of specific forms of ownership and financing. For example, the *keiretsu* in Japan offers substantial influence and coordination among companies; the *Hausbank* financing system in Germany provides a bank with insider information and influence on companies; and Islamic finance is difficult to compare with forms of financing in Western countries. The question then is whether such transactions are economically similar to the concepts underlying the development of global standards or if they should be covered by separate standards. That is, errors would occur either if different transactions are recorded similarly or if they are indeed similar but recorded differently. Moreover, it may be difficult to clearly define the economic substance without having an unintended impact on other transactions, such as generating structuring opportunities.

4.2 Efficiency of standard setting

A major potential benefit of global accounting standards lies in the broad knowledge, experience, and expertise that can be considered and used in the process of developing standards. Setting global standards involves people from many different countries and it pulls together ideas and views from constituents worldwide. If standards are developed in a joint convergence effort, for example by the IASB and the FASB, the expertise of both large standard setters is brought to the table. Ideally, the resulting standards should then be of higher quality. The discussion of technical issues is facilitated by organizations such as the International Forum of Accounting Standard Setters (IFASS), which replaced the National Standard Setters (NSS) forum, and the Consultative Forum of Standard Setters (CFSS) that is organized within the European Financial Reporting Group (EFRAG).

Joint standard setting reduces the total cost of standard setting in the economy because of economies of scale. It avoids parallel efforts to develop standards and allows standard setters to build on expertise from others. Standards that have proved effective can be adopted and standards that did not work very well can be avoided or improved. Despite this broader set of expertise, converged standards tend to persist, as it is difficult to innovate, experiment, or simply change standards that are widely applied in practice. It is clearly not desirable to use a large part of the world as 'beta testers' of new standards; hence, changing converged standards significantly has a high cost and slows down change.

Given the existence of a global standard setter, incentives for countries to maintain their own national accounting standard setters decrease because it is costly, but the marginal benefit diminishes. The IASB emphasizes potential benefits of national standard setters to avoid undermining their existence. It argues that their contribution can be to bring to the IASB's attention specific issues that it should consider, to ensure consistent interpretation and application of standards, to provide feedback on implementation issues, and many more. The IASB also cooperates with individual national standard setters on particular projects.

Diminishing influence of a single national standard setter has led to the establishment of regional groups of standard setters. In the EU, the EFRAG assumes an important role in the formal endorsement process of IFRS. In addition, it undertakes pro-active projects to provide input into conceptual accounting issues. More recently, the Asian-Oceanian Standard-Setters Group (AOSSG) and the Group of Latin-American Standard-Setters (GLASS) were formed. The IASB regards these groups as the main channels of cooperation with national standard setters, as it becomes increasingly difficult for the IASB to talk to each standard setter separately. It remains to be seen how this hierarchical system of aggregating communication to the IASB will work in practice.

4.3 Politics of standard setting

Involvement of many people and different organizations in standard setting also has disadvantages. Accounting is not a technical discipline in a sense that there is a 'true' accounting, which must only be discovered; accounting is driven by objectives and requires trade-offs in achieving the objectives. Therefore, constituents may have very different views on issues: they vary in their background and experience; they may have a hidden political agenda (including perhaps to preserve the status quo); and the like. Moreover, the political power and influence of constituents may vary across countries.

Attempting to listen to all constituents is likely to slow down or paralyse standard setting because the groups of people whose views are not supported oppose the standard.[16] The quality of accounting standards can even decrease if a global standard setter avoids generating opposition to a standard and tries to please everyone by adopting lax or ambivalent standards. Alternatively, a global standard setter may be induced to consider every aspect in a new standard, which can make it difficult to discern the principle or can lead to complex and rules-based standards. Consequently, the objective of providing global high-quality standards may be compromised.

Accounting standard setting has traditionally been a target for political influence. The main reason is that accounting redistributes wealth and a new accounting standard may benefit some stakeholders at the cost of others. Political influence can be exerted by governance mechanisms imposed on the standard setter, such as monitoring boards, degree of delegation, veto power, and more subtly, financing the standard setter, particularly if it is a private body. Public lobbying and lobbying behind closed doors are other means to influence standard setters' decisions. As a result, accounting standards can include compromises and exceptions, which contradict the conceptual basis. Examples for political interference in the recent past are the recognition of changes in the fair value of financial instruments in income or directly in equity (other comprehensive income); the expensing of management stock options in income or only disclosure; and the smoothing of pension liabilities with a device known as the corridor approach.

Political pressure increases with the importance of the IASB's standards. Countries may want to gain more influence in the IFRS Foundation (IFRSF) and the IASB.[17] For example, a report to the European Parliament argues that the decision to adopt IFRS in the EU has turned IASB into a quasi-regulator and this fact would require several measures to change the governance structure of the IFRSF.[18] The IFRSF reacted with a review of the constitution that eventually established a monitoring group with representatives of public authorities and international organizations as a second oversight body besides the trustees. Recognizing the fact that political influence is increasingly important, the new chairman of the IASB as of 2011 was a former politician.

It is an open issue if standards developed by a global standard setter are more or less susceptible to political influence than those of national standard setters. One may argue that lobbying effectiveness reduces for at least two reasons:

- the likelihood that lobbying succeeds in affecting a standard is reduced if there are many divergent interests globally, so that there will be less lobbying impact. For example, it becomes more difficult to have an effect on standard setting if the issue arises only in one or few jurisdictions; and
- the de facto power of the global standard setter increases with increasing acceptance worldwide, so pressure by national political powers is less effective.

However, a global standard setter is vulnerable to political pressure by a major country (or group of countries) that threatens to withdraw support and perhaps develops its own accounting standards or derivatives of the global standard. For example, the EU as the 'prime' consumer of IFRS through its mandatory IFRS adoption influenced standards heavily, particularly when it comes to standards that lean more to US GAAP. In 2006, the IASB proposed the adoption of SFAS 131 on operating segments essentially word by word. After little resistance, the draft was enacted as IFRS 8 in the same year. However, the endorsement by the EU was controversial as members of the European Parliament resisted an 'Americanization' of IFRS and finally accepted it only under the provision that it be reviewed within two years after becoming effective. Indeed, the IASB is currently undertaking a post-implementation review of IFRS 8. As another example, in the wake of the financial crisis 2008, the EU threatened to write its own standard on financial instruments to facilitate reclassification out of categories that require fair value measurement into cost-based measurement, arguing that European banks should not be subject to stricter rules than US banks. The IASB reacted with a hasty amendment to IAS 39 that was passed within three or so days ignoring the due process, and the EU endorsed the amendment within another three days.

The final result of a convergence process depends on the willingness of countries to give up some of their sovereignty with respect to setting accounting standards and on the power of other countries. For example, Simmons (2001) argues that accounting standards for cross-listing pose low negative externalities to a large country such as the US, but induce high incentives for others to follow them. This would suggest little movement by the US to adopt international accounting standards. On the other hand, Posner (2010) describes a path dependency of institutional configurations and regulatory capacities that eventually made IFRS rather than US GAAP *the* international accounting standard. Véron (2007) calls the move of the EU the 'global accounting experiment', as the full consequences are not yet known.

5. Dimensions of convergence

Convergence describes the process of bringing closer together accounting standards across countries. It comprises a broad spectrum ranging from harmonization of standards to standardization by employing uniform standards. From an economic point of view, convergence is desirable if the benefits are greater than the costs in the long run. Therefore, one would expect convergence (to a certain degree) to occur in some settings, but not in others. It is difficult to quantify many of the benefits and costs, although it is possible to make statements on changes in net benefits and trends. For example, it is well known that the benefits of standardization increase with the adoption of the standards due to network benefits.[19] Switching costs of firms and institutions in a country are important, but are a one-time effect that needs to be traded off against the long-term net benefits of a change. In this section, I review the degree and the potential scope of convergence and discuss mandatory or voluntary adoption options.

5.1 Degree of convergence

There are several aspects that affect the degree of convergence of standards. One aspect is the flexibility of the converged standard. The harmonization in the EU was shaped by accounting directives that included dozens of options, which were essentially taken from local GAAP in case countries could not find a compromise.[20] Therefore, the success of the harmonization was low, as countries were usually able to continue with the standards with which they were accustomed prior to the directives. This example shows that it is possible to formally converge to a common standard, as long as it is flexible enough. Flexibility can occur through explicit options or principles that are sufficiently high-level so as to allow various interpretations. However, in this way formal convergence happens without bringing convergence of financial reporting practice, which also illustrates that convergence and quality are different, and sometimes countervailing, concepts. The IASB follows a different strategy: IFRS includes high-quality, tight standards with relatively few options. Converging with IFRS, therefore, implies significant change in the reporting practice and makes it harder to achieve.[21]

There are several ways to converge with IFRS.[22] The most natural way is that a country simply incorporates IFRS without any qualification. The main problem with this route is that for most countries it is not feasible to give away authority to set accounting standards to a foreign private body such as the IASB. The solution is the establishment of a formal endorsement mechanism, which includes a review of the standards and an approval decision.

Some countries incorporate IFRS within their local standards. For example, Australia adopts IFRS as part of Australian Accounting Standards. The Australian standard setter makes sure that complying with Australian Accounting Standards ensures compliance with IFRS. Again, the reference in financial reports is to Australian standards rather than to IFRS directly. The EU's endorsement process requires amending the EU regulation. This process is lengthy, not least because of the translation of the standard into the official EU languages. It involves several European bodies besides the European Commission: three committees, one technical, one political, and one that overviews the process; further, it requires votes in the European Parliament and the Council. The involvement of many different institutions increases the likelihood that a standard is not endorsed, which then creates a local version of IFRS. The EU, indeed, has carved out a specific hedge accounting rule so that the European IFRSs are not compliant with the full IFRSs.[23] Financial reports in the EU refer to 'IFRSs as endorsed by the EU'. An endorsement process allows inclusion of country-specific amendments and modifications, but hinders full convergence with IFRS and may induce confusion among users of financial statements, thus reducing the potential benefits of global standards. Moreover, an endorsement process is time-consuming and can cause a delay in the incorporation of a new standard. The SEC staff proposed a further endorsement process, labelled 'condorsement' (SEC 2011), which involves a lengthy transition period over which US GAAP would converge to IFRS before IFRS is fully incorporated.

Convergence can also bring different sets of standards closer together. Indeed, this is probably the original use of the term 'convergence' – albeit without achieving full compliance. The IASB works to persuade countries to adopt IFRS as they are. There are some large countries that have not endorsed IFRS yet. With two of them, the US and Japan, the IASB has set up long-term convergence projects. In a Memorandum of Understanding (MoU) in 2002, known as the Norwalk Agreement, the IASB and the FASB agreed to make their standards fully compatible and to coordinate the future development of standards. The Memorandum does not explicitly talk about 'convergence'; however, in the MoU 2006 the boards reaffirmed their commitment to IFRS and US GAAP convergence, thus using the term 'convergence'. The MoU shaped much of the work programme of the IASB over the last few years, including the development of new standards on major themes such as financial instruments, leases, and revenue recognition. The FASB has been highly successful (perhaps too successful for some observers) in shaping new standards and gearing them towards its own thinking.

The history of the convergence project also reveals difficulties that the two boards have with achieving full convergence. One example is the development of a new standard on financial instruments. Probably influenced by the EU, the IASB hurried to develop a new standard, IFRS 9, as response to the financial crisis in 2008, and organized the project in a piecemeal approach. In contrast, the FASB took longer, but offered a full-fledged draft of a new standard. Despite the overall convergence objective, the draft standards differ substantially, particularly on the impairment for financial instruments carried at cost. Another example is the development of a new standard on business combinations. Here, the two boards were successful in agreeing to a common standard but, nevertheless, the IASB introduced a new option for the measurement of goodwill of non-controlling interests into IFRS 3 that is not available under US GAAP. The reason arguably was that several IASB members were uncomfortable with the full goodwill approach.

In 2007, the IASB and the Accounting Standards Board of Japan (ASBJ) signed the Tokyo Agreement, in which both boards 'share the belief that convergence towards high quality accounting standards will greatly benefit capital markets around the world' and seek to eliminate major differences in their standards. Japan has less influence on the resulting, converged standards than the US, which is evident from the work programme of the IASB that contains several joint projects with the FASB, but none with the AJSB. Therefore, convergence of IFRS and Japanese GAAP is more of a one-way street where Japan, similar to other national standard setters, influences the development of IFRS more indirectly through other channels.

The IASB is working with other large countries to reform their local accounting standards in a direction that is in compliance with IFRS. For example, China follows a 'continuous convergence process'[24] to reduce differences between Chinese standards and IFRS.

Countries can converge to IFRS in a one-sided effort. This is particularly likely if the global standards incorporate a standard on an accounting issue that is deemed of higher quality than the local standard. In contrast to 'official' convergence projects, convergence occurs on a non-systematic basis. For example, German GAAP was amended significantly in 2009 by enactment of the *Bilanzrechtsmodernisierungsgesetz* (BilMoG). Many of the new rules were influenced by IFRS, for example the recognition of development costs (which, however, are only optional), the discounting of long-term provisions, and the application of the temporary concept for deferred taxes. Earlier proposals for inclusion of the fair value measurement for certain financial instruments were so controversial that they were not included in the final law.

Finally, a minimal form of convergence is achieved by keeping local GAAP but providing additional disclosures that help users to assess how the financial statements would look like if the company had adopted IFRS. Reconciliation is a common means of additional disclosures, but it is costly to companies that then have to prepare their financial statements under two different accounting standards. A broad description of differences between local GAAP and IFRS without providing figures can give international users a sense of which items in the financial statements would be affected by applying different standards. Additional disclosures offer only limited benefits of convergence, but can be a starting point towards stronger forms of convergence.

5.2 Scope of convergence

Figure 13.1 depicts different categories of companies, for which benefits and costs of convergence of accounting standards towards IFRS are likely to be different. Convergence has occurred for listed companies, driven by the globalization of capital markets. Multinational companies are another group that is likely to benefit most from convergence. Indeed, IFRS focuses on capital market participants, and the EU requires IFRS for listed firms only (but with the option for other firms to report under IFRS). Listed companies and multinational companies overlap to a great extent, and they are usually also large companies.

The next category includes private companies that have a strong international orientation, such as private equity funding or trade relationships internationally. They benefit from convergence, but to a lower extent than listed companies. Finally, locally oriented companies do not reap benefits from convergence of accounting standards across countries, but incur potential costs, for example due to a misfit of the global standard with their country-specific institutional and economic setting. In particular, small and medium-sized companies (SMEs) are unlikely to benefit strongly from global standards.

This statement does not contradict the fact that the IASB developed IFRS for SMEs in 2009. This is a self-contained standard based on full IFRS. Compared with full IFRS it is less complex and tries to adjust to the needs of smaller companies. For example, IFRS for SMEs do not cover certain issues deemed irrelevant for SMEs; they contain fewer and simpler options, including some deviations from full IFRS; and they require significantly less disclosures. Interestingly, IFRS for

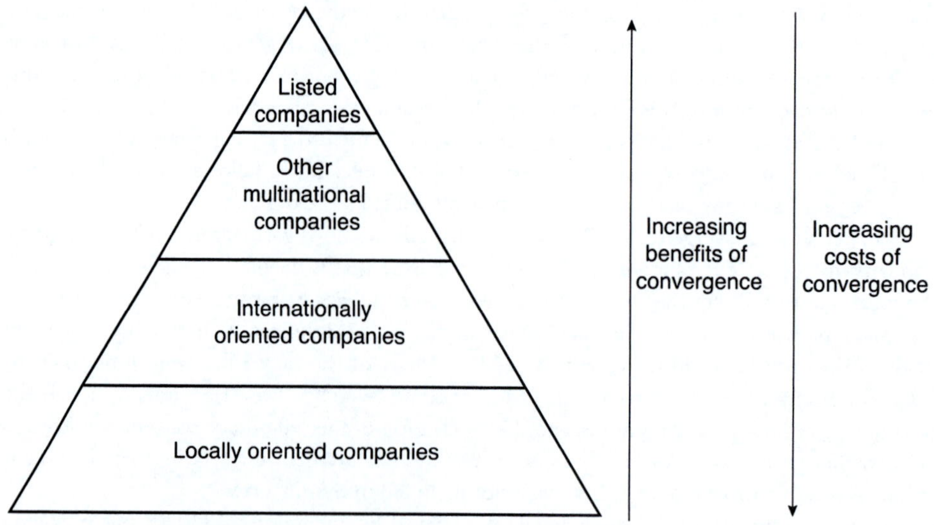

Figure 13.1 Benefits and costs of convergence for categories of companies

SMEs derive from the same conceptual framework as full IFRS, despite the fact that the uses of financial statements are starkly different for listed companies and SMEs, particularly the weight associated with informing investors and stewardship uses of accounting information. However, the main reason for developing IFRS for SMEs has not been to bring convergence across countries, but to offer less-developed countries a set of high-quality accounting standards, which they can adopt.

A similar observation holds for public sector accounting, where the International Public Sector Accounting Standards Board (IPSASB) develops IPSAS for use in public sector entities. IPSAS are based on IFRS, but adjust them to such entities and usually lag the development of IFRS somewhat. The IPSASB has the strategic goal of converging IPSAS with IFRS. Again, the demand for IPSAS arises because there do not exist many well-developed and high-quality standards for public sector entities.

Convergence differs according to the kind of financial information. IFRS is generally applicable to consolidated (group) financial statements,[25] because they are considered the primary financial information for investors. However, most jurisdictions require other financial information in addition to consolidated statements. These include:

- separate financial statements – these often serve as a basis for dividend distribution restrictions, equity capital requirements, bankruptcy indication, and other company law and governance triggers. For example, EU regulation requires companies in the EU to prepare separate financial statements in compliance with (harmonized) local GAAP, and offers member states the option to require or allow separate statements according to IFRS. Around half of the member states give companies that option, the rest do not.
- tax reporting – determination of income taxes is based on financial statements, which can either use IFRS, local GAAP, or be based on specific tax rules that are detached from GAAP. Interestingly, the EU has been working on a common tax base since 2001 and issued a proposal for a directive on a Common Consolidated Corporate Tax Base (CCCTB) in 2011. It aims at introducing a single system for computing taxable income in the EU and its allocation to the member states, but does not address the corporate tax rate. This should alleviate the fiscal impediments of over-taxation and double taxation and should reduce administrative and compliance costs. Since the proposal has strong implications for the tax revenue raised in the member states, it has been controversial, and the proposed CCCTB is optional and not compulsory for corporations.
- regulatory financial reports – financial statements are also used as a basis for capital adequacy requirements for banks and insurance companies. The Basel framework by the Bank of International Settlement and Solvency directives by the EU are attempts to bring convergence of these requirements. Here, the main driver for convergence is globalization of the banking and insurance industry, particularly regarding competition and possible contagion effects, as witnessed in the recent financial crises. In regulated industries it is common to base rate regulation on financial information, which often requires companies to follow specific rules.
- management accounting – companies have full discretion to design their management accounting and internal reporting systems. While they usually use the financial accounting system as a basis, they often make adjustments to determine key numbers to support management decisions. The demand for converged management accounting systems is low – a benefit can derive from rolling out the management reporting system to subsidiaries in different countries.

If, and to the extent that, companies need to prepare several kinds of financial information, they incur the cost of maintaining them. Convergence between them within a company can reduce this cost significantly. Therefore, companies may have incentives to select among options that are useful for more than one purpose or minimize the number of adjustments they make to the information systems.

5.3 Mandatory or voluntary adoption

The analysis of benefits and costs of convergence does not differentiate whether adoption of converged standards is mandatory in a country or voluntary. Comparability is highest if companies that are in the same group (e.g. listing, industry, analyst peer group) use the same standards. Mandatory adoption is clearly preferable in this sense, but it does not take into account benefits and costs on the firm level. There may be firms that incur a net cost of applying converged standards. From a welfare perspective, mandatory adoption is preferable if the total benefits of comparability are higher than the total costs. Presumably the result of this trade-off depends on the size and the institutions in each country.

The IASB seeks acceptance of IFRS in countries worldwide. Acceptance can mean mandatory compliance with IFRS or companies being allowed to choose whether to comply with IFRS. For example, the regulation that adopted IFRS in the EU requires listed companies to report under IFRS in their consolidated statements and provides an option for member states to require or allow other companies to use IFRS in their consolidated statements or to use IFRS in separate financial statements. The options enacted in the member states vary significantly,[26] providing evidence of different net benefits of a convergence with IFRS on the level below that of listed firms.

Convergence can occur on the country level, which has the advantage that the standards can be mandated and enforced by the institutions in the respective country. To avoid the legal system, a company would have to move its headquarters or incorporation into another country that has a different legal system. An alternative is convergence on the stock exchanges level. In this case, exchanges require IFRS within their contractual listing requirements. Companies can choose to be listed on a particular stock exchange or market segment. At the other end of the spectrum is the firm level: companies can decide to prepare financial statements in accordance with IFRS, with the caveat that they may be required to prepare a second set of financial statements to conform with the local law, which is a costly undertaking. Indeed, voluntary adoption was the driver for several countries accepting IFRS consolidated statements to replace consolidated statements under local GAAP. Leuz (2010) proposes the creation of a global player segment, which would comprise companies that apply the same accounting standards (IFRS) and are subject to the same enforcement mechanisms and have similar reporting incentives. This institutional environment should be provided by a supra-national body, such as, for example, IOSCO or ESMA. This proposal does not require countries' institutional settings to converge in order to generate a measurable benefit of converged accounting standards. Companies would be able to self-select into this superior institutional environment and reap the economic benefits associated with global financial reporting.

The voluntary adoption model is not restricted to a single global standard. Alternatively, it can allow for competition among global standards. Competition among standards offers some benefits over a standard setting monopoly, but also some costs.[27] To realize benefits of competition among standards the candidate standards should be sufficiently different; competition among converged standards is pointless. Benefits stem from the fact that there are several competing accounting theories that lead to stark differences in financial reporting, such as the prevalence of the asset–liability or the revenue–expense approach or different measurement concepts. Mixing them in a single set of standards may lead to a result worse than having companies choose which concept fits their needs better. Competition is likely to increase innovation in accounting standard setting and to reduce the susceptibility of the standard setters to capture by political influence. Moreover, the market shares of the standards can indicate the quality of the standards. Disadvantages relative to a single standard are the lower comparability across companies and reduced benefits from standardization; moreover, standard setting is more costly. Ray (2011) identifies economic settings in which uniform standards or a choice among few standards is preferable. Bertomeu and Cheynel (2013) show that having two standard setters can improve welfare due to more company information being available in the capital market. This result also suggests that competition among standards does not inevitably lead to a race to the bottom, but can go to the top.[28]

6. Conclusions

'The creation of a truly global set of accounting standards is a long-held dream for many. … a global accounting language is likely to end up with some distinctly different national dialects' (Reilly 2011, p. 873). This chapter has examined benefits and costs of convergence of accounting standards, mainly using the historic case of the convergence with, and adoption of, IFRS. This case also illustrates the abundance of dimensions convergence can take and the importance of institutions and incentives to achieve convergence of financial reporting in practice. It also provides insights into the politics of accounting standards.

It is remarkable how successful the IASB has been in promoting IFRS globally in a relatively short period. Unsurprisingly, it has not achieved full convergence, and will perhaps never do so. Also, research has documented mixed results on the economic effects. But it has shown that more emphasis should be put on convergence of institutions relating to accounting if convergence should be achieved. Indeed, there are many efforts underway to harmonize auditing, corporate governance, and enforcement. On the other hand, it is clear that convergence to IFRS benefits a small segment of companies that are internationally oriented, so there are limits to convergence.

Finally, the analysis should remind us that there is no 'correct' accounting per se, but accounting is driven by the objectives of financial reporting and has economic effects. There are many different ways of accounting for transactions and events and of providing information to users of financial statements. Therefore, whether and how much convergence is really desirable is a challenging question.

Notes

Helpful comments by Christian Groß are gratefully acknowledged.

1 See, e.g., Nobes and Parker (2010).
2 For a detailed account of the history of the IASC and IASB respectively see Camfferman and Zeff (2007) and Zeff (2012).
3 In the 1990s, the G4+1 Group of standard setters (Australia, Canada, New Zealand, the UK, and the USA) worked on a convergence of accounting standards at least for Anglo-American countries. It disbanded in 2001 with the establishment of the IASB.
4 This does not suggest that convergence is more important than quality; in fact, it is probably the opposite (see Jamal *et al.* 2010).
5 See, e.g., Benston *et al.* (2006), pp. 6–14.
6 See, e.g., SEC (2003) and Hail *et al.* (2010a).
7 See SEC (2008), pp. 11–18.
8 See, e.g., Ball *et al.* (2003) and Daske *et al.* (2008).

9 See, e.g., Walker (2010).
10 For example, La Porta *et al.* (2000) describe the influence of legal families on investor protection. See also Leuz (2010) for a clustering of institutional variables.
11 Schipper (2005) predicts an increasing demand for implementation guidance. Interestingly, global audit firms provide voluminous commentary books with their views of the application of IFRSs.
12 Dahlgren and Nilsson (2012) provide several examples of the difficulties of translating IFRS into European languages.
13 See Berger (2010), pp. 28–9.
14 For more background information see Benston *et al.* (2006), pp. 243–54.
15 Only excerpts from this database are publicly available.
16 In contrast, Perry and Nölke (2006) argue that the IASB was able to rapidly promote and introduce fair value measurement because it is a transnational private authority and did not require as much political process.
17 The IFRSF also has incentives to grow and increase influence. See Wagenhofer (2009).
18 See Committee on Economic and Monetary Affairs (2008).
19 Ramanna and Sletten (2012) find that perceived network benefits explain the staggered adoption of IFRS around the world and also find that network benefits are more important for smaller countries. See also Währisch (2001) for an analysis of network effects.
20 The Fourth Directive (separate accounts) includes some 60 and the Seventh Directive (consolidated accounts) some 50 options. See Benston *et al.* (2006), pp. 136, 141–5.
21 However, Daske *et al.* (2013) show that even within the group of IFRS adopters some firms make few changes and adopt IFRSs more as a label rather than increasing their commitment to transparency.
22 See, e.g., SEC (2011), Hail *et al.* (2010b).
23 The significance of this carve-out is marginal. A study by ICAEW (2007, p. 78) identified eight banks in the EU that have used it.
24 See Michel Prada, Chairman of the IFRS Foundation Trustees, in a speech delivered in Frankfurt on 27 June 2012 (www.ifrs.org/Alerts/Conference/MP+Frankfurt+speech+June+2012).
25 IAS 27 and IAS 28 contain few standards for separate financial statements; and the discussion about the definition of a reporting entity in the conceptual framework clearly shows that separate financial statements are not in the focus of the IASB.
26 See the Implementation of the IAS Regulation (1606/2002) in the EU and EEA provided by the EU as of July 2010 (http://ec.europa.eu/internal_market/accounting/docs/ias/ias-use-of-options2010_en.pdf).
27 See, e.g., Dye and Sunder (2001), Sunder (2002, 2009), Benston *et al* (2003, 2006), Walker (2010).
28 See also Huddart *et al.* (1999) for the case of exchange level competition.

Bibliography

Ball, R., A. Robin and J.S. Wu (2003) 'Incentives versus Standards: Properties of Accounting Income in Four East Asian Countries', *Journal of Accounting and Economics* 36: 235–70.

Barth, M.E., W.R. Landsman, M. Lang and C. Williams (2012) 'Are IFRS-based and US GAAP-based Accounting Amounts Comparable?', *Journal of Accounting and Economics* 54: 68–93.

Benston, G., M. Bromwich, R.E. Litan and A. Wagenhofer (2003) *Following the Money: The Enron Failure and the State of Corporate Disclosure*, Washington, DC: Brookings Institution Press.

Benston, G., M. Bromwich, R.E. Litan and A. Wagenhofer (2006) *Worldwide Financial Reporting: The Development and Future of Accounting Standards*, New York and Oxford: Oxford University Press.

Berger, A. (2010) 'The Development and Status of Enforcement in the European Union', *Accounting in Europe* 7: 15–35.

Bertomeu, J. and E. Cheynel (2013) 'Toward Positive Theory of Disclosure Regulation: In Search of Institutional Foundations', *The Accounting Review* 88: 789–824.

Brochet, F., A.D. Jagolinzer and E.J. Riedl (2012) 'Mandatory IFRS Adoption and Financial Statement Comparability', Working paper, Harvard University.

Camfferman, K. and S.A. Zeff (2007) *Financial Reporting and Global Capital Markets: A History of the International Accounting Standards Committee 1973–2000*, Oxford: Oxford University Press.

Cascino, S. and J. Gassen (2011) 'Comparability Effects of Mandatory IFRS Adoption', Working paper, Humboldt-Universität zu Berlin.

Christensen, H.B., L. Hail and C. Leuz (2013) 'Mandatory IFRS Reporting and Changes in Enforcement', Working paper, University of Chicago.

Committee on Economic and Monetary Affairs (2008) 'Report on International Financial Reporting Standards (IFRS) and the Governance of the International Accounting Standards Board (IASB)', European Parliament, 5 February.

Dahlgren, J. and S.-A. Nilsson (2012) 'Can Translations Achieve Comparability? The Case of Translating IFRSs into Swedish', *Accounting in Europe* 9: 39–59.

Daske, H., L. Hail, C. Leuz and R. Verdi (2008) 'Mandatory IFRS Reporting around the World: Early Evidence on the Economic Consequences', *Journal of Accounting Research* 46: 1085–142.

Daske, H., L. Hail, C. Leuz and R. Verdi (2013) 'Adopting a Label: Heterogeneity in the Economic Consequences around IAS/IFRS Adoptions', *Journal of Accounting Research* 51: 495–547.

De Franco, G., S.P. Kothari and R.S. Verdi (2011) 'The Benefits of Financial Statement Comparability', *Journal of Accounting Research* 49: 895–931.

Dye, R.A. and S. Sunder (2001) 'Why Not Allow FASB and IASB Standards to Compete in the US?', *Accounting Horizons* 15: 257–71.

Hail, L., C. Leuz and P. Wysocki (2010a) 'Global Accounting Convergence and the Potential Adoption of IFRS by the US, Part I: Conceptual Underpinnings and Economic Analysis', *Accounting Horizons* 24: 355–94.

Hail, L., C. Leuz and P. Wysocki (2010b) 'Global Accounting Convergence and the Potential Adoption of IFRS by the US, Part II: Political Factors and Future Scenarios for US Accounting Standards', *Accounting Horizons* 24: 567–88.

Huddart, S., J. Hughes and M. Brunnermeier (1999) 'Disclosure Requirements and Stock Exchange Listing Choice in an International Context', *Journal of Accounting and Economics* 26: 237–69.

IASB (2010) *The Conceptual Framework for Financial Reporting 2010*, London: International Accounting Standards Board.

ICAEW (2007) *EU Implementation of IFRS and the Fair Value Directive*, London: The Institute of Chartered Accountants in England and Wales.

Jamal, K., R. Bloomfield, T.E. Christensen, R.H. Colson, S. Moehrle, J. Ohlson, S. Penman, T. Stober, S. Sunder and R.L. Watts (2010) 'A Research-based Perspective on the SEC's Proposed Rule: Roadmap for the Potential Use of Financial Statements Prepared in Accordance with International Financial Reporting Standards (IFRS) by US Issuers', *Accounting Horizons* 24: 139–47.

Khurana, I.K. and P.N. Michas (2011) 'Mandatory IFRS Adoption and the US Home Bias', *Accounting Horizons* 25: 729–53.

Kim, S., P. Kraft and S. Ryan (2012) 'Financial Statement Comparability and Credit Risk', Working paper, New York University.

Kvaal, E. and C.W. Nobes (2010) 'International Differences in IFRS Policy Choice: A Research Note', *Accounting and Business Research* 40: 173–87.

Kvaal, E. and C.W. Nobes (2012) 'IFRS Policy Changes and the Continuation of National Patterns of IFRS Practice', *European Accounting Review* 21: 343–71.

La Porta, R., F. Lopez-de-Silanes, A. Shleifer and R. Vishny (2000) 'Investor Protection and Corporate Governance', *Journal of Financial Economics* 58: 3–27.

Lang, M.H., M.G. Maffett and E.L. Owens (2010) 'Earnings Comovement and Accounting Comparability: The Effects of Mandatory IFRS Adoption', Working paper, University of Rochester.

Leuz, C. (2010) 'Different Approaches to Corporate Reporting Regulation: How Jurisdictions Differ and Why', *Accounting and Business Research* 40: 229–56.

Nobes, C.W. and R.B. Parker (2010) *Comparative International Accounting*, 11th edn, Harlow: Prentice Hall.

Perry, J. and A. Nölke (2006) 'The Political Economy of International Accounting Standards', *Review of International Political Economy* 13: 559–86.

Posner, E. (2010) 'Sequence as Explanation: The International Politics of Accounting Standards', *Review of International Political Economy* 17: 639–64.

PricewaterhouseCoopers (2002) *2005: Ready or Not*, London: PricewaterhouseCoopers.

Ramanna, K. and E. Sletten (2012) 'Network Effects in Countries' Adoption of IFRS', Working paper, Harvard University.

Ray, K. (2011) 'One Size Fits All? Costs and Benefits of Uniform Accounting Standards', Working paper, Georgetown University.

Reilly, D. (2011) 'Convergence Flaws', *Accounting Horizons* 25: 873–77.

Schipper, K. (2005) 'The Introduction of International Accounting Standards in Europe: Implications for International Convergence', *European Accounting Review* 14: 101–26.

Schultz, J.J. and T.J. Lopez (2001) 'The Impact of National Influence on Accounting Estimates: Implications for International Accounting Standard-Setters', *International Journal of Accounting* 36: 271–90.

SEC (2003) 'Study Pursuant to Section 108(d) of the Sarbanes-Oxley Act of 2002 on the Adoption by the United States Financial Reporting System of a Principles-Based Accounting System', July, Washington, DC: Securities and Exchange Commission.

SEC (2008) 'Roadmap for the Potential Use of Financial Statements Prepared in Accordance With International Financial Reporting Standards by US Issuers', Release No. 33-8982, Washington, DC: Securities and Exchange Commission.

SEC (2010) 'Commission Statement in Support of Convergence and Global Accounting', Release No. 33-9109, Washington, DC: Securities and Exchange Commission.

SEC (2011) 'Work Plan for the Consideration of Incorporating International Financial Reporting Standards into the Financial Reporting System for US Issuers: Exploring a Possible Method of Incorporation', Staff Paper, May, Washington, DC: Securities and Exchange Commission.

Simmons, B.A. (2001) 'The International Politics of Harmonization: The Case of Capital Market Regulation', *International Organization* 55: 589–620.

Stecher, J. and J. Suijs (2012) 'Hail, Procrustes! Harmonized Accounting Standards as a Procrustean Bed', *Journal of Accounting and Public Policy* 31: 341–55.

Sunder, S. (2002) 'Regulatory Competition Among Accounting Standards Within and Across International Boundaries', *Journal of Accounting and Public Policy* 21: 219–34.

Sunder, S. (2009) 'IFRS and the Accounting Consensus', *Accounting Horizons* 23: 101–11.

Sunder, S. (2011) 'IFRS Monopoly: The Pied Piper of Financial Reporting', *Accounting and Business Research* 41: 291–306.

Véron, N. (2007) *The Global Accounting Experiment*, Brussels: Bruegel Blueprint Series.

Wagenhofer, A. (2009) 'Global Accounting Standards: Reality and Ambitions', *Accounting Research Journal* 22: 68–80.

Währisch, M. (2001) *The Evolution of International Accounting Systems: Accounting System Adoptions by Firms from a Network Perspective*, Frankfurt and New York: Peter Lang.

Walker, M. (2010) 'Accounting for Varieties of Capitalism: The Case Against a Single Set of Global Accounting Standards', *British Accounting Review* 42: 137–52.

Yip, R.W.Y. and D. Young (2012) 'Does Mandatory IFRS Adoption Improve Information Comparability?', *The Accounting Review* 87: 1767–89.

Zeff, S.A. (2012) 'The Evolution of the IASC into the IASB and the Challenges it Faces', *The Accounting Review* 87: 807–37.

14

The Role of Conceptual Frameworks in Accounting Standard-Setting

Carien van Mourik and Peter Walton

1. Introduction and definition

In the world of IFRS, conceptual frameworks occupy a prominent role, and yet, outside of Anglophone countries, the use of conceptual frameworks in standard-setting is a relatively recent phenomenon inspired by the FASB and IASB Conceptual Frameworks. For example, the Accounting Standards Board of Japan's Conceptual Framework dates from 2006, and in Islamic accounting the Conceptual Framework of the Accounting and Auditing Organisation for Islamic Financial Institutions (AAOIFI) is even more recent. Evidently therefore the use of an explicit conceptual framework is a choice rather than a necessity. In this chapter we will first define what we mean by a conceptual framework, then review the literature that considers the usefulness or otherwise of such a framework. After that we will review the evolution of the conceptual framework, the current IASB framework and finally the role that it plays in the world of IFRS.

Macve (1981, p. 9) wrote:

> The role of a 'conceptual framework' is to provide a structure for thinking about what is 'better' accounting and financial reporting. It is a theoretical endeavour with the practical aim of clarifying the objectives of financial reporting, and how alternative practices are likely to help achieve those objectives. Whether as a company director, a chief accountant, an auditor or an accounting standard-setter, one cannot make a rational choice of accounting procedures without some framework of principle.

Carsberg (1984: 25) defines a conceptual framework as:

> A conceptual framework comprises a set of basic principles that command general support and can be used to help with detailed decisions by increasing the likelihood of consistency and reducing the costs of analysis. In financial reporting, a conceptual framework is expected to help with decisions by standard-setters and others about how accounting measurements should be made, what information should be included in published reports, and how the information should be displayed.

Carsberg points out that everyone who writes about the objectives of financial reporting, and considers income measurement and related issues, is in effect discussing a conceptual framework and authoritative analyses of financial reporting such as Paton and Littleton (1940) address the same subject area without calling it a conceptual framework.

The IASB's Conceptual Framework, originally entitled the *Framework for the Preparation and Presentation of Financial Statements*, but changed in 2010 to *Conceptual Framework for Financial Reporting*, which is again in the process of revision has its origins in problems with US standard-setting in the 1960s. The US standard-setting institutions were substantially changed with the creation in 1973 of the FASB as an independent standard-setter, and the FASB was mandated to develop a conceptual framework as part of its standard-setting process. Carsberg (1984, p. 27) notes that people thought that, if they could reach agreement on a conceptual framework, appropriate decisions would be clearer and people with vested interests would find greater difficulty in resisting them. The idea was that accounting–technical considerations would override political considerations in standard setting. For this purpose, the structure and substance of the conceptual framework would need to be coherent and theoretically sound, and its concepts internally consistent and applicable in practice. This chapter concerns the conceptual framework within this narrower focus of a tool for standard-setting, and eventually, preparation of financial reports.

1.1 The need for a conceptual framework in standard-setting

Standard-setting arrangements differ between countries and cultures, and have emerged and evolved at different times in different economies. The comparative international accounting literature (notably Nobes, 1984) shows that there are two separate streams of development in financial reporting in industrialized countries, an Anglo-Saxon stream and a Continental European stream. In the Anglo-Saxon group, standard-setting has typically evolved through arrangements where the private sector, and particularly the accounting profession, has been responsible for writing detailed rules, within an overarching statute law constraint. However, in the Continental European group, the tradition has been for the state to specify detailed accounting standards within a Commercial Code. Continental European countries have not evolved conceptual frameworks for standard-setting as such. While statute law may well set out the objectives of the law-makers, there is typically no appeal to accounting concepts as such.

Hoarau (1995) contrasts US standard-setting with the French model (one of two key models in the continental European group). He notes (p. 225): 'The composition and functioning of the standard-setting organisation is founded on multidisciplinary cooperation and the representation of the widest possible range of different users of accounting'. He adds that this forces the government to seek consensus and compromise between competing interests. He also points out that a governmental process of standard-setting 'is by its very nature discontinuous in terms of the government orders or other statutes which give accounting standards … the force of the law'. He emphasizes the link to corporate taxation as another important factor.

The conceptual framework which is the subject of this chapter is typically something that is associated more with Anglo-Saxon standard-setting, operating in a private sector context. It is not associated with countries whose system is more law and taxation based, which could be said to operate on a basis of achieving pragmatic, consensual solutions to individual problems without regard to any concept other than appropriate regulation of the economy. Another possibly significant factor is that the Anglo-Saxon standard-setting world until relatively recently saw accounting standard-setting as simply a technical issue. It was only in the late 1970s and

1980s that the literature started to acknowledge that standards had economic consequences. The potential social and financial consequences of standard-setting were not considered previously and its function of making political choices was not seen (see Chapter 17).

Pacter (1983: 76) points out that the American Institute of Certified Public Accountants (AICPA) had as early as 1958 called for the evolution of concepts that would 'provide a meaningful foundation for the development of principles and the development of rules or other guides for the application of principles in specific situations'. Carsberg (1984: 27) identifies a number of reasons for using a conceptual framework in standard-setting. He wrote: 'The first purpose in embarking on the conceptual framework project is to facilitate decisions on controversial issues'. He added that it also avoided wasted efforts in that standard-setters did not need to go over the same ground on each project, and it helped to generate consistency in standards. He also thought that 'an agreed conceptual framework should enable practitioners to make decisions on more issues themselves and avoid the need for so many detailed standards'.

This last point is a significant difference between the FASB and the IASB. The US framework is intended only for use by standard-setters to guide their decision-making. It does not figure in their authoritative literature – it is not part of the US Accounting Standards Codification. However, under IFRS, the conceptual framework is intended to be a tool for preparers and auditors as well. IAS 8 *Accounting Policies, Changes in Accounting Estimates and Errors* specifically provides that where there is no IFRS that addresses a particular transaction, or which can be analogized to, the preparer should look to the conceptual framework. As Gélard (2010) underlines, the IASB framework is intended to be a working tool that helps preparers and auditors flesh out principles-based standards.

Burlaud and Colasse (2011: 28) suggest that there is another aspect to the conceptual framework: 'the use of a conceptual framework by a standard-setter contributes to building it a reputation for competence and gives it substantial legitimacy'. There is also a body of work in the literature on professions that suggests that the more 'technical' the cognitive base of a professional group is perceived to be, the higher is the professional standing of that group. One could argue that a possible factor in explaining why Anglo-Saxon private sector standard-setters have conceptual frameworks, and Continental European standard-setters do not, is that the latter are able to enact their standards through national law, while the former cannot, and must appeal to other forms of authority.

1.2 Criticism of the use of a conceptual framework

Burlaud and Colasse (2011: 27) are critical of a number of aspects of the IASB's use of the conceptual framework. They also point out that the statement of objectives of financial reporting is 'highly political in character since it amounts to making a choice as to the governance of the company'. The French academics comment 'it may therefore seem surprising that such a declaration should emanate from a group of technical experts with no political legitimacy'.

They note that the IASB framework privileges the investor, and that it assumes that as the investor runs the most risks, information that meets their needs will meet the needs of others. Burlaud and Colasse (ibid.: 32) comment that this analysis is questionable and ask whether employees do not run higher risks, and whether the needs of all users are necessarily homogeneous. They add that 'investors do not constitute a homogeneous category and vary in their interests, the level of risk they run, their access to information and, in the end, their accounting information needs'.

Van Mourik (2010) notes that IFRS are used in a wide variety of institutional environments worldwide and suggests that providing information useful for investors provides too narrow a focus. She reviews seven assumptions that underlie the IASB conceptual framework and concludes that it focuses entirely on the economic functions of financial reporting and neglects its claim to satisfy a public interest because:

- it does not provide evidence of stewardship, even though the discharge of managers by shareholders is a formal part of the annual meeting in many countries;
- it does not provide accountability to the general public regarding public and private costs and benefits;
- it does not provide information about added value and how this has been distributed over its stakeholders; and
- it does not discuss protection and reconciliation of conflicting economic interests of all stakeholders.

She summarizes that financial accounting and reporting fulfil both economic and social functions, but the latter are ignored by the IASB.

A criticism of the way in which the US framework was constructed is that it favours an approach of measuring resources and claims on them as the starting point of recognition and measurement. The implicit assumption was that performance and income ought to be measured as the change in net assets from one period to the next (except for those changes resulting from transactions with the shareholders). In other words, the FASB implicitly adopted a balance sheet approach to the determination of income. This is a not uncontroversial assumption, but is addressed somewhat ambiguously in the original FASB framework.

Indeed, ambiguity could be said to be another weakness of conceptual frameworks in general. The underlying idea of the framework is to have high-level principles which are made operational in accounting standards. The principles are meant to give consistency to the standards, but the higher the level of abstraction from the operational, the more ambiguous the framework is likely to become, and the more difficult to operationalize.

Macve (1981) was commissioned by the UK Accounting Standards Committee to 'review current literature and opinion in the UK, US and elsewhere with a view to forming preliminary conclusions as to the possibilities of developing an agreed conceptual framework for setting accounting standards and the nature of such a framework' (ibid.: 3). This study remains one of the most authoritative critiques of the idea of using a conceptual framework. More recent critiques include Christensen (2010), which was commented and elaborated upon by Macve (2010).

Macve (1981: 11) notes that there are inherent limitations to what financial statements can show. 'There is no unambiguous or correct definition of "income" and "value" on which to base measures of profit and net assets.' He points to an 'absence of comprehensiveness' because it is not possible to reflect all the attributes concerning an entity's value and changes in its value. There will be a need to make allocations and estimates of the future which require subjective judgements (irrespective of the performance measurement and income concept adopted).

He says that there is general agreement that financial statements should be useful, but there is uncertainty about how accounting information is used and why. He suggests there is a variety of needs – 'different users will have different needs for accounting information depending on the situations and decisions they face, their level of understanding, and the alternative sources of information available to them' (ibid.: 11). In addition:

> the different individuals and groups involved with financial reporting … often have conflicting economic interests, and any decisions about accounting practices (which will affect

them all) have to be made after weighing up the consequences for these different parties and what their respective rights are (ibid.).

He comments that these problems make financial reporting and the establishment of a conceptual framework a political as well as a technical matter. Macve concludes:

> Accounting theory cannot give complete, precise answers to accounting problems. The history of the development of accounting suggests that it serves many purposes reasonably well, rather than any one purpose very well. It therefore seems unlikely that searching for an agreed conceptual framework of theory in abstraction from individual problems of disclosure and measurement will be successful (ibid.: 13–14).

2. The IASB conceptual framework

Leaving aside the argument that any discussion of the objectives of financial reporting is in effect a conceptual framework discussion, the history of the development of elaborated conceptual frameworks in standard-setting starts in the US.

2.1 The US framework

Zeff (forthcoming) reviews the evolution of the idea that the objective of financial reporting is to provide decision-useful information to investors. He notes that George O. May (senior partner in Price Waterhouse) gave advice to the New York Stock Exchange in 1932 that referred to both stewardship (the traditional orientation) and decision-making as objectives. He analyses a great deal of literature in the succeeding years which show a range of views on the objectives of financial reporting and the users of statements. He says:

> the earliest exponent of the decision-usefulness approach to accounting theory and standard setting was George Staubus, an accounting professor at the University of California, Berkeley. He first developed the approach in his doctoral thesis, 'An Accounting Concept of Revenue', completed in 1954 at the University of Chicago (ibid.).

He expanded on this in subsequent publications. Zeff adds: 'The first sign of institutional acceptance of the decision-usefulness objective was in *A Statement of Basic Accounting Theory* (*ASOBAT*) issued by a nine-member American Accounting Association (AAA) committee in 1966' (ibid.).

Pacter (1983) wrote that the Accounting Principles Board (APB), formed in 1959, had been urged to work on concepts as well as specific standards. Zeff notes that in 1970 the APB did indeed issue its non-mandatory Statement no 4 *Basic Concepts and Accounting Principles Underlying Financial Statements of Business Enterprises* which said that the basic purpose of financial accounting and financial statements was to provide quantitative financial information about a business enterprise that was useful to statement users, particularly owners and creditors, in making economic decisions.

However, the APB was relatively short-lived. As Meek (2003: 68) notes:

> The APB was criticised almost from its beginning. One of its objectives was to establish broad accounting principles, but too many of its decisions were ad hoc in nature and … focused on specific problems. The APB had trouble producing opinions that were consistent internally and across one another.

As a consequence the AICPA in 1971 set up two committees to review standard-setting. The Wheat Committee reviewed the standard-setting institution and its recommendations resulted in the creation of the FASB in 1973. The second committee, chaired by Robert Trueblood, was to consider the objectives of financial statements (Pacter, 1983) and its report (the 'Trueblood Report': AICPA, 1973) was published in 1973. Pacter reports:

> The members and staff of the FASB were mindful that its predecessor was criticised for not having made adequate progress toward developing a normative set of objectives and concepts for corporate financial reporting. And so, among the seven projects on the FASB's initial technical agenda was one that encompassed the objectives of financial reporting … work on the FASB's objectives project began with a consideration of the Trueblood study group's report (Pacter, 1983: 78).

The FASB issued a series of Statements of Financial Accounting Concepts, starting with SFAC 1 *Objectives of Financial Reporting by Business Enterprises* in 1978. It issued SFAC 2 *Qualitative Characteristics of Accounting Information* and SFAC 3 *The Elements of Financial Statements of Business Enterprises* (replaced in 1985 by SFAC 6) in 1980. SFAC 5 *Recognition and Measurement in Financial Statements of Business Enterprises* was issued in 1984 (SFAC 4 addressed the objectives of reporting by non-profit organisations).

2.2 The IASC's 1989 framework

Cairns (2001: 3) says that the decision-usefulness concept was included in the IASC's first standard: IAS 1 *Disclosure of accounting policies* issued in 1974. There was some call for the IASC to follow the US and work on a conceptual framework, but Cairns says:

> The IASC believed, however, that its constituency was far more likely to criticise it for gaps in its standards rather than its failure to develop a conceptual framework. Therefore, it was not until the early 1980s that the first seeds of the framework were sown (ibid.: 4).

The IASC started work in 1982 on a limited project to examine some aspects of the objectives of financial statements. It produced separate documents dealing with different aspects but in 1986 decided to work on a full conceptual framework. Cairns writes:

> In its new project the IASC was able to draw on the published concepts statements of the FASB and work in progress of the standard setting bodies in Australia and Canada. The FASB's concepts statements had been used in all the building block projects [pursued by the IASC] and were familiar to all members of the steering committee. Australia was contemporaneously developing its statements of accounting concepts while Canada was also developing its financial statement concepts (ibid.: 7).

The IASC also examined the concepts underlying financial reporting in Japan, continental Europe, and a range of developing and newly industrialized countries. While none of these countries had published a conceptual framework in a similar form to that of the FASB or that proposed by Canada, Australia and the IASC, there were clearly concepts or principles underpinning their accounting requirements

The final document was issued in 1989. Cairns reports (ibid.: 8) that the IASC considered whether stewardship or accountability should be an objective, but concluded that users were not interested in these for their own sake but wanted information to make decisions about management performance. The IASC also considered whether to make any reference to the true and fair view (a UK concept extended to the EU by the Fourth Company law Directive; see Chapter 17), but decided against it. A number of countries said they did not know what it meant, and it had not been used elsewhere by the IASC.

Although the 1989 IASC Conceptual Framework[1] certainly appears to give priority to the information needs of investors as providers of risk capital, Cairns (2001: 8) says that the 1989 IASC framework did not focus on investor needs, as some assert. He points out that the IASC framework identifies a number of users, without giving precedence to any, but does suggest that information that satisfies the needs of providers of risk capital will meet many of the needs of other users. He adds that, like the US framework, the IASC framework bases the recognition of assets, liabilities and income round the definitions of asset and liability, but contests that this implies a balance sheet orientation:

> Rather, the IASC believed (and still believes) that it is impossible to define income and expenses without including in those definitions the definitions of assets and liabilities – none of the critics of the IASC's approach or the similar approach adopted by some national standard-setting bodies have proposed operational definitions of income and expenses which are independent of the definitions of assets and liabilities (Cairns, 2001: 9).

2.3 Convergence with the FASB

In 2004 the IASB agreed to start a joint project with the FASB to update and converge their conceptual frameworks. The argument was that if their objective was to converge their standards, it was appropriate that there should be a common conceptual framework which underpinned the standards. In 2010 the boards issued final versions of the objectives of financial reporting (Chapter 1) and the qualitative characteristics (Chapter 3), and the project was suspended while they concentrated on finalizing their financial crisis-related projects.

The IASC framework talked about financial statements and not financial reporting, which is a wider concept, but the IASB agreed to move to the US use of 'financial reporting'. However, some IASB members (notably Sir David Tweedie and Professor Geoff Whittington, who gave an alternative view in the exposure draft) wanted stewardship to be part of the objectives. A similar view was held by Benston *et al.* (2007: 231–2) in their critique of the FASB's (2006) Preliminary View of the objective of financial reporting and the qualitative characteristics in the conceptual framework. Nevertheless, the FASB was firmly against this, asking what information would be provided under a stewardship approach that was not provided under a decision-useful for investors approach. The 2010 objectives are expressed as follows:

> [OB2] The objective of general purpose financial reporting is to provide financial information about the reporting entity that is useful to existing and potential investors, lenders, and other creditors in making decisions about providing resources to the entity. Those decisions involve buying, selling, or holding equity and debt instruments and providing or settling loans and other forms of credit (IASB, 2010a).

However, paragraph OB4 does add:

> To assess an entity's prospects for future net cash inflows, existing and potential investors, lenders, and other creditors need information about the resources of the entity, claims against the entity, and how efficiently and effectively the entity's management and governing board have discharged their responsibilities to use the entity's resources (ibid.).

When the project staff worked on the qualitative characteristics of financial reporting, it was decided that the original formulation did not give any clue as to how the main characteristics interacted. They tried to design a flowchart that would take the standard-setter (or other user) through a series of steps which in effect prioritized the different characteristics. In the end they abandoned this and moved to a formulation where they have fundamental characteristics (that financial reporting must satisfy) and 'enhancing' characteristics which would lead one to choose between alternatives.

A contentious issue in this area is the use of the word 'reliability' in the old US framework. This said that the primary characteristics should be relevance and reliability, but then defined reliability as meaning a faithful representation of what the number purported to represent. However, many constituents have taken reliability to mean verifiability, i.e. that a reliable number is one that can be independently checked and verified. Board members argued that, given the essentially subjective nature of estimates used in financial reporting, they did not want to constrain estimates to those that could be verified. They have tried to make this issue clear by using the term 'representational faithfulness' as a fundamental characteristic instead of reliability, and identifying verifiability as an enhancing characteristic.

Between 2004 and 2010 the project staff did extensive work on the elements of financial reporting, measurement and the reporting entity. In reviewing the elements, the intention was not to change the recognition approach but to consider whether the wording should be refined in any way. However, staff found it very difficult to get beyond the existing definition of an asset without changing the underlying notion, and the financial crisis put pressure on staff time so this aspect was shelved, but not before the boards had debated alternative formulations. The existing definition talks about an asset being probable future cash flows. The boards raised the issue that sometimes the value of an asset was that the entity had rights to prevent other people accessing the asset. Such an asset (e.g. an unused trademark) would not generate cash flows directly, but would enhance the flows to other assets. They also discussed whether what was being recognized was the actual asset or the *right* to the asset.

The old frameworks define a liability as the opposite of an asset, and equity as the difference between the two. The boards debated, without coming to any conclusion, whether it was possible to have a definition of a liability that was independent of the definition of an asset, and whether the same might be possible for equity.

The existing IASC/IASB framework says very little about measurement, which was also a problematic issue for the FASB's old framework. The boards decided that they wanted to address the subject thoroughly. The staff of the Canadian Accounting Standards Board produced a discussion paper, but this seemed to advocate fair value for everything and was not taken up by the FASB and IASB. FASB staff then had a number of attempts to draft a measurement chapter, all of which fell foul of the board members. One particular analysis that emerged was that in measuring assets one should distinguish between those that generated cash flows directly (e.g. an investment property or a financial instrument) and those that generated cash flows indirectly, needing a combination with other assets and labour inputs (e.g. a manufacturing facility, retail premises, etc.).

The boards also did some work on the reporting entity. They issued a Discussion Paper (IASB, 2008) which asked thirteen questions covering four topics:

- whether or not the reporting entity concept should be limited to legal entities, and whether or not the entity should be described rather than precisely defined;
- consideration of three approaches to determining the composition of a group reporting entity: the controlling entity model (ibid.: Pars. 64–79), the common control model (ibid.: Pars. 80–95) and the risks and rewards model (ibid. Pars. 96–105) which the IASB preferred;
- whether to follow the parent company approach to consolidated financial statements (proportionate consolidation reflecting the proprietors' perspective where non-controlling interests are shown as liabilities) or the entity approach (full consolidation method reflecting the reporting entity's perspective where no distinction is drawn between controlling and non-controlling interests). This third topic also included the question of whether parent company financial statements should be precluded or not; and
- the fourth issue concerned issues related to definitions of control.

The IASB's subsequent Exposure Draft ED/2010/2, for which comments were to be received by 16 July 2010, described the reporting entity as:

> a circumscribed area of economic activities whose financial information has the potential to be useful to existing and potential equity investors, lenders and other creditors who cannot directly obtain the information they need in making decisions about providing resources to the entity and in assessing whether the management and the governing board of that entity have made efficient and effective use of the resources provided. The reporting entity concept is intended to further this objective (IASB, ED/2010/2: RE2).

In a letter dated 15 July 2010, the European Financial Reporting Advisory Group (EFRAG) responded to the Exposure Draft:

> We consider that the perspective from which the financial statements are presented is critical and should be discussed in the conceptual framework. Clarifying the 'perspective' is important in assessing how to resolve accounting policy issues and is central to considering how to satisfy the objective of financial reporting. Accordingly, we think it is necessary to carry out an in-depth analysis of the implications of adopting either (the proprietary or the entity) perspective and to ensure they are properly debated.

However, all of these phases of the project were suspended in light of the need to focus resources on the financial crisis. At the time of writing (2012) the IASB has made the tentative decision to abandon the joint conceptual framework project in favour of finalizing its own framework improvements independently of the FASB. At an IASB meeting, ironically being held at the FASB's board room in Connecticut during a week of joint meetings, the staff proposed that, following an extensive review of the IASB's future agenda, which had involved many constituents, finalizing the framework should be the next priority once the financial crisis projects were completed. The suggestion was that the IASB would do its own work on the elements of financial reporting, measurement, presentation and disclosure. The presentation part would go beyond the existing framework and would also involve defining the role of Other Comprehensive Income. The disclosure part would be completely new, but would aim to develop some disclosure framework and would extend to interim statements. The work on the reporting entity (Chapter 2) would be finalized.

2.4 The 2010 conceptual framework

The IASB decided in 2010 that the two parts of the framework that had been revised, the objectives and the qualitative characteristics, should be published and be bolted on to the 1989 framework, with the latter amended as necessary to reflect the update. So currently the official IASB Conceptual Framework is a hybrid of the 2010 update and the 1989 original. The significant aspects of the 1989 framework that have not been revised are the elements of the financial statements, their recognition and measurement, and the concepts of capital and capital maintenance. The other work the IASB plans to do will go well beyond what is in the 1989 version, while, based on the previous debates, the asset definition is not likely to be changed significantly.

Chapter 1 addresses the objectives of general purpose financial reporting which, as discussed above, is to provide information about the reporting entity that is useful to existing and potential investors, lenders and other creditors in making decisions about providing resources to the entity. The sentence in the 1989 IASC Conceptual Framework referring to the information needs of the providers of risk capital has been removed from the 2010 IASB Conceptual Framework. However, in spite of the ambiguity of the terms used in the IASB Conceptual Framework, the IFRS Foundation's Report on the Trustees' Strategy Review (IFRS Foundation 2011: 11) leaves no doubt that the IASB is committed first and foremost to protecting the interests and information needs of investors in capital markets.

The chapter goes on to detail that investors' decisions depend on their expectations of future returns, which in turn depend on 'their assessment of the amount, timing and uncertainty of (the prospects for) future net cash inflows to the entity' (OB3). There is a subtlety here, not always understood by students of the earlier framework, that the financial statements relate to the *entity*'s cash flows, but the investor is looking to estimate future cash flows to the *investor*, which will be dividends, interest and capital gains, so the decision-making is a two step process.

The conceptual framework places stress on the notion of *general purpose* financial reporting, which it says is aimed at those who do not have the power to require the entity to provide information directly. Consequently management is considered to be outside the scope. The chapter also notes that financial reports cannot give all the information needed to make decisions, and that different users will have different and possibly conflicting needs.

Financial reports should give information about the entity's resources and the claims against them but should also give information about transactions and other events that change the entity's resources and claims against it. 'Both types of information provide useful input for decisions about providing resources to an entity' (OB12).

The 1989 framework did not define the reporting entity, but Chapter 2 of the new conceptual framework is intended to provide an operational definition of a group reporting entity and has been left blank. The revised qualitative characteristics of financial reporting are Chapter 3 of the new conceptual framework. Reflecting the move from 'financial statements' to 'financial reporting', the new chapter notes that the qualitative characteristics apply to any information supplied to investors, including forward-looking information. There is a cost constraint that pervades all financial reporting (QC3) – the cost of providing the information must not exceed the expected benefits (QC35).

As discussed above, the chapter identifies fundamental characteristics and enhancing characteristics. The fundamental characteristics are relevance, materiality and representational faithfulness. Relevance is defined as the information being capable of making a difference to decisions, which occurs if information has predictive or confirmatory qualities, or both. Some people would argue that the most useful information is sometimes forward looking, or informative about the market value of the net assets of the firm.

The document describes representational faithfulness as follows:

> Financial reports represent economic phenomena in words and numbers. To be useful, financial information must not only represent relevant phenomena, but it must also faithfully represent the phenomena that it purports to represent. To be a perfectly faithful representation, a depiction would have three characteristics. It would be *complete*, *neutral* and *free from error*. Of course, perfection is seldom, if ever, achievable. The Board's objective is to maximise those qualities to the extent possible [italics in original] (QC12).

The enhancing characteristics are comparability, verifiability, timeliness and understandability. These are largely self-explanatory. The chapter says that financial reports are intended for people who have a reasonable knowledge of business and economic activities and who review and analyse the information diligently. It notes that sometimes phenomena are inherently complex and cannot be made easy to understand. This section is silent on the degree of accounting knowledge as such that a user might be expected to have, but does say a user may on occasion have to call for expert advice. The subject is slightly controversial because critics say that IFRS are too complex and produce information that is not understandable, but it is not clear what level of knowledge should be required.

The qualitative characteristics section also discusses materiality. This is a threshold quality in as far as reports should include all material information and no immaterial information. The definition is linked to that of relevance:

> Information is material if omitting it or misstating it could influence decisions that users make on the basis of financial information about a specific reporting entity. In other words, materiality is an entity-specific aspect of relevance based on the nature or magnitude, or both, of the items to which the information relates in the context of an individual entity's financial report (QC11).

Materiality is a difficult issue for preparers, auditors and standard-setters. There is a growing feeling that financial reports are too lengthy because preparers are reluctant to exercise their judgment about the materiality of the information. Preparers argue that, if they apply materiality, they then have to justify the judgement to their auditors which involves extra work – it is simpler just not to exercise judgement. The IASB has a policy of not mentioning materiality in individual standards, even if the exercise of a materiality judgment may be particularly relevant.

The final key section of the framework is the definition of the elements. As mentioned, the definition of an asset is the cornerstone, and the definition of the liability is the opposite of the asset, with equity being a residual of the asset and liability measurement process. An asset is a resource controlled by the entity as a result of past events and from which future benefits are expected to flow to the entity. Its recognition is constrained by two further factors:

- it must be probable (more likely than not) that future economic benefits will flow to the entity; and
- the item must have a cost or value that can be measured with reliability (it is complete, neutral and free from error).

Although the definition of an asset seems simple, the combination of required factors – control, past event, probable inflows, reliable measurement of cost – provides a relatively strict test. Advertising cannot be treated as an asset, for example, because its effects cannot be controlled, client loyalty cannot be measured.

The definition of a liability is that it is a present obligation of the entity arising from past events, the settlement of which is expected to result in an outflow of resources from the entity. The requirement for there to be a triggering past event is a key issue in prohibiting the creation of provisions that are excessively prudent in nature – you cannot, for example, provide for restructuring while it is just a board decision and no event has taken place.

This part of the conceptual framework also discusses income and expense. It raises the question of the difference between revenue and gains and between expenses and losses, suggesting that revenues and expenses arise from transactions in the ordinary course of business whereas gains (increases in economic benefits). For example, these could be the result of advantageous increases in the market price of assets and advantageous decreases in the market price of liabilities, when items are measured at fair value. Conversely, losses are the result of disadvantageous increases in the market price of liabilities and decreases in the market price of assets. Income is recognized when an increase in assets or a decrease in liabilities takes place, expenses are recognized when there is a decrease in future expected benefits or an increase in future expected cash outflows.

3. The uses of the conceptual framework

As discussed earlier in this chapter, there are two primary uses of this kind of conceptual framework. First, there is the use of the framework by standard-setters to guide them in setting standards, and, second, there is the use by preparers and auditors to guide them in the choice of specific accounting policies for use in the particular entity.

3.1 A guide for standard-setters

The FASB Conceptual Framework has its origins in a desire to make US standards more consistent and provide a rationale for resisting pressure from constituents. It is clear that the standard-setter uses the framework in writing standards, and the preparer and auditor concern themselves only with the standards, and not the concepts supposedly underpinning it. The IASB, however, sees the framework as being both a guide for standard-setting and a tool for preparers and auditors. The IASB constitution specifies that the standard-setters must set standards that are based on the conceptual framework. A piece of content analysis of documents reporting the IASB's debates (Walton 2009) shows that references to the conceptual framework figure frequently in debate. The conceptual framework is also referred to often in the Basis for Conclusions to new standards (the Basis for Conclusions as its title suggests provides the board's rationale for the choices it has made).

In practice the way in which the board expects staff to analyse a topic is to ask if there is any change in the assets or liabilities of the entity, and, if the answer is affirmative, to carry out further analysis of the change to determine if there is income or expense. The effects of this approach can be seen in the new revenue recognition standard, IFRS 14, which starts from the point of a contract being signed and asks if there exist from that moment any assets or liabilities. The board concluded there was an asset in the right to receive the revenue from the contract and a liability to provide the good or service specified in the contract, which the board calls a performance obligation. The standard requires the asset and liability to be recognized at inception of the contract – which is a significant departure from the traditional approach of not recognizing executory contracts in the financial reports, unless they are deemed onerous (loss-making). Revenue is then released under the new standard as performance obligations are satisfied.

The conceptual framework says the financial reports should show the resources of the entity (the right to receive payment in this case) and claims against the entity (the obligation to deliver a good or service). When there is a change in either of these assets and liabilities, this flows through the income statement. The revenue recognition standard is a clear application of the conceptual framework to a central operation in accounting. However, the application is flawed – the asset and liability are not measured independently. The standard specifies that the liability is measured by taking the revenue amount specified in the contract and allocating it to the performance obligations.

In a wholesale application of the framework, the asset would be measured at contract price, and the performance obligation at whatever was the cost of satisfying the obligation (i.e. expected future outflows). The IASB and FASB (it was a joint project) did indeed discuss that for a very long time, but they came up with objections that measuring the performance obligation separately would normally release a profit (at least the part of the price that was supposed to cover selling costs) at the time of signing the contract. Of course the normal requirement is to release profit only on realization, and the standard-setters thought that a strict application of the framework would open the door to earnings manipulation. There was also the question of whether the performance obligation should be measured at an entity-specific value (more opportunities for manipulation) or fair value (but how do you measure that in this case, and what if the entity-specific cost is actually higher than the market?). Finally, how did you know that the difference between performance obligation and selling price was all profit? The standard-setters settled for specifying that the liability was measured at the selling price, so there would be no profit at inception. They were 'comfortable' with that situation – a qualitative characteristic not specified in the conceptual framework, but frequently mentioned by IASB members.

The use of an asset and liability starting point to addressing any accounting question leads to an assumption that the IASB favours a balance sheet approach over an income statement approach to the determination of income. This is a very old and fundamental issue (for example see Chapters 2, 3 and 4 of this book), and is only really an issue if the measurement basis is something other than historical cost, such as where the measurement of assets, liabilities and, as a consequence, income is based on market price changes rather than realized transactions or events. If the standard-setter takes a balance sheet approach and uses a current value measurement, then there will be changes in the values of assets and liabilities each period that arise from market changes and not transactions and these will normally be recorded in income (or indeed Other Comprehensive Income). Some IASB members have asserted, as did the Secretary General of its predecessor (Cairns 2001: 9), that basing the income statement on changes in assets and liabilities is conceptually superior and therefore the only clear way of defining profit and loss. However, both the transactions approach and the balance sheet approach to the determination of income have advantages and disadvantages related to relevance, reliability, practical application, and auditability, and there is little *evidence* of the conceptual superiority of one concept over the other.

3.2 Its use by preparers and auditors

The IASB Conceptual Framework includes a page on its purpose and status, this confirms that in addition to being used by the standard-setter, the framework is intended (unlike the FASB framework):

- to assist preparers of financial statements in applying IFRSs and in dealing with topics that have yet to form the subject of an IFRS;
- to assist auditors in forming an opinion on whether financial statements comply with IFRSs; and
- to assist users of financial statements in interpreting the information contained in financial statements prepared in compliance with IFRSs

This intention is given concrete force by IAS 8 *Accounting Policies, Changes in Estimates and Errors*. The IASB revised this standard in 2003, as part of their overhaul of the legacy standards they took over from the IASC. In that revision they included a hierarchy to guide preparers in their choice of accounting policies. The standard says that if an IFRS addresses a particular transaction, then it should be followed. However, if there is no IFRS on the subject, then the preparer should be guided in their choice of policy by the qualitative characteristics, and should look (a) to see whether an existing IFRS can be analogized to, if not (b) should devise an accounting policy based on the conceptual framework, and (c) may look at recent pronouncements by national standard-setters who use a similar framework.

A number of writers, including former IASB member Gilbert Gélard (2010), insist on the idea that the conceptual framework plays a significant role in helping preparers and auditors in adapting IFRS to specific transactions and circumstances. They argue that IFRS are necessarily more oriented towards principles than detailed rules because they are applied in many different legal, social and economic environments, and that the framework should be used by the entity to work out how to apply the standards to their transactions. We have not been able to find any research evidence on this subject, and we acknowledge that evaluating how people make decisions is a notoriously difficult issue to research.

4. Conclusion

This chapter has aimed to explore the origins of conceptual frameworks in accounting, the evolution of the IASB's framework and its use by standard-setters and constituents. The chapter notes that any discussion of the objectives and nature of financial reporting might be considered to be a conceptual framework discussion, but the specific issue of having a formalized conceptual framework as a tool in standard-setting emerged in the US and crystallized with the Trueblood Report (AICPA, 1973), followed from 1978 by a series of concepts statements issued by the FASB (Pacter, 1983). The objective of providing information that was useful for investors' decisions also emerged in the US (Zeff, forthcoming) and superseded traditional approaches such as considering the statements as monitoring stewardship or providing accountability.

The US framework is organized in separate parts which address primarily the objectives, qualitative characteristics and elements of financial reporting. The IASC built the decision-usefulness objective into its first standard (1974) and issued a number of separate documents addressing different aspects but subsequently decided to issue a single framework document which emerged in 1989. This was amended over the period 2004–2010 in an effort to update and align with the FASB, although some work was abandoned under pressure to give priority to financial crisis projects. The IASB finalized its revised objectives and qualitative characteristics in 2010 and plans to work on updating and extending the rest of the 1989 framework.

The IASB does make frequent reference to the framework in its deliberations, and in particular analyses transactions from the perspective of changes in assets and liabilities. Critics say performance is based on income generation not asset valuation, but the standard-setter says you can only reliably measure income by looking at the changes in resources and claims against them. The IASB mandates the use of the framework by preparers to apply IFRS in particular situations or to develop accounting policies consistent with IFRS where no relevant IFRS exists.

Note

1 As it subsequently appears in the IASB literature.

Bibliography

AICPA (1973) *The Objectives of Financial Statements* (Trueblood Report) New York: American Institute of Certified Public Accountants

Benston, G.J., Carmichael, D.R., Demski, J.S., Dharan, B.G., Jamal, K., Laux, R, Rajgopal, S. and Vrana, G. (2007) 'The FASB's Conceptual Framework: A Critical Analysis'. *Accounting Horizons* 21:2, 229–38.

Burlaud, A. and Colasse, B. (2011) 'International Accounting Standardisation: Is Politics Back?' *Accounting in Europe* 8:1, 23–48

Cairns, D. (2001) 'The Conceptual Framework: The International Experience'. Working paper, available at www.cairns.co.uk.

Carsberg, B. (1984) 'The Quest for a Conceptual Framework for Financial Reporting', in Carsberg, B. and S. Dev (eds) *External Financial Reporting*. London: Prentice Hall International, London School of Economics and Political Science, pp. 25–39

Christensen, J. (2010) 'Conceptual Frameworks of Accounting from an Information Perspective'. *Accounting and Business Research* 40:3 287–99

Gélard, G. (2010) 'Du bon usage d'un cadre conceptuel amélioré'. *Revue Française de Comptabilité* 437 November

Hoarau, C. (1995) 'International Accounting Harmonisation: American Hegemony or Mutual Recognition with Benchmarks'. *Accounting in Europe* 4:2, 217–34

IASB (2001) *Framework for the Preparation and Presentation of Financial Statements.* (April) London: International Accounting Standards Board

IASB (2008) *Discussion Paper Preliminary Views on an Improved Conceptual Framework for Financial Reporting: The Reporting Entity.* (May) London: International Accounting Standards Board

IASB (2010a) *The Conceptual Framework for Financial Reporting.* (September) London: International Accounting Standards Board

IASB (2010b) 'International Accounting Standards Board'. London: International Accounting Standards Board

IFRS Foundation (2011) *Report of the Trustees' Strategy Review, IFRSs as the Global Standard: Setting a Strategy for the Foundation's Second Decade.* (April) London: International Financial Reporting Standards Foundation

IFRS Foundation (2012), *IFRSs as Global Standards: Setting a Strategy for the Foundation's Second Decade.* February, London: International Financial Reporting Standards Foundation

Macve, R. (1981) *A Conceptual Framework for Financial Accounting and Reporting: The Possibilities for an Agreed Structure.* London: ICAEW

Macve, R. (2010) 'Conceptual Frameworks of Accounting: Some Brief Reflections on Theory and Practice'. *Accounting and Business Research* 40:3, 303–8

Meek, G. (2003) 'Accounting in the United States', in Walton, P., Haller, A. and Raffournier, B. (eds) *International Accounting*, 2nd edn, London: Thomson

Nobes, C. (1984) *International Classification of Financial Reporting*. London: Croom Helm

Pacter, P. (1983) 'The Conceptual Framework: Make No Mystique About It'. *Journal of Accountancy* July, 76–88

Paton, W.A. and A.C. Littleton (1940) *An Introduction to Corporate Accounting Standards*, Monograph no 3, New York: American Accounting Association

Van Mourik, C. (2010) 'The Legitimacy of the Assumptions on which the IASB Conceptual Framework is Based: An Institutional Perspective'. Working Paper, Open University

Walton, P. (2009) 'Les délibérations de l'IASB en 2002 et 2003: une analyse statistique'. *Comptabilité-Contrôle-Audit* 15:1, 35–54

Zeff, S. (Forthcoming) 'The Objectives of Financial Reporting: A Critical History'. *Accounting and Business Research*

15

The Application of IFRS Across Different Institutional Environments

Bernard Raffournier

The International Financial Reporting Standards (formerly known as International Accounting Standards) are now widely used in several parts of the world. This chapter describes how these standards have diffused and evaluates their impact on accounting quality, as well as their economic consequences. It also examines why, despite the adoption of common accounting standards, certain national characteristics persist, before considering several issues that the IASB will have to face in the near future.

1. The diffusion of IFRS

1.1 The pre-2005 period

Although the IASC was created in 1973, international accounting standards were rarely applied until the beginning of the 2000s. The reason is that in each country IAS were in conflict with domestic GAAP, whose application was mandatory. To circumvent this obstacle, some companies tried to prepare financial statements complying with both sets of standards. They took advantage of options allowed by national GAAP to select treatments required by international standards, which allowed them to claim compliance, at least partial, with IAS/IFRS. This possibility was suppressed in 1999, with the adoption of revised IAS 1 which stipulates that, for periods starting on or after 1 July 1998, financial statements cannot be described as complying with IAS if they do not comply with all the requirements of each applicable standard.

The other solution available to firms that were anxious to apply IAS/IFRS was to prepare accounts complying with these standards in addition to official financial statements established according to domestic GAAP. This option has rarely been used, probably due to its cost and the confusion that it would have generated among users of financial statements. Indeed, it would be difficult to explain that the same economic reality can result in two distinct pictures whereas each set of standards is aimed at giving a true and fair view of the enterprise. Rapidly it became clear that the diffusion of IAS/IFRS into the financial reporting practices of enterprises would require a change in national regulations. This change took two forms.

In 2000, the International Organization of Securities Commissions (IOSCO) recommended that its members allow large companies to use IAS in the preparation of their financial statements for cross-border offerings and listings. Although this recommendation was not fully unrestricted (national stock exchanges could still require reconciliations with local GAAP), this initiative played a major role in the widespread acceptance of IAS at the world level. In application of this directive, the London Stock Exchange and the Frankfurt Stock Exchange authorized foreign issuers to apply IAS instead of national rules as soon as 2000. Similar dispositions were adopted in France and Italy but they never entered into force (Delvaille *et al.*, 2005).

It is in Europe that the main initiatives toward IFRS adoption took place. This geographical area has long been characterized by a large variety of accounting rules and practices, which is a consequence of the coexistence of the two major accounting traditions, Anglo-Saxon and Continental European. In this context, the need for an international harmonization of accounting practices was particularly imperious. The first step toward IAS adoption took place in 1995, when the European Commission decided to cooperate with the IASC in order to achieve conformity with the IAS and the EU Directives (Haller, 2002). The practical consequence was the introduction, in several member states, of provisions allowing the use of IAS as an alternative to local GAAP for the preparation of the consolidated financial statements of listed companies.

This initiative resulted in a slight increase of companies using IAS. According to a study based on the 1999 annual report (i.e. after the introduction of the requirement that companies claiming for conformity with IAS must comply with all IAS requirements), the rate of IAS adoption among EU listed companies was 4.5 per cent (Cuijpers and Buijink, 2005). However, most IAS adopters were in Germany (44 per cent) and Austria (20 per cent). By contrast, UK companies were particularly reluctant to adopt IAS.

A necessary condition for companies to voluntarily comply with IFRS is that the expected advantages outweigh the costs of adoption. Due to the pre-eminence they give to fund providers, IAS/IFRS clearly pertain to the Anglo-Saxon view of accounting. By switching to IFRS, companies from Continental Europe could hope that the reliability of their financial statements will be improved, which should attract more foreign investors and reduce their financing costs. British companies were less enthusiastic given the relative proximity of UK GAAP and IFRS.

Nevertheless, all companies of the same country were far from adopting IFRS spontaneously, which suggests that a voluntary change of accounting standards was contingent upon individual incentives. In order to identify these incentives, Dumontier and Raffournier (1998) compared the characteristics of Swiss companies that were applying IAS with those that were using domestic GAAP. The Swiss case is particularly favourable to such a study because Switzerland has long been a poorly regulated country with regard to accounting. It was only in 1984 that the national standard setting body was created and its standards were very permissive. In this context, the advantages that could be expected from IAS adoption were substantial. The empirical study based on data from 1994 reveals that companies applying IAS were larger, more internationally diversified, less capital intensive and had a more diffuse ownership.

Cuijpers and Buijink (2005) conducted a similar research at European level. Comparing firms that were using IAS in 1999 with those using local GAAP, they found that IAS adopters were larger, more likely to be listed on a US stock exchange, and had more geographically dispersed operations. These results are confirmed by Renders and Gaeremynck (2007) who found that in Europe, large companies with a Big 5 auditor, a low ownership concentration and whose securities are listed on more stock exchanges had a higher rate of early compliance with IFRS. Taken together, these studies suggest that pressures from outside markets are a key driver for voluntary IAS/IFRS adoption.

Contrary to previous studies that are based on listed firms, Francis *et al.* (2008) examined IAS adoption by private companies. Their study uses data collected in late 1999 and early 2000 and involves 3,722 entities from 56 countries. IAS adopters are characterized by higher growth opportunities, more foreign ownership and greater external financing needs. These firms also are larger, more engaged in exports and more often organized as limited liability corporations. These results must nevertheless be taken with prudence given the high proportion of emerging countries in the sample (the most represented countries are Thailand, Russia, Poland, Estonia, Brazil and Turkey). It is not obvious that incentives to IFRS adoption are the same in emerging and more developed economies.

Because incentives to IFRS adoption are mainly individual, it could not have been expected that all European companies would spontaneously change their accounting standards, even after the removal of institutional obstacles that remained in some countries. On the contrary, the acceptance of IFRS-based financial statements by European stock exchanges resulted in two-tier financial reporting with, in the same country, the coexistence of companies applying IAS and others that were still using domestic GAAP. Moreover, as IAS adopters were concentrated in a limited geographical area (Germanic countries essentially), comparisons between firms from different parts of Europe had not really been made easier. The European Commission therefore came to the conclusion that the standardization of financial information that was a prerequisite to the establishment of the Single Market made it necessary to impose the adoption of IFRS. As a result, the Commission decided in 2000 that all EU listed companies would have to prepare their consolidated financial statements in conformity with IFRS from 2005 onwards (Commission of the European Communities, 2000).

1.2 The situation since 2005

The EU decision to make IFRS mandatory for all European listed companies was a major historical event since its objective was to standardize the financial reporting practices of more than 7,000 firms. It also made IFRS the most widely accepted accounting standards in the world. This decision considerably reinforced the legitimacy of IFRS and definitively established the IASB as the unchallenged reference for standard setting.

The European example was followed by several major countries which in turn adopted the IFRS so that, at the beginning of 2012, 92 countries require the use of IFRS for their domestic listed companies (Table 15.1). Nevertheless it is worth noting that, in some cases, standards that have been adopted as IFRS are not exactly in accordance with those published by the IASB.

Table 15.1 Acceptance of IFRS by countries (as of February 2012)

	Domestic listed companies	*Domestic unlisted companies*
IFRS required for all	92	25
IFRS required for some	5	30
IFRS permitted	25	44
Subtotal	122	99
IFRS not permitted	31	36
Total	153	135

Source: Deloitte (www.iasplus.com/country/useias.htm)

This widespread acceptance of IFRS substantially modified the balance of power between the IASB and the US authorities (SEC and FASB). Although the use of IFRS is still prohibited for US firms, the Securities and Exchange Commission (SEC) decided in 2008 that foreign companies preparing their financial statements in accordance with IFRS will no longer have to reconcile their accounting figures with the amounts that would have been obtained using US GAAP. This decision was effective for periods ending after 15 November 2007.

Countries that adopt IFRS transfer their national standard setting to a supranational private organisation on which they generally have little influence.[1] They do so because they expect advantages from this loss of sovereignty. According to the IASB, the objective of financial reporting is 'to provide financial information about the reporting entity that is useful to existing and potential investors, lenders and other creditors in making decisions about providing resources to the entity' (IASB, 2010 p. 9). This acknowledged pre-eminence of fund providers contrasts with the Continental European view of accounting under which financial statements must satisfy the information needs of a variety of stakeholders (shareholders, creditors, employees, customers, the state, etc.).

Due to this financial orientation, the advantages of IFRS adoption should be particularly substantial for developing or transitional economies and countries that do not share the Anglo-Saxon view of accounting. Through the adoption of IFRS, emerging economies can inexpensively endow themselves with a set of recognized standards that are in line with the investors' needs, which should help them collect funds from private investors or public international organisations. For developed countries, the replacement of former domestic GAAP by more investor-oriented accounting standards should increase the international visibility of their firms.

According to Hope *et al.* (2006), two categories of countries should have incentives to adopt IFRS: those with relatively weak investor-protection mechanisms and those that are opening up their capital markets. For the former, IFRS adoption should reduce the expropriation risk by majority shareholders. For countries of the latter category, the adoption of IFRS should increase access to financial markets and attract new investors. The empirical analysis support these predictions: countries that have adopted IFRS prior to 2005 or 2006 exhibit poorer disclosure rules and anti-director rights; they also provide better access to their stock market for international investors than jurisdictions that did not adopt IFRS.

Judge *et al.* (2010) used a sociological approach. In accordance with the institutional theory, they consider that the adoption of IFRS by many jurisdictions throughout the world may be a consequence of political or economical pressures from international bodies such as the International Monetary Fund (coercive isomorphism). IFRS adoption may also be motivated by a wish of imitation (mimetic isomorphism) or be a consequence of the sharing of common values by deciders in different countries (normative isomorphism). Their empirical analysis based on 132 countries reveals that IFRS-adopting jurisdictions tend to have a higher level of foreign aid, import more than other countries and have a more highly educated population. The authors interpret these findings as supporting the three forms of isomorphism.

2. The effects of IFRS adoption on accounting quality

2.1 The comparability of accounting figures

The prime objective of IFRS adoption is to increase the cross-border comparability of accounting figures. In 2000, the European Commission wrote:

> There are currently many different financial reporting rules and differing interpretations based on distinct traditions within the European Union. Unless reform is undertaken,

> inconsistencies – many of them of major importance – will continue. European financial reporting will remain fragmented, thereby hampering the development of a deep liquid single EU capital market (Commission of the European Communities, 2000, p. 3).

In as much as IFRS generally admit less options than domestic GAAP that they have replaced, their adoption should also result in an increase of comparability within each country. Strangely, there is still little evidence on the impact of IFRS adoption on within and between country reporting comparability.

To date, the most comprehensive study is that of Jones and Finley (2011). It measures the evolution of the dispersion of accounting numbers for a sample of European and Australian firms before and after the mandatory adoption of IFRS by both countries. The authors calculated about twenty financial ratios for the years 2006 and 1994–2004 and observed that, for most of them, the coefficient of variation was significantly lower in 2006 than in the pre-IFRS period. This suggests that IFRS adoption has reduced the dispersion of accounting figures and thus increased within-country comparability.

In a study involving companies from the UK and Australia, Cairns *et al.* (2011) tested whether mandatory IFRS adoption has improved within and between country comparability for a set of policy choices requiring or permitting fair value measurement. The evidence is mixed as the authors conclude that within and between country comparability has increased for property, plant and equipment, derivatives and share-based payments, but decreased for financial assets and liabilities due to the use of the fair value option instead of amortized cost.

2.2 Earnings management

IFRS are probably the most complete and detailed set of accounting standards after US GAAP. As with any standard, they cannot be applied to practical cases without resorting to estimations, in particular where impairment of assets or provisions are concerned. Managers can use this relative incompleteness of accounting standards to manipulate accounting figures, particularly earnings, which gives rise to what is generally called 'earnings management', a behaviour defined by Healy and Wahlen (1999, p. 368):

> Earnings management occurs when managers use judgement in financial reporting and in structuring transactions to alter financial reports to either mislead some stakeholders about the underlying economic performance of the company or to influence contractual outcomes that depend on reported accounting numbers.

Earnings management can take several forms. Some manipulations are purely one-off, as those aimed at increasing earnings prior to the issuance of securities, or meet a given level of performance (analysts forecasts, for example). Other manipulations are multi-periodic, as income smoothing whose purpose is to reduce earnings volatility and accordingly the perceived risk of securities, or 'big bath', a manipulation consisting in recording large losses in a particular year to generate hidden reserves that can be recognized as profits in subsequent years.

Earnings management is not punished with the same strength in all jurisdictions. In some countries, it is permitted, or even encouraged, as in the Germanic area (Germany, Switzerland, Austria) where, before IFRS adoption, companies could legally create hidden reserves. In most non-Anglo-Saxon countries, the strong link between accounting and tax rules creates incentives to manipulate earnings, at least in parent-only financial statements. For the IASB on the contrary, earnings management cannot be accepted, as it is in contradiction to the objective of 'faithful representation' (IASB, 2010, p. 18). Outside the Anglo-Saxon world, one should thus observe less earnings management after the switch to IFRS. Several studies have tried to test this prediction in diverse environments.

Barth *et al.* (2008) measured the earnings management practices of a sample of companies that have voluntarily adopted IFRS between 1994 and 2003. They observed that earnings manipulations were significantly less frequent after IFRS adoption than before. It is worth noting that, although the study covers 21 countries, 72 per cent of sample firms come from Switzerland, Germany or China. Van Tendeloo and Vanstraelen (2005) conducted a study based on German data only. Contrary to Barth *et al.* (2008), they did not find differences with regard to earnings management for firms that had adopted IFRS and those that were still using domestic GAAP in the years 1999–2001.

Studies on mandatory IFRS adoption are not more corroborating. In a research covering Australia, France and the UK, Jeanjean and Stolowy (2008) do not note a decline in the pervasiveness of earnings management after the introduction of IFRS. For France, they even find an increase of earnings manipulations, contrary to Zéghal *et al.* (2011) for whom IFRS adoption is associated with a decrease in earnings management practices.

Results obtained at the European level are also inconclusive. On the one hand, a study by Callao and Jarne (2010) on 1,408 firms from 11 EU member states shows that earnings management has intensified since the adoption of IFRS. On the other, Chen *et al.* (2010) report a decrease in earnings management towards a target and a lower magnitude of discretionary accruals but more earnings smoothing after IFRS adoption. This latter research suggests that the transition to IFRS may have different effects on various types of earnings management.

2.3 Timeliness

To be useful to decision taking, accounting information must not only be relevant, it should also be available in due time. Timeliness is thus a key dimension of accounting quality. According to the IASB (2010, p. 21) 'timeliness means having information available to decision-makers in time to be capable of influencing their decisions'. This definition is too general for empirical studies. The proxy generally used to make it operational is the frequency of large losses. This choice is based on the assumption that managers are reluctant to report losses. Rather than recognizing them as they occur, they would probably prefer to defer losses to future periods, with the hope that they will be offset by future earnings. Because IFRS are more investor-oriented than most non Anglo-Saxon domestic GAAP, their adoption should result in more timely accounting information, that is in a higher frequency of large losses.

In their study on voluntary IAS adoption, Barth *et al.* (2008) provide evidence consistent with this prediction. Adversely, Chen *et al.* (2010) in the European Union and Paananen and Lin (2009) in Germany found that the adoption of IFRS was associated with a lower percentage of losses, which suggests that IFRS have not improved the timeliness of accounting data.

2.4 Value relevance

According to the IFRS and, more generally, the Anglo-Saxon view of accounting, the purpose of accounting is to provide information useful for decision taking by investors. If, as expected, accounting data are relevant for company valuation, they should be highly correlated with market values. Accordingly value relevance is often defined as the ability of accounting data to summarize information impounded in market prices (Francis and Schipper, 1999). Value relevance can thus be assessed by regressing accounting data with their market equivalents. Two types of models are currently used. Price models relate equity to the market value of shares with an equation such as:

$$P_{it} = \alpha_i + \beta_{1i} B_{it} + \varepsilon_{it}$$
$$\text{or } P_{it} = \alpha_i + \beta_{1i} B_{it} + \beta_{2i} E_{it} + \varepsilon_{it}$$

where P_{it} = price of share i at time t

B_{it} = book value per share i at time t

E_{it} = earnings per share i at time t

Alternatively, return models measure the association between earnings per share and market returns:

$$R_{it} = \alpha_i + \beta_{1i} E_{it} + \varepsilon_{it}$$
$$\text{or } R_{it} = \alpha_i + \beta_{1i} E_{it} + \beta_{2i} \Delta E_{it} + \varepsilon_{it}$$

where R_{it} = market return of share i at time t

E_{it} = earnings per share i at time t

ΔE_{it} = change in earnings per share i at time t

In both cases, coefficients β capture the value relevance of each accounting figure, whereas the coefficient of determination of the equation (R^2) indicates the value relevance of the whole set of accounting data included in the equation.

Since IFRS are more market-oriented than most previous national GAAP, the value relevance of accounting data should be higher after their adoption. As for other dimensions of accounting quality, the evidence is mixed. On the one hand, Barth *et al.* (2008) find that companies that have voluntarily adopted IFRS exhibit higher value relevance after adoption than before. Similar results were obtained for mandatory IFRS adoption in China (Liu *et al.*, 2011) and Romania (Filip and Raffournier, 2010). On the other hand, Aubert and Grudnitski (2011) find no increase in value relevance in any EU country after IFRS adoption. Karampinis and Hevas (2011) obtain a similar result in the case of Greece.

In a study covering five major European countries, Devalle *et al.* (2010) note that the impact of IFRS differs according to the stock exchange considered. The value relevance of accounting data increased due to the adoption of IFRS in France and the UK, but decreased in Germany, Spain, and Italy. Evidence of a negative impact of IFRS on value relevance in Germany was also found by Paananen and Lin (2009).

No clear conclusion can be drawn from the results of empirical studies. In some countries, the quality of accounting information seems to have increased after IFRS adoption, whereas in other jurisdictions, the change had no impact. A possible explanation of this conflicting evidence is that certain domestic GAAP were already close to IFRS, whereas others were very different from IASB standards.

3. The economic consequences of IFRS adoption

In the EU, the underlying objective of IFRS adoption was to make European securities more attractive to extra-European investors and allow the growth of European stock exchanges which, at the beginning of the century, were around half the size of US capital markets (Commission of the European Communities, 2000). The adoption of IFRS was expected to reduce information processing costs faced by foreign investors by making it less costly to analyze foreign financial statements. Several studies have tried to evaluate the impact of IFRS adoption on the financial market and foreign investments.

3.1 Consequences on capital markets

3.1.1 Information asymmetry

A crucial market characteristic is informational efficiency, i.e. the capacity of prices to reflect all available information at any time. When information is unequally spread over participants, those who have superior information may use it to obtain a better price at the expense of other investors. Information asymmetry is thus detrimental to market efficiency.

To the extent that IFRS require larger disclosure and are more investor-oriented than most national GAAP they replace, their adoption should result in a decrease of information asymmetry on the concerned financial markets. Several authors have tried to test this prediction. As information asymmetry cannot be directly observed, these studies are based on proxies. The most commonly used proxy is the bid–ask spread, i.e. the difference between the bid price and the asked price of a security at a given point of time. Bid–ask spread can be interpreted as a measure of information asymmetry in as much as it should theoretically be nil if buyers and sellers had the same information regarding future earnings.

In Germany, Gassen and Sellhorn (2006) showed that companies that voluntarily adopted IFRS between 1998 and 2004 experienced a sharp decline in bid–ask spread. Similar results were obtained by Fabiano (2006) in Switzerland. With regard to mandatory adoption, a study by Platikanova and Nobes (2006) covering 15 European countries reveals a significant fall in bid–ask spread in 2005, as compared to 2003. Nevertheless, there are important differences among countries, which suggests that the impact of IFRS adoption on information asymmetry depends also on national characteristics.

3.1.2 Analysts forecasts

IFRS adoption should facilitate the work of financial analysts. If, as expected, the switch to IFRS results in lower information asymmetry, more timely accounting information and less earnings management, forecasting future earnings should be easier after the change of standards. Analyst forecasts should thus be more accurate and less dispersed after IFRS adoption than before. Several empirical studies have tried to test these predictions.

Ashbaugh and Pincus (2001) examined 80 non-US companies claiming to comply with IAS in the years 1990–93. They observed that, for these firms, the switch to IFRS was associated with a significant decrease in analyst forecast errors. Nevertheless, this finding must be interpreted with prudence given that, at the time of the study, firms could claim for IAS compliance without respecting all IAS requirements.

Two recent studies concern the adoption of IFRS by the European Union in 2005. Jiao *et al.* (2012) document increased forecast accuracy and less dispersion after the switch to IFRS. Byard *et al.* (2011) obtain similar evidence but only for firms domiciled in countries with specific characteristics. A wider study including the EU as well as other countries that have made IFRS mandatory (Australia, Hong Kong, Philippines, Singapore, South Africa, Switzerland) shows that IFRS adoption improves the accuracy of forecasts made by foreign analysts but not those of domestic professionals (Tan *et al.*, 2011). This finding is interesting as it suggests that forecast quality depends less on accounting standards than on the analysts' proximity with enterprises.

3.1.3 Market liquidity

The increased quality of accounting information resulting from IFRS adoption, in particular the expected reduction in information asymmetry, should reassure market participants and incite them to invest more in listed companies. As a result, the security market should become more liquid. In the EU, increasing the liquidity of the Single Market was acknowledged as the primary motivation of IFRS adoption (Commission of the European Communities, 2000).

Daske *et al.* (2008) examined the effect of mandatory IFRS adoption in 26 countries. Using four proxies for market liquidity, they found that market liquidity increased after IFRS adoption. In the same vein, Landsman *et al.* (2012) report that firms from countries that have adopted IFRS experience a greater increase of abnormal trading volume in the days surrounding earnings announcements than firms from other countries.

Globally, empirical studies tend to show that IFRS adoption has reduced information asymmetry, increased market liquidity and made earnings forecasts easier. It remains to be seen whether this improvement in the functioning of markets has benefited companies.

3.2 Consequence on foreign investments

According to financial theory, investors should invest in foreign companies to diversify their risk internationally. Despite that, there is evidence that most portfolios are overinvested in domestic securities.[2] This home bias is generally interpreted as a consequence of information costs that investors have to face when they invest in foreign countries. Beneish and Yohn (2008) distinguish three types of information costs that are associated with foreign investment:

- information processing costs;
- costs resulting from the uncertainty about the quality of financial reporting; and
- about the distribution of future cash flows.

Information processing costs are the costs of becoming familiar with the financial statements of foreign companies. These costs are reinforced by the investors' perception that they are less competent in interpreting financial statements of foreign companies. The more foreign accounting standards deviate from the investor's domestic GAAP, the higher these costs are. The adoption of common internationally recognized accounting standards as IFRS should reduce the cost of analysing foreign financial statements and make foreign investors more confident in their ability to correctly interpret these statements. As IFRS are recognized as high quality standards, of higher quality at least than most national GAAP they have replaced, their adoption should also reduce costs associated with the uncertainty about the quality of foreign financial statements.

The third category of costs results from the view that domestic investors have an information advantage over foreigners with regard to the distribution of companies' future cash flows. This argument reflects the idea that local investors are better informed about the risk-return characteristics of domestic securities because of higher proximity with local companies. Given that the whole set of information available on a company largely exceeds what is likely to be disclosed in financial statements, IFRS adoption should normally not challenge the informational advantage of local investors. Nevertheless, to the extent that IFRS disclosure requirements are higher than those of most former local GAAP, IFRS adoption may result in public disclosure of information that otherwise would not be available to foreign investors.

The switch to IFRS should reduce the information costs of foreign investors and consequently incite them to invest more outside their boundaries. Empirical studies are consistent with this prediction. In a study covering 29 countries, Covrig *et al.* (2007) found that average foreign mutual fund ownership was significantly higher among firms that had voluntarily adopted IAS. They also found that the level of foreign investments was particularly high among IAS adopters located in poor information environments. Similarly, Shima and Gordon (2011) document that US foreign equity investment is associated with IFRS adoption, at least in strong regulatory environments. Concerning debt financing, Kim *et al.* (2007) report that voluntary IAS adopters attract more foreign lenders from the international loan market than firms that are using domestic GAAP.

3.3 Consequence on the cost of capital

The increased quality of accounting information and the reduction in information asymmetry resulting from the switch to IFRS should lower the perceived risk of securities. As a consequence, the claims of investors should, *ceteris paribus*, be less after IFRS adoption than before. The switch to IFRS should thus be associated with a decrease in the financing cost of companies. From a firm's point of view, this impact on the cost of capital is probably the main criteria measuring the benefits of IFRS adoption.

The cost of capital is the average cost of all financings used by a company. It encompasses the cost of equity capital and the cost of borrowings. Nevertheless, most studies have focused on the first component. In Europe, neither Daske (2006) nor Cuijpers and Buijink (2005) found evidence of a lower cost of equity capital for voluntary IAS adopters. By contrast, Daske *et al.* (2008) and Li (2010) document a decrease in firms' cost of equity capital after IFRS mandatory adoption. The only study on the cost of debt was made by Kim *et al.* (2007). It reports that lenders charge significantly lower loan rates to IAS adopters than they do to non-adopters.

4. IFRS adoption and national characteristics

Several empirical studies on the effects of IFRS adoption document important country differences. This suggests that the impact of accounting standards is contingent on the context in which they are applied, in particular on local institutional characteristics. Before considering the influence of national features, it is useful to examine the level of IFRS compliance in countries that have adopted IASB standards.

4.1 The degree of IFRS compliance

It could be expected that mandatory adoption of IFRS in Europe and some other parts of the world would result in a standardization of accounting practices in the concerned countries. As mentioned above, IFRS adoption seems to have improved the international comparability of financial statements. Nevertheless, the standardization process has not been complete, as evidenced by empirical research.

Several studies document significant noncompliance with the disclosure requirements of IFRS among firms that voluntarily adopted IFRS. Hodgdon *et al.* (2008), for example, examined the level of compliance for a sample of firms that claimed to comply with the disclosure requirements of IFRS in 1999–2000. They found an average compliance score of 68 per cent and an extreme dispersion of observations, with score values ranging from 4 per cent to 96 per cent. The decision to make IFRS mandatory did not solve the problem, as Tsalavoutas (2011) shows that, in 2005, certain IASB standards were still poorly respected in Greece, in particular those that differed the most from previous Greek GAAP.

Several authors examined whether noncompliance has an impact on the benefits resulting from IFRS adoption. Hodgdon *et al.* (2008) in particular have shown that analyst forecast errors are inversely related to the level of compliance with IFRS. But it is probably Daske *et al.* (2007) who made the most comprehensive study on this issue. These authors examined a set of companies that had voluntarily adopted IAS/IFRS between 1998 and 2004. Using several measures of IFRS compliance, they split the sample firms into two categories: serious and 'label' adopters. Only the former exhibited a decrease in their cost of capital and bid–ask spread following the switch to IAS/IFRS. What is particularly interesting in this finding is that it suggests that market participants are able to distinguish between firms that really conform to IFRS and those that comply only superficially with these standards. The rest of this section is devoted to an examination of national characteristics that may create incentives to fully comply with IFRS.

4.2 The legal and regulatory environment

Legal systems can be classified in two categories: common law and code (or civil) law.[3] These categories differ in the importance they give to the rights of private property owners versus the state. Code law is traditionally viewed as emphasizing the rights of the state to a higher degree than common law (Beck *et al.*, 2003). Numerous studies document the influence of the legal system on accounting quality. Ball *et al.* (2000), for example, find that accounting income is more timely in common law than in code law countries. Nevertheless, the code/common classes are not homogeneous and partitioning countries with reference to this only criterion would hide important differences within each category. It is thus preferable to abandon the classical code/common law dichotomy to more precisely distinguish the diverse dimensions of legal systems.

One of these dimensions is shareholder protection. The interests of shareholders are not equally protected in all legal systems (La Porta *et al.*, 1998). Because non-compliance with IFRS is detrimental to shareholders, it should be less frequent in countries characterized with a high level of shareholder protection. Moreover, in jurisdictions that actively protect shareholders, domestic GAAP were probably less different from IFRS than in other countries. In these jurisdictions, the transition to IFRS has probably represented a less fundamental change than in countries with low shareholder protection. One can thus predict that compliance with IFRS is higher in environments characterized with high investor protection.

Strong legal rules are a necessary condition to guarantee that the rights of shareholders are protected, but not a sufficient one. Legal rules may remain largely ineffective without proper enforcement. Furthermore, a solid system of legal enforcement can also substitute for weak rules since active and well-functioning courts can rescue investors abused by managers (La Porta *et al.*, 1998). The influence of law enforcement is supported by numerous studies dealing with various aspects of accounting quality (e.g. Bushman and Piotroski, 2006; DeFond *et al.*, 2007). Assuming that a high level of law enforcement increases the likelihood that legal provisions aimed at protecting shareholders are really respected, a positive association between law enforcement and IFRS compliance can be expected. Consistent with this prediction, Daske *et al.* (2008) document that the increase in liquidity and equity valuations following mandatory IFRS adoption is restricted to countries with strict enforcement regimes.

4.3 Other influences

4.3.1 Corporate governance quality

Law is not the only source of protection for investors. Efficient corporate governance practices may also reduce the level of expropriation by insiders. Durnev and Kim (2005), for example, show that firms with better governance are valued higher on stock markets, especially where legal investor protection is weak, which suggests that efficient corporate governance practices may be a substitute for poor legal environments.

In recent years, the rights of shareholders have been considerably strengthened with the adoption of corporate governance rules. In a survey ordered by the European Commission, Gregory and Simmelkjaer (2002) identify 35 documents that qualify as corporate governance codes. They also note that most EU member states have at least one code document. In a limited number of countries (Germany and Sweden), corporate governance provisions have been included in company law, but in most European states they take the form of codes of best practices whose application is voluntary or enforced by stock exchange authorities.

There is a growing body of research on the influence of corporate governance characteristics on accounting quality. The proportion of outside directors in particular was found as being positively related to earnings timeliness (Beekes *et al.*, 2004) and negatively associated with earnings management (Klein, 2002). To the extent that IFRS adoption increases accounting quality, IFRS compliance and corporate governance characteristics should also be associated. More precisely, one can predict that firms subject to high quality corporate governance mechanisms exhibit higher levels of IFRS compliance. Unfortunately, this hypothesis has not yet been empirically tested.

4.3.2 Auditors

Many studies have investigated the impact of auditor type on various aspects of accounting quality. They generally report a positive association between accounting quality and the size of audit firm. The traditional interpretation is that large audit firms are more independent of their clients than smaller auditors. Accordingly, they can more easily oppose GAAP violations, earnings management or creative accounting.

Big 4 audit firms have largely anticipated IFRS adoption. Well before IFRS implementation, they developed training programmes and audit controls specifically for IFRS audits (Street, 2002). Since such investments are costly, smaller audit firms could not be expected to have the same level of IFRS expertise as Big 4, at least in the early years of IFRS application. In support of this argument, several studies document that compliance with IFRS is higher in companies audited by a large audit firm (Glaum and Street, 2003; Hodgdon *et al.*, 2009).

4.3.3 The financial system

It is traditional to oppose bank- and market-oriented financial systems. In the former, banks are the main providers of company financing, whereas, in the latter, companies generally prefer raising funds from the security market. In market-oriented countries, the large number of shareholders generates a high demand for accounting quality, in particular more timely incorporation of economic income in accounting earnings. Inversely, in bank-oriented countries, the demand for high-quality accounting data is lower because information asymmetry is more likely to be resolved through insider communications with management (Ball *et al.*, 2000). Since IFRS are supposed to provide information of better quality than most domestic GAAP, the demand for IFRS compliance should be higher in market-oriented financial environments than in bank-oriented countries. This conjecture has not yet been formally tested but several empirical studies provide evidence consistent with it. Leuz *et al.* (2003) and Burgstahler *et al.* (2006) for example have shown that earnings management is less prevalent in countries with large and highly developed equity markets than in bank-oriented economies.

5. Issues for the future

Since the beginning of the twenty-first century, the IASB has emerged as the key player in international accounting standard setting. Its standards have been adopted or are on the point of being adopted by a large number of countries. Its only competitor, the US Financial Accounting Standard Board, seems to have given up the idea of imposing its standards beyond the US boundaries; it now works with the IASB on joint projects in order to arrive at convergence of US GAAP and IFRS, which should, at an undefined horizon, result in IFRS adoption by the US authorities. Despite these successes, the IASB is faced with several problems it will have to address in the next years in order to hold its authority.

5.1 The proliferation of 'local IFRS'

According to the IASB, a company cannot claim compliance with IFRS unless it complies with all the requirements of IFRS (IAS 1, § 16). Nevertheless several empirical studies provide evidence of partial compliance, in particular where enforcement mechanisms are insufficient or ineffective. However, noncompliance is not always a consequence of management opportunism. Even in countries that are claiming IFRS adoption, rules may exist that prevent full application of these standards. Moreover, some countries have developed local versions of IFRS that differ from IASB standards on specific points.

In some cases, new standards must pass an agreement process whose length is variable before being applicable. In the EU, IFRS are enforceable only after they have been approved by the European Commission. The agreement process gives political authorities the power to refuse any standard that could go against their interests or be unsuitable for the local context. The threat of non-adoption may also help them obtain changes in a standard project. By refusing to adopt the initial version of IAS 39, the EU obtained a revision of this standard (Bengtsson, 2011). Of course, only countries or groups of countries whose political or economical weight is substantial can effectively exert pressure on the IASB.

Rather than adopting IFRS as such, some countries preferred to integrate them into their own regulations. In some jurisdictions (Australia, New Zealand, Korea), IFRS have been copied with no significant change, so that domestic GAAP can be seen as 'IFRS-equivalents'. But in other cases (China, Philippines, Singapore), substantial differences remain. Sometimes also, IFRS have been taken as they stood at a point in time and no updating has since been made (Uruguay, Venezuela).[4]

The proliferation of local versions of IFRS is dangerous because it makes it possible for financial statements to be presented as complying with IFRS despite significant deviations from IASB standards. The 'IFRS-equivalent' concept itself is unclear, as there is no indicator that can be used to measure the degree of equivalence with IFRS and decide from what level the 'IFRS-equivalent' label may be granted. IFRS are unanimously recognized as high quality standards. It would be regrettable if their image were altered due to the proliferation of ersatz copies that would usurp their name. As the owner of the 'IFRS' brand name, the IASB would be well advised to oppose the development of more or less faithful imitations.

5.2 The resistance to IFRS

Despite their wide diffusion, IFRS are still subject to criticisms from practitioners, academicians and politicians. Some of them are technical, others are political. The former are based mainly on an alleged excessive use of fair value. IFRS are accused of resorting too much to fair value for valuation purposes. This criticism was particularly strong at the beginning of the last financial crisis, when some observers did not hesitate to allege that IFRS played a significant role in the 2008 credit crunch. We will not discuss this point as many articles have been written on this issue (André *et al.,* 2009; Laux and Leuz, 2009; Magnan, 2009); moreover this book devotes a full chapter to fair value. We will thus focus on political criticisms that have rarely been taken up by the literature in English. These criticisms turn on the market orientation of IFRS and an alleged lack of legitimacy for the IASB.

5.2.1 The market orientation of IFRS

IFRS are representative of the Anglo-Saxon view of accounting which considers that the primary objective of financial reporting is to provide information useful to investors. This pre-eminence of funds providers is explicitly acknowledged by the new conceptual framework which stipulates that 'the objective of general purpose financial reporting is to provide financial information about the reporting entity that is useful to existing and potential investors, lenders and other creditors in making decisions about providing resources to the entity' (IASB, 2010, § OB2).

In Continental Europe, especially in France, many people challenge this investor orientation. They consider that there are many potential users of accounting information (employees, suppliers, customers, the state, the society in general) and that accounting should not favour one category at the expense of others. More fundamentally, some people express the view that accounting reflects a certain conception of the enterprise (Burlaud and Colasse, 2011) and that recognizing investors as privileged users of financial reporting amounts to favouring them in the sharing of the wealth created by the firm (Chiapello and Medjad, 2009). Capron (2005), for example, notes that in Anglo-Saxon countries expenses are generally classified by function, which makes the calculation of value added more difficult than when they are classified by nature, as in most European countries. He fears that even if both presentations are presently admitted, the use of IFRS will progressively result in the extinction of the classification by nature and consequently delete the debate on value added sharing. Because of their investor orientation, IFRS are often perceived in Continental Europe as the Trojan Horse of financial capitalism.

5.2.2 The IASB legitimacy

For a long time, the IASB had only a proposal role; its standards served as a reference for the production of national GAAP but had no coercive nature. In the early 2000s, when some countries or groups of countries decided to make IFRS mandatory for listed companies, the IASB changed its status, switching from a simple technical organization to a supranational standard setter.

In the Anglo-Saxon world, this evolution did not generate strong opposition as it is usual in these countries for the state to entrust private organizations with the task of regulating technical issues. In Continental Europe by contrast, several voices were raised, blaming authorities for giving up a part of their sovereignty. Reactions to this privatization of standard setting were particularly strong in France and, to a lesser extent, in Germany, probably because in these two countries accounting regulation was previously endorsed by law (Chiapello and Medjad, 2009).

The IASB was criticized mainly for an alleged lack of legitimacy. According to Burlaud and Colasse (2011), the IASB is not legitimate because Board members are not democratically elected. In defence of the IASB, Gélard and Pigé (2011) retort that a democratic election is not the only way to acquire legitimacy. For them, IFRS take their legitimacy from the decision of the European Commission, a democratic entity, to endorse these standards.

The criticisms on legitimacy are reinforced by the domination that large audit firms exert on the IASB. As noted by Chiapello and Medjad (2009), most Board members are former auditors and the Big 4 are the primary IASB contributors in terms of expertise. Irrespective of their origin, IASB Board members have thus a common professional experience and an Anglo-Saxon accounting culture (Burlaud and Colasse, 2011), which makes them unable to faithfully reflect the variety of accounting traditions.

This controversy on IASB legitimacy highlights the opposition between two opposed views of accounting. In the Anglo-Saxon world, accounting falls within economics and the purpose of financial reporting is to reflect the economic reality as well as possible. As a technical matter, it is quite natural to leave its regulation to people with the highest technical expertise, i.e. professionals (chartered accountants). In Continental Europe, by contrast, accounting is at the heart of distributive mechanisms among stakeholders: shareholders, lenders, employees, the state, etc. (Chiapello and Medjad, 2009). Because wealth sharing is a political issue, financial reporting must be regulated by democratically elected representatives. It is for that reason that the main provisions of accounting regulation are included in the law. In Continental Europe, the intrusion of IFRS amounts to a cultural revolution that dramatically goes against the way financial reporting and accounting regulation are perceived. Because these beliefs are deeply anchored in national culture, criticisms of IFRS are not likely to weaken. The IASB should thus take them into account, notably by widening the professional origin of Board members, if it feels desirable to enhance public adherence to IFRS outside the Anglo-Saxon world.

5.4 The influence of politicians

As long as the IASB was a private organization whose decisions had no immediate consequence on the financial statements of companies it was not submitted to intense scrutiny from politicians. But, since it has acquired the status of standard setter in several countries, the IASB has had to face increased political pressures. The main evidence of these pressures is the decision taken in 2008 to allow the reclassification of certain financial instruments. According to IAS 39, the valuation mode of financial assets depends mainly on the category to which they have been allocated at acquisition: those considered as held for trading or available for sale being shown at fair value. Until then, the IASB had always opposed category changes, given the earnings management opportunities that these reclassifications would allow. In autumn 2008, the subprime crisis and the collapse of Lehman Brothers caused a crisis of confidence among market participants. As a result, the market price of most securities declined. Because many financial assets were measured at fair value, ratios used for bank regulation deteriorated, which prevented banks from lending funds and amplified the credit crunch. To limit the economic consequences of the crisis, the EU urged the IASB to modify its standard. In response, the IASB waived its due process procedure and urgently issued an amendment to IAS 39, allowing the reclassification of financial assets that had to be measured at fair value.

This decision was harmful to the IASB in as much at it provides evidence that the international standard setter is likely to give in to political pressures, provided they come from powerful institutions. Since then, political organizations such as the European Parliament and the G20 have stepped into the breach and claim to have their say in the elaboration of IFRS and IASB functioning (Bengtsson, 2011). The IASB independence vis-à-vis politicians is now called into question. It is all the more regrettable since political independence constitutes one of IASB main assets. If so many countries have left the IASB to elaborate their accounting standards, it is precisely because it is an international organization that was not submitted to the influence of some country or other. One cannot imagine for example that China would have adopted US GAAP or the European Directives. Some detractors of IFRS now take advantage of this precedent to argue that the IASB is under the influence of the EU and that IFRS are in fact European standards, which of course considerably reduces their chance of being adopted elsewhere, particularly in the US. If the IASB intends to keep its status as a unique international standard setter, it should reassert its independence from any political power and reaffirm that its unfortunate decision of 2008 will be unique.

Notes

1 Only the US, the European Union and some major countries can, through their direct or indirect representatives on the Board, really influence IASB decisions.

2 Ahearne *et al.* (2004) for example document that by 2000, US investors held approximately 88 per cent of their funds in US equities.

3 Common law has an English origin, which explains that common law countries are members of the former British Empire. In code law countries, the legal system was inspired by France, Germany or Scandinavian states (La Porta *et al.*, 1997).

4 This information is extracted from Deloitte's IASPlus website: www.iasplus.com/en/resources/use-of-ifrs.

Bibliography

Ahearne, A. G., Griever, W. L. and Warnock, F. E. (2004) 'Information Costs and Home Bias: An Analysis of US Holdings of Foreign Equities'. *Journal of International Economics*, 62(2), 313–36.

André, P., Cazavan-Jeny, A., Dick, W., Richard, C. and Walton, P. (2009) 'Fair Value Accounting and the Banking Crisis in 2008: Shooting the Messenger'. *Accounting in Europe*, 6(1), 3–24.

Ashbaugh, H. and Pincus, M. (2001) 'Domestic Accounting Standards, International Accounting Standards, and the Predictability of Earnings'. *Journal of Accounting Research*, 39(3), 417–34.

Aubert, F. and Grudnitski, G. (2011) 'The Impact and Importance of Mandatory Adoption of International Financial Reporting Standards in Europe'. *Journal of International Financial Management and Accounting*, 22(1), 1–26.

Ball, R., Kothari, S. P. and Robin, A. (2000) 'The Effect of International Institutional Factors on Properties of Accounting Earnings', *Journal of Accounting and Economics*, 29(1), 1–51.

Barth, M. E., Landsman, W. R. and Lang, M. H. (2008) 'International Accounting Standards and Accounting Quality'. *Journal of Accounting Research*, 46(3), 467–98.

Beck, T., Demirgüç-Kunt, A. and Levine, R. (2003) 'Law and Finance: Why Does Legal Origin Matter?' *Journal of Comparative Economics*, 31(4), 653–75.

Beekes, W., Pope, P. and Young, S. (2004) 'The Link Between Earnings Timeliness, Earnings Conservatism and Board Composition: Evidence from the UK'. *Corporate governance: An International Review*, 12(1), 47–59.

Beneish, M. D. and Yohn, T. L. (2008) 'Information Friction and investor Home Bias: A Perspective on the Effect of Global IFRS Adoption on the Extent of Equity Home Bias'. *Journal of Accounting and Public Policy*, 27(6), 433–43.

Bengtsson, E. (2011) 'Repoliticalization of Accounting Standard Setting: The IASB, the EU and the Global Financial Crisis'. *Critical Perspectives on Accounting*, 22(6), 567–80.

Burgstahler, D.C., Hail, L. and Leuz, C. (2006) 'The Importance of Reporting Incentives: Earnings Management in European Private and Public Firms'. *The Accounting Review*, 81(5), 983–1016.

Burlaud, A. and Colasse, B. (2011) 'International Accounting Standardisation: Is Politics Back?'. *Accounting in Europe*, 8(1), 23–47.

Bushman, R.M. and Piotroski, J. D. (2006) 'Financial Reporting Incentives for Conservative Accounting: The Influence of Legal and Political Institutions'. *Journal of Accounting and Economics*, 42(1–2), 17–148.

Byard, D., Li, Y. and Yu, Y. (2011) 'The Effect of Mandatory IFRS Adoption on Financial Analysts' Information Environment'. *Journal of Accounting Research*, 49(1), 69–96.

Cairns, D., Massoudi, D., Taplin, R. and Tarca, A. (2011) 'IFRS Fair Value Measurement and Accounting Policy Choice in the United Kingdom and Australia'. *The British Accounting Review*, 43(1), 1–21.

Callao, S. and Jarne, J. I. (2010) 'Have IFRS Affected Earnings Management in the European Union?'. *Accounting in Europe*, 7(2), 159–89.

Capron, M. (2005) 'Les enjeux de la mise en œuvre des normes comptables internationales', in Capron, M. (ed.) *Les normes comptables internationales, instruments du capitalisme financier*, Paris: La Découverte, pp. 5–26.

Chen, H., Tang, Q. Jiang, Y. and Lin, Z. (2010) 'The Role of International Financial Reporting Standards in Accounting Quality: Evidence from the European Union'. *Journal of International Financial Management and Accounting*, 21(3), 220–78.

Chiapello, E., and Medjad, K. (2009) 'An Unprecedented Privatisation of Mandatory Standard-Setting: The Case of European Accounting Policy' *Critical Perspectives on Accounting*, 20(4), 448–68.

Commission of the European Communities (2000) *Communication from the Commission to the Council and the European Parliament – EU Financial Reporting Strategy: The Way Forward*. Brussels: Commission of the European Communities.

Covrig, V. M., Defond, M. L. and Hung, M. (2007) 'Home Bias, Foreign Mutual Fund Holdings, and the Voluntary Adoption of International Accounting Standards'. *Journal of Accounting Research*, 45(1), 41–70.

Cuijpers, R. and Buijink, W. (2005) 'Voluntary Adoption of Non-local GAAP in the European Union: A Study of Determinants and Consequences'. *European Accounting Review*, 14(3), 487–524.

Daske, H. (2006) 'Economic Benefits of Adopting IFRS or US-GAAP: Have the Expected Costs of Equity Capital Really Decreased?'. *Journal of Business Finance and Accounting*, 33(3–4), 329–73.

Daske, H., Hail, L., Leuz, C. and Verdi, R. (2007) 'Adopting a Label: Heterogeneity in the Economic Consequences of IFRS Adoptions'. Working paper available on ssrn.com.

Daske, H., Hail, L., Leuz, C. and Verdi, R. (2008) 'Mandatory IFRS Reporting Around the World: Early Evidence on the Economic Consequences'. *Journal of Accounting Research*, 46(5), 1085–142.

DeFond, M., Hung, M., and Trezevant, R. (2007) 'Investor Protection and the Information Content of Annual Earnings Announcements: International Evidence'. *Journal of Accounting and Economics*, 43(1), 37–67.

Delvaille, P., Ebbers, G. and Saccon, C. (2005) 'International Financial Reporting Convergence: Evidence from Three Continental European Countries'. *Accounting in Europe*, 2, 137–64.

Devalle, A., Onali, E. and Magarini, R. (2010) 'Assessing the Value Relevance of Accounting Data after the Introduction of IFRS in Europe'. *Journal of International Financial Management and Accounting*, 21(2), 85–119.

Dumontier, P. and Raffournier, B. (1998) 'Why Firms Comply with IAS: An Empirical Analysis with Swiss Data'. *Journal of International Financial Management and Accounting*, 9(3), 216–45.

Durnev, A. and Kim, E.H. (2005) 'To Steal or not to Steal: Firm Attributes, Legal Environment, and Valuation'. *The Journal of Finance*, 60(3), 1461–93.

Fabiano, J. (2006) 'Relationship Between Cost of Capital and International Accounting Standards for Swiss Companies'. Working paper available on ssrn.com.

Filip., A. and Raffournier, B. (2010) 'The Value Relevance of Earnings in a Transition Economy: The Case of Romania'. *The International Journal of Accounting*, 45(1), 77–103.

Francis, J. and Schipper, K (1999) 'Have Financial Statements Lost their Relevance?'. *Journal of Accounting Research*, 37(2), 319–52.

Francis, J.R., Kurana, I.K., Martin, X. and Pereira, R. (2008) 'The Role of Firm-Specific Incentives and Country Factors in Explaining Voluntary IAS Adoptions: Evidence from Private Firms'. *European Accounting Review*, 17(2), 331–60.

Gassen, J. and Sellhorn, T. (2006) 'Applying IFRS in Germany: Determinants and Consequences'. Working paper available on ssrn.com.

Gélard, G., and Pigé, B. (2011) 'Normalisation comptable internationale et légitimité: Commentaires sur "Normalisation comptable internationale – le retour du politique ?"'. *Comptabilité Contrôle Audit*, 17(3), 87–99.

Glaum, M. and Street, D.L. (2003) 'Compliance with the Disclosure Requirements of Germany's New Market: IAS versus US GAAP'. *Journal of International Financial Management and Accounting*, 12(1), 64–100.

Gregory, H.J., and Simmelkjaer, R.T. (2002) *Comparative Study of Corporate Governance Codes Relevant to the European Union and its Member States*', London: Weil, Gotshal & Manges LLP, available at http://ec.europa.eu/internal_market/company/docs/corpgov/corp-gov-codes-rpt-part1_en.pdf.

Haller, A. (2002) 'Financial Accounting Developments in the European Union: Past Events and Future Prospects'. *The European Accounting Review*, 11(1), 153–90.

Healy, P. M. and Wahlen, J. M. (1999) 'A Review of the Earnings Management Literature and its Implications for Standard Setting'. *Accounting Horizons*, 13(4), 365–83.

Hodgdon, C., Tondkar, R. H., Harless, D. W. and Adhikari, A. (2008) 'Compliance with IFRS Disclosure Requirements and Individual Analysts' Forecast Errors'. *Journal of International Accounting, Auditing and Taxation*, 17(1), 1–13.

Hodgdon, C., Tondkar, R.H., Adhikari, A. and Harless, D.W. (2009) 'Compliance with International Financial Reporting Standards and Auditor Choice: New Evidence on the Importance of the Statutory Audit'. *The International Journal of Accounting*, 44(1), 33–55.

Hope, O.-K., Jin, J. and Kang, T. (2006) 'Empirical Evidence on Jurisdictions that Adopt IFRS.' *Journal of International Accounting Research*, 5(2), 1–20.

IASB (2010) *The Conceptual Framework for Financial Reporting 2010*. London: IASB.

Jeanjean, T. and Stolowy, H. (2008) 'Do Accounting Standards Matter? An Exploratory Analysis of Earnings Management Before and After IFRS Adoption'. *Journal of Accounting and Public Policy*, 27(6), 480–94.

Jiao, T., Koning, M., Mertens, G. and Roosenboom, P. (2012) 'Mandatory IFRS Adoption and its Impact on Analysts' Forecasts'. *International Review of Financial Analysis*, 21(1), 56–63.

Jones, S. and Finley, A. (2011) 'Have IFRS Made a Difference to Intra-country Financial Reporting Diversity?'. *The British Accounting Review*, 43(1), 22–38.

Judge, W., Li, S. and Pinsker, R. (2010) 'National Adoption of International Accounting Standards: An Institutional Perspective'. *Corporate Governance: An International Review*, 18(3), 161–74.

Karampinis, N. I. and Hevas, D. L. (2011) 'Mandating IFRS in an Unfavorable Environment: The Greek Experience'. *The International Journal of Accounting*, 46(3), 304–32.

Kim, J.-B., Tsui, J. S. L. and Yi, C. H. (2007) 'The Voluntary Adoption of International Accounting Standards and Loan Contracting around the World'. Working paper available on www.ssrn.com.

Klein, A. (2002) 'Audit Committee, Board of Director Characteristics, and Earnings Management'. *Journal of Accounting and Economics*, 33(3), 375–400.

Landsman, W. R., Maydew, E. L. and Thornock, J. R. (2012) 'The Information Content of Annual Earnings Announcements and Mandatory Adoption of IFRS'. *Journal of Accounting and Economics*, 53(1–2), 34–54.

La Porta, R., Lopez-de-Silanes, F. and Shleifer, A. (1997) 'Legal Determinants of External Finance'. *The Journal of Finance*, 52(3), 1131–50.

La Porta, R., Lopez-de-Silanes, F. and Shleifer, A. (1998) 'Law and Finance'. *Journal of Political Economy*, 106(6), 1113–55.

Laux, C. and Leuz, C. (2009) 'The Crisis of Fair-value Accounting: Making Sense of the Recent Debate'. *Accounting, Organizations and Society*, 34(6–7), 826–34.

Leuz, C., Nanda, D. and Wysocki, P.D. (2003) 'Earnings Management and Investor Protection: An International Comparison'. *Journal of Financial Economics*, 69(3), 505–27.

Li, S. (2010) 'Does Mandatory Adoption of International Financial Reporting Standards in the European Union Reduce the Cost of Equity Capital?'. *The Accounting Review*, 85(2), 607–36.

Liu, C., Yao, L. J. Hu, N. and Liu, L. (2011) 'The Impact of IFRS on Accounting Quality in a Regulated Market: An Empirical Study of China'. *Journal of Accounting, Auditing and Finance*, 26(4), 659–76.

Magnan, M. (2009) 'Fair Value Accounting and the Financial Crisis: Messenger or Contributor?'. *Accounting Perspectives*, 8(3), 189–213.

Paananen, M. and Lin, H. (2009) 'The Development of Accounting Quality of IAS and IFRS over Time: The Case of Germany'. *Journal of International Accounting Research*, 8(1), 31–55.

Platikanova, P. and Nobes, C. (2006) 'Was the Introduction of IFRS in Europe Value-relevant?'. Working paper available on www.ssrn.com.

Renders, A. and Gaeremynck, A. (2007) 'The Impact of Legal and Voluntary Investor Protection on the Early Adoption of International Financial Reporting Standards (IFRS)'. *De Economist*, 155(1), 49–72.

Shima, K. M. and Gordon, E. A. (2011) 'IFRS and the Regulatory Environment: The Case of US Investor Allocation Choice'. *Journal of Accounting and Public Policy*, 30(5), 481–500.

Street, D.L. (2002) 'Large Firms Envision Worldwide Convergence of Standards'. *Accounting Horizons*, 16(3), 215–18.

Tan, H., Wang, S. and Welker, M. (2011) 'Analyst Following and Forecast Accuracy after Mandated IFRS Adoptions'. *Journal of Accounting Research*, 49(5), 1307–57.

Tsalavoutas, I. (2011) 'Transition to IFRS and Compliance with Mandatory Disclosure Requirements: What is the Signal?'. *Advances in Accounting, Incorporating Advances in International Accounting*, 27, 390–405.

Van Tendeloo, B. and Vanstraelen, A. (2005) 'Earnings Management under German GAAP versus IFRS'. *European Accounting Review*, 14(1), 155–80.

Zéghal, D., Chtourou, S. and Sellami, Y. M. (2011) 'An Analysis of the Effect of Mandatory Adoption of IAS/IFRS on Earnings Management'. *Journal of International Accounting, Auditing and Taxation*, 20(1), 61–72.

Part 4

Institutional Aspects of (International) Financial Reporting Regulation

16

The International Accounting Standards Board

Kees Camfferman

1. Introduction

As should be clear from a perusal of the other contributions in this volume, the International Accounting Standards Board (IASB) has undoubtedly become one of the key international actors in financial reporting regulation. It is hardly possible to discuss any contemporary issue in financial accounting and financial reporting without reference to the IASB and its International Financial Reporting Standards (IFRS). But the IASB, which began operations in 2001, could not have obtained this degree of recognition without the foundations laid by its predecessor body, the International Accounting Standards Committee (IASC). A quarter-century after its founding in 1973, the steady work of the IASC resulted in the fairly complete body of International Accounting Standards (IAS), which could stand comparison with national standards in most developed countries. By 2000, IAS had obtained a distinct foothold in financial reporting practice, not only because several national standard setters were converging their national standards with IAS, but also because a few hundred listed companies, mainly but not exclusively in Europe, had adopted IAS directly in the hope of improving their access to international capital markets. But with all due recognition of the achievements of the IASC, it may be said that after the IASB took over from the IASC the significance of IAS (known since 2001 as IFRS) increased to entirely new levels, and also probably far beyond what most participants and observers expected at the time the IASB came into being.

As long as the IASC was in existence, International Accounting Standards had typically been thought of as existing side by side with national standards. They might serve as a source of inspiration for the development of these national standards (whose further development might in turn also inspire the further development of IAS), and they might on a voluntary basis be adopted as a substitute or complement of national standards by the subset of companies seeking cross-border listings. However, it was not expected that they would supplant national standards, at least not in the more developed economies. After 2000, however, the latter prospect quite suddenly became much more realistic.

The main impetus for this change in perspective came from the announcement, in 2000, by the European Commission, of a plan to require the use of IAS in the consolidated financial statements of all listed companies in the European Union (EU), starting in 2005. This was followed soon after by similar policy changes in Hong Kong, Australia and New Zealand, and later in the decade in other significant economies including Canada, Brazil and South Korea. Many smaller countries also took steps towards the use of IFRS in one form or another, with the result that the IASB could soon claim that 'more than a hundred' countries were using IFRS.[1]

Meanwhile, several major countries have drawn closer to IFRS, without yet committing themselves to full adoption. In 2007, the United States Securities and Exchange Commission (SEC) decided that it would henceforth accept IFRS-based financial statements prepared by foreign registrants without a reconciliation of the key numbers to US Generally Accepted Accounting Principles (US GAAP). The lifting of this 20-F reconciliation had for many years been the IASC's ultimate objective. Yet, as soon as it was reached, the SEC continued without pause to raise the far more fundamental question of the use of IFRS instead of US GAAP by listed companies domiciled in the US. In 2009, Japan announced that its listed companies would be allowed to use IFRS rather than Japanese GAAP in their consolidated financial statements, and that it was contemplating mandatory use of IFRS by all listed companies. And, while China has so far ruled out direct applicability of IFRS for its listed companies, it has undertaken a major convergence effort with the result that its claim that Chinese accounting standards are, since 2007, 'substantially converged' with IFRS is widely accepted.

At the time when this chapter was completed (the early summer of 2012), the US SEC had not announced its final policy decision on domestic use of IFRS, and it is clear that significant second thoughts have arisen in the US about the desirability of a radical move towards IFRS. It is also clear that US hesitation has already eroded support for mandatory use of IFRS in Japan, and that the SEC's eventual decision will have a significant impact, positive or negative, on support for IFRS elsewhere in the world. This uncertainty about the future does not detract at all from the earlier observation that the significance of IFRS has grown spectacularly over the last decade, and far beyond original expectations. The main focus of this chapter is therefore on how the IASB as an organization has responded to this rapid and profound change in the role accorded to its standards by jurisdictions around the world.

The chapter is organized as follows. Section 2 reviews the replacement of the IASC by the IASB and the basic design choices made for the new organization at that time. Section 3 discusses how the original structure of the organization has functioned and has been modified over time, in response to the changes in the IASB's environment and significance, outlined above. As will be seen, the main tension has been between the independence of the standard-setting function, ingrained in the original design, and the need for some kind of accountability following from the quasi-legal status attributed to IFRS in many jurisdictions. Section 4 essentially discusses the same question, but shifts the focus from the organizational structure of the IASB to its due process for setting standards, where one sees a similar tension between independence and the need for broad involvement and the ability to demonstrate responsiveness to constituents' concerns. Section 5 provides an impression of how the IASB's technical work has reflected its changing environment. Section 6 concludes with a brief outlook.

This chapter should be read as an overview in which most issues can only be touched upon. For further reading, the footnotes provide selective references to the voluminous literature that has developed on the IASB.

2. Reform of the IASC and the IASB's original design

One of the essential features of the IASC was that it was created and, in a sense, owned by the accountancy profession. At the initiative of the Institute of Chartered Accountants in England and Wales, professional accountancy bodies from ten countries had agreed in 1973 to create the IASC.[2] The 'committee' (subsequently referred to as the Board) was therefore composed of delegates representing these founding organizations. When these delegations voted to publish an exposure draft or standard, it could in principle be assumed that their vote represented the view of the sponsoring organization, even though in practice there was considerable variety in the degree to which the delegations consulted their home base or received instructions. This dependence on the accountancy profession was not fundamentally changed by subsequent modifications. Delegations from other than the founding organizations were admitted on a rotation basis, including, as time went by, a minority of delegations from other than professional associations of accountants, such as a delegation of financial analysts, delegations representing financial executives and (Swiss) companies using IAS. In 1981 agreement was reached that all organizations sending delegations to the Board would be appointed for fixed terms by the Council of the International Federation of Accountants (IFAC), even though the selection of the actual delegates remained the responsibility of the Board member bodies. Until the end of the IASC, a strong majority of delegations continued to come from accountancy bodies, which also financed a large proportion of the IASC's budget.

During the 1990s, pressure for reform began to build up in a way that mirrored the evolution of accounting standard setting in particularly the English-language countries represented on the Board. Generally speaking, accounting-standard setting in the US, the UK and Australia had begun as an activity of the accountancy profession, but over time the responsibility for standards shifted to bodies set apart from the profession. The archetype of this approach to standard setting was the US Financial Accounting Standards Board (FASB), created, like the IASC, in 1973. The FASB was a fully independent private-sector organization, with a Board consisting of full-time technical experts, who were expressly expected not to represent any particular interest or constituency, and who were supported by a sizeable technical and research staff.

Pressure for change of the IASC came from various directions. Some members of Board delegations believed that a further enhancement of the quality of IAS was possible only when the organization shifted away from a representational basis towards an independent expert basis. Politically, the Asian financial crisis brought reform of the global financial architecture on the agenda. Although the IASC itself did not come under fire as a result of the crisis – its standards were rather seen as part of the solution – shoring up its independence by cutting the direct link between the IASC and the accountancy profession probably looked like a good idea in this context. But, most directly, the US SEC made it increasingly clear that acceptance of IAS for purposes of listing in the US required that the standards be set in a process that the SEC could be comfortable with. And it was not a secret that the SEC was by and large comfortable with the FASB model. The European Union, which during the 1990s increasingly saw IAS as the key to its own future policies on accounting regulation, was quite happy to see the IASC cut loose from the accountancy profession, but it was among the strongest champions of a representative model in which the work of the technical experts setting the standards would in one way or the other be subject to approval by people whose authority could be traced to a clear legal and political mandate.

The end of the sharp debate was that the SEC essentially imposed the FASB's structure on the reformed IASC. At that time, late in 1999, the SEC held all the high cards. European companies were queuing up to list in the United States, and there was strong pressure to allow US GAAP to become the de facto standard for these larger European corporations. There was no political will to create a European alternative to US GAAP, and IAS was the only hope for a set of standards that might become acceptable in the US without actually being set in the US.

As a result, early in 2001 the IASB took the place of the IASC. Although the IASB was not a carbon copy of the FASB, it shared many of its basic features.[3] Like the FASB, the IASB, as described in its initial constitution, was set up as a completely independent, private-sector organization. The organization was controlled by a foundation, the International Accounting Standards Committee Foundation (IASCF), which had its counterpart in the US Financial Accounting Foundation (FAF). The IASCF was governed by 19 trustees, all of whom held or had held senior private-sector or regulatory positions. While the trustees were drawn from a range of countries with the aim of achieving a prescribed geographical balance, they were explicitly not meant to be representatives of these countries but to be committed to act in the public interest. The initial trustees were chosen by an ad hoc nominating committee. The independence of the organization was apparent in that subsequent vacancies among the trustees were to be filled by the trustees themselves, in a process of co-optation. The trustees' first chairman (2000–2005) was Paul Volcker, the former chairman of the US Federal Reserve Board. Volcker fully shared the SEC's view of the importance of independent standard setting, and his international standing made him a formidable defender of the IASB.

The IASCF trustees were responsible for raising funds and for appointing the standard setting Board itself. This Board was to consist of twelve full-time members and two part-time members. This composition had been the subject of much debate. The SEC preferred a small, purely full-time Board like the seven-member FASB. While the eventual number of IASB Board members, as well as the two part-time members, represented a degree of compromise, the SEC's fundamental preferences were clearly reflected. This was certainly true with respect to the absence of any geographical criteria for Board members, whose 'foremost qualification' was described as 'technical expertise' (IASCF constitution, para. 24). The Board's chairman during its first decade (2001–11) was Sir David Tweedie, who had been the UK Accounting Standards Board (ASB)'s full-time chairman for the preceding ten years. Although the ASB was certainly not identical to the FASB, Tweedie did represent the new breed of professional standard setters that was in the ascendant over the older volunteer approach. A large proportion of the other initial IASB Board members were also professional or semi-professional standard setters who had been active in national standard setters and/or the IASC. In that respect, the initial Board was quite homogeneous, and able to make a flying start: most members had known each other before, sometimes for many years, they shared a similar view of the issues that needed to be dealt with, and had enough experience among them to define projects quickly and move rapidly towards answers which some of them had already been considering or debating among themselves for a long time.

The Board was not left to develop its standards alone. It was assisted by a staff appointed under the authority of the Board chairman, who doubled as the organization's chief executive officer. The IASB inherited a small technical staff of about half a dozen people from the IASC. Over the years, this was built up to about 25 technical staff in 2005 and around 50 by the end of the decade. This was another point where the IASB began to resemble the FASB: whereas, prior to 2000, no standard setter in the world came anywhere near the FASB in terms of staff resources, around 2010 the IASB and the FASB had become far more evenly matched in this respect.

The trustees also appointed, according to the constitution, a Standards Advisory Council (SAC), a broadly composed consultative group which was to meet regularly with the Board to discuss its agenda and ongoing projects. Although the constitution specified a composition of 'about thirty members' (para. 42), the initial SAC had no fewer than forty-nine members. While this obviously meant that a wide range of backgrounds was present, it made the SAC a little unwieldy. The Board, the trustees and the SAC itself would struggle somewhat over the following years to find the most effective composition and role for this advisory body. While the SAC had a counterpart in the Financial Accounting Standards Advisory Council (FASAC) attached to the

FASB, any US influence in this respect had already made itself felt at a much earlier stage; the inclusion of the SAC in the initial IASB organization was seen as a continuation of a Consultative Group convened by the IASC since 1981.

Something similar was true of the final component of the IASB organization, which was the Standing Interpretations Committee (SIC), a body of part-time members charged with recommending interpretative pronouncements on narrowly defined issues, based on the existing standards. The IASB inherited the SIC (modified in 2002 to become the International Financial Reporting Interpretations Committee, IFRIC) from the IASC, which had created it in 1996. Here the US influence was a little more recent and perhaps a little more direct; at that time, it was not a secret that the SEC favoured the creation of an interpretations body for the IASC somewhat like the Emerging Issues Task Force attached to the FASB.

3. Subsequent evolution of the organizational structure

The original design of an independent, mainly full-time Board, solely responsible for setting standards and overseen by a group of part-time trustees, has not been fundamentally altered, so far. However, as the IASB's standards rapidly gained in significance, becoming mandatory or at least optional for ever greater numbers of companies in ever more countries, inevitably an almost continuous debate arose about the governance of this private-sector organization acquiring quasi-legislative powers in many jurisdictions.[4] Initially, the centre of gravity of this debate was in the European Union, as companies there began to realize that from 2005 onwards they would be obliged to apply a set of accounting standards that many of them had until then hardly considered in any detail, and which differed in many respects from existing national standards. When these companies contacted the IASB to call for changes in the International Accounting Standards which the IASB had inherited from the IASC, they soon discovered that the IASB was determined to set its own standard setting priorities. This was true in particular for the standard on financial instruments, IAS 39.[5] In 2001 the IASB began a project to make limited improvements to this standard. It left important issues, including most of the hedge accounting rules, outside the scope of this project, even though many banks and corporate preparers believed that IAS 39 contained fundamental flaws in this area. Although the IASB was willing to make more changes to IAS 39 than it had originally planned, it rejected certain demands of the banks as inconsistent with the accounting principles enshrined in its conceptual framework. The resulting conflict between parts of the European banking sector and the IASB rapidly acquired a political dimension as the decision to 'endorse' IAS 39 for use within the European Union still had to be taken. The European Commission was responsible for managing the EU's 'endorsement' process and initially had been sanguine that it, as the IASB's first and most important 'customer', would find the IASB attentive to its wishes. Now it was caught in the middle between member state governments, mobilized by their financial institutions, and an obstinately independent IASB, which refused to sacrifice what it believed to be its principles. The conflict was temporarily resolved in 2004, when IAS 39 was endorsed for use in the European Union with two 'carve-outs'.[6]

Whereas with IAS 39 the IASB was essentially criticized for refusing to act, in other early projects it was seen by some to move too far, too fast. The IASB's initial projects on insurance, performance reporting and share-based payments caused considerable concern and resentment among reporting companies that the IASB was trying to impose radical changes in financial reporting without an adequate mandate.

Meanwhile, the IASCF trustees had started their first five-yearly review of the IASB's constitution, as required by that constitution itself. Many interest groups, guided by their recently gained impression that the IASB was unwilling to listen to reporting companies and too willing to propose radical change, used the occasion to revive the central issue of the debate over the restructuring of the IASC. The question was raised whether the IASB should not move towards a more representative model, as opposed to an independent-expert model. The IASCF trustees, still chaired by Paul Volcker, continued to believe that the model put in place in 2001 was basically sound and were willing to make minor modifications only. In taking this position, they took note of the fact that the US SEC still had to decide whether to allow foreign registrants to list on the basis of IFRS, without reconciliation. The SEC did not hide its view that, apart from the quality of the standards themselves, it regarded the independence of the IASB as an essential element of the package on which it would base its decision. The SEC followed the heavily politicized debates over IAS 39 attentively, looking for signs of undue political influence on the Board's technical work.

As a result, the IASCF trustees merely proposed some fine-tuning of the constitution in their final report on the constitution review, issued in July 2005.[7] They rejected the idea of geographical membership quota for Board members, presumably to avoid any suggestion that Board members represented particular jurisdictions or regions. The trustees also reaffirmed the Board's exclusive right to set its own technical agenda, even though they strengthened the language describing their own oversight role. However, they modified the criteria for Board membership, making 'professional competence and practical experience' the primary criterion, rather than 'technical expertise'. In doing so, they presumably signalled that they had heard the recurrent complaint that the Board members were not only independent-minded, but also too intent on the conceptual purity of their standards, as opposed to the needs and possibilities of actual reporting practice. Similarly, the fact that the voting threshold to approve final standards was raised from 8 to 9 out of 14 votes could be read as a suggestion that the Board should be slightly more careful to introduce change without sufficient support. A final change was that the trustees created a high-level Trustee Appointment Advisory Group, which was to review proposed appointments of new trustees. The actual appointment decisions were firmly reserved for the trustees, and therefore the essentially private-sector nature of the organization was unchanged. Yet the Advisory Group, consisting of ex-officio members such as the managing director of the International Monetary Fund and the presidents of the World Bank and the European Central Bank, was a first small step towards formally embedding the IASB into a structure of global public accountability.

Given the relatively limited changes effected by the first constitution review, it is not surprising that the central questions surrounding the IASB's governance did not go away. The removal of the 20-F reconciliation requirement by the SEC in 2007,[8] and the fact that it immediately put the use of IFRS by domestic companies on its agenda, considerably raised the stakes as it made the prospect that the IASB might truly become the global standard setter suddenly seem much more realistic. The SEC itself began to reflect on the kind of relationship it should maintain with the IASB in order to fulfil its own responsibilities towards the US capital market.[9] In Japan, where receptiveness towards the idea of an eventual adoption of IFRS greatly increased in view of the developments in the United States, existing concerns that voices from Japan were insufficiently heard at the IASB led to demands for enhanced governance.[10] In the European Union, strident demands for more accountability and democratic legitimacy of the IASB were emanating from the European Parliament, which had gained additional powers in the process of endorsing IFRS for use in the EU.[11] All of these factors were strengthened by the fact that, as before, the IASB's technical work did not fail to provoke controversy.

In March 2008, the trustees, now under the chairmanship of the former Dutch finance minister Gerrit Zalm (2008–10) embarked upon their second five-yearly review of the IASCF constitution, but they identified two issues for priority treatment: public accountability and the composition of the IASB Board. Both issues were settled rapidly, with changes in the constitution agreed in January 2009. With respect to the Board, the kind of geographical quota that the SEC had forcefully opposed when the IASC was restructured were now introduced. In a Board expanded to 16 members, North America, Europe and Asia/Oceania were now to have four members each, with two more coming from Africa and South America (one each), and the other two from any area. That this change was now acceptable was presumably partly due to turnover among the trustees: not only had the chairmanship changed hands, but by early 2007 the terms of all but one of the original 19 trustees had ended.[12] Another factor may have been that the SEC, now that it was contemplating the adoption of IFRS in the United States, began to see merit in ensuring at least a minimum of US Board membership.

The second change introduced in 2009 was the creation of a Monitoring Board, initially composed of the chairs of IOSCO's Emerging Market Committee and Technical Committee, the commissioner of Japan's Financial Services Agency, the chairman of the SEC and the European commissioner responsible for the internal market portfolio. Compared to the Trustee Appointment Advisory Group, which it replaced, the Monitoring Board included organizations with much more direct responsibilities for regulating financial reporting. It was presented as 'a formal link between the Trustees and public authorities. This relationship seeks to replicate, on an international basis, the link between accounting standard-setters and those public authorities that have generally overseen accounting standard-setters.'[13] Also in contrast to the Advisory Group, the Monitoring Board was not a part of the IASB organization. Rather, it was an autonomous group, to which the IASC Foundation trustees ceded certain powers. As the trustees' chairman Gerrit Zalm used to joke: 'we were involved when the Monitoring Board was created, but once it's created we're lost ... We created our own god'.[14] The most important power was the Monitoring Board's right to approve the appointment of new trustees. This again was a significant step, given that only a few years earlier the trustees had strongly asserted their exclusive authority to make such appointments. In addition, the Monitoring Board assumed the more general responsibility of reviewing the trustees' discharge of their duties according to the constitution.

That the Monitoring Board could take on a life of its own was suggested during 2010, when the trustees sought a successor to the IASB's first chairman, David Tweedie. Although the Monitoring Board's mandate was clearly limited to approving the appointment of trustees, it was reported that the Monitoring Board actively involved itself in the selection of the new Board chairman.[15] Also in 2010, the Monitoring Board began, at its own initiative, a review of the governance arrangements of the IASC Foundation (since 2010 known as the IFRS Foundation), around the same time that the trustees began a major strategy review for the IASB's second decade. Although the Monitoring Board and the Trustees emphasized that they were committed to coordinate their activities, there could be no doubt that the Monitoring Board had become an important actor in its own right. In the February 2012 report with which the Monitoring Board concluded its governance study, it stated, among other things, that it was seeking a formal role for itself in future Board chairman appointments, even though the actual decision would remain with the trustees. And, while reaffirming the importance of the IASB Board's independence in technical matters, the Monitoring Board clarified that, if it refers an issue to the IASB for consideration, it will expect a persuasive justification from the IASB if it were to decide not to put the issue on its agenda.[16]

Other significant changes in the IASB's setup occurred more gradually over the decade. One change related to the composition of the Board itself. This took some time, because the trustees essentially decided to reappoint all of the initial members who indicated that they wished to serve a second term. As a result, it was not until 2009 that the remaining group of original

Board members became a minority in the Board. The last three of the original Board members, including Chairman Tweedie, left the Board in June 2011. As indicated above, the initial Board was a tight-knit, fairly homogeneous group of people, representing extensive standard-setting experience. In later years, and probably reflecting the modified membership criteria introduced in 2005, the range of backgrounds in the Board became somewhat more diverse, as more users and members with a regulatory background were appointed. The appointment of Hans Hoogervorst, a former finance minister and securities regulator in the Netherlands, to succeed David Tweedie as chairman of the Board can presumably be seen as part of that trend: the Board became a broader and perhaps more politically attuned body, probably expecting to rely more heavily on its staff for technical expertise.

A second important gradual change related to the IASB's funding.[17] In its first years, the IASB had been financed by voluntary contributions. These came, foremost, from the Big-5 audit firms (as they were, before the demise of Arthur Andersen) and then from a wide range of individual contributors, mainly business entities, and mainly from Europe, the United States and Japan. These contributions were actively solicited by the trustees. This was in fact the funding model of the FASB, which since 1973 had relied on voluntary contributions, apart from revenue from publications, as its main source of income. For the FASB, however, this changed in 2002 with the Sarbanes–Oxley Act, which provided for funding through mandatory contributions from listed companies. The kind of post-Enron scepticism over accounting-standard setting underlying this change also raised questions about the IASB's approach to financing. Already at an early stage, the trustees began to consider the possibility of more stable funding mechanisms that would appear to be less prejudicial to the IASB's independence. However, this required putting collective funding schemes in place in many individual countries, where the trustees had to rely on the cooperation of local governments or regulatory bodies. Despite this difficulty, over time a variety of mandatory or voluntary national contribution schemes were set up in a number of countries, making the IASB less dependent on the willingness of individual donors to continue their contributions.

4. The evolution of the standard-setting process

The two main themes with respect to the evolution of the IASB's standard-setting process are the gradual elaboration of this process in response to the kind of pressures for responsiveness and accountability mentioned in the previous section, and the evolving relations between the IASB and national standard setters, in particular the US Financial Accounting Standards Board.

The 'due process' of the IASB, as documented in its initial constitution, largely reflected the practices of its predecessor, the IASC. At the heart of the process was the exposure draft system as developed by the US standard setter in the 1950s and adopted by most of the accounting standard setters set up in other countries from the 1960s onwards. In this system, the public circulation of exposure drafts gave interested parties at least one occasion to provide written comments on proposed standards or changes in standards.[18] The IASC had already elaborated on this basic formula by issuing, for important projects, a discussion paper as a first-stage due process document, before proceeding to a formal exposure draft. In addition, the IASC had installed steering committees for most projects, manned by volunteers drawn from a mixture of relevant professional backgrounds. The IASC in its final years had also tentatively begun to add a 'basis for conclusions' to its standards, to explain how the Board had made its decisions and dealt with comments received in the exposure stage.

The IASB continued with most of these procedures, although it dispensed with the steering committees. Under the IASC, these had sometimes played a leading role in developing and drafting the standards, but the new IASB clearly believed that this was the responsibility of the Board and its staff. The new IASB Board did form some working groups with a purely advisory role, but until 2004 their role was hardly conspicuous.

The difficulties over IAS 39, alluded to above, including the controversies over the European endorsement of IFRS, prompted the Board to take a more active role in organizing consultations with interested parties, starting with a series of roundtables on financial instruments held in March 2003. During 2004, a raft of working groups was established to advise the Board on various projects. Both Board members and trustees became conscious that a successful defence of the independence of the Board required the IASB to be able to demonstrate a high degree of transparency and responsiveness to concerns of constituents, in the context of a clearly defined and meticulously observed due process. This resulted in a number of further modifications, including the publication of a due process handbook in 2006, the establishment of a due process committee of trustees, actively overseeing the Board's adherence to due process, and improved transparency through webcasts and wider distribution of the Board's agenda papers and near-final drafts of standards. As a result, the IASB was proud to announce that in 2007 it received a top ranking in a global survey of NGO accountability.[19] Currently the IASB, in addition to holding ad hoc consultations and roundtables is going through an annual cycle of consultations which includes one or more meetings each with the Standards Advisory Council (currently known as IFRS Advisory Council), with advisory groups of users and preparers,[20] with European standard setters,[21] with the Accounting Standards Board of Japan and with an annual gathering of standard setters known as the World Standard Setters meeting.[22]

Nevertheless, demands for more due process enhancements continue to be heard. Particularly from Europe, the IASB has been pressed to justify its standards by undertaking impact or effect studies, even though the objective and methodology of such studies remain a matter of debate. Other recent due process enhancements that are still under development include the issuance of feedback statements in addition to the bases for conclusions, and the performance of post-implementation reviews of new standards.

Against this background, the IASB's most conspicuous departure from its own due process stands out as an isolated incident: in October 2008, the trustees allowed the Board to modify IAS 39 with immediate and even retroactive effect, without any exposure or formal consultation. This change was made under great political pressure from, again, the European Union, as certain European banks in the tumultuous weeks following the collapse of Lehman Brothers clamoured to be allowed to reclassify certain financial instruments and thus avoid reporting losses, in line with corresponding provisions in US GAAP. The subsequent consensus that this amendment should not set a precedent illustrated the extent to which the world had learned to accept, at least in ordinary circumstances, the principle of independent accounting standard setting.

While the previous paragraphs looked at the Board as a standard setter operating on its own, the IASB's cooperation with national standard setters formed an essential element of its technical activities. In the discussions preceding the transformation of the IASC into the IASB, the new international standard setter was conceived as a first among equals: the centre of a circle of strong national standard setters, with which it would cooperate on the further development and gradual convergence of international standards and the various sets of national standards. Such a conception was quite natural in the 1990s, given that there were few countries which had abandoned national standard setting altogether in favour of international standards. Moreover, there was an active group of standard setters from English-speaking countries, known as the G4, which at some point began to look like a potential rival to the IASC.[23] In this light, the IASB's initial constitution provided for special relationships between the IASB and a number of what came to be known as liaison-standard setters, who turned out to be the five members of the G4 (the standard setters from Australia, Canada, the UK and the US to which subsequently the New Zealand standard setter had been added) plus the standard setters from France, Germany and Japan. In the early years, these standard setters had what might be called a privileged position, in the sense that they had exclusive access to IASB agenda papers, held regular meetings with the IASB and, in the case of some of them, undertook joint projects with the IASB.

However, the position of the Australian, New Zealand and European liaison standard setters was soon substantially weakened when it became clear that listed companies in their countries would in a few years be adopting IFRS, so that these standard setters would lose the responsibility to set standards for this most prestigious segment of companies. Simultaneously, it soon became clear that the IASB intended to give the highest priority to working with the US FASB, as the IASB still had its eyes on the prize of access to US capital markets on the basis of IFRS, without reconciliation. In October 2002, the IASB and the FASB announced their so-called Norwalk Agreement, in which they indicated in rather general terms their intention to cooperate in the development of accounting standards. Despite the general tone, the Norwalk Agreement did mark a clear shift in the IASB's cooperation with national standard setters: for many years, the bilateral relationship in which the IASB and the FASB pursued the mutual 'convergence' of their standards would be the dominant factor in the IASB's technical work. For other standard setters, including the Accounting Standard Board of Japan, 'convergence' acquired the more limited meaning of adjusting national standards to IFRS, mainly on a unilateral basis.

The increasingly close cooperation between the IASB and the FASB raised both operational and fundamental due process issues. In operational terms, the Boards had to develop an effective working relationship to reach joint decisions. In doing so, they had to deal with practical complications such as the different sizes of the two Boards (seven or even five FASB members, all living near Norwalk, Connecticut, versus 14 or 15 IASB members,[24] many of whom still commuted to London from all over the world to attend Board meetings), the different meeting schedules (once a week for the FASB, once a month for the IASB), and the different sizes and degrees of experience of their staff. Some difficulties could be overcome by technology, including increasing use of video-conferencing. But this did not by itself help the Boards to cope with basically different approaches to standard setting, often characterized, perhaps with over-simplification, as rules-based versus principles-based. There was also the question of whether both Boards, by seeking consensus, were not in effect giving the other Board a veto over their decisions. Could this be reconciled with their mandates and their due process? Many of the IASB's European constituents, at any rate, were not convinced that the IASB was always giving proper attention to their needs. Particularly smaller companies, which had no interest in overseas listings, often perceived the IASB as making many changes to standards that they had not asked for, in pursuit of 'convergence for the sake of convergence'.

In the European Union, those who would seek to counterbalance or at least complement the American influence on the IASB's technical work have sometimes looked to the European Financial Reporting Advisory Group (EFRAG), which was set up in 2001 to assist the European Commission in the process of endorsing IFRS. EFRAG, while not a standard setter in its own right, has increasingly sought to play a pro-active role in the IASB's deliberations. More recently, standard setters in other regions have formed the Asian–Oceanian Standard-Setters Group (AOSSG) and the Group of Latin American Accounting Standard-Setters (GLASS), with similar aims of becoming strong regional interlocutors of the IASB. While the IASB has welcomed the creation of such regional groupings, it is too early to say what impact they will have on the future development of IFRS. At any rate, and contrary to some initial expectations, the advent of the IASB has so far not meant the end of most national standard setters, although their future role vis-à-vis the IASB continues to be a matter of debate.[25]

5. The IASB's technical work

For several reasons, it is not so easy to obtain a quick overview of the IASB's technical work between 2001 and 2012. One simple reason is that the IASB has not used a consistent numbering or coding system to identify its exposure drafts or final pronouncements, which makes it easy to lose track of the many smaller changes the IASB has continuously been making to existing standards. A more fundamental phenomenon is that the IASB has rather actively managed its agenda, frequently adding, splitting, phasing, combining, suspending or refocusing projects. For many years, the number of projects continued to grow. The IASB's initial agenda, established in July 2001, contained 9 projects, whereas the October 2008 work plan listed more than 25 active projects or separately managed phases of projects, not counting a number of planned or suspended projects and research projects. While counting heterogeneous objects such as IASB technical projects is of limited use, the numbers do indicate something of the magnitude of the task that the Board set itself and those of its constituents who felt obliged to keep abreast of all these developments.

The IASB did not start with a blank sheet of paper, but inherited the body of standards produced by the IASC. At its first meeting, the IASB passed a resolution that all the existing International Accounting Standards would remain applicable until amended or withdrawn. Although most Board members would be able to point out many deficiencies in these standards, the body of IAS already had significant features that would often be seen as typical for the IASB. The IASB has often been perceived as an advocate of fair value accounting, yet most of the applications of fair value in IFRS as of 2012 could already be found in the standards developed by the IASC prior to 2001. Similarly, the IASB's fundamental balance sheet approach was already introduced in the conceptual framework drawn up by the IASC in 1989 and which the IASB inherited unchanged.[26] As a result, the IASB's work during its first decade has oscillated between the need to maintain and improve inherited standards and the desire to develop entirely new ones.

Prior to 2004, a substantial part of the IASB's energy was absorbed by an omnibus 'Improvements' project to make minor amendments to a range of standards, as well as by a separate project to improve the financial instruments standards IAS 32 and 39. In undertaking these projects, the IASB was looking with one eye to the United States, continuing the IASC's strategy of making IFRS the passport to cross-border listings, and with the other to Europe and Australia, for whom the IASB believed it needed to provide a 'stable platform' of standards for massive first-time adoption in 2005.

As indicated above, the initial project to amend the financial instruments standard IAS 39 caused considerable difficulties, not least because of disagreement over what the scope of the project should be. The IASB maintained that it was just making limited improvements to a standard it had inherited from the IASC. Some constituents found that hard to square with the Board's proposal to introduce of a full fair value option which seemed to pave the way towards the much more radical reform of the standard which at least some Board members were known to favour. And, if the IASB was willing to do that, why did it initially refuse to discuss some aspects of hedge accounting?

In addition to making improvements, the IASB embarked from the start on more ambitious 'leadership' projects, but with limited success. Its initial project to develop a standard on insurance contracts, inherited from the IASC, was still not concluded after all the initial Board members had left the Board in 2011.[27] Similar problems befell a project to radically change the presentation of performance in the financial statements. The impression that the Board was about to abolish net income provoked such opposition, not least in Japan, that the project was effectively abandoned at the end of 2003.[28] An early success was scored with IFRS 2 (2003) on share-based payment. Where the FASB in the 1990s had succumbed to heavy industry lobbying, the IASB succeeded in issuing a standard requiring the expensing of employee stock options and other share-based payments, thus allowing the FASB to follow suit in the next few years.

Following the 2002 Norwalk Agreement, convergence with US GAAP became more and more the dominant factor in the IASB's technical work. Initially, the emphasis was on short-term convergence projects, in which both the IASB and the FASB sought 'quick wins' by adopting elements of existing standards of the other Board. This proved more difficult than expected. On the IASB side, only a few significant projects of this kind were actually finished in what might be called a short term. One concerned the removal of an optional treatment from IAS 23, on borrowing costs (2007). Two others took the form of new standards: IFRS 5 (2004), on discontinued operations, and IFRS 8 (2006), on operating segments, both of which reflected the corresponding US standards. Being a disclosure standard, IFRS 8 did nothing to reduce the reconciling differences between US GAAP and IFRS earnings and shareholders' equity, but because it was an almost verbatim copy of the US standard it did provide the occasion for the European Parliament to take a highly critical look at the IASB. By temporarily blocking the endorsement process of the standard, it asserted its right to be heard and lent its weight to demands for more accountability and improved due process at the IASB.[29]

Gradually, the IASB and the FASB shifted their attention away from short-term convergence towards joint projects to develop new standards from scratch. An early example was a project on the application of the purchase method to account for business combinations. This project actually predated the Norwalk Agreement and resulted in a set of revised standards in 2008. In 2004, both Boards agreed to work jointly on a new conceptual framework. By 2012, only one out of eight phases identified for this project had been completed. The completed phase resulted in new chapters on the relatively uncontroversial topics of the objectives of financial reporting and qualitative characteristics of financial information, leaving fundamental questions of recognition and measurement for later consideration.

To prepare the way for the SEC's dropping of the reconciliation requirement in 2007, the two Boards drew up a Memorandum of Understanding in February 2006 in which they reasserted their commitment to convergence of IFRS and US GAAP. In contrast to the Norwalk Agreement, this MoU contained an explicit agenda of existing and expected future projects, with general indications of progress to be expected by 2008. When the SEC turned its attention to adoption of IFRS for use by domestic US companies, the two Boards began work on an updated MoU, which was published in September 2008. In this version, a general target of 2010/11 began to appear for completion of most of the very ambitious convergence agenda. At that point in time, the convergence agenda included most of the IASB's active projects, including highly controversial or complex topics such as financial statement presentation (the successor to the earlier ill-fated performance reporting project), revenue recognition and leases. The target date appeared to be keyed to the SEC's 'roadmap' rule proposal, issued in November 2008, which envisaged the possibility of required used of IFRS by US issuers as early as 2014.

The financial crisis erupting with full severity in the autumn of 2008 provided the IASB both with challenges and opportunities. After surviving the initial political storm over the alleged role of its accounting standards in causing or acerbating the crisis,[30] and after satisfying some of its critics on this point by making a swift reclassification amendment to IAS 39 (see above), the IASB profited from the crisis: the G20 made a strong call for short-term action to improve accounting standards on financial instruments, and it underlined the importance of the medium-term objective of a 'single high-quality global set of standards'. This allowed the IASB to pursue its convergence agenda at full speed and to make rapid progress on developing a new standard on recognition and measurement of financial instruments to replace IAS 39. The IASB had always seen IAS 39 as an interim solution and in 2004 it had added a project to its agenda to develop a new standard. By the time of the 2006 MoU, this had become a joint project with the FASB, but until 2008 nothing more than a discussion paper had been produced. Early in 2009, however, the IASB apparently saw an opportunity to benefit from the sense of urgency caused by the crisis. It decided to move the project forward at full speed and succeeded in issuing the core of a new standard, IFRS 9, before the end of 2009. In the process it lost the FASB, which, under similar pressures as the IASB, had chosen a somewhat different course for revising its standards on financial instruments. But by the end of 2009, some of the IASB's constituents had come to the conclusion that a new standard on financial instruments was not, after all, needed immediately. Contrary to initial expectations, the European Commission made it known that it was not going to propose IFRS 9 for endorsement before the remaining components of the standard were in place. These remaining components included thorny issues such as impairment of financial instruments and hedge accounting, on which the IASB now began to work at its more usual pace. By 2012, IFRS 9 was not yet complete, and the mandatory application date of the extant part of the standard had been postponed to 2015.

The years 2009 and 2010 were years of intense activity at the IASB, not only because of the financial crisis but also because of the rush to complete the convergence agenda. Whereas the Board had traditionally met once a month, it now planned many additional meetings. The number of joint meetings with the FASB, either in person or by video-link, also increased. Nevertheless, it became ever clearer that the ambitious plans of the 2008 MoU could not all be realized. From 2009 onwards, the signs multiplied that many interested parties in the US were having second thoughts about the adoption of IFRS. The SEC missed its self-imposed deadline of coming forward with a clear proposal on the use of IFRS by domestic companies before the end of 2011. The SEC's reticence removed an important rationale underlying the target date in the 2008 MoU, which in turn may have weakened the FASB's determination to complete the MoU projects in time. For the IASB, however, mid-2011 remained an important date, as it marked the end of the terms of the last original Board members, including Chairman Tweedie.

Some projects were indeed finished in time, including one on joint ventures (joint arrangements) and one on consolidation and special-purpose entities, of which the origins could be traced back to 2002. A project on the revision of IAS 12, on income taxes, which had begun life as a post-Norwalk short-term convergence project and which since had gone through several mutations in scope and objectives, could only be finished in time by restricting it to a limited amendment. But the financial statement presentation project was essentially dropped. It had revived old suspicions that the IASB and the FASB were bent on abolishing the traditional income concept based on the realization principle in favour of comprehensive income, and the resulting resistance made timely completion unrealistic. As projects were completed or sidelined one by one, only four major projects remained on the IASB's agenda by mid-2011: leases, revenue recognition, insurance contracts and financial instruments. None of the four were completed by that time, though.

While convergence with US GAAP has unquestionably been the dominant factor in the IASB's agenda, it would be incorrect to infer that the IASB has been oblivious to the needs of other jurisdictions. For example, the IASB amended its standards on financial instruments in response to requests from Europe and New Zealand, where significant numbers of reporting entities had the legal form of a cooperative. Due to the original wording of the standards these were at risk of having to report that they had no equity at all. Another example is that the IASB undertook to undo an earlier change it had made to IAS 24, on related party transactions, when it appeared that this would cause significant problems in China due to the prevalence of state-owned entities. But perhaps the most significant project that the IASB undertook without reference to the United States was its standard for small- and medium-sized entities, issued in 2009. (See also Chapter 21 in this volume.) So far, there simply is no counterpart of this kind of 'little GAAP' in the United States, and the IASB developed the standard mainly with a view to the reporting needs of companies in developing and emerging economies.

6. Outlook

As this chapter is written, the biggest question mark hanging over the IASB is undoubtedly the long-awaited decision by the SEC on the future role of IFRS in reporting by domestic listed companies in the US. If the United States were to embrace IFRS, or commit to do so at a specified point in the future, it would seem that there is little left to stop the IASB from becoming the global standard setter. In that case, one would expect most other major economies, including Japan, to follow the lead of the US. On the other hand, a clear reaffirmation by the SEC of the continued importance of national accounting standards (US GAAP) might encourage other jurisdictions to reconsider their stance on IFRS as well. Conceivably, this could lead to a reversal of some of the harmonization and unification of accounting standards around the world achieved during the last two decades. The IASB, assuming it would survive in the process, would again become a standard setter among national or regional standard setters, not unlike the IASC of the 1990s.

Yet, regardless of what the SEC decides, the United States has in important respects already become a two-standards country. US investors in US securities markets have learned to accept foreign issuers reporting under IFRS without reconciliation. Many US subsidiaries of foreign parents use IFRS, which means that these consolidation standards are no longer exclusively a matter for highly trained specialists but are rapidly becoming part of mainstream accounting education. More generally, even if the IASB does not become the single global standard setter, it seems likely that it has already contributed to a structural reduction of global accounting diversity. One might, for instance, envisage the European Union developing its own accounting standards at some point in the future, but all the complaints about IFRS so far have not kindled any noticeable desire to revert to a situation of 27 national accounting standards for listed companies. Worldwide, the experience with IFRS seems to have brought home the advantages of having at least a common set of accounting concepts. Even though the world may not agree on the recycling of components of other comprehensive income or the usefulness of level-three fair value numbers, it has become quite easy to set up a meaningful and precise discussion of such issues across almost any set of national borders.

Another point that seems independent of the SEC's decision is that it does seem likely that the exclusive bilateral cooperation of the FASB and the IASB is drawing to a close, and that this will prove to have been an episode in the history of the IASB rather than a structural feature. The extensive agenda consultations that the IASB has undertaken in 2011 are by themselves a sign that it is looking more widely than a focus on US GAAP convergence,[31] and the responses to the consultation suggest that many of the IASB's constituents outside of North America are no longer willing to support a unique role for the FASB in developing IFRS.[32]

Beyond this negative consensus, however, there are as yet not many signs that the world has made up its mind about what kind of global standards it wants. While the IASB may have to bear some of the blame for some of the controversies its projects have instigated, sometimes its work has merely brought to light an existing diversity of views on basic questions. Should standards remain at a general level or contain detailed application guidance? Should they aim to be neutral representations of given economic phenomena or should they explicitly take the economic consequences of accounting, including perhaps the concerns of prudential regulators, into account?

With such a continuing diversity of views, which will be expressed in an already quite elaborate due process, it is hard to see the IASB making fast progress in developing new standards. In the past decade, many projects have already suffered severe delays, and in some cases where the IASB was able to act swiftly it was helped by specific circumstances (such as Enron in the case of IFRS 2 on share-based payment, and the financial crisis in the case of IFRS 9).

Finally, given the likelihood of enduring controversy around IFRS, the question of the IASB's governance will continue to be raised. The current Monitoring Board is likely to be an interim solution, if only because important jurisdictions such as China are not yet represented. As its composition broadens, its powers relative to those of the IFRS Foundation trustees will continue to be discussed.

Notes

1 In his 'Report of the Chairman' included in the IASCF's *Annual Report,* David Tweedie did not give a total number in 2001 and 2002. In the 2003 report he mentioned 'more than ninety countries' that would permit or require the use of IFRS starting 1 January 2005. The corresponding numbers in the next years were '99' (2004), 'a hundred' (2005), 'more than a hundred' (2006). Throughout the past decade, detailed information about the progress of IFRS in jurisdictions around the world has been logged on the Deloitte website www.iasplus.com, which also appears to have been the source of the numbers reported by the IASB.

2 This section draws mainly on the extensive treatments of the IASC's history, including its restructuring into the IASB, in Kirsch (2006) and Camfferman and Zeff (2007). Zeff (2012) discusses both the IASC and the IASB, including many points addressed in this chapter.

3 A discussion of the initial set-up of the IASB by its first chairman and director of operations can be found in Tweedie and Seidenstein (2005).

4 See Véron (2007) for an influential analysis of these issues. See for further extensive discussion Zimmermann *et al.* (2008) and Botzem (2012).

5 A discussion of the early stages of the revision of IAS 39 can be found in Walton (2004).

6 For a review of the evolution of the European Union's policies and processes with respect to IFRS by senior members of the European Commission staff, see Van Hulle (2004) and Schaub (2005). The latter publication also includes some comments on the carve-outs.

7 'Changes in the IASCF constitution: report of the IASC Foundation trustees', July 2005.

8 See Erchinger and Melcher (2007) for a review of the process towards the elimination of the reconciliation requirement.

9 Securities and Exchange Commission, 'Concept Release on Allowing US Issuers to Prepare Financial Statements in Accordance with International Financial Reporting Standards', 7 August 2007, pp. 23–4.

10 E.g. 'Future directions of accounting standards in Japan: the next step towards a single set of accounting standards', report by Nippon Keidanren, 14 October 2008 (English summary accessible at www.keidanren.or.jp).

11 See the report to the European Parliament by Alexander Radwan, MEP, 'Report on International Financial Reporting Standards (IFRS) and the Governance of the International Accounting Standards Board (IASB)', 5 February 2008 (A6-0032/2008) and Parliament's related resolution of 9 October 2008 (T6_PA(2008)0469), both accessible at www.europarl.europa.eu.

12 The one exception was Philip Laskawy. His term was effectively extended to allow him to serve as acting chairman when Volcker's successor, Tommaso Padoa-Schioppa, resigned in May 2006, after just five months in office, to become Italy's Economy and Finance Minister. Zalm took over from Laskawy in January 2008.

13 IASC Foundation constitution, February 2009, paragraph 18.

14 Transcript of Monitoring Board and IASCF trustees meeting, 1 April 2010, accessible at www.iosco.org/monitoring_board.
15 'New Chairman for IASB', *World Accounting Report,* November 2010.
16 IFRS Foundation Monitoring Board, 'Final Report on the Review of the IFRS Foundation's Governance', 9 February 2012. Accessible at www.iosco.org/monitoring_board.
17 See Larson and Kenny (2011) for a more extensive discussion of the IASB's funding.
18 Studies of the IASB's due process in action have tended to focus on comment letter analysis. Examples include Jorissen *et al.* (2006) and Hansen (2011).
19 According to the 2007 *Global Accountability Report* issued by One World Trust. See IASB press release of 2 December 2007.
20 An 'Analyst Representative Group' with which the IASB began meeting in 2004 has developed into the current 'Capital Markets Advisory Committee'. Similarly, meetings with a group European CFO's beginning in 2004 eventually led to the current Global Preparers Forum. Neither group is formally part of the IASB organization.
21 The IASB meets periodically with the chair of the Technical Expert Group of the European Financial Reporting Advisory Group (EFRAG) together with the chairs of the French, German, Italian and UK standard setters who are non-voting members of EFRAG.
22 The World Standard Setters (WSS) have been meeting since November 2002, and are convened by the IASB. In addition, there has been since 2005 a separate cycle of meetings known as National Standard Setters (NSS). The IASB attends, but does not convene, the NSS meetings.
23 See Street (2005) for a more extensive discussion of the G4.
24 In 2008, the size of the FASB was reduced to five members. It was restored to seven in 2010. The IASB had, by mid-2012, not yet reached its full complement of 16 members as allowed by the constitution revised in 2009.
25 See Stevenson (2010) for the views of the Chairman of the Australian Accounting Standards Board. Stevenson had also served as the IASB Technical Director. Contrasting examples of how national standard setters are redefining their roles can be found in the 'Plan stratégique 2011–2012' of the French Authorité des normes comptables (accessible at www.anc.gouv.fr) and the UK ASB's January 2012 proposals on 'The future of financial reporting in the UK and Ireland' (accessible at www.frc.org.uk).
26 Whittington (2008) contains important reflections on the IASB's use of its conceptual framework by a former Board member. For another Board member's perspective on the framework project see McGregor and Street (2007).
27 For a review of the early stages of the insurance contracts project, see Dickinson (2003).
28 Barker (2004) is a review of some of the issues by the IASB project manager for this project.
29 See Crawford *et al.* (2010) for a discussion of the IFRS 8 episode.
30 On this discussion, see for instance André *et al.* (2009).
31 See the IASB's 'Request for views: agenda consultation 2011' (July 2011).
32 See the analysis of comment letters on the agenda consultation by the IASB's staff, agenda paper 5A for the IASB meeting of 25 January 2012, paras 48–51.

Bibliography

André, Paul, Anne Cazavan-Jeny, Wolfgang Dick, Chrystelle Richard and Peter Walton, 'Fair Value Accounting and the Banking Crisis in 2008: Shooting the Messenger', *Accounting in Europe,* 6 (2009), 3–24.

Barker, Richard, 'Reporting Financial Performance', *Accounting Horizons,* 18: 2 (June 2004), 157–72.

Botzem, Sebastian, *The Politics of Accounting Regulation: Organizing Transnational Standard Setting in Financial Reporting* (Cheltenham: Edward Elgar, 2012).

Camfferman, Kees and Stephen A. Zeff, *Financial Reporting and Global Capital Markets: A History of the International Accounting Standards Committee, 1973–2001* (Oxford: Oxford University Press, 2007).

Crawford, Louise, Christine Helliar and David Power, *Politics or Accounting Principles: Why Was IFRS 8 So Controversial?* (London: ICAEW Centre for Business Performance, 2010).

Dickinson, Gerry, 'The Search for an International Accounting Standard for Insurance: Report to the Accountancy Task Force of the Geneva Association', *The Geneva Papers on Risk and Insurance,* 28: 2 (April 2003), 151–75.

Erchinger, Holger and Winfried Melcher, 'Convergence between US GAAP and IFRS: Acceptance of IFRS by the US Securities and Exchange Commission (SEC)', *Accounting in Europe,* 4 (2007), 123–39.

Hansen, Thomas Bowe, 'Lobbying of the IASB: An Empirical Investigation', *Journal of International Accounting Research*, 10: 2 (2011), 57–75.

Jorissen, Ann, Nadine Lybaert and Katrien Van de Poel, 'Lobbying Towards a Global Standard Setter: Do National Characteristics Matter? An Analysis of the Comment Letters Written to the IASB', in Greg N. Gregoriou and Mohamed Gaber (eds) *International Accounting: Standards, Regulations, and Financial Reporting* (Oxford/Burlington: Elsevier, 2006), 1–40.

Kirsch, R.J., *The International Accounting Standards Committee: A Political History* (London: Wolters Kluwer, 2006).

Larson, Robert K., and Sara York Kenny, 'The Financing of the IASB: An Analysis of Donor Diversity', *Journal of International Accounting, Auditing and Taxation*, 20: 1, (2011), 1–19.

McGregor, Warren and Donna L. Street, 'IASB and FASB Face Challenges in Pursuit of Joint Conceptual Framework', *Journal of International Financial Management and Accounting*, 18: 1 (2007), 39–51.

Schaub, Alexander, 'The Use of International Accounting Standards in the European Union', *Northwestern Journal of International Law & Business*, 25: 3 (Spring 2005), 609–29.

Stevenson, Kevin M., 'Commentary: IFRS and the Domestic Standard Setter: Is the Mourning Period Over?', *Australian Accounting Review*, 54: 20 (2010), 308–12.

Street, Donna L., *Inside G4+1: The Working Group's Role in the Evolution of the International Accounting Standard Setting Process* (London: ICAEW Centre for Business Performance, 2005).

Tweedie, David and Thomas R. Seidenstein, 'Setting a Global Standard: The Case for Accounting Convergence', *Northwestern Journal of International Law & Business*, 25: 3 (Spring 2005), 589–608.

Van Hulle, Karel, 'From Accounting Directives to International Accounting Standards', in Christian Leuz, Dieter Pfaff and Anthony Hopwood (eds) *The Economics and Politics of Accounting: International Perspectives on Research Trends, Policy, and Practice* (Oxford: Oxford University Press, 2004), 349–75.

Véron, Nicolas, *The Global Accounting Experiment*, Bruegel Blueprint Series 2 (Brussels: Bruegel, 2007).

Walton, Peter, 'IAS 39: Where Different Accounting Models Collide', *Accounting in Europe*, 1 (September 2004), 5–16.

Whittington, Geoffrey, 'Fair value and the IASB/FASB Conceptual Framework Project: An Alternative View', *Abacus*, 44: 2 (June 2008), 139–68.

Zeff, Stephen A., 'The Evolution of the IASC into the IASB, and the Challenges it Faces', *The Accounting Review*, 87: 3 (2012), 807–38.

Zimmermann, Jochen, Jörg R. Werner, and Philipp B. Volmer, *Global Governance in Accounting: Rebalancing Private Power and Private Commitment* (Basingstoke and New York: Palgrave Macmillan, 2008).

17

Influences on the Standard-Setting and Regulatory Process

Lisa Baudot and Peter Walton

1. Introduction

An accounting standard-setter writes standards that impact numerous interested parties, including governments, institutions and organizations, industry groups and individual users of financial accounting information. As a consequence the standard-setter is surrounded by groups that would like to influence standard-setting in a way which meets their particular goals and needs for information. The standard-setter itself also has interests that come into play, such as the need to create and maintain legitimacy in fulfilling its standard-setting functions. Maintaining legitimacy as a standard-setter often involves retaining governmental support and credibility with interested parties. In the case of an organization such as the International Accounting Standards Board (IASB), which is a free-standing private-sector body not funded by government, its existence depends upon institutions and businesses being willing to finance it and on regulators being willing to use its standards. Therefore, the potential for interested groups to influence standard-setting arises from multiple sources and directions.

The purpose of this chapter is two-fold. First, this chapter introduces the nature of standard-setting influence as distinguished in the academic research literature. Here, influence has been studied primarily as observable participation in the process of standard-setting and, much less so, as less overt outside pressures on standard-setting structures and relations. In introducing the academic perspectives and the importance of considering both we attempt to demonstrate the multiple sources from and directions in which influence on standard-setting can potentially flow. Following on from this, the second part of this chapter takes the development of international accounting structures and regulations in the European Union (EU) as an exemplar through which to demonstrate these sources and directions and show not only how the nature of standard-setting influence affects standard-setting but how standard-setting affects the nature of influence.

1.1 Nature of standard-setting influence

Accounting research offers theoretical perspectives and empirical evidence about influences on accounting standard-setting and regulatory processes from the perspective of observable participation in the standard-setting process as well as from the perspective of less overt, but perhaps more compelling, examples of influencing standard-setting.

1.1.1 Influence as participation in standard-setting due process

The majority of research theorizes about the influence of various participants in the due process of accounting standard-setting largely from the standpoint of classical economic and regulatory theory. Such a perspective assumes rational, and therefore self-interested, choice to participate by an interested party. Extending from the economics of regulation theory (Downs, 1957; Stigler, 1971), participation choice research presumes the underlying incentive to participate to be dependent on the benefits expected to accrue from participation less the costs incurred to participate (Watts and Zimmerman, 1978; Sutton, 1984). According to Sutton (1984), where the costs of participating exceed the expected benefits, an interested party is assumed to abstain from participation despite being affected by a proposed accounting standard or change. In other words, those affected by a proposed standard or proposed change will choose to participate in attempt to influence the standard in a way that benefits them but only if the benefits they anticipate outweigh the costs they incur to participate. Often, this is seen to imply that the larger the interested party, the more likely they will be to participate as they will have more to gain (or lose) and greater resources to cover costs of participation.

While the theory of the economics of regulation provides the basis for the majority of accounting research, participation can also be considered through another view often referred to as the 'coalitions of interest' perspective (Haring, 1979; Brown, 1981). This perspective looks to extend the study of participation from the orientation of understanding individual participant decisions to an orientation towards understanding the participation of groups or collectives and the relative influence of those groups on standard-setting decisions. While not contesting the rational decision making view, a collective perspective necessitates a consideration of factors including the potentially evolving and competing logics of different groups and the consensus or conflict both within and between these groups.

Accounting research on the standard-setting process is primarily focused on the choice to participate in a particular standard by different categories of interested parties with presumably different sets of preferences and attributes. In terms of understanding the participation choices of different groups, accounting focuses on the decision of individuals or groups to participate, the frequency of participation and the mode of participation.

Early research examined participation choice in the due process of standard-setting primarily in the context of single issue, single-country studies. These studies were conducted in the domestic, and largely Anglo-Saxon, standard-setting environment of the UK and US with few exceptions (e.g. Watts and Zimmerman, 1978; Schalow, 1995; Weetman *et al.*, 1996; Georgiou, 2002). Following these studies, a number of single-issue, multi-country studies analysed international accounting standard-setting by the IASC and later the IASB (Kenny and Larson, 1993, 1995; MacArthur, 1996).

Single-issue studies analyse participation by interested parties by focusing on one particular standard offering the advantage of simplicity in identifying and measuring participation given the particular attributes of a standard and of the participants. However, this same simplicity also represents a disadvantage in that participation might be better understood by taking a longer view and considering which attributes of standards may drive participation as well as considering the possibility of strategic participation by participants with certain attributes over time.

Researchers attempt to overcome the perceived limitations of single-issue studies by employing a multi-issue approach which involves studying participation on more than one issue over a period of time. Multi-issue studies have been conducted in a single-country setting (Puro, 1984; MacArthur, 1988; Tandy and Wilburn, 1992; Saemann, 1999) and more recently in a multi-country setting which involved participation in the study of international accounting standard-setting under the IASC or IASB (Larson, 2002; Kwok and Sharp, 2005; Larson, 2007; Jorissen *et al.*, 2012).

Many studies choose to focus on one interest group at a time; primarily the financial statement preparers and auditors (e.g. Watts and Zimmerman, 1978; Puro, 1984; Schalow, 1995; MacArthur, 1996; Larson, 1997; Georgiou, 2002) since they appear, at least in the studies of Anglo-Saxon standard-setting, to participate to a greater extent than other interested parties. However, a focus only on preparers and auditors, despite representing significant interest groups, ignores the participation of users (i.e. institutional investors, financial analysts, etc.) industry/trade associations, advisory groups (i.e. the European Financial Reporting Advisory Group, EFRAG), and national standard-setting bodies. The participation of certain groups has also been studied in the literature on coalitions of influence in standard-setting (*accounting firms*: Haring, 1979; Puro, 1985; Mezias and Chung, 1989; Hussein and Ketz, 1980; Brown, 1981; *preparers:* Brown and Feroz, 1992; Saemann, 1995; *users*: Brown, 1981, Saemann, 1999). Results are, however, inconclusive as to the actual extent of influence of coalitions.

Finally, the majority of participation research has been conducted through reference to comment letters issued in response to FASB or IASC/IASB discussion papers (e.g. Watts and Zimmerman, 1978; Georgiou, 2002), interpretations (e.g. Larson, 2002; Larson, 2007) and most often to exposure drafts (e.g. Puro, 1984; MacArthur, 1988; Tandy and Wilburn, 1992; Kenny and Larson, 1995; Larson, 1997; Saemann, 1999). These comments letters are publicly available (i.e. observable) and represent a formal method for participants to express their accounting preferences. Further, a focus on comment letters submitted during one phase of due process neglects consideration of the choice to participate at several points in the due process of standard-setting or not at all.

While participation in due process provides interested parties with an opportunity to indicate their preferences, there remain many open questions as to the how these interested parties attempt to, and the extent to which they actually do, influence the outcome of the standard-setting process both through comment letter submission and otherwise. Further, certain critical aspects of influence such as political and institutional pressures appear not to be considered. These aspects will be discussed in the next section.

1.1.2 Influence as outside pressures on standard-setting structures and relations

In addition to influence as participation in due process, the literature also acknowledges accounting standard-setting influence as political and institutional pressure exerted on standard-setting structures and relations. Similar to the perspectives on influence through participation in due process, political influence (sometimes called the 'politics of standard-setting') can be defined in terms of the self-interested considerations or assertions put forth by a range of parties affected by accounting standard-setting (e.g. Watts and Zimmerman, 1978; Sutton, 1984; Weetman *et al.*, 1996; Zeff, 2002). However, a political perspective goes one step further to emphasize how accounting standard-setting both shapes and is shaped by power relations existing in the society and environment in which standards-setting occurs (e.g. Arnold and Sikka, 2001; Martinez-Diaz, 2005; Perry and Nolke, 2005). These power relations occur between and within different levels including that of the transnational or national-state and government regulatory level, the organizational level (national accounting standard-setters, advisory bodies, professional and industry associations) and at the constituent level (i.e. individual business and investor interests).

In addition, influence on accounting standard-setting and power relations is affected by institutional pressures where institutions represent formal systems, organizations and regulations and the informal norms, values and shared meanings that underlie them. For example, formal systems influencing standard-setting and power relations include economic systems, political systems, legal systems and the organizational structures which support them (e.g. Tamm-Hallstrom, 2004; Botzem and Quack, 2006; Botzem, 2012). On the other hand, informal norms, values and shared meanings influencing standard-setting and power relations derive from long-established beliefs and behaviours which determine the nature of economic, political, and legal systems and regulations (e.g. Robson, 1991; Young, 1994, 1996, 2003, 2006; Robson and Young, 2009). As such, one can see how institutions themselves can deploy different types of pressures for change or conformity on both standard-setters and interested parties in the standard-setting process.

The great difficulty in assessing what outside pressures come into play on a particular issue is that it may be impossible to see influence being exerted. This may be because pressure is exercised through conversations and leaves no trace, and it may also be that people conceal the fact that influence has been exercised. By way of example, cases in which private meetings have taken place during which certain proposals have been encouraged or discouraged are known to exist but remain confidential. As such, it is impossible to say how widespread is the impulse to conceal the exercise of influence, but even the IASB when meeting in public, and mentioning pressure from outside, tends to suppress the identity of the source.

Further, the existence of influence is also treated differently in different cultures. In the Anglo-Saxon accounting world, the literature until the 1970s tended to suggest that setting accounting standards was a purely technical issue. It was only with Zeff (1978) and Burchell *et al.* (1985) that the literature started to acknowledge that accounting standards had economic consequences and were influenced by behavioural considerations. This contrasts with France where the state, when it created the first national standard-setter in 1946, acknowledged the existence of diverse economic impacts and deliberately set out to include vested interests in the standard-setting process (Scheid and Walton, 1992, p. 115).

The consideration of political and institutional pressures reveals how the seemingly technical act of accounting standard-setting is embedded in and influenced by its environment (e.g. Young, 1994, 1996, 2003, 2006; Botzem and Quack, 2006; Botzem, 2012). As such, understanding influences on accounting standard-setting entails taking a comprehensive view of the complex and on-going interactions and power struggles between a diversity of participants affected by standard-setting set within the context of the social, economic and political environment at the time.

The rest of this chapter aims to illustrate the complexity of these interactions through the emergence and evolution of international accounting regulations in the European Union (EU) and the EU's role in the development of IASB standards. The EU was selected as a focal point for this chapter as it played a central role in the emergence of international accounting regulations and their eventual adoption. Its mechanisms are also relatively transparent and therefore provide an opportunity to see different interests operating to try to influence standard-setting. Given that it is itself an international organization, it also provides additional opportunities to observe competing national interests. However, we would emphasize that we are using the EU as an example of the kinds of influence that are likely to play out in any standard-setting process and not because we believe the EU is particularly active in this way.

The next two sections set international standard-setting within its context by outlining a brief history of the emergence and evolution of international accounting regulations within the EU. As will be shown, the interactions of numerous individual nation-states, regulatory bodies, standard-setting organizations, and constituents are critical to the story and demonstrate the dense network of actors and influence which exists in international standard-setting. The last two sections then highlight a number of examples of this network of actors and influence at work in the development of international standards.

2. Emergence of the international accounting structures and regulations in the EU

The development of a set of common accounting standards and its adoption by various national economic systems has been promoted as having important implications for the internationalization of the operations of multinational firms, of governance practices, and of trade flows within the global economy. This 'internationalization project' is often perceived as the outcropping of a more general mission based on a belief in the value of free trade, the elimination of state controls over capital, and economic restructuring of controls such as deregulation and privatisation (Suddaby *et al.*, 2007). As capital markets became increasingly international, the need for a common international language of accounting was advanced as encouraging greater comparability of firms based in different countries but traded in the same capital market (Whittington, 2005). Confusion, uncertainty, inefficiency, and an increased cost of capital were additional reasons put forth as existing when diverse practices were followed and therefore justifying the development of financial statements using a comparable set of (international) accounting standards. The following sections describe the influence of various interested parties in the emergence of international accounting structures and regulations in the EU.

2.1 EU harmonization programme

The EU, at that time consisting of only six countries, embarked in the 1960s on a programme of accounting harmonization which it considered a necessary part of a company law harmonization programme designed to permit the free movement of goods and services across national boundaries. One of the principal instruments of that programme was the Fourth Company Law Directive (1978) which laid out the form and content for individual company financial statements. This directive went through three major drafts, the first of which, issued in 1971 was based largely on the German 1965 Aktiengesetz (Alexander, 1993). Some authors suggest that this first draft was one of the motivations behind the creation of the IASC (Bocqueraz and Walton, 2006). The UK, Ireland and Denmark were in an advanced stage of preparation to become members of the EU, which took place in 1973. However, British accountants were extremely perturbed at the possibility of having to comply with the 1971 draft of the Fourth Directive, and some people (including the president of the American Institute of Certified Public Accountants who was directly involved) thought that this was in the mind of the British accountants who participated in setting up the International Accounting Standards Committee (IASC), the predecessor body to the IASB. The suggestion is they wanted an alternative purveyor of authoritative transnational standards to act as a counter-balance to the EU. We would underline that this example also illustrates the difficulty of proving that influence has been exerted.

In fact the British and Irish opposition to using the 1971 draft Fourth Directive found a different outlet. The EU agreed to modify the 1971 draft, and the next draft, published in 1974 after the UK, Denmark and Ireland had become member states, included a number of features drawn from British and Irish accounting requirements. In particular the 1974 draft included the requirement that the financial statements must give a true and fair view of the company's financial situation – a core UK requirement since 1947. Hopwood (1990) suggests that the UK and Ireland thought the clause which says that the rules can be set aside if it is necessary to give a true and fair view (this is known as the 'true and fair override') would allow them not to apply the German rules if they did not want to.

The Germans, of course, did not like the override, which breached a principle of German law. The final version of the directive, published in 1978, watered it down slightly by saying that if following the rules did not give a true and fair view, the company should make additional disclosures, and only if that was not sufficient should a rule be overridden. However, the directive is a good example of what happens when different interests collide. The statute says that financial statements must give a true and fair view (UK and Irish requirement) and be prepared following the best principles of accounting (German requirement). It contains numerous optional treatments which were admitted to allow member states not to have to make radical changes. A particularly obvious example is the required formats, which allow four different income statement presentations and two different balance sheet layouts.

The drafting of the fourth directive is also an illustration of the difficulty of disentangling national government interests from private interests. The directives were drafted by a committee consisting of member states' representatives (today's Accounting Regulatory Committee is the descendant of the directive drafting committees). The member states, however, might send along a civil servant and someone from the accounting profession as a technical adviser. A concrete example is Paul Rutteman, who has written about his involvement, as a technical partner in a large international firm and representing the UK professional bodies, in drafting the Seventh Directive, much of which was influenced by the relevant international accounting standard (Rutteman, 1984).

2.2 The end of regional harmonization

Harmonization of financial reporting proved to be a very unwieldy thing. A directive has to be incorporated into national law. When countries amended their company law to reflect the Fourth and Seventh Directives, they typically bolted it on to existing law, so that no two member states actually had the same requirements. On top of that individual states were sometimes slow to adopt a directive (Italy was the last member state to adopt the Fourth Directive, doing so in 1992, 14 years after it was issued and 25 years after work started on drafting it). Germany also had problems and evolved a practical expedient that the true and fair view applied to the notes to the accounts but not the main statements, which had to follow best accounting principles. Many smaller companies in Germany did not like to make all the disclosures required, so there was a massive non-compliance with filing requirements. Failure to file resulted in only a small fine.

The European Commission organized a conference to review harmonization in 1990, and the participants showed little enthusiasm for further improvement. In 1995 the Commission issued a key policy statement, saying that it would abandon regional harmonization and encouraging member states to align their reporting requirements for consolidated financial statements on International Accounting Standards (IAS). The head of accounting at the European Commission throughout this period was Karel van Hulle. He analysed the situation (van Hulle, 2004) as being that many European companies were preparing a second set of financial statements according to US GAAP or IAS. 'This requirement was extremely burdensome and led to confusion about the 'correct numbers' (ibid., p. 355) and the Commission examined four alternatives.

The first was a mutual recognition agreement with the US, but the options in the directives meant that there was no comparability within Europe in how the directives were applied, and mutual recognition with the US 'was not a realistic proposition'. A second solution considered was to allow certain large listed companies to be excluded from the directives and allowed to choose another comprehensive basis of accounting. Van Hulle notes that this raised a number of difficult questions, including how to determine the scope of the exclusion. It would involve each member state amending their company law, and abandoning any idea of a homogeneous approach to reporting.

The Commission considered updating the directives, but thought that it would be difficult to decide which issues should be revised, and that member states would want to reopen old issues that they had disagreed with before. The process would take a long time, and the revisions would be out of date before they were published. Another solution would have been to create a Europe-wide standard-setter, but this would have required legislation, and would take both time and money as well as creating a third layer of accounting between international and national.

Van Hulle says:

> The Commission saw no need to develop European standards for the sake of having European standards when other solutions were equally satisfactory. It was also clear a more flexible framework was needed, one that could respond rapidly to current and future developments (ibid., p. 357).

The solution chosen was to recommend that member states aligned their future requirements on those of the IASC. The preference for IAS was justified by the fact that, through the IASC agreement with IOSCO, there was 'a real possibility that in the not too distant future the major securities regulators of the world would accept financial statements based on an agreed set of IAS' (ibid., p. 358). Van Hulle adds that the Commission did not advocate using US GAAP because these had been developed without any European input and were designed to satisfy the needs of the American capital market. The 1995 statement preferring IAS stipulated that these should be followed, as long as they were in conformity with the EU accounting directives. The Commission had also just taken up observer status at meetings of the IASC (Camfferman and Zeff, 2007, pp. 228–9).

The 1995 Communication says that the EU expected to influence the content of international standards by organizing a combined input to the IASC through the 'Contact Committee' (a committee of member state representatives that addressed issues arising out of the accounting directives), although van Hulle (2004, p. 359) notes that individual member states such as France, Germany, the UK and the Netherlands, who were on the IASC board, frequently took different positions from each other and from the Commission's position. The 1995 Communication describes its approach as being 'organized in a pragmatic way' which will 'minimise costs' (ibid., p. 7). It also underlines that the future focus is on consolidated accounts. It says an approach 'including individual accounts would be more likely to run into controversy, since these are in many Member States directly related to reporting for tax purposes'.

This is indicative of the nature of the political compromise between the Commission and the member states. One of the most obvious failures of EU harmonization is in the field of taxation. Despite the central tenet of freedom of movement between member states, and the development of a common currency, harmonized taxation, which would enormously help freedom of movement by companies and economic management, has never advanced. As the 1995 Communication points out, in many states the accounts of individual companies also provide the basis for tax assessment. This is one of the reasons for resistance to accounting directives. The political compromise offered by the Commission was that it would leave member states to regulate individual company accounts and the related taxation issues, while the Commission would encourage the use of international standards which had the potential to provide harmonization in consolidated accounts (which have no impact on taxation).

2.3 The IAS regulation

The 1995 Communication was to have unexpected consequences. Having recommended IAS as the basis of future development, the standards were then caught up in the initiative to build a single capital market in the EU. The Financial Services Action Plan on the creation of a single financial market in the EU (European Commission, 1999, p. 7) noted the objectives the Commission wished to achieve in the area of accounting were 'the twin objectives of comparable financial reporting and alignment on international best practice'. The FSAP noted 'Comparable, transparent and reliable financial information is fundamental for an efficient and integrated capital market' and added:

> Capital-raising does not stop at the Union's frontiers: our companies may also need to raise finance on international capital markets. Solutions to enhance comparability within the EU market must mirror developments in internationally accepted best practice. At the present juncture, International Accounting Standards (IAS) seem the most appropriate bench-mark for a single set of financial reporting requirements which will also enable companies (which wish to do so) to raise capital on international markets.

This was followed by the Commission's Communication 'EU Financial Reporting Strategy - the way forward' (European Commission, 2000) which announced the Commission's intention to require EU listed companies to use international accounting standards. Before the issue of this document the EU had been involved in a hard-fought debate with the IASC over the future shape of the IASB. Camfferman and Zeff (2007) devote a whole chapter to this key issue with significant implications for the governance of the future standard-setter. Camfferman and Zeff say (ibid., p. 433) that the EU strongly opposed the structure that was eventually decided upon. They preferred a larger, geographically representative body, while the SEC preferred a smaller, professional board modelled on the FASB.

3. Evolution of international accounting structures and regulation in the EU

This next section looks at how the EU organized itself to adopt IFRS, and the various influences on standard-setting that have occurred in the first decade of the IASB's existence.

3.1 The EU endorsement mechanism

Despite having lost the argument about the structure of the IASB, the Commission went ahead with its announcement of a move to IFRS. In terms of governance, the communication said, 'This strategy will need to take full account of public policy interests' (COM (2000) 359: 7). It proposed that public oversight would be provided through the endorsement function, which would consist of a technical level and a political level. There was no mention of seeking any role in the governance of the IASB.

However, it suggested that objections to international standards in the endorsement process would be 'probably infrequent' and noted:

> To avoid such a situation concerns about emerging IAS will need to be expressed at the earliest stage in the IASC's drafting process. Indeed, the Union will need to develop internal coordination at all stages of the IAS standard setting process not least to influence the debate. The endorsement mechanism can help coordinate the European position within the IASC (ibid., p. 8).

The Commission decided to require adoption of IFRS through a Regulation, which had to be applied throughout the EU without transposition into national law, to ensure that adoption was uniform. The so-called 'IAS Regulation' (2002-1606) required IFRS to become part of European law through a process known as 'comitology'. A committee of representatives of all the member states is given the power to endorse IFRS into European law. As van Hulle (2004, p. 366) points out, while most people agreed that the choice of IFRS was right, there was considerable opposition to handing over control of accounting standards to a private body: 'Doing so would not conform to the democratic traditions of member states'. There had to be an endorsement system, but 'it was unthinkable that an IAS adopted by the IASB would then need to be re-negotiated at the EU level.'

In order to minimize this possibility, a number of safeguards were put in place. Although the Commission was not given a seat on the IASB, and observer status no longer existed in the new structure, the Commission expected to maintain close links with the IASB and had a seat on what is now the IFRS Advisory Council. The second safeguard was to create a system so that European interests were consulted as early as possible in the standard-setting process. Van Hulle remarks (ibid., p. 367) that there was a high likelihood of different positions being expressed by individual member states and the EU needed to do something to ensure that European interests spoke with a single voice. 'The best way to prevent a possible rejection of an IAS by the EU would be to ensure that there had been proper input from the very beginning and that all arguments had been properly discussed.'

The European Financial Reporting Advisory Group (EFRAG) came into existence. 'This body was set up by the main parties interested in financial reporting (industry, accounting profession, standard-setters, stock exchanges, financial analysts)' (ibid., p. 367). In fact the body not only represented as many people with a probable desire to influence IFRS as possible, but they were also asked to pay for the privilege. EFRAG was set up to run at no cost to the EU. Mr van Hulle approached the Federation of European Accountants (FEE – the long-standing regional body for the profession) to set up EFRAG. FEE then approached other Europe-wide lobbying or representative organizations to participate. The supporters of the organization, who also have seats on its supervisory board, include Business Europe, the European Banking Federation and the European Insurance and Reinsurance Federation.

The fundamental part of the EU endorsement process is that EFRAG interacts with the IASB during the standard-setting process, and aims to coordinate European inputs to that process. When a final standard is issued by the IASB, EFRAG then provides the Commission with a technical assessment (known as its 'endorsement advice'). A later addition is that a further committee, the Standards Advice Review Group (SARG) assesses the EFRAG endorsement to ensure it has not been unduly affected by any one interest group. The Commission puts the standard in front of the Accounting Regulatory Committee (ARC - representatives of the 27 member states) who decide whether or not to endorse it. Informally, the ARC expects a two-thirds majority voting in favour for an endorsement to be made. Over time the procedure has been extended, with the European Parliament having the right to comment on an endorsement during a three-month

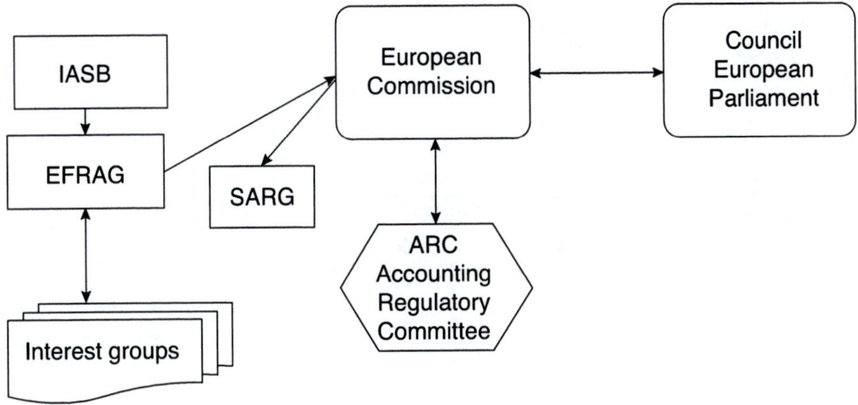

Figure 17.1 EU adoption of IFRS

period after the decision has been made. At the end of the procedure, the Commission submits the decision to the European Council of Ministers for final endorsement (see Figure 17.1).

It can be seen that the EU endorsement mechanism provides one forum for business, the profession and other commercially interested people to give their views, and another for governments. However, the first one includes national standard-setters who may be close to government, and, in the second one, national representatives may have been influenced by their constituents. When EFRAG was set up, the expectation was that the EU would accept IAS/IFRS as issued by the IASB. In an interview, the first chairman of EFRAG, Johan van Helleman, said: 'There is a strong feeling that we should take IFRS as they are. We could provide negative advice to the European Commission, but that should be a very great exception' (WAR, 2001b). However, as we will examine below, the endorsement process provides many opportunities for influence to be exercised. In 2012, the SEC staff in their report on possible US use of IFRS recommend having an endorsement mechanism because:

> an endorsement process may allow a jurisdiction to exert more influence over the standard-setting process because the threat of a potential rejection of a proposed accounting standard may influence the IASB decision on the scope of the accounting standard, how to account for a particular transaction, or the timing of the completion of an accounting standard-setting project (SEC, 2012, p. 3).

3.2 The monitoring board

If, as van Hulle (2004) says, the Commission was initially prepared not to have any direct influence over the IASB, this position changed fairly soon. In 2005 Irish accountant Charlie McCreevy took over the reins as Commissioner for DG Markt (Internal market), which is responsible for financial reporting, and at once organized a meeting with the IASB chairman to discuss a greater role for Europe in IASB governance (WAR, 2005a). The Commissioner, and the European Parliament, repeatedly emphasized that the IASB was not accountable to anyone, and that the countries that used its standards had no oversight of its functioning, which was not acceptable. Oversight was provided by the Trustees of the IFRS Foundation, and Trustees alone were responsible for appointing new Trustees.

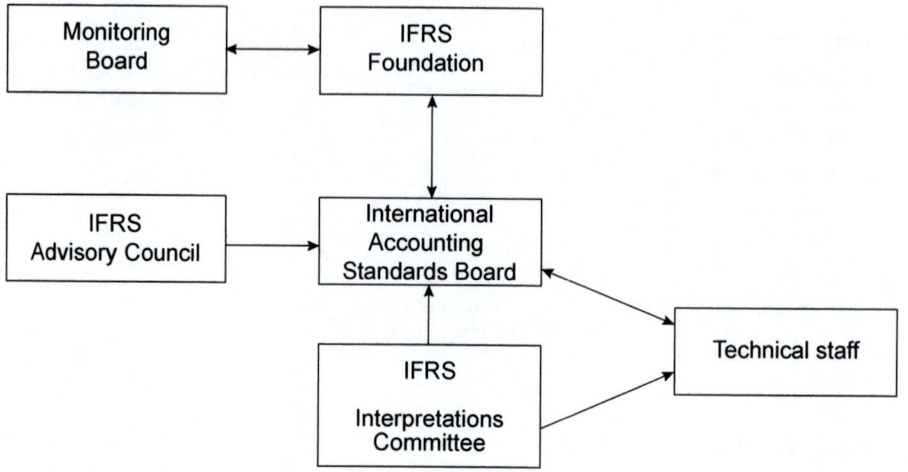

Figure 17.2 The structure of the IFRS Foundation

The Trustees subsequently reviewed the IASB constitution (which is done on a systematic basis) and created a new oversight body, the Monitoring Board, which would have no direct link with the IASB, but which would have the right to review all decisions made by the Trustees. The Monitoring Board came into existence in 2009 and consisted of five members: the European Commissioner responsible for the Internal Market, the chairman of the SEC, the chairman of the Japanese Financial Services Agency and two representatives of IOSCO. A process had been created which provided direct influence on the major decisions concerning the standard-setter, albeit excluding in theory the technical decisions (see Figure 17.2).

One of the key areas where the Monitoring Board has since exercised its influence was in the appointment of the new chairman of the IASB. Sir David Tweedie's two terms came to an end in June 2011. The Trustees proposed Ian Mackintosh, an experienced Australian accounting regulator, who was then chairman of the UK Accounting Standards Board. The Monitoring Board refused to confirm the appointment, apparently at the instigation of the European Commission, and the Monitoring Board's then chairman, Hans Hoogervorst, a non-accountant, was given the post. Mr Mackintosh was appointed as vice-chairman.

In the following two sections we will look at a series of examples of the network of actors and influence at work in the EU concerning the development of international accounting standards as such. The first deals with financial instruments, and the second other technical accounting issues.

4. Financial instruments

How to account for financial instruments has been a controversial and complex issue for more than two decades. The central issue is that instruments that have little or no cost at inception may bind a company into substantial potential gains or losses of which no indication is given on a historical cost measurement basis. Traditionally accounting has used current market value as a surrogate when historical cost is not available or not relevant, and that was proposed for financial instruments, but with the criticisms that (a) it imports market volatility into the financial statements, (b) the current market position is not necessarily any indication of the value at which a transaction will be realised, and (c) current market values are only available for a limited number of items, and estimates lack the objectivity claimed as an advantage for fair value.

4.1 IAS 39 and the JWG draft

The IASC's financial instruments project started in 1988 and resulted in the approval of IAS 39, a 'temporary' standard, in December 1998 as a last ditch move to complete the IASC's development programme agreed with IOSCO (Cairns *et al.,* 2002, pp. 364–70). The IASC had agreed in 1997 to participate in a project initiated by a group of Anglo-Saxon standard-setters to develop a single internationally agreed financial instruments standard. This group set up what was called the Joint Working Group (JWG) and included Australia, Canada, Japan, New Zealand, the USA and then Germany, France, the UK and the Nordic Federation. The JWG produced a draft standard which was intended to replace the 'temporary' IAS 39. However, although the French had participated in the development of the proposal, when it was unveiled in December 2000 it was greeted with much opposition in France; the French participants in the JWG therefore withdrew their approval, and the successor to IAS 39 went no further.

One of the difficulties in EU adoption of IFRS was that the ARC had to endorse all the pre-existing IFRS, which also implied that EFRAG needed to prepare endorsement advice, an enormous task for a fledgling organization. Eventually it was agreed that IAS 39 and IAS 32 would be deferred and addressed separately, after adoption of the other standards in 2003.

4.2 The Chirac letter

In July 2003 the French president, Jacques Chirac, wrote to Romano Prodi, president of the European Commission, asking him to review the adoption of IFRS in general and IAS 39 in particular. The letter talks about the excessive importance given to market value which creates volatility in the financial statements. Mr Chirac said adoption of IAS 39 'would have negative consequences for financial stability'. He also said: 'It seems to me essential that the European Union, the Commission and the Member States should have more weight in the elaboration of standards by the IASB'. It is generally believed that this overtly political intervention was motivated by French banks, who throughout the development of IAS 39 had taken a strong role in the accounting committee of the European Banking Federation in opposing the standard.

4.3 Macro-hedging requirements

When the IASB came into existence it went through the formal process of confirming all the IASC's standards, but in the light of reluctance on the part of some board members to endorse what they saw as flawed standards, the IASB also agreed to undertake an 'improvements' programme to address known problem areas without redebating the underlying standards. IAS 39 was put into this programme, and the IASB was asked by the European Banking Federation to grant more flexibility in accounting for macro-hedges.

Essentially the issue was that IAS 39 has an anti-abuse stance on hedge accounting (Hague, 2004). A concern when it was written was that companies would designate hedging instruments retrospectively to achieve desired performance effects. The standard therefore requires that hedges are designated at inception on an instrument by instrument basis. However, the banks argue that much of their hedging is not done instrument to instrument but by portfolios, and that often they aim to hedge only a part of the risk. This is referred to as 'macro-hedging'. A committee of IASB members, under pressure from the Commission, and European bankers spent something like two years discussing how IAS 39 could be amended to provide some relief. The IASB did provide relief but the bankers said that what was afforded was inoperable.

4.4 The fair value option

Another problem raised by bankers was that of an 'accounting mismatch' between liabilities held at fair value and assets which economically were held to back the liability, but were accounted for at historical cost: the accounting did not reflect the economics. The IASB eventually provided a solution for this that was known as the 'fair value option'. The fundamental notion was that the IASB believed that accounting for financial instruments at fair value always gave better information for investors. Therefore it was prepared to allow preparers an option to use fair value if they wished to.

This proposal was exposed for comment in the normal way and subsequently redebated and finalized, after which the IASB received a letter from the European Central Bank saying that it opposed the fair value option. It believed that this would allow banks to inflate their assets for prudential regulation purposes and it was not prepared to allow this. Despite the fact that due process had been completed, the IASB reopened the subject and, in consultation with the European Central Bank, introduced restrictions on the use of the option.

4.5 The carve-out

It was clear that IAS 39 was going to be the most difficult legacy standard to be endorsed by the ARC. In the first instance EFRAG was unable to give endorsement advice. EFRAG's voting arrangements put obstacles in the way of the organization disagreeing with a standard. Approval required only a simple majority of those voting, while a recommendation not to endorse required a two-thirds super-majority. In between those two positions, EFRAG simply did not give advice one way or the other. Six members of the eleven member EFRAG Technical Expert Group had dissenting opinions on IAS 39. They claimed the standard did not have the qualities required by the IAS Regulation and did not give a true and fair view (Walton, 2004, p. 6).

There was a danger that IAS 39 would not be endorsed. Karel van Hulle (making a presentation at an event to mark the tenth birthday of EFRAG), reported in WAR (2011) said that the Commission had devised the idea of the carve-out. The IAS Regulation (2002-1606) says the ARC must either reject or accept a standard, it does not allow for changing the standard. However, the Commission asked themselves if they had the power to remove something and decided that they did, which was a better solution than rejecting a core standard. In Mr van Hulle's view, had they not come up with the carve-out they would not have reached the tenth birthday of EFRAG.

The EU's Accounting Regulatory Committee (ARC) voted on 1 October 2004 to approve IAS 39, minus the provisions on fair value and portfolio hedging of core deposits. This has subsequently been known as the carve-out.

4.6 Reclassification of financial instruments

The 2007 financial crisis generated a major confrontation between the EU and the IASB. IAS 39 provides four classifications of financial instruments depending on the preparer's business intentions for the instrument. To prevent profit manipulation by retrospective designation, the standard requires classification to be done at inception, thereafter it is irrevocable. This requirement was stressed by the state of the financial markets: instruments held in the 'available for sale' category have to be valued at fair value, but because of the reluctance of people to trade (liquidity preference) market values were less than the expected contractual cash flows of some assets. Financial institutions wanted to reclassify from available for sale to 'held to maturity' on the basis that they would realize more cash by holding the asset and it would not be valued at fair value.

The details of the political manoeuvres are given in André *et al.* (2009). Essentially the French government persuaded the European Commission to draft a further carve-out from IAS 39 which would remove the prohibition on reclassification. In October 2008 the Council of Ministers then told the IASB that it must amend IAS 39 to allow reclassification, or the ARC would apply its carve-out. The IASB took emergency powers to amend the standard as the Commission asked. Sir David Tweedie subsequently commented that in amending the standard the IASB were able to insert disclosure requirements about any reclassification, which would protect investors. The ARC could only remove clauses, it could not add anything.

4.7 Non-endorsement of IFRS 9

A by-product of the October 2008 reclassification confrontation was the EU insistence that the IASB rush out a replacement standard by the end of 2009. The IASB was already working on a two-classification model for financial assets. It was well aware that a complete replacement of IAS 39 within a one-year time frame was impossible, so it opted for a phased replacement of IAS 39 by IFRS 9. It duly completed the financial asset part of IFRS 9 and this was issued in final form early in 2010, with an implementation date of 2013. However, when this was put forward to the ARC by the Commission, the German delegation voted against it, and persuaded a sufficient minority to follow them, so IFRS 9 was not endorsed into European law, despite the Council of Ministers having expressly asked for that in 2008.

The explanation given is that there had been a change in the composition of the German coalition government in the interim, which had placed a new team in the Ministry of Justice, which is responsible for financial reporting. The new team were unwilling to endorse IFRS 9 without knowing what the rest of the standard would look like, even though all parts would have been submitted individually. The application date of IFRS 9 was initially January 2013, but the IASB put this back to January 2015 once it was clear that all parts would not be completed by then. At the time of writing, there remains a clear risk that the official application date will arrive before the ARC endorses the standard.

Another consequence of the 2008 crisis was, as mentioned above, that IFRS 9 would be issued on a phased basis. There are now three versions of IFRS 9, those of 2010 (financial assets), 2011 (financial assets and liabilities) and 2013 (financial assets and liabilities, and general hedge accounting). Outside of the EU preparers can use any of these three or just stay with IAS 39. This has a very negative effect on the comparability of financial statements.

4.8 An exception to debt/equity classification

The dividing line between debt and equity is one of the most difficult and crucial issues in regulation. IAS 32 *Financial Instruments: Presentation* takes a restrictive but clear view that any financial instrument that *requires* the reporting entity to make a payment to the holder is debt and not equity. In 2008 the IASB modified this for certain securities. The problem that gave rise to this was first raised by New Zealand farm cooperatives, but the issue also arises with partnerships and the German standard-setter took an active role in finding a solution because the jurisdiction has legal vehicles that include limited partners. We are therefore including it at the end of the financial instruments section for the sake of completeness.

The technical issue is that in some corporate forms equity-holders are required, if they wish to cease to participate, to sell their stake back to the reporting entity, and the entity is required to purchase them. Under IAS 32, such an arrangement causes the instrument to be treated as a liability. In the case of a cooperative, for example, this may mean that (a) all its equity is classified as debt, and (b) that every period in which it makes a profit causes the liability to be increased, which generates a loss.

The IASB was sympathetic to the problem and an amendment to IAS 32 was passed, allowing such instruments to be classified as equity, while setting restrictions on the use of this exception. The existence of this requirement was subsequently to be one of the complicating factors in the attempt to reach a joint standard with the FASB on distinguishing equity instruments from debt instruments. That project has been shelved indefinitely after numerous attempts to devise a workable formula.

5. Other technical issues

Although financial instruments has been one of the most difficult areas for standard-setters, particularly during a period of prolonged financial crisis, they have not been the only source of constituent problems for the IASB and the EU. In this area the work of the IFRS Interpretations Committee (formerly the International Financial Reporting Interpretations Committee – IFRIC) has also been subject to the exercise of competing interests.

5.1 Emissions trading schemes

One of the issues that the IASB was slow to address in relation to preparing for the 2005 switch to IFRS by the EU was the need for some guidance on how to account for the emissions trading scheme that the EU had initiated. This scheme provides for companies that emit greenhouse gases to be given a reducing annual allowance for authorized emissions. Companies exceeding their allowance have to buy more, those not using their allowance can sell on the market. The IASB chose to ask IFRIC to issue an Interpretation, rather than set out to write a new standard.

The consequence of this was that the guidance could only be on how to apply existing standards. The result was IFRIC 3 *Emission Rights* which provided guidance based on IAS 38 *Intangible Assets*, IAS 37 *Provisions* and IAS 20 *Government Grants*. Essentially the Interpretation said that allowances should be recognized as an intangible when acquired, and measured at fair value, and that the obligation to surrender the rights should be recognized progressively as emissions took place, being measured at fair value also.

European constituents thought this was a counter-intuitive solution, since the use of fair value measurement at different times meant that the allowance received and the allowance subsequently surrendered could be measured differently, giving rise to a profit or loss. Economically there was neither a profit nor a loss. EFRAG consistently produced negative comments on the Interpretation and in 2005 gave negative endorsement advice to the Commission (WAR, 2005c). The IASB withdrew the Interpretation. This is actually the only time that EFRAG has, to date, refused to endorse an IASB pronouncement. It did not produce the shockwaves that would have been feared five years' earlier, when EFRAG was being designed.

5.2 Concessions

A similar situation presented itself with IFRIC 12 *Service Concession Arrangements*. The IASB's agenda was heavily committed, but IFRS had no rules for accounting for government and similar concessions, a type of transaction that was not common in the Anglo-Saxon accounting world, but was significant in a number of European countries. These are arrangements whereby, for example, the government grants a contract to a private sector company to build infrastructure, such as a motorway, and the company subsequently operates the motorway, either for a fee or through levying tolls. The IASB was reluctant to address this as a standard-setting issue and passed it to IFRIC to say how existing standards should be applied.

There was much debate about the issues lasting several years, but IFRIC 12 ruled that, where ownership of the infrastructure asset passed to the government sponsor in return for the right to raise future revenue, the concession operator should recognize an intangible. This brought considerable opposition, notably from Spain, where concession operators would find themselves showing intangible assets where previously they had recognized a tangible. They argued that this would have significant economic consequences because banks would apply less favourable lending rules for an intangible as compared to a tangible asset.

EFRAG spent a long time debating this issue, and it seemed in January 2007 that there was not an absolute majority for giving favourable endorsement advice. EFRAG had further meetings and finally issued a favourable endorsement in March, accompanied by dissents from three out of twelve TEG members (WAR, 2007). Spain also opposed endorsement of the Interpretation by the ARC, but was unable to muster a blocking minority.

5.3 Statement of comprehensive income

The IASB and FASB had embarked upon a joint process to revise financial statement presentation. This was split into phases, and in the first phase, both standard-setters were to introduce a Statement of Comprehensive Income to replace the Income Statement as well as that part of the Statement of Changes in Equity that addresses those changes in equity that are not exchanges with shareholders. The IASB already had an optional statement, the Statement of Recognized Income and Expense, which was little used. It issued an exposure draft in 2008 mandating a single statement of comprehensive income. This caused negative feedback from companies, particularly in Europe.

The IASB was puzzled by the response because it considered that it was not asking for any disclosure of information that was not already provided in the financial statements. However, it was clear that companies thought that analysts would look at the comprehensive income number for the year instead of the operating profit as the basis for forecasts. The corporate reaction raises an interesting question as to how efficient capital markets are in incorporating publicly available information.

At a public standard-setting meeting in November 2005, the IASB noted the strong opposition, especially from the European Round Table of Industrialists, and conceded that the statement could be broken into two parts, operating income and other comprehensive income, to be shown on separate pages (WAR, 2005b). Deputy Chairman Tom Jones is reported as saying that a fight over two pages instead of one was not something the IASB needed.

5.4 IFRS 8 operating segments

An extreme example of political intervention in standard-setting occurred with IFRS 8: the standard was endorsed by the ARC, and therefore was ready to enter European law, when the European Parliament intervened to try to stop it. It took the European Commission a great deal of effort to persuade the Parliament eventually to drop its opposition.

IFRS 8 was an example of what the FASB and IASB called 'short term convergence'. This was a scheme, now dropped, whereby if one standard-setter had a more recent standard on a subject where both had a standard, the other would adopt the later one as being more up to date. The IASB's standard, IAS 14, had originally been issued in 1981 along similar lines to US and Canadian standards. But the FASB had subsequently revised its requirements with a new standard, SFAS 131. The US standard moved to an approach known as 'through the eyes of management'. Where the earlier standards had mandated a split of selected consolidated information across industrial and geographical segments, the new standard said that the segment information should be what was used by the Chief Operating Decision-Maker (CODM) for management purposes.

The fundamental idea was that previous segment information was often a compliance exercise involving the preparation of data broken out from the consolidated statements and not reflecting how the company saw its activities. The SFAS 131 argument was that information used for decision-making by management was more useful for investors (and reduced information asymmetry). The argument against this approach was that (a) the figures were not necessarily GAAP-based, and (b) they were not comparable between companies. US research tended to show that post-SFAS 131 more segments were actually reported by companies.

The IASB decided, in conjunction with the FASB and the SEC, that convergence on segments was desirable, and that the more recent US standard should be used. IFRS 8 is in effect SFAS 131, amended for different vocabulary used by the two standard-setters. An exposure draft was issued in 2006 and the final standard early in 2007. After endorsement by the ARC, the European Parliament has a three-month window in which to comment, if it wishes to. In this case British investment analysts lobbied the Economic and Monetary Affairs Committee of the European Parliament, saying that IFRS 8 would result in worse information for investors. The Commission and the Parliament agreed that the three-month window would be extended, both institutions would prepare studies, and Parliament would debate the issue later in the year.

Parliament commissioned Nicolas Véron from the Bruegel Institute to write a report. This was released in September and claimed that the IASB had ignored 'widespread negative sentiment' and that there were insufficient safeguards to ensure that segments reflected economic reality and conveyed a proper understanding of risks. He recommended that the EU should not adopt the standard. The Commission, for its part, had put out a questionnaire to assess the probable effects of the standard. Its report, European Commission (2007), concluded that the management approach had an overall positive effect on the quality of information, gave increased usefulness and relevance and appropriately addressed the needs of global users of financial information. The European Parliament finally agreed to endorse the standard in November 2007.

5.5 IFRS 10 implementation date

The IASB issued three related standards, IFRS 10 to IFRS 12 in 2011 for application from January 2013. IFRS 10 is a major standard dealing with consolidation, while 11 and 12 address accounting for joint arrangements and disclosures concerning activities with related companies. The IASB also decided to work on an amendment to IFRS 10 in order to specifically exempt from consolidation subsidiaries of investment companies that were managed on a fair value basis as an investment and not as a part of the parent's operations. IFRS 10 has slightly changed the basis on which a consolidation decision is made, and the investment company exemption would avoid financial institutions having to consolidate as operating subsidiaries their investment funds. These are to be accounted for at fair value. The accounting for joint arrangements and the new disclosures called for a different approach to joint ventures.

While EFRAG accepted the standards, it firmly believed that the implementation date should be a year later, because its constituents had told it that they needed time to obtain the necessary additional information and to reassess previous consolidation decisions. They also feared that the investment company exemption would not be available by January 2013 and some investees could potentially be treated as operating subsidiaries for one year. They wrote to the IASB in late 2011 to ask the IASB to reconsider, which it duly did, but noted that (a) the standards were part of the IASB's commitment to the G20, and (b) some countries had already adopted the standards early.

EFRAG subsequently gave positive endorsement advice to the European Commission, but at the same time recommended that the application date should be January 2014 and not 2013. The ARC, meeting in June 2012, followed the recommendation, and so the three standards have an application date in Europe which is different to that of the IFRS as issued by the IASB.

The standard is still the subject of discussion, however, since the European Securities and Markets Authority (ESMA), the Commission's stock exchange oversight body, has subsequently expressed concerns about how the standard is being applied, and in 2011 asked the IASB to give further guidance on the identity of the CODM – which the IASB refused to do.

6. Conclusion

This chapter is not an attempt to go deeply into the workings of different influences on accounting standard-setting, but rather it presents a sequence of events which took place over a long period and are intended as an example of how some influences can be seen to operate on standard-setting. The example we have chosen relates:

- to the emergence and evolution of international accounting structures and regulations in the EU in general; and
- to the EU presence in the development of specific IASB standards, to demonstrate that there are numerous institutional influences at work in the standard-setting process and these are rarely absent.

The chapter builds on the previous work of Walton (2009) in suggesting that a number of workings of influence exist by nature of the EU's institutional arrangements for accounting regulation. More specifically, this chapter represents an early attempt to show that the institutional arrangements created by the EU in support of a single financial market and common set of financial reporting standards present numerous opportunities for influence to be exerted, both by those institutions and by other institutions and individuals who wish to influence standard-setting outcomes.

We envision that if an historical account of the presence of American capital market interests in the emergence and evolution of international accounting structures and regulations and the development of specific IASB standards, or more particularly standards undergoing convergence with US GAAP, had been referenced as an exemplar, our conclusion would have likely been similar – that institutional arrangements supporting of global financial markets and global accounting standards have generated numerous opportunities for influence by American capital market interests.

Bibliography

Alexander, D. (1993) 'A European True and Fair View?' *European Accounting Review* 2:1 59–80

André, P., Cazavan-Jeny, A., Dick, W., Richard, C. and Walton, P. (2009) 'Fair Value Accounting and the Banking Crisis in 2008: Shooting the Messenger'. *Accounting in Europe* 6, 3–24.

Arnold, P., Sikka, P. (2001) 'Globalization and the State–Profession Relationship: The Case of the Bank of Credit and Commerce International'. *Accounting, Organizations and Society* 26, 475–99.

Bocqueraz, C. and Walton, P. (2006) 'Creating a Supranational Institution: The Role of the Individual and the Mood of the Times'. *Accounting History* 11:3, 271–88

Botzem, S. (2012) *The Politics of Accounting Regulation: Organizing Transnational Standard Setting in Financial Reporting*. Cheltenham and Northampton, MA: Edward Elgar.

Botzem, S. and Quack, S. (2006) 'Contested Rules and Shifting Boundaries: International Standard Setting in Accounting', in M.-L. Djelic and Sahlin-Andersson, K. (eds) *Transnational Governance; Institutional Dynamics of Regulation*. Cambridge: Cambridge University Press, pp. 266–86.

Brown, P. (1981) 'A Descriptive Analysis of Select Input Bases of the Financial Accounting Standards Board'. *Journal of Accounting Research* 19, 232–46.

Brown, P. and Feroz, E. (1992) 'Does the FASB Listen to Corporations?'. *Journal of Business Finance and Accounting* 19:5, 715–31.

Burchell, S., Clubb, C. and Hopwood, A. (1985) 'Accounting in its Social Context: Towards a History of Value Added in the United Kingdom'. *Accounting, Organizations, and Society* 10:4, 381–413.

Cairns, D., Creighton, B. and Daniels, A. (2002) *Applying International Accounting Standards* (3rd edn). London: Tolley.

Camfferman, K., and Zeff, S. (2007) *Financial Reporting and Global Capital Markets: A History of the International Accounting Standards Committee, 1973–2000*. Oxford: Oxford University Press.

Downs, A. (1957) 'An Economic Theory of Political Action in a Democracy'. *The Journal of Political Economy* 65:2, 135–50.

European Commission (1995) *Accounting Harmonisation: A New Strategy vis-à-vis International Harmonisation*. European Commission Communication COM (1995) 508.

European Commission (1999) *Financial Services: Implementing the Framework for Financial Markets – Action Plan*. European Commission Communication, 11 May, COM (1999) 232.

European Commission (2000) *EU Financial Reporting: The Way Forward*. European Commission Communication COM (2000) 359.

European Commission (2007) *Endorsement of IFRS 8 Operating Segments: Analysis of Potential Effects*. European Commission MARKT F3 D.

Georgiou, G. (2002) 'Corporate Non-participation in the ASB Standard-setting Process'. *European Accounting Review* 11:4, 699–722.

Hague, I.P.N (2004) 'IAS 39: Underlying Principles'. *Accounting in Europe* 1, 21–6.

Haring, J.R. (1979) 'Accounting Rules and "The Accounting Establishment"'. *Journal of Business* 52, 507–19.

Hopwood, A. (1990) 'Ambiguity, Knowledge and Territorial Claims: Some Observations on the Doctrine of Substance over Form'. *British Accounting Review* March.

Hussein, M.E. and Ketz, J.E. (1980) 'Ruling Elites of the FASB: A Study of the Big Eight'. *Journal of Accounting, Auditing and Finance*, 354–67.

Jorissen, A., Lybaert, N., Orens, R. and van der Tas, L. (2012) 'Formal Participation in the IASB's Due Process of Standard Setting: A Multi-issue/Multi-period Analysis'. *European Accounting Review* 21:4, 693–729.

Kenny, S.Y. and Larson, R. (1993) 'Lobbying Behavior and the Development of International Accounting Standards'. *European Accounting Review* 3, 531–54.

Kenny, S.Y. and Larson, R. (1995) 'The Development of International Accounting Standards: An Analysis of Constituent Participation in Standard Setting'. *International Journal of Accounting* 30, 283–301.

Kwok, W. and Sharp, D. (2005) 'Power and International Accounting Standard Setting: Evidence from Segment Reporting and Intangible Assets Projects'. *Accounting, Auditing and Accountability Journal* 18:1, 74–99.

Larson, R. (1997) 'Corporate Lobbying of the International Accounting Standards Committee'. *Journal of International Financial Management and Accounting* 8, 176–203.
Larson, R. (2002) 'The IASC's Search for Legitimacy: An Analysis of the IASC's Standing Interpretations Committee'. *Advances in International Accounting* 15, 79–120.
Larson, R. (2007) 'Constituent Participation and the IASB's International Financial Reporting Interpretations Committee'. *Accounting in Europe* 4:2, 207–54.
MacArthur, J. (1988) 'Some Implications of Auditor and Client Lobbying Activities: A Comparative Analysis'. *Accounting and Business Research* 19:73, 56–64.
MacArthur, J. (1996) 'An Investigation into the Influence of Cultural Factors in the International Lobbying of the International Accounting Standards Committee: The Case of E32, Comparability of Financial Statements'. *International Journal of Accounting* 31, 213–37.
Martinez-Diaz, L. (2005) 'Strategic Interests and Improvising Regulators: Explaining the IASC's Rise to Global Influence, 1973–2001'. *Business and Politics* 7:3, 1–26.
Mezias, M. and Chung, S. (1989) *Due Process and Participation at the FASB: A Study of the Comment Period.* Morristown, NJ: Financial Executives Research Foundation.
Perry, J. and Nolke, A. (2005) 'International Accounting Standard Setting: A Network Approach'. *Business and Politics* 7:3.
Puro, M. (1984) 'Audit Firm Lobbying Before the Financial Accounting Standards Board: An Empirical Study'. *Journal of Accounting Research* 22:2, 624–46.
Puro, M. (1985) 'Do Large Accounting Firms Collude in the Standards-setting Process?'. *Journal of Accounting, Auditing, and Finance* 8, 165–77.
Robson, K. (1991) 'On the Arenas of Accounting Change: The Process of Translation'. *Accounting, Organizations and Society* 16:5–6, 547–70.
Robson, K. and Young, J. (2009) 'Socio-Political Studies of Financial Reporting and Standard-Setting', in C. Chapman, D. Cooper, P. Miller (eds) *Accounting, Organizations and Institutions: Essays in Honour of Anthony Hopwood* Oxford: Oxford University Press, pp. 341–66 .
Rutteman, P. (1984) *The EEC Accounting Directives and their Effects.* Cardiff: University College Cardiff Press
Saemann, G. (1995) 'The Accounting Standard-setting Due Process, Corporate Consensus, and FASB Responsiveness: Employers' Accounting for Pensions'. *Journal of Accounting, Auditing and Finance* 10:3, 555–64.
Saemann, G. (1999) 'An Examination of Comment Letters Filed in the US Financial Accounting Standard-setting Process by Institutional Interest Groups'. *Abacus* 35:1, 1–28.
Schalow, C. (1995) 'Participation Choice: The Exposure Draft for Postretirement Benefits Other Than Pensions'. *Accounting Horizons* 9:1, 27–41.
Scheid, J.-C. and Walton, P. (1992) *European Financial Reporting: France.* London: Routledge.
SEC (2012) *Work Plan for the Consideration of Incorporating International Financial Reporting Standards into the Financial Reporting System for US Issuers: Final Staff Report.* Washington, DC: Office of the Chief Accountant, Securities and Exchange Commission.
Stigler, G. (1971) 'The Theory of Economic Regulation'. *Bell Journal of Economics and Management Science* (Spring), 2–21.
Suddaby, R., Cooper, D. and Greenwood, R. (2007) ' Transnational Regulation of Professional Services: Governance Dynamics of Field Level Organizational Change'. *Accounting, Organizations and Society* 32:4–5, 333–62.
Sutton, T. (1984) 'Lobbying of Accounting Standard-setting Bodies in the US and the UK: A Downsian Analysis'. *Accounting, Organizations and Society* 9:1, 81–95.
Tamm-Hallstrom, K. (2004) *Organizing International Standardization: ISO and the IASC in Question of Authority.* Cheltenham: Edward Elgar.
Tandy, P. and Wilburn, N. (1992) 'Constituent Participation in Standard-setting: The FASB's First 100 Statements'. *Accounting Horizons* 6:2, 47–58.
Van Hulle, K. (2004) 'From Accounting Directives to International Accounting Standards', in Leuz, C., Pfaff, D. and Hopwood, A. (eds) *The Economics and Politics of Accounting: International Perspectives on Trends, Policy and Practice.* Oxford, Oxford University Press
Véron, N. (2007) 'EU Adoption of the IFRS 8 Standard on Operating Segments', Report to Economic and Monetary Affairs Committee of the European Parliament.
Walton, P. (1997) 'The True and Fair View and the Drafting of the Fourth Directive'. *European Accounting Review* 6:4, 721–30.

Walton, P. (2004) 'IAS 39: Where Different Accounting Models Collide'. *Accounting in Europe* 1, 5–16.
Walton, P. (2009) 'European Adoption of IFRS: A Poisoned Chalice?'. *EAA Newsletter* 27 2009-03, 11–15.
WAR (2001a) 'IASB Work Programme'. *World Accounting Report* May, 10–12.
WAR (2001b) 'An International Career'. *World Accounting Report* November, 15.
WAR (2004) 'Carve Out Approved'. *World Accounting Report* November, 3–4.
WAR (2005a) 'McCreevy and Tweedie debate IASB'. *World Accounting Report* February, 3–4.
WAR (2005b) 'Rejection of IFRIC 3'. *World Accounting Report* June, 5.
WAR (2005c) 'Concession on single statement'. *World Accounting Report* December, 2.
WAR (2007) 'Service concession arrangements'. *World Accounting Report* April, 6.
WAR (2011) 'EFRAG celebrates birthday in style'. *World Accounting Report* November, 9–12.
Watts, R. and Zimmerman, J. (1978) 'Towards a Positive Theory of the Determination of Accounting Standards'. *Accounting Review* 53:1, 112–34.
Weetman, P., Davie, E. and Collins, W. (1996) 'Lobbying on Accounting Issues: Preparer/User Imbalance in the Case of the Operating and Financial Review'. *Accounting, Auditing and Accountability Journal* 8:1, 59–76.
Whittington, G. (2005) 'The Adoption of International Accounting Standards in the European Union'. *European Accounting Review* 14:1, 127–53.
Young, J. (1994) 'Outlining Regulatory Space: Agenda Issues and the FASB'. *Accounting, Organizations and Society* 19:1, 83–109.
Young, J. (1996) 'Institutional Thinking: The Case of Financial Instruments'. *Accounting, Organizations and Society* 21:5, 487–512.
Young, J. (2003) 'Constructing, Persuading and Silencing: The Rhetoric of Accounting Standards'. *Accounting, Organizations and Society* 28, 621–638.
Young, J. (2006) 'Making Up Users'. *Accounting, Organizations and Society* 31, 579–600.
Zeff, S. (1978) 'The Rise of "Economic Consequences"'. *Journal of Accountancy* 106 (December), 56–63.
Zeff, S. (2002) '"Political" Lobbying on Proposed Standards: A Challenge to the IASB'. *Accounting Horizons* 16:1, 43–54.

18

Stock Exchanges and International Financial Reporting

Philippe Danjou

1. Introduction: globalization of trade and financial markets led to the internationalization of accounting standards

> Accounting practices and standards play an increasingly central role in intermediating information in capital markets and shaping business behaviour. Thus, the decision made by the European Union in the early 2000s to abandon national accounting standards for its listed companies and adopt instead the International Financial Reporting Standards (IFRS) can be considered among the most momentous of financial market policy initiatives of the past few decades. The EU decision also had a key influence in triggering similar moves to adopt IFRS in a number of jurisdictions, including China, Australia, Canada, South Korea, and possibly Japan and India as well in the near future. Even the United States, which in the past half-century had led many developments in accounting, is now considering recognition of IFRS as an acceptable set of standards for at least some of the companies listed on its markets (Véron, 2007: vi).

Globalization of financial markets is part of a wider phenomenon of globalization of national economies. The rapid growth of the international trade in goods and services which really took off around the middle of the twentieth century was accompanied by substantial increases in international capital flows. Between 1970 and 2000 the value of world exports of goods and services increased twenty-fold and was supported by a fifty-fold increase in foreign direct investment (source UNCTAD). Realizing that there were opportunities to accelerate their own growth, many countries, among which the developing economies, have modified their legislation with a view to reducing legal barriers and making it easier to attract foreign capital. At the same time, the leading corporations in Europe and the USA which were faced with limited opportunities for growth on their domestic markets decided to develop internationally through direct investments or mergers and acquisitions. As a cash settlement of the acquisitions was often too onerous, many transactions were effected through exchanges of shares which frequently entailed the admission of the newly issued shares to trading on a foreign market. The differences in the accounting regimes applicable to the parties to such transactions became more visible and

Table 18.1 Global market capitalization 2010 (in trillion of US$)

Geographical area	*2001 (rounded amount)*	*2001 (percentage)*	*2010 (rounded amount)*	*2010 (percentage)*
USA	14	52	17	30
Americas excl. USA	1	3.7	5	9
Europe, Africa & Middle East	8	30	15	27
Asia excl. China	3	11	10	18
China	1	3.7	8	15

Source: World Federation of Exchanges, market capitalization by region
www.world-exchanges.org/files/statistics/excel/Ts2%20Market%20cap.XLS (accessed on 30 September, 2012)

created unnecessary costs and efforts to explain differences to investors and sometimes reconcile between the different sets of standards.

Table 18.1 summarizes the globalization of the financial markets and the development of significant financial markets in the developing economies as follows:

- In 2001, the USA accounted for 52 per cent of the global market capitalization (totalling approximately 28 trillion US $), followed by Europe at 30 per cent and Asia (excluding China) at 11 per cent. With a market capitalization of some one trillion US$, China accounted for only 3.7 per cent of the total.
- In 2010, the total market capitalization reached some 55 trillion US$, but the US market share had fallen to 30 per cent, Europe's share to 27 per cent. The share of Asia excluding China has increased to 18 per cent and the share of China to 15 per cent of the total. The remaining share (9 per cent) relates to the Americas excluding USA, which did not figure in the league ten years earlier.

More and more, the development of businesses and the financing of projects draw their funding from the capital markets. Capital markets offer unique investment opportunities for the private and institutional investors. The development of international trade and the globalization of cultures make cross border investments a natural behaviour.

> In the process of the developing globalization of financial markets seen over recent decades, both technological advances and financial innovation played a key role. In the past few decades, information systems have become able to compute and store more data more rapidly. Telecommunications networks have extended their ramifications and augmented their capacity while more reliable data exchange protocols have made it possible to connect computing machines in more efficient ways. As a result, cross-border financial deals have become both easier and more secure, effectively lowering the barrier constituted by distance, be it determined by geography or other factors.[1]

However, whereas the growing use of English as the language of business made it easier to invest internationally, a significant impediment to this evolution was the heterogeneity of the financial communication languages used on the different financial markets. The demand for a single, internationally accepted financial reporting language became more and more pressing. International Accounting Standards (IAS) which had been developed steadily since 1973 by the IASC represented a real opportunity. In this chapter, we will explain the key roles played by the European Union and by the International Organization of Securities Commissions towards the adoption of a high quality, single set of accounting standards to be used globally in reporting financial information to providers of capital. Over the past decade, significant progress has been made: as of this year (2012), two-thirds of G20 members require the use of IFRSs, and decisions are expected from the USA and Japan regarding the accounting standards to be followed by their domestic issuers. Table 18.2 provides information about the use of IFRS in the world as of March 2012.

Table 18.2 The use of IFRS in the world as of March 2012 for the countries belonging to the G20

Country	*Status for listed companies as of December 2011*
Argentina	Required for fiscal years beginning on or after 1 January 2012
Australia	Required for all private sector reporting entities and as the basis for public sector reporting since 2005
Brazil	Required for consolidated financial statements of banks and listed companies from 31 December 2010 and for individual company accounts progressively since January 2008
Canada	Required from 1 January 2011 for all listed entities and permitted for private sector entities including not-for-profit organisations
China	Substantially converged national standards
European Union	All member states of the EU are required to use IFRSs as adopted by the EU for listed companies since 2005
France	Required via EU adoption and implementation process since 2005
Germany	Required via EU adoption and implementation process since 2005
India	India is converging with IFRSs at a date to be confirmed
Indonesia	Convergence process ongoing; a decision about a target date for full compliance with IFRSs is expected to be made in 2012
Italy	Required via EU adoption and implementation process since 2005
Japan	Permitted from 2010 for a number of international companies; decision about mandatory adoption by 2016 expected around 2012
Mexico	Required from 2012
Republic of Korea	Required from 2011
Russia	Required from 2012
Saudi Arabia	Required for banking and insurance companies. Full convergence with IFRSs currently under consideration
South Africa	Required for listed entities since 2005
Turkey	Required for listed entities since 2005
United Kingdom	Required via EU adoption and implementation process since 2005
United States	Allowed for foreign issuers in the US since 2007; target date for substantial convergence with IFRSs is 2011 and decision about possible adoption for US companies expected in 2011

Source: IFRS Foundation website www.ifrs.org/Use+around+the+world/Use+around+the+world.htm (accessed 30 September 2012)

Note: More than 100 jurisdictions in the world require or permit the use of IFRS for the preparation of financial statements of listed companies and certain public interest entities (financial institutions and insurance companies). A detailed analysis by jurisdiction is available on the web site iasplus.com maintained by Deloitte: www.iasplus.com/Plone/en/resources/use-of-ifrs

The current global framework of financial reporting under IFRS is relatively complex and requires an understanding of the roles played by a number of actors and numerous types of legislation. At the risk of oversimplifying the picture, I would describe it as follows:

- Within the EU, the basic elements of legislation concerning listed entities can be found in documents covering various aspects of the information provided by them to the investors:
  - regulations concerning the information to be provided when securities are offered to the public (e.g. in the EU, the Prospectus Directive 2010/73/EU[2]);
  - regulations concerning the periodic and punctual information to be published by issuers (in the EU, it is to be found in the Transparency Directive 2004/109/EC[3])
  - regulations concerning the manner in which periodic financial statements are to be prepared (in the EU, the 4th and 7th Accounting directives[4] and the IAS Regulation);
  - regulations concerning the auditing of the financial statements (in the EU, the 4th and 7th Directives as amended by Directive 2006/46/EC[5] on statutory audits of annual and consolidated accounts);
  - other regulations or codes of conduct relating to internal controls and aspects of corporate governance;
  - regulations concerning accepted market practices, the definition of inside information, market integrity and market manipulation (Commission Directive 2003/124/EC and Directive 2003/6/EC of the European Parliament and the Council[6]); and
  - in addition, a very important legislative text was published by the European Union in 2004: the Markets in Financial Instruments Directive 2004/39/EC[7] (known as 'MiFID') as subsequently amended, is a European Union law that provides harmonized regulation for investment services across the 30 member states of the European Economic Area (the 27 member states of the European Union plus Iceland, Norway and Liechtenstein). The main objectives of the Directive are to increase competition and consumer protection in investment services. As of the effective date, 1 November 2007, it replaced the Investment Services Directive.
- 'Preparers' of financial statements are the entities ('Issuers') who issue financial instruments (equity or debt instruments) listed on financial markets and present their financial statements under the applicable accounting standards. More and more often, they report under IFRS either because they are required to do so by their national accounting requirements, or on a voluntary basis. In addition to listed issuers, certain public interest entities or regulated entities such as financial institutions or insurance companies are often required to use IFRS. The application of IFRS is either general, i.e. for all financial statements published (parent-only company accounts and consolidated financial statements) or, more often, partial, which means that only the consolidated financial statements are presented in accordance with IFRS. When issuers do not report under IFRS, they either follow national GAAP (e.g. US GAAP or Japanese GAAP) or, when permitted, they use the other accounting framework which has de facto been recognized as internationally acceptable, the US GAAP. When the 'parent only' financial statements are not prepared according to IFRS, they follow the applicable national standards, which in the EU are somewhat harmonized (at least in terms of formats of presentation) on the basis of the 4th Directive.
- The standard setters who publish the accounting standards applicable are the national standard setters (e.g. the French ANC, the UK Accounting Standards Board, the US Financial Accounting Standards Board) and the international standard setter IASB together with its interpretation Committee IFRIC. The structures of the IASB and its parent organization

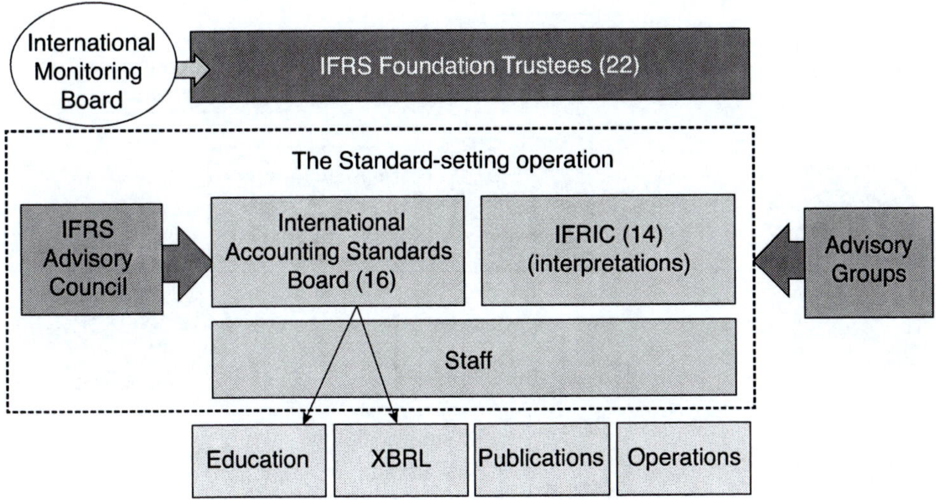

Figure 18.1 The structure of the IFRS Foundation

the IFRS Foundation are illustrated in Figure 18.1. Since 2002, IASB and FASB have been working together with a view to converge their two sets of standards but there are still a number of significant differences between the two.

- In many jurisdictions, there is an endorsement mechanism (see Figure 18.2) which involves public authorities and gives to the accounting standards the force of law. This is the case for instance in the USA, where the US SEC recognizes the FASB and its pronouncements as the mandatory regime applicable to the US issuers. It is also the case in the European Union where the IASB is recognized as the international standard setter and the organization responsible for developing the standards, but where its output is incorporated into the EU legislation through endorsement decisions which become the applicable law when they are published in the Official Journal of the EU.
- The endorsement mechanism sometimes involves official expert committees to advise the responsible public authority about the acceptability of the standards issued by the accounting standard setter. In Europe, those committees are the Accounting Regulatory Committee (ARC) and the European Financial Reporting Advisory Group (EFRAG).
- The authorities in charge of the surveillance of financial markets and investors' protection are as of today the national securities commissions (e.g. the US SEC, the German BAFIN, the French AMF). Their roles usually consist of approving the listing of securities and admission documents (prospectuses) which contain financial information as prescribed by the applicable legislation. Quite often, they are also tasked with the enforcement of the proper application by issuers of the accounting requirements applicable in their respective jurisdiction. The enforcement mechanisms usually involve a domestic issuer following domestic GAAP and a domestic enforcement agency. But more and more there are situations where an issuer is listed on several national markets, with the result that the enforcement may involve several national agencies. Furthermore, with the growing use of IFRS as accounting standards applied internationally, domestic agencies have to enforce international standards in addition to their domestically applicable standards. International cooperation in the area of enforcement has become a necessity so as to avoid divergent

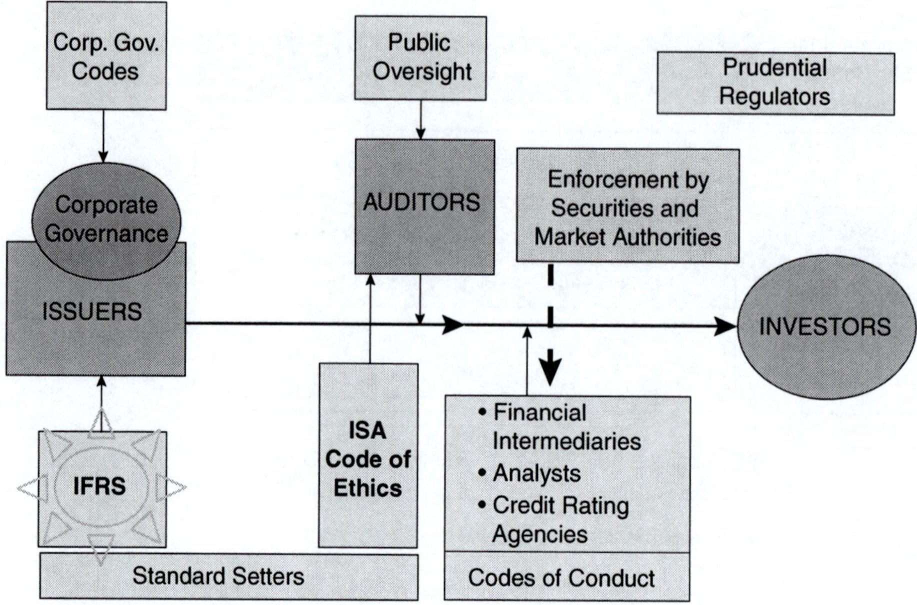

Figure 18.2 The financial information chain and the related actors and frameworks of reference

application of IFRS. As a consequence of this international cooperation on enforcement (which is conducted mainly within the European Union, and, albeit to a lesser degree, on a worldwide basis under the IOSCO) the interaction between enforcement agencies and the international standard setter has developed steadily.

The quality of the financial information provided by issuers to investors depends on many factors and the interaction of several classes of actors: management and directors of the issuers, auditors, enforcement authorities, financial intermediaries, as illustrated in Figure 18.3. Each class of actor follows its applicable regulations and standards of reference, or codes of conduct.

In this chapter, we will describe the roles of each key regulatory authority and the policies they have been following over the past decade in relation to promoting international accounting harmonization, and how they have organized the support system after the adoption of IFRS. We will also explain the roles of the committees who intervene in the adoption of IFRS promulgated by the International Accounting Standards Board and how they interact with the standard setter and with the other regulatory authorities. Most of the contents will be factual and based on publicly available data.

2. The situation of financial reporting that prevailed on regulated capital markets before the adoption of IFRS: the Tower of Babel and resulting investors' confusion

Prior to 2005, there was a large variety of accounting standards used by listed companies. In Europe, they most often used the national GAAP which were only partly harmonized on the basis of the 4th and 7th EU Accounting directives. Many large German companies, which were listed in the USA in addition to German markets, reported under US GAAP, as did a few French companies. Swiss companies reported either under International Accounting Standards (IAS) or

US GAAP as well as under Swiss GAAP. Often, such companies presented two sets of financial statements prepared under the different GAAP. However, in total only a handful of companies reported on the basis of IAS.

Outside the EU, US companies reported under US GAAP, while their Canadian neighbours reported either under US or Canadian GAAP. Japanese companies reported under Japan GAAP, while some of the more international ones used US GAAP:

- *US SEC required US GAAP or a reconciliation of financial information to US GAAP until 2007:* As many companies sought a listing on US markets to tap capital from US investors, at a time when the US markets were the deepest and most liquid ones, the SEC only accepted registration statements prepared under US GAAP, or required a full reconciliation from the financial statements prepared under the domestic GAAP to US GAAP. This was a costly and complex exercise and created a certain amount of confusion as the investors were presented with two sets of financial data, often giving quite different pictures of the financial situation and performance of the entity. Further, many of them asserted that such additional information was of little use to investors, as very few of them asked questions about the reconciling items during investors meetings. Was this reconciliation from national GAAP to US GAAP really useful? It seems that to a large extent it was required because the SEC did not trust the quality of the GAAP used by foreign registrants and wanted the reconciliation to provide a 'fair presentation' as required under US standards and by this means be able to verify the quality of the underlying financial data.

  For example in 1998, Daimler Benz AG took over the Chrysler Corp. through a public offering of shares exchange. Daimler Benz AG had to prepare a reconciliation from its financial statements prepared under German GAAP to US GAAP, and the huge amounts that showed up in the reconciliation table were widely commented at the time in the financial press. Many investors were shocked to discover the extent to which different accounting standards could give a contrasted picture of the financial situation.
- *The relative lack of regulatory action by stock market enterprises:* It is rather surprising to note that in this context, the stock market enterprises (the 'bourses') were relatively inactive and let the supervisory authorities initiate the reforms of accounting standards. A search on the web site of the World Federation of Exchanges did not return any results about accounting standards prior to 2007, in which year its annual meeting[8] included a round table discussion about accounting standards convergence (WFE, 2007).

3. IOSCO's policies on financial reporting and their outcomes 1995–2000

3.1 Background information about the International Organization of Securities Commissions

The International Organization of Securities Commissions (IOSCO) was created in 1983 with the decision to change from an inter-American regional association (created in 1974) into a global cooperative body. Eleven securities regulatory agencies from North and South America took this decision in April 1983 at a meeting in Quito, Ecuador. In 1984, securities regulators from France, Indonesia, Korea and the United Kingdom were the first agencies to join the organization from outside the Americas.

Today IOSCO is recognized as the international standard setter for securities markets. Its membership regulates more than 95 per cent of the world's securities markets and it is the primary international cooperative forum for securities market regulatory agencies. IOSCO members are drawn from, and regulate, over 100 jurisdictions and its membership continues to grow.

IOSCO provides comprehensive technical assistance to its members, in particular those which regulate emerging securities markets.

In 1998 IOSCO adopted a comprehensive set of Objectives and Principles of Securities Regulation (IOSCO Principles), which is recognized as the international regulatory benchmark for all securities markets. In 2003 the organization endorsed a comprehensive methodology (IOSCO Principles Assessment Methodology) that enables an objective assessment of the level of implementation of the IOSCO Principles in the jurisdictions of its members and the development of practical action plans to correct identified deficiencies.

In 2002 IOSCO adopted a multilateral memorandum of understanding (IOSCO MMoU) designed to facilitate cross-border enforcement and exchange of information among international securities regulators. Then in 2005 IOSCO endorsed the IOSCO MMoU as the benchmark for international cooperation among securities regulators and set out clear strategic objectives to expand the network of IOSCO MMoU signatories by 2010. It approved as an operational priority the effective implementation - in particular within its membership - of the IOSCO Principles and of the IOSCO MMoU, which are considered primary instruments in facilitating cross-border cooperation, reducing global systemic risk, protecting investors and ensuring fair and efficient securities markets.

The member agencies currently assembled together in the International Organization of Securities Commissions have resolved, through its permanent structures, which include a General Secretariat:

- to cooperate in developing, implementing and promoting adherence to internationally recognized and consistent standards of regulation, oversight and enforcement in order to protect investors, maintain fair, efficient and transparent markets, and seek to address systemic risks;
- to enhance investor protection and promote investor confidence in the integrity of securities markets, through strengthened information exchange and cooperation in enforcement against misconduct and in supervision of markets and market intermediaries; and
- to exchange information at both global and regional levels on their respective experiences in order to assist the development of markets, strengthen market infrastructure and implement appropriate regulation.

The IOSCO's Executive Committee has established two specialized working committees. the first one, the Technical Committee, is made up of eighteen agencies that regulate some of the world's larger, more developed and internationalized markets. Its objective is to review major regulatory issues related to international securities and futures transactions and to coordinate practical responses to these concerns. The work of the committee is divided into the following six major functional subject areas:

- multinational disclosure and accounting;
- regulation of secondary markets;
- regulation of market intermediaries;

- enforcement and the exchange of information;
- investment management; and
- credit rating agencies.

The Technical Committee is responsible for the co-ordination of international cooperation on the regulation of securities transactions. It was intended that the Committee would gather experts from member countries to review regulatory problems related to the issue and trading of international securities and propose practical solutions to these problems. The Technical Committee consists of senior representatives from securities commissions or stock exchanges with an active interest in international securities trading. The member regulatory bodies are from the following countries: Australia, Canada, (Ontario and Quebec), France, Germany, Hong Kong, Italy, Japan, the Netherlands, Sweden, Switzerland, the United Kingdom and the United States.

The second specialized committee, the Emerging Markets Committee, endeavours to promote the development and improvement of efficiency of emerging securities and futures markets by establishing principles and minimum standards; preparing training programmes for members' staff; and facilitating the exchange of information and transfer of technology and expertise

At the occasion of the next annual conference held in May 2012, a new organizational structure, the principles of which were approved by the President's Committee,[9] was implemented. A Transitional Board is to be set up for two years, tasked with preparing a new organization chart with a single committee regrouping the Executive, Technical and Emerging Markets committees.

3.2 Monitoring of IAS and encouraging further progress to reduce options and improve transparency

The first indication about IOSCO's policies in the field of accounting standards harmonization can be found in a September 1989 report[10] on International Equity Offers which noted that:

> Globalisation of the financial markets has facilitated distribution of capital market products in multiple jurisdictions both by public offers and private placements. This benefits issuers, by increasing competition and reducing costs of capital. Investors also benefit from greatly enhanced investments opportunities, as does the world economy, by promoting efficiency of capital allocation.
>
> Internationalised financial markets present substantial challenges to the financial and securities regulators in each market. To maximise the benefits of internationalisation, regulators must co-operate to protect the soundness and integrity of the world's capital markets and to reduce unnecessary costs involved in compliance with redundant, conflicting or inconsistent regulation (IOSCO, 1989: 3).
>
> The differences in disclosure requirements, particularly with respect to financial statements, and audit practice present major obstacles to international equity offers. While there is some evolution of disclosure practice towards using a single, common prospectus in international equity offers involving offers to the public, differing requirements for financial statements (particularly with respect to accounting and auditing standards) in various jurisdictions may persuade issuers to make the offer on a private basis to avoid the problem of co-ordination of disclosure requirements (IOSCO, 1989: 7).

In response to the problems identified, the Working Party reached six basic conclusions and recommendations one of which deals directly with the harmonization of standards so as to allow issuers to prepare a single set of disclosures:

Disclosure/harmonization

a) Efficiency of the capital raising process would be greatly enhanced by permitting issuers to prepare one disclosure document for use in each jurisdiction in which it chooses to sell securities. There appear to be several ways of reaching that goal:
   - Standards could be harmonized among jurisdictions; jurisdictions could accept the disclosure document prepared in accordance with the home country (predominant market) requirements, which, while not the same, are sufficiently based on the same model with the same regulatory purposes to be deemed to provide investors with adequate disclosure.
   - It is recommended that regulators be encouraged, where consistent with their legal mandate and the goal of investor protection, to facilitate the use of single disclosure documents, whether by harmonization of standards, reciprocity or otherwise.

b) A critical factor in the evolution of reliance on a single disclosure document is acceptance of financial statements in multiple jurisdictions. Development or recognition of adequate internationally acceptable accounting, auditing and independence standards would greatly facilitate the development of the use of a single disclosure document. The recommendations of the IOSCO Working Party No. 2 on Accounting and Auditing Standards will be an important contribution to the development of these standards (IOSCO, 1989: 8).

Five years later, the recommendation had seen some implementation as indicated by the following abstract from the Report of the Chairman of the Working Party presented in October 1994 at the IOSCO Annual Meeting in Tokyo:

> Working Party No. 1 and its Subcommittee on Accounting and Auditing have focused their efforts for the last year on international accounting standards and international auditing standards. Significant progress has been made in the area of international accounting standards. In the area of international audit standards, on the other hand, developments have been disappointing.
>
> The goal of the Working Party's efforts in the International Accounting Standards area is the implementation of the second recommendation included in the Working Party's 1989 Report on Cross Border Equity Offerings. That recommendation, which was endorsed by IOSCO at its Annual Meeting in Santiago, Chile November 1990 stated:
>
>> A critical factor in the evolution of reliance on a single disclosure document is the acceptability of financial statements in multiple jurisdictions. Developments, or recognition, of adequate internationally acceptable accounting, auditing and independence standards would greatly facilitate the development of the use of a single disclosure document.
>
> The Working Party's plan of work, ratified by the Technical Committee in June 1993, provides for the Working Party to:
>
> 1. Continue to review and comment on each international standard during each phase of its development by the IASC.

> 2. Identify for the IASC those standards that will be reviewed by the Working Group in determining whether it can recommend to the Technical Committee that there is an acceptable comprehensive body of International Accounting Principles that could be used in cross-border offerings. The goal would be to enumerate those standards for the IASC no later than the end of 1993.
> 3. Advise the IASC of the Working Party's views with respect to each standard as finalized. The view will be determined by consensus. If there is not a consensus on a final standard, the Working Group would not express a view on the final standard, but would transmit to the IASC opinions expressed in the meeting, which will be considered in finalizing standards by the IASC. The timing will be dictated by the IASC.
> 4. Upon the IASC's completion of the comprehensive body of standards identified as indicated in paragraph (2), to advise the Technical Committee as to the Working Party's recommendation with respect to the use of such standards in cross-border offerings.
>
> Thus, a recommendation by the Working Party to endorse IASC standards will be based on a consideration of a comprehensive body of core accounting standards (IOSCO, 1994: 1–2).

By letter dated 16 August 1993 to the IASC, the IOSCO Working Party identified those core standards it found to be necessary components of a comprehensive set of international accounting standards. From 1996 onwards, IOSCO had sent observers to the IASC Board meetings and a working relationship established, with a view to accelerate the improvements to IASs that IOSCO had identified. A complete analysis of the relationship between IOSCO and IASC is developed by Kirsch (2006).

The May 2000 Sydney resolution on the use of IAS's core standards[11]

This important resolution, which really created a worldwide impetus for the adoption of IASs, is to be found in the Report of the Technical Committee of IOSCO:

> The Technical Committee has received and approved for publication the following report. This report summarizes the work of its Working Group on Multinational Accounting and Disclosure (the Working Party) assessing the accounting standards published by the International Accounting Standards Committee (IASC).
>
> After considering this report, the Technical Committee recommends to IOSCO members the use of 30 selected IASC standards for cross-border listings and offerings by multinational enterprises, as supplemented in the manner described in this report (i.e., reconciliation, supplemental disclosure and interpretation), where necessary to address outstanding substantive issues at a national or regional level. These 30 standards and their related interpretations are referred to in this report as the 'IASC 2000 standards' [and are listed in Appendix A].

[...]

> Those supplemental treatments are:
>
> - reconciliation: requiring reconciliation of certain items to show the effect of applying a different accounting method, in contrast with the method applied under IASC standards;

- disclosure: requiring additional disclosures, either in the presentation of the financial statements or in the footnotes; and
- interpretation: specifying use of a particular alternative provided in an IASC standard, or a particular interpretation in cases where the IASC standard is unclear or silent.

In addition, as part of national or regional specific requirements, waivers may be envisaged of particular aspects of an IASC standard, without requiring that the effect of the accounting method used be reconciled to the effect of applying the IASC method. The use of waivers should be restricted to exceptional circumstances such as issues identified by a domestic regulator when a specific IASC standard is contrary to domestic or regional regulation. The concerns identified and the expected supplemental treatments are described in the report entitled *IASC Standards – Assessment Report* 4 (Assessment Report).

IOSCO notes that a body of accounting standards like the IASC standards must continue to evolve in order to address existing and emerging issues. IOSCO's recommendation assumes that IOSCO will continue to be involved in the IASC work and structure and that the IASC will continue to develop its body of standards. IOSCO strongly urges the IASC in its future work programme to address the concerns identified in the Assessment Report, in particular, future projects (IOSCO, 2000).

IOSCO supports the setting up of IASB and encourages further convergence of accounting standards

IOSCO had been a member of the Strategy Working Party (SWP) formed in 1996 to review the future strategy of IASC. Mr Ed Waitzer, a former chair of IOSCO's Technical Committee, was appointed chairman of the SWP (Kirsch, 2006: 340–41). After lengthy discussions, which culminated with the approval of the new structures for the forthcoming IASB and the Foundation, at a meeting in December 1999 the Board of IASC appointed a Nominating Committee (NC) to select the first Trustees of the Foundation. Members of the NC included Mr Michel Prada,[12] the then Chair of IOSCO's Technical Committee and three other senior representatives of markets authorities (US SEC, represented by its chairman Arthur Levitt, who was appointed chair of the NC, the chair of the UK FSA and the chair of the Hong Kong SFC). The 'old' IASC held its last meeting in December 2000 and was 'decommissioned' in March 2001, at which time the new Constitution of the IFRS Foundation came into operation.

The Final Communiqué[13] of the 27th Annual Conference of IOSCO held in May 2002 included the following comments:

> Following up on its *Resolution Concerning the Use of IASC Standards for the Purpose of Facilitating Multinational Securities Offerings and Cross Border Listings* adopted by the Presidents' Committee in May 2000, IOSCO conducted a survey of the acceptance of International Accounting Standards by IOSCO members. The results indicate that many jurisdictions permit incoming issuers to use IAS, and others are actively working towards this end.
>
> Moreover, since May 2000, there have been a number of developments promoting the use of IAS. These include: (i) the decision of the EU Council of Ministers (ECOFIN Council) requiring the use of IAS by 2005; (ii) the completion of the reconstitution of the IASB into a full-time independent standard setter; and (iii) the formation of the Committee of European Securities Regulators with a special sub-group devoted to these issues. Looking ahead, to further these efforts, IOSCO encourages the IASB and national standard setters to work cooperatively and expeditiously to achieve convergence in order to facilitate

cross-border offerings and listings and encourages regulators to address the broader issues of consistent interpretation, application and enforcement.

3.3 IOSCO's other activities aimed at improving financial reporting

IOSCO has also been active, through its Standing Committee (ex Working Party) on Multinational Disclosure and Accounting, on strengthening the quality of audits performed on the issuers' financial statements and the independence of auditors. For instance, in 2002 IOSCO issued two policy documents:

- Principles of Auditor Independence and the role of Corporate Governance in Monitoring an Auditor's Independence;[14] and
- Principles for Auditor Oversight.[15]

It is noteworthy that those policy statements influenced the creation of auditors' oversight agencies in different jurisdictions, for instance the Public Company Accounting Oversight Board[16] in the USA, or the Haut Conseil du Commissariat aux Comptes[17] in France.

In June 2009, IOSCO issued a Statement endorsing the International Auditing Standards revized as a result of the IAASB's 'clarity project':[18]

> IOSCO has long encouraged efforts around a set of internationally developed auditing standards through the work of the International Auditing and Assurance Standards Board (IAASB), the private-sector standard setting body that develops International Standards on Auditing (ISAs).For the last several years the IAASB has carried out a project to restructure and improve the body of ISAs (known as the 'Clarity Project'). IOSCO has encouraged these efforts, as noted in its 9 November 2007 Statement on International Auditing Standards. The IAASB has now announced the completion of this work and the release of the clarified ISAs. IOSCO welcomes achievement of this milestone.
>
> IOSCO endorses the replacement of the previous ISAs with the new standards, noting the improvements that have resulted from clarifying the ISA requirements. IOSCO looks forward to continued progress in terms of the translation, education and other efforts by many to facilitate global audit practices as well as the continuous improvement of ISAs over time.

3.4 IOSCO's participation in the IFRS Foundation's Monitoring Board

In April 2009, acknowledging the need to improve the public accountability of the IFRS Foundation (which at the time was named the IASC Foundation – IASCF), the Trustees of the Foundation and the authorities responsible internationally for the oversight of the major financial markets decided to establish a Monitoring Board to establish a formal relationship between capital markets authorities and the IASCF in order to facilitate the ability of capital markets authorities that allow or require the use of IFRS in their jurisdictions to effectively discharge their mandates relating to investor protection, market integrity and capital formation.

The Charter of the IASCF Monitoring Board is available on the website of IOSCO[19] which hosts all documents regarding the activities of this Board. IOSCO's representatives[20] currently have two seats on the Monitoring Board (MB). The structure of the IFRS Foundation is illustrated in Figure 18.1 (above). A key responsibility of the Monitoring Board is to ratify the appointment of the Foundation's trustees, who report to it on the activities of the Foundation. A Memorandum of Understanding has been signed between the Foundation and the members of the MB to further describe the purpose and duties of the MB and the oversight of the IASB's due process.

4. The EU regulation 1606/2002 on IFRS, a final outcome of the 1999 Financial Services Action Plan

The roots of the European Commission's Internal Market Directorate's policy are to be found in a 1995 Communication[21] titled 'Accounting Harmonization: a new strategy vis-à-vis international harmonization' which includes the following important statement:

> The approach proposed in the present communication consists of putting the Union's weight behind the international harmonisation process which is already well under way in the International Accounting Standards Committee (IASC). The objective of this process is to establish a set of standards which will be accepted in capital markets world-wide.
>
> The Union must at the same time preserve its own achievements in the direction of harmonisation, which are a fundamental part of internal market law. It therefore needs to take steps to ensure that existing international standards (IAS) are consistent with the Community's Directives and that IAS which remain to be formulated remain compatible with Community law.

The ideas contained in this document gained support, probably as a result of the concurrence of the views with those professed by IOSCO, and were politically endorsed in 1999.

4.1 The FSAP

Originally adopted in May 1999, the Commission's *Implementing the Framework for Financial Services Action Plan (FSAP)*[22] was designed to open up a single market for financial services in the EU. It comprized 42 measures designed to harmonize the Member States' rules on securities, banking, insurance, mortgages, pensions and other forms of financial transactions:

> The wide consultations undertaken over the past 12 months, the Resolution of the European Parliament and the work of the FSPG[23] have confirmed that a fresh impetus is called for to harvest the undeniable opportunities offered by the single financial market and the single European currency. The present action plan consolidates the issues which have emerged from the Commission communication, as fleshed out by the FSPG discussions. In respect of most of the following actions, the Commission has already the occasion to confirm or announce its intention to proceed with initiatives as they have emerged from these discussions. Essentially action is envisaged under three headings: wholesale markets; retail markets, and sound supervisory structures. The Framework plan … provides the detailed basis for this work, which should build on efforts undertaken in other formal or informal bodies where appropriate (COM (1999)232, 11.05.99: p. 5).
>
> **Financial reporting**
>
> Comparable, transparent and reliable financial information is fundamental for an efficient and integrated capital market. Lack of comparability will discourage cross-border investment

> because of uncertainty as regards the credibility of financial statements. FSPG discussions pinpointed the urgent need for solutions which give companies the option of raising capital throughout the EU using financial statements prepared on the basis of a single set of financial reporting requirements. Capital-raising does not stop at the Union's frontiers: our companies may also need to raise finance on international capital markets. Solutions to enhance comparability within the EU market must mirror developments in internationally accepted best practice. At the present juncture, International Accounting Standards (IAS) seem the most appropriate bench-mark for a single set of financial reporting requirements which will enable companies (which wish to do so) to raise capital on international markets. In the same way, International Standards on Auditing appear to be the minimum which should be satisfied in order to give credibility to published financial statements (COM (1999)232, 11.05.99: p. 7).

More specifically, the FSAP contained the following recommendation:

> Discussions in the FSPG have triggered an important debate on how the twin objectives of comparable financial reporting and alignment on international best practice can be simultaneously achieved. Consideration is currently being given to a possible solution which would provide companies with an option (as the sole alternative to preparing financial statements in accordance with national laws transposing EU accounting Directives) to publish financial statements on the basis of IAS standards. The objective of comparability in financial reporting will be secured by excluding national deviations from IAS for companies exercising this option. A screening mechanism will be required in order to ensure that IAS output conforms with EU rules and corresponds fully with EU public policy concerns. Securities markets supervisors could be associated to this task. These issues will be amplified in a Commission Communication to be published by the end of 1999, which will prefigure amendments of the 4th and 7th Company Law Directives. Auditing issues will be addressed in a separate Commission Recommendation (COM (1999)232, 11.05.99: p. 7).

This FSAP was implemented actively by the Commission, but further analysis showed that creating an 'IAS option' was not the best solution to guarantee comparability.

The Lisbon European Council of 23–24 March 2000 had emphasized the need to accelerate completion of the internal market for financial services, set the deadline of 2005 to implement the Commission's Financial Services Action Plan and urged that steps be taken to enhance the comparability of financial statements prepared by publicly traded companies. On 13 June 2000, the Commission published a Communication: 'EU Financial Reporting Strategy: the way forward' in which it was proposed that all publicly traded Community companies prepare their consolidated financial statements in accordance with one single set of accounting standards, namely International Accounting Standards (IAS), at the latest by 2005.

4.2 The adoption of the IAS regulation

On 8 June 2002, The Council of the European Union adopted an 'IAS Regulation'[24] requiring listed companies, including banks and insurance companies, to prepare their consolidated accounts in accordance with International Accounting Standards (IAS) from 2005 onwards. Member States could defer application until 2007 for those companies that were listed both in the EU and elsewhere and that currently used US GAAP (or other GAAP) as their primary basis of accounting, as well as for companies that had only publicly traded debt securities. The goal of the Regulation was to eliminate barriers to cross-border trading in securities by ensuring that company accounts throughout the EU were reliable, transparent, and comparable. The Regulation had the force of law without requiring transposition into national legislation. However, 'to ensure appropriate political oversight', the Regulation established a new EU mechanism to 'assess IASs to give them legal endorsement' before they can be used in Europe. Member States had the option of extending the requirements of the Regulation to unlisted companies and to the production of individual accounts. The Recital #3 acknowledged that harmonization on the sole basis of the Accounting Directives had failed and was not a viable solution going forward:

> Council Directive 78/660/EEC of 25 July 1978 on the annual accounts of certain types of companies, Council Directive 83/349/EEC of 13 June 1983 on consolidated accounts, Council Directive 86/635/EEC of 8 December 1986 on the annual accounts and consolidated accounts of banks and other financial institutions and Council Directive 91/674/EEC on the annual accounts and consolidated accounts of insurance companies are also addressed to publicly traded Community companies. The reporting requirements set out in these Directives cannot ensure the high level of transparency and comparability of financial reporting from all publicly traded Community companies which is a necessary condition for building an integrated capital market which operates effectively, smoothly and efficiently. It is therefore necessary to supplement the legal framework applicable to publicly traded companies.

The Recital #2 to the Regulation explained clearly the goal of the European Union to work towards worldwide standards, not solely to adopt common EU standards:

> In order to contribute to a better functioning of the internal market, publicly traded companies must be required to apply a single set of high quality international accounting standards for the preparation of their consolidated financial statements. Furthermore, it is important that the financial reporting standards applied by Community companies participating in financial markets are accepted internationally and are truly global standards. This implies an increasing convergence of accounting standards currently used internationally with the ultimate objective of achieving a single set of global accounting standards.

Because the Regulation resulted in accounting standards being given the force of law, it was necessary to clearly identify those standards. Hence, Article 2 of the Regulation stipulates that:

> For the purpose of this Regulation, 'international accounting standards' shall mean International Accounting Standards (IAS), International Financial Reporting Standards (IFRS) and related interpretations (SIC-IFRIC interpretations), subsequent amendments to those standards and related interpretations, future standards and related interpretations issued or adopted by the International Accounting Standards Board (IASB).

This article clearly established the legitimacy of the newly established IASB as the organism that would publish the standards to be followed by European listed companies. However, as the IFRS Foundation which hosts the IASB is a private entity without official legitimacy, Europe found it necessary to give a legal endorsement to the standards proposed by IASB and established the following criteria and procedure:

> Article 3 – Adoption and use of international accounting standards

1. In accordance with the procedure laid down in Article 6(2), the Commission shall decide on the applicability within the Community of international accounting standards.
2. The international accounting standards can only be adopted if:
   - they are not contrary to the principle set out in Article 2(3) of Directive 78/660/EEC and in Article 16(3) of Directive 83/349/EEC and are conducive to the European public good; and,
   - they meet the criteria of understandability, relevance, reliability and comparability required of the financial information needed for making economic decisions and assessing the stewardship of management.
3. At the latest by 31 December 2002, the Commission shall, in accordance with the procedure laid down in Article 6(2), decide on the applicability within the Community of the international accounting standards in existence upon entry into force of this Regulation.
4. Adopted international accounting standards shall be published in full in each of the official languages of the Community, as a Commission regulation, in the Official Journal of the European Communities.

In a first endorsement Regulation[25] EC/1725/2003, the European Commission adopted 'en bloc' a series of IASs and SICs that were extant at 1 September 2002. IAS 32 and 39 were not part of the first set. A further Regulation 2238/2004 adopted all extant and updated standards except IAS 32 and 39. On 19 November 2004, just in time for the preparation of the first set of IFRS accounts, the Commission published a Regulation[26] 2086/2004 endorsing IAS 32 and 39 with an exceptional and of temporary nature exclusion (referred to in common language as 'the carve out') of certain paragraphs of IAS 39 relating to the Fair Value Option[27] and Hedge accounting. An explanatory memorandum[28] on 'the carve out' has been posted by the Commission.

4.3 The ARC

Article 6 – Committee Procedure

The Commission shall be assisted by an accounting regulatory committee hereinafter referred to as 'the Committee'. The Accounting Regulatory Committee (ARC) is composed of representatives from Member States and is chaired by the European Commission. The Committee has been set up by the Commission in accordance with the requirements contained in Article 6 of the IAS Regulation 1606/2002. The function of the Committee is a regulatory one and consists in providing an opinion on the Commission proposals to adopt an international accounting standard as envisaged under Article 3 of the Regulation. Members of the ARC are usually the representatives of the Members states' ministries competent for accounting matters. The decisions of the Commission and of the ARC are taken after consideration of 'endorsement advice' provided by the European Financial Reporting Advisory Committee (hereafter EFRAG).

4.4 The EFRAG

The IAS Regulation foresees an accounting technical committee which shall provide support and expertise to the Commission in the assessment of international accounting standards. The committee is called the European Financial Reporting Advisory Group (EFRAG). The function of the Committee is a regulatory one and consists in providing an opinion on the Commission proposals to adopt an international accounting standard as envisaged under Article 3 of the Regulation:

> EFRAG was set up in 2001 to assist the European Commission in the endorsement of International Financial Reporting Standards (IFRS), as issued by the International Accounting Standards Board (IASB) by providing advice on the technical quality of IFRS. EFRAG is a private sector body set up by the European organisations prominent in European capital markets, known collectively as the 'Member Organisations'.

In March 2006, EFRAG's role was formalized in a Working Arrangement with the European Commission, which states that 'EFRAG will provide advice to the Commission on all issues relating to the application of IFRS in the EU.' EFRAG is funded by the Member body organizations which pay subscriptions on a half-yearly basis and by voluntary contributions. In addition, EFRAG receives since 2010 financial support from the European Union - DG Internal Market and Services. EFRAG operates through a Technical Expert Group (EFRAG TEG),which makes its decisions independently of the EFRAG Supervisory Board and all other interests. The 12 voting members of EFRAG TEG were selected from throughout Europe and come from a variety of backgrounds. The chairmen of the French, German, Italian and UK Standard Setters are non-voting members of EFRAG TEG. Representatives of the European Commission and ESMA attend EFRAG TEG meetings as observers. EFRAG's role is both proactive and reactive. In particular it:

- provides advice to the European Commission on the endorsement of new or amended IFRSs and IFRS interpretations;
- comments on proposed IFRSs and IFRS interpretations, IASB discussion papers and other consultative documents;
- attends various IASB Working Group meetings as observers;
- maintains regular contacts with the IASB through meetings with its chairman. IASB Board members and senior staff participate in each EFRAG TEG meeting;
- works closely with European National Standard Setters (NSS) on various activities designed to encourage debate in Europe on accounting matters, in order to develop European views on issues of importance and enhance the quality of Europe's input to the IASB;
- meets quarterly with the European National Standard Setters (NSS) to exchange views;
- meets quarterly with European User representatives in the EFRAG User Panel; and
- participates in the World Standard Setters meetings (organized by the IASB).

The members of EFRAG TEG are appointed by the EFRAG Supervisory Board. The EFRAG Supervisory Board looks primarily to the qualifications of the EFRAG TEG candidates in terms of knowledge and experience and endeavours to ensure a broad geographical balance, together with experience from preparers, the accounting profession, users and academics.

4.5 Endorsement status as of 31 March 2012

EFRAG maintains on its web site an up to date report[29] on the endorsement status of IFRS and IFRIC's applicable in the EU.

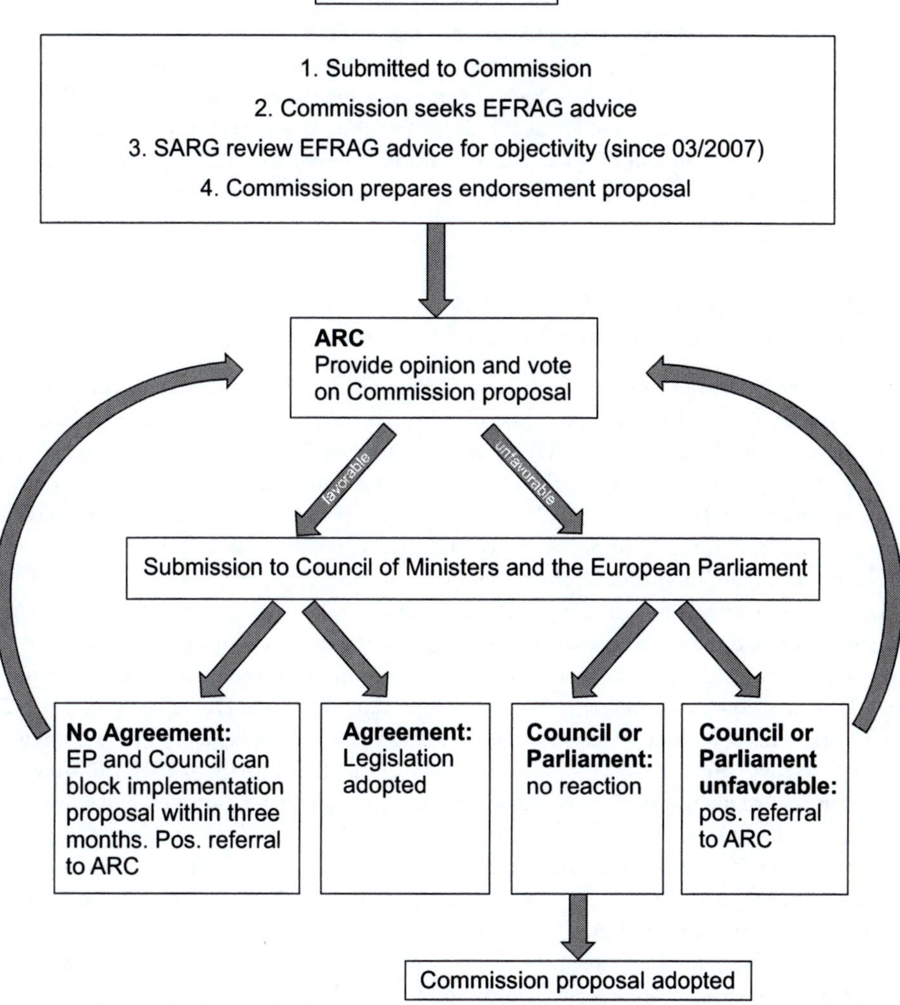

ARC (Accounting Regulatory Committee): Advisory body composed of representatives of the Member State and representatives of the Commission. It approves implementing measures by qualified majority under the so-called Comitology procedure.

Comitology: When implementing powers are given to the Commission, it must act in conjunction with committee(s) of national civil servants (here ARC) who has the power to block the Commission and refer the matter to the Council.

Comitology reform: Prior to the reform the EP had no right to block implementing measures – only the comitology committee(s) could do so, and if they did, the proposal was referred to the Council alone.

Figure 18.3 The EU endorsement mechanism

The report contains an overview per issued standard and interpretation, listing the date of the endorsement date and the date the endorsed standard/interpretation was published in the Official Journal of the European Union. The report further provides an overview of standards and interpretations pending endorsement and the dates EFRAG is expected to issue its advice, and of the corresponding ARC voting. Except for IAS 39 which was the subject of a partial 'carve out' of its provisions relating to hedge accounting and the fair value option, all IFRS and IFRIC which are currently in effect at the date of writing this Chapter have been endorsed by the Commission. The IAS 39 carve out is said to be 'temporary' and subsequently, the fair value option carve out was resolved through Commission Regulation[30] (EC) No 1864/2005 of 15 November 2005.

4.6 Mutual recognition of GAAP: EU' s decisions regarding the equivalence of accounting standards followed in certain ('third country') jurisdictions

According to the Prospectus and Transparency Directives, financial statements presented by issuers from outside the EU should be prepared in accordance with IFRS or equivalent accounting standards. Article 23(4) of (Transparency) Directive 2004/109/EC requires the Commission to set up a mechanism for the determination of the equivalence of the information required under this Directive. The Commission is required to adopt measures to establish general equivalence criteria regarding accounting standards relevant to issuers of more than one country. Article 23(4) of Directive 2004/109/EC also requires the Commission to take decisions in relation to the equivalence of accounting standards used by third country issuers, and enables the Commission to allow the use of third country accounting standards during an appropriate transitional period. Given the close interconnection of the information required under Directive 2004/109/EC with the information required under Directive 2003/71/EC, it is appropriate that the same criteria for determination of equivalence apply in the framework of both Directives. Accordingly, Commission Regulation (EC) No 1569/2007 laid down the conditions for acceptance of third country accounting standards for a limited period expiring on 31 December 2011:

In December 2008 the Commission adopted a Decision and a Regulation,[31] which identified as equivalent to IFRS the US GAAP and Japanese GAAP, and accepted financial statements from companies using GAAP of China, Canada, India and South Korea within the EU on a temporary basis, until no later than 31 December 2011. Since 1 January 2009 listed companies can report using IFRS (as adopted by the EU) in the aforementioned countries, while companies from these countries listed in the EU can report using their national accounting standards.[32]

The Commission evaluated the usefulness and functioning of the equivalence mechanism and concluded that it should be extended for a period of 3 years until 31 December 2014. Since the period for which the Commission had put in place conditions for granting equivalence to the Generally Accepted Accounting Principles (GAAP) of third countries expired on 31 December 2011, this Regulation should apply from 1 January 2012. This is necessary in order to provide legal certainty to issuers from the relevant third countries listed in the Union and avoid the risk that they might have to reconcile their financial statements with International Financial Reporting Standards (IFRS). The provision of retroactivity thus alleviates any potential additional burden on the issuers concerned.[33]

5. The situation regarding the issuers of securities on US capital markets

5.1 Overall policy of the US Securities and Exchange Commission (SEC)

The SEC has taken a number of steps to explore the use of International Financial Reporting Standards (IFRS) in the United States. This includes allowing foreign private issuers in the US to use IFRS in their filings with the SEC without preparing reconciliation to US GAAP and considering the use of IFRS by US issuers. The SEC also engages in dialogue with international counterparts regarding emerging accounting issues and interpretations through its membership in IOSCO and dialogue with the Committee of European Securities Regulators (CESR), now replaced by ESMA (see below Section 5.2). The SEC has been a strong supporter as well of the International Accounting Standards Board (IASB), the standard setting body that promulgates IFRS, including through the SEC's membership in the IASCF Monitoring Board.

The SEC actively supports the efforts made by IASB and FASB to converge their accounting standards. According to a press release[34] issued in December 2009 in reaction to the publication by the two standard setters of an updated Memorandum of Understanding:

> Today, the Financial Accounting Standards Board (FASB) and the International Accounting Standards Board (IASB) issued a statement reaffirming the Boards' commitment to improving International Financial Reporting Standards (IFRS) and U.S. Generally Accepted Accounting Principles (US GAAP). In the statement the IASB and the FASB described their plans to strengthen their efforts for completing the major projects in their Memorandum of Understanding (MoU) by 2011. The publication of this statement is intended to provide an understanding of the progress that is being made by the Boards on these projects and to address public concerns regarding the potential of the two Boards to reach different conclusions in the major projects in the MoU. The respective oversight bodies of the IASB and the FASB also issued a statement fully supporting the efforts of the IASB and the FASB in reaching improved and converged global accounting standards.

5.2 The SEC's 2007 decision to allow foreign private issuers to report under IFRS without reconciliation to US GAAP

Noting that convergence efforts between IASB and FASB had reduced the number of differences between the two accounting frameworks, and responding to mounting pressure from Europe for a mutual recognition of applicable standards in relation to the admission of foreign issuers on their respective markets, the US Securities and Exchange Commission adopted at the end of 2007 a rule[35] that allows Foreign Private Issuers to present their financial statements in accordance with IFRS published by the IASB:

> The Commission is adopting rules to accept from foreign private issuers in their filings with the Commission financial statements prepared in accordance with International Financial Reporting Standards ('IFRS') as issued by the International Accounting Standards Board ('IASB') without reconciliation to generally accepted accounting principles ('GAAP') as used in the United States. To implement this, we are adopting amendments to Form 20-F, conforming changes to Regulation S-X, and conforming amendments to other regulations, forms and rules under the Securities Act and the Securities Exchange

> Act. Current requirements regarding the reconciliation to U.S. GAAP do not change for a foreign private issuer that files its financial statements with the Commission using a basis of accounting other than IFRS as issued by the IASB. The effective date is March 4, 2008.

It should be noted that in the last sentence, the SEC makes it clear that financial statements which do not fully conform to the IFRSs as issued by the IASB (for instance, where reference is made to IFRS as modified by jurisdiction X, or subject to a 'carve out' of certain IFRS provisions) will not benefit from this rule. EU issuers have therefore to assert compliance with (full) IFRS and cannot make use of the 'carve out' decided by the European Commission when it endorsed IAS 39. This also makes it very important that the EU endorsement process does not create undue delays as compared to the effective dates decided by IASB for its standards.

5.3 *Towards allowing or requiring the use of IFRS for US domestic issuers?*

In 2008, the SEC published[36] a 'Roadmap for the potential use of financial statements prepared in accordance with IFRS by US issuers':

> The Securities and Exchange Commission ('Commission') is proposing a Roadmap for the potential use of financial statements prepared in accordance with International Financial Reporting Standards ('IFRS') as issued by the International Accounting Standards Board by U.S. issuers for purposes of their filings with the Commission. This Roadmap sets forth several milestones that, if achieved, could lead to the required use of IFRS by U.S. issuers in 2014 if the Commission believes it to be in the public interest and for the protection of investors. This Roadmap also includes discussion of various areas of consideration for market participants related to the eventual use of IFRS in the United States. As part of the Roadmap, the Commission is proposing amendments to various regulations, rules and forms that would permit early use of IFRS by a limited number of U.S. issuers where this would enhance the comparability of financial information to investors. Only an issuer whose industry uses IFRS as the basis of financial reporting more than any other set of standards would be eligible to elect to use IFRS, beginning with filings in 2010.

However, as of the date of writing this chapter of the book, no decision for the implementation of the Roadmap has yet been announced. The staff of the Office of the Chief Accountant has prepared several reports on the subject.

The SEC had indicated it would make a decision on incorporation of international financial reporting standards in 2011. Then, on 5 December, James Kroeker, the agency's chief accountant, said SEC staff needed 'a measure of a few additional months time' to issue a final report. At the same time, staff accountants are devising an approach for commissioners to weigh as they studied the issue of IFRS's future in the United States. At the time, Kroeker said, 'I can't give you a precise schedule, but what I can tell you is we will do so carefully and thoughtfully, being guided by an ideal that produces the maximum benefit for the investing public and the capital markets.' The issue has the potential to be politically sensitive. The US Congress may choose to hold hearings on IFRSs and time is running out for the SEC to consider the IFRS question in advance of the upcoming presidential election in November 2012. The European Commission has expressed some frustration at the lack of decision by the SEC. In a speech pronounced[37] in February 2011, Mr Jonathan Faull, Director General of Internal Market Directorate, at the occasion of a conference on accounting and auditing, said:

> But now, it is not only about European companies: the need for a common language is a global one. The G20 called for convergence in accounting standards. And the Commission wants to work further with the IASB to support that commitment. In particular, we look forward to the US SEC's forthcoming decision on the use of IFRS, due in 2011. From a wider perspective, this is an essential element of global reform. Why? Because if accounting standards are different, then capital requirements become different too. But in any case, whatever the US decides to do about IFRS, differences between US accounting and IFRS will narrow this year, thanks to the ongoing convergence project between the two sets of standards.
>
> Convergence represents a massive challenge but it should not be at the expense of quality, which should remain the primary driver of the IASB's work. It is essential that the standard setter responds fully to the concerns that have been expressed by stakeholders. If a few more months are required to develop high quality solutions, then let's make use of the revised deadline set by the G-20 (December 2011)! I am of the firm opinion that this would not put the broader convergence agenda at risk.
>
> Looking at the longer term, convergence is not an end in itself. It is only a means to facilitate the adoption of a single set of globally-accepted accounting standards, in line with G-20 recommendations. And of course, this is not just about the US. The purpose is to have as many jurisdictions as possible on board.

5.4 Convergence efforts between IASB and FASB and improvements to the accounting standards are encouraged by the European Commission, the SEC and by the G20 political leaders

A common set of high quality global standards has been a priority of both the IASB and the FASB and the objective of having IFRS accepted globally is a key element of the IFRS Foundation's mission statement: 'to develop a single set of high quality, understandable, enforceable and globally accepted international financial reporting standards (IFRSs) through its standard-setting body, the IASB'. In September 2002 the IASB and the FASB agreed to work together, in consultation with other national and regional bodies, to remove the differences between international standards and US GAAP. This decision was embodied in a Memorandum of Understanding (MoU) between the boards known as the Norwalk Agreement. The boards' commitment was further strengthened in 2006 when the IASB and FASB set specific milestones to be reached by 2008 ('A roadmap for convergence 2006–2008'):

A Roadmap for Convergence Between IFRSs and US GAAP 2006–2008: Memorandum of Understanding between the FASB and the IASB - 27 February 2006.

> At their meetings in April and October 2005, the FASB and the IASB reaffirmed their commitment to the convergence of US generally accepted accounting principles (US GAAP) and International Financial Reporting Standards (IFRS). A common set of high quality global standards remains the long-term strategic priority of both the FASB and the IASB.
>
> The FASB and the IASB recognise the relevance of the roadmap for the removal of the need for the reconciliation requirement for non-US companies that use IFRSs and are registered in the United States. It has been noted that the removal of this reconciliation

requirement would depend on, among other things, the effective implementation of IFRSs in financial statements across companies and jurisdictions, and measurable progress in addressing priority issues on the IASB-FASB convergence programme. Therefore, the ability to meet the objective set out by the roadmap depends upon the efforts and actions of many parties—including companies, auditors, investors, standard setters and regulators.

The FASB and the IASB recognise that their contribution to achieving the objective regarding reconciliation requirements is continued and measurable progress on the FASB-IASB convergence programme. Both boards have affirmed their commitment to making such progress. Recent discussions by the FASB and the IASB regarding their approach to the convergence programme indicated agreement on the following guidelines:

- Convergence of accounting standards can best be achieved through the development of high quality, common standards over time.
- Trying to eliminate differences between two standards that are in need of significant improvement is not the best use of the FASB's and the IASB's resources—instead, a new common standard should be developed that improves the financial information reported to investors.
- Serving the needs of investors means that the boards should seek to converge by replacing weaker standards with stronger standards.[38]

In 2008 the two boards issued an update to the MoU, which identified a series of priorities and milestones, emphasising the goal of joint projects to produce common, principle-based standards. The updated plan set up the objectives for the period 2008–11. At the end of 2011, although significant progress has been achieved on several joint projects, a number of important ones are still being deliberated by the two Boards (Financial Instruments, Lease Contracts, Revenue Recognition, Insurance Contracts).

Response to the Recommendations of the G20 leaders

As part of the action plan adopted in response to the financial crisis that erupted in 2007, the Group of 20 Leaders (G20) called for standard-setters to 're-double' their efforts to complete convergence in global accounting standards. On 2 April 2009, the G20 published a report[39] (G20, 2009) assessing the progress against each of the 47 actions set out in the Washington Action Plan that formed part of their commitment to reform the financial sector. The progress report included a range of reforms to be undertaken by regulators, credit rating agencies and standard-setters. The text of the recommendation in relation to accounting standard is as follows:

> We have agreed that the accounting standard setters should improve standards for the valuation of financial instruments based on their liquidity and investors' holding horizons, while reaffirming the framework of fair value accounting.
>
> We also welcome the FSF recommendations on pro-cyclicality that address accounting issues. We have agreed that accounting standard setters should take action by the end of 2009 to:

- reduce the complexity of accounting standards for financial instruments;
- strengthen accounting recognition of loan-loss provisions by incorporating a broader range of credit information;

- improve accounting standards for provisioning, off-balance sheet exposures and valuation uncertainty;
- achieve clarity and consistency in the application of valuation standards internationally, working with supervisors;
- make significant progress towards a single set of high quality global accounting standards; and,
- within the framework of the independent accounting standard setting process, improve involvement of stakeholders, including prudential regulators and emerging markets, through the IASB's constitutional review.

Following this request, in November 2009 the IASB and the FASB published a progress report describing an intensification of their work programme, including the hosting of monthly joint board meetings and to provide quarterly updates on their progress on convergence projects.

At subsequent summits in Pittsburgh (2009), Toronto (2010), Seoul (2010) and Cannes (2011) the G20 leaders reaffirmed their support for a single set of global accounting standards and for the completion of convergence of international and US accounting standards in pursuit of that objective. Furthermore, the G20 leaders called on the IASB to further enhance cooperation with stakeholders, with particular emphasis on support for emerging economies and within the context of their independent standard-setting framework.

The IASB publishes at regular intervals a report detailing the status of its standard-setting efforts in response to the G20 recommendation. In April 2012 the IASB and FASB published a joint progress report for the Financial Stability Board Plenary on Accounting Convergence,[40] in which they describe the progress made on financial instruments, including a joint expected loss impairment ('provisioning') approach and a more converged approach to classification and measurement.

6. Organizing consistent application and enforcement of accounting standards

6.1 The European Commission's policies on consistent interpretation and enforcement

The short lived EU roundtable on consistent implementation of IFRS

From the very early days of the transition to IFRS, the European Commission and CESR (the forerunner of ESMA) were concerned that the full benefits of adopting IFRS would be reaped only if there was a consistent application and enforcement of the standards, and that a system where the standards are principles-based and include only a limited amount of detailed guidance was not yet successfully tested. The Commission relied on CESR regarding the enforcement and encouraged the publication of the Standards on Enforcement and the establishment of a coordination mechanism (see below). However it also felt it necessary to provide a forum where certain interpretation issues could be discussed and resolved ahead of the publication of financial statements. There was also a perception that IFRIC was not sufficiently responsive to the questions put to it. The Commission organized a series of roundtable meetings which were attended by the accounting firms, representatives from CESR and from IFRIC. After a couple of years, this was discontinued as preparers and the accountants indicated there was no evidence of a real need.

Recent evolutions of the role of IFRIC under the new IFRS Foundation strategy

In February 2012, the Trustees of the IFRS Foundation, the oversight body of the IASB, concluded their review of the strategy of the IFRS Foundation. The review was initiated at the end of 2010 as the IFRS Foundation was entering its second decade of existence and was a result of the IFRS Foundation's second Constitution Review that was completed in early 2010. The Trustees' strategy review sought to articulate a clear strategy and vision for the organization by considering the mission, governance, standard-setting process and financing of the IFRS Foundation. The report asserts that the success of IFRSs (and the objective of global standards) requires consistency and faithfulness in the application of IFRSs. The Trustees reached the following conclusions:

> In pursuing its mission, the IFRS Foundation has a vested interest in helping to ensure the consistent application of IFRSs internationally. The Foundation should pursue that objective in the following ways:
>
> - The IASB, as the standard-setter, should issue standards that are clear, understandable and enforceable. The IASB will provide guidance on its standards that is consistent with a principle-based approach to standard-setting.
> - Application guidance and examples should be provided when it is necessary to understand and implement the principles in a consistent manner.
> - The IASB will work with a network of securities regulators, audit regulators, standard-setters, regional bodies involved with accounting standard-setting, accounting bodies and other stakeholders to identify where divergence in practice occurs across borders.
> - Where divergence in practice could be resolved through an improvement in the standard or an Interpretation, the IASB or the IFRS Interpretations Committee will act accordingly.
> - The IFRS Foundation, through its education and content services, should undertake activities aimed at promoting consistent application.
> - The IASB, in partnership with relevant authorities, will identify jurisdictions where IFRSs are being modified and, in these circumstances, encourage transparent reporting of such divergences at the jurisdictional level.
> - The IFRS Foundation will seek the assistance of the relevant public authorities to achieve this objective.
>
> Among the tools available to the IFRS Foundation in its efforts to ensure consistent application are: the IFRS Interpretations Committee, to identify emerging areas of divergence across borders before they become entrenched practice, to refer issues to the IASB when standards require improvement, and to issue Interpretations within a principle-based environment. In the second decade, the Interpretations Committee will probably play a more active role, in close co-ordination with the IASB (IFRS Foundation, 2012a: A5).

Both the IASB and IFRIC are currently implementing the organizational changes necessary to give effect to those recommendations. On 2 May 2012, the Trustees of the IFRS Foundation published[41] recommendations on efficiency and effectiveness of the IFRS Interpretation Committee, with the key objective of the Committee being equipped with 'a broader range of tools', 'enabled to be more responsive to requests for assistance' and having 'to deal with a wider range of requests'.

6.2 The EU authorities responsible for enforcement: from FESCO to ESMA

6.2.1 FESCO

Cooperation between authorities responsible for financial markets in the EU began rather informally in the late 1990s through a discussion forum: the FESCO (Forum of European Securities Commissions). The press release issued by the French COB[42] on 9 December 1997 reads:

> The implementation of the European Directives in the financial field, and the forthcoming introduction of the Euro, imply an increasing integration of financial activities in Europe.
>
> Considering that investor protection, that efficiency, integrity and transparency of markets and that the overall safety of the financial system are fundamental to achieving sound and stable financial markets, 17of the statutory Securities Commissions of the Member States of the European Economic Area (EEA),during their meeting in Paris on December 8, 1997, have adopted a Charter creating the Forum of European Securities Commissions (FESCO).
>
> By doing so, the members of FESCO have expressed their resolution to adhere, both in principle and in practice, to the commitments stated in the Charter, and in particular:
>
> - to share their experience and work together to facilitate the fair and efficient realisation of the European Single Market in financial services;
> - to unite their efforts in order to develop common regulatory standards in respect of the supervision of financial activities or markets concerning aspects that are not harmonized by the existing European Directives and where a common approach is appropriate; and
> - to provide, to the extent permitted by law, the broadest possible mutual assistance and to strengthen cross-border cooperation so as to enhance market surveillance and effective enforcement against abuse.

In 2000, FESCO decided to focus on the harmonization of financial reporting in the context of the European plans to create a single financial market:

> FESCO has decided to create an expert group on Accounting, chaired by Henrik Bjerre Nielsen, Director General of the Finanstilsynet of Danemark. This group will explore institutional and substantial issues in relation to accounting standards, and in particular to the implementation and enforcement of IAS in the EEA. FESCO is taking up the challenge posed by the communication of the European Commission 'EU Financial Reporting Strategy: the way forward', which makes clear securities regulators must play an important role in the implementation and the consistent enforcement of IAS throughout the EEA (FESCO, 2000).[43]

6.2.2 CESR

A few years later, in response to the rapid developments of the European Commission's plans to implement its single financial market strategy, and following the recommendations of the Baron Lamfalussy Report,[44] the authorities decided to strengthen and make their cooperation arrangements more institutional. They established a Committee of European Securities Regulators to replace the Forum:

CESR was established as an independent committee of European securities regulators. All undertakings, standards, commitments and work agreed within the Forum of the European Securities Commissions (FESCO) will be taken over by CESR. The role of this Committee is to:

- Improve co-ordination among securities regulators;
- Act as an advisory group to assist the EU Commission, in particular in its preparation of draft implementing measures in the field of securities;
- Work to ensure more consistent and timely day to day implementation of community legislation in the member states.

The Committee was established under the terms of the European Commission's decision of 6 June 2001 (2001/1501/EC). It is one of the committees envisaged in the 'final report of the group of Wisemen on the regulation of European securities markets'. The report itself was endorsed by the Stockholm European Council Resolution. Each Member State of the European Union has one member on the Committee. The members are nominated by the Members States and are the Heads of the national public authorities competent in the field of securities. The Committee of European Securities Regulators met the first time, in Paris, on Tuesday 11 September 2001.

At about the same time, two other 'Level-3 committees' of the European Union foreseen in the 'Lamfalussy process' were created: the Committee of European Banking Supervisors (CEBS) and the Committee of European Insurance and Occupational Pensions Supervisors (CEIOPS).

6.2.3 A brief overview of the Lamfalussy process

The 'Lamfalussy process', named after Baron Alexandre Lamfalussy, is a four-level process that has been adopted in the EU for the development, implementation and enforcement of EU legislation regarding financial markets. It was first established in relation to the securities markets and later extended to cover banking, insurance and occupational pensions, and UCITS:

- At Level 1, the European Parliament and the Council adopt, following proposals from the Commission, legislative acts (Directives and Regulations) establishing core or essential principles. For instance, the EU Transparency Directive, the EU Regulations on Prospectus and on the use of IAS are Level 1 documents.
- At Level 2, the Commission, assisted by Committees in accordance with comitology procedures (for instance, the European Securities Committee or the Accounting Regulatory Committee) and advized at Level 3 by networks of national regulatory agencies, adopts technical measures to implement the Level 1 essential principles.
- Level 3 involves work on implementation by the networks (e.g, CESR, CEBS and CEIOPS), including the development of common approaches and dissemination of best practices through the issuance of standards, recommendations and other forms of guidance.
- Level 4 deals with compliance and enforcement of Level 1 and 2 principles and implementation texts.

The Lamfalussy Report had identified the following key priorities to be adopted and brought into effect at the latest by the end of 2003:

- a single prospectus for issuers, with a mandatory shelf registration system;

- modernization of admission to listing requirements and introduction of a clear distinction between admission to listing and trading;
- generalization of the home country principle (mutual recognition) for wholesale markets, including a clear definition of the professional investor;
- modernization and expansion of investment rules for investment funds and pension funds;
- adoption of International Accounting Standards; and
- a single passport for recognized stock markets (on the basis of the home country control principle).

6.2.4 CESRFin and EECS

As the adoption of the IFRS was decided by the European Union in 2002, CESR immediately identified the need to monitor the change over from the national GAAP being used so far to the new accounting framework. There were concerns that, absent a coordinated and orderly transition, the change in accounting standards could generate reporting errors, disrupt investors' analyses of financial data, and create severe market confusion. Also, the Regulation 1606/2002 called in particular for CESR to have a role in developing standards for enforcement. Recital n. 16 of the regulation says:

> A proper and rigorous enforcement regime is key to underpinning investors' confidence in financial markets. Member States, by virtue of Article 10 of the Treaty, are required to take appropriate measures to ensure compliance with international accounting standards. The Commission intends to liaise with Member States, notably through the Committee of European Securities Regulators (CESR), to develop a common approach to enforcement.

On this basis, CESR established a permanent working committee CESRFin tasked with the monitoring of the transition to IFRS and developing a harmonized enforcement regime. CESRFin's Work Plan, which was approved by CESR in January 2002, includes the development of principles, guidelines and standards in the areas of:

- definition of enforcement;
- selection techniques;
- powers to be attributed to the enforcers; and
- cross-border listings and offerings.

The standards on enforcement

In March 2003, CESR published[45] the first Standard on Financial Information, which defines the purpose of enforcement, the instruments and documents to which it applies, the required characteristics of enforcement authorities, and the methods of enforcement. The 21 principles contained in this Standard #1 are still in force today, insofar as they have been adopted without change by ESMA, the successor to CESR.

In April 2004, CESR released its Standard #2 on the coordination of enforcement of financial information.[46] According to the press release:

> The standards adopted will contribute to the creation within Europe of robust and consistent enforcement of the internationally recognised set of accounting standards (as published

by the International Accounting Standards Board and endorsed by the European Commission) to be implemented by 2005. This will therefore deliver greater consistency of accounting treatment across Europe and will ensure a level playing field.

The key principles introduced by Standard # 2 include:

- discussion of enforcement decisions and experiences within a formalized structure which will involve CESR Members and delegated authorities that are non-securities regulators, for example, stock exchanges, or national review panels ('European Enforcers Co-ordination Sessions' – EECS).
- the principle that all supervisors should take into account existing decisions taken by EU National Enforcers.
- additionally, CESR proposes that where practicable within constraints of time and confidentiality, discussions with other EU National Enforcers should take place before significant decisions are taken.
- the development of a database as a practical reference tool which sets out decisions taken by EU National Enforcers, to provide a record of previous decisions reached in particular cases. The database of enforcement decisions will set out the principles upon which decisions have been taken by EU National Enforcers.

The mechanism of the enforcement data base and the criteria for the publication of enforcement decisions will be described further down.

6.2.5 Organizing an orderly transition from national GAAP to reporting under IFRS, so as to limit disruptions to investors

Regarding the transition from national accounting standards to IFRS, CESR issued in December 2003 a 'Recommendation[47] for additional guidance regarding the transition to IFRS'. This Recommendation contained several proposals whereby European listed Companies can be encouraged to provide markets with appropriate and useful information during the transition phase from local accounting standards to International Financial Reporting Standards (IFRS). Those recommendations relate primarily to:

- what type of information could usefully be published before the year of transition in relation with the changeover to the IFRS framework;
- the accounting framework to be used by issuers when interim financial information is published during the financial year beginning on or after 1 January 2005; and
- how to achieve comparability of information published for the year 2005 with preceding periods.

The context of this Recommendation was explained by CESR as follows:

> In view of the unusual importance of this complete change in accounting principles and its potential impacts on financial markets, CESR believes that useful guidance should be provided by its Members regarding the financial information that has to be published by European listed companies during the transition phase (starting at the date of adoption of the IAS Regulation) in order to:
>
> - contribute to the successful implementation of this process;

- foster the presentation of comparable information among companies during the transition phase; and
- promote a framework such that the information published is relevant and as understandable as possible by investors.

> Indeed, it is probable that, anticipating the importance of the event represented by the mandatory application of IAS/IFRS as from 1 January 2005, many investors and financial analysts will be impatient to assess the real impact of the transition for listed companies. Around the turning point, accounting information will often be analysed in terms of its forthcoming significance under IAS/IFRS (CESR, 2003b: §3).

The Recommendation addressed the annual and interim financial statements that would be published during period from 2003 to the end of 2005, during which national accounting standards would remain applicable.

> The change towards IAS/IFRS implies a complex process that could usefully be accompanied by a particular effort of financial communication in order to prepare gradually the market to assess its impact on the consolidated financial statements. CESR has identified four different milestones in the transition process that coincide with the publication of the 2003 annual financial statements, 2004 annual financial statements, 2005 interim financial statements and 2005 annual financial statements (CESR, 2003b: §11).

It should be noted that, as CESR had no direct regulatory power regarding the application of European legislation, it could only encourage its member organizations to act in a coordinated way. This is acknowledged in the text of the Recommendation:

> The present document is clearly a recommendation from CESR Members to themselves to encourage listed companies to adopt the proposed disclosure guidelines.
>
> Although each national regulator could decide to go beyond and require full or partial compliance with this guidance, CESR believes that a recommendation is sufficient at this stage in order to meet two objectives. The first objective is to keep the distinction between standards provided by EU regulations and directives in the area of financial reporting (notably through endorsement of IASB's standards) and additional guidance provided by CESR Members. The second objective is that the recommendation remains at the level of principles whose primary aim is to foster listed companies to adopt proper communication policies during the transition process with sufficient flexibility and not to create detailed reporting rules, in terms of timing and content of such reporting (CESR, 2003b: §6 and §7).

There is sufficient evidence that this approach was efficient as practically all CESR members issued their own guidance or regulations applicable to the issuers under their authority, based on the Recommendation.

6.2.6 ESMA

The European Securities and Markets Authority was established on 1 January 2011 to succeed CESR by the EU Regulation 1095/2010.[48] The decision gave full effect to the conclusions of the Lamfalussy report mentioned above and to the further conclusions of a High-Level Group chaired by Mr Jacques de Larosière. The High-Level Group recommended that the supervisory framework be strengthened to reduce the risk and severity of future financial crises. It recommended reforms to the structure of supervision of the financial sector in the Union. The group also concluded that a European System of Financial Supervisors should be created, comprising three European Supervisory Authorities, one for the banking sector, one for the securities sector and one for the insurance and occupational pensions sector and recommended the creation of a European Systemic Risk Council.

As a matter of fact, a European Banking Authority (EBA) and a European Insurance and Occupational Pensions Authority (EIOPA) were established at the same time as ESMA to replace respectively CEBS and CEIOPS. The first Recital to the 1095/2010 Regulation states that:

> The financial crisis in 2007 and 2008 exposed important shortcomings in financial supervision, both in particular cases and in relation to the financial system as a whole. Nationally based supervisory models have lagged behind financial globalisation and the integrated and interconnected reality of European financial markets, in which many financial institutions operate across borders. The crisis exposed shortcomings in the areas of cooperation, coordination, consistent application of Union law and trust between national supervisors.

ESMA has been given a greater role in Level 2 in drafting what can be considered as subordinate acts (known as delegated acts and implementing acts). Delegated acts are concerned more with the substantive content of the legislative requirement, for example setting out what authorization information firms must provide to competent authorities, whilst implementing acts are similar to executive measures giving effect to the substantive requirements, this might include for example, standard forms, templates and procedures for communicating information or processes between competent authorities.

At Level 3, ESMA will develop guidelines and recommendations with a view to establishing consistent, efficient and effective supervisory practices within the European System of Financial Supervision, and to ensure the common, uniform and consistent application of Union Law. The guidelines and recommendations are addressed to competent authorities or financial market participants. Whilst not legally binding, these have been strengthened under ESMA and competent authorities must now make every effort to comply and must explain if they do not intend to comply. Financial market participants can also be required to report publicly whether they comply. ESMA will also take other steps under Level 3 to ensure supervisory convergence.

At Level 4, a fast track procedure has been introduced by the Regulation establishing ESMA. On this basis, ESMA now has a new role. At the request of a national competent authority, the European Parliament, Council, Commission or the Stakeholder Group, ESMA can be requested to launch an enquiry and can issue a recommendation addressed to the national authority, within two months of launching its investigation. ESMA will also be able to launch investigations on its own initiative. The Commission will also be able to follow its usual procedures for referring a case against the Member State to the Court of Justice.

ESMA has organized itself around a number of working committees. One of them is of particular relevance to the area of financial reporting. The Corporate Reporting Standing Committee conducts all ESMA's work on issues related to accounting, audit, periodic reporting and storage of regulated information. In particular, it:

- pro-actively monitors and influences regulatory developments in the area of accounting and auditing, including an active monitoring of the EU endorsement process of international standards and the work of relevant EU accounting and/or auditing Committees;

- coordinates the activities of National Enforcers from the European Economic Area relating to the enforcement of compliance with IFRS. Notably this includes:
  - Analysis and discussion of individual enforcement decisions under IFRS and emerging financial reporting issues under IFRS.
  - Identifying issues which are not covered by financial reporting standards or which may be affected by conflicting interpretations for referral to standard-setting or interpretative bodies such as the IASB and IFRIC.
  - Facilitating the exchange of views and sharing of experiences on methods for supervising the financial information of companies offering publicly securities and/or having these securities listed on an EU regulated market.
- pro-actively monitors and influences developments relating to periodic financial reporting under the Transparency Directive; and
- establishes and maintains appropriate relationships with securities regulators from major capital markets outside Europe, to foster operational cooperation between EU and non-EU regulators on the competences in the remit of the Standing Committee.

An example of ESMA's activities regarding the consistent application of IFRS, and of its interaction with IASB, can be found in the Public Statement[49] on Sovereign Debt in IFRS financial statements, issued on 25 November 2011 following letters exchanged between the Chairmen of IASB and ESMA. It should also be noted here that ESMA has been given a role that CESR did not have: ESMA is exclusively responsible for the registration and supervision of Credit Rating Agencies in the European Union. In addition, ESMA also carries out policy work to prepare future legislation, such as regulatory technical standards, and guidelines. This work is undertaken through the CRA technical committee, which has representatives from all the national competent authorities.

6.2.7 Publication by the European Enforcers Coordination Sessions (EECS) of selected enforcement decisions

EECS is a forum which has been working under the oversight of CESR (now ESMA) and brings together all EU National Enforcers of financial information. The enforcers meet to exchange views and discuss experiences of enforcement of IFRS. A key function of EECS is the analysis and discussion of decisions taken by independent EU National Enforcers in respect of financial statements published by issuers with securities traded on a regulated market and who prepare their financial statements in accordance with IFRS. The purpose of this is to increase convergence amongst enforcers' activities across Europe. ESMA regularly publishes extracts from the EECS database of enforcement decisions contributing to provide greater transparency for market participants on application of standards that they consider useful. A selection of enforcement decisions published by ESMA, as well as periodic reports on the enforcement activities at the level of the European Economic Area, can be found on its web site.[50] The report on enforcement activities for 2010 says:

> As a result of IFRS enforcement activities in 2010, around 20 per cent of the approximately 700 actions taken in Europe have been subject to coordination at EECS level. The accounting issues giving rise to actions arose in all areas covered under IFRS, and most frequently related to: recognition, measurement and disclosures of financial instruments, application of new requirements for operating segments, disclosure on impairment of non-financial

assets, measurement and presentation of non-current assets held for sale and discontinued operations or aspects related to share-based payments. A range of topics has also been discussed with representatives of the IFRS Interpretations Committee (IFRS IC), as part of the regular feedback EECS is providing to the IFRS IC (ESMA, 2011a).

6.3 Was the transition from national GAAP to IFRS successful?

A report[51] for the European Commission was published in October 2007 by the ICAEW: 'EU Implementation of IFRS and the Fair Value Directive', whose objectives were defined as follows:

> The objectives of the study of EU implementation of IFRS and the Fair Value Directive are to provide the European Commission with:
>
> - a general analysis of the first year of application of IFRS in the EU so that DG Internal Market has the necessary information to carry out an evaluation of the functioning of the IAS Regulation and to feed into discussions in the Accounting Regulatory Committee on how the IAS Regulation has worked in practice; and
> - information on the application of the modernised Accounting Directives, especially provisions related to fair value accounting in the Fourth Company Law Directive 78/660/EEC as amended by the Fair Value Directive so that DG Internal Market has the necessary information to carry out a review of these provisions (ICAEW, 2007: 5).

The key findings regarding the transition to IFRS were the following:

> The IAS Regulation has been effective in achieving the core objective of all publicly traded entities preparing consolidated financial statements in accordance with IFRS-EU, subject to the deferral of implementation in some countries to 2007 for entities with only debt securities admitted to trading or those entities listed on a non-EU market and using internationally accepted standards.

The roundtable discussions and interviews highlighted the fact that the journey from national GAAP to IFRS had varied enormously in different jurisdictions. At one extreme, in some countries IFRS had been used widely by large companies for many years, and for those companies at least, the transition was a fairly low key affair. In other countries, there was no experience of IFRS application and national GAAP bore no resemblance to international standards, resulting in tremendous challenges for all parties involved in the financial reporting process. The quality of financial reporting under national GAAP was acknowledged to have varied, and it was mentioned that SEC registrants were better equipped than others to make the transition. It was also apparent that the level of economic development and governance environments found in each jurisdiction had a major bearing on the process. In short the concept of a single transition to IFRS in the EU 2005 was shown to be of limited usefulness, even in the narrow context of publicly traded companies.

Against this background, the message from the roundtables was broadly consistent, and substantially confirmed the findings of the on-line survey. In particular, IFRS implementation had been challenging, but successful, as evidenced by a lack of material problems uncovered with the 2005 numbers during the process of preparing financial information for 2006 and the absence of any general loss of confidence in financial reporting. It was reported that larger companies especially had prepared early, and had devoted considerable resources to educating and training their boards, staff and investors. The contribution of the IASB to this process, in making necessary improvements to IFRS in time for 2005 application, was referred to.

It was also emphasised by several participants that the experience of smaller quoted companies was often very different from larger companies. Resources available to manage the transition and to deal with ongoing changes were far more limited, preparation tended to be undertaken at a later stage, and it was much less likely that the company or their auditors had prior experience of IFRS. Nonetheless, it was pointed out that there was little evidence of problems being identified with initial IFRS numbers in the second year of reporting under the IAS Regulation (ICAEW, 2007).

With regards to the role of regulators in the process of transition to IFRS, the ICAEW noted that:

> European regulators, along with other stakeholder groups, play a key role in ensuring that IFRS are applied with a degree of consistency appropriate in the context of principles based accounting standards. Our discussions with some securities regulators and our reviews of reports and correspondence confirm our view that the consolidated financial statements of Sample 1 companies generally comply with IFRS-EU, IFRS or both. They also confirm that there are issues which require further attention by companies, including disclosures regarding accounting policies and key judgements made by management, but that none of these issues are sufficiently major to undermine the level of compliance with IFRS-EU or IFRS (ICAEW, 2007).

Another report was commissioned from Ineum Consulting and published[52] in December 2008. It concluded that the overall quality of IFRS financial statements had improved in 2006 in comparison with 2005. However, the application of IFRS by small and medium-sized listed companies posed specific problems and the choice of presentation options for the format of the financial statements remained influenced by national accounting cultures. Overall, disclosures had improved but there remained room for improvement of disclosures on judgments and estimates. The communication of additional non-GAAP performance measures was not prevalent and 84 per cent of companies commented their net IFRS results in their management report, thus contradicting a view expressed by some that IFRS measures are not widely used by management.

7. Financial reporting standards in the EU for entities traded on non-regulated securities markets and for non–listed entities

It is important to note that the IAS Regulation applies in a mandatory way only to issuers whose financial instruments are listed on a regulated market, a notion which differs from that of an organized trading facility. The scope of the Regulation is as follows:

- mandatory for preparation of the consolidated financial statements as determined under the 7th Directive;
- if, at the balance sheet date, the securities of the entity are admitted to trading on a regulated market of any Member State within the meaning of Article 1(13) of Council Directive 93/22/EEC of 10 May 1993 on investment services in the securities field.

The Directive on Investment Services (ISD), which was later on replaced by the MIFID Directive (see above), provides criteria for a regulated market:

> it shall function regularly, be characterized by the fact that regulations issued by the competent authority define the conditions for the operations of and access to that market, and it requires compliance with all the reporting and transparency requirements laid down pursuant to articles 20 and 21 of the ISD.

The ISD requires each Member State to draw a list of those markets that fulfil the above conditions. As a result, each competent authority in cooperation with the stock market enterprises decides the regulations which apply to each domestic market and classifies the markets as either regulated or unregulated vis-à-vis the ISD. In the case of NYSE-Euronext, it operates Euronext Securities Markets in Amsterdam, Brussels, Lisbon, London and Paris via its five Euronext Market Undertakings (market operators). These Euronext Securities Markets are Regulated Markets within the meaning of the MIFID. NYSE-Euronext also operates Alternext markets in Paris, Amsterdam and Brussels, which under the scope of article 4(1)(15) of the MIFID are 'organized multilateral trading facilities'. The harmonized 'Alternext Markets Rule Book'[53] prescribes that the financial statements of the issuer admitted on one of the markets shall be prepared, consolidated where applicable, in accordance with IFRS (if allowed by its National Regulations) or with the accounting standards applicable in the country of its registered office. So, there is an IFRS option but no requirement to follow IFRS.

In addition, Paris and Brussels operate 'free markets' (marche libre and delisted securities market) which are also non-regulated multilateral trading facilities. Their functioning is governed by 'organization memoranda'[54] which indicate that the accounting requirements of the entities admitted to trading are 'those determined by their legal form', i.e. by the national accounting requirements applicable to any legal entity.

The IAS Regulation also contains a series of Member States options to extend the use of IFRS beyond the mandatory application to the consolidated financial statements of entities listed on a regulated market. Those options[55] are:

- to require or permit the application of IFRS in preparing individual (parent company) accounts of those entities required to follow IFRS for the preparation of the consolidated accounts;
- to require or permit the application of IFRS in the preparation of consolidated accounts by entities not listed on a regulated market; and
- to require or permit the application of IFRS in preparing individual (parent company) accounts of the entities not listed on a regulated market.

A study on the application of Member States options regarding the use of IFRS is available on the European Commission's website.[56] A broad conclusion to be drawn from the survey could be that the application of IFRS beyond the mandatory requirement is usually permitted for consolidated accounts but still limited for non listed companies, with a majority (18 out of 27) of Member States allowing an alignment of the accounting standards for annual and consolidated accounts of the entities listed on a regulated market, and a vast majority (25 out of 27) permitting IFRS to be used in lieu of the national GAAP for the preparation of consolidated accounts of non listed companies. For those Member States (11 out of 27) who are reluctant to extend the use of IFRS to annual accounts of non listed companies, an explanation often given is the strong linkage between the profit basis for income tax calculations and the profit or loss determined according to national GAAP.

8. Conclusion

On the basis of this factual review of the evolution of policies and regulatory authorities since 1995, it is in my opinion clear that the successful globalization of IFRS was the result of the combined actions of IOSCO and the European Commission. In the key year of 2000, both the EU and IOSCO took the decisions that put international accounting standards on the launching ramp. The 2002–5 transition period coincided with the introduction of a coherent framework of legislation for the admission to trading of securities and the organization of the supporting enforcement mechanisms. The new IFRS Foundation was created to replace the IASCF following a model borrowed from the one that existed in the USA (the technical Board FASB being overseen by the Financial Accounting Foundation) and this structure, which was improved continuously and endorsed by the public authorities, gave the IASB the credibility necessary to be recognized as a worldwide standard-setter.

The use of IFRS has now reached the critical mass. Nearly a half of the companies in the Global 500 league published by *Fortune* magazine now report under IFRS. The large investors get used to utilize IFRS financial data and there is no evidence that their needs are not served adequately. The continued support of the G20 leaders to the convergence of financial regulations make it likely that at some point in the future, the jurisdictions who are still hesitant will take a positive decision to move beyond the mutual recognition of standards and fully adopt IFRS. It may well take a number of years, but as we say in my home country '*Paris ne s'est pas fait en un jour.*'

Please note that this chapter was written in April 2012 and that further developments have not been taken into account.

Notes

1 Speech by Professor Otmar Issing, 12 September 2000, Ottobeuren. www.ecb.int/press/key/date/2000/html/sp000912_2.en.html (accessed 30 September 2012)
2 http://eur-lex.europa.eu/LexUriServ/LexUriServ.do?uri=OJ:L:2010:327:0001:0012:EN:PDF
3 http://eur-lex.europa.eu/LexUriServ/LexUriServ.do?uri=OJ:L:2004:390:0038:0057:EN:PDF
4 http://eur-lex.europa.eu/LexUriServ/LexUriServ.do?uri=CELEX:01983L0349-20090716:EN:NOT
5 http://eur-lex.europa.eu/LexUriServ/LexUriServ.do?uri=CONSLEG:1983L0349:20090716:EN:PDF
6 http://eur-lex.europa.eu/LexUriServ/LexUriServ.do?uri=CELEX:32003L0124:EN:NOT
7 http://eur-lex.europa.eu/LexUriServ/LexUriServ.do?uri=OJ:L:2004:145:0001:0044:EN:PDF
8 www.world-exchanges.org/files/statistics/excel/Notes per cent20on per cent20the per cent20Proceedings per cent20- per cent202007 per cent20Annual per cent20Meeting.pdf
9 www.iosco.org/library/statements/pdf/statements-19.pdf
10 www.iosco.org/library/pubdocs/pdf/IOSCOPD2.pdf
11 www.iosco.org/library/pubdocs/pdf/IOSCOPD109.pdf
12 Effective 1 January 2012, Mr Prada was appointed Chairman of the Trustees of the IFRS Foundation.
13 www.iosco.org/news/pdf/IOSCONEWS5-English.pdf
14 www.iosco.org/library/pubdocs/pdf/IOSCOPD133.pdf
15 www.iosco.org/library/pubdocs/pdf/IOSCOPD134.pdf
16 http://pcaobus.org/Pages/default.aspx
17 www.h3c.org/
18 www.iosco.org/library/statements/pdf/statements-7.pdf
19 www.iosco.org/monitoring_board/pdf/Monitoring_Board_Charter.pdf
20 The chair of the Technical Committee and the chair of the Emerging Markets Committee.

21 COM 95 (508) EN.
22 http://ec.europa.eu/internal_market/finances/docs/actionplan/index/action_en.pdf
23 The Financial Services Policy Group (FSPG) was established in 1998 by the Commission to update rules governing financial trade among Member States; it consisted of representatives of the EU finance ministers.
24 http://eur-lex.europa.eu/LexUriServ/LexUriServ.do?uri=OJ:L:2002:243:0001:0004:EN:PDF
25 http://eur-lex.europa.eu/LexUriServ/LexUriServ.do?uri=CELEX:32003R1725:EN:HTML
26 http://eur-lex.europa.eu/LexUriServ/LexUriServ.do?uri=OJ:L:2004:363:0001:0065:EN:PDF
27 The exclusion of the parts of IAS 39 dealing with the Fair Value Option (FVO) was rescinded on 15 November 2005 by Regulation 1864/2005 following IASB's 2004 decision to propose restrictions to, and additional related disclosures, on the use of the FVO and subsequent discussions with the European central bank and the Basel Committee of banking supervisors.
28 http://ec.europa.eu/internal_market/accounting/docs/ias/explanatory-memo-2004-09-ias39-proposal_en.pdf
29 www.efrag.org/Front/c1-306/Endorsement-Status-Report_EN.aspx
30 http://eur-lex.europa.eu/LexUriServ/LexUriServ.do?uri=CELEX:32005R1864:EN:NOT
31 http://eur-lex.europa.eu/LexUriServ/LexUriServ.do?uri=OJ:L:2012:103:0011:0012:EN:PDF
32 http://ec.europa.eu/internal_market/accounting/third_countries/index_en.htm
33 http://eur-lex.europa.eu/LexUriServ/LexUriServ.do?uri=OJ:L:2012:103:0011:0012:EN:PDF
34 www.sec.gov/news/press/2009/2009-237.htm
35 www.sec.gov/rules/final/2007/33-8879.pdf
36 www.sec.gov/rules/proposed/2008/33-8982.pdf
37 http://ec.europa.eu/commission_2010-2014/barnier/docs/jf__speech09022011_en.pdf
38 www.fasb.org/news/memorandum.pdf
39 www.g20.utoronto.ca/2009/2009ifi.html
40 www.financialstabilityboard.org/publications/r_120420d.pdf
41 www.ifrs.org/Alerts/PressRelease/IC+review+May+2012.htm
42 www.amf-france.org/documents/general/83_1.pdf
43 www.esma.europa.eu/system/files/00_094b.pdf
44 http://ec.europa.eu/internal_market/securities/docs/lamfalussy/wisemen/final-report-wise-men_en.pdf
45 www.esma.europa.eu/system/files/03_073.pdf
46 www.esma.europa.eu/system/files/04_157.pdf
47 www.esma.europa.eu/system/files/03_323e.pdf
48 www.esma.europa.eu/system/files/Reg_716_2010_ESMA.pdf
49 www.esma.europa.eu/system/files/2011_397.pdf
50 www.esma.europa.eu/page/IFRS-Enforcement
51 http://ec.europa.eu/internal_market/accounting/docs/studies/2007-eu_implementation_of_ifrs.pdf
52 http://ec.europa.eu/internal_market/accounting/docs/studies/2009-report_en.pdf
53 https://europeanequities.nyx.com/sites/europeanequities.nyx.com/files/nyse_alternext_rules_en_1501210.pdf
54 https://europeanequities.nyx.com/sites/europeanequities.nyx.com/files/Organisation_memorandum_-_consolidated_version_effective_on_March_29_2010.pdf
55 Additionally, Member States were permitted to defer to 2007 the mandatory application of IFRS by entities whose debt securities only were admitted on a regulated market.
56 http://ec.europa.eu/internal_market/accounting/docs/ias/ias-use-of-options_en.pdf

Bibliography

Communications, directives and regulations issued by the European Commission

Communication of the Commission (1995) *Accounting Harmonisation: A New Strategy Vis-à-vis International Harmonisation*, COM95 (508) EN Available at http://ec.europa.eu/internal_market/accounting/docs/com-95-508/com-95-508_en.pdf (accessed 1 October 2012)

Communication of the Commission (1999) *Financial Services: Implementing The Framework for Financial Markets: Action Plan,* COM(1999)232. Available at http://ec.europa.eu/internal_market/finances/docs/actionplan/index/action_en.pdf (accessed 1 October 2012)

Communication of the Commission (2004) *Explanatory Memorandum of the Commission Services on the Proposal for a Regulation Adopting IAS 39.* 24 September 2004. Available at http://ec.europa.eu/internal_market/accounting/docs/ias/explanatory-memo-2004-09-ias39-proposal_en.pdf (accessed 1 October 2012)

Council Directive 93/22/EEC on Investment Services in the Securities Field. 10 May 1993. Available at http://eur-lex.europa.eu/LexUriServ/LexUriServ.do?uri=CONSLEG:1993L0022:19980926:EN:PDF (accessed 2 October 2012)

Directive 2003/6/EC of the European Parliament and the Council of the European Union, of 28 January 2003. Available at http://eur-lex.europa.eu/LexUriServ/LexUriServ.do?uri=CELEX:32003L0006:EN:NOT (accessed 1 October 2012)

Directive 2003/124/EC of the European Parliament and the Council of the European Union, of 22 December 2003. Available at http://eur-lex.europa.eu/LexUriServ/LexUriServ.do?uri=CELEX:32003L0124:EN:NOT (accessed 1 October 2012)

Directive 2004/39/EC of the European Parliament and the Council of the European Union, of 21 April 2004. Available at http://eur-lex.europa.eu/LexUriServ/LexUriServ.do?uri=OJ:L:2004:145:0001:0001:EN:PDF (accessed 1 October 2012)

Directive2004/109/EC of the European Parliament and the Council of the European Union, of 15 December 2004. Available at http://eur-lex.europa.eu/LexUriServ/LexUriServ.do?uri=OJ:L:2004:390:0038:0057:EN:PDF (accessed on 1 October 2012)

Directive 2006/43/EC of the European Parliament and the Council of the European Union, of 17 May 2006. Available at http://eur-lex.europa.eu/LexUriServ/LexUriServ.do?uri=CONSLEG:2006L0043:20080321:EN:PDF (accessed 1 October 2012)

Directive 2010/73/EU of the European Parliament and the Council of the European Union, 24 November 2010. Available at http://eur-lex.europa.eu/LexUriServ/LexUriServ.do?uri=OJ:L:2010:327:0001:0012:EN:PDF (accessed 1 October 2012)

Fourth Directive of the Council of the European Communities 78/660/EEC. Available at http://eur-lex.europa.eu/LexUriServ/LexUriServ.do?uri=CELEX:31978L0660:EN:NOT (accessed on 1 October 2012)

Seventh Directive of the Council of the European Communities 83/349/EEC. Available at http://eur-lex.europa.eu/LexUriServ/LexUriServ.do?uri=CELEX:31983L0349:EN:NOT (accessed on 1 October 2012)

Regulation (EC) No 1606/2002 of the European Parliament and the Council of the European Union, 19 July 2002. Available at http://eur-lex.europa.eu/LexUriServ/LexUriServ.do?uri=OJ:L:2002:243:0001:0004:EN:PDF (accessed 1 October 2012)

Regulation (EC) No 1095/2010 of the European Parliament and the Council of the European Union, 24 November 2010. Available at www.esma.europa.eu/system/files/Reg_716_2010_ESMA.pdf (accessed 2 October 2012)

Commission Regulation (EC) No 1725/2003 of the European Parliament and the Council of the European Union, 29 September 2003. Available at http://eur-lex.europa.eu/LexUriServ/LexUriServ.do?uri=CELEX:32003R1725:EN:HTML (accessed 1 October 2012)

Commission Regulation (EC) No 2086/2004 of the European Parliament and the Council of the European Union, 19 November 2004. Available at http://eur-lex.europa.eu/LexUriServ/LexUriServ.do?uri=CELEX:32004R2086:EN:NOT (accessed 1 October 2012)

Commission Regulation (EC) No 1864/2005 of the European Parliament and the Council of the European Union, 15 November 2005. Available at http://eur-lex.europa.eu/LexUriServ/LexUriServ.do?uri=CELEX:32005R1864:EN:NOT (accessed 1 October 2012)

Commission Delegated Regulation (EC) No 310/2012 of the European Parliament and the Council of the European Union, 21 December 2011. Available at http://eur-lex.europa.eu/LexUriServ/LexUriServ.do?uri=OJ:L:2012:103:0011:0012:EN:PDF (accessed 1 October 2012)

IOSCO Reports and Statements

IOSCO (1989) 'International Equity Offers, Summary Report. International Organisation of Securities Commissions', September. Available at www.iosco.org/library/pubdocs/pdf/IOSCOPD2.pdf (accessed 30 September 2012)

IOSCO (1994) 'Report on Disclosure and Accounting' Report of the Technical Committee of IOSCO, October 1994. Available at www.iosco.org/library/pubdocs/pdf/IOSCOPD39.pdf

IOSCO (2000) 'IASC Standards Assessment Report. Report of the Technical Committee of the International Organisation of Securities Commissions, International Organisation of Securities Commissions', September. Available at www.iosco.org/library/pubdocs/pdf/IOSCOPD109.pdf (accessed 30 September 2012)

IOSCO (2002a) 'Principles of Auditor Independence and the Role of Corporate Governance in Monitoring an Auditor's Independence: A Statement of the Technical Committee of the International Organisation of Securities Commissions', October. Available at www.iosco.org/library/pubdocs/pdf/IOSCOPD133.pdf (accessed 1 October, 2012)

IOSCO (2002b) 'Principles for Auditor Oversight: A Statement of the Technical Committee of the International Organisation of Securities Commissions', October. Available at www.iosco.org/library/pubdocs/pdf/IOSCOPD134.pdf (accessed 1 October, 2012)

IOSCO (2007) 'Final Communiqué of the 27th Annual Conference of the International Organization of the Securities Commissions'. Available at www.iosco.org/news/pdf/IOSCONEWS5-English.pdf (accessed 1 October 2012)

IOSCO (2009a) 'Media Statement: IOSCO Statement on International Auditing Standards', 11 June. Available at www.iosco.org/library/statements/pdf/statements-7.pdf (accessed 1 October 2012)

IOSCO (2009b) 'Charter of the IASCF Monitoring Board'. Available at www.iosco.org/monitoring_board/pdf/Monitoring_Board_Charter.pdf (accessed 1 October 2012)

IOSCO (2011) 'Media Statement: Final Update 36th Annual Conference of the International Organization of the Securities Commissions'. Available at www.iosco.org/library/statements/pdf/statements-19.pdf (accessed 1 October 2012)

Other References

CESR (2003a) 'Standard No. 1 on Financial Information: Enforcement of Standards on Financial Information in Europe'. Paris: Committee of European Securities Regulators, March. Available at www.esma.europa.eu/system/files/03_073.pdf (accessed 2 October 2012)

CESR (2003b) 'European Regulation on the Application of IFRS in 2005: Recommendation for Additional Guidance Regarding the Transition to IFRS'. Paris: Committee of European Securities Regulators, December. Available at www.esma.europa.eu/system/files/03_323e.pdf (accessed 2 October 2012)

CESR (2004) 'Press Release: Co-ordinating Enforcement of Financial Information'. Paris: Committee of European Securities Regulators, 22 April. Available at www.esma.europa.eu/system/files/04_157.pdf (accessed 2 October 2012)

COB (1997) 'Press Release: The Creation of the Forum of European Securities Commissions (FESCO)'. Paris: Commission des opération de bourse, 9 December. Available at www.amf-france.org/documents/general/83_1.pdf (accessed 2 October 2012)

Committee of Wise Men (2001) 'Final Report of the Committee of Wise Men on the Regulation of European Securities Markets'. Brussels, 15 February. Mandated by the European Union's Ministers of Economic and Finance Ministers (ECOFIN) on 17 July 2000. Available at http://ec.europa.eu/internal_market/securities/docs/lamfalussy/wisemen/final-report-wise-men_en.pdf (accessed 2 October 2012)

ESMA (2011a) 'Activity Report on IFRS Enforcement in 2010'. European Securities and Markets Authority, 21 October. Available at www.esma.europa.eu/system/files/2011_355.pdf (accessed 2 October 2012)

ESMA (2011b) 'Public Statement: Sovereign Debt in IFRS Financial Statements. European Securities and Markets Authority', 25 November. Available at www.esma.europa.eu/system/files/2011_397.pdf (accessed 2 October 2012)

European Commission (2012) 'Results of a study on the implementation of the IAS Regulation (1606/2002) in the EU and EAA'. 7 February. Available at ec.europa.eu/internal_market/accounting/docs/ias/ias-use-of-options_en.pdf (accessed 2 October 2012)

FASB/IASB (2002) 'Memorandum of Understanding "The Norwalk Agreement"'. Available at www.fasb.org/news/memorandum.pdf (accessed 1 October 2012)

Faull, J. (2011) 'Financial Reporting and Auditing: A Time for Change?' Keynote address. Available at ec.europa.eu/commission_2010-2014/barnier/docs/jf__speech09022011_en.pdf (accessed 1 October 2012)

FESCO (2000) 'Press Release: FESCO Proposes New Common Regulatory Responses for the European Single Market for Financial Services'. Forum of European Securities Commissions, 25 September. Available at www.esma.europa.eu/system/files/00_094b.pdf (accessed 2 October 2000).

G20 (2009) 'Global Plan Annex: Declaration on Strengthening the Financial System'. 2 April. Available at www.g20.utoronto.ca/2009/2009ifi.html (accessed 1 October 2012)

IASB/FASB (2012) 'Joint Update Note from the IASB and FASB on Accounting Convergence'. Available at www.financialstabilityboard.org/publications/r_120420d.pdf (accessed 2 October 2012)

ICAEW (2007) *EU Implementation of IFRS and the Fair Value Directive: A Report for the European Commission*. London: Institute of Chartered Accountants in England and Wales, October. Available at http://ec.europa.eu/internal_market/accounting/docs/studies/2007-eu_implementation_of_ifrs.pdf (accessed 2 October 2012)

IFRS Foundation (2012a) 'IFRSs as the Global Standards: Setting a Strategy for the Next Decade', February. London: IFRS Foundation.

IFRS Foundation (2012b) 'Report on the Trustees' Review of Efficiency and Effectiveness of the IFRS Interpretations Committee', May. London: IFRS Foundation.

Ineum Consulting (2008) 'Evaluation of the Application of IFRS in the 2006 Financial Statements of EU Companies: Report to the European Commission'. December. Available at http://ec.europa.eu/internal_market/accounting/docs/studies/2009-report_en.pdf (accessed 2 October 2012)

Kirsch, R.J. (2006) *The International Standards Committee: A Political History*. London: Wolters Kluwers

NYSE Euronext (2010) 'Organisation Memorandum: Marché Libre and Delisted Securities Market'. 29 March. Available at https://europeanequities.nyx.com/sites/europeanequities.nyx.com/files/Organisation_memorandum_-_consolidated_version_effective_on_March_29_2010.pdf (accessed 2 October 2012)

NYSE Euronext (2012) 'Alternext Markets Rule Book'. Available at https://europeanequities.nyx.com/sites/europeanequities.nyx.com/files/nyse_alternext_rules_en_1501210.pdf (accessed 2 October 2012)

Securities and Exchange Commission (2007) 'Acceptance from Private Foreign Issuers of Financial Statements Prepared in Accordance With International Financial Reporting Standards Without Reconciliation to US GAAP'. Available at www.sec.gov/rules/final/2007/33-8879.pdf (accessed 1 October 2012)

Securities and Exchange Commission (2008) 'Roadmap for the Potential Use of Financial Statements Prepared in Accordance with International Financial Reporting Standards by US Issues'. Available at www.sec.gov/rules/proposed/2008/33-8982.pdf (accessed 1 October 2012)

Véron, N. (2007) 'The Global Accounting Experiment'. Bruegel Blueprint series, April. Available at http://aei.pitt.edu/8354/1/BP2_accounting.pdf (accessed 30 September, 2012)

WFE (2007) '2007 Annual Meeting: Notes on the Proceedings'. World Federation of Exchanges. Available at www.world-exchanges.org/files/statistics/excel/Notes%20on%20the%20Proceedings%20-%202007%20Annual%20Meeting.pdf (accessed 1 October 2012)

19

Auditors and International Financial Reporting

Kathryn Cearns

1. Introduction

The early to mid-nineteenth century saw the genesis of all the major accounting firms we know of today, including the 'Big 4' – Deloitte Touche Tomatsu (Deloitte), Ernst & Young (E&Y), KPMG and PricewaterhouseCoopers (PwC) – and many of the other international network firms. The histories of these firms are intertwined with the nascent development of the accounting profession in the UK (the ICAEW was established from its founding societies in 1880, for example), the USA and Canada and elsewhere, and their births and subsequent developments are startlingly similar in terms of where they started life, the type of men who founded them, what entrenched their establishment amongst a raft of similar small firms of accountants and their accelerated growth through acquisitions and mergers, particularly from the late 1960s. Before then (since 1856), UK law limited the number of partners in any general partnership to 20. Once this limitation was repealed in the Companies Act of 1967, the firms grew exponentially. In fact the extent to which the large firms grew through mergers and acquisitions was so great that it is almost impossible to fit the family tree of the antecedents of any one of the firms on one piece of paper.[1]

Without the internationalization of the auditing and accounting profession as reflected in the history of the large firms, the calls for international accounting and auditing standards would probably have been weaker and longer in coming, and certainly more difficult to achieve given the significant cost and time involved. For these firms, enormously successful in tracking the needs of their multinational clients, international standards that transcend national regulation are greatly to their advantage in terms of risk management, client service delivery and the establishment and maintenance of their brand and match their truly global coverage. The more fragmented voices of the financial statement user community – shareholders and their proxies, including analysts and fund managers, as well as creditors and their proxies, including credit rating agencies and bank lenders – would probably have got there in the end (not that the end has yet been reached, of course, although significant progress has been made), but it might have taken rather longer.

In addition, the firms have effectively acted as a cost diffuser and absorber as they have incurred substantial costs in dealing with both direct and indirect adoption of IFRS across the globe. As their clients moved to IFRS the costs have been passed on to them, but in a more efficient fashion than if each company had needed to undertake all the preparation itself. Tokar (2005) has written of the substantial efforts KPMG undertook in dealing with the increasing prevalence of IFRS, and these reflect similar work of the other large firms, but it is also interesting to note, as discussed further below, how the rise in IFRS has affected how the big firms operate in order to achieve consistency of application across the world.

2. The rise of the 'supra-national' audit firm networks

As noted above, the histories of the largest firms show great similarities in terms of timing of birth and growth, means of expansion and establishment of their brand. Although each of the Big 4 now operate using various different legal structures (which are in many cases still developing and change periodically due to regulatory and other impetuses) their overall structure is very similar in substance.

In the case of each of the Big 4 firms, their last merger may often have been their biggest but it was only the final one of many that preceded it. The following gives a potted history of some of the earliest origins of each of the Big 4 and a summary of their development. Not all the limbs of each firm are mentioned, but the following should be sufficient to give an overview.

2.1 A brief history

2.1.1 Deloitte[2]

The main founders of the firm as it currently stands were William Welch Deloitte and Sir George Touche (as well as Nobuzo Tohmatsu in Japan and Philip Ross in Canada).

William Welch Deloitte, born in 1818, opened his own offices in Basinghall Street in London in 1845. It was the creation of joint stock companies that offered the first real opportunity to establish the modern audit function, and Deloitte made his name in dealing with the major 'bubble' industry of the day, namely railways. He became auditor of the Great Western Railway and uncovered a fraud at the Great Northern Railway. He set up new accounting systems, both for railways and hotels. By the time of his retirement in 1897, from the firm that was by then Deloitte, Plender, Griffiths & Co, he was the oldest practising accountant and had been in business the longest. He was an early president of the ICAEW and his successor firms were also instrumental in establishing PwC. In 1952, Deloitte's firm in the United States merged with Haskins & Sells.

George (subsequently Sir George) Touche was born in Edinburgh in 1861 and apprenticed to A. T. Niven, Chartered Accountant of the same city. His move to London in 1883 was to the firm of Broads, Paterson & May where he apparently uncovered a fraud on his first ever assignment. Sir George made his early reputation through involvement with, and effectively helping to clean up, the investment trusts sector – so another 'bubble' sector was a driver for progress in the auditing profession. In 1889 he was appointed Secretary of the Industrial and General Trust. In these early days of investment trusts there was much poor practice. Britain in the late nineteenth century was the largest creditor nation, with capital flowing out all over the world. Investment trusts raised equity to invest in portfolios of investments, but also raised debt through debentures. The Barings Crisis in the 1890s badly damaged the sector, causing permanent reductions of capital due to losses. Sir George Touche helped to restore the sector to health, with others such as Robert Fleming.

Sir George founded his own firm, George A. Touche & Co., in 1899, and in 1900 Touche, Niven & Co was founded in the USA. There were further forays internationally, including Java and Buenos Aires, but the world wars interrupted the business of these outposts. More successfully, in 1911 George A. Touche & Co. opened in Canada, and subsequently expanded across the country.

It is worth noting in passing that the US firm was involved in one of the early substantial pieces of litigation relating to audit negligence, known as the Ultramares case, in the mid-1920s and early 1930s. This effectively established many important principles as applied to audit, including proximity and the establishment of a duty of care to third parties, upon which current audit negligence case law is based.[3]

In 1958 the Canadian firm of P. S. Ross & Sons, founded by Philip Ross in the mid-nineteenth century, merged with George A. Touche & Co. to become Ross, Touche & Co. in Canada and in 1960 the US, Canadian and UK firms merged and began trading under the same name of Touche, Ross, Bailey & Smart. In 1990 the firm merged with Spicer & Oppenheimer, and an international merger was effected, also in 1990, between Deloitte Haskins & Sells and Touche Ross to form Deloitte & Touche. Confusingly, the UK Deloitte firm and some others instead merged with Coopers & Lybrand to form Coopers & Lybrand Deloitte, which subsequently dropped 'Deloitte' and merged with Price Waterhouse to form PwC. In 2002 the UK practice of Arthur Andersen joined Deloitte following the collapse of Arthur Andersen (AA). In addition, AA's practices in Belgium, Brazil, Canada, Mexico, the Netherlands, Portugal and Spain also agreed to merge with Deloitte (most of the remainder of AA's practices going to E&Y as mentioned below).

2.1.2 Ernst & Young[4]

The mid-nineteenth century also saw the foundation of the main predecessor firms of Ernst & Young and perhaps the main names of note were Arthur Young and Alwin C. Ernst, although both these names are from the US branches of the organization.

Beginning first with the main UK branch, however, in 1849 Harding & Pullein was founded in England and joined by Frederick Whinney, who subsequently became a partner in 1859. The firm was subsequently renamed Whinney, Smith and Whinney.

Arthur Young was born in 1863 in Glasgow (yet another Scot at the forefront of the new profession), qualifying in law but moving on to an interest in finance. He moved to the USA to pursue an interest in accounting, starting his first firm, Stuart and Young, in Chicago in 1894. In 1906 Arthur and his brother Stanley founded Arthur Young & Company, which in 1924 allied itself with Broad Paterson & Co. in England. In 1944 the firm Clarkson Gordon & Company, which had expanded into management consulting, joined forces with Arthur Young & Co.

It is worth noting the origins of some of the other predecessor firms that began life as early as the 1820s and eventually, via mergers and changes of name, joined up with Arthur Young in the 1950s, 1960s and 1970s. Many of their founders and partners originated in Glasgow and Edinburgh and the names include James McClelland, Alexander Moore, James Haldane, Richard Brown, John Graham and Peter Rintoul – a remarkably strong element of the firm thus deriving from Scotland.

Alwin C. Ernst was born in 1881 and started work as a bookkeeper, then with his brother Theodore he formed Ernst & Ernst in Cleveland in 1903. The firm joined forces with Whinney, Smith & Whinney in 1924, again around the time that it became more obviously advantageous to have cross-Atlantic links to service clients expanding overseas.

Eventually in 1979 Ernst & Whinney was formed, creating a broadly Anglo-American firm, and in the same year Arthur Young's European offices joined several large local European firms which all became members of Arthur Young International. Finally in 1989 Arthur Young merged with Ernst & Whinney to create Ernst & Young (E&Y).

Although that was apparently the last big merger,[5] E&Y's size was also augmented in 2002 during the fallout from the failure of Arthur Andersen & Co. E&Y took over many of the AA practices internationally, although not those in the UK, China or the Netherlands. In addition, in 2010 E&Y acquired the Brazilian practice of Grant Thornton.

2.1.3 KPMG[6]

KPMG's antecedents appear to have come rather later to the field than those of the other big firms, but the firm made up for it by being one of the earliest to undertake a so-called 'mega merger'.

In 1870 William Barclay Peat formed William Barclay Peat & Co. in London (although predecessor firms in the names of Robert Fletcher & Co. and R. Mackay & Co. had existed since 1867). In 1877 accountancy firm Thomson McLintock opened an office in Glasgow and in 1911 William Barclay Peat & Co. and Marwick Mitchell & Co. merged to form Peat Marwick Mitchell & Co., later known as Peat Marwick.

Perhaps in contrast to the other firms, there was a strong continental flavour from practices that joined from mainland Europe, which in places had almost an equally long history as the UK and US firms. In 1917 Piet Klijnveld opened his accounting firm in Amsterdam, later merging with Kraayenhof to form Klynveld Kraayenhof & Co.

In 1979 Klynveld Kraayenhof & Co. (Netherlands), Thomson McLintock and Deutsche Treuhandgesellschaft (Germany) formed KMG (Klynveld Main Goerdeler) as a grouping of independent national practices to create a European-based international firm. Then in 1987 KMG and Peat Marwick joined forces in the first mega-merger of large accounting firms and formed a firm called KPMG in the US (and most of the rest of the world), but called Peat Marwick McLintock in the UK. By 1999 the firm was known as KPMG worldwide.

As already noted, in 1997 KPMG and E&Y announced a merger following that which had formed PwC. Lack of regulatory approval, as well as other reasons, later led the KPMG/E&Y tie-up to be abandoned.

2.1.4 PricewaterhouseCoopers[7]

Now the biggest professional services firm in the world by revenues, PwC's was the last 'mega merger' to be successfully effected, between Price Waterhouse and Coopers & Lybrand. Like the other firms discussed above, the two firms each had histories dating back to the nineteenth century.

On the Coopers & Lybrand side, in 1854 William Cooper founded an accountancy practice in London, which became Cooper Brothers seven years later when his three brothers joined. In 1898, Robert H. Montgomery, William M. Lybrand, Adam A. Ross Jr and his brother T. Edward Ross formed Lybrand, Ross Brothers and Montgomery in the USA.

In 1957 Cooper Brothers, Lybrand, Ross Bros & Montgomery and a Canadian firm McDonald, Currie and Co., agreed to adopt the name Coopers & Lybrand in international practice. In 1973 the three member firms in the UK, US and Canada changed their names to Coopers & Lybrand. In 1990 in certain countries including the UK Coopers & Lybrand merged with Deloitte Haskins & Sells to become Coopers & Lybrand Deloitte, in 1992 renamed Coopers & Lybrand.

On the Price Waterhouse side of things, Samuel Lowell Price founded an accountancy practice in London in 1849, going into partnership with William Hopkins Holyland and Edwin Waterhouse in 1865. Holyland left shortly after and the firm was known from 1874 as Price, Waterhouse & Co.

By the late nineteenth century, Price Waterhouse had gained significant recognition as an accounting firm. As a result of growing trade between the UK and the USA, Price Waterhouse opened an office in New York in 1890 and the American firm expanded quickly. The original British firm opened offices elsewhere in the UK and worldwide, each time establishing a separate partnership in each country. Thus the worldwide practice of PW was a federation of collaborating firms that had grown organically rather than being the result of an international merger.

PW and Arthur Andersen discussed a merger in 1989 but the negotiations failed mainly because of conflicts of interest such as Andersen's strong commercial links with IBM and PW's audit of the same. Finally, in 1998 Price Waterhouse merged with Coopers & Lybrand to form PwC. In 2002, the Hong Kong and China practices of Arthur Andersen joined PwC (most of AA joining E&Y as noted above).

2.2 Lessons from history

The history of the Big 4 – and the other major firms such as BDO, Grant Thornton and Baker Tilly – bear some remarkable similarities. The main founding firms usually had their birth in the UK and/or North America at roughly the same time, as global trade expanded rapidly across empires and commonwealths, hampered only temporarily it seems by intervening world wars. International expansion was needed to follow the clients and their money and links were often established early on, particularly between English-speaking, common law jurisdictions. Unlike the more ancient professions such as law or medicine, accountancy and audit practice, in its much more recent infancy, could transcend national regulation and boundaries using the universal language of finance – for them, national regulation came later. Within the UK, Scotland was at the forefront of the establishment of the accountancy profession:

> Stacey [*English Accountancy,* 1954] suggests that historically accountancy divides itself into three periods. First there is the period which covered the detailed and concise records of transactions and estates which existed and developed through Roman times to the Middle Ages. There is then the period of merchant capitalism which runs through to the industrial revolution and saw the introduction of double entry bookkeeping. Finally there is the period from the nineteenth century to the present time when the profession of accountancy emerged. This last period probably started in the second half of the century for England but ... it was a little earlier for Scotland (White, 2003).

The need for assurance and a better approach to accounting grew as joint stock companies began to be permitted by law during the nineteenth century and the position of creditors became, as a consequence, more precarious. But, in addition, wider pools of equity investors were not directly involved in the management of the business and demanded more and better information with some direct assurance. As we still find today, the case for accounting and audit – and the reform thereof – was frequently linked to major scandals when investors and creditors were unable to verify the accounts produced by 'asset bubble' companies such as railroads and investment trusts. The accountants who pioneered the practice of accounting and audit and founded major accounting firms were often responsible for cleaning up some of these scandals and instituting better practice:

> The development of a UK railway system coincided with the growth of factories and cities. The 1840s saw the beginning of 'railway mania' that some compare to the dotcom revolution at the end of the twentieth century. The development of the railway companies preceded the developments in company law and specific railway legislation was introduced imposing greater public controls on the larger railway companies. These included

> the requirements for audit and as one accountant at the time [Frederick Whinney, The Accountant, 2 July 1887] said, 'The rail mania of 1845 brought us a very great acquisition of business not only in audits, but also in winding-up of companies' (White, 2003).

As the accounting firms were developing in competition with each other, the founders wished to be seen as professionals who could work together for the public interest. The rise of the professional accountancy bodies was the result, leading to an enhanced status for those who might earlier have been dismissed as mere bookkeepers. The UK institutes in their current form developed in many cases from regional bodies. For example the ICAEW, which received its Royal Charter in 1880, was the result of a merger between predecessor societies in Liverpool, London, Sheffield and Manchester, as well as the Society of Accountants in England, but these had all been founded only in the 1870s. The American Institute of Public Certified Accountants was founded in 1887 and the Canadian Institute of Certified Accountants formally in 1902. As noted above, these were all preceded by the development of the profession in Scotland (arising probably from the different legal approaches to certain issues there), and the first Scottish accountants then emigrated to other parts of the world where they could grow their businesses:

> The interchange of ideas and experience amongst men pursuing the same techniques and concept of ethics was eventually bound to bring about closer co-operation. The Society of Accountants in Edinburgh was formed in 1853 and received a Royal Charter in 1854. The Institute of Accountants and Actuaries in Glasgow was formed in 1853 and received a Royal Charter in 1855. The Society of Accountants in Aberdeen was formed and incorporated by Royal Charter in 1867 (White, 2003).

The need to be in partnership and the inability to limit liability meant that firms had to be ingenious to grow nationally and internationally. Until restrictions were removed on the number of partners permitted in a general partnership, for example, alliances between separate firms could not lead to full merger, so different formats were used to achieve synergies and cooperative working.[8] The removal of the partner limit, as well as moves to deregulate financial services generally, led to a surge of growth from the late 1960s and early 1970s that has given us the huge firms we have today.

2.3 The current state of affairs

That brings us neatly to the current formation of the big firms. In contrast to the point made above about the power of a more recently developed profession to take paths to international cooperation not open to older professions, the hand of national regulation has weighed on the firms in certain ways such that it has usually been necessary to maintain a separate entity (whether partnership or corporate entity) in each jurisdiction of operation. This is particularly true of audit. Although anyone can call themselves an accountant, in most countries certain activities are regulated, including audit and insolvency practice, and where regulation is national there is a need to establish a nationally delineated firm to be regulated.

This has not been entirely to the detriment of the firms: liability leakage across a network is a major risk factor and this can be prevented more easily if liabilities can be isolated within national practices, restricting the risk of vicarious liabilities for the acts of other national practices within a network. In extremis, national practices can be abandoned and a new national practice established or taken over from another firm. For example, PwC's affiliated practice in Japan, ChuoAoyama Audit Corporation, was temporarily stripped of its licence to practice in 2006 following the collapse of cosmetics company Kanebo and action by the Japanese courts and the Financial Services Agency of Japan. This led to the establishment of a new firm there, PricewaterhouseCoopers Aarata, and the old firm was effectively abandoned. Similarly Grant Thornton International dropped its Italian practice after the discovery of the Parmalat fraud.

Range of practice areas

The other major development over the past half a century has been the growing scope and breadth of the activities undertaken by the large accounting firms, in particular into consulting services, ranging from major computing and business process advice to actuarial and surveying services. Regulators (and some clients) became nervous in the 1990s that the firms were providing such a wide range of services that there was a risk that the central function of audit, a key governance plank underpinning markets and built into both corporate and securities laws in highly regulated markets, would become a poor relation. Although the primary concern was direct conflicts of interest where many different services were provided to audit clients, there was particular concern that the independence of the auditor would be undermined by commercial pressures to keep clients happy.

Matters were somewhat brought to a head after the Enron scandal and the collapse of Arthur Andersen, as well as some of the other scandals that came out around the same time, including WorldCom, Adelphia and Tyco. The USA passed the Sarbanes–Oxley Act of 2002 ('SOX'), which sought to address some of the major weaknesses identified in corporate governance and which also introduced new standards for those auditing large publicly listed companies. This involved, inter alia, the establishment of a new Public Company Accounting Oversight Board to oversee the audit firms, including inspecting their work and with the ability to discipline them. SOX has been contentious for a number of reasons, mainly on the grounds that it introduced huge complexity, the cost of which is not justified by the benefits it introduced. Nevertheless, it has survived legal challenge[9] and other countries have introduced similar legislation. Title II of SOX covers auditor independence and, among other things, restricts the non-audit services, including consulting, that auditors can offer to their clients. There had been SEC rules before SOX, but the SOX rules were a step up in stringency.

As a consequence of the pressure which culminated in SOX (which was under discussion well before it was finally passed, so it had been signalled for some time), most of the big firms sold their consultancy practices or spun them off in the early 2000s; only Deloitte retained theirs (although Deloitte France spun off its consultancy practice as Ineum Consulting, now part of Kurt Salmon). These consultancies were to some extent focussed on implementing complex integrated hardware and software solutions for clients and were in competition with other businesses supplying the same services. As the opportunities to outsource ERP (enterprise resource planning) systems to clients increased, so did potential conflicts of interest with the audit side of the firm, as noted above, and problems arose in demonstrating audit independence. The questions were about perceptions of independence, not just independence in fact.

E&Y was the first mover, when in 2000 it sold its consulting business to Cap Gemini, the French IT consultancy group, forming Cap Gemini Ernst & Young, which was subsequently renamed Capgemini. The deal was for approximately $11bn of stock in the French business. In 2002, after various abortive attempts to sell or float its consultancy, PwC sold its consultancy business for approximately $3.9bn in cash and stocks to IBM. In 2001 KPMG divested its US consulting arm through an initial public offering of KPMG Consulting Inc (subsequently BearingPoint Inc, which filed for Chapter 11 bankruptcy protection in 2009 only to be purchased subsequently by Deloitte). The UK and Dutch KPMG consulting businesses were sold in 2002 to Atos Origin.

Contractual non-compete restrictions following divestment of their consulting businesses meant that the big audit firms could not venture back onto the same playing field as their former businesses. The firms were in any case apparently already moving into different areas of consulting and leaving, at least to some extent, the field of major IT infrastructure for other competitors. Even as the non-compete restrictions fell away, but probably in any case as a matter of choice, all the firms have moved into and expanded activities that might be labelled as 'consultancy' because they are not part of their core audit/assurance, insolvency or tax work. Some of these activities are useful adjuncts to audit work, for example the major firms have either developed or purchased actuarial practices, which means they have the necessary expertise to hand when dealing with major insurance or pension clients. Other types of business include property companies (Deloitte bought Drivas Jonas in the UK in 2010) and most recently the firms have been moving into the sustainability consulting field. SOX itself, somewhat ironically, provided significant opportunities for the large firms in helping clients to comply with the rules affecting companies, particularly on internal controls (section 404 of SOX)

Most of the firms also run recruitment and HR businesses, and offer risk management and governance services, thus delivering a very wide range of business services. This has not all been plain sailing: forays into some fields have proved rather less successful or come up against regulatory barriers, and the firms have sold or abandoned the businesses they bought or created. The most obvious example, at least in the UK, was the attempt to create associated law practices in the 1990s (although legal restrictions at the time meant that the law firms had to be owned and run by lawyers). The idea of a 'one stop shop' service at the very large end of the market, with the big audit firms supplying both financial and legal services, did not find much favour with clients, fell foul of regulatory moves to restrict non-audit services, and perhaps also underestimated the brand power of the large incumbent legal practices. The legal firms owned or allied to the big audit firms were gradually closed or sold off, for example, KLegal, the KPMG-associated legal practice, was closed in 2003 (and the firm also sold its Disputes Advisory Practice to FTI Consulting). Tite & Lewis moved from E&Y to merge with Lawrence Graham in 2004. Bucking the trend, however, PwC Legal LLP still exists. In addition, some business lines have proved problematic for regulatory and brand reasons, for example the aggressive sale of tax products has come under scrutiny: KPMG was the subject of a deferred prosecution agreement in the USA in 2005–8 after admitting criminal wrongdoing in creating fraudulent tax shelters to help wealthy clients avoid taxes.

In spite of the odd failure, however, what is striking is the range of business lines into which the large audit practices have moved, successfully combining a wide variety of types of professional service under the same powerful brand and creating synergies and risk management benefits for their audit and capital markets service lines. Regulators may have concerns about the impact on audit – and possibly other regulated activities – but as a business model it has proved extremely successful as clients have welcomed both the depth and breadth of service delivery.

In any case, in the last few years the firms have shifted the focus of their non-audit services to non-audit clients, in reaction to the increasing regulatory scrutiny of audit independence and deference to client concerns.[10] There are those who wish to see the firms provide even fewer non-audit services to clients, in order to ensure auditor independence, although these risk destabilizing capital market transactions where the auditors are usually the best placed to do financial due diligence in a way that is fairly well-aligned with their audit function. There are also those with continuing concerns about the range of activities the firms carry out, even if these are all directed at non-audit clients, and who therefore wish to see 'audit only' firms, as if some kind of functional purity would make audits better and safer. The reverse may be true, however, and proposals along these lines, particularly from the European Commission,[11] risk undermining the entire business model of the firms and hence undermining quality at the top end of the audit market.

Current legal and business structures

The current legal and business structures have to some extent evolved as a reaction to regulatory and litigation threats. As is often pointed out (rather accusingly), none of the big firms is one unified business in the way that corporate multinationals operate, by way of ownership and control; rather they each operate as a form of network of firms that voluntarily work together under the same name and branding. The criticism of this approach should perhaps be directed more at the national regulatory and statutory rules over audit firms, which often prevent forms of ownership of national firms that take power away from nationally registered auditors. While these structures allow some benefit to the firms in preventing liabilities leakage across different jurisdictions – vicarious liability is avoided because individual firms within networks cannot obligate each other – that position is constantly under threat, particularly in the USA where attempts are frequently made to draw in the worldwide practices as parties to national litigation (an argument advanced, for example, in the litigation against BDO over Banco Espiritu Santo). In spite of this, some of the firms have demonstrated a desire and willingness to become more integrated.

Deloitte's member firms are all members of a UK private company limited by guarantee, by which means they associate with each other while being separate legal entities regulated by their own national authorities. The network was previously organised through a Swiss Verein. E&Y use EY Global to set policies and practice, but with client work performed by the network firms. It is managed regionally as well, over the Americas, Asia, Japan and finally Europe, Middle East, India and Africa. KPMG operates its network through a Swiss co-operative, but there has also been some recent movement to regionalize from 2007 with the formation of KPMG Europe LLP (a UK limited liability partnership), of which many of the firm's major European practices are members, although they still retain their separate legal structures. PwC uses a UK limited company as its international umbrella vehicle with much the same function as that of the other firms. So although the specific legal vehicles may vary, the overall structures adopted by the large firms are very similar in substance.

In terms of business lines, there are similarities, but in the main the choice of where specific business lines are located in the overall structure may be a matter of history. PwC runs across three main business lines: assurance services, tax advisory and advisory (the latter encompassing most of the consulting businesses). KPMG similarly offers audit, tax and advisory, but with some differences as to what sits where within that structure. E&Y splits some areas out further under the headings of assurance services, tax services, advisory services and transaction advisory services. Deloitte arguably has a slightly different business line structure covering audit and enterprise risk services, consulting, financial advisory, tax and other services.

The range of activity across the firms is thus substantial and gives credence to the tendency for the firms to identify themselves as 'professional services' firms rather than audit or accountancy firms. Nevertheless, auditing and the assurance services most closely related to audit continue to underpin their brands. The ability of the firms to maintain those brands across the world is in no small part due to their internationalization of internal compliance manuals and standards. Their approach both to accounting and auditing has in turn and over time given great impetus to the external development of international standards.

3. Internationalization of auditing and accounting standards

The push to internationalize standards is familiar in a wide range of activity, some driven by absolute necessity – how flight control systems operate, for example – and others by market demand. In the case of accounting and auditing, the increase in global capital flows and growth of multinational companies are two of the factors that have driven the desire to harmonize. The role of the large audit firms in this process reflects those drivers.

3.1 IFAC and the forum of firms

The drive to internationalization outlined above moved to a new level as the accountancy profession started to react to the needs of supra-national audit firms which in turn were reacting to the needs of their multinational clients. The International Federation of Accountants (IFAC) was established in 1977 at the 11th World Congress of Accountants. It is a membership body of professional accountancy bodies and now has 167 members and associates in 127 countries and jurisdictions worldwide.[12] Box 19.1 shows IFAC's original 12-point programme.

Box 19.1
IFAC's original 12-point programme

The following 12-point work programme was established at the inaugural meetings of the IFAC Assembly and of the Council in Munich, Germany in October 1977. These 12 points guided IFAC committees and staff through the first five years of operation. Many elements of this work program are still relevant today.

Develop statements which serve as guidelines for international and auditing guidelines.

Establish the basic principles which should be included in the code of ethics of any member body of IFAC and to refine or elaborate on such principles as deemed appropriate.

Determine the requirements and develop programs for the professional education and training of accountants.

Collect, analyse, research and disseminate information on the management of public accounting practices to assist practitioners in more effectively conducting their practices.

Evaluate, develop and report on financial management and other management techniques and procedures.

Undertake other studies of value to accountants, such as a possible study on the legal liabilities of auditors.

Foster closer relationships with users of financial statements including preparers, trade unions, financial institutions, industry, governments and others.

Maintain good relations with regional organizations and explore the potential for establishing other regional organizations, as well as assisting in their organizations and development.

Establish regular communications among the members of IFAC and other interested organizations, principally through an IFAC Newsletter.

Organize and promote the exchange of technical information, educational materials and professional publications, and other literature emanating from member bodies.

Organize and conduct an international congress of accountants approximately every five years.

Seek to expand the membership of IFAC.

Source: www.ifac.org/about-ifac/organization-overview/history, accessed 30 May 2012.

In recognition of the importance of the major audit networks in supporting the development of international auditing standards, the Forum of Firms was formally established by IFAC in 2001. Although membership is open to any firm or network that puts itself forward and which meets the relevant criteria, and a network's suitability is effectively self-certified, this mechanism pulls together and binds the largest global firms into an association that requires adherence to international auditing and quality control standards. For IFAC, this mechanism cements the biggest audit firms into the profession at an international level, giving great advantages in terms of engagement in IFAC's work, including standard setting. The advantage to the member firms may be less obvious, yet undoubtedly it offers them a quality marque that gives a proto-regulatory reason for following international auditing (and quality control and ethics) standards which are beneficial to the firms, but which they would struggle to set themselves acting in concert due to a lack of perceived independence and, perhaps more recently, cartel concerns, and which might well otherwise be resisted by clients in less regulated jurisdictions.

It is notable that, although the Forum of Firms requires adherence to international auditing and quality control standards, as well as its Code of Ethics, its objective includes a reference to financial reporting more generally: 'The objective of the Forum is to promote consistent and high quality standards of financial reporting and auditing practices world-wide.'[13] Box 19.2 shows the IFAC Forum of Firms, membership requirements and obligations.

Box 19.2
IFAC Forum of Firms, membership requirements and obligations

Membership in the Forum is open to networks and firms of all sizes that conduct, or have an interest in conducting, transnational audits; promote the consistent application of high-quality audit practices and standards worldwide; support convergence of national audit standards with the International Standards on Auditing (ISAs); and commit to meeting the Forum's membership obligations.

The Forum's membership obligations require that members:

- maintain quality control standards in accordance with the International Standard on Quality Control (ISQC 1) issued by the IAASB in addition to relevant national quality control standards;
- conduct, to the extent not prohibited by national regulation, regular globally coordinated internal quality assurance reviews;
- have policies and methodologies for the conduct of transnational audits that are based, to the extent practicable, on the International Standards on Auditing (ISAs) issued by the IAASB;
- have policies and methodologies that conform to the IESBA Code of Ethics for Professional Accountants and national codes of ethics; and
- agree to submit to the Secretary of the Forum an annual report, in an approved format, indicating that it meets the membership obligations set forth above.

International networks of firms practising under the same name or whose member firms are otherwise closely identified with one another, such as through common elements in their name, will be expected to join as one organization.

Source: www.ifac.org/about-ifac/forum-firms, accessed 30 May 2012

What this has effectively done is to allow the large international audit networks both to support and take advantage of international auditing standards that otherwise would have no regulatory or legal basis because auditing standards have been until now usually set by national regulators or sometimes national professional bodies, where there are any national standards at all. The large audit networks will thus overlay local auditing standards or rules with those international standards to which they have signed up through IFAC's Forum of Firms. In jurisdictions where auditing standards are non-existent or relatively undeveloped, this raises the bar of audit quality and helps the firms maintain their brand. In places where the national standards are well developed and relatively sophisticated, they may be quite close to the international version or even go beyond them, but the overall commitment to high quality standards is maintained. Depending on the level of local regulatory enforcement of auditors, local or national rules will in theory trump an ISA when the two are in conflict. This is unlikely to be a problem in most jurisdictions, however, as it is rare for there to be an impediment to carrying out additional procedures.[14]

3.2 ISAs and their interaction with national rules and standards

The International Auditing and Assurance Standards Board (IAASB) was founded in March 1978. Formerly known as the International Auditing Practices Committee (IAPC), the IAPC's initial work focused on three areas: object and scope of audits of financial statements, engagement letters and general auditing guidelines. The IAPC's guidelines were subsequently reconfigured as International Standards on Auditing (ISAs) in 1991.

Following a comprehensive review of the IAPC, it was reconstituted in 2002 as the International Auditing and Assurance Standards Board (IAASB). Subsequent reforms followed in order to strengthen its standard-setting processes, and in 2004 the IAASB began what it called the Clarity Project, a comprehensive programme to enhance the ISAs. The aim of this programme was to a great extent to ensure the acceptability of the standards to regulatory enforcement agencies around the world, particularly in the USA. The International Organization of Securities Commisions (IOSCO) was influential in this debate,[15] as it has been on the improvements necessary to IFRS to make them acceptable to world stock markets and their regulators; the IASC duly followed the advice given to improve the relevant standards that were found wanting.[16] Box 19.3 shows the IAASB: Changes resulting from the Clarity Project.

The IAASB and IFAC recognised that the ISAs would never achieve widespread formal endorsement at national and regional levels unless the relevant audit and/or securities regulators believed them to be enforceable. This was in spite of the fact that, as already noted, ISAs were already effectively being used for major company audits throughout the world through the Forum of Firms agreement. Here the path of auditing and accounting standards has diverged: the IASB's standards had to be accepted by regulators in major capital markets countries to be used by publicly-quoted companies; whereas the IAASB standards could be imposed as an overarching layer of good practice over any standards at national level, with official endorsement coming after the event as ISAs gained in reputation and acceptance. On this basis, arguably, ISAs have an easier ride towards global adoption, but this also reflects the more contentious nature of accounting standards due to the wider number of stakeholders with vested interests. So far, in comparison to the IASB's situation, there have been very few calls for changing the governance over the IAASB, which while under the auspices of a Public Interest Oversight Board is nevertheless still housed in the organization, IFAC, whose members represent the auditing profession.

Box 19.3
IAASB: Changes resulting from the Clarity Project

Improvements arising from the Clarity Project broadly compromise the following:

identifying the auditor's overall objectives when conducting an audit in accordance with ISAs;

setting an objective in each ISA and establishing the auditor's obligation in relation to that objective;

clarifying the obligations imposed on auditors by the requirements of the ISAs and the language used to communicate such requirements;

eliminating any possible ambiguity about the requirements an auditor needs to fulfill; and

improving the overall readability and understandability of the ISAs through structural and drafting improvements.

Auditors and others should look to ISA 200, Overall Objectives of the Independent Auditor and the Conduct of an Audit in Accordance with International Standards on Auditing, for assistance in understanding the purpose and scope of an audit. This ISA sets out how the objectives, requirements, and guidance in all ISAs are to be understood.

Source: www.ifac.org/auditing-assurance/clarity-center, accessed 31 May 2012

3.3 International accounting standards as an underpinning for international audit

It may be a fairly obvious statement to make that one of the difficulties in promulgating International Standards on Auditing is the fact that there is no global set of accounting standards to which the ISAs can refer in relation to what constitutes a suitable accounting framework such that an ISA-based audit may be carried out. This problem is tackled by the ISAs, although not necessarily completely overcome, by classifying two types of 'applicable financial reporting framework', namely a 'fair presentation framework' and a 'compliance framework'. Under the former, there is either an explicit or implicit acknowledgement that additional disclosures may be required beyond the specified rules, and it is explicitly stated that departure from those rules is permitted in order to give a fair presentation. In a compliance framework, these criteria are absent.[17]

Some form of accounting framework is thus a necessity for an ISA audit, because otherwise the audit opinion has no anchor in what is expected by users of the financial statements, and some attempt has been made to account for different histories and traditions. (Other criteria are also imposed by ISAs, in particular the requirement for management of the auditee company to acknowledge its responsibility for the financial statements and internal controls and to undertake to give all information and explanations to the auditor.) The more that accounting standards are converged and harmonised across the world, the more ISAs can also be uniformly applied. It may be argued that differences in accounting framework are less of an issue in this context than, say, management culture or corporate governance in a jurisdiction, but the adoption of international accounting standards in a country will often give a signal about the desire for transparency and international acceptability.

3.4 Audit firm risk management and the desire to harmonize standards

One of the most important contributors to the brand of the large audit practices is the great technical depth and breadth that underpins their service delivery, although this is also a defensive mechanism against litigation and regulatory actions that would otherwise cost the firms dearly. It naturally follows, therefore, that the advent of international standards, both in financial reporting and auditing, plays greatly to the benefit of supra-national auditors. To the extent that staff can be trained in one set of standards to service the needs of the largest multinational clients, but at the same time those standards are also applied in servicing national companies, costs are reduced in terms of training. In addition, risk exposures are reduced, because the firms can, through their network agreements, impose consistency of interpretation and application.

This is not to say the increasing dominance of IFRS has been a painless process for the large firms and it has led to changes in the way they operate across the national firms that make up their networks. In some ways, in the short term, it also leads to additional risk:

> The widespread adoption of IFRSs, both directly and indirectly via convergence of national requirements, presents a number of challenges for auditors both as individuals and as firms. ... the challenges can be much greater for countries that opt for direct adoption of IFRSs, since there is no corresponding single international regulatory framework or infrastructure built around IFRS, and companies and their auditors often are required to make wholesale changes to their financial reporting practices (Tokar, 2005).

4. Influence of audit on financial reporting standards development

The output of financial reporting standards has to be capable of audit. Nevertheless, until relatively recently there has been little formal liaison between accounting and auditing standard setters. Where the influence has come it has generally been through the direct involvement of auditors or former auditors as members of relevant standard setting boards who, through their experience of auditing financial information, will tend to consider the capacity of that information to be audited in a satisfactory manner. There are those who would argue that this may have a deadening effect on the development of accounting standards and hold back innovation. In the past 10–15 years, however, there have been significant developments in accounting standards, particularly in relation to pensions, financial instruments and share-based payment, which are arguably harder to audit, and yet auditing standards and practices have developed to deal with these significant changes and the auditors or former auditors involved in their development did not object (or at least, not for long once they had got used to a new idea). In addition, auditors have not been on their own in setting accounting standards; they tend to be accompanied by colleagues with experience of preparing financial statements (the 'preparer' community), academics, analysts and other investor representatives, credit-rating agencies and others from the 'user' community. Thus the voice of the auditor has been only one voice in the development of accounting standards, albeit a powerful one.

More recently, the IASB has begun to liaise more formally with the IAASB. Representatives meet on a regular basis and better communication will presumably be beneficial to both. It remains to be seen how much this affects the standard setting of either board. It may be that the IASB will be swayed by the views of auditors about the 'auditability' of the financial statements produced under IFRS. For example, the question currently under consideration by the IASB of moving from an incurred loss to an expected loss model for loan impairments is likely to cause greater difficulty for auditors where management expectations will need to be judged. Having said that, however, the first constituents that need a reasonable level of certainty about what goes into the financial statements is the preparers of the financial statements: how will directors know they can stand by the information they have put out if it is too subjective or otherwise unreliable?[18] In terms of influencing in the other direction, this may be limited as the pressure on audit seems now to be coming from those who wish to have assurance on information that is not in the historical financial statements, namely forward-looking information, risk disclosures and key performance indicators. Auditing standard setters may therefore be focussed more on how assurance might be given in other areas rather than on the financial statements, and the IAASB's recent issuance of a standard of assurance on greenhouse gas statements is an example of this.

It has generally been the audit firms, rather than the formal audit standard setting bodies, that have arguably had much more impact on IFRS. As well as developing their own internal approach to applying IFRS worldwide, in terms of training and risk management, they publish generic guidance to clients and the wider market. They also take some of the decisions necessary to promote consistent application:

> These discussions and comparisons [with local GAAPs] also strengthened the acceptance within the KPMG network of firms of IFRSs as a separate body of standards with its own interpretations that should not be stretched to accommodate inconsistent existing national practices. Seeking to accommodate inconsistent national practices turns IFRSs into a reference framework rather than an independent body of standards for direct application (Tokar, 2005).

Overall, this has meant that the firms have had to coordinate their views on IFRS, including on particular accounting treatments and commenting on proposed standards to the IASB, in a way they had not done before. This has led to greater centralization of technical decision-making, but it has also required consensus-building mechanisms to be developed in the firms as the use of IFRS, as indicated above, has to be implemented properly at national level; simply imposing views from the centre is unlikely to be successful in the longer term:

> [T]he expectation is that KPMG member engagement teams will endorse the approach illustrated in every audit around the world. Therefore, it was very important that the positions taken reflect the consensus view of the member firms (Tokar, 2005).

5. Factors militating against internationalization of audit and financial reporting

Anyone who has been involved in the tortuous process by which IFRS are endorsed in the EU and waited in vain for the USA to commit itself to applying IFRS for domestic issuers while telling everyone else what IFRS should look like, will recognize that the introduction of international accounting standards is not plain sailing. The huge success story of IFRS adoption over the past few years masks some problems which are only now coming to the fore. Some of these problems are inevitable and predictable barriers to the internationalization of standards. How can accounting practices which have been developed and applied over considerable periods of time, which are affected by local history, culture and regulatory frameworks, give way to an absolutely consistent application of international standards? As Nicolas Véron has convincingly argued,[19] however, some of the problems are not technical but political and arise from powerful vested interests realizing after the event that their hold over these rules becomes much more tenuous as standard setting moves from a national to an international stage.

5.1 Local practice, culture and legal/regulatory frameworks

In the UK, perhaps ironically, accounting standards originally developed because members of the accountancy profession in business felt that they were at the mercy of their auditors in deciding how their results should be calculated and presented. Company law dictated (and still does) that financial statements must be produced on a true and fair basis and that these must be audited. The financial statements acted as a means of reporting to shareholders but also, to the extent the company had limited liability, as a mechanism for creditor protection. There was a call by business members of the ICAEW to start a process of codification of accounting rules so that business people could be masters of their own information, if not their fate. Only later did the stewardship imperative of reporting to shareholders and the creditor protection measures become augmented by the provisions of securities law, requiring information for markets where shares in companies are traded.

In the USA, by contrast, accounting standards developed as a direct result of securities laws introduced following the Wall Street Crash and related problems. There is, to European eyes at least, surprisingly little provision of rules for accounting for small companies, with very different views on creditor protection and stewardship reporting to shareholders about management performance. With very different views of corporate governance in the USA, the buy/hold/sell decision-making of investors is the primary focus.

As we have already seen in some of the history of the large audit firms, some of their founders were also the progenitors of the accountancy institutes that allowed accountants in both business and practice to come together to formulate some of the early accounting standards. Only later, as potential conflicts of interest became more pronounced, did standard setting tend to move into structures independent of the profession, such as the UK Accounting Standards Board and the US Financial Accounting Standards Board. In such cases it has nevertheless been vital to the production of successful standards, capable of practical application, to pull in as members of the standard setters those with direct experience of application, whether through audit, preparation or use of financial statements.

In some countries in Europe, accounting has developed on a more legalistic basis, tied to the taxation and distribution systems. In others, the route has been more focussed on shareholder information for stewardship and decision-making purposes, which tends to be more closely aligned to the UK and US positions. But Europe has since the 1970s had accounting directives that have to some extent unified accounting, although they have had to encompass the different legal and regulatory developments within the EU. With the advent of IFRS and the decision to adopt them into law for all listed companies in the EU in 2002, which took effect in 2005, the EU moved to a position where securities law took a more international approach focussing on investor needs, and now IFRS are embedded in the main aspects of securities law in the EU, namely the Prospectus and Transparency Directives.[20] While adoption of IFRS is permitted for unlisted companies as a member state option, the take up of the option is frequently indicative of the history of accounting in each state: those with a tax and distribution-based system, usually entirely based on historical cost, tend not to permit the use of IFRS (including France and Germany); others with less of a legalistic approach to accounting, with a shareholder-centric approach, tend to permit use of IFRS. (States with no real private sector accounting history at all, such as the former Communist states, tend to leap straight to IFRS for all, often on a mandatory basis.)

There is also an issue about those left behind by the IFRS world. As discussed below, some EU countries choose not to permit unlisted companies to use IFRS. This means that a split is developing in the accounting profession between IFRS and non-IFRS practitioners, which may vary from country to country. In the UK the unlisted sector is about to move away from UK GAAP (which has become an unhappy mixture of old UK standards and adopted IFRS standards) onto an IFRS-based approach. Its basis is the IFRS for SMEs, although this is being modified quite substantially for a variety of reasons, including maintaining consistency with the law, which in Europe is extremely detailed.[21] One of the drivers for the change discussed by the UK Accounting Standards Board is the fact that the UK accountancy profession now tends to base all its training on IFRS, not on UK GAAP, and this causes additional costs and problems for companies and audit firms that straddle both the listed/quoted sector (which includes the AIM [Alternative Investment Market]) and the unlisted market or those just focussed on the unlisted market. The UK profession has broadly welcomed this move to alignment of local rules with IFRS, with mechanisms that allow helpful relaxation of disclosure rules for subsidiaries, for example. The expectation that this will be pushed down to the smallest companies, albeit in an even more simplified form. In contrast, the divergence in practice between IFRS and non-IFRS reporting in other countries may fade over time or may grow to be a permanent fault line in the accounting profession.

5.2 Regulatory and political intervention

The IASB is not able to enforce its own standards or require them to be followed: only governments or regional blocs such as the EU are able to do so through their own laws. There will always be the temptation, therefore, to alter the standards in some way. The drivers for such amendments come in a variety of guises. Powerful regulators may wish to amend the accounting rules to suit their regulatory purpose. Bank regulators, for example, may wish to impose additional provisioning on top of IFRS requirements, something that arguably happened in Spain through 'dynamic provisioning' and which some bank regulators would still like to impose following the financial crisis. Political interventions tend to be the result of lobbying by those who believe that proposed new accounting rules are detrimental to their business, often because they would lead to significant changes in practice. The 'carve out' of IAS 39 has been a running sore in the debate on accounting in Europe, but there are also problems on the horizon in the form of accounting in regulated industries.

Inevitably there are many who resent the loss of national control over standard setting. Experience suggests, however, that a move to adopt international standards is beneficial to the functioning of capital allocation, allowing companies to 'brand' their financial information as meeting internationally accepted criteria and giving users much better information. Although application may not be entirely consistent, the fact that companies are broadly using one framework for delivering financial statements and that framework is widely understood is seen to be beneficial. It might be argued, therefore, that those who seek to amend the standards locally will lose much of the benefit of international standards; but, on the other hand, such deviations from the standards are likely to fall away over time as countries recognize the benefit and value of international comparability.

It should also be recognized that, although IFRS is subject to threats to deviate from the standards and risks of different local application, political interference has been just as much of a problem for national standard setting. In the USA, the FASB was forced to make its standard on share-based payment, SFAS 123, voluntary as to recognition and measurement, due to substantial political pressure, whereas a mandatory standard was successfully introduced by the IASB in the form of IFRS 2. (There have also been controversies in the UK over PFI [Private Finance Initiative] accounting and pensions accounting which also involved some political pressure on the UK standard setter.) Whereas some argue that the IASB is unaccountable in comparison with national standard setters, others would suggest it has had some notable successes. Moreover, the fact that the IASB has no application or enforcement rights means that it has no choice but to garner widespread support for its standards through due process and continual outreach to its key stakeholders, proper post-implementation reviews and engagement and dialogue with dissenters.

5.3 Regionalization

The balance between different regional interests is changing over time in relation to international standards. This is true in both accounting and auditing and is partly a function of the changing economic circumstances of different regions, which at the moment are in a great state of flux.

North America's deep and liquid capital markets have in many ways been the cradle of standard setting. Their influence is still great in terms of the level of sophistication of their legal and regulatory framework and the strength of the rule of law. But their share of the world's stock market capitalization is declining and their model is under threat from rising powers elsewhere, particularly China.

Europe's push for a single internal market in the EU should have provided a counterbalance to the US model. But in terms of accounting and auditing, the EU remains fragmented, divided by different cultural and legal norms, which EU-wide laws tend to paper over but do little to harmonize. The recent debates over changes to the EU Accounting Directives have shown just how divided that view is; some in Europe advocate going back to historical cost accounting (and so aligning accounting with tax and capital maintenance rules) with no permitted use of current values at all, including both revaluations of property and fair value of financial derivatives (which would thus remain off balance sheet). In contrast, others have embraced a model that provides more current value information for users of financial statements. Although a pan-European private sector body, the European Financial Reporting Advisory Board (EFRAG), works to draw EU views together to respond to the IASB as well as advising the European Commission on adoption of IFRS into EU law, strong differences of opinion remain. Some undoubtedly view the standards as something to be negotiated over, as with any law, rather than as a final result of a due process.

Where the US influence will possibly be further counterbalanced is in groupings forming in the Asia-Pacific region. Many countries, including Japan and China, have welcomed the advent of IFRS and have realised the need to invest in their own infrastructure in order to take part in the IFRS debate, so significantly raising their game on the international stage. They have also started to cooperate and coordinate with each other, increasing the possibility of developing joint positions on major accounting and auditing issues. Some emerging economies are starting to do the same, and regional groupings in Africa, for example, are beginning to form.

6. Summary and conclusions

The large audit firms have grown over the past century into some of the most successful businesses in the world, capable of acting as one globally and yet regulated and owned on a national basis. Their beginnings and histories bear striking similarities. Their global presence has acted as a catalyst of and mechanism for internationalization of accounting and auditing standard setting. Their risk management and internal processes act, at least to some extent, as a force for consistent application of IFRS as well as local GAAP, often above and beyond that achieved by regulatory means, and generally the internationalization of both accounting and auditing standard setting is directly beneficial to them.

They are under intense regulatory scrutiny as a result of the financial crisis. That regulatory action will affect their business models is a given, but they have in the past dealt with these successfully and indeed operate in highly regulated environments. There is a danger, however, that regulatory action that damages their businesses to too great an extent might actually undermine their function in the world's capital markets, weakening audit quality and the brands that create trust in companies coming to markets around the world. A fundamental debate about what society wants from corporate reporting and the role of audit within that would be a better place to start in producing a case for change.

Notes

1 I am hugely indebted to the work of Peter Boys, BA FCA and the results thereof that he makes freely available on the ICAEW website in relation to the history and family trees of the large accountancy practices. See www.icaew.com/en/library/subject-gateways/accounting-history/resources/whats-in-a-name/preface%20and%20introduction#introduction.
2 I am grateful to William Touche for allowing me access to some early histories of his forbears and those others instrumental in the history of the firm.
3 *Ultramares Corporation v Touche et al.*, 174 N.E. 441 (1932).
4 My thanks to Allister Wilson of Ernst&Young. Certain information is taken from the Ernst & Young website at www.ey.com/US/en/About-us/Our-history and http://www.ey.com/US/en/About-us/Our-history/About-us-Our-history-timeline. Other information is from the work of Peter Boys, as noted above.
5 An attempt was made in 1997 to merge with KPMG (following the merger of Price Waterhouse and Coopers & Lybrand) but this was eventually abandoned for various reasons, including anti-trust issues.
6 My thanks to Lynn Pearcy of KPMG. As well as the Roger White text cited below, certain information is also derived from 'Winstbury' (1977).
7 My thanks to Pauline Wallace of PwC. Information is derived from 'Jones' (1995) and from the work of Peter Boys, noted above.
8 Although the limit on the number of partners (20) was removed in the UK through the 1967 Companies Act, there are countries where such restrictions still prevail, such as India.
9 *Free Enterprise Fund v. Public Company Accounting Oversight Board,* 561 US (2010).
10 See for example the report by Audit Analytics in 2008 at www.thecaq.org/publicpolicy/pdfs/AuditAnalytic_Non-Audit_Fee_5YrRprt_3-6-08.pdf. This indicates that the proportion of fees paid to the auditors of accelerated filers in the USA fell from an average of 50 per cent to under 20 per cent between 2002 and 2006.
11 See COM (2011) 779 final, 2011/0359 (COD) dates 30 November 2011 at http://ec.europa.eu/internal_market/auditing/docs/reform/regulation_en.pdf.
12 www.ifac.org/about-ifac/organization-overview/history, accessed 30 May 2012.
13 Forum of Firms Constitution as at September 2011, available at www.ifac.org/sites/default/files/callouts/Forum%20of%20Firms%20Constitution-September%205,%202011-FINAL.pdf, accessed 30 May 2012.
14 Where directors' duties and the rules to disclose information to auditors vary from country to country, auditors seek to impose the rights to information required by the ISAs through the contract of engagement and associated management representations.
15 See www.iosco.org/library/statements/pdf/statements-7.pdf.
16 See www.iosco.org/library/pubdocs/pdf/IOSCOPD182.pdf.
17 See ISA 200 *Overall objectives of the independent auditor,* para 13.
18 See the ICAEW document *Changes to financial reporting and audit practice* (May 2009) for further debate on this point.
19 For example in *Keeping the Promise of Global Accounting Standards* (July 2011), Bruegel Policy Brief.
20 Directives 2004/109/EC and 2003/71/EC respectively.
21 See www.frc.org.uk/asb/press/pub2702.html for further details.

Bibliography

ICAEW (2009) *Changes to Financial Reporting and Audit Practice.* (May) London: Institute of Chartered Accountants in England and Wales

Jones, E. (1995) *True and Fair: A History of Price Waterhouse.* London: Hamish Hamilton.

Tokar, M. (2005) 'Convergence and the Implementation of a Single Set of Global Standards: The Real- life Challenge'. *Accounting in Europe* 2: 47–68.

Véron, N. (2011) 'Keeping the Promise of Global Accounting Standards'. Bruegel Policy Brief 2011/05. (July) Available at www.bruegel.org/publications/publication-detail/publication/575-keeping-the-promise-of-global-accounting-standards/.

White, R. (2003) *Peats to KPMG: Gracious Family to Global Firm.* Natural (privately published).

Winstbury, R. (1977) *Thomson McLintock & Co: The First Hundred Years.* London: Seeley, Service & Co.

20

Multinational Corporations and IFRS

Malcolm Cheetham, Manfred Kaeser and Juliane Scheinert

1. Introduction

For the assessment of the impact of IFRS on multinational corporations (MNC) one is tempted to take a narrow view and to think of the burden of increasingly complex standards and increased disclosure requirements which often are only for compliance purposes with little additional value to the users. However, the comparison of today's financial statements with the ones presented twenty or thirty years ago clearly shows the progress made in the area of financial reporting. Many terms and concepts have been created and have become common accounting language, such as goodwill, fair value less costs to sell, value in use, and which now have a very clear common definition.

This longer term view gives hope that the difficulties companies have faced with the changes in accounting standards is the price to be paid for constant improvements which will ultimately result in high quality financial reports. Rome was not built in a day. Such massive undertaking, such as building international accounting standards, cannot be done without pain and effort from all participants. As a Swiss-based multinational company in the pharmaceuticals industry, Novartis is directly impacted by the changes in the accounting standards. Like its peers, the company has to live up to high standards in terms of quality of its products and ethical behavior in a global and transparent environment. The compliance with rules and regulations for financial reporting just as with other standards is expected. Therefore, Novartis is keen to actively participate in the project of developing high quality accounting standards.

2. MNCs' participation in, or influence on, international accounting standard setting

Novartis's participation in the standard setting process happens in various ways: the company's involvement in the standard setting process of the IASB; exchange of information with other pharmaceutical companies on the European and global levels; and intensive discussion with other preparers within Switzerland. The involvement of entities in the standard setting process is important as it helps companies to take ownership in the development of requirements for financial statements. If they can participate in new IFRS standards they are in a better position to understand where financial reporting is heading and to adjust systems and procedures on time to cope with new reporting requirements.

2.1 Involvement in the standard setting process of the IASB

The IASB itself offers various possibilities for participation in the due diligence process. The most common form is the comment letter on exposure drafts in which Novartis tries to provide the business view on new standards or on amendments to existing ones. Novartis considers this an important tool especially where it considers that the proposed changes do not add value or the changes could even provide a misleading picture. This means that Novartis does not issue comment letters in the company's name on all standards which are exposed but works together with peer companies within the pharmaceutical industry or with other preparers in Switzerland. When these comment letters cover all Novartis issues, it does not generally produce another comment letter just to repeat the issues already covered by others.

IASB outreach sessions, or field-tests, which are organized from time to time and where Novartis participates whenever possible, is an efficient form of involvement as it permits a dialog with the IASB staff and allows for a better understanding of the proposed changes. There are mutual benefits for both IASB staff and the preparers and users when issues can be discussed in these outreach sessions face-to-face on the basis of specific transactions.

A significant number of the IASB Board members and some of its staff also meet several times a year with representatives of companies that have an interest in the development of IFRSs at meetings known as the Global Preparers Forum, normally at the Board's offices in London. Currently one of the 16 members of this forum is the Chief Accounting Officer of Novartis. The purpose of the Global Preparers Forum is to provide input into concepts and proposals that the IASB is developing and offer advice to the IASB on the practical implications of its intended proposals for preparers of financial statements.

Last, but not least, the conferences and workshops organized by the IFRS Foundation as part of its education initiatives are a valuable source for entities to provide continued professional education to associates working in the finance and reporting departments. The information and the material received through these conferences can be used internally to train management at all levels of the organization in a continued process of improvement of technical accounting knowledge.

2.2 Discussions with peer companies within the same industry

Representatives of multinational pharmaceutical companies meet on a regular basis to discuss the implications of proposed or newly implemented accounting standards. These discussions are often driven by auditors, who have a vested interest in a common interpretation of accounting standards and a common solution for practical issues within the industry. There are also industry specific congresses on accounting and reporting issues where a wide range of speakers from the audit profession, enforcement bodies and consultants present their involvement and their views on changes in accounting standards.

2.3 Discussions with other preparers

In Switzerland, SwissHoldings, which is an association representing the interests of Swiss industrial and service groups, has a subgroup on accounting and financial reporting. This subgroup pro-actively monitors developments and trends regarding IFRS, provides feedback statements to the IASB, and supports principles-based standards based on well-defined and clear rules. This feedback is normally in the form of comment letters on proposed changes to the accounting standards. In other countries, our peer companies work with similar local associations and with the national standard setters to represent the interests of their constituents in the development of IFRS.

On a European level, Novartis also participates in the technical discussions organized by the EFRAG (the European Financial Reporting Advisory Group) on the implications of new accounting standards.

2.4 Particular situation of Swiss multinational companies

Switzerland, even though a relatively small country with only approximately 8 million inhabitants, is nevertheless home to a substantial number of world-renowned companies in the fields of banking, insurance, pharmaceuticals, luxury goods and food processing, to name just a few areas. At the end of 2011 it had three companies listed in the top 50 worldwide companies by market capitalization according to the *Financial Times*.

Due to the importance of these Swiss MNCs on the world scene there has been an increasing need for these companies to be considered on a level playing field financially with their peer companies from especially Anglo-Saxon countries with a long history of producing high quality financial statements for the use of investors, Swiss companies therefore participated at a very early stage in the development of the IAS (International Accounting Standards – now IFRS). This was due to the lack of local regulations in Switzerland. A law to mandate companies to establish consolidated accounts was only presented by the government to the Swiss Parliament in 1983, becoming effective only in 1992. During this period, Swiss companies had a keen interest in developing accounting standards which would help the production of their consolidated accounts. When the presentation of consolidated accounts became mandatory, many Swiss companies established their accounts based on IAS. They could have based them also on the Swiss GAAP or on US GAAP. However, many companies considered that IAS provided a better framework than the local GAAP, which was more adequate for small and medium-size companies, or US GAAP, which was considered to be too focused on the US business and legal environment.

2.5 MNCs' participation: conclusion

The exchange of information between companies during the standard setting process has a benefit which goes far beyond the shared view on specific accounting issues. It intensifies the dialog between entities across the globe and allows entities an insight into alternative methods on how to face the challenges of industry in particular and of the financial community in general. It fosters discussions on systems, procedures and organizational structures which otherwise may not take place. These intense discussions also prepare the ground for a consistent application of new accounting standards once they have been adopted.

In summary, IASB generally follows due process which allows companies to assess implications of new accounting standards and to provide feedback on their concerns. However, some accounting standards or specific disclosure requirements which are presently written for a particular industry such as the financial services industry do not provide useful information in other industries and therefore reduce the relevance of financial statements in those other industries and as a result often reduce financial reports under IFRS to a mere compliance exercise. For example, IFRS 13 on fair value measurement prescribes that for quoted instruments the market price is the basis of their fair value. As long as a single share or a single debt instrument is the unit of account this concept makes sense. However, in certain circumstances, for example in a business combination, the unit of account is not a single share, but an entire stake. Due to the existence of minority discounts and control premiums the value of an entire stake might be different from the market price of a single share multiplied by the number of acquired shares. The concept underlying IFRS 13 ignores such situations even though IFRS 3, the relevant standard for business combinations, explicitly accepts this situation. The result of this is that currently there is a conflict between the measurement guidance in IFRS 3 and IFRS 13, which could be due to the fact that IFRS 13 was written mainly to address the issues related to specific transactions in the financial services industry.

3. Financial reporting in Multinational Corporations (MNCs) before and after the adoption of IFRS

The evolution of accounting standards, and of IFRS in particular, has changed the financial accounting and reporting departments of MNCs. Accounting and reporting managers have increasingly become business partners who are involved at a very early stage in strategic decisions such as acquisitions, divestments and reorganizations in order to understand and assess the impact of these transactions on the financial statements. This has changed the accounting department from performing backward-looking compliance tasks towards business partnering, helping to create or preserve value. For example, the requirement to perform a purchase price allocation for a business combination forces accountants to identify the key value drivers of a business. It is not sufficient just to determine that a certain transaction is strategically appealing. Instead the strategic rationale has to be quantified and the value of the entire transaction has to be split between the net identifiable assets of the acquiree and its future growth platform. As a result, the expected future value creation of the combined business is expressed in terms of future earnings and helps to quantify the strategic rationale. As a result certain proposed transactions might not be entered into in the first place.

Novartis's predecessor companies, Sandoz and Ciba, carried out the adoption of IAS (now IFRS) in the early 1990s. IAS was much simpler in those days so that the most important impact of its adoption was the alignment of internal management reporting with external financial reporting. This concentration on one set of accounts brought a higher focus on externally published financial results and thereby contributed to the overall quality of the financial statements. However, the adoption of IAS also brought with it the need to educate finance associates on the existing standards and keep them up to date on ongoing changes.

As a result of the Novartis listing at the US SEC in May 2000, a reconciliation from IAS to US GAAP had to be provided for the Group's net income and equity. This reconciliation was provided from the date of the listing until the discontinuance of this requirement at the end of 2006. Although there were considerable differences between IAS and US GAAP during this period, the information provided with this reconciliation did not attract much attention from the financial community because the differences were clearly related to the different accounting standards and were of a non-cash nature. Fortunately, this extremely onerous requirement was removed which shows that even the US SEC shares the preparers' concerns about the cost–benefit analysis of financial reporting. See Table 20.1, which shows the details of the US GAAP reconciliation for 2006 and 2005.

Table 20.1 Novartis US GAAP reconciliation for the periods ending 31 December 2006 and 2005

	2006 *USD millions*	*2005* *USD millions*
Net income from continuing operations under IAS/IFRS	**7,019**	**6,072**
US GAAP adjustments:		
Available-for-sale securities	–114	278
Inventory	103	20
Associated companies		–6
Intangible assets	–1,743	–1,238
Property, plant and equipment	58	53
Pensions and other post-employment benefits	–198	–181
Deferred taxes	125	178
Share-based compensation	–5	–44
Non-controlling interests	–27	–11
Others	–68	
Net income from continuing operations under US GAAP	**5,150**	**5,121**
Net income from discontinuing operations under US GAAP	114	69
Net income under US GAAP	**5,264**	**5,190**
Earnings per share under US GAAP		
- Continuing operations earnings per share (USD)	2.19	2.19
- Discontinuing operations earnings per share (USD)	0.05	0.03
- Total earnings per share (USD)	2.24	2.22
Diluted earnings per share under US GAAP		
- Continuing operations diluted earnings per share (USD)	2.18	2.19
- Discontinuing operations diluted earnings per share (USD)	0.05	0.03
- Total diluted earnings per share (USD)	2.23	2.22

(Continued)

Table 20.1 Continued

	31 Dec. 2006 USD millions	*31 Dec. 2005 USD millions*
Equity under IAS/IFRS	**41,294**	**33,164**
US GAAP adjustments:		
Available-for-sale securities	–37	–24
Inventory	–11	–23
Associated companies	–307	25
Intangible assets	1,349	4,092
Property, plant and equipment	–436	–409
Pensions and other post-employment benefits	15	3,133
Deferred taxes	130	–1,438
Share-based compensation	–186	–96
Non-controlling interests	–183	–174
Others	61	
Net assets related to discontinuing operations	–19	50
Total US GAAP adjustments	376	5,136
Equity under US GAAP	**41,670**	**38,300**

4. Opportunities that IFRS offers to Multinational Corporations

The advantages offered by IFRS to MNCs go far beyond the preparation and presentation of financial statements. As discussed above, IFRS have significantly contributed to turning the accounting departments into business partners. IFRS have also created the base for a more intensive exchange of information on accounting and financial reporting between all interested parties.

4.1 Single global accounting standard increases quality of reporting

The IFRS have made a significant contribution to the quality of today's financial statements. The global footprint of IFRS has made it much easier for MNC to recruit skilled local accounting specialists who understand international accounting standards as well as local regulations. Without the introduction of IFRS it would have been difficult to achieve the same level of common understanding of technical accounting matters within the MNC.

The wider base of common understanding of technical accounting also facilitates the exchange of information between peer companies and a proactive identification of accounting issues and the development of commonly accepted and high-quality accounting solutions for industry specific issues. This common base also enables frequent benchmarking of a company's accounts against those of competitors, which potentially leads to incremental improvements to produce higher quality information.

The importance of IFRS to today's global businesses also requires IFRS to keep its momentum for continuous improvement by leveraging the input from preparers, regulators, auditors, researchers, and analysts from across the world. During the due process for new standards the proposed principles are challenged and tested by people with diverse backgrounds, both geographically and industry specific, which helps to create robust principles. However, there are situations in which the standard setter is not able to cope with the substantial amount of input and is therefore forced to focus on a certain industry which seems to be most affected. This may lead to inappropriate solutions for other industries.

4.2 Basis for a global process and control framework within a multinational group

Historically, due to the diversity of local accounting standards, there were often diverse practices in place within MNCs to convert local accounts into their group accounts, prepared using a single set of accounting rules. The acceptance of IFRS in many jurisdictions enables MNCs to standardize the process around producing statutory and group accounts thereby strengthening the related internal controls. One example is the establishment of a global Chart of Accounts (C.A.). If such a C.A. had to reflect the needs of different accounting rules in the various jurisdictions, the sheer volume of the accounts to be covered would impair the ability to maintain and understand the C.A. However, if the C.A. is based on a global accounting standard, local specialties may still need to be addressed, but there is a higher likelihood a specific requirement in one jurisdiction being essentially the same as in another jurisdiction, so that one local account is needed instead of two.

5. Challenges that IFRS presents to Multinational Corporations

5.1 Introduction

IFRS prescribes the production of financial statements based on theoretically coherent models. However, the drive for consistency between the various standards sometimes requires entities to present issues in a very complex way as shown below.

5.2 Complexity of standards impairs communication with stakeholders

As principle-based standards, IFRS accounting guidance is usually founded on well-established theoretical concept. However, theoretical concepts are usually based on simplified assumptions, thereby reducing the complexity often encountered in practice. As long as the different aspects of the complexity can be explained by the theory underlying the respective IFRS standard, the implementation of the standards usually leads to appropriate results. However, not all economic aspects of certain transactions may be covered by the concept of the applicable standard. In some cases, the theoretical concept even leads to counterintuitive results. This impairs the understandability of a company's financial reports. Often such issues are addressed by voluminous disclosure on certain transactions, which can be difficult to understand. Even if all transactions of a business fitted well into a specific accounting framework, the amount of additional disclosures to be provided to explain the details is often enormous. Important facts and circumstances are typically buried somewhere in these notes and are not easy to detect. Analysts often call companies with specific questions to which the answer is already provided in the notes. Extensive disclosures do not always help to increase transparency but can even decrease it. As a result, the financial statements can no longer be used as a communication tool; instead their preparation becomes more of a compliance exercise.

The following are some examples of situations in which theoretically sound concepts lead to results which are difficult to communicate.

a) Deferred tax on unrealized intercompany inventory profit at the buyer's tax rate

According to IAS 12 deferred tax assets and liabilities have to be measured using the tax rate and the tax base consistent with the expected manner of recovery. This requires the application of the buyer's tax rate when setting up a deferred tax on the elimination of unrealised intercompany profits in inventory in consolidated accounts. As shown below this may lead to anomalies in the income tax recognized in the consolidated accounts:

> *Example:* Subsidiary A resides in a tax jurisdiction with a tax rate of 20 percent and sells products intercompany which remain in subsidiary B's inventory. Subsidiary B is domiciled in a tax jurisdiction with an applicable tax rate of 30 percent. Subsidiary A generates a profit taxable of CU 100 on the transaction which is fixed at 20 percent (CU 20). As this is an intercompany transaction the profit gets eliminated in the consolidated accounts. One would expect that the current tax expense of CU 20 is offset by an equal deferred tax income on the unrealized profit eliminated on consolidation. However, this is not the case as the buyer's tax rate has to be used to calculate the deferred tax income (ie. CU 30). As this is different from the seller's tax there is a net tax income of CU 10 recorded on the consolidation.

The theoretical rationale is embedded in the standard's principle that the deferred tax rate should be based on the expected manner of recovery: the buyer (subsidiary B) carries the inventory; accounting and tax base in the buyer's accounts is equal to the purchase price. However, for the consolidated accounts the unrealized intercompany profit embedded in the inventory is eliminated. This creates a difference between the accounting base and the tax base on which a deferred tax asset has to be set up. As the asset is recovered through the third-party sale of the inventory by subsidiary B, the higher tax rate of subsidiary B has to be applied to calculate deferred taxes.

As shown, this concept results in a net deferred income tax income expense on intercompany transactions, if the seller and buyer are subject to different tax rates. This is a counterintuitive result and not straightforward to explain to management and investors.

b) Difference in accounting for contingent consideration for assets acquired as part of a business or on a standalone basis

An asset can be acquired on a standalone basis or as part of a business in a business combination. Although the economic value of the asset is the same, some potentially significant differences might arise in the accounting where there is contingent consideration to be paid on the outcome of a future event. These differences are of particular importance if the acquisition is of a single asset in a transaction which needs to be treated as a business combination. This is the case if an asset is acquired along with employees and contracts so that the definition of a business (requiring inputs, processes, and outputs) is deemed to be fulfilled.

In a business combination the asset, on initial recognition, is valued at its fair value less costs to sell. In a single asset purchase transaction, the asset is valued at the consideration exchanged for the single asset plus transaction costs. Barring transaction costs, the two values should be equal in theory, an assumption which usually holds true as long as the consideration is not contingent on future events. For transactions with contingent considerations, IFRS 3 requires that the fair value of the contingency payment is part of the consideration to be allocated to the identifiable assets and liabilities. If there is only a single identifiable asset in the transaction, the contingency payment is implicitly allocated to the asset. Any change to the fair value of the contingent consideration after initial recognition is recognized in profit and loss. In contrast under the relevant guidance for a single asset transaction, all payments are only recognized as part of the cost base if and when they become due. In the specific case outlined above, it may be possible to structure the transaction to achieve the required accounting treatment. As a result, where there is discretion as to whether an asset is purchased in a single asset transaction or in a business combination there is a possibility for accounting arbitrage. This is of great importance in the pharmaceutical industry where acquisitions often involve intangible assets and where contingent consideration occurs frequently in the form of very substantial milestone payments dependent on the development success of a drug.

The reason for the treatment under IFRS 3 is that the agreement of the acquirer to make contingent payments as the obligating event at the time of the acquisition. Therefore the fair value of the contingency has to be included in the transaction price. Further, IFRS 3 explains that changes in the fair value of the contingency should be recognized in profit and loss as laying out that they are usually due to post-acquisition events and should therefore not impact the fair values assigned to assets or liabilities at the acquisition date. Although this theoretical rationale is valid in many situations, in particular when the contingency relates to the future performance of a group of assets, it leads to the following result for the acquisition of a single not ready for use asset structured as a business combination. Failure of the development asset results in an income due to the reversal of the probable amount for the contingent consideration whereas success of the development asset usually results in an expense due to the increase in the amount of the probable contingent consideration. Furthermore, in the case of success the contingent payments represent costs of bringing the asset to the location and condition necessary for it to be capable of operating in the manner intended by management. As an asset is created, these costs should be fully capitalized and not recognized in profit and loss.

c) Technical goodwill arising in a business consideration

Another difficult point to explain is the creation of 'technical' goodwill in a business combination. In many tax jurisdictions the amortization of an asset acquired in a share deal is not tax deductible, while the amortization of an asset acquired in an asset deal is tax deductible. Accordingly, the price a buyer is willing to pay for an asset acquired in a share deal is lower than in an asset deal as the tax amortization benefit, i.e. the value of tax deductibility of the asset amortization, is not available. However, IFRS 3 requires that the fair value of an asset acquired in a business combination should be determined as if it were acquired on a standalone basis. Therefore the tax amortization benefit needs to be included in the asset value. While the theoretical concept has merit, it leads to a benefit being capitalized as part of the asset, which the acquiring entity is not able to realize in its ongoing operations. On an aggregated level this impact is more than offset by a deferred tax liability which has to be set up for the difference between the tax and the asset value. However, as this deferred tax liability cannot be discounted per IAS 12 it is higher than the tax amortization benefit, which is discounted. This leads to so called 'technical' goodwill that arises in a business combination performed through share transaction and which does not occur in a single asset transaction and which is difficult to explain:

> *Example:* A single asset was identified in a business combination and the consideration paid for the business/asset was CU 100. The tax amortization benefit increased the asset value

by CU 20, i.e. an asset of CU 120 was recognized. The related deferred tax liability is CU 25. The difference of 5 resulting from the difference between the tax amortization benefit of CU 20 and the deferred tax liability of CU 25 is due to not discounting the deferred tax liability. Accordingly, net identifiable assets are CU 95, so that a goodwill of 5 arises, which can only be explained by the fact that deferred tax liabilities are not discounted. The reason given in IAS 12 for not discounting deferred taxes is that a detailed schedule of the timing of the reversal of each difference would be required, which is considered to be too complex to produce in many cases. In the situation described above, however, it would not be complex to arrive at a reversal schedule, but it is complex to explain the accounting result of not discounting deferred taxes.

5.3 Need for "core" figures to provide useful information

IFRS aims to provide a correct theoretical approach to present activities in the reporting period. The underlying concepts are often complex and not well understood by non-experts. Furthermore, even disclosure requirements often lead to voluminous disclosures as explained above and often fail to address the requirements of investors in, for example, forecasting an entity's business activities. For example, IFRS does not provide a concept for separating recurring business income/expense from exceptional income/expenses. However, investors request such information as it allows a detailed analyses of the underlying business performance and sustainable cash flows. In order to address this need, companies are increasingly developing their own analyses of income and expenses. Unfortunately, the method to present such "non-core" items of income and expense is not unified across companies. Table 20.2 shows the Novartis presentation of its core results for 2011.

Table 20.2 Novartis presentation of core results for 2011

2011	*IFRS results*	*Amortization of intangible assets*	*Impairments*	*Acquisition-related divestment gains, restructuring and integration charges*	*Exceptional items*	*Core results*
Gross profit	40,392	2,918	278	5	246	43,839
Operating income	10,998	3,028	1,224	148	511	15,909
Income before taxes	10,773	3,238	1,224	148	552	15,935
Taxes	–1,528					–2,445
Net income	9,245					13,490
Basic earnings per share (USD)	3.83					5.57

(Continued)

2011	*IFRS results*	*Amortization of intangible assets*	*Impairments*	*Acquisition-related divestment gains, restructuring and integration charges*	*Exceptional items*	*Core results*
The following are adjustments to arrive at Core Gross Profit:						
Net sales	58,566				117	58,683
Cost of Goods Sold	−18,983	2,918	278	5	129	−15,653
The following are adjustments to arrive at Core Operating Income:						
Marketing & Sales	−15,079				2	−15,077
Research & Development	−9,583	905	31		90	−9,239
General & Administration	−2,970	13				−2,957
Other income	1,354		−3	−102	−806	443
Other expense	−3,116	4	608	245	1,159	−1,100
The following are adjustments to arrive at Core Income before taxes:						
Income from associated companies	528	210			41	779

Note: All figures given are in USD millions

5.4 Frequency of change

IFRS standards are subject to constant changes and principle-based guidance does not by nature provide implementation rules. It is up to the preparer to interpret and implement a principle. Often there is no single interpretation of a principle, which means, for example, the application of a new or changed standard by the user and a regulator may differ. Stability of interpretation is often only reached after a number of years. Frequent material changes to the IFRS accounting guidance therefore lead to recurring application "uncertainty." Furthermore, by the time stakeholders have developed a full understanding of an IFRS standard it has often been revised, so that it is often very challenging for users to obtain a complete understanding of the financial statements. This is also increasingly undermining the acceptance of IFRS in many parts of the world.

5.5 Summary comments

In summary, there is increasing concern about the extensive disclosure requirements of some standards which are mainly relevant for the core business of a few specific industries but need to be applied to the same extent by all other preparers. In these cases the disclosures often do not provide additional useful information to the user of the financial statements and, therefore, possibly in various cases, result in a compliance exercise with little added value (e.g. standards on financial instruments which mainly focus on the banking industry).

Some changes contemplated by the standard setter such as the implementation of the direct cash flow method, or the changes in the leasing standard which could result in the capitalization of all financial leases, may have a good theoretical justification and would result in a better way of reporting. However, the implementation of these requirements would lead to extensive costs (e.g. re-engineering of IT systems and processes) in particular in a multinational environment, which may not be justified by the expected benefits. A suggestion for dealing with this situation is to consider emphasising more the importance of relevance and materiality in the IFRS framework. Information which is not used by management for running the business and is not useful to the financial community, should not be provided in the notes.

21

The IFRS for SMEs

Paul Pacter

Good financial reporting makes investing and lending more efficient. Historically financial reporting standards were developed by each country individually. Sometimes they were set by government, in other cases by the accounting profession, and, in still other cases, by an independent board. National standards made sense when companies raised money, and investors looked for investment opportunities, only in their home country.

But a huge change has occurred in the past 35 years – the globalization of the world's capital markets. Now, investors seek investment opportunities all over the world, and companies look for capital at the lowest price anywhere. Almost daily we read about cross-border mergers, and individual investors can turn on their computer and buy stocks on securities markets worldwide.

In globalized capital markets, accounting differences make financial reports less understandable and complicate comparisons that investors and creditors want to make, hindering the efficient allocation of capital. This is true equally for equity capital and debt capital, and also for large companies and small ones.

1. Why have global accounting standards?

High quality global financial reporting standards – carefully applied and rigorously enforced – benefit capital providers by:

- presenting financial information that is understandable, both domestically and across borders;
- enhancing comparability between entities; and
- raising the level of confidence that capital providers can have in the financial statements they receive.

Global standards also benefit companies that seek capital by:

- reducing compliance costs;
- enabling access to international or overseas sources of capital by providing financial information in an understandable 'global language'; and
- removing other uncertainties that affect their cost of capital.

Global standards also improve consistency in audit quality and facilitate education and training and software development. In contrast, if financial reporting is country specific then home-grown training materials, audit methodologies, and application software must be developed from scratch. In 1973, the accounting standard setters in nine countries acknowledged the need for global accounting standards by jointly creating the International Accounting Standards Committee (IASC), predecessor of the International Accounting Standards Board (IASB). The IASC was a part-time body that produced a series of International Accounting Standards (IASs 1 to 41). However, by 2000, there were only a limited number of voluntary adoptions of IASs by listed companies, and very few adoptions by unlisted companies.

In 2001, the IASC was reorganized to become the full-time IASB. The IASB's objective is to develop a single set of high quality, understandable, enforceable, and globally accepted financial reporting standards based on clearly articulated principles. The IASB is an independent 16-member board, overseen by a geographically and professionally diverse body of trustees of the IFRS Foundation, and publicly accountable to a monitoring board of public capital market authorities. In developing its standards, the IASB follows a thorough, open, participatory, and transparent due process. The IASB engages with investors, regulators, business leaders, and the global accountancy profession at every stage of the process.

By early 2013, the IASB had produced the first 13 in its series of International Financial Reporting Standards (IFRSs) and has also improved virtually every one of the IASs that it inherited. By that date, as well, IFRSs had been adopted as a requirement for listed companies in over 100 countries. Europe was the catalyst for global adoptions of IFRSs – deciding in 2002 to make the use of IFRSs mandatory in the consolidated financial statements of companies listed on regulated European securities markets starting in 2005. Once Europe made the decision, dozens of other countries followed. And many other countries that did not adopt IFRSs directly have instead converged their national standards with IFRSs.

2. Why a global standard for SMEs?

This growing use of IFRSs around the world (directly or via national convergence) occurred at the same time as IFRSs themselves were greatly expanded, made more rigorous and more detailed, and (by addressing tough issues) made more complex. Not surprisingly, small companies began expressing concerns that those complex and detailed standards were beyond their needs and capabilities – and the resulting financial statements, while suitable for investors in listed companies, were not aimed at the kinds of credit and lending decisions that most users of the financial statements of small companies have to make. And, the little companies said, the volume and complexity of required disclosures is burdensome and excessive.

In late 2003, the IASB decided to develop a separate standard for smaller companies in response to overwhelming demand from regulators, standard-setters, small businesses, and auditors in both developed and emerging economies across the globe. Lenders, vendors, customers, rating agencies, venture capitalists, and outside investors all use the financial statements of SMEs to make credit, lending, and investment decisions. Often, those are cross-border decisions. High-quality, comparable information, tailored to their needs, is important to them. There is, therefore, a public interest in sound and transparent financial reporting by small companies.

In most countries in the world, all or most SMEs are required by law or government regulation to prepare and publish general purpose financial statements – and, in many jurisdictions, to have them audited. (General purpose financial statements are described in Section 9.1 of this chapter.) In the European Union there are around 25 million business entities (including corporations, partnerships, proprietorships, and co-ops) of which, by law, around 5 million must publish general purpose financial statements; 6 million in Brazil and 800,000 in Hong Kong must prepare financial statements. And so on in most countries.

A few are different. In the United States there are around 25 million businesses of which only a relative handful (perhaps 25,000) have a statutory requirement to prepare general purpose financial statements based on US generally accepted accounting principles (GAAP). The rest are free not to prepare financial statements at all or to use other financial reporting frameworks (with disclosure). Australia is similar to the United States in that only listed and the very largest unlisted companies must prepare general purpose financial statements.

It is not the IASB or the accounting profession who impose financial reporting obligations in jurisdictions around the world – it is legislators and regulators. Their goal is to protect the public interest by having good information available to capital providers and others.

SMEs do not usually have the capabilities to comply with all of the complexities of full IFRSs, which include many detailed disclosures designed to meet the needs of public capital markets. Nor do SMEs often have the resources to hire outside experts to help them comply. A further reality in some jurisdictions is that the quality of implementation of full IFRSs (or converged local equivalents) needs improvement. That is particularly true in the case of small companies and developing countries. Some jurisdictions have developed their own SME standards applicable to non-public companies. Often, however, those have serious limitations from a user perspective, are not readily understood by lenders and other capital providers, particularly across borders, have limited support (e.g. textbooks and software), and sometimes are weakly enforced. For example:

- Many national GAAPs for small companies today do not require a cash flow statement, even though the great majority of bank lenders and short-term creditors say the cash flow statement is essential to them.
- Often under national SME GAAPs, relatively short-term obligations are off the balance sheet entirely – for example, by measuring derivatives at cost (which is nil) or by not recognizing them at all, and by ignoring deferred tax, employee benefit, and warranty obligations.
- Some national standards for SMEs do not require SMEs to recognize impairments of both financial and non-financial assets on a timely basis, leading to overstatements of assets.
- Some national standards for SMEs recognize all factorings of receivables as sales rather than collateralized loans without regard to the extent of credit risk that the SME may have retained.
- Often related party disclosures are minimal under national SME GAAPs.

Capital providers want transparency. They know how to assess and balance both good news and bad news. What they abhor (and impose a price for) is uncertainty.

3. Full IFRSs include a few differences for non-public entities

Even before the IASB decided to develop an International Financial Reporting Standard for Small and Medium-sized Entities (IFRS for SMEs), full IFRSs included several differences for entities whose securities are not publicly traded. These were (and are):

- IAS 14 *Segment Reporting* requires disclosure of segment information only by entities whose debt or equity instruments are traded or being registered for trading in a public market. IFRS 8 *Operating Segments,* which replaced IAS 14 effective in 2009, similarly is mandatory only for public companies;
- IAS 27 *Consolidated and Separate Financial Statements* exempts some parent entities from preparing consolidated financial statements if (a) the parent itself is a subsidiary of an IFRS parent and (b) its debt or equity instruments are not traded or being registered for trading in a public market. Similar exemptions were in IAS 28 *Investments in Associates* and IAS 31 *Interests in Joint Ventures.* Those standards were recently amended or replaced by IFRS 10 *Consolidated Financial Statements* and IFRS 11 *Joint Arrangements.* The new standards continued the exemptions that were in the old standards; and
- IAS 33 *Earnings per Share* requires presentation of earnings per share data only by entities whose ordinary shares or potential ordinary shares are publicly traded or being registered for trading.

4. Development of the IFRS for SMEs

In late 2003 the IASB began a project to develop a separate, simplified IFRS for SMEs. That standard was issued six years later, in July 2009. In developing the IFRS for SMEs the IASB consulted extensively worldwide. A working group of nearly 40 SME experts advised the IASB on the structure and content of the SME standard at various stages in its development. The exposure draft of the IFRS, published in 2007, was translated into five languages to assist SMEs in responding to the proposals. More than 50 round-table meetings and seminars were held to receive direct feedback, and the draft IFRS was field-tested by 116 SMEs in 20 countries. As a result, further simplifications were achieved in the final document. Key steps leading to issuance of the IFRS for SMEs were:

- July 2003: IASB deliberations began, having carried forward the project from the former IASC agenda.
- June 2004: publication of the discussion paper *Preliminary Views on Accounting Standards for Small and Medium-sized Entities*; comment deadline was 24 September 2004.
- April 2005: staff questionnaire on *Possible Recognition and Measurement Modifications for Small and Medium-sized Entities (SMEs).*
- October 2005: public round-table discussions with the Board on recognition and measurement simplifications.
- July 2003 to February 2007: deliberation of the issues by the Board at 31 public Board meetings.
- August 2006: a complete staff draft of the exposure draft (ED) was posted on the IASB website.
- November 2006: a revised staff draft was posted on the IASB website.
- February 2007: publication of the ED (English language); comment deadline was 30 November 2007.

- April–September 2007: translations of the ED into four languages were posted subsequently.
- April 2007: publication of a staff overview of the ED on the IASB's website.
- June 2007: field-testing of the ED with the participation of 116 small companies in 20 countries.
- November 2007: end of the comment period; 162 comment letters received.
- March to April 2008: staff present to the Board an overview of the main issues raised in the comment letters and field tests.
- April 2008: working group submits comprehensive recommendations for possible changes to the ED.
- May 2008 to April 2009: Board redeliberations of the proposals in the ED at 13 public Board meetings.
- April 2009: Board decides that the name of the final standard will be International Financial Reporting Standard for Small and Medium-sized Entities (IFRS for SMEs), as proposed in the ED.
- June 2009: 13 Board members vote in favour, 1 dissenting opinion.
- July 2009: publication of the IFRS for SMEs.

5. Initial thinking of the board at the beginning of the project

At the beginning of the process, a large minority of the IASB Board members were skeptical about the need for any simplifications of principles for recognizing and measuring assets and liabilities in SME financial statements. On the one hand, Board members believed that the same concepts of financial reporting are appropriate for all entities regardless of public accountability – particularly the concepts for recognizing and measuring assets, liabilities, income, and expenses. This suggested that a single set of accounting standards should be suitable for all entities, although it would not rule out disclosure differences based on users' needs and cost–benefit considerations. On the other hand, the Board acknowledged that differences in the types and needs of users of SMEs' financial statements, as well as limitations in, and the cost of, the accounting expertise available to SMEs, suggested that a separate standard for SMEs is appropriate. The preliminary views of the Board, published in a June 2004 discussion paper, included the following:

- There were no recognition or measurement simplifications, only disclosure simplifications.
- If the IFRS for SMEs does not address a particular accounting recognition or measurement issue that is addressed in full IFRSs, the entity would be required to look to full IFRSs to resolve that issue (sometimes called a 'mandatory fallback' to full IFRSs).
- An entity using the IFRS for SMEs may elect to follow a treatment permitted in full IFRSs that differs from the treatment in the IFRS for SMEs (sometimes called an 'optional fallback' to full IFRSs).
- Assent of all owners would be required to use IFRS for SMEs.
- A subsidiary, associate, or joint venture must use full IFRSs if its parent or principal investor uses full IFRSs (ie, the investee would not be eligible to use the IFRS for SMEs).
- An entity that is economically significant in its home country must use full IFRSs.
- An entity that is a public utility or that provides an essential public service must use full IFRSs.
- Organize the SME standard by the same IAS/IFRS statement number and sequence as full IFRS, not by topic.

After considering the responses to the discussion paper, the Board's views on all of the above changed significantly. In the final IFRS for SMEs:

- many of the principles for recognizing and measuring assets, liabilities, income, and expense in full IFRSs have been simplified, mainly on two grounds:
  - the need by users of SME financial statements for information that helps them assess short-term cash flows, liquidity, and solvency. These users ask: If I lend money to the SME, will they be able to pay back the principal and interest when due? And if I sell goods or services to the SME on credit, will they be able to pay the invoice when I send it? Unlike equity investors in public capital markets, they are not concerned with forecasting earnings and share prices or with long-term forecasts in general.
  - the capabilities and resources available to SMEs;
- disclosures have been significantly reduced as compared to full IFRSs;
- there are no mandatory fallbacks to full IFRS. If the SME standard does not address an issue, management is permitted but not required to consider the requirements and guidance in full IFRSs;
- the IFRS for SMEs is organized topically;
- assent of all owners is not required to use the IFRS for SMEs;
- a subsidiary, associate, or joint venture may use the IFRS for SMEs in its separate financial statements even if its parent or investor uses full IFRSs;
- an entity that is economically significant in its home country is not restricted from using the IFRS for SMEs; and
- an entity that is a public utility or that provides an essential public service is not restricted from using the IFRS for SMEs.

6. Most contentious issues

In developing the IFRS for SMEs, the following were some of the more contentious technical issues:

- income taxes – whether SMEs should recognize deferred taxes;
- consolidation – whether it should be required;
- goodwill – whether to amortize or just have an annual impairment test as in full IFRSs;
- cash flow statement – whether it should be required for SMEs;
- micro entities – whether a separate standard is needed;
- financial instruments – which ones should be measured at amortized cost, and whether fair value or amortized cost should be the default measurement category;
- share-based payment – whether SMEs should recognize share-based payment transactions, such as share options given to employees;
- defined benefit pension plans – whether to require accrual of the unfunded liability and by what method;
- whether to allow an SME to choose any recognition or measurement option allowed in full IFRSs; and
- the name of standard – IFRS for SMEs? IFRS for Private Entities? IFRS for Non-publicly Accountable Entities?

7. Final IFRS for SMEs

The IFRS for SMEs is divided into 35 sections, plus a preface and a glossary. The sections are organized topically – starting with scope, concepts, and basic principles, and then financial statement presentation, balance sheet, income statement, and other issues – as in Table 21.1.

Table 21.1 The sections of the IFRS for SMEs

Section No.	*Section title*
1	Small and medium-sized entities
2	Concepts and pervasive principles
3	Financial statement presentation
4	Statement of financial position
5	Statement of comprehensive income and income statement
6	Statement of changes in equity and statement of income and retained earnings
7	Statement of cash flows
8	Notes to the financial statements
9	Consolidated and separate financial statements
10	Accounting policies, estimates and errors
11	Basic financial instruments
12	Other financial instruments issues
13	Inventories
14	Investments in associates
15	Investments in joint ventures
16	Investment property
17	Property, plant and equipment
18	Intangible assets other than goodwill
19	Business combinations and goodwill
20	Leases
21	Provisions and contingencies: Appendix – guidance on recognising and measuring provisions
22	Liabilities and equity: Appendix – example of the issuer's accounting for convertible debt
23	Revenue: Appendix – examples of revenue recognition under the principles in Section 23
24	Government grants
25	Borrowing costs
26	Share-based payment
27	Impairment of assets
28	Employee benefits
29	Income tax

(*Continued*)

Table 21.1 Continued

Section No.	*Section title*
30	Foreign currency translation
31	Hyperinflation
32	Events after the end of the reporting period
33	Related party disclosures
34	Specialised activities
35	Transition to the IFRS for SMEs

Source: The full text of the standard in multiple languages is available for download without charge from http://go.ifrs.org/IFRSforSMEs

The IFRS for SMEs is accompanied by two separate booklets, one setting out the basis for the Board's conclusions and the other containing illustrative financial statements and a presentation and disclosure checklist. For full IFRSs, the main standards section is available for free download from the IASB's website, but not the implementation guidance (such as illustrative financial statements) or the basis for conclusions. For the IFRS for SMEs, all of its components are available for free download, in English and many other languages.

8. How the IFRS for SMEs differs from full IFRSs

The IFRS for SMEs is tailored for small companies. It is organized by topic and focuses on the needs of lenders, creditors, and other users of SME financial statements who are primarily interested in information about cash flows, liquidity, and solvency. It takes into account the costs to SMEs and the capabilities of SMEs to prepare financial information. And compared with full IFRSs, and many national requirements, the IFRS for SMEs is less complex in a number of ways; for example it has only 230 pages, compared with over 3,000 in the full IFRSs.

8.1 Five types of simplification

The IFRS for SMEs reflects five types of simplification compared with full IFRSs:

- some topics in full IFRSs are omitted because they are not relevant to typical SMEs;
- some accounting policy options in full IFRSs are not allowed because a more simplified method is available to SMEs;
- many of the recognition and measurement principles that are in full IFRSs have been simplified;
- substantially fewer disclosures are required (a reduction of roughly 90 per cent from full IFRSs); and
- the text of full IFRSs has been redrafted in 'plain English' for easier understandability and translation.

Sections 8.2 to 8.5 of this chapter give more detail on those simplifications. Note that those sections outline the simplifications made to full IFRSs at the time the IFRS for SMEs was issued in July 2009. Since then several new and revised IFRSs have been issued, including IFRSs 9 to 13, IFRIC 19 and 20, and amendments to many existing standards. Most of the new and revised IFRSs are not yet effective (although they do allow for early adoption). However, when they do become effective, and as full IFRSs continue to be updated, the differences between full IFRSs and the IFRS for SMEs outlined in 8.2 to 8.5 will change.

8.2 Omitted topics

The IFRS for SMEs does not address the following topics that are covered in full IFRSs:

- earnings per share;
- interim financial reporting;
- segment reporting; and
- special accounting for assets held for sale.

8.3 Options in full IFRSs eliminated in the IFRS for SMEs

Examples of complex options in full IFRSs that have been eliminated in the IFRS for SMEs include:

- financial instrument options, including available-for-sale, held-to-maturity, and fair value options;
- the revaluation model for property, plant, and equipment;
- the revaluation model for intangible assets;
- proportionate consolidation for investments in jointly-controlled entities (the Board has recently eliminated proportionate consolidation for investments in jointly-controlled entities in full IFRSs effective 2013);
- for investment property, measurement is driven by circumstances rather than allowing an accounting policy choice between the cost and fair value models; and
- various options for government grants.

8.4 Recognition and measurement simplifications

The main simplifications to the recognition and measurement principles in full IFRSs include:

- *Financial instruments:*
  - Financial instruments meeting specified criteria are measured at cost or amortized cost. All others are measured at fair value through profit or loss. This avoids the inherent complexities of classifying financial instruments into four categories, such as assessing management's intentions and dealing with 'tainting provisions' regarding classification of financial assets as held to maturity;
  - the IFRS for SMEs establishes a simple principle for derecognition. The 'pass-through' and 'continuing involvement' tests in full IFRSs are dropped;
- *Hedge accounting requirements*: including the detailed calculations, are simplified and tailored for SMEs;
- *Goodwill and other indefinite-life intangible assets:* always amortized over their estimated useful lives (presumed to be ten years if useful life cannot be estimated reliably). An impairment test is performed only if there is an indication of impairment (full IFRSs would require the test annually);

- *Investments in associates and joint ventures:* can be measured at cost unless there is a published price quotation (in which case fair value must be used unless the equity method is used for all investments);
- *Research and development costs:* must be recognized as expenses when incurred;
- *Borrowing costs:* must be recognized as expenses when incurred;
- *Property, plant and equipment and intangible assets:* residual value, useful life, and depreciation method for items of property, plant, and equipment, and amortisation period/method for intangible assets, need to be reviewed only if there is an indication they may have changed since the most recent annual reporting date (full IFRSs would require an annual review);
- *Defined benefit plans:*
  - all past service cost must be recognized immediately in profit or loss;
  - all actuarial gains and losses must be recognized immediately either in profit of loss or other comprehensive income;
  - an entity is required to use the projected unit credit method to measure its defined benefit obligation and the related expense only if it is possible to do so without undue cost or effort. Otherwise, the IFRS for SMEs provides for a simplified measurement model;
- *Income tax:* requirements follow the approach set out in the Board's ED Income Tax, published in March 2009, which proposed a simplified replacement for IAS 12 Income Taxes. The IASB has decided not to finalize that ED for full IFRSs;
- *Non-current assets and disposal groups held for sale:* no separate held-for-sale classification. Instead, holding an asset (or group of assets) for sale is an impairment indicator;
- *Biological assets:* the fair value through profit or loss model is required only for biological assets for which fair value is readily determinable without undue cost or effort. SMEs follow the cost-depreciation-impairment model for all other biological assets; and
- *Equity-settled share-based payment:* the directors' best estimate of the fair value of the equity-settled share-based payment is used to measure the expense if observable market prices are not available.

8.5 Disclosure simplifications

The disclosure requirements in the IFRS for SMEs are substantially reduced when compared with full IFRSs. In quantified terms, there has been a roughly 90 per cent reduction in the number of required disclosures. The reasons for the reductions are of four principal types:

- Some disclosures are not included because they relate to topics covered in full IFRSs that are omitted from the IFRS for SMEs.
- Some disclosures are not included because they relate to recognition and measurement principles in full IFRSs that were replaced by simplifications in the IFRS for SMEs.
- Some disclosures are not included because they relate to options in full IFRSs that are not included in the IFRS for SMEs.
- Some disclosures are not included on the basis of users' needs or cost–benefit considerations.

Assessing disclosures on the basis of users' needs was not easy, because users of financial statements tend to favour more, rather than fewer, disclosures. The Board was guided by the following broad principles:

- Users of the financial statements of SMEs are particularly interested in information about short-term cash flows and about obligations, commitments, or contingencies, whether or not recognized as liabilities. Disclosures in full IFRSs that provide this sort of information are necessary for SMEs as well;

- Users of the financial statements of SMEs are particularly interested in information about liquidity and solvency. Disclosures in full IFRSs that provide this sort of information are necessary for SMEs as well;
- Information on key judgments and assumptions made by management, and other key sources of estimation uncertainty that that have the most significant effect on the amounts recognized in the financial statements;
- Information about an entity's accounting policy choices is important for SMEs;
- Disaggregations of amounts presented in SMEs' financial statements are important for an understanding of those statements; and
- Some disclosures in full IFRSs are more relevant to investment decisions in public capital markets than to the transactions and other events and conditions encountered by typical SMEs.

9. Who can use the IFRS for SMEs?

The IFRS for SMEs sets out a simple principle to identify which companies are eligible to use the standard: The IFRS for SMEs is appropriate for an entity that does not have public accountability and that is required by law or regulation, or chooses, to prepare general purpose financial statements (GPFS).

9.1 General purpose financial statements

GPFS are directed to the general financial information needs of a wide range of users, including outside investors, lenders and other creditors, and other external decision makers who are not in a position to demand reports tailored to meet their particular information needs. GPFS present financial position, results of operations, cash flows, and changes in equity. An independent auditor is able to express an opinion on whether GPFS present fairly the financial position, results of operations, and cash flows of the reporting entity.

GPFS are aimed at financial statement users who are external to the company. While owner-managers of an SME will almost certainly find the information in IFRS for SMEs financial statements useful, they are not the principal audience for which the financial statements are intended. Neither full IFRSs nor the IFRS for SMEs are designed to provide the kind of management accounting information that owners and key managers need to run their business.

Nor can the IFRS for SMEs directly provide information about taxable income in a particular jurisdiction. Tax authorities have the power to demand whatever information they need to meet their statutory tax assessment and collection obligations. Nonetheless, profit or loss determined in conformity with the IFRS for SMEs can serve as the starting point for determining taxable profit in a given jurisdiction by means of a reconciliation that is easily developed at a national level.

9.2 Public accountability

An entity has public accountability (and therefore should use full IFRSs) if:

- its debt or equity instruments are traded in a public market or it is in the process of issuing such instruments publicly; or

- it holds assets in a fiduciary capacity for a broad group of outsiders as one of its primary businesses. This is typically the case for banks, credit unions, insurance companies, securities brokers/dealers, mutual funds, and investment banks.

Therefore, in simple terms, any private company that is not a financial institution is eligible to use the standard as far as the IASB is concerned. Of course, it is up to the government or the accounting profession in each jurisdiction to decide who should use the IFRS for SMEs, whether it is mandatory or optional, and if optional what the alternatives are.

The IASB's definition of SMEs does not include quantified size criteria for determining what is a small or medium-sized entity. IFRSs are used in over 100 countries. The Board concluded that it is not feasible to develop quantified size tests that would be applicable and long-lasting in all of those countries. This is consistent with the Board's general principle-based approach to standard-setting.

In deciding which entities should be required or permitted to use the IFRS for SMEs, jurisdictions may choose to prescribe quantified size criteria. Similarly, a jurisdiction may decide that certain categories of entities should be required to use full IFRSs rather than the IFRS for SMEs, for example, entities that are economically significant in that country, entities that are public utilities or that perform an essential public service, or entities that are subsidiaries of parent companies that use full IFRSs.

Section 15 of this chapter discusses the suitability of the IFRS for SMEs for micro-sized entities – those with fewer than, say, five or ten employees.

9.3 IASB's definition differs from other SME definitions

Many national governments and regulators have developed their own definitions of a small or medium-sized entity for various purposes, often for matters of economic development and national statistics gathering rather than financial reporting purposes. Similarly some regional and international non-governmental bodies have developed their own definitions. The IFRS for SMEs is clear that its definition of SME is solely for the purpose of determining eligibility to use the IFRS for SMEs. While most of the national jurisdictions that have adopted the IFRS for SMEs have used the IASB's eligibility criteria without modification, some have added size tests or other restrictions as to the use of the IFRS for SMEs.

10. Benefits of adoption of the IFRS for SMEs

Why would an SME want to adopt it? The number one reason is improved access to capital. SMEs consistently complain that 'my business is successful and growing, yet it is very hard to get a bank loan or other credit'. The lenders, on the other hand, respond 'we do not understand or have confidence in the reported financial figures'. Improved financial reporting is aimed at helping SMEs get loans and credit and/or helping to reduce the price they have to pay for that capital.

Other benefits of the IFRS for SMEs include:

- improved comparability with other companies in the same jurisdiction and across borders;
- improved quality of reporting as compared to many existing national GAAPs for SMEs;
- reduced burden for entities in jurisdictions where full IFRSs or full national GAAP are now required;

- training materials, workshops, Q&As, newsletters, and other implementation support from the IASB (discussed in Section 13 of this chapter); and
- availability of textbooks, computer software, and commercial training programmes.

11. IFRS for SMEs has influenced full IFRSs

Interestingly, the IFRS for SMEs has actually influenced changes to full IFRSs in a few instances. Here are examples of decisions the Board made in the IFRS for SMEs that subsequently also became changes to full IFRSs:

- Financial instruments (IFRS 9 *Financial Instruments*, issued May 2011):
  - Two categories – no held-to-maturity or available-for-sale (AFS) categories (though for 'political' reasons IFRS 9 ended up with a limited AFS option for equity instruments);
  - Classification is based on the cash flow characteristics of a debt instrument (held only to collect contractual interest and principal versus held for other purposes);
  - No bifurcation of derivatives;
- Defined benefit post-employment benefits (IAS 19 *Employee Benefits*, revised June 2011):
  - Actuarial gains and losses through P&L or comprehensive income; no corridor approach or other deferral mechanism;
  - Past service cost through P&L;
- Elimination of proportionate consolidation for jointly controlled entities (IFRS 11 *Joint Arrangements*, issued May 2011).

12. Who is using the IFRS for SMEs?

The IFRS for SMEs was issued in July 2009. Today, just three years later, over 80 jurisdictions have adopted it or announced plans to do so in the next several years. Very few of those have made any amendments to its contents whatsoever, and most allow or require all SMEs to use it. Of course, a company following an amended standard cannot assert compliance with the IFRS for SMEs – thereby losing a principal benefit of following a globally recognized standard. The following is a summary of jurisdictions using the IFRS for SMEs (includes several jurisdictions that have made slight amendments to the standard):

- South America: Argentina, Bolivia, Brazil, Chile, Colombia, Ecuador, Guyana, Peru, Suriname, Venezuela.
- Caribbean: Antigua and Barbuda, Aruba, Bermuda, Bahamas, Barbados, Cayman, Dominica, Dominican Republic, Guadeloupe, Jamaica, Montserrat, St Kitts-Nevis, St Lucia, Trinidad.
- Central America: Belize, Costa Rica, El Salvador, Guatemala, Honduras, Nicaragua, Panama.
- Africa: Botswana, Egypt, Ethiopia, Ghana, Kenya, Lesotho, Malawi, Mauritius, Namibia, Nigeria, Sierra Leone, South Africa, Swaziland, Tanzania, Uganda, Zambia, Zimbabwe.
- Asia-Oceania: Bangladesh, Cambodia, Fiji, Hong Kong, Malaysia, Myanmar, Nepal, Philippines, Samoa, Singapore, Sri Lanka, Tonga.
- Middle East: Jordan, Lebanon, Palestine, Qatar.
- Eurasia: Azerbaijan, Kyrgyzstan, Moldova, Turkey.
- Europe – non-EU: Bosnia, Macedonia, Switzerland.

- Europe – European Union: Estania, Ireland and UK have adopted (Ireland and UK with some modifications). Companies in the European Union are required to follow the EU Accounting Directives. The European Commission has done a comparison of the IFRS for SMEs with the Directives and has identified just two substantive (and minor) differences. However, to date the EU has not acted to adopt or endorse the IFRS for SMEs. The European Commission has consulted on the IFRS for SMEs and found that 19 Member States favour a member state option to permit or require the IFRS for SMEs, while six oppose. The United Kingdom and Ireland have proposed to replace their national Financial Reporting Standards with the IFRS for SMEs with some modifications including those to eliminate the conflicts with the Directives.
- North America: available for use in United States, Canada (limited use so far).

13. Implementation support

The IASB has a whole new constituency for the IFRS for SMEs, many countries where, up to now, SMEs have followed a very simple local GAAP. In recognition of this, the IASB and the IFRS Foundation are working intensively to support the smooth and rigorous implementation of the IFRS for SMEs. Historically, the IASB has not provided this degree of implementation support for full IFRSs, whereas IFRS for SMEs was accompanied by implementation support that we are providing including:

- an integrated set of illustrative financial statements (with money amounts and notes) and a presentation and disclosure checklist;
- translations of the standard and the accompanying documents (see Section 13.1 of this chapter);
- comprehensive training materials in several languages (Section 13.2);
- three-day regional training workshops held worldwide focusing on developing countries and emerging economies (Section 13.3);
- an SME Implementation Group (SMEIG) has been set up to support international adoption (Section 13.4);
- free monthly IFRS for SMEs Update newsletter (Section 13.5);
- a comprehensive IFRS for SMEs section on the IASB's website (Section 13.6);
- an executive briefing booklet (Section 13.7);
- IASB members and staff have made many presentations about the IFRS for SMEs both to encourage adoption and to explain the standard (Section 13.8);
- IFRS for SMEs XBRL taxonomy (Section 13.9); and
- links to download the IFRS for SMEs materials mentioned above and others, e.g. presentation slides from the training workshops, webcasts, and other materials without charge on the IASB's website (Section 13.10).

13.1 Translations

The standard has already been translated into 18 languages, and others are in process, as follows:

- completed: Albanian, Arabic, Armenian, Bosnian, Chinese (simplified), Croatian, Czech, Estonian, French, German, Hebrew, Italian, Japanese, Kazakh, Khmer, Lithuanian, Macedonian, Mongolian, Polish, Portuguese, Romanian, Russian, Serbian, Spanish, Turkish, Ukranian;
- proposed or in discussion: Georgian.

13.2 Training materials

The IFRS Foundation's Education Initiative has developed self-study training materials with hundreds of guidance examples, available for free download in PDF format. There is one training module for each of the 35 sections of the IFRS for SMEs – nearly 2,000 pages of material in all.

Each module has the complete text of the section, with each paragraph annotated with commentary and numerical examples. Also, at the end of the module is a comparison with full IFRSs, discussion of significant estimates and judgements required in applying the section, a quiz (with answers), and two case studies (with solutions).

The training materials are written initially in English. So far they have been translated into Arabic, Russian, Spanish, and Turkish, with more translations to come.

13.3 Training workshops

In 2010 the IASB and the IFRS Foundation began a series of 'train the trainers' workshops on the IFRS for SMEs, many organized in conjunction with the World Bank. These are regional in the sense that participants in each workshop come from a number of countries. They are generally three days with eight classroom hours per day. The IFRS Foundation and the IASB provide the training materials and two instructors (without charge other than reimbursement of travel expenses). A regional accountancy body or other organization handles all of the arrangements.

To date workshops have been held in the following countries (listed in chronological order): Malaysia, India, Tanzania, Egypt, Brazil, Panama, Nordic countries, Caribbean, Singapore, Kazakhstan, Turkey, Gambia, Argentina, Myanmar, Dubai, Kenya, Barbados, Bosnia, Chile, Cameroon (French West Africa), Bangladesh, Indonesia, and Abu Dhabi. Together, over 2,500 participants from 105 countries have attended those workshops. As a condition for participating, each participant is asked to commit to organize at least one IFRS for SMEs train the trainers workshop in their home country. Many have already done so, resulting in enormous leverage to the IASB's training efforts. Table 21.2 presents a detailed outline of the three-day workshop curriculum.

Table 21.3 summarizes the number of slides in each of the 20 PowerPoint presentations used for the workshops (24 classroom hours). Those slides are available for free download from the IASB's website in several languages. The IASB encourages others to use these PowerPoints in their own training programmes.

Table 21.2 Curriculum for a typical IFRS for SMEs train the trainers workshop

	Day 1	*Day 2*	*Day 3*
08:00-10:00	1.1 Details of workshop 1.2 Overview of the IFRS for SMEs: Bullet points covering all of Sections 1-35, including highlight of differences with full IFRSs	2.1 Financial instruments: Section 11 and Section 12 Financial Instruments Section 22 Liabilities and Equity	3.1 Liabilities: Section 20 Leases Section 21 Provisions Section 28 Employee benefits 3.4 Quiz-case discussion on liabilities
10:00-10:30	Tea/coffee break	Tea/coffee break	Tea/coffee break
10:30-11:30	1.3 Scope and concepts: Section 1 Definition of an SME Section 2 Concepts	2.1 Financial instruments continued: Section 12 Financial instruments Portion of Section 30 dealing with foreign currency hedging	3.2 Liabilities, continued: Section 29 Income taxes

(*Continued*)

Table 21.2 Continued

	Day 1	*Day 2*	*Day 3*
11:30-12:30	1.4 Quiz-case discussion on scope and concepts	2.2 Quiz-case discussion on financial instruments	3.3 Quiz-case discussion on income taxes
12:30-13:30	Lunch	Lunch	Lunch
13:30-15:30	1.5 Financial statement presentation: Sections 3 to 8 Financial statement presentation Section 10 Accounting policies, estimates, and errors Section 32 Events after year end Section 33 Related party disclosures Those portions of Section 30 relating to functional currency and presentation currency 1.7(a) Quiz-case discussion on financial statement presentation	2.3 Assets: Section 13 Inventories Section 17 Property, plant, and equipment Section 18 Intangible assets Section 27 Impairment of assets	3.5 Other issues: Section 9 Consolidation Section 19 Business combinations Section 30 Foreign operations 3.8 Quiz-case discussion on consolidation and business combinations
15:30-16:00	Tea/coffee break	Tea/coffee break	Tea/coffee break
16:00-17:00	1.6 Revenue: Section 23 Revenue	2.4 Assets, continued: Section 14 Associates Section 15 Joint ventures Section 16 Investment property	3.6 Other issues: Section 35 Transition to the IFRS for SMEs
17:00-18:00	1.7(b) Quiz-case discussion on revenue	2.5 Quiz-case discussion on assets	3.7 Quiz-case discussion on transition

*These numbers (1.1, 1.2, and so on) represent the PowerPoint files available for download from http://www.ifrs.org/IFRS+for+SMEs/SME+Workshops.htm

Notes: There are no separate workshop sessions covering the following sections of the IFRS for SMEs. However, those sections are covered as part of the overview in the first session of day one.

- Section 24 Government grants
- Section 25 Borrowing costs
- Section 26 Share-based payment
- Section 34 Specialized industries

Table 21.3 PowerPoint slides used in three-day IFRS for SMEs train the trainers workshops

PPT Module	*Topic*	*Number of Slides*
1.1 and 1.2	Details of workshop and overview	83
1.3	Scope and concepts	30
1.4	Quiz on scope and concepts	25
1.5	Financial statement presentation	138
1.6	Revenue	44
1.7a	Quiz on financial statement presentation	58
1.7b	Quiz on revenue	24

(*Continued*)

Table 21.3 Continued

PPT Module	*Topic*	*Number of Slides*
2.1	Financial instruments	74
2.2	Quiz on financial instruments	69
2.3	Assets	98
2.4	Investments	50
2.5	Quiz on assets	42
3.1	Liabilities	95
3.2	Income tax	31
3.3	Quiz on income tax	19
3.4	Quiz on liabilities	36
3.5	Other issues	68
3.6	Transition to IFRS for SMEs	37
3.7	Quiz on transition	22
3.8	Quiz on other issues	32
	TOTAL SLIDES	1,075

All of these PowerPoint slide sets are available for download without charge from www.ifrs.org/IFRS+for+SMEs/SME+Workshops.htm

13.4 SME Implementation Group (SMEIG)

In September 2010, the Trustees of the IFRS Foundation appointed an SME Implementation Group (SMEIG) following a public call for nominations. Its 22 members have two main responsibilities:

- to develop and publish questions and answers as non-mandatory guidance for implementing the IFRS for SMEs; and
- to make recommendations to the IASB regarding possible amendments to the IFRS for SMEs as part of a comprehensive post-implementation review of the standard that got underway in the second half of 2012.

The terms of reference and operating procedures of the SMEIG were approved by the Trustees in January 2010. The process for issuing Q&As is outlined in Box 21.1.

Q&As published by the SMEIG are non-mandatory guidance intended to help those who use the IFRS for SMEs to think about specific accounting questions. The Q&As relate only to the IFRS for SMEs and are not intended to modify in any way the application of full IFRSs. This is made clear in the Q&As.

When the IASB issued the IFRS for SMEs in 2009, it made a commitment to undertake a post-implementation review of the standard. That review got under way in late 2012. The review includes a request for public comments on amendments that should be considered for the IFRS for SMEs. As part of the review, the IASB will also consider incorporating Q&As into the revised IFRS for SMEs. For that reason, it is unlikely that the SMEIG will issue many, if any, additional draft Q&As before the comprehensive review is completed. And the need for any further Q&As on an ongoing basis is being assessed as part of the review.

Box 21.1
SMEIG process for issuing Q&As

The SMEIG follows a rigorous due process in developing Q&As. The process is set out in the *Terms of Reference and Operating Procedures for the SME Implementation Group*, approved by the Trustees of the IFRS Foundation in January 2010. That document is available for download without charge from www.ifrs.org/IFRS+for+SMEs/Implementation+Group.htm

Briefly described, the process involves the following steps:

1. *Identification of issues* Based on issues communicated to the IASB by users of the IFRS for SMEs.
2. *Deciding whether to publish a Q&A* Staff prepare an analysis of each submitted question with a recommendation on whether it should be addressed by a Q&A (based on established criteria set out in the Terms of Reference and Operating Procedures of the SMEIG) and if the recommendation is to develop a Q&A, what the staff's recommended answer would be and why. Staff send their recommendations to members of the SMEIG by email. SMEIG members have 30 days to respond in writing to the staff on (a) whether the SMEIG member agrees with the staff recommendation on the need for a Q&A, and (b) if the recommendation is to publish a Q&A, whether the SMEIG member agrees with the substance of the staff's proposed answer and, if not, what the SMEIG member's answer would be and why.
3. *Reaching a tentative consensus* Staff prepare a summary of the views of SMEIG members. A tentative consensus is reached on the need for a Q&A if a simple majority of SMEIG members agree with the staff recommendation. Similarly, a tentative consensus is reached on the substance of the staff's proposed answer for a Q&A if a simple majority of SMEIG members agree with the staff recommendation. If a tentative consensus is reached that a Q&A is needed and on the substance of the answer, staff prepare a draft Q&A. The draft Q&A will include the SMEIG's reasons for reaching the answer that it did.
4. *The IASB reviews the draft Q&A* Members of the IASB have access to all of the communications within the SMEIG leading to development of the draft Q&A. The draft Q&A is circulated to the members of the IASB for their review. The draft Q&A is released for public comment unless four or more IASB members object within a week of being informed of its completion ('negative clearance').
5. *Public comments invited on the tentative consensus* The draft Q&A is posted on the IASB's website for public comment for a period of 60 days (this has been increased in practice from the 30 days set out in the Terms of Reference and Operating Procedures of the SMEIG due to requests from respondents). Staff prepare an analysis of comments received. Staff make recommendations for changes to the draft Q&A, if any, and send them to SMEIG members with a request for approval of a final Q&A. SMEIG members have 30 days to respond.
6. *Reaching a final consensus* Staff prepare a summary of the views of SMEIG members. A consensus is reached on the final Q&A if a simple majority of SMEIG members agree with the staff recommendation.
7. *The IASB reviews the final Q&A* Members of the IASB have access to all of the communications within the SMEIG leading to development of the final Q&A, and to the public

(*Continued*)

comments on a draft Q&A. When the SMEIG has reached a consensus on a final Q&A, it is circulated to members of the IASB by email. If four or more IASB members object to the consensus within 15 days of being informed of its completion, it is placed on the agenda of a public meeting of the IASB for discussion and a formal vote to approve publication. If no more than three IASB members object to the consensus within 15 days of being informed of its completion, the Q&A is published on the IASB's website. Approved Q&As are informal guidance and not mandatory standards. Therefore, they are published in the name of the SMEIG, not the IASB. This status is noted in each Q&A.

13.5 Free monthly newsletter

In March 2010, the IASB began publishing a free monthly IFRS for SMEs Update newsletter. There are now over 13,000 subscribers. It is a staff summary of news relating to the IFRS for SMEs. Each issue includes an update on translations of the IFRS for SMEs, new Q&As and draft Q&As being developed by the SMEIG, newly posted training materials, upcoming workshops, recent national adoptions, and news about the comprehensive review of the IFRS for SMEs. There are hyperlinks to download materials and to other useful information. Subscribers also receive periodic email alerts about IFRS for SMEs news, such as new Q&As and draft Q&As.

13.6 IFRS for SMEs web pages

The IASB's website includes a separate section dedicated to the IFRS for SMEs. Major sub-sections are:

- Project history;
- Training material;
- Webcasts;
- Q&As;
- IFRS for SMEs Update;
- Presentations about the SMEs;
- Train the trainers workshops;
- Access the IFRS for SMEs;
- SME Implementation Group;
- Non-English resources;
- Comprehensive Review 2012–14; and
- Guidance for micro-sized entities.

13.7 Executive briefing booklet

The IASB has published an eight-page executive briefing booklet entitled *A Guide to the IFRS for SMEs*. It is written for lenders, creditors, owner-managers, and others who use SME financial statements. In non-technical language, it covers:

- What is the IFRS for SMEs?
- Who is it aimed at?
- How does it differ from full IFRSs?

- Who is planning to use it?
- Implementation support from the IASB.

It is updated periodically and is available for free download in PDF format and in printed form.

13.8 Downloadable presentations

The IASB's website includes many PowerPoint presentations about the IFRS for SMEs, of various lengths and in multiple languages, which are available without charge for use by others who are making presentations about the IFRS for SMEs.

13.9 XBRL

The IFRS Taxonomy is the representation of IFRSs in XBRL – (eXtensible Business Reporting Language). XBRL was developed to provide a common, electronic format for business and financial reporting. The IFRS Taxonomy covers both full IFRSs and the IFRS for SMEs. The Taxonomy contains tags for all of the disclosures in the IFRS for SMEs.

13.10 Links to download IFRS for SMEs materials for free

In addition to making the standard itself available for free, a great deal of information about the IFRS for SMEs is available without charge for download from the IASB website. Here are some links:

- IFRS for SMEs web pages on IASB's website: www.ifrs.org/IFRS+for+SMEs/IFRS+for+SMEs.htm
- IFRS for SMEs (full standard in English and translations): http://go.ifrs.org/IFRSforSMEs
- Training materials (35 modules, multiple languages): http://go.ifrs.org/smetraining
- PowerPoint training modules (20 PPTs, multiple languages): http://go.ifrs.org/trainingppts
- Board and staff presentations (multiple languages): http://go.ifrs.org/presentations
- IFRS for SMEs Update newsletter: http://go.ifrs.org/smeupdate
- SMEIG Q&As and comprehensive review: http://go.ifrs.org/smeig
- Executive briefing booklet: www.ifrs.org/IFRS+for+SMEs/IFRS+for+SMEs.htm
- XBRL: www.ifrs.org/XBRL/IFRS+Taxonomy/IFRS+Taxonomy.htm

14. Plans for updating the IFRS for SMEs

When the IASB issued the IFRS for SMEs in mid-2009, it stated that it planned to consider amendments to the IFRS for SMEs approximately once every three years. The initial review is a comprehensive review of the standard that will enable the IASB to assess the first two years' experience in implementing the standard (2010 and 2011). The review got under way in the second half of 2012. The SMEIG is taking the lead in the review. The SMEIG will make recommendations to the IASB on whether to amend the IFRS for SMEs:

- to incorporate issues that were addressed in the Q&As;
- to reflect other implementation issues that were not addressed by Q&As; and
- for new and amended IFRSs that were approved since the IFRS for SMEs was issued.

Table 21.4 shows the estimated timetable for the review.

Table 21.4 Estimated timetable for the review of IFRS for SMEs

2H 2012	Review gets underway. SMEIG prepares an invitation to comment. The public are invited to make recommendations on possible amendments and encouraged to give their reasoning.
1H 2013	The SMEIG reviews responses to the invitation to comment and makes recommendations to the Board on possible amendments.
1H 2013	The Board deliberates amendments and develops and approves an Exposure Draft (ED) of proposals.
2H 2013	The SMEIG reviews responses to the ED and makes recommendations to the Board.
2H 2013	The Board deliberates amendments to proposals in the ED and agrees on final revisions to IFRS for SMEs.
2H 2013 or 1H 2014	The Board publishes final revisions to the IFRS for SMEs.
2014 or, more likely, 2015	Effective date of revisions.

Even before the review had begun, users of the IFRS for SMEs had called to the IASB's attention a small number of implementation issues. Those included suggestions to:

- revise the principles in Section 29 *Income Tax* to be the same as IAS 12. Currently, Section 29 has fewer exemptions than IAS 12, and it does not reflect a recent amendment to IAS 12 that contains a presumption that recovery of the carrying amount of an investment property measured at fair value through profit and loss is through sale of the asset;
- allow revaluation of property, plant and equipment (otherwise debt seems excessive);
- allow capitalization of development cost; and
- allow capitalization of borrowing cost.

It is not a 'given' that significant changes will be made to the IFRS for SMEs as a result of the comprehensive triennial reviews. When it was issued, the IFRS for SMEs reflected many simplifications of the principles in full IFRSs for recognizing and measuring assets, liabilities, income, and expenses, as well as substantial disclosure reductions. The IASB does not intend that changes to full IFRSs adopted after the IFRS for SMEs were issued will automatically be 'pushed down' to the IFRS for SMEs. Those changes will be considered on their merits in the context of the needs and capabilities of small and medium-sized companies.

15. Suitability of the IFRS for SMEs for micro entities

The Board said – and it is my personal view as well – that the IFRS for SMEs is suitable for any entity without public accountability (regardless of size) that is required by law or regulation, or chooses, to prepare general purpose financial statements (GPFS). GPFS provide information to lenders, creditors, investors, and other financial statement users who are external to the company. They help bring about the efficient allocation and pricing of capital in an economy. GPFS are described in Section 9.1 above.

It is not the IASB that mandates which companies must prepare GPFS. That decision is made by local legislators and regulators based on their assessment of the public interest in having good financial information available that can be used for sound investing, lending, and credit decisions and in the interest of economic development. Micro entities are tiny private companies with fewer than say, five or ten employees. Even before thinking about whether the IFRS for SMEs is suitable for such entities, a jurisdiction must address and resolve an even more fundamental question: whether those companies should be required by law or regulation to prepare GPFS at all. Answering that question involves balancing the societal benefit of having good financial information about small companies available publicly with the costs imposed on small companies to provide that information. That is a government decision, not the IASB's.

If a parliament or a regulator has demanded that micro-sized companies prepare GPFS, the next decision is which standards should be followed in preparing the GPFS. Possibilities include full IFRSs or full national GAAP applicable to publicly traded companies, a simple local standard for SMEs, the 'SMEGA Level 3' standard adopted by UNCTAD,[1] or the IFRS for SMEs. In reaching that decision, a jurisdiction must bear in mind that a huge issue for micro-sized companies is access to capital. Companies of that size consistently lament their inability to borrow money even though their products or services are selling well and they have lots of opportunities to grow. The banks and other capital providers, on the other hand, say – to put it bluntly – we don't understand or have confidence in the financial statements. So there is a big role for the IFRS for SMEs in filling this information gap, even for micros.

Some micro-sized companies may look at the 230-page IFRS for SMEs and find it daunting. Actually, for most micros, a good number of the sections of the standard may have no relevance at all. And, even in those sections that do have relevance, some of the specific principles or topics may not affect most micros. Even so, the IASB is currently developing simplified guidance to assist a micro-sized entity in applying the IFRS for SMEs.

16. Use of the IFRS for SMEs in emerging economies

The previous section of this chapter discusses the suitability of the IFRS for SMEs for micro-sized entities. The issues regarding its suitability in emerging economies are similar:

- In many emerging economies, full IFRSs (and national equivalents of full IFRSs) are being pushed down to all small entities through national adoption or convergence.
- Training and enforcement of full IFRSs and national equivalents are inadequate.
- The IFRS for SMEs is less complex solution tailored to meet the needs of lenders and creditors who provide capital to SMEs.
- Fair value measurements under full IFRSs are a particular concern in emerging economies. The IFRS for SMEs requires considerably fewer fair value measurements than full IFRSs.

The IASB and the IFRS Foundation have recognized the special needs of emerging economies by providing a wide range of implementation support including many regional training workshops most of which have been conducted in emerging economies. Better financial reporting should improve the ability of small companies in emerging economies to gain access to finance. This, in turn, leads to more successful businesses, more job creation, and reduction in poverty.

17. Use of the IFRS for SMEs by not-for-profit entities and government-owned SMEs

Are not-for-profit entities permitted to use the IFRS for SMEs? What about government-owned SMEs? The IFRS for SMEs does not prohibit not-for-profit SMEs or government-owned

SMEs from using the standard. Receiving donations or tax payments from the public does not make an entity publicly accountable provided that those assets are not held to directly benefit the specific donor or taxpayer. Generally this is not the case, and money donated or paid immediately becomes an asset of the non-profit SME or government-owned SME to be employed in its primary business (e.g. the charitable activities or the provision of public services).

However, a not-for-profit SME or government-owned SME that is considering using the IFRS for SMEs must bear in mind that the standard does not provide any specific guidance on how to apply the principles to some issues important to their financial reporting. These issues include:

- recognizing revenue from restricted contributions;
- recognizing revenue from tax assessments and payments;
- presenting the operating statement; and
- recognizing and measuring impairment and consumption of some assets such as museum collections, parks, and public infrastructure.

18. Personal 'regrets'

As the principal author of the IFRS for SMEs, I have occasionally been asked whether there are aspects of the original standard I would change if the content of the IFRS for SMEs had been solely my own decision, rather than that of the IASB. The IFRS for SMEs was the collective effort of the Board and the staff, not one individual. I am quite satisfied with how the standard turned out. And the comprehensive review of the standard currently under way will ferret out potential tweaks to improve the standard. Still, if we had had more time before issuing the IFRS for SMEs in July 2009, there are two matters that I might have wanted to discuss further: income taxes and eligibility.

The most difficult topic on which to get Board agreement was income tax. The standard was ready to go into production (typesetting, and so forth) when the Board was still debating Section 29 in April 2009. Our constituents were also divided. The staff recommendation at several stages in the project was for a taxes payable approach (i.e. no deferred taxes), with appropriate disclosure. That was not adopted. The Board also gave serious consideration to a timing difference approach (which focuses on the differences between profit or loss and taxable profit rather than on differences between asset and liability carrying amounts and tax bases). But we ended up with a full temporary difference approach pretty close to the one in IAS 12. Moreover, the temporary difference approach we ended up with was the one proposed in the IASB's March 2009 exposure draft *Income Taxes* that the Board has subsequently decided to abandon. So if I could make one change to the standard it would be to rethink accounting for income taxes. Still, for most SMEs, recognition of deferred taxes seems to be straightforward. The Board has had few implementation questions so far.

There's another area where I would have seriously considered a change – though I think most of my colleagues on the IASB would disagree. I would leave it up to each individual jurisdiction to decide whether small publicly traded companies can use the IFRS for SMEs. While the IFRS for SMEs is not designed for established public securities markets, the reality in many smaller countries is that the quality of implementation of full IFRSs by smaller listed companies leaves something to be desired. And, often, enforcement mechanisms are not in place. If the legislators or regulators in such a country believe that the investor's interest and the public interest are best served by allowing small listed companies to use the IFRS for SMEs, I would leave the decision in their hands.

19. Assessing the IFRS for SMEs

In addition to the IASB, others want to assess the IFRS for SMEs from a variety of perspectives, including regulators, standard-setters, and educators. In that regard, the IFRS for SMEs offers many opportunities for study. Here are some research ideas:

- Analyse the nature and magnitude of the changes to SMEs' financial statements on adoption of the IFRS for SMEs:
  - identify which financial statement items were the main ones affected;
  - the overall effect on income and equity; and
  - the different effects on different types of companies, for example based on industry or size or geography.
- Analyse which accounting policy choices were made where options are available in the IFRS for SMEs, and why.
- If SMEs had a choice of some other accounting framework instead of the IFRS for SMEs (e.g. full IFRS or local GAAP), examine why they chose the IFRS for SMEs.
- Analyse difficulties encountered in switching from previous GAAP to IFRS for SMEs.
- Analyse the ways SMEs planned and executed the transition, costs involved, extent to which they relied on outside help (e.g. from auditors), and lessons learned.
- Identify whether accounting quality has improved since adoption of the IFRS for SMEs.
- Analyse reactions of bank lenders and rating agencies to the new type of financial information they are receiving.
- Explore whether cost of debt financing has decreased since adoption of the IFRS for SMEs.

20. In conclusion

The general purpose financial statements of SMEs are used in making financing decisions by lenders, vendors, customers, venture capitalists, and other outside investors, as well as by rating agencies, governments, and others external to the entity. That is why there is a public interest in sound and transparent financial reporting by small companies. And there is a payback for the small company: improved access to capital.

The IASB issued the IFRS for SMEs with confidence that it will result in better quality reporting by small companies without undue burden, meet the needs of their lenders and creditors, and be understood across borders. If capital providers understand and have confidence in the financial figures, an SME's ability to obtain the capital it needs improves, and its cost of capital is reduced. In addition, where customers, suppliers, and others have greater confidence to do business with the SME, there will be a positive impact on the company's operations. Ultimately, this will lead to overall benefits of the economy in which the SME operates.

Notes

1 SMEGA Level 3 is titled *Accounting and Financial Reporting Guidelines for Small and Medium-sized Enterprises*. It was published by the United Nations Conference on Trade and Development (UNCTAD) in 2009 and contains 9 pages of accounting standards and 11 pages of model financial statements. The financial statements prepared using SMEGA Level 3 are not general purpose financial statements. UNCTAD's website is www.unctad.org.

Part 5

Social and Economic Aspects of (International) Financial Reporting Regulation

22

Socio-Economic Consequences of IFRSs

Soledad Moya

1. Introduction

The objective of this chapter is to outline a map of the literature on possible social and economic consequences of the adoption and implementation of IFRSs. Although probably older, the concept of economic consequences gained prominence in the late 1970s after publications by Wyatt (1977), Rappaport (1977) and Zeff (1978). Zeff (1978: p. 56) defined economic consequences as the impact of accounting reports on the decision-making behavior of business, government, unions, investors and creditors.

In the US, the Financial Accounting Standards Board (FASB) adopted the idea that the effects of individual financial reporting standards needed to be analyzed (Rappaport, 1977). At present, however, owing to the adoption of IFRSs in the EU in 2005 and since then in many other countries worldwide,[1] we may face global socio-economic effects and, therefore, the IASB is also faced with the challenge of considering the economic consequences of individual IFRSs (Schipper, 2010) and perhaps even IFRS as a whole. Hence, the discussion on socio-economic consequences could be making a come-back. Since 2002, extant literature can be found devoted to the consequences of IFRS for the main attributes of financial information quality, that is, studies on the effects of the adoption of IFRS on the qualitative characteristics of financial information such as transparency, timeliness or comparability (e.g. Barth *et al.*, 2008; Daske *et al.*, 2008; Cascino and Gassen, 2012). Those effects could be classified as "intended" following Brüeggemann *et al.*'s (2011) classification because IFRS adoption is expected to have a positive effect on the quality of financial information.

However, there are other effects, economic or social, that require much more theoretical and empirical study, and that can be classified as unintended ones (Brüeggemann *et al.*, 2011). Some examples of these are effects on contracting, on business analysis or even on social issues beyond the numbers, such as effects on corporate social responsibility or country level effects for emerging economies. The debate about consequences of international accounting standards and the development of effects analysis is therefore relevant currently. Since IFRSs have become the key for globalization in accounting regulation, the effects derived from their implementation are a necessary issue for analysis and there is a call for research in the subject. Regulators are aware of the need for conducting effects analysis of accounting standards and are introducing, in their due process, additional steps that consider them. The IASB had already in 2008 included in its *Due Process Handbook* a specific section entitled Impact Analysis where it is said that, in forming its judgement on the evaluation of impact, the IASB will consider costs incurred by preparers and by users and also the benefits of better economic decision making. The European Financial Reporting Advisory Group (EFRAG), together with the Accounting Standards Board (ASB) and some national standard setters issued a discussion paper on the necessity of conducting effects analysis of accounting standards. The questions discussed are whether this effect analysis should be done, how it should be done and by whom. Some debate and responses to this Discussion Paper can be found in Haller *et al.* (2012).

Additionally, there is a general call for research on the subject as regulators recognize that, although perhaps they should be responsible for the development of these analyses, some help from academia is sure going to be very helpful. In this sense, the paper by Trombetta *et al.* (2012) shows how academic research can assist regulators and standards setters in evaluating *ex ante* and *ex post* the effects of corporate financial reporting and disclosure regulation.

Therefore the objective of this chapter is to outline a map of possible social and economic effects, many already intensively studied in the literature and others where there is still much to be done, which may help us to understand and make advances in the study of these effects. To do so, in Section 2 we go back in time and look for the moment when the so called "economic consequences" first appeared in the literature. Then, we will discuss the economic consequences of IFRSs in business, financial and capital markets (Section 3) and the social consequences (Section 4) the adoption and implementation of IFRSs may have. Finally, Section 5 looks forward to possible challenges still to come.

2. The origin and substance of the theory that accounting standards and regulation have social and economic consequences

2.1 Some conceptual issues: the definition of economic and social consequences

Several authors identified economic consequences in the seventies, for example Rappaport (1977) or Wyatt (1977) referred to the subject in some early papers between 1975 and 1980. Rappaport, stated that, already at that moment, there was a growing recognition that the setting of financial accounting needed to be viewed more broadly than simply from a technical accounting perspective. It was not enough to be an expert accountant, it was also necessary to appreciate the environment in which accounting functions and of the impact that accounting decisions had on that environment. This expanded view of standard setting came from an increasing recognition that the legislation of accounting standards involved a potential redistribution of wealth, imposing restrictions or costs on some while conferring benefits to others.

Wyatt (1977) affirmed that, historically, accounting standards had been based in a greater measure on technical accounting considerations that on the potential economic and social ramifications they might expect to have. In his opinion, as a result, the central issue of standard setters' considerations had often been how best to report the effects of completed transactions. However, he also affirmed that, more recently, accounting standards setters seemed to have become aware of the economic and social ramifications of the standards to be adopted.

Although both Rappaport and Wyatt did already refer to the consequences of accounting standards, one of the first definitions of the term "economic consequences" is generally attributed to Zeff. In this sense, Zeff (1978: 56) refers to them as "the impact of accounting reports on the decision-making behavior of business, government, unions, investors and creditors". And what would accompany this definition would be, implicitly, that accounting discussions (not yet standard setters) should take into account what kind of effects can be derived from financial reporting.

At that moment, therefore, the thought of economic consequences derived from the accounting process meant a revolution. Up to then, accounting standards had been thought to be neutral or, at least, nobody had realized that both users and preparers could be adversely affected for the accounting standard process.

2.2 The FASB and its role as the first accounting regulator to "care" about economic consequences

At the moment of the first recognition of economic consequences as an issue for analysis, FASB had a key role in the development of accounting standards and, therefore, in the possible consideration of those consequences. Rappaport (1977) explains how, at that moment, FASB had three strategic options for the definition of its role in this issue:

- The "conceptual framework strategy" was based on the assumption that a well-founded framework can make a significant contribution to the development of a field of study, for it serves to organize and integrate knowledge into a systematic whole.
- The "economic impact strategy", considered that FASB should incorporate potential economic impacts into its deliberation process. This strategy would be based on the premise that while there would always be some disagreement on any proposed standard, the FASB would remain viable only if the process by which it reaches decisions was seen to be both comprehensive and equitable by the groups affected.
- The "mixed strategy" was based on a mixture of the previous two, that is, working under the conceptual framework and also considering economic impacts of accounting standards. This third strategy would mean that the FASB should not take any measurement or disclosure initiative whose consequences would be likely to be contrary to the apparent social and economic policies being pursued by the government.

FASB seems to have chosen the third one and considers both the conceptual framework and the economic consequences. To give an idea of how "impacting" that new thought was, at that moment the FASB started asking for research papers on the effects of several standards that were being discussed at the time. And perhaps it is then when the notion of economic consequences of accounting standards was born. This does not mean that before the 1970s there was no consideration of economic consequences of accounting standards; in fact, Zeff (1978) cites very interesting examples of economic consequences which occurred after the adoption of new USA standards issued by the Accounting Principles Board (APB). However, the "formal" thinking about economic consequences can be undoubtedly situated between 1975 and 1980.

One example of early studies on economic consequences would be the paper by Imhoff and Thomas (1988). In their paper, they examined capital structure changes to investigate the impact of SFAS No. 13 on lessees. This accounting standard essentially rearranged capital leases disclosures from footnotes to the balance sheet and they studied whether this mandated capitalization substantially altered key accounting ratios. Their results documented a systematic substitution from capital leases to operating leases and nonlease sources of financing. In addition, lessees appeared to reduce book leverage by increasing equity and reducing conventional debt.

2.3 The implementation of IFRS in Europe: a relevant step in the "globalization" of socio-economic consequences

We have introduced the development of the economic consequences of accounting standards concept, without referring specifically to the IFRS as those first definitions and studies were intimately related to US GAAP and FASB as the first regulator to consider those issues. The IFRS came into force in Europe on 1 January 2005. After that moment, all European quoted companies have to use IFRS in their consolidated financial reporting. For the rest, EU countries have the option to either require or permit IFRSs. Some countries, such as Spain, have already implemented new Spanish GAAP based on IFRS for all reporting entities, while other countries, such as Germany or France, are still making use of local GAAP although, in Germany, IFRS application is permitted.

Apart from the adoption in Europe, IFRS are being permitted or adopted by other jurisdictions outside Europe. We can mention here, for example, the ambitious project born in 2002 with the Norwalk Agreement signed between the FASB and the IASB. In this agreement each regulator acknowledged their commitment to the development of high-quality, compatible accounting standards that could be used for both domestic and cross-border financial reporting. At that meeting, both the FASB and IASB pleaded to use their biggest efforts to (a) make their existing financial reporting standards fully compatible as soon as is practicable and (b) to coordinate their future work programs to ensure that once achieved, compatibility was maintained.

In 2002, when the agreement was signed and the 2005 effective date of IFRS implementation for all Europe was already quite close, it seemed important to enhance a convergence process that would allow multinational companies to move easily between different countries. These movements would be much easier if a common or closer accounting regulation was agreed for financial reporting. In fact, a very relevant process took place in 2007 when the SEC eliminated its requirement for international companies to reconcile financial statements prepared under the IFRS to generally accepted accounting principles in the United States. This created an unprecedented situation of two co-existing financial reporting standards in the US. At that moment it seemed that US companies might be tempted to drop US GAAP entirely, which had been unimaginable. However, it is important to note that, recently, the convergence process seems to be at risk, In this sense experts from both regulators' bodies have stated that increasing politicization of the accounting process and tensions over sovereignty are making it harder to achieve.

Apart from the US, IFRS are also extending to many countries throughout the world. For example, many countries in South America and Asia have already adopted or are considering adopting IFRS.[2] Considering all that has been said so far, we can see how IFRS implementation and the consequences of accounting standards is not a local or regional issue at all but a global one where a great part of the world is, or is going to be, involved.

3. Economic consequences: the impact of IFRSs in business, financial and capital markets

There have been many transformations in the accounting standards setting process in the world since the first authors talked about economic consequences. However, the substance is mainly the same: if we accept that accounting standards may have an impact on the distribution of wealth, an analysis of the consequences needs to be included in the process. But what are these consequences? In recent years, and particularly since the adoption of IFRS in Europe, many studies have been published related to the economic consequences of IFRS adoption. In Brüeggemann *et al.* (2011) we can find a summary of those studies. These authors provide a really interesting review of most of the work done in relation to the economic consequences of IFRS and they classify economic impacts into two different categories: intended and unintended consequences. Intended consequences would be, following the authors, those derived from the IASB Conceptual Framework. That is, those related to the fundamental characteristics of accounting information. In this sense, accounting standards would try to "improve" attributes related to accounting quality such as relevance or comparability. These intended consequences are intimately related with the "informative" role of accounting information and apart from intended we consider them desirable.

The unintended ones would be relative to the contractual role of accounting. That is, accounting standards play a key role in how companies and stakeholders define their relationships and in this sense the change in an accounting rule may lead to changes in the way the different parties react and contract. This second focus runs parallel to the positive accounting theory and the effect of accounting standards on stakeholders' behavior (Holthaussen and Leftwich, 1983).

Additionally, these unintended consequences can also be desirable or non-desirable. If an accounting standard leads to lower cost of capital, this would be an unintended but desirable economic consequence. On the contrary, if a new accounting standard leads to stricter debt covenants or even to a worsening of the relative position of a company, in terms of performance or leverage, from our point of view it would be an unintended but also an undesirable economic consequence. It is interesting to note, as Brüeggeman *et al.* (2011) point out, that the two fundamental roles of financial reporting are not necessarily compatible with each other. And they provide some examples such as Gassen (2008) were the information role of accounting information is negatively related to its contracting role.

There are some other possible classifications for the effects of accounting standards. In Haller *et al.* (2012) another classification is provided based on the entities affected. They classify effects into the following categories:

- effects on the providers of capital (positive or negative);
- effects on reporting entities (positive or negative);
- other micro effects; and
- other macro effects.

There is a certain parallelism between this classification and the one we are using based in Brüeggemann *et al.* (2011), as our accounting effects would be those related to providers of capital, our business analysis, contracting effects and compliance costs could be considered as reporting entity's effects and we also consider some micro and macro effects.

3.1 Accounting effects: consequences relative to the main attributes of financial information according to the IASB framework

The purpose of the IFRS implementation is based on the basic assumption that they will lead to an improvement in transparency and also in comparability so that capital will move easily among markets. The IASB Conceptual Framework issued in 2010 refers to the qualitative characteristics of financial information and cites relevance, comparability, faithful information, verifiability, timeliness and understandability as the main attributes of financial reporting. The conceptual framework declares that financial information is useful when it is relevant and represents faithfully what it purports to represent. It also adds that the usefulness of financial information is enhanced if it is comparable, verifiable, timely and understandable. All these characteristics would design the "informative" role of accounting mentioned before. Therefore, most empirical research has been devoted to analyze whether, effectively, this informative role of financial reporting improves with IFRS adoption. It would be considered an intended consequence following Brüeggemann *et al.* (2011).

One of the most cited studies is Barth *et al.* (2008). These authors conducted a study for more than 20 European countries and analyzed the effects of IFRS in transparency, timeliness and value relevance. They conclude that there is a positive effect of the IFRS in the quality of financial information, even though they cannot prove absolute causality due to the obvious presence of some other influencing factors such as incentives and macroeconomic issues. Another study by Morais and Curto (2009) tries to determine if the value relevance of European listed companies increased after IFRS. Their results show that the value relevance of financial information during the period companies applied mandatory IAS 7 IFRS is higher than for the period during which they applied local standards.

Another very interesting study is that conducted by Daske *et al.* (2008). In their paper they analyze the effects on market liquidity, cost of capital and Tobin's *q* of IFRS adoption for a sample of 26 countries. They find that, on average, market liquidity increases but cost of capital decreases. However, they find that the effect is not the same for all countries and depends on enforcement or incentives for transparency.

Although as we have just seen there are studies that show a positive relationship between IFRS adoption and earnings quality, we find also some studies that do not confirm that, at least not for all the desirable attributes of accounting information. In this sense we can cite the study of JeanJean and Stolowy (2008) where they analyze the effect of mandatory introduction of IFRS on earnings quality, and particularly on earnings management, in Australia, France and the UK. They find that the pervasiveness of earnings management did not decline after the IFRS implementation and that, in fact, it increased for France. They concluded that sharing rules was not a sufficient condition to create a common business language and again enforcement and incentives played an important role in the effect for financial reporting characteristics. Lambert *et al.* (2007) show how the directional impact of high quality accounting information on the cost of capital is ambiguous and in the same line we have the paper by García Osma and Pope (2009) who examined earnings management attributes across 30 countries before and after mandatory IFRS adoption. Their results indicate that reporting incentives such as the enforcement or the investor protection rules play a dominant role in the determination of earnings quality.

Disclosure is also an issue to be considered as it is related to transparency, informativeness and quality of financial information. Mariusz *et al.* (2012) examine changes in segment disclosure after the introduction of IFRS 8 in Australia and document that a substantial number of firms increased the number of segments reported, although for multiple segments firms, which did not change the number of segments disclosed, they document a reduction in the amount of information disclosed.

In relation to comparability, an example can be found in Cascino and Gassen (2012) where they try to contribute to the debate whether IFRSs increase comparability or else this expectation will be dependent on the incentives of companies. Using two comparability indexes they conclude that the overall comparability effect of mandatory IFRS adoption is marginal at best. They also find that firm, region and country level incentives systematically shape accounting compliance.

We can see then how research in the economic consequences in relation to financial information attributes seems to be inconclusive and the only qualitative characteristic in which researchers agree is value relevance as all studies seem to find a positive relationship between IFRS adoption and the increase in the value relevance of accounting information.

There are also studies revealing that having good quality standards does not necessarily mean that we will have good quality financial reporting outcomes. For example, Ball *et al.* (2003) showed how financial reporting quality was low in Hong Kong, Malaysia, Singapore and Thailand despite presumably high-quality standards because the institutional structure provided incentive to issue low-quality financial statements. In this sense, they argue that countries that want to increase financial reporting quality have to think about changes in manager and auditor incentives and other institutional features and that those may be even more important than having high quality accounting regulation.

Also in 2003, Leuz *et al.* (2003) examined the extent of earning management across three different types of economy:

1. outsider economies with large stock markets, dispersed ownership, strong investor rights and strong legal enforcement (Singapore, Hong Kong, Malaysia, UK, Norway, Canada, Australia and the US);
2. insider economies with less well-developed stock markets, concentrated ownership, weak investor rights but strong legal enforcement (Austria, Taiwan, Germany, Switzerland and Sweden); and
3. economies that are similar to the insider economies but with weak legal enforcement (Thailand, Greece, Korea, Spain and India).

They found increasing earnings management as they moved from economies in 1 to economies in 3 showing that institutional forces such as the extent of investor protection could substantially shape financial reporting outcomes.

As stated by Holthausen (2009: 459), the question is whether it is feasible to identify the most important determinants of financial disclosure quality at country level. We have seen in previous paragraphs how legal enforcement can play a key role in the quality of financial reporting outcomes so it is not only the quality of financial regulation that will lead to more quality accounting but also a set of country characteristics that take advantage of these higher quality accounting standards.

3.2 Business analysis effects

Changes in accounting regulation can also modify decisions made upon business analysis. If financial reporting is based on the accounting standards, modifications on presentation or valuation rules will modify financial statements and therefore can affect business analysis.

Many examples of this effect can be found in the literature. For example, in Fitó *et al.* (2012) the authors analyze the impact of IFRS adoption in Spain. They study the effect of the IFRS introduction in accounting variables and ratios and find that the effect has been significant for most of the variables and for some or the ratios, basically those related to the company's structure. In relation to the performance ratios, they find significant differences for earnings per share. Similar studies can be found for other European countries, such as Sweden (Lantto and Sahlström, 2009) or Germany (Hung and Subramanyam, 2007). Results reported show that, in general, there is a significant impact on the analysis of financial statements due to the implementation of IFRS, although this change generally varies by country, depending on the differences between local GAAP before transition and IFRS.

Some more specific examples can be found in recent times of proposed modifications of IFRS regulation that may affect, if issued, business analysis and therefore the process of decision making. The IASB has issued a new draft on leases which introduces significant changes in the way operating leases should be recognized and measured in the financial statements. This draft was issued in August 2010 and it is currently under discussion. Current IFRS do not require operating leases capitalization and recognizes them as an expense in the year they are accrued (IAS 17, para. 33). However, the exposure draft proposes capitalization of those operating leases in the Statement of Financial Position of companies so that users are provided with a complete and understandable picture of an entity's leasing activities.

The main advantage of this new proposal is that users of financial information will be able to know about assets controlled by the companies which, at the moment, are off balance sheet amounts. However, some disadvantages expected, basically for preparers, would be the economic effects derived from this new inclusion and the complexity added. So in this case we could be facing some economic consequences which are partly intended (the benefits for informativeness and transparency) and the costs for preparers, both from an implementation and an analysis point of view.

The IASB proposal for operating leases has received nearly 1,000 comment letters (290 answers after the consulting process in 2009 and 760 after the 2010 draft) from individuals, auditors, private companies and other institutions, some supporting and some complaining about the project. It is interesting to note that approximately half of the letter writers supported the project based on the increasing quality of the information argument. Amongst the complaints, the issues most mentioned are the ballooning effect in the balance sheets (so that issue is seen as an advantage by some and as an inconvenience for others), economic effects such as leverage, and compliance costs and complexity derived from implementation.

Prior literature on the impact of new accounting standards shows how the potential magnitude of the effect can be measured by means of the analysis of key ratios. Beattie *et al.* (1998) and Fülbier *et al.* (2008) demonstrate that the capitalization of operating leases can have a significant impact on financial ratios which, at the same time, may lead to relevant economic consequences related to the financial structure, financial contracts and performance of companies affected. For Spain, Fitó *et al.* (2011) have conducted an *ex ante* research study trying to predict, using the capitalization method, the effect on financial ratios of operating leases capitalization in Spanish companies. The results indicate a significant increase in their leverage positions and this may affect their capital structure, debt covenants and their relative position in the market. They also find significant effects for both Return on Equity and Return on Assets, which means that the proposal does not only affect the presentation of items in the balance sheet and static measures such as gearing, but also the "real" performance of the company (ROA) and the return for shareholders (ROE).

3.3 Contracting effects

We can read in the IASB Conceptual Framework that the general purpose of financial reporting is to provide financial information about the reporting entity that is useful in making decisions and in assessing whether the management and the governing board of that entity have made efficient and effective use of the resources provided (IASB, 2010: para. 1). So the second fundamental role of financial reporting is to make management accountable for the company's resources.

This second role brings into the economic consequences literature the stewardship theory where managers are administrators of the company's wealth and act in the best way they can to protect it. This theory opposes the agency theory which considers the conflict of interests between managers and shareholders and regards accounting information as a control for managers to ensure that their own interests do not prevail among those of the shareholders. The stewardship theory supports exactly the opposite. Managers are not destroyers of the company and what they really try to do is to manage the company as honestly and efficiently as possible in order to benefit shareholders. If these assumptions are correct, accounting standards should allow them to do a better job, making management easier and facilitating the decision-making process.

Consistent with this stewardship role of accounting, contracts between the firm and its stakeholders are frequently based on financial accounting numbers (Brüeggemann *et al.*, 2011). Some examples of contracting would be related to lending agreements or management compensation contracts. These economic consequences that can be considered as unintended have not been as much studied in the literature. However, some examples can be found, for example in Wu and Zang (2009). These authors find that IFRS adoption is associated with the firm's internal performance evaluation and, in particular, with increases in the sensitivities of CEO turnover and employee layoffs to accounting earnings. However, it is interesting to note that those authors base their assumption on the improvement of those informational benefits of IFRS adoption but we have seen so far how there seems to be consensus only for market relevance while evidence for transparency, comparability or disclosure seems to be inconclusive.

IFRS could also induce economic consequences through adjustments in debt conditions. In fact, and in relation to the business analysis section, if companies see their leverage ratios altered due to a change in an accounting standard, it is fairly possible that debt contracting is more restricted or even that firms may have to renegotiate part of the debt. There are, however, scarce studies that have worked on this subject, for example Christensen *et al.* (2009), where they provide indirect evidence of a relationship between IFRS adoption and wealth transfers between lenders and shareholders by means of the impact on debt covenants.

An additional effect could be derived from the previous one related to the capital structure of the reporting entities. As Imhoff showed already in 1983 for US GAAP and financial leases capitalization, changes in the recognition of leases (in that study he was referring to capital leases) modified in some cases firms' capital structure as many of them moved from capital leases to operating leases in order not to include them in their balance sheets. With the proposal of operating leases capitalization, it could happen again that firms switched to another source of financing trying to avoid the recognition, as a liability, of their future operating leases payments.

There are some other contracts that can be affected by the IFRS adoption. Some examples could be dividends payout, management compensation contracts or even tax agreements. Literature on the subject is scarce still but sure that, in the future, there will be a development of this research area as regulators must know about all the effects that can be derived from the issuing of new standards.

3.4 Compliance costs

The incorporation of new standards may have an important effect on the costs of compliance for preparers. With the 2005 IFRS adoption, jurisdictions adopting IFRS had to move to a different conceptual framework and new standards that meant a lot of training and need of expertise for companies. In Spain, for example, an extraordinary call for accounting and the new regulation courses came from small and medium-sized companies at the time of understanding and therefore being able to adapt to the new Spanish Accounting Standards based on IFRS. Big companies often rely on their auditors for the compliance with new standards and regulations.

But not only when adopting IFRS as their general regulatory body do the reporting entities have compliance costs. Also, when a new standard is issued, if presentation of financial statements, measurement or disclosure is substantially affected, they will face important costs of adaptation. In this sense and as we have said in the previous section it is interesting to note how the Exposure Draft issued by the IASB in relation to the Operating Leases received more than 1,000 comment letters from individuals, auditors and firms, many of which complained about the costs of compliance. This last issue, about complexity, seems to be a very recurrent one, often related with the imprecision that users find in the definitions and contents of the exposed draft.

4. Social consequences as the impact of IFRSs implementation beyond business: the impact for individuals and other stakeholders

There is scarce literature on social impacts and we have not yet found a definition. From our point of view, social consequences are those that cannot be quantified and that affect social aspects of business, both at a micro- and at a macroeconomic level. From a micro perspective, changes in accounting regulation may determine disclosures about social issues and corporate social responsibility. An example can be found in the actual move towards the development of the integrated reporting, meaning that annual accounts have to incorporate not only economic but social information. Also from a micro perspective, we can refer to the lobbying process generated by accounting standards.

From a macroeconomic point of view, if there are effects at country level that cannot be quantified specifically we could refer to macro social effects. As stated by Biondi (2011) our socio-economies are a figurative construct that is deeply embedded in accounting. He adds that accounting, as a straightforward routine, may have greater significance than is usually acknowledged, under which the main stakeholders (such as financees and financed in the global financial markets) and the other stakeholders such as employees, labor unions, environmentalists and developing countries may also be affected in different ways, either positively or negatively.

Traditionally, quite a lot of attention has been paid to the socio-political analysis of economic statistics but that is not the case with accounting. Biondi suggests several reasons for this fact:

- Accounting appears more neutral, mechanical, procedural and objective than economic statistics which makes it appear as less manipulative and more apolitical than statistics.
- Accounting appears lifeless and plain boring and has traditionally been considered as unintellectual and trivial in human life.
- Despite this monotonousness, accounting requires some degree of technical knowledge if one wants to make use of it and be able to discuss it.

All these factors may have led to non-consideration of socio-political issues of accounting standards. However, accounting is a social and a political issue from the moment that it affects business and people.

4.1 Impact on corporate social responsibility

When we talk about impact of accounting standards on corporate social responsibility we are referring to what in the literature is described as green accounting, which can be defined as that part of accounting that tries to account for environment issues reflecting not only economic but also social impacts of regulation.

In recent times we have seen an increase in the awareness on the part of corporate entities that they should give something back to society. An entity that fails to make a positive contribution to society will be perceived as being socially irresponsible. The corporate social reports which have now become an annual report in addition to the traditional financial report, are one of the instruments used to demonstrate that entities care about social information. In this sense, Idowu and Towler (2004) look at corporate social responsibility (CRS) reports of different companies across different industries in the UK. They show how there are two distinct practices adopted when reporting on CSR matters. Some companies issue separate reports for their CSR activities whilst others devote a section in their annual reports for providing information on these activities. The study also notes that all companies in the survey recognize the enormous benefits that can emanate from making known their CSR policies and activities.

Accounting regulation can, therefore, contribute a lot to the provision and disclosure of social information. The new trend toward the integrated reporting, defined as a new corporate report where both financial and social information are disclosed and related to each other, is an example of the impact that accounting standards may have in the development of green accounting.

4.2 The lobbying process of accounting standards

Sutton (1984) affirms that an accounting standard setting process is a political lobbying one and, as such, it offers potential participants several opportunities and means by which they can influence its outcomes. Both FASB and IASB have often gone through a lobbying process when an accounting standard is released for discussion. As an example, it can be said that both the project on operating leases cited in previous sections and the one on revenue recognition that both regulators are working on in a joint manner, have received around 1,000 comment letters each, which can give us an idea of the impacts expected from these changes of regulation, if finally issued.

The lobbying process is often related to the economic consequences of the standards, as mentioned in previous paragraphs, but we consider the lobbying process itself a social consequence of standards, as it makes individuals, preparers and users react and opine themselves about proposals that are going to make a change in their personal or business lives. In this sense, we definitely do not consider accounting to be boring or non-political when it has the capability of provoking so much response.

4.3 Impacts at a macroeconomic level: country-level studies

The globalization process is not only affecting Europe (and US eventually due to the homogenization process in progress). Many countries outside Europe have been or will be impacted by this new world of accounting homogenization. There is some literature about how this globalization process is viewed from emerging countries.

A very interesting study is that of Gallhofer *et al.* (2011), where they interview Syrian accountants, exploring how they perceive globalization's actual and potential impacts. They show how Syrian professionals perceive globalization as Anglo-American and imperialistic in character. They point out some challenges facing the Syrian profession, including competition in accountancy from international firms that threatens to impact upon local jobs, the need to adopt and enforce international standards of accounting in Syria and related changes required in training to achieve integration in the global order. However, they also see globalization as having positive dimensions that may improve their lives and the profession.

Another interesting reference would be that of China, where the globalization process is presented as an occasion of growth. In this sense, Suzuki *et al.* (2007) state that since 2000, international accounting, as a common language on business and a mode of governance, has become widely disseminated in China and has become an indispensable infrastructure of its socio-economy. Our main conclusion here is that more research is needed for potential impacts at country level and about the relationship between jurisdictions. Surveys and personal interviews are bound to be particularly useful if we want to know about the feelings and reactions towards the globalization of financial reporting.

5. Challenges in gauging the socio-economic impact that IFRSs do seem to have: how to define and measure benefits and costs?

Two regulators are playing a key role in this globalization process. The first and most important one is IASB, the body which issues IFRS and is therefore responsible for the development of a body of high quality standards. The other is EFRAG, the European body in charge of assisting the European Commission in the endorsement of IFRS, and the IASB by providing advice on the technical quality of IFRS.

5.1 The incorporation of "economic consequences" into the IASB due process: the effects analysis

Regulators are aware of the need for conducting effects analysis of accounting standards and are introducing, in their due process, additional steps that take into consideration the effects derived from the new standards.

For the IASB, a relevant step was taken in 2008 when the *Due Process Handbook* for IASB was issued by the International Accounting Standards Committee Foundation (IASCF). This document includes a specific reference to the effects analysis process. It states that, after publication of IFRS, the IASB will prepare an analysis of the likely effects and this information will be provided to jurisdictions that adopt IFRSs. The analysis will attempt to assess the likely effects of the new IFRS (para. 50) on: the financial statements of preparers, compliance costs for users, cost of analysis for users, comparability costs and quality and usefulness effects.

This paragraph refers basically to the intended consequences related to usefulness and quality of information and also consequences for users as those derived from the business analysis and implementation costs. The IASB does not go beyond those effects and therefore does not include other unintended consequences than those related to the contracting role of accounting.

An example of the work that IASB has been doing would be the publication of the IFRS 11 Effects Analysis in July 2011. In the document, we can find two sections dedicated to effects analysis, one with the financial statements effects and the other with the cost–benefit analysis (CBA). This cost–benefit analysis is a qualitative one, where IASB separates costs and benefits for users and for preparers. There are only some quantitative references related to concrete examples of reporting entities.

5.2 The role of EFRAG in the effects analysis process

EFRAG, the Accounting Standards Board (ASB) and some national standard setters have issued a discussion paper on the necessity of conducting effects analysis of accounting standards[3]. The questions discussed are whether this effect analysis should be done, how it should-be done and who should do it.

The Discussion Paper was quite a preliminary one and several comment letters were received in response. The European Accounting Association's Financial Reporting Standards Committee (FRSC) responded to the document and their conclusions can be found in Haller *et al.* (2012).

The EFRAG document does not contain guidance for the implementation of an effects analysis procedure and is still defining what an effect analysis is, what effects should be considered and who should perform this analysis. In this sense, the paper by Trombetta *et al.* (2012) as an additional part of the response of FRSC to EFRAG's Discussion Paper, shows how academic research can assist regulators and standards setters in evaluating *ex ante* and *ex post* the effects of corporate financial reporting and disclosure regulation.

5.3 Future prospects for the consideration of socio economic consequences of accounting standards

The impact analysis of accounting standards has definitely come onto the agenda of regulators. Both IASB and EFRAG know that jurisdictions which have already incorporated IFRSs into their legal framework, or which are about to do so, may require some impact assessment before a new IFRS is brought into law and probably also afterwards, so they are making efforts for the recognition and consideration of those effects.

There are, therefore, some questions open for debate. One would be in relation to the responsibility of the effect analysis. The IASB is, probably, in the first term responsible for it but engaged with other regulators, the academia and the reporting entities. That is, IASB would be responsible for the consideration of those effect studies, but is IASB responsible for their contents? Or would it be better if an independent party was in charge? In recent times IASB has made some open calls for research into subjects related to the adoption or implementation of new standards. Following these calls, academia or the reporting entities could be very helpful in the development of these studies and providing conclusions that may be useful for jurisdictions that are future adopters.

Another question is whether EFRAG is also responsible for the performing of effect analysis. We understand that they are from the moment that they have a regulatory commitment, and that IFRS as adopted in Europe can have differences with the original IFRS. However, and following from what has been said for IASB, EFRAG should be accompanied by other regulators.

What about the effects that should be considered? In this paper we have mapped the main social and economic consequences derived from IFRS implementation. Of course, there may be others that have not yet been considered but the question is whether they should all be considered by regulators. Or should they only focus on those that are strictly related to their objectives, basically to the benefits (or not) of economic decision making resulting from improved financial reporting? From our point of view regulators should consider as many effects as possible, as long as it is reasonable and assumable. That is, apart from the effects on the attributes on financial information and therefore in the information quality, taking into consideration other effects such as those in the business analysis, in the contracting relations and in compliance costs, can help jurisdictions and reporting entities to be aware of the changes that they may be compelled to face.

Another open question is what type of effect analysis should be carried out? Should it be a cost–benefit analysis? Should it be quantitative in nature or else qualitative? We believe that the answer will depend on the nature of the standard to be brought to law. We will be able to carry out quantitative analysis for the predicted impact, on leverage or return, of the capitalization of operating leases, but, for the revenue recognition project (IASB, 2011a) probably only qualitative analysis will be possible as the impact cannot be accounted for in terms of change in accounting variables or ratios. We believe that, if it is possible to carry out a quantitative analysis of the predicted or the *ex post* impact, it would be desirable. However, a qualitative cost–benefit analysis would also be very useful, as we can see for example in the IFRS 11 effects analysis carried out by IFRS.

6. Conclusions

The debate about consequences of international accounting standards and the development of effects analysis is ongoing. Since IFRS have become the key for globalization in accounting regulation, the effects derived from their implementation are a necessary issue for analysis. Regulators are aware of the need for conducting effects analysis of accounting standards and are introducing, in their due process, additional steps that take into consideration the effects derived from the new standards. Additionally, there is a general call for research on the subject as regulators recognize that, although they should, perhaps, be responsible for the development of these analyses, some help from academia would be helpful.

In this paper we have tried to outline a map of possible effects, both social and economic, due to IFRS adoption, which may help us to understand and to advance in the study of these effects. Some have already been quite intensively studied in the literature while others still have a lot to be done.

The economic consequences of IFRS adoption relate basically to the effect on the main attributes of financial information as stated by the IASB Conceptual Framework, the impact on business analysis and in contracting relationships. We have seen how there is abundant literature on the subject, although mainly focused in the category devoted to financial information quality. IFRS has generated an intended and desirable effect in the value relevance of accounting information. However, attributes as transparency or comparability do not seem to improve in a clear and straightforward way as research is inconclusive about it and it looks as if enforcement and reporting incentives should play a determinant role in the success of the IFRS adoption in terms of incrementing information quality. In this sense we advocate that wider studies should be conducted to try and test the improvement or not of qualitative characteristics of financial reporting as it is one of the expected effects of regulators.

For the business analysis, empirical research both *ex ante* or *ex post* shows how, in a general way, IFRS adoption has incorporated significant effects both for leverage and liquidity positions and for performance analysis. Those economic consequences can be intended or not and also desirable or not depending on the direction of the effects provoked.

There are also some effects derived from the contracting role of accounting. Again we get unintended consequences that may be desirable or not. If IFRS adoption leads to easier or better lending agreements or improvements in the design of performance incentives, this will be an unintended but desirable consequence. However, if the new standards lead to stricter conditions for reporting entities, changes in their financial structure or worsening of their relative positions, then those would be unintended but also undesirable consequences. There are many other examples of contracts that can be affected by the IFRS adoption, such as dividends payout, management compensation contracts or even tax agreements. Literature on the subject is scarce so there is much work to do in this area.

We have also considered the social consequences of IFRS adoption. Literature here too is scarce and is not generally to be found in accounting journals but rather in social sciences literature. When we relate to social consequences we consider issues such as green accounting and corporate social responsibility, the lobbying process or, more at a macroeconomic level, country-level impacts. We have seen how new standards generate at times huge amounts of responses both in support of or against the proposal. We definitely do not consider accounting to be boring or non political when it has the capability of provoking so much response. In our opinion, there is a need for studies on those social consequences in order to determine how individuals, businesses or countries are affected beyond the numbers. Also more research is needed for the potential impacts at country level and about the relationship between jurisdictions. Surveys and personal interviews are bound to be particularly useful if we want to know about feelings and reactions towards the globalization of financial reporting.

Regulators have included the effects analysis in their agenda and we have seen how both IASB and EFRAG are incorporating this issue in their future projects. However, several questions remain related to who should be responsible for the effect analysis studies, what effects should be considered and what kind of analysis should be carried forward. In this sense, we believe that regulators are responsible for the incorporation of this step as a compulsory one in the process of standard setting, but they should not do this alone and should count on academic expertise and knowledge and the opinions of reporting entities affected by the changes. Studies should cover as many of the effects as possible. Apart from the effects on the attributes of financial information and therefore on the quality of financial information, considering other effects, such as those in the business analysis, in the contracting relations and in compliance costs, can help jurisdictions and reporting entities to be aware of the changes that they may be compelled to face. As for the type of analysis, we believe that both qualitative and quantitative studies can be very useful for making jurisdictions aware of the impact of IFRSs.

Some 35 years ago, Zeff (1978) asserted that the economic consequences of accounting standards were going to be the most challenging accounting issues of the 1970s, for the US and FASB. Now, in the new era of globalized international accounting standards, it is time for a reconsideration. The incorporation of IFRSs in Europe in 2005 and the expansion to a major part of the world has brought significant changes to the accounting standard processes. New consequences, both social and economic, are affecting financial information stakeholders, from the reporting entities as preparers, to users such as investors or creditors, but also to social accounting and country relationships. It is time therefore to reconsider those issues if we want the process of international accounting standards globalization to be a success.

Notes

1 See www.iasplus.com for detail of IFRS implementation by country.

2 Updated information about the process of IFRS adoption worldwide is available at www.iasplus.com.

3 EFRAG (2011) "Considering the Effects of Accounting Standards". Discussion Paper.

Bibliography

Ball, R., Robin, A. and Wu, J. (2003) "Incentives versus Standards: Properties in Accounting Income in Four East Asian Countries". *Journal of Accounting and Economics*, 36, 235–70.

Barth, M., Landsman, W. and Lang, M. (2008) "International Accounting Standards and Accounting Quality". *Journal of Accounting Research*, 46, 3, 467–98.

Beattie, V., Edwards, K. and Goodacre, A., (1998) "The Impact of Constructive Operating Lease Capitalization on Key Accounting Ratios". *Accounting and Business Research*, 28, 233–54.

Biondi, Y. and Suzuki, T. (2007) "Socio-economic Impacts of International Accounting Standards: An Introduction". *Socio Economic Review*, 5, 585–602.

Brüeggemann, U., Hitz, J.M. and Sellhorn, T (2011) *Intended and Unintended Consequences of Mandatory IFRS Adoption: Review of Extant Evidence and Suggestions for Future Research*. Denver, CO: American Accounting Association.

Cascino, S. and Gassen, J. (2012) "Comparability Effects of Mandatory IFRS Adoption: SFB 649". Discussion Paper 2012-009. Berlin: Humboldt University.

Christensen, H., Lee, E. and Walker, M. (2009) "Do IFRS Reconciliations Convey Information? The Effect at Debt Contracting". *Journal of Accounting Research* 47: 1167–1199

Czernkowski, R.M., Bugeja, M. and Moran, D. (2012) *Did IFRS 8 Increase Segment Disclosure?* Ljubliana: European Accounting Association.

Daske, H., Hail, L., Leuz, C. and Verdi, R. (2008) "Mandatory IFRS Reporting Around the Word: Early Evidence on the Economic Consequences". *Journal of Accounting Research*, 46: 5, 1085–142.

Fito, M.A., Moya, S. and Orgaz, N. (2011) *Considering the Effects of Operating Leases Capitalization in Key Financial Ratios*. Bamberg: EUFIN.

Fito, M.A., Gomez, F. and Moya, S. (2012) "Choices in IFRS Adoption in Spain: Determinants and Consequences". *Accounting in Europe*, 9:1, 61–83.

Fülbier, R., Lirio, J. and Pferdehirt, M. (2008) "Impact of Lease Capitalization on Financial Ratios of Listed German Companies". *Schmalenbach Business Review*, 60, 122–44.

Gallhofer, S., Haslam, J. and Kamla, R. (2011) "The Accountancy Profession and the Ambiquities of Globalization in a Post-colonial, Middle Eastern and Islamic Context: Perceptions of Accountants in Syria". *Critical Perspectives on Accounting*, 22, 4, 376–95.

García Osma, B. and Pope, P. F. (2009) "Earnings Quality Effects of Mandatory IFRS Adoption". Working paper, Universidad Autónoma de Madrid and Lancaster University.

Gassen, J. (2008) "Are Stewardship and Valuation Usefulness Compatible or Alternative Objectives of Financial Accounting?". Working paper. Berlin: Humboldt University .

Haller, A., Nobes, C., Cairns, D., Hjelstrom, A., Moya, S., Page, M. and Walton, P. (2012) "The Effects of Accounting Standards: Accounting in Europe". *Accounting in Europe* 9, 113–26.

Holthausen, R.W. (2009) "Accounting Standards, Financial Reporting Outcomes and Enforcement". *Journal of Accounting Research*, 47, 447–58.

Holthausen, R.W. and Leftwich, R.W. (1983) "The Economic Consequences of Accounting Choice". *Journal of Accounting and Economics*, 5, 77–117.

Hung, M. and Subramanyam, K.R. (2007) "Financial Statements Effects of Adopting International Accounting Standards: The Case of Germany". *Review of Accounting Studies*, 12: 4, 623–71.

IASB (2010) "Leases: Exposure Draft ED/2010/9", August, London: International Accounting Standards Board.

IASB (2011a) "'Effects Analysis'. IFRS 11 Joint Arrangements and Disclosures for Joint Arrangements included in IFRS 12 Disclosure of Interests in Other Entities", July, London: International Accounting Standards Board.

IASB (2011b) "'Re-exposure Draft', ED/2011/6. Revenues from Contracts with Customers", November, London: International Accounting Standards Board.

IASCF (2008) *Due Process Handbook for the International Accounting Standards Board*, London: International Accounting Standards Board.

Idowu, S. and Towler, B. (2004) "A Comparative Study of the Contents of Corporate Social Responsibility Reports of UK Companies", *Management of Environmental Quality: An International Journal*, 15: 4, 420–37 .

Imhoff, E.A. and Thomas, J.K. (1988) "Economic Consequences of Accounting Standards: The Lease Disclosure Rule Change". *Journal of Accounting and Economics*, 10, 277–310.

Jeanjean, T. and Stolowy, H. (2008) "Do Accounting Standards Matter? An Exploratory Analysis of Earnings Management Before and After". *Journal of Accounting and Public Policy*, 27: 6, 480–94.

Lambert, R., Leuz, C. and Verrecchia, R. (2007) "Accounting Information, Disclosure, and the Cost of Capital". *Journal of Accounting Research*, 45: 2, 385–420.

Lantto, A. and Sahlström, P. (2009) "Impact of International Financial Reporting Standard Adoption on Key Financial Ratios". *Accounting and Finance*, 49, 341–61.

Leuz, C., Nanda, D. and Wysocki, P. (2003) "Earnings Management and Investor Protection: An International Comparison". *Journal of Financial Economics*, 9, 505–27.

Morais, A. I. and J. D. Curto (2009) "Mandatory Adoption of IASB Standards: Value Relevance and Country-specific Factors", *Australian Accounting Review* 19: 2, 128–43.

Rappaport, A. (1977) "Economic Impact of Accounting Standards: Implication for the IASB". *Journal of Accountancy* 143, 89.

Schipper, K. (2010), "How Can We Measure the Costs and Benefits of Changes in Financial Reporting Standards?". *Accounting and Business Research*, 40: 309–27.

Sutton, T.G. (1984) "Lobbying of Accounting Standard Setting Bodies in the UK and the USA: A Downsian Analysis". *Accounting, Organizations and Society*, 9, 1.

Suzuki, T., Yan, Y. and Chen, B. (2007) "Accounting for the Growth And Transformation of Chinese Business and the Chinese Economy: Implications for Transitional and Development Economics". *Socio Economic Review*, 5: 4, 665–94.

Trombetta, M., Wagenhofer, A. and Wysocky, P. (2012) "The Usefulness of Accounting Research in Understanding the Effects of Accounting Standards", *Accounting in Europe*, 9: 2, 127-146

Wu, J. and Zang, I. (2009) "The Voluntary Adoption of Internationally Recognized Accounting Standards and Firm Internal Performance Evaluation". *The Accounting Review*, 84, 1281–309.

Wyatt, A. (1977) "The Economic Impact of Financial Accounting Standards". *Journal of Accountancy*, 144, 92.

Zeff, S.A. (1978) "The Rise of 'Economic Consequences'". *Journal of Accountancy*, December.

23

Turf Wars or Missionary Zeal: IFRS, IFAC, The World Bank and the IMF

Rachel Baskerville

1. Introduction

In 1829, Daniel Tyerman and George Bennet arrived back in London after an eight-year trip around the world, having been ordered to report to the London Missionary Society on gospel observance, standards and conditions of a worldwide network of missionary stations. The importance of the adaptation of the missionary workers to local cultures and political conditions was key to each local success. Yet their comprehensive report (39 pamphlet volumes) was largely forgotten a decade after completion (Hiney, 2001, p. 313).

In 1999, two bodies with a similar evangelical zeal, but for a worldwide markets gospel, and standards of market behaviour, launched assessments of observance of standards relevant to 'private and financial sector development and stability'. This initiative, by the IMF and the World Bank, peaked at 148 reports in 2003, down to 85 per annum by 2005. The bundle of 'Reports of the Observance of Standards and Codes' (ROSCs)[1] had mixed results, as expressed in the views from users and market participants. By the end of 2011 most of the IMF's 188 member countries had completed one or more ROSC assessments, 1,273 ROSCs had been produced, of which about 63 per cent were published.[2] There was often an eight-month or so period after completion before agreement on the ROSC, if at all, and the 'shelf-life' was sometimes only one year (IMF and the World Bank, 2005, 2011).

The tepid response by users of the benefits of these ROSCs is not unexpected. Such global initiatives to support the operations of quasi-integrated international financial markets move inexorably over a range of unique cultural landscapes: countries where tax laws are idiosyncratically distinctive; countries where the EU and others support retention and growth of local languages; countries seeking self rule and respect for choices of political structures and operations.

The utility of the ROSC project has not been unquestioned in the past decade; for example, Rojas-Suarez (2002) asked why it was that Argentina, with four official ROSCs and four self-assessments published on the IMF website, and therefore one of the developing countries most involved with the ROSC's process, was experiencing what appeared to be one of the deepest and lengthiest crises in recent history:

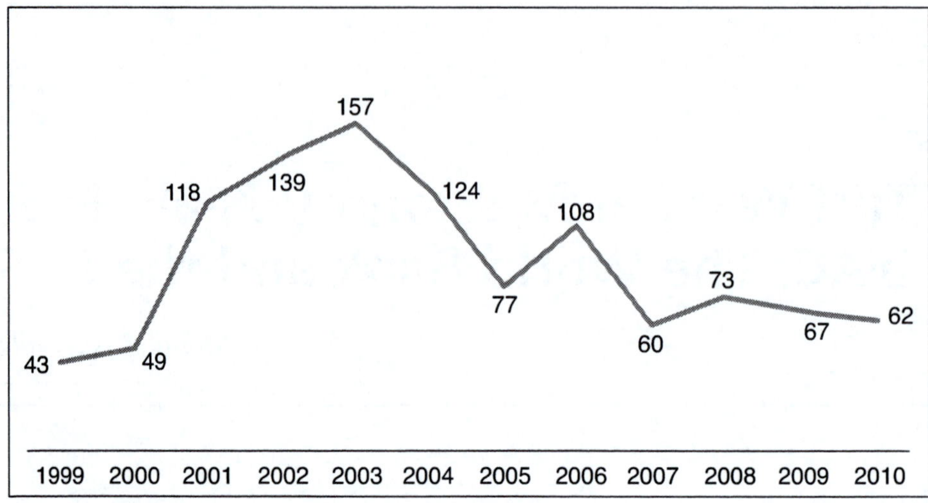

Figure 23.1 ROSC completion per annum, 1999–2010

> [W]hy did a positive assessment by the IMF/World Bank about progress in the implementation of four standards not shield the country against the eruption of a financial crisis? ... [I]t is not difficult to predict that this episode will be used over and over again by those who are skeptic about the usefulness of the standards (Rojas-Suarez, 2002, p.12).

It is not clear to any educated reader whether or not the governance boards of global entities such as the World Bank and the IMF believe that a common good of humanity is achieved in increasingly efficient operations of financial markets. However, it is clear that there are ardent views held by staff members in such entities who appear to fervently believe that relief from poverty can be best achieved though efficient operations of financial markets. A more cynical gloss on the increased involvement of the World Bank and IMF in standard setting activities might suggest 'market capture' of these institutions by standard setting and monitoring organisations (such as IFRS.org[3]), which are in need of more diverse funding sources. Perhaps they seek capital from the IMF and the World Bank in exchange for their steady advocacy and monitoring of accounting and auditing standards to enhance the operations of financial markets to ensure financial stability and growth; funding movements will be further discussed in this chapter. The last decade of progress on this shows little sign of the desired standardization and there are repeated calls for better monitoring and regulation to support IFRS, as documented in other chapters in this book.

The imperative towards a scheme of international financial architecture with the involvement of the IMF and the World Bank had its roots in the mid 1990s, when questions arose about how to prevent the financial chaos which developed as a result of Mexico's devaluation of the peso in 1994. Then the widespread financial crisis in Asia in 1997/8 lead to more direct action (Wade, 2009). 'Financial stability' began to be seen as a potential problem in a rapid globalizing world. There were varying explanations of the Asian crisis and many different ideas as to how such a crisis could be prevented in the future' (Humphrey *et al.,* 2009, p. 811 referring to Muchhala, 2007, and Rahman, 1998). Some blame was laid at the door of the IMF for having exacerbated the crisis (Weisbrot, 2007) but the need to improve financial capital flows worldwide led to the establishment of the Financial Stability Forum in 1999, its key mandate being to 'set up this system of standards' (Humphrey *et al.*, 2009, p. 811).

According to Hegarty *et al.* (2004, p.15), suggested impediments to successful implementation included a lack of globally consistent quality of audit by the big audit firms, and the lack of a 'comprehensive framework of principles for the regulation of accounting and auditing'. In many countries what was required was an institutional framework into which standards could fit. 'The "standards–surveillance–compliance" regime was to be seriously applied on a global basis, and not 'just' for emerging and developing economies' (Humphrey *et al.*, 2009, p. 812). With the G20 increasingly involved in many aspects of governance of global economies, the old dichotomy between emerging economies that were 'clients' of the IMF and international standard setters, and the developed industrial states, especially the UK and USA who were the 'masters' of the system, appeared to be breaking down (ibid.).

This chapter offers some analysis of the historic role of the UN, the educational activities of the OECD, and current level of activities of the World Bank and the IMF with regards to standard setting. In order to do this, this chapter describes some details of these four organizations (Section 2), and then offers a brief review of:

- spheres of influence: existing sources of a variety of standards, and a brief reflection on the accountability of trans-national actors (Sections 3 and 4);
- 'under the radar': that some in-house IFRS and research publications appear to ignore the World Bank and IMF (Section 5);
- five observed levels of involvement in standard setting activities by these international actors (Section 6);
- IFAC and IFRS organizational relationships with IMF and World Bank as observed from their annual reports (Section 7); and
- the chapter concludes with Discussion (Section 8).

2. The international organizations

The United Nations

The United Nations (UN) is an international organization founded in 1945 after the Second World War by 51 countries committed to maintaining international peace and security, developing friendly relations among nations and promoting social progress, better living standards and human rights. The UN has four main purposes and, with the World Bank, shares a primary mission, being the relief of poverty. These purposes are:

- to keep peace throughout the world;
- to develop friendly relations among nations;
- to help nations work together to improve the lives of poor people, to conquer hunger, disease and illiteracy, and to encourage respect for each other's rights and freedoms; and
- to be a centre for harmonizing the actions of nations to achieve these goals.[4]

The involvement of the UN in accounting standard issues was in earlier years through the activities of UNCTAD (the United Nations Conference on Trade and Development), which included the earlier work of the Commission on Transnational Corporations. In 1973 the

United Nations Economic and Social Council had charged a 'Group of Eminent Persons' with the task of advising on matters related to transnational corporations. After seeking stakeholder views this body recommended:

- permanent programme of work and a Centre be established to study transnational corporations and related policy issues; and
- the creation of a Commission on Transnational Corporations, to which the Centre was to report. The Commission provided the intergovernmental forum on transnational corporations while the Centre undertook a programme of information gathering, research and policy analysis, technical assistance, and consensus-building to support the work of the Commission.[5]

Thus the UN Commission on Transnational Corporations (TNCs) began functioning in 1974 with three objectives:

- to further understanding of the political, economic, social, and legal effects of TNC activity, especially in developing countries;
- to secure international arrangements that promote the positive contributions of TNCs to national development goals and world economic growth while controlling and eliminating their negative effects; and
- to strengthen the negotiating capacity of host countries, in particular the developing countries, in their dealings with transnational corporations (ibid.).

This body lasted for 17 years. The UNCTC was dissolved in 1993 as part of the reorganization of the UN's economic sector, and the programme on TNCs was transferred to UNCTAD. A snapshot of its subsequent activities can be observed from looking at the agendas and work papers, e.g. at the meeting on 1 July 1996, representatives of 50 member states of UNCTAD were present, including all major economic powers, but the only standard setters present were from the Accounting and Auditing Organization for Islamic Financial Institutions, two Canadian professional bodies (from CICA and CGAC), the Chartered Association of Certified Accountants (now known as ACCA) and the International Accounting Standards Committee.[6] The elected governing body did not include any Anglo-Saxon delegates. It appears to have continued to work in various projects to encourage the use of IFRS in countries outside the Anglo-Saxon/Western power blocs.

For example, a 2008 report suggested that it is likely that the IFRS for SMEs may not be suitable for smaller enterprises, as such enterprises may not produce general-purpose financial statements, and proposed that a three-tiered structure be followed to reflect user needs and the cost–benefit assessment of the optimal level of reporting. This did not refer to the IFRS for SMEs but instead jumped from a second tier (applying to 'significant' but non-issuer business enterprises) to their third tier:

> This level would apply to smaller enterprises that are often owner-managed and have no or few employees. The approach proposed is simplified accruals-based accounting, closely linked to cash transactions. National regulators may permit a derogation for newly formed businesses or new entrants to the formal economy to use cash accounting for a limited time (UNCTAD, 2008, p. 2).

The Organization for Economic Cooperation and Development (OECD)

The OECD, formed in 1960, currently has twenty-nine of the world's most developed, industrialized countries as its members. A valuable contribution of the OECD is its surveys of accounting practices in member countries and its assessment of the diversity or conformity of such practices. Its Working Group on Accounting Standards supports efforts by regional, national, and international bodies promoting accounting harmonization. In 1998, the OECD issued 'Principles of Corporate Governance' that support the development of high-quality, internationally recognized standards that can serve to improve the comparability of information between countries.

The OECD appears to be involved by organizing conferences on accruals, government financial statistics and IPSASB standards, e.g. the 12th annual OECD public sector accruals symposium was held on 8–9 March 2012 in Paris. The meeting was chaired by Michel Prada, President of the Public Sector Accounting Standards Council of France and included reports from the:

- International Public Sector Accounting Standards Board;
- International Accounting Standards Board;
- Statistics Department of the International Monetary Fund (IMF);
- Statistical Office of the European Commission (EUROSTAT); and
- accounting standard setting boards in individual countries.

The OECD 50th anniversary vision statement noted that it would:

> continue to help countries develop policies together to promote economic growth and healthy labour markets, boost investment and trade, support sustainable development, raise living standards, and improve the functioning of markets ... The 2008–09 financial and economic crisis underscored the increased complexity and interconnectedness of today's world, the on-going central importance of growth and employment, as well as the need for more effective regulation of the financial sector and enhanced co-operation to address common concerns.[7]

The World Bank

The World Bank, created in 1944, appears initially to have consisted of the IBRD and the International Development Association (IDA). Its objectives used to be stated as a broad portfolio's focus on 'social sector lending projects, poverty alleviation, debt relief and good governance' ('About Us', www.worldbank.org in 2011). This has more recently been simplified to: 'At the World Bank, we have made the world's most pressing development issue – to reduce global poverty – our mission.'

However, on the Home page the heading: 'Five Agencies, One Group' is used by the World Bank to explain its structure. The World Bank Group consists of five organizations. A user may click on any of the icons at the bottom of the home page and move to the different websites. The earlier 'WorldBankGroup.org' URL no longer exists, and a web-surfer is automatically taken to worldbank.org (which also contains annual reports for the IBRD and the IDA). The function of these five bodies as described on the World Bank home page is as follows:

- The International Bank for Reconstruction and Development (IBRD; aka the World Bank) 'lends to governments of middle-income and creditworthy low-income countries'. It was established in 1946 with 32 shareholding countries, $7.7 billion in capital, and headquarters in the USA in its first year.

- The International Development Association (IDA) established in 1960, 'provides interest-free loans—called credits— and grants to governments of the poorest countries'. In time, IDA countries became the IFC's main focus.
- The International Finance Corporation (IFC), established in 1956, 'provides loans, equity and technical assistance to stimulate private sector investment in developing countries'.
- The Multilateral Investment Guarantee Agency (MIGA) was established in 1988. Its purpose, as described on the World Bank home page, is to provide guarantees against losses caused by non-commercial risks to investors in developing countries. On MIGA's own home page its mission is to promote foreign direct investment into developing countries to 'help support economic growth, reduce poverty, and improve people's lives'.
- The International Centre for Settlement of Investment Disputes (ICSID) Convention was established in 1966 'inspired by the desire to increase cross-border flows of private capital' (ICSID, About Us). It is described on the World Bank home page as 'providing international facilities for conciliation and arbitration of investment disputes'. The Administrative Council, the governing body of ICSID, is comprised of one representative of each of the 157 ICSID Contracting States that are signatories to the Convention. Although the income statements appear to invariably result in zero earnings (neither profit nor loss), it is noted that:

  > After the completion of an arbitration/conciliation proceeding, if it is determined that there is an excess of advances and investment income over expenditures for the proceedings, the surplus is refunded to the parties in proportion to the amounts advanced by each party to the Centre (ICSID Annual Report 2011, p. 59).

The World Bank advances to the ICSID were $US1.57 million in the 2011 financial year, relative to total assets and liabilities both being $US 22.4 million (i.e. no equity component on the Balance sheet). In addition to the above five entities, the World Bank/IBRD includes the three-member World Bank Inspection Panel, formed in 1993, and described as:

> an independent, 'bottom-up' accountability and recourse mechanism that investigates IBRD/IDA financed projects to determine whether the Bank has complied with its operational policies and procedures (including social and environmental safeguards), and to address related issues of harm (www.worldbank.org/inspectionpanel, Home page).

While there is much mention throughout the annual report of accountability, there is none specifically in relation to financial reporting accountability to stakeholders; it is more in relation to processes and procedures.

The IBRD, the IFC and the IDA have one Board for governance, whereas MIGA has a separate Board. However, the representatives of the USA, Japan, Germany, France and the UK are the same on both bodies. There are a further twenty directors presenting various collations and voting blocks. In addition to the five executive directors shared with the IBRD, the IDA and the IFC, MIGA adds a representative for China. In MIGA, the other voting coalitions are much smaller, there are 19 other directors, and Russia and Saudi Arabia do not form a coalition with anyone else, unlike their coalitions operational in the World Bank and IFC. The integrated nature of these other entities to the operations of the World Bank is noted by other writers, e.g. Annisette, 2004, although her analysis focuses on the IRBD alone. She noted:

> The IDA was established to make 'soft' loans to the world's poorest countries unable to afford the IBRD's terms. Although it has a different source of funds, and country

> eligibility for its loans is not the same as the IBRD it is not a separate institution, but rather, a separate account managed by the officers of the IBRD. The IFC on the other hand makes loans exclusively for private enterprise in Bank borrowing countries. In addition to providing credit to local companies the IFC has helped many transnational corporations to establish themselves in developing countries. Finally the MIGA was established for the purpose of encouraging direct foreign investment in developing countries (Annisette, 2004, p. 305).

The size of financial activities of four of these largest entities is described in the MIGA annual report as:

> The World Bank Group committed $57.3 billion in fiscal year 2011. The World Bank, comprising IDA and IBRD, committed $43 billion in loans and grants to its member countries. Of this, IDA commitments to the world's poorest countries were $16.3 billion. IFC committed $12.2 billion and mobilized an additional $6.5 billion for private sector development in developing countries. $4.9 billion of the total went to IDA countries. MIGA issued $2.1 billion in guarantees in support of investments in developing countries (MIGA Annual Report 2011, p. 7).

The IMF (International Monetary Fund)

The IMF has two well-differentiated roles:

> First, a regulatory role, which comes from its capacity to design conditionality, exercise surveillance on the economy of its members and oversee compliance with members' obligation to collaborate with the Fund to assure 'orderly exchange arrangements and to promote a stable system of exchange rates'. Second, a lending role, which comes from its capacity to serve as a multilateral pool of reserves meant to 'give confidence to members by making the general resources of the Fund temporarily available', so as to help them correct their [balance of payments] problems while promoting 'high levels of employment and real income' and 'without resorting to measures destructive of national or international prosperity' (Torres, 2007, p. 17).

The IMF came into existence in 1945, and now describes itself on its website as:

> The International Monetary Fund (IMF) is an organization of 188 countries, working to foster global monetary cooperation, secure financial stability, facilitate international trade, promote high employment and sustainable economic growth, and reduce poverty around the world.

However, Woods and Lombardi (2006) find it astonishing that there are virtually no mechanisms to hold accountable elected directors of the IMF (those representing 'constituencies' of countries that gather to have a seat at the Board). The situation for appointed directors (those appointed by countries that enjoy their own seat at the Board, i.e. the USA, Japan, Germany, France, the UK, China, Russia and Saudi Arabia) is somewhat different, as in some cases (e.g. the USA) their appointment has to be approved by the legislature. The European Union countries act individually within the IMF, but 'coordinately'. As Woods and Lombardi (ibid.) note, the EU countries form a coalition with a Brussels permanent sub-committee on the IMF. Together they hold 32.18 per cent of the votes.

The IMF's capacity to influence its key members' policies through its advice, and to give confidence to potential borrowers by offering opportune and meaningful financial assistance in case of trouble, was questioned by Torres (2007). He suggested that the governance structure appears inconsistent with its multilateral nature, is dysfunctional to its purposes, and there is an ideological bias in its policy advice. This prevents the IMF from being responsive to stakeholders; the current reform process is 'tinkering on the margins' and might well fail to bring the desired additional credibility and effectiveness to the IMF. Similarly, Tan (2006) offered an analysis of the IMF's operational framework and political programme at what he terms 'the most crucial juncture in its institutional history'. This view was derived from his analysis of four recent publications on the Bretton Woods institutions, and focused on how commentators perceive and address the current 'crisis of legitimacy' affecting the IMF and the World Bank, a crisis which may be one driver to more involvement with other transnational actors.

3. Spheres of influence

In the decade since the 2002 'Conference on Financing for Development: Regional Challenges and the Regional Development Banks at the Institute for International Economics' there has been an increase in co-ordination only between those involved in international standard setting processes and developments, with the ROSC activities offering a detailed country-by-country assessments. After that 2002 Conference, analysis by Rojas-Suarez (2002) indicated the extant regulatory institutions shown in Table 23.1.

Table 23.1 Key standards for sound financial systems

Subject Area	*Key Standard*	*Issuing Body*
Macroeconomic Policy and Data Transparency		
Monetary and Financial Policy Transparency	Code of Good Practices on Transparency in Monetary and Financial Policies	IMF
Fiscal Policy Transparency	Code of Good Practices on Fiscal Transparency	IMF
Data Dissemination	Special Data Dissemination Standard (SDDS) General Data Dissemination System (GDDS)	IMF
Institutional Market Infrastructure		
Insolvency	Principles and Guidelines on Effective Insolvency and Creditor Rights Systems	World Bank
Corporate Governance	Principles of Corporate Governance	OECD
Accounting	International Accounting Standards (IAS)	IASB
Auditing	International Standards on Auditing (ISA)	IFAC
Payment and Settlement	Core Principles for Systemically Important Payment Systems	CPSS
Market Integrity	The Forty Recommendations of the Financial Action Task Force on Money Laundering	FATF
Financial Regulation and Supervision		
Banking Supervision	Core Principles for Effective Banking Supervision	BCBS
Securities Regulation	Objectives and Principles of Securities Regulation	IOSCO
Insurance Supervision	Insurance Core Principle	IAIS

Alan Richardson offers an analysis of a part of the networks of these organizations, and suggests that:

> among the international bodies, the Basel Committee emerges as holding a pivotal role linking the IFAC committees and the organizations centred on the World Bank and IOSCO. The Basel Committee was the first of the World Bank cluster of organizations to liaise with the accounting standard-setting bodies when they asked the IASC to develop standards for bank financial statements in 1976 (Richardson, 2009, p. 584).

In his analysis of Canadian standards setting networks, Richardson described this network as consisting of '61 organizations clustered into four 'factions',' i.e. a group of densely interconnected bodies, consisting of:

- a domestic securities regulator's cluster (linked to the Canadian Securities administrators);
- an IOSCO/World Bank cluster;
- an IFAC/Basel cluster; and
- a domestic accounting and auditing standard setting cluster (linked to the CICA).

Richardson's analysis thus expanded the conceptions of accounting and auditing standards setting process in Canada to include a diversity of 'centers of calculation' linked together in 'networks of rule' (Rose and Miller, 1992). Standard setting can thus be observed to be embedded in a network structure with multiple influences (Richardson, 2009, p. 585). This is similar to the analysis by Humphrey *et al.* (2009) of global auditing regulation in which they described three, rather than four, influential entities/groupings. However, they move the Basle Committee into the IOSCO/WORLD bank cluster. Their clusters are:

- IFAC;
- international regulators: World Bank, IOSCO, the International Association of Insurance Supervisors, the Basel Committee on Banking Supervision and the European Commission; and
- the large multinational audit firms.

All three groups have interlocking relationships with each other (Humphrey *et al.*, 2009, pp. 813–4).

It is noticeable that the majority of such entities are essentially private institutions. As asked by Jonsson (2008), who is entitled to hold such powerful entities accountable? He notes the soft blurring of the public/private boundaries, and the need to conceive of democracy in novel terms. It is observed by many specialists in this field that the engagement of international actors in, for example, standards setting activities may lead to more cumbersome and less responsive decision making (Jonsson, 2008, p. 88). Much literature on private authority in global governance takes as its common point of departure the notion

> that authority has to do with legitimized power, which is not monopolized by state actors . . . regulatory tools outside the state-centric sphere are not legally binding regulations (hard law) but rather variants of soft law, such as standards, rankings and monitoring frames and codes of conduct (ibid.).

Because we are now in the area of the global 'soft law' for standards in accounting, this may require higher levels of accountability by those setting these standards than in earlier eras when each local professional body was accountable to its members and the state for the standards and financial market development.

4. Accountability

Categorization of these spheres of influence, and the roles of transnational actors, both draw attention to the nature of accountability by multinational bodies, the World Bank and IMF in particular. Woods and Narlikar (2001) observed that many such global entities are trying to bolster that accountability through enhancing transparency and accounting. Eight years ago the websites and links to their annual reports on line were always slow, indirect at times, and even obscure in some cases (Baskerville and Huckstep, 2009). There has certainly been an observable shift in access to online financial reporting by these entities in the past five years.

But whether or not there has been a more fundamental shift in accountability since the Woods and Narlikar (2001) study remains to be analysed. They had concluded that there are still gaps between the World Bank, the IMF and the WTO regarding their accountability, due to their structure not being suited to new stakeholders, their work programmes expanding faster than their accountability efforts, and possibly due to a gap between 'legitimacy and accountability in international economic governance' (ibid., p. 582). And as Barnett and Finnemore (1999, p. 700) pointed out, the same rules that define bureaucracies for such entities, and make them powerful, can also make them 'unresponsive to their environments, obsessed with their own rules at the expense of primary missions, and ultimately lead to inefficient self-defeating behavior'. Given such a range of studies in these entities, and the understandings of accountability or lack thereof, it is surprising that their importance is overlooked.

5. Under the radar

In contrast to research described so far in this chapter, there is another surprisingly large body of research pertaining to the activities of IFRS and IFAC which does not refer at all to the involvement of the World Bank and the IMF. For example in the IFRS (2006) 'Statement of Best Practice: Working Relationships between the IASB and other Accounting Standard-Setters' they did not consider the World Bank or the IMF. Instead they suggested that 'other accounting standard-setters' refers to organizations that have responsibility for setting accounting standards at a national level, including those whose responsibilities include but are broader than convergence with or adoption of IFRSs, and at an international level, specifically the International Public Sector Accounting Standards Board. It also includes those organizations that have responsibility for, and those with a direct role in facilitating, the setting of accounting standards across a number of countries in a region. It was instead addressing timing, feedback, agenda setting, education, etc., between the IASB and national standard setters or those implementing and monitoring application of IFRS.

More scholarly articles, such as the examination of IFRS diffusion by Chua and Taylor (2008), have documented the inexorable rise of IFRS standards and offered an alternative explanation for the origin and diffusion of IFRS that incorporates social and political factors, but contain no consideration of the role of the World Bank and the IMF. Another recent piece of scholarship by Donna Street, when she interviewed those most closely involved in the events in the decade before the establishment of the IASB, concluded the G4 served as a key catalyst for change, but did not consider the role of the IMF and World Bank. Given that such sterling research ignores connections or spheres of influence of the World Bank and the IMF, an analysis was undertaken examining the annual reports and websites of both these bodies.

6. Five levels of involvement

The following analysis postulates five levels of involvement by the World Bank and IMF in standard setting policies. First, when large entities such as the World Bank and the IMF issue their own guidance. Choi and Mueller (1978) noted that the International Finance Corporation (IFC), part of the World Bank Group, was in the practice of issuing special instruction booklets on the format of financial statements presented to the IFC, as well as guidance on the appropriate underlying accounting standards and principles (ibid., p. 105).

Second, supporting monitoring implementation of IFRS and IAS either by themselves or by proxy. The role of the ROSCs has already been discussed in this chapter, whereas monitoring of the proper application of IFRS is essentially an audit function. Therefore one might anticipate a focus of activity on the regulation and proper functioning of audit. The regulation of audit is undertaken by the IAASB, funded through IFAC.

Third, noting their own compliance in the adoption of accrual accounting with the appropriate standards. For example, the United Nations with its 193 member states is the most representative of all the global bodies and, in terms of its own reporting, has adopted accrual accounting and International Public Sector Accounting Standards. This is paralleled by the IFAC 2011 Annual Report: they note their financial statements have been prepared in accordance with International Public Sector Accounting Standards. This is in contrast to:

- the World Bank (2011) Annual Report, which noted that their financial statements have been prepared in conformity with the accounting principles generally accepted in the United States of America (US GAAP); and
- both the IFRS 2010 Annual Report (who note their financial statements have been prepared in accordance with International Financial Reporting Standards), and the IMF 2011 Annual Report, who note their 'consolidated financial statements of the General Department are prepared in accordance with International Financial Reporting Standards (IFRS) issued by the International Accounting Standards Board (IASB)'.

Fourth, enhancing the profile and/or the legitimating of IFRS and IFAC by cross reference on websites. In order to get an indication of this exercise, a count was undertaken (April 2012) using search engines on each of the websites, as indicated in Table 23.2 and Figure 23.2. This method of indicating stakeholder salience is a simple indicator to offer a snapshot of the extent to which the stakeholder relations are or are not reciprocated. For example, searching for the acronym IASC turned up 990 results in the World Bank URL, but none on MIGA.

In the reverse process, when a search was made for reference to the acronyms representing these stakeholders on the IFRS and IPSAS websites, the results were as shown in Table 23.3, Table 23.4 and Figure 23.3.

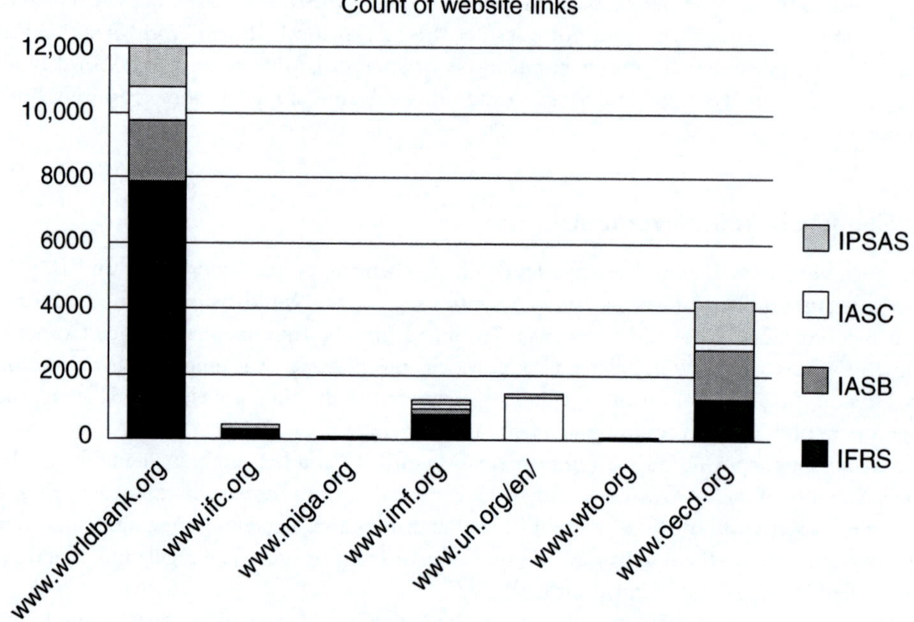

Figure 23.2 Cross referencing on website URLs as at April 2012

Table 23.2 Cross referencing on website URLs as at April 2012

	IFRS	*IASB*	*IASC*	*IPSAS*	*Total:*
www.worldbank.org	7910	1870	990	1200	11970
www.ifc.org	407	40	17	0	464
www.miga.org	55	22	0	0	77
www.imf.org	855	168	55	126	1204
www.un.org/en/	23	45	1250	168	1486
www.wto.org	24	7	16	3	50
www.oecd.org	1280	1540	211	1270	4301

Table 23.3 Cross referencing on IFRS and IFAC websites as at April 2012

	World Bank	*IFC*	*MIGA*	*IMF*	*United Nations*	*WTO*	*OECD*
www.ifrs.org	595	7	0	48	81	10	21
www.ifac.org	99	1	0	9	44	0	17

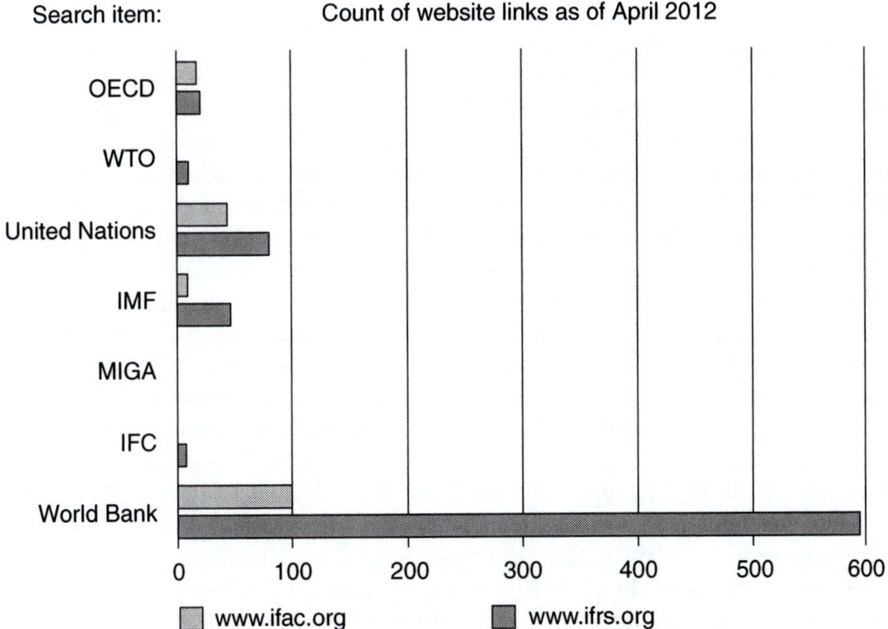

Figure 23.3 Cross referencing on IFRS and IFAC websites as at April 2012

It is clear from these two tables and figures that the most cross referencing occurs on the World Bank linkages, even though the ROSC was a joint IMF/World Bank programme.

This now leads to the fifth level of involvement, that of funding support. The World Bank and the IMF do not have representatives on the IFAC and IASB Boards. However, it can be observed from an inspection of the Annual Reports of the IFAC and IFRS/IASB that there is involvement in that direction as reported by the IFAC and IFRS/IASB. This is covered in Section 6.

7. IFAC and IFRS foundation's relationship with IMF and World Bank

The relationship of IFAC with IMF and World Bank from annual report disclosures

For at least the past five years, the IMF and the World Bank are listed as organizations with which IFAC has 'regulatory relationships' in the IFAC annual report. However, there is no detail about the money coming from them to IFAC. Total revenues for IFAC for 2011 were $25.9 million, of which 52 per cent is from 'membership dues', but there is no breakdown, i.e. it is not possible to determine the amount provided from the World Bank exactly. A further 37 per cent is from the Forum of Firms.

IFAC has a long history of cooperation with the World Bank, for example in 2005 it developed a strategy that emphasized the commitment to the public interest, a mandate to build an 'investment climate of trust', and a role in contributing to economic growth and stability.

In 2002, IFAC and a group of six international financial institutions – the Basel Committee on Banking Supervision, the European Commission, the Financial Stability Board, the International Association of Insurance Supervisors, the International Organization of Securities Commissions, and the World Bank (the Monitoring Group) – began a dialogue about 'the importance of high-quality audits of financial statements and the need to restore and enhance public confidence in financial reporting and auditing. The result of this dialogue was the 'IFAC Reforms'. The IFAC Reforms changed the structure and processes for the auditing, ethics, and education standard-setting boards supported by IFAC, and called for the Monitoring Group to perform a five-year review of their implementation' (IFAC Annual Report).

The manner in which IFAC aimed to meet these commitments has, for a long time, been through Auditing and Public Sector (including governmental reporting) standards. In the 2004–6 report by the president of IFAC, Graham Ward, he noted that IFAC had sponsored a Workshop for both the government and corporate sectors, funded together with the World Bank and African development bank. The World Bank and African development bank contributed $261,819 to this Workshop.

During 2005, the funding support for the Public Interest Oversight Board (PIOB) of IFAC included monies from the World Bank and USA Federal Reserve Board (USA) with support to the PIOB totalling $478,289. In 2006 the figure had more than doubled to $1,047,363 (IFAC Annual Report 2006, p. 47). In the 2007 Annual Report, IFAC supported the PIOB to the tune of $1.56 million which included $90,000 from the World Bank and others.

From 2010, IFAC began acknowledging in its Annual Report its input into the World Bank Reports on Observance of Standards and Codes (ROSCs); these ROSCs had been undertaken on 14 countries that year. In 2010, the Monitoring Group issued its 'Review of the IFAC Reforms:– Final Report', which stated that virtually all of the changes called for by the IFAC Reforms had been implemented. It also acknowledged that the initial implementation of the IFAC Reforms had been a significant undertaking, and recognized the 'numerous achievements with respect to their implementation'. Finally, the Report identified a number of near-term actions for IFAC and the standard-setting boards it supports, focused on further enhancing diversity, transparency, and accountability (IFAC 2010, p. 19, n.1).

The IPSASB (International Public Sector Accounting Setter Board) also conducted a survey to determine the level of implementation of IPSASs (International Public Sector Accounting Standards) by World Bank list of economies. Initial results from the survey showed that of 209 World Bank economies, approximately one third were either adopting or making plans to adopt IPSAS or have standards in place that are broadly consistent with IPSASs.

The relationship of the IFRS foundation with the IMF and the World Bank from annual report disclosures

It is clear from the IFRS Annual Reports as to the identity of stakeholders who have long-term funding commitments to IFRS, e.g. specific countries in the EU, as well as an EU commitment of €4 million a year for 2011–13. Both the World Bank and the IMF were identified separately, 10 years ago, as supporting organizations. But their support more recently is unclear. In the 2008 Annual Report the organizations and individuals consulted during the IFRS Constitution Review proposals mentioned that the president of the World Bank was a member of the monitoring group, but there is no mention of the IMF.

In 2010 the large 'International Accounting firms' donated $US8.4 million a year to core funding of FIRS.org, whereas the amount from various 'Central banks and International organizations' is only $US.5 million a year (IFRS Annual Report 2010). So from the Annual Reports of IFRS, there is apparently little direct involvement, and the lack of research based on their involvement may be unsurprising.

8. Discussion and conclusion

There are at least three understandings or interpretations of the above data, whilst bearing in mind that the current equilibrium could be undermined quite easily, almost as a sleight of hand, if those in charge of global financial architecture see it as important that IFRS should move from being controlled by high level accounting technicians, and use their financial muscle to affect a shift in the ultimate control of IFRS. The largely unsubstantiated claim that IFRS caused the Global Financial Crisis is one nail in this coffin. Alternative readings may include that the above evidence points to:

- a successful and gradual merging of objectives and monitoring outputs whereby the IMF, World Bank, IFAC and IFRS all gain from synergies. Funding support for IFAC and IFRS is continued and may increase as their missions and objectives morph through consanguity with the large global entities, although remaining seemingly independent to outsiders; or
- a turf war, with IFRS and IFAC wishing to remain in control of the development of standards. They may allow the World Bank and IMF a 'tolerable' level of observer or voting rights in lesser activities, but remain wary of being any more a part of the World Bank/IMF grouping; or
- the World Bank and the IMF eyeing the apparent successful distancing from the Global protest movement and Occupy Wall Street events by IFAC and IFRS, and the World Bank and IMF are wishing to align to smaller, less politicized bodies. IFAC and IFRS, meanwhile, are careful to steer clear of claiming any panacea for financial instability and lack of economic growth, and advocate IFRS adoption as a process, not a solution.

As Tamm Hallström (2004) points out, the quest for authority is an imperative for private standard setters. But the extent to which this needs to be accompanied by a missionary-like zeal for worldwide compliance with one set of financial standards to ensure maximum market efficiency remains a belief, rather than a fact. For IFRS, reliance on approval and acceptance by private actors such as preparers, users, or third parties (e.g. banks or rating agencies) is not enough. International standards need to be permitted and usually endorsed by public actors, especially the EU and IOSCO. That explains not only the powerful role of IOSCO, but also the relevance of coming to terms with the EU (Martinez-Diaz, 2005). Contrary to the self-regulatory rhetoric dominant in the accounting field, state recognition remains a central requirement for the IFRS success. Even the early diffusion of IAS in developing countries is to be attributed to the World Bank's development agenda and less to the convincing content of the standards (Camfferman and Zeff, 2007, pp. 441f.). But passing the 'chokepoint of public recognition' requires a broad approach and Tamm Hallström (2004, p. 138ff.) distinguishes four general strategies to achieve compliance with the standards: positive self-marketing, establishment of suitable procedures, cooperation with reference organizations, and ultimately the persuasion of private and public authorities. The latter two of these strategies can be observed within the foregoing analysis in this chapter.

Tamm Hallström identifies organizing principles that Camfferman and Zeff have also elaborated on without, however, identifying them in analytical terms. Each of these principles refers to an actor group 'important in the standard-setting activity' (ibid., p. 141). She sees the organizational structure as reflecting the relative weight of interest groups and the necessity to secure external recognition for the enforcement of privately drafted standards in the global arena (Botzem and Quack 2009, p. 994).

> In addition, the openness of the IASB to regulatory, supervisory and business communities is also becoming an issue of debate (FSF, 2009). The severe challenges the IASB is facing today would come as a surprise to many readers who rely only on Camfferman and Zeff's account of the IASC as a success story. In fact, these events could have been hardly foreseen if one would follow the others in their uncritical stance towards professional self-regulation (Botzem and Quack 2009, p. 997).

The IFRS strategies are not wholly driven by an attempt to provide coordination solutions for the global allocation of capital and a belief in maximizing the efficiency of capital market operations. The need to ensure proper application, widespread support among accounting firms, and monitoring through transparent audit reporting are all essential to the continuation of the IFRS brand.

The ongoing evolution of a relationship between the IMF, World Bank, IFAC and IFRS will no doubt be further energized by financial cycles and collapses. It is hoped that the zeal attached to the mandated adoption in World Bank conditions will, in fact, prevent the worst effects of economic downturns on second and third world economies, or at least offer some protection. Unfortunately, we can be sure these downturns will happen again even after the current cycle has passed. But those most interested in accounting regulation do need to be clear to themselves whether we need to accept the missionary zeal for worldwide IFRS adoption and increasing World Bank involvement regardless of cultural specificity and regulatory landscapes, or to observe it as a turf war of major consequences if not separated out for analysis and informed debate. This chapter offers a starting point to some such considerations.

Notes

1 www.worldbank.org/ifa/rosc.html, accessed 12 May 2012
2 www.imf.org/external/np/exr/facts/sc.htm, accessed 12 May 2012
3 IFRS.org is the moniker by which the IASB decided to promote its 'brand' from 2010
4 www.un.org/en/aboutun/index.shtml, accessed 20 June 2012
5 www.benchpost.com/unctc/ accessed 5 July 2012
6 http://unctad.org/en/Docs/tbitncac1d10.en.pdf accessed 5 July 2012
7 www.oecd.org/dataoecd/36/44/48064973.pdf accessed 30 April 2012

Bibliography

Annisette, M. (2004) 'The True Nature of the World Bank'. *Critical Perspectives on Accounting* 15(3): 303–23.

Barnett, M.N., and Finnemore, M. (1999) 'The Politics, Power and Pathologies of International Organizations'. *International Organization* 53(4): 699–732.

Baskerville, R.F. and Huckstep, W. (2009) 'The Financial Reporting Accountability of the Global Economic Multilaterals', paper presented to the 6th International Critical Management Studies Conference, Warwick, July 2009.

Botzem, S. and Quack, S. (2009) '(No) Limits to Anglo-American Accounting? Reconstructing the History of the International Accounting Standards Committee: A Review Article'. *Accounting, Organizations and Society* 34: 988–98.

Camfferman, K. and Zeff, S.A. (2007) *Financial Reporting and Global Capital Markets: A History of the International Accounting Standards Committee 1973–2000*. Oxford: Oxford University Press.

Choi, F.D.S and Mueller, G.G. (1978) *An Introduction to Multinational Accounting*. Englewood Cliffs, NJ: Prentice-Hall.

Chua, Wai Fong and Taylor, S.L. (2008) 'The Rise and Rise of IFRS: An Examination of IFRS Diffusion'. *Journal of Accounting and Public Policy* 27: 462–73.

FSF (2009) 'Report of the Financial Stability Forum on Addressing Procyclicality in the Financial System', available at www.fsforum.org/ publications/r_0904a.pdf.

Hegarty, J., Gielen, F. and Hirata-Barros, A.C. (2004) 'Implementation of International Accounting and Auditing Standards Lessons Learned from the World Bank's Accounting and Auditing ROSC Program', September, available at www.worldbank.org/ifa/LessonsLearned_ROSC_AA.pdf.

Hiney, T. (2001) *On the Missionary Trail: The Classic Georgian Adventure of Two Englishmen, Sent on a Journal around the World 1821–1829*. London: Vintage Books.

Humphrey, C., Loft, A. and Woods, M. (2009) 'The Global Audit Profession and the International Financial Architecture: Understanding Regulatory Relationships at a Time of Financial Crisis'. *Accounting, Organizations and Society* 34(6–7): 810–25.

IFAC (2006) *Annual Report 2006*, available at www.ifac.org/publications-resources/2006-ifac-annual-report, accessed 14 March 2013.

IFAC (2010) *Annual Report 2010*, available at www.ifac.org/publications-resources/ifac-2010-annual-report, accessed 14 March 2013.

IFAC (2011) *Annual Report 2011*, available at www.ifac.org/publications-resources/ifac-2011-annual-report, accessed 14 March 2013.

IFRS (2010) *Annual Report 2010*, available at www.ifrs.org/The-organisation/Governance-and-accountability/Annual-reports/Pages/2010Annual-Report.aspx, accessed 14 March 2013.

IMF (2011) *Annual Report 2011*, available at www.imf.org/external/pubs/ft/ar/2011/eng/index.htm, accessed 14 March 2013.

IMF and the World Bank (2005) *The Standards and Codes Initiative: Is It Effective? And How Can It Be Improved?*, prepared by the staffs of the International Monetary Fund and World Bank, approved by M. Allen and D. M. Leipziger, 1 July, available at www.worldbank.org/ifa/ROSC%20review%202005.pdf, accessed 14 March 2013.

IMF and the World Bank (2011) *Review of the Standards and Codes Initiative*, prepared by the staffs of the International Monetary Fund and World Bank approved by R. Moghadam (IMF) and J. Devan (World Bank), 16 February, available at www.imf.org/external/np/pp/eng/2011/021611a.pdf, accessed 14 March 2013.

Jonsson, C. (2008) 'Democracy beyond Nation State: Transnational Actors and Global Governance'. *Statsvetenskaplig Tidskrift*, 110(1): 83–97, available at www.transdemos.se/publications/transdemos StvTidskr.pdf.

Martinez-Diaz, L. (2005) 'Strategic Experts and Improvising Regulators: Explaining the IASC's Rise to Global Influence, 1973–2001'. *Business and Politics* 7(3) Art. 3.

Muchhala, B. (ed.) (2007) *Ten Years After: Revisiting the Asian Financial Crisis*. Washington, DC: Woodrow Wilson International Center for Scholars.

OECD (2011) *OECD 50th Anniversary Vision Statement*, meeting of the OECD Council at ministerial level, Paris, 25–26 May, available at www.oecd.org/dataoecd/36/44/48064973.pdf accessed 30 April 2012.

Rahman, Z. (1998) 'The Role of Accounting in the East Asian Financial Crisis: Lessons Learned'. *Transnational Corporations* 7: 1–51.

Richardson, Alan J. (2009) 'Regulatory Networks for Accounting and Auditing Standards: A Social Network Analysis of Canadian and International Standard-setting', *Accounting, Organizations and Society* 34: 571–88.

Rojas-Suarez, Liliana (2002) *International Standards for Strengthening Financial Systems: Can Regional Development Banks Address Developing Countries Concerns?* Address to the Conference on Financing for Development: Regional Challenges and the Regional Development Banks at the Institute for International Economics, 19 February, available at www.new-rules.org/storage/documents/ffd/rojas-suarez-2.pdf accessed 14 March 2013.

Rose, N., and Miller, P. (1992) 'Political Power Beyond the State: Problematics of Government'. *British Journal of Sociology* 43(2): 173–205.

Street, Donna L. (2006) 'The G4's Role in the Evolution of the International Accounting Standard Setting Process and Partnership with the IASB', *Journal of International Accounting, Auditing and Taxation* 15: 109–26.

Tamm Hallström, K. (2004) *Organizing International Standardization: ISO and the IASC in Quest of Authority*. Cheltenham: Edward Elgar.

Tan, C. (2006) 'Reform or Reinvent? The IMF at a Crossroads'. *Global Governance* 12(4): 507–22.
Torres, H. R. (2007) 'Reforming the International Monetary Fund: Why its Legitimacy is at Stake'. *Journal of International Economic Law* 10: 443–60.
UN (n.d.) 'About Us', available at www.un.org/en/aboutun/index.shtml.
UNCTAD (2008) *Accounting and Financial Reporting Guidelines for Small and Medium-sized Enterprises (SMEGA)*, Intergovernmental Working Group of Experts on International Standards of Accounting and Reporting, Twenty-fifth session, Geneva, 4–6 November, available at http://unctad.org/en/docs/c2isard50_en.pdf accessed 31 July 2012.
Wade, R. H. (2009) 'Accountability Gone Wrong: The World Bank, Non-governmental Organizations and the US Government in a Fight over China'. *New Political Economy* 14(1): 25–48.
Weisbrot, M. (2007) 'Ten Years After: The Lasting Impact of the Asian Financial Crisis', in Muchhala, B. (ed.) *Ten Years After: Revisiting the Asian Financial Crisis*. Washington, DC: Woodrow Wilson International Center for Scholars, pp. 105–18.
Woods, N., and Lombardi D. (2006) 'Uneven Patterns of Governance: How Developing Countries are Represented in the IMF'. *Review of International Political Economy* 13(3): 480–515.
Woods, N., and Narlikar, A. (2001) 'Governance and the Limits of Accountability: The WTO, the IMF, and the World Bank'. *International Social Science Journal* 53(170): 569–83.
World Bank (2011) 'Annual Report 2011', available at http://web.worldbank.org/WBSITE/EXTERNAL/EXTABOUTUS/EXTANNREP/EXTANNREP2011/0,,contentMDK:22969490~menuPK:8121330~pagePK:64168427~piPK:64168435~theSitePK:8070617,00.html, accessed 14 March 2013.

24

Accounting Regulation in Emerging Markets and Newly Industrializing Countries

Ahsan Habib

1. Introduction

This chapter provides an overview of financial reporting regulation in emerging markets and newly industrializing countries (NICs). Emerging markets are characterized by social or business activity undergoing a rapid growth and industrialization process, assisted by government policies favoring economic liberalization and the adoption of a free-market system (Hoskisson *et al.*, 2000). NICs are countries having economies that have not yet reached developed status but have, in a macroeconomic sense, outpaced their developing counterparts (Wikipedia). The emerging market and NIC share of world gross domestic product (GDP) stood at 38 per cent in 2010, twice that in 1990. Measuring GDP at purchasing-power parity, emerging market countries actually overtook the developed world in 2008. Emerging economies attracted over half of all inflows of foreign direct investment (FDI), courtesy of these countries' fast-growing domestic markets (*The Economist*, 2011). The exact number of emerging market countries is difficult to identify precisely, since the numbers change with time. The big emerging market economies are Brazil, China, Egypt, India, Indonesia, Mexico, Philippines, Poland, Russia, and Turkey.

The spectacular economic growth registered by emerging market countries and NICs invites the question of the role of financial reporting in promoting such phenomenal growth. Financial reporting provides the primary source of independently verified information to the capital providers about the performance of managers (Sloan, 2001). This facilitates efficient resource allocation decisions by signalling changing investment opportunities to managers and outside investors, disciplining self-interested managers to invest in value-maximizing projects, and reducing firms' cost of capital (Bushman and Piotroski, 2006). Bushman and Smith (2001: 304) argue that the efficiency of capital allocation depends upon:

> the extent to which managers identify value creating and destroying opportunities, the extent to which managers are motivated to allocate capital to value creating investments and withdraw capital from value destroying investments, and the extent to which capital is available to invest in value creating opportunities.

The financial reporting system, particularly financial accounting information, is expected to facilitate capital allocation decisions through any of these channels.

The efficient functioning of the financial reporting system, however, is contingent upon identifying the financial reporting objectives and developing a rigorous set of accounting standards that is compatible with those reporting objectives, as well as upon certain institutional factors (e.g. corporate governance, the existence and enforcement of laws governing investor protection and disclosure standards) that ensure strict enforcement of accounting standards. Emerging markets and NICs provide some very diverse and interesting insights into these issues when compared with their developed country counterparts. For example, many of the emerging market countries and NICs inherited their accounting systems from another country, but are themselves characterized by quite different reporting incentives. Additionally, most have adopted, or are going to adopt, a common set of financial reporting standards, International Financial Reporting Standards (IFRSs), designed to promote better transparency and international comparability. However, there remain serious concerns as to the applicability of a common set of reporting standards in the emerging economies and NICs, and as to whether such standards can be strictly enforced in these countries (Briston, 1978; Samuels and Oliga, 1982; Perera, 1989). Although the current structure of the International Accounting Standards Board (IASB) allows a close engagement with stakeholders around the world, the design of the reforms has usually been led by lawmakers in Europe or the United States. Consequently, representatives from emerging markets and NICs are asked to undertake sometimes costly accounting and auditing reforms which are necessitated because of crises that occur outside of their own countries (Fortin *et al.*, 2010).

This chapter proceeds as follows: Section 2 discusses the financial reporting objectives in emerging markets and NICs and how they differ from their developed country counterparts. Section 3 describes the accounting standard-setting issues for these countries with a particular emphasis on the adoption of IFRSs. Section 4 analyses the broader effect of the financial reporting regime on economic growth in emerging markets and NICs. Finally, Section 5 concludes the chapter.

2. Objectives of financial reporting in emerging markets and NICs

2.1 Financial reporting objectives in the leading conceptual frameworks

The objectives of financial reporting outlined in the leading conceptual frameworks primarily reflect user needs for accounting information, as in these illustrations:

- The primary users of general purpose financial reporting are present and potential investors, lenders and other creditors, who use that information to make decisions about buying, selling or holding equity or debt instruments and providing or settling loans or other forms of credit (OB2) (*The International Accounting Standards Board (IASB) Conceptual Framework*).
- The objective of general purpose financial reporting is to provide financial information about the reporting entity that is useful to existing and potential investors, lenders, and other creditors in making decisions about providing resources to the entity. Those decisions involve buying, selling, or holding equity and debt instruments and providing or settling loans and other forms of credit (OB2) (*Financial Accounting Standards Board (FASB) Conceptual Framework*).

The theoretical argument supporting such an objective stems from the fact that information asymmetry between corporate managers and investors requires the former to provide financial statements prepared following generally accepted accounting principles, so that investors can assess the performance of the management group with respect to the efficient use of their resources (Jensen and Meckling, 1976).

A contracting-based argument for the provision of financial reporting considers organizations as a contracting intermediary. All parties contracting with the firm demand information about the firm's ability to meet its contractual obligations. This contracting structure of the firm creates the fundamental demand for financial reporting and disclosure in an economy. This demand, however, is not homogeneous since published financial statements and other corporate disclosures play important economic roles in short- and long-term debt markets, in equity markets, in the evaluation and compensation of management, in labor markets, in informing major customers and suppliers, and in a variety of economic contexts. These heterogeneous uses affect the properties of the optimal accounting system and of the optimal accounting information supplied by it. Any analysis of accounting and disclosure infrastructure requirements must pay attention to heterogeneous sources of demand and cannot be restricted to the equity market (Ball, 2001).

Such a heterogeneous demand and the consequent supply of accounting information varies between the 'common law' versus the 'code law' models of financial reporting (Ball *et al.* 2003).[1] Common law reporting practices are grounded in a 'shareholder' model of reporting which assumes that ownership dispersion creates information asymmetry and thus provides opportunities for professional managers (who manage the organizations but do not control them) to deceive outside investors (who own the organizations but do not manage them). Corporate governance rights are meant to be exercised by the shareholders, and information asymmetries in these countries are more efficiently resolved through public disclosures which generate a stronger demand for published financial statements (Ali and Hwang, 2000). US and UK financial reporting practices are illustrative of common law reporting regimes. Code law countries, on the other hand, rely more on a 'stakeholder' model of governance, where information asymmetries are resolved through 'insider' communication with stakeholder representatives. Such characteristics generate a lower demand for publicly available financial statement disclosures (Ball *et al.*, 2003). China, a code law country, is illustrative of this proposition.

2.2 Unique financial reporting objectives in the emerging markets and NICs

China installed a highly centralized planned economy following the Soviet Union's socialist principles. Such a state-dominated economy encouraged the development of uniform accounting systems (UASs) serving the needs of the state for economic planning and control. These UASs were charts of accounts and detailed explanations as to how and when to use the accounts, plus detailed rules or regulations for costing, profit distribution, depreciation, and other matters. UASs used principles, concepts, and methods quite different from those widely used in market-based economies. The UASs incorporated no elements of a market economy. A nationwide hierarchical network of financial reporting was maintained through which financial statements prepared by individual companies were aggregated all the way up to the central government. The Chinese Ministry of Finance developed a conceptual framework entitled 'Accounting Standards for Business Enterprises', in 1992. The document asserts that financial accounting and reporting:

- should meet the information requirements for macroeconomic management;
- should allow relevant parties to assess the financial position and operating results of the business; and
- should meet the information needs of business management.

It is interesting that the information needs of macroeconomic management are given priority over the decision-making needs of individual investors (Xiao and Pan, 1997; Graham and Li, 1997; Zhou, 1988).

The ownership structure of Chinese listed firms is significantly different from that of the USA or European countries. A typical Chinese company comprises three predominant groups of shareholders: the state, 'legal persons/institutions', and individuals. A distinct feature that separated the Chinese stock market from those of other countries was the creation of a split-share structure consisting of non tradable share (NTS) holders and tradable share (TS) holders.[2] This split-share structure was established in the early 1990s upon the formation of the Shanghai and Shenzhen Stock Exchanges, was intended to help raise finance for state-owned enterprises (SOEs), while retaining state control over their operation (Green *et al.*, 2010). This split-share structure constrained significantly the tradability of NTS held by the state and 'legal persons', and effectively gave the government absolute control over joint stock companies. The split-share structure arrangement has been the alleged cause of severe agency problems between controlling shareholders (NTS holders) and minority shareholders (TS holders) because of weak managerial incentives for acting in the best interest of the public shareholders, among other reasons (CSRC, 2005). Considering this split-share structure as an obstacle to the efficient functioning of the Chinese capital market, the Chinese government launched a split-share structure reform to convert publicly listed firms' NTS to TS, with the expectation that demand for publicly disclosed accounting information would increase. Green *et al.* (2010) find that both mandatory and voluntary disclosures improved in the post-reform period for firms completing this reform when compared to a matched control group of companies that had not commenced the reform. Jiang and Habib (2012) document an increase in earnings informativeness in the post-reform period attributed to the increased tradability of shares resulting from this reform.

Greece provides another example where the conventional financial reporting objectives, which are focused on the needs of investors who actively manage their portfolios in the capital markets, may not be suitable. In Greece, despite the unrestricted movement of capital between Greece and other EU nations, banks are the prominent mode of finance (Tzovas, 2006; Anagnostopoulos and Buckland, 2007). This environment encourages financial reporting that protects the interests of the creditors. By establishing a close relationship with many companies, and by owning part of a firm's capital, banks are in a position to directly obtain relevant information without having to rely on publicly disclosed accounting information (Ballas *et al.*, 2010).

Other emerging markets and NICs have financial reporting objectives which are not aligned with the reporting incentives. This is particularly the case for countries that inherited a foreign reporting system from colonial rule. For example, India, Bangladesh, and Pakistan inherited shareholder-oriented reporting objectives of British colonial origin without actually having the necessary institutional environments in terms of capital market size, maturity, activity and opportunity to diversify. For example, the capital market of Bangladesh fails to provide shareholders the opportunities to diversify risks through stock trading, because the market is driven, not by fundamental information, but rather by irrational behaviour (see section 2.3 for an example). Weak investor protection, absence of litigation, and lack of incentives for auditors to provide high quality audits result in financial statements that are not very informative for shareholders. In addition, family ownership of the organizations in these countries is dominant, and family managers tend to be less constrained by disciplinary forces and are more entrenched (Fan and Wong, 2002; Morck *et al.*, 1988).

In Latin American countries investors, banks, and other lenders rarely use financial statements to determine creditworthiness. Instead, family or personal ties, or high collateral requirements, replace financial information and market discipline in determining the prospective borrowers (Fortin *et al.*, 2010: 96). Fan and Wong (2002) find that controlling-family shareholders in East Asian countries tend to take advantage of flexibility and discretion over accounting choice and auditor selection to distort the firm's true earnings performance.

The financial reporting objectives espoused in the IASB and FASB Conceptual Frameworks assume the presence of active markets where transactions are conducted at arm's length. However, one of the significant features of emerging market economies and NICs is the dominance of business groups which simulate an internal capital market. Granovetter (2005) argues that business groups emerge because of market failures and poor-quality legal and regulatory institutions. The role of such groups is to internalize transactions, in the absence of legal safeguards guaranteeing transactions between unaffiliated firms (Khanna and Palepu, 1997). In a recent comprehensive meta-analytic review of the impact of business group affiliation, Carney *et al.* (2011) find that, although business group affiliation diminishes firm performance in general, this is less so in countries with underdeveloped financial and labour market institutions. However, Sarkar *et al.* (2011) find that insider control exacerbates opportunistic earnings management in India, and this is more pronounced for group-affiliated firms compared to their standalone counterparts. Controlling insiders may be reluctant to provide disclosures that will make them less able to consume private benefits, even when such disclosures increase firm value and reduce the cost of capital. From a policy perspective, designing accounting standards and reporting regulations without considering this dominant form of ownership structure may lead to 'unexpected or ineffective' policy outcomes (Leuz and Wysocki, 2008).

2.3 Financial reporting objectives and capital markets

The conceptual frameworks developed by the IASB and the FASB emphasize the information provision role of financial statements for, among other things, buying, selling or holding equity or debt instruments which are carried out through organized stock markets. One of the most important functions of stock markets involves efficient allocation of capital by channelling scarce capital into businesses that need it most and withdrawing it from negative net present value projects. Markets also allow investors to trade their shares for liquidity purposes. Theory suggests that management-prepared financial statements should play a vital role for the efficient functioning of capital markets since financial reporting provides the primary source of independently verified information to the capital providers about the performance of managers (Sloan, 2001). However, such an association between the two is not obvious in some of the emerging markets and NICs.

Emerging markets vary widely with respect to the size and functioning of the stock markets. Two of the largest emerging markets, India and China, had about 5,034 and 2,063 listed companies respectively on their stock exchanges by the end of 2010. Interestingly, the number of listed companies in the Indian Stock Exchange is the largest in the world. Another emerging economy country, Thailand, shows hardly any variation in the number of listed companies over time. Market capitalization, too, varies significantly, with the Shanghai Stock Exchange alone recording a market capitalization of $2,804bn at the end of June 2011, much larger than that recorded by the Indian Stock Exchange market capitalization of $1,506bn (WFE, 2012). Table 24.1 provides a summary overview of some of the stock market indicators for some emerging market countries and NICs.

The extent to which this variation in capital market development is affected by public and private enforcement of regulatory mechanisms is an issue for policy-making at international development agencies (Jackson and Roe, 2009). These law enforcement institutions should be regarded as more important than investor protection laws (DeFond and Hung, 2004). The intensity of securities regulation can be measured by securities regulation costs as a fraction of GDP (Jackson, 2007; Coffee, 2007; Jackson and Roe, 2009). These authors document that the amount of public resources devoted to financial regulation is significantly higher in the common law countries compared to their code law counterparts (the estimation is based on major industrialized

Table 24.1 Some key stock market indicators

Panel A: Number of listed companies including foreign companies on select emerging markets and NICs stock exchanges

Exchange	*1990*	*1995*	*2000*	*2001*	*2002*	*2003*	*2004*	*2005*	*2006*	*2007*	*2008*	*2009*	*2010*
Americas													
Brazilian SE	579	544	467	441	412	391	388	381	350	404	392	386	381
Mexican Exchange	390	185	177	172	169	237	326	326	335	367	373	406	427
Santiago SE (Chile)	216	282	261	249	246	240	240	246	246	241	238	236	231
Asia – Pacific													
Bombay SE	NA	NA	NA	NA	NA	NA	4,730	4,763	4,796	4,887	4,921	4,955	5,034
Indonesia SE	123	237	286	315	331	333	331	336	344	383	396	398	420
National SE India	NA	NA	NA	1,041	916	911	957	1,034	1,156	1,330	1,406	1,453	1,552
Philippines SE	153	205	230	232	234	236	235	237	239	244	246	248	253
Shanghai SE	NA	NA	NA	646	715	780	837	833	842	860	864	870	894
Shenzhen SE	NA	NA	NA	508	508	505	536	544	579	670	740	830	1,169
Thailand SE	159	416	381	385	398	420	463	504	518	523	525	535	541
Europe – Africa													
Egyptian Exchange	NA	NA	NA	NA	NA	NA	795	744	595	435	373	313	228
Istanbul SE	110	205	316	311	289	285	297	304	316	319	317	315	339
Johannesburg SE	769	638	606	532	451	411	389	373	389	411	411	396	397
Moscow SE	NA	NA	NA	NA	NA	NA	NA	161	193	207	233	234	245

Panel B: Domestic market capitalization (in USD million)

Exchange	*2000*	*2001*	*2002*	*2003*	*2004*	*2005*	*2006*	*2007*	*2008*	*2009*	*2010*
Americas											
Brazilian SE	226,152	186,238	121,641	226,358	330,347	474,647	710,247.4	1,369,711	591,966	1,337,247	1,545,566
Mexican Exchange	125,204	126,258	103,941	122,533	171,940	239,128	348,345.1	397,725	234,055	352,045	454,345
Santiago SE	60,400	56,310	49,828	87,508	116,924	136,493	174,418.8	212,910	131,808	230,732	341,799
Asia – Pacific											
Bombay SE	NA	NA	130,390	278,663	386,321	553,074	818,878.6	1,819,101	647,205	1,306,520	1,631,830
Indonesia SE	26,813	22,998	30,067	54,659	73,251	81,428	138,886.4	211,693	98,761	214,942	360,388
National SE India	NA	NA	112,454	252,893	363,276	515,972	774,115.6	1,660,097	600,282	1,224,806	1,596,625
Philippines SE	25,261	20,606	18,197	23,191	28,602	39,818	68,269.8	102,853	52,031	86,349	157,321
Shanghai SE	NA	NA	306,444	360,106	314,316	286,190	917,507.5	3,694,348	1,425,354	2,704,779	2,716,470
Shenzhen SE	NA	NA	156,648	152,872	133,405	115,662	227,947.3	784,519	353,430	868,374	1,311,370
Thailand SE	29,217	35,950	45,406	119,017	115,390	123,885	140,161.3	197,129	103,128	176,956	277,732
Europe - Africa											
Egyptian SE	NA	NA	NA	NA	38,533	79,509	93,496.4	139,274	85,978	91,207	84,277
Istanbul SE	69,659	47,150	34,217	68,379	98,299	161,538	162,398.9	286,572	118,328	233,997	307,052
Johannesburg SE	131,321	84,344	116,544	260,748	442,526	549,310	711,232.3	828,185	482,700	799,024	925,007
Moscow SE	NA	48,503	58,888	137,611	153,323	266,425	886,516.9	1,221,530	337,089	736,307	949,149

Table 24.2 Resource-based securities law enforcement data

Countries	*Staff per million of population*	*Budget per billion US$ of GDP*	*Public enforcement index*
Brazil	2.68	31,729	0.58
Chile	9.93	66,093	0.60
Egypt	3.65	–	0.30
Greece	12.16	60,111	0.32
India	0.43	–	0.67
Mexico	5.19	49,864	0.35
Pakistan	2.36		0.58
Peru	5.32	108,353	0.78
Philippines	4.29	65,848	0.83
Thailand	6.52	83,985	0.72
Poland	4.64	22,661	–
Turkey	6.17	58,893	0.63
USA	23.75	83,232	0.90
UK	19.04	80,902	0.68
Australia	34.44	89,217	0.90

Source: Jackson and Roe (2009), Table 2.

Note: Formal public enforcement equals the arithmetic mean of: (1) supervisor characteristics index; (2) its rule-making power index; (3) its investigative powers index; (4) orders authority index; and (5) criminal authority index, as per La Porta, Lopez-de-Silanes and Shleifer (2006).

developed countries). Table 24.2 reproduces some key indicators of resource-based regulatory intensity measures for some emerging markets and NICs from Jackson and Roe (2009).

To benchmark these numbers against the three developed countries, the input measures for the USA, the UK and Australia are also provided. Australia devotes about 35 staff per million of population to the oversight of securities regulation issues. The comparable figure for Brazil is only three.[3] Individual country studies, however, provide some evidence that regulatory sanctions by securities regulators in emerging economy countries convey valuable information. For example, Chen *et al.* (2005) find that the enforcement actions initiated by the CSRC generate negative market returns, an observation that attests to the credibility of the CSRC.

Although a well-functioning stock market has been positively linked with economic growth (e.g, Levine and Zervos, 1998; Arestis *et al.*, 2001; Beck and Levine, 2002), the role of a reliable financial reporting system in promoting a well-functioning stock market is questionable in many of the emerging markets and NICs. The recent spate of roller coaster behaviour for the Dhaka Stock Exchange (DSE) index in Bangladesh is a case in point. The market index rose by a staggering 22 per cent on a single day on 16 November 2009 because of the listing of a mobile phone company. But, by the end of 2010, it was well known that the capital markets of Bangladesh were well overvalued and overheated and they fell by 285 points on 13 December 2010, and then again by a further 551 points, the largest single day fall in the history of the DSE. The index then stood at around 8,000. The market regulatory authority, the Securities and Exchange Commission, together with the Bangladesh Bank, had relaxed its earlier conservative measures (Bangladesh Bank allowed banks to invest a tenth of their total liabilities) to boost confidence in the marketplace. However, opportunists took full advantage of this and expropriated retail investors' money. The market stood at around 5,500 index points in October 2011 from 8,900 a year previously and now stands at 3,534 index points. The market appears to be driven by news that is not directly relevant to company-level financial reporting. Another emerging economy market, Vietnam, is a case in point. Although market capitalization of Vietnamese stock exchanges as a percentage of GDP remains very high (39.2 per cent in 2010), the demand for financial reporting in making prudent stock trading decisions is very low. Only a third of investors analyse financial information before making investment decisions. About 40 per cent of investors are investing on basic information, and the rest invest based on what others do (Chu, 2010).

Taken together, the discussion above provides an alternative perspective on financial reporting objectives when compared to mainstream reporting objectives in providing information for decision-usefulness. Emerging markets and NICs institutional environments are characterized by the dominance of business group and family ownership structures, a feature that diminishes the role of publicly available financial information. Stock markets in some of the emerging market countries fail to perform the role of allocating capital efficiently, instead being used by powerful people to expropriate resources.

3. Accounting standard setting in emerging markets and NICs and IFRS adoption

3.1 Importance of Accounting Standards

Underpinning a system of reliable financial information is a framework of sound accounting, auditing, and reporting practices. This framework must be built using rigorous standards for accounting and auditing, skilled accountants and auditors capable of implementing those standards, and a robust enforcement regime that penalizes non-compliance (Fortin *et al.*, 2010). Financial reporting standards ensure the preparation of understandable, relevant, reliable and comparable financial statements providing information in a timely manner, with a conscious trade-off between their costs and benefits. Capital markets function more efficiently and corporate governance and regulation are more effective with credible financial reporting aided by a rigorous set of accounting standards. La Porta *et al.* (1998: 1140) suggest:

> For investors to know anything about the company they invest in, basic accounting standards are needed to render company disclosures interpretable. Even more important, contracts between managers and investors typically rely on the verifiability in courts of some measures of firms' income or assets. If a bond covenant stipulates immediate repayment when income falls below a certain level, this level of income must be verifiable for the bond contract to be enforceable even in court in principle. Accounting standards might then be necessary for financial contracting, especially if investors' rights are weak.

However, countries worldwide vary significantly with respect to the development, implementation and enforcement of accounting standards. The market-oriented common law countries rely on private sector standard setting initiatives, while the code law countries seem to accept state dominance in setting financial reporting standards. Countries that were under British colonial rule for a substantial period of time tend to use the British Company Act for the preparation of financial statements (e.g. Malaysia, India, and Pakistan). However, in most cases, the Act lacks clarity with regard to statutory requirements on disclosures in the financial statements of incorporated companies: (see World Bank, 2003, Report on the Observance of Standards and Codes (ROSC)). External auditing is mandatory, with shareholders appointing statutory auditors. Auditor rotation policy is common and, unlike the practice in South Korea, joint auditing is not required for the listed companies.

Countries that were under non-UK colonial rule developed their financial reporting differently. For example, Mexico was colonized by Spain, a code law country, but its accounting and auditing practices have been influenced by the US GAAP, and generally accepted auditing standards (GAAS). The main reason for this trend has been the importance of foreign direct investment from the United States, as well as a trend among large Mexican publicly traded corporations towards listing in the world's largest stock exchanges in the USA (ROSC, Mexico, see World Bank, 2004). Brazil, a code law country, entrusts the Securities Commission (CVM) and stock exchanges with responsibility for developing financial reporting standards, instead of its professional accounting bodies. The Corporations Law of 1976 prescribes the accounting and financial reporting requirements for corporations. Financial statements are required to be audited by auditors registered with the Central Bank of Brazil and the Securities Commission. This is in contrast to cases where auditors need to be registered with the professional accounting body of that particular country. Under the Corporations Law, the board of directors is responsible for appointing and dismissing independent auditors.

3.2 The current trend among emerging market and NICs towards adopting IFRSs

Despite these significant differences in financial reporting regulation and audit profession development among emerging markets and NICs, one common theme that binds these countries together is their commitment to the adoption of IFRSs as the relevant accounting standards. For example, Malaysia and Indonesia have expressed their intention to fully converge their domestic accounting standards and Malaysian financial reporting standards with IFRSs. The generally accepted accounting principles in Thailand (Thai GAAP) are based on the International Accounting Standards (IASs) and IFRSs. The Russian Ministry of Finance endorsed almost all of the existing IFRSs, the Standards Interpretation Committee (SIC) and the International Financial Reporting Standards Interpretation Committee (IFRIC) interpretations for use in Russia at the end of 2011 (IASplus.com).

The rationales for adopting IFRSs as one common reporting standard are well understood. Proponents argue that the adoption of a single set of reporting standards would be particularly beneficial for emerging markets and NICs as it would:

- eliminate or reduce set-up costs in developing national accounting standards;
- attract foreign investment by the provision of comparable financial statements;
- improve the perceived quality and status of financial reports; and
- reduce the cost to firms of preparing financial statements (Nobes and Parker, 2006).

An additional incentive for emerging economies to adopt IFRSs is to attract foreign direct investment (FDI). One of the major factors that hinder the ability of many developing and emerging market countries to attract FDI is the lack of a credible reporting system. Adoption of a common set of reporting standards may partially alleviate that problem.[4] However, opponents argue that accounting and accountability problems are unique to emerging market and NICs and donor agencies should collaborate more closely with the recipient country to ensure that their assistance is delivered only in accordance with the respective national accounting development plans (Wallace and Briston, 1993).

However, the adoption of IFRSs can be regarded as a first step only. Financial reporting quality is influenced by several institutional factors, other than the quality of accounting standards, that affect the demand for and the supply of financial information, such as firm and country-level corporate governance, and the legal system. Ball *et al.* (2003) believe that although it is not surprising to see academic and professional accounting literatures replete with discussions on the characteristics of both accounting standards (e.g. costs and benefits associated with a particular accounting standard) and standard setting authorities, and on the variation of standards across countries, that's not the end of the story. They are of the opinion that this focus on standards is

> substantially and misleadingly incomplete, because financial reporting practice under a given set of standards is sensitive to the *incentives of the managers and auditors* responsible for financial statement preparation. Preparer incentives depend on the interplay between market and political forces in the reporting jurisdiction [italics added].

Firms' reporting incentives are shaped by many factors, including the country's legal institutions (e.g. the rule of law), the strength of the enforcement regime (e.g. auditing), capital market forces (e.g. the need to raise external capital), product market competition, and a firm's compensation, ownership and governance structure along with its operating characteristics (Hail *et al.*, 2010).

Emerging markets and NICs provide a rich laboratory for testing the incompatibilities that could arise from IFRS adoption because the reporting incentives faced by these countries are unlikely to be addressed by IFRSs. For example, Ball *et al.* (2003) use the example of four East Asian countries which imported their accounting standards from the USA, the UK and the IASB, but do not necessarily produce financial statements that share the reporting qualities envisioned by these standards. The institutional environment relevant to the application of these standards in the four countries studied is not compatible with the environment in which USA, UK, and international standards are developed. Research documents that these East Asian countries do not encourage timely recognition of economic losses, which is a crucial element of high quality financial reporting (Ball *et al.*, 2000, 2003).

3.3 Challenges associated with the successful implementation of IFRSs in emerging market countries and NICs

It is important to understand that a single set of accounting standards does not necessarily guarantee the comparability of firms' reporting practices even when the enforcement of standards is very high. Reporting comparability is unlikely to occur as long as firms' reporting incentives differ. Therefore the wholesale adoption of IFRSs will bring little benefit as long as standard setters fail to incorporate variations in reporting incentives across countries in their IFRS adoption processes. IFRS adoption will necessitate major changes in supporting institutions, as outlined by Ball (2001: 128):

> An economically efficient public financial reporting and disclosure system requires … the training an audit profession of adequate numbers, professional ability, and independence from managers to certify reliably the quality of financial statements; separating as far as possible the systems of public financial reporting and corporate income taxation, so that tax objectives do not distort financial information; reforming the structure of corporate ownership and governance to achieve an open-market process with a genuine demand for reliable public information; establishing a system for setting and maintaining high-quality, independent accounting standards; and, perhaps most important of all, establishing an effective, independent legal system for detecting and penalizing fraud, manipulation, and failure to comply with standards of accounting and other disclosure, including provision for private litigation by stockholders and lenders who are adversely affected by deficient financial reporting and disclosure.

Many of the emerging markets and NICs encounter serious problems in initiating and sustaining the institutional changes required for the successful implementation of IFRSs.

Bangladesh, for example, has long been using IASs as the domestic accounting standards for listed companies. However, mere adoption does not guarantee successful implementation of IASs, because supportive institutional requirements are lacking. For example, an independent and competent audit profession required for successful implementation IAS/IFRSs-based reporting system is in short supply. The professional accounting institute, the Institute of Chartered Accountants of Bangladesh (ICAB) has failed to enforce its self-regulatory monitoring to improve audit quality in Bangladesh (Mir and Rahaman, 2005). Kabir *et al.* (2011) document that even Big 4-affiliated audit firms in Bangladesh fail to provide high-quality audits. This is not surprising given the lack of market demand for quality differentiated audits and a strong monitoring and enforcement regime in this country. Empirical studies from Greece show that auditors, irrespective of their Big N affiliation, fail to prevent earnings management and do not provide qualified opinions in response to managerial opportunistic behaviour in the post-IFRS regime, because of lack of incentives (Tsipouridou and Spathis, 2012).[5]

Another major challenge facing auditors with IFRS adoption relates to a substantial increase in audit risk, because auditors now have to verify more managerial judgments in the principles-based standard setting approach pursued by the IASB. Careful consideration needs to be directed at the professional accounting education systems in these countries, to assess the adequacy of auditor training in facing this challenge.

Another obstacle for the successful implementation of IFRSs in the emerging markets and NICs relates to the IASB's increasing emphasis on a fair value measurement system. The fair value concept originates in economies in which firms engage in arm's length exchanges and, thus fair value is oriented towards providing relevant information to facilitate such exchanges. However, emerging economies and NICs are characterized by an institutional environment where business transactions are often carried out within social and political networks; a feature that mitigates the benefits of a fair value-based accounting system. He *et al.* (2012) document fair value-induced earnings management practices among firms that have strong incentives to avoid reporting losses for regulatory purposes. Their findings suggest that 'intended benefits of improved transparency through [fair value accounting] FVA implementation may fail to materialize or, worse, unintended consequences such as more earnings management may arise' (ibid., p. 3).

The success of IFRS implementation also hinges on the presence of strong regulatory institutions (e.g. securities commissions, courts) and an environment with a high litigation risk. Litigation risk motivates managers to disclose their bad decisions and report their losses in a timely fashion. It also motivates auditors to ensure the transparency of financial statements (Ball, 2001). In the absence of an efficient system of private detection, and the penalization of inadequate disclosure and reporting, other institutional changes will not bring the desired benefits. An example of a low litigation environment in China follows (Liu *et al.*, 2010: 4):

> While Chinese listed companies are subject to litigation risk for misrepresentation of financial statements, it is highly unlikely that they will be sued by investors. Less than ten firms have been sued since China's two stock exchanges were established in 1990, and most of the cases involving those 10 firms are not related to auditing issues … According to the Supreme Court's *Judicial Interpretation* of January 2002, investors are not allowed to file litigation against a listed company without the CSRC first issuing a penalty announcement, even the listed company's financial statements are widely believed to be fraudulent.

A similar low litigation risk environment exists in India where only 10 per cent of Indian listed companies have purchased a directors' and officers' liability insurance (D&O), although this number is rising since some spectacular high-tech corporate collapses in India. There has also been a spike in claims brought by shareholders in 2010, some 42 per cent. The actions arise out of mergers, takeovers, and financial disclosures (Sharma, 2010).

Fortin *et al.* (2010) identify some key challenges associated with the successful adoption of IFRSs in Latin American countries, some of which are considered as big emerging market countries. For effective and sustained implementation of the IFRSs, Fortin *et al.* (2010: 78–9) recommend that:

> the scope of application of IFRS should be limited to companies in which there is a public interest; ample transition time should be allowed for effective implementation of the standards; and an adequate mechanism for ensuring that "local IFRS" keep pace with new [IASB] standards and amendments … is required. Finally … it becomes increasingly important for [Latin American] countries to be actively engaged in the international standard-setting process, which means reviewing exposure drafts for key standards and submitting detailed comments to the IASB.

Many Latin American countries fail to adequately address these concerns.[6]

IFRS application is seen to offer the greatest advantage where countries have vibrant stock markets, demanding high quality financial reporting for the efficient allocation of capital. However, some emerging economy countries don't see the benefit of having stock exchanges. For example, the government authorities of Brunei have assessed the suitability and the need for Brunei to establish its own stock market, but opined against it. The institutional environment of Brunei is such that it appears to be easier for local companies to obtain their capital through private equity, commercial bank loans or government loan schemes (*The Brunei Times*, 2011). What is interesting though, is that Brunei has revised relevant sections of the Companies Act and made IFRS mandatory for all limited companies since 2002. Why, then, would Brunei require IFRS compliance, even though the institutional environment of that country may demand a lesser emphasis on published financial statements? Ball (2001) believes that the well-known signalling model of Spence (1973) provides a plausible answer. Ball (2001: 166–7) reasons that:

> it is essentially costless to [signal with respect to the adoption of IASs]. . . If there is no cost of signaling quality, all rational actors signal that they are high quality, so the signal loses its discriminatory informativeness. The cost to a country of adopting IAS as its accounting is economically trivial, provided it changes little else. The claim that using IAS is cheaper than using domestic standards even implies a negative signaling cost. The predicted consequence is that low-quality countries will seek to hide among high-quality countries by adopting IAS, while at the same time continuing to issue low-quality financial statements.

Lasmin (2011) offers an institutional perspective on the adoption of IFRSs by emerging market countries and NICs. The need to be socially accepted by the global community is sometimes paramount, so that the decision to adopt IFRS might not be triggered by economic reasoning alone. Most developing countries have to accept IFRS partly because of their limited ability to produce a legitimate set of standards, and partly because of their dependence on these organizations. This acceptance explains why developing countries tend to follow similar set of accounting practices to legitimize their dependence (DiMaggio and Powell, 1983).

Taken together, the discussion in this section shows that a sound and reliable financial reporting system relies critically on the successful application of a set of standards suitable to the economic environment of individual countries. However, emerging market countries and NICs rely heavily on accounting standards developed in the Western world, which ignore the unique incentives faced by these countries. Even if the adoption of IFRS can be defended on the grounds that such adoption will increase reporting comparabilities and will affect FDI positively, these countries may lack crucial institutional support, such as a strong regulatory enforcement system and a competent and independent audit profession and, consequently, may fail to achieve the benefits to be expected from IFRS adoption.

4. Financial reporting systems and economic development in emerging markets and NICs

4.1 Financial reporting and economic growth

Do financial reporting systems impact economic growth of a country? There are considerable debates on the macro effect of financial development, a very important component of which is the financial reporting system. Lucas (1988) suggests that the role of financial intermediation in economic growth has been over-emphasized. Levine *et al.* (2000), on the other hand, show that financial development matters for economic growth. Wurgler (2000) refines this stream of research by investigating the role of financial development on capital allocation efficiency (this measure is not a direct proxy for economic growth) and finds that countries with well-developed financial intermediaries improve capital allocation efficiency. Whether financial reporting makes a positive contribution to capital allocation efficiency is investigated by Habib (2008), who finds support for this proposition.

Figure 24.1 provides an integrated depiction of the factors likely to affect a country's financial reporting regime and the ways a reporting regime might affect economic growth. There are three channels through which a high quality financial reporting regime could affect economic growth:

- better identification of good vs. bad projects;
- discipline on project selection and expropriation by managers; and
- reduction in information asymmetries.

The role of timely and credible disclosures is integral to the efficient functioning of these three channels. Corporate disclosures play a critical role in the efficient functioning of capital markets by mitigating agency conflicts among managers, majority shareholders and minority shareholders (Healy and Palepu, 2001: 406). Voluntary disclosures by management and disclosures mandated by regulations are the two primary communication vehicles shaping the corporate information environment (Beyer *et al.*, 2011: 297). The authors document that about 66 per cent of the accounting-based information explaining quarterly return variance is provided by voluntary disclosures, followed by analysts with 22 per cent, and then by mandatory disclosures.

However, it can also be argued that financial reporting quality is unrelated to economic growth. Some real world examples also support this argument. For example, big emerging economy countries like China, India, and Brazil do not have a very high quality reporting regime (Bushman and Smith, 2001; ROSC, at World Bank), yet over the past decade these countries have enjoyed phenomenal economic growth. One plausible explanation could be that these economies may be characterized more as 'insider' economies because of the prevalence of business groups, requiring less reliance on published financial reporting.

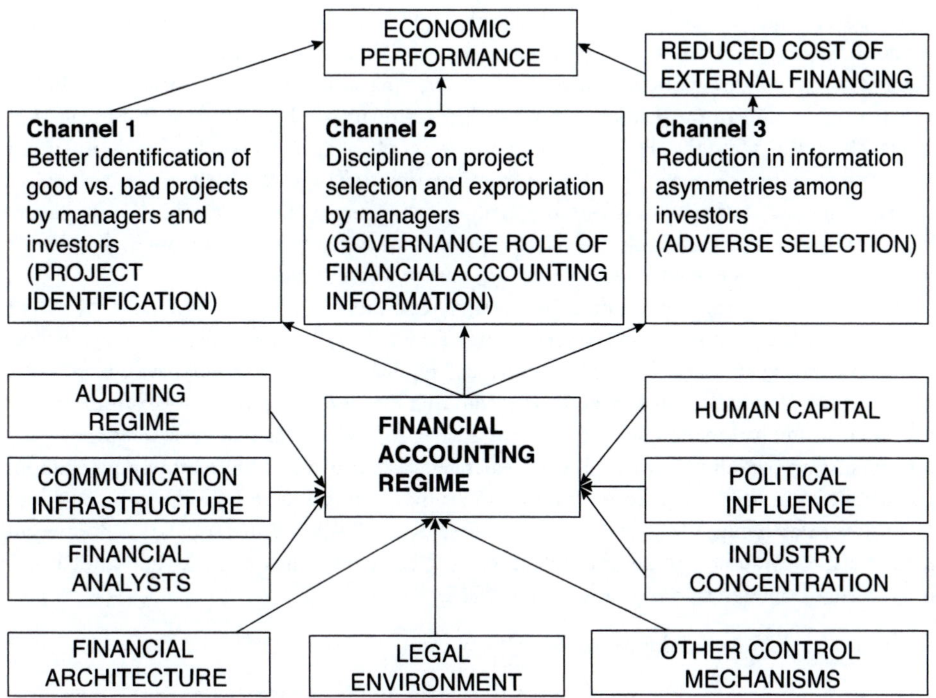

Figure 24.1 Financial reporting environment

Source: Habib (2008, p. 6), adapted from Bushman and Smith (2001, Figure 1, p. 294 and Figure 2, p. 306).

4.2 Financial reporting characteristic and growth in emerging market countries and NICs

In emerging markets and NICs, the role of corporate disclosures in promoting economic growth has seldom been systematically examined. Francis *et al.* (2005) examine the effect of external financing dependence on the incentive to make disclosures, and the consequent effect on the cost of capital, using a sample of non-US countries that included some emerging economy countries. Although the authors document a negative association between corporate disclosures and the cost of capital, the findings required a cautious interpretation because of the old sample period (1993–5) and the aggregate nature of the findings. Lopes and de Alencar (2010) used a more recent disclosure data set (1998–2005) from Brazil and document that increased disclosures reduce cost of capital. However, this finding holds only for firms with low analyst coverage and low ownership concentration. Many of the emerging economy countries do not have the strong financial analyst community that is present in the USA and the UK. Furthermore, emerging market countries and NICs are characterized by ownership concentration by family and business group affiliates.[7] Therefore, it would be premature to conclude that disclosures will reduce cost of capital in emerging markets and NICs in general and, thus, promote economic growth through a reduction in information asymmetry.

Financial accounting information is also likely to affect economic growth indirectly by performing a corporate governance role, since 'Financial accounting provides a rich set of credible variables that support a wide range of enforceable contractual arrangements and that form a basis for outsiders to monitor and discipline the investment decisions and statements of firms' managers' (Bushman *et al.*, 2011: 2). One of the desirable characteristics of an informative reporting environment is timely loss recognition (TLR) which requires early recognition of economic losses compared to economic gain (Basu, 1997). Managers know that TLR will force them to disclose value-destroying investments triggering intervention by outside stakeholders and, hence, discourage them from making such investments in the first place (Bushman *et al.*, 2011). The authors find that TLR disciplines investment by managers who face declining investment opportunities. However, it is not evident from the study whether such a benefit accrues to emerging markets and NICs too. Because many of the emerging markets and NICs are plagued with weak property rights (high risk of expropriation of assets by states), the disciplinary role of financial reporting is likely to be weakened (Bushman and Piotroski, 2006).

A financial reporting environment, however, is not created in a vacuum but, rather, is affected by a host of other institutional characteristics (see Figure 24.1). For example, a high quality audit contributes positively to the creation of a financial reporting system that will have a ripple effect on economic growth. Rigorously audited accounting data provide better information for identifying good and bad investments, disciplining managers, and reducing adverse selection among investors (Bushman and Smith, 2001). Research suggests that many of the emerging economy countries do not have adequate audit profession infrastructure, which may affect the credibility of financial statements.[8] Michas (2011) consulted ROSC reports, and summarized emerging market economy audit profession development (APD) under four categories and a total of 13 indicators. A brief description follows (ibid.: 1742):

Category 1 Auditor Education

(i) Are universities' accounting educational curriculum standards the same for all universities?
(ii) Are auditors required to perform on a professional examination before being licensed to practice as an auditor?
(iii) Are accountants required to gain professional experience before being licensed as an auditor?
(iv) Are auditors required to fulfil continuing education requirements on an annual basis?

Category 2 Auditing Standards

(v) To what extent are the country's auditing standards consistent with International Standards on Auditing?

Category 3 Auditor Independence

(vi) Are auditors in the country prohibited from both preparing and auditing a client's financial statements?
(vii) What is the level of liability faced by auditors in the country?
(viii) Are company audit committees responsible for appointing listed companies' external auditors?
(ix) Is auditor rotation required for external auditors of listed companies?
(x) Has the audit profession adopted the ethics code of the International Federation of Accountants?

Category 4 Auditor Oversight

(xi) Are auditors required to register with or be licensed by a central governing organization, either public or private?
(xii) What type of auditor practice reviews are mandatory within the country?
(xiii) Does an organization within the country consistently issue published audit implementation guidelines?

Michas then scored these categories from a minimum of 0.00 to a maximum of 1.00 and termed this an APD score. Michas revealed a wide variation among the emerging market countries' APD scores. For example, Brazil scored an APD of 0.73 out of a possible 1.00, whereas her South American neighbouring nations exhibited a dismal picture (e.g. Chile and Columbia scored an APD of 0.22 and 0.06 respectively). India and Mexico scored around 0.60, which is not very impressive.

Although the discussion on the possible channels through which accounting information can help foster economic growth is important, there is very little evidence on the effect of these channels on economic growth, particularly for emerging countries and NICs. Wurgler (2000) used the sensitivity of capital investments to value-added as a proxy for economic growth and showed that emerging market countries perform much worse on the efficiency index compared to their developed country counterparts. For example, India, Chile, and Mexico had a capital allocation efficiency index of 0.10, 0.29, and 0.34 respectively compared to 0.99 and 0.84 for Germany and Austria respectively. Interestingly, these three emerging countries also scored much less on financial reporting quality than their developed country counterparts. Li and Shroff (2009) show that industries plagued with information uncertainties grow faster in countries with better quality financial reporting. Their approach considers specific channels through which financial reporting could affect economic growth.

To summarize, the controversy surrounding the role of financial reporting in promoting economic growth in countries is more acute for emerging market countries and NICs because their institutional environment does not seem to be conducive to the development of a better quality financial reporting regime. However, many of these countries have registered spectacular growth over the last decade; an anomaly that requires a more probing investigation.

5. Concluding remarks

This chapter provides an overview on the financial reporting environment in the emerging markets and NICs. The review has been organized around:

- financial reporting objectives;
- accounting standard setting and IFRS adoption; and
- the role of financial reporting in the economic development of these countries.

These countries offer an interesting platform to compare mainstream financial reporting objectives which focus mainly on the provision of decision-useful information to dispersed shareholders (FASB and ISAB Conceptual Frameworks). Stock markets play an important role for the demand of publicly available information since markets allow retail investors to trade for liquidity using accounting information. However, the institutional environment in the emerging markets and NICs is characterized by the dominance of business groups with family ownership: a feature that reduces the demand for published financial information. Although the size of the stock markets in many of these emerging economies is quite large, regulatory enforcement to protect minority investors is weak compared to their developed market counterparts, making stock markets a less reliable institution for promoting efficient allocation of capital.

Domestic standard setting organizations in many of the emerging market countries and NICs have adopted standards developed in other parts of the world without modifying the standards to suit the local economic environment. This has downplayed the role of an efficient reporting regime, characterized by a strong conceptual framework and rigorous accounting standards, in fostering economic growth. Increased globalization has left no other choice for these countries but to adopt IFRSs. However, the lack of a concomitant development of institutional arrangements for enforcing these standards has remained a matter of much concern. Finally, the role of financial reporting in promoting economic growth in the emerging market countries and NICs is far from being settled. Many of these countries have registered a spectacular growth over the last two decades but the role of the financial reporting regime in promoting such growth has not received much attention.

Notes

1 The argument for a legal influence on accounting practices can be traced back at least to Seidler (1967: 776) who suggested that 'the fundamental similarity in the results of the legalistic approach to the determination of accounting principles in civil law countries, such as Turkey and Italy, can be contrasted with the patterns found in common law countries such as England and the United States'. A stream of very influential research by La Porta *et al.* (1997, 1998, 2000) and parallel research by Rajan and Zingales (1998), Levine (1997), and Levine *et al.* (2000) has established that a country's legal system primarily predisposes a country towards its principal systems of finance. In particular, common law countries provide strong investor protection, which in turn is responsible for the development of strong equity markets (La Porta *et al.*, 1997: 1141–2).

2 Companies in China could issue three categories of shares. A-shares are denominated in local currency and are available to domestic investors only and traded on the Shanghai and Shenzhen Stock Exchanges. B-shares are foreign currency-denominated and are initially tailored for foreign investors. H-shares refer to the shares of companies incorporated in mainland China that are traded on the Hong Kong Stock Exchange. Firms that issue B-shares or H-shares can also issue A-shares (dual listing). Prior to China's split-share structure reform, domestic A-shares were divided into NTS and TS. NTS holders represent the government, hold roughly a two-thirds majority, and manage the firms, while TS holders exert little power to affect the decisions made by NTS holders (Yeh *et al.*, 2009).

3 See Table 2 of Jackson and Roe (2009: 214–15). Academic work on the superiority of public versus private enforcement mechanisms provides mixed evidence. La Porta *et al.* (2006) find that private enforcement of investor protection via both disclosure and private liability rules is directly associated with financial market development, but public enforcement is not. Jackson and Roe (2009), on the other hand, find that public enforcement is as important as disclosure, and more important than private liability rules, in explaining financial market outcomes around the world.

4 Akisik (2008) reveals empirically that emerging market and transition economy countries with better reporting systems and corporate governance structures attracted more FDI.

5 Iatridis and Rouvolis (2010) examined the post-adoption effects of the implementation of IFRS in Greece and found that the effects in the official year of adoption appeared to be unfavourable but improved significantly in the subsequent period. Karampinis and Hevas (2011) found IFRS had made only a minor impact on the value relevance and conditional conservatism of accounting income.

6 One notable exception is Chile, which was the first large country in the Latin American region to adopt IFRS in full for reporting periods beginning on or after 1 January 2009. This decision, however, was taken in late 2006, by Chile's Superintendency of Securities and Insurance (SVS). To successfully implement IFRS, the SVS set up a clear and comprehensive section on IFRS on its website, issued ten circulars dealing with IFRS adoption, and conducted two surveys of securities issuers to assess their degree of preparedness for implementation (Fortin *et al.*, 2010: 86).

7 For example, the average percentage of shares owned by the three largest shareholders is 66.4 per cent for Brazil from 2004 to 2008. The comparable figure for Chile is 69.2 per cent, Czech Republic 81 per cent and Poland 59.3 per cent (Aguilera *et al.*, 2012).

8 Fan and Wong (2005), however, provide another perspective on the governance role of auditing in East Asian countries. They find that firms with ownership-induced agency problems employ high quality auditors and this is particularly pronounced for firms that raise equities frequently.

Bibliography

Aguilera, R.V., de Castro, L.R.A., Lee, J.H. and You, J. (2012) 'Corporate Governance in Emerging Markets', in G. Morgan and R. Whitley (eds) *Capitalisms and Capitalism in the 21st Century*. Oxford: Oxford University Press, pp. 319–44.

Akisik, O. (2008) 'Accounting Standards, Corporate Governance, and Foreign Direct Investments: The Experience of Emerging Market Economies'. *Research in Accounting in Emerging Economies*, 8, 157–87.

Ali, A. and Hwang, L.-S. (2000) 'Country-specific Factors Related to Financial Reporting and the Value Relevance Of Accounting Data'. *Journal of Accounting Research*, 38(1), 1–21.

Anagnostopoulos, I. and Buckland, R. (2007) 'Bank Accounting and Bank Value: Harmonizing (D)Effects of a Common Accounting Culture?' *Journal of Financial Regulation and Compliance*, 15(4), 360–80.

Arestis, P., Demetriades, P. and Luintel, K. (2001) 'Financial Development and Economic Growth: The Role of Stock Markets'. *Journal of Money Credit and Banking*, 33, 16–41.

Ball, R. (2001) 'Infrastructure Requirements for an Economically Efficient System of Public Financial Reporting and Disclosure.' *Brookings-Wharton Papers on Financial Services*, 127–69.

Ball, R, Kothari, S.P. and Robin, A. (2000) 'The Effect Of International Institutional Factors on Properties of Accounting Earnings'. *Journal of Accounting and Economics*, 29 (1), 1–51.

Ball, R, Robin, A. and Wu, J.S. (2003) 'Incentives versus Standards: Properties of Accounting Income in Four East Asian Countries'. *Journal of Accounting and Economics*, 36, 235–70.

Ballas, A.A., Skoutela, D. and Tzovas, C.A. (2010) 'The Relevance of IFRS to an Emerging Market: Evidence from Greece'. *Managerial Finance*, 36(10), 931–48.

Basu, S. (1997) 'The Conservatism Principle and the Asymmetric Timeliness of Earnings'. *Journal of Accounting and Economics*, 24(3), 3–37.

Beck, T. and Levine, R. (2002) 'Stock Markets, Banks and Growth: Panel Evidence'. NBER Working paper 9082, Cambridge, 1–23.

Beyer, A., Cohen, D.A., Lys, T.Z. and Walther, B.R. (2011) 'The Financial Reporting Environment: Review of the Recent Literature'. *Journal of Accounting and Economics*, 50, 296–343.

Briston, R.J. (1978) 'The Evolution of Accounting in Developing Countries'. *International Journal of Accounting Education and Research*, 14, 105–20.

Brunei Times, The (2011) 'Need to Build Brunei Stock Exchange: Bandar Seri Begawan', 6 March, available at www.bt.com.bn/news-national/2011/03/06/need-build-brunei-stock-exchange, accessed 14 March 2012.

Bushman, R.M. and Piotroski, J.D. (2006) 'Financial Reporting Incentives for Conservative Accounting: The Influence of Legal and Political Institutions'. *Journal of Accounting and Economics*, 42(1–2), 107–48.

Bushman, R. M. and Smith, A.J. (2001) 'Financial Accounting Information and Corporate Governance'. *Journal of Accounting and Economics*, 32(1–3), 237–333.

Bushman, R.M., Smith, A.J. and Piotroski, J.D. (2011) 'Capital Allocation and Timely Accounting Recognition of Economic Losses'. *Journal of Business, Finance and Accounting*, 38 (1–2), 1–33.

Carney, M., Gedajlovic, E.R., Heugens, P.M.A.R., Van Essen, M. and Oosterhout, Van. (2011) 'Business Group Affiliation, Performance, Context, and Strategy: A Meta-analysis'. *Academy of Management Journal*, 54(3), 437–60.

Chen, G., Firth, M., Gao, D.N. and Rui, O.M. (2007) 'Is China's Regulatory Agency a Toothless Tiger? Evidence from Enforcement Actions'. *Journal of Accounting and Public Policy*, 24, 451–88.

China Congress (2004) 'Guidelines on Promoting Reform, Opening-up and Steady Development of China's Capital Market'. *China Congress*, No.3.

Chu, K. (2010) 'Vietnam's Stock Market has Come Far in its First 10 Years', *USA Today*, 22 August, available at www.usatoday.com/money/markets/2010-08-22-vietnam-stocks_N.htm, accessed 20 February 2012.

Coffee, J.C. (2007) 'Law and the Market: The Impact of Enforcement'. Working paper, Columbia University.

CSRC (2005) *Circular on Further Promoting Reform of Listed Companies Share Split Structure*. The China Securities Regulatory Commission, No. 46.

DeFond, M.L. and Hung, M. (2004) 'Investor Protection and Corporate Governance: Evidence from Worldwide CEO Turnover'. *Journal of Accounting Research*, 42(2), 269–312.

DiMaggio, P. J. and Powell, W. W. (1983) 'The Iron Cage Revisited: Institutional Isomorphism and Collective Rationality in Organizational Fields'. *American Sociological Review*, 48, 147–60.

Economist, The (2011) 'Why the Tail Wags the Dog? Emerging Economies Now Have Greater Heft on Many Measures than Developed Ones', 6 August, available at www.economist.com/node/21525373, accessed 18 March 2012.

Fan, J.H. and Wong, T.J. (2002) 'Corporate Ownership Structure and the Informativeness of Accounting Earnings in East Asia'. *Journal of Accounting and Economics*, 33(3), 401–25.

Fan, J.H. and Wong, T.J. (2005) 'Do External Auditors Perform a Corporate Governance Role in Emerging Markets? Evidence from East Asia'. *Journal of Accounting Research*, 43(1), 35–72.

FASB (2006) 'Preliminary Views: Conceptual Framework for Financial Reporting'. Financial Accounting Series 1260-001, Financial Accounting Standards Board. Available at: http://72,3,243.42/draft/pv_conceptual_framework.pdf.

Fortin, H., Barros, A.C.H. and Cutler, K. (2010) *Accounting for Growth in Latin America and the Caribbean: Improving Corporate Financial Reporting to Support Regional Economic Development.* Washington, DC: The World Bank.

Francis, J. R., Khurana, I. K. and Pereira, R. (2005) 'Disclosure Incentives and Effects on Cost of Capital Around the World'. *The Accounting Review*, 80(4), 1125–62.

Graham, L.E. and Li, C. (1997) 'Cultural and Economic Influences on Current Accounting Standards in the People's Republic of China'. *The International Journal of Accounting*, 32(3), 247–78.

Granovetter, M. (2005) 'Business Groups and Social Organization'. In N. J. Smelser and R. Swedberg (eds) *The Handbook of Economic Sociology* (2nd edn), 429–450. Princeton, NJ: Princeton University Press.

Green, W., Morris, R.D. and Tang, H. (2010) 'The Split Equity Reform and Corporate Financial Transparency in China'. *Accounting Research Journal*, 23(1), 20–48.

Habib, A. (2008) 'Corporate Transparency, Financial Development and the Allocation of Capital: Empirical Evidence'. *ABACUS*, 44(1), 1–21.

Hail, L., Leuz, C. and Wysocki, P. (2010) 'Global Accounting Convergence and the Potential Adoption of IFRS by the US (Part I): Conceptual Underpinnings and Economic Analysis'. *Accounting Horizons*, 24 (3), 355–94.

He, X., Wong, T.J. and Young, D. (2012) 'Challenges for Implementation of Fair Value Accounting in Emerging Markets: Evidence from China'. *Contemporary Accounting Research*, forthcoming.

Healy, P. and Palepu, K. (2001) 'Information Asymmetry, Corporate Disclosure, and the Capital Markets: A Review of the Empirical Disclosure Literature'. *Journal of Accounting and Economics*, 31(1–3), 405–40.

Hoskisson, R. E., Eden, L., Lau, C. M. and Wright, M. (2000) 'Strategy in Emerging Economies'. *Academy of Management Journal*, 41(3), 249–67.

Iatridis, G. and Rouvolis, S. (2010) 'The Post-Adoption Effects of the Implementation of International Financial Reporting Standards in Greece.' *Journal of International Accounting, Auditing and Taxation*, 19(1), 55–65.

Jackson, H.E. (2007) 'Variation in the Intensity of Financial Regulation: Preliminary Evidence and Potential Implications'. *Yale Journal on Regulation*, 24, 253–91.

Jackson, H.E. and Roe, M.J. (2009) 'Public and Private Enforcement of Securities Laws: Resource-based Evidence'. *Journal of Financial Economics*, 93, 207–38.

Jensen, M. C. and Meckling, W. H. (1976) 'Theory of the Firm, Managerial Behavior, Agency Costs,and Ownership Structure'. *Journal of Financial Economics*, 3(4), 305–60.

Jiang, H. and Habib, A. (2012) 'Split Share Structure Reform and Earnings Informativeness in China'. *Corporate Ownership and Control Journal*, 10(1), 499–514.

Kabir, M.H., Sharma, D., Islam, A. and Salat, A. (2011) 'Big 4 Auditor Affiliation and Accruals Quality in Bangladesh'. *Managerial Auditing Journal*, 26(2), 161–81.

Karampinis, N. I. and Hevas, D. L. (2011) 'Mandating IFRS in an Unfavourable Environment: The Greek Experience'. *The International Journal of Accounting*, 46(3), 304–32.

Khanna, T. and Palepu, K. (1997) 'Why Focused Strategies May Be Wrong for Emerging Markets'. *Harvard Business Review*, 75(4), 41–51.

La Porta, R., Lopez-de-Silanes, F. Shleifer, A. and Vishny, R. (1997) 'Legal Determinants of External Finance'. *Journal of Finance*, 52(3), 1131–50.

La Porta, R., Lopez-de-Silanes, F. Shleifer, A. and Vishny, R. (1998) 'Law and Finance'. *Journal of Political Economy*, 106(6), 1113–55.

La Porta, R., Lopez-de-Silanes, F. Shleifer, A. and Vishny, R. (2000) 'Investor Protection and Corporate Governance'. *Journal of Financial Economics*, 58(1–2), 3–27.

La Porta, R., Lopez-de-Silanes, F. and Shleifer, A. (2006) 'What Works in Securities Laws?'. *Journal of Finance*, 61, 1–32.

Lasmin, D. (2011) 'An Institutional Perspective on International Financial Reporting Standards Adoption in Developing Countries'. *Academy of Accounting and Financial Studies Journal*, 15(2) (Special issue), 61–71.

Leuz, C. and Wysocki, P. (2008) 'Economic Consequences of Financial Reporting and Disclosure Regulation: A Review and Suggestions for Future Research'. Working paper, MIT Sloan School of Management.

Levine, R. (1997) 'Financial Development and Economic Growth: Views and Agenda'. *Journal of Economic Literature*, 35, 688–726.

Levine, R. and Zervos, S. (1998) 'Stock Markets, Banks and Economic Growth'. *American Economic Review*, 88, 537–58.
Levine, R., Loayza, N. and Beck, T. (2000) 'Financial Intermediation and Growth: Causality and Causes'. *Journal of Monetary Economics*, 46(1), 31–77.
Li, F. and Shroff, N. O. (2009) 'Financial Reporting Quality and Economic Growth'. Working paper, University of Michigan.
Liu, F., Su, X. and Wei, M. (2010) 'The Insurance Effect of Auditing in a Regulated and Low Litigation Risk Market: An Empirical Analysis of Big 4 Clients in China'. Working paper, City University of Hong Kong and Sun Yat-sen University.
Lopes, A.B. and de Alencar, R.C. (2010) 'Disclosure and Cost Of Equity Capital in Emerging Markets: The Brazilian Case'. *The International Journal of Accounting*, 45, 443–64.
Lucas, R. E., Jr. (1988) 'On the Mechanics of Economic Development'. *Journal of Monetary Economics*, 22(1), 3–42.
Michas, P.N. (2011) 'The Importance of Audit Profession Development in Emerging Market Countries'. *The Accounting Review*, 86(5), 1731–64.
Mir, M.Z. and Rahaman, A.S. (2005) 'The Adoption of International Accounting Standards in Bangladesh: An Exploration of Rationale and Process'. *Accounting, Auditing & Accountability Journal*, 18(6), 816–41.
Morck, R., Shleifer, A. and Vishny, R. (1988) 'Management Ownership and Market Valuation: An Empirical Analysis'. *Journal of Financial Economics*, 58(1–2), 215–60.
Nobes, C. and Parker, R.H. (2006) *Comparative International Accounting*. Harlow and New York: Financial Times.
Perera, M.B.H. (1989) 'Accounting in Developing Countries: A Case for Localized Uniformity'. *British Accounting Review*, 21, 141–58.
Rajan, R.G. and Zingales, L. (2003) 'The Great Reversals: The Politics of Financial Development in the Twentieth Century'. *Journal of Financial Economics*, 69(1), 5–50.
Ramanna, K. and Sleten, E. (2009) 'Why Do Countries Adopt International Financial Reporting Standards?'. Working paper, Harvard Business School and MIT.
Samuels, J.M and Oliga, J.C. (1982) 'Accounting Standards in Developing Countries'. *International Journal of Accounting Education and Research*, Fall, 66–88.
Sarkar, J., Sarkar, S. and Sen, K. (2011) 'Insider Control, Group Affiliation and Earnings Management in Emerging Economies: Evidence from India'. Working paper, Indira Gandhi Institute of Development Research.
Seidler, L.J. (1967) 'International Accounting: The Ultimate Theory Course'. *The Accounting Review*, 42(4), 775–81.
Sharma, N. (2010) *Insurance and Reinsurance Directors' and Officers' Liability Issues in India*. Ince & Co.
Sloan, R. G. (2001) 'Financial Accounting and Corporate Governance: A Discussion'. *Journal of Accounting and Economics*, 32(1–3), 335–47.
Spence, M. (1973) 'Job Market Signaling'. *Quarterly Journal of Economics*, 87(3), 355–74.
Tsipouridou, M. and Spathis, C. (2012) 'Earnings Management and the Role of Auditors in an Unusual IFRS Context: The Case of Greece'. *Journal of International Accounting, Auditing and Taxation*, 21, 62–78.
Tzovas, C. (2006) 'Factors Influencing a Firm's Accounting Policy Decisions when Tax Accounting and Financial Accounting Coincide'. *Managerial Auditing Journal*, 21(4), 372–86.
Wallace, R. and Briston, R. (1993) 'Improving the Accounting Infrastructure in Developing Countries'. *Research in Third World Accounting*, 2, 201–24.
WFE (2012) 'World Federation of Exchanges', available at www.world-exchanges.org/statistics/time-series, accessed 2 March 2012.
World Bank (n.d.) 'Reports on the Observance of Standards and Codes, Accounting and Auditing', (ROSC A&A) available at www.worldbank.org/ifa/rosc_aa.html.
Wurgler, J. (2000) 'Financial Markets and the Allocation of Capital'. *Journal of Financial Economics*, 58(1–2), 187–214.
Xiao, Z. and Pan, A. (1997) 'Developing Accounting Standards on the Basis of a Conceptual Framework by the Chinese Government'. *The International Journal of Accounting*, 32(3), 279–99.
Yeh, Y.-H., Shu, P.-G., Lee, T.-S. and Su, Y.-H. (2009) 'Non-tradable Share Reform and Corporate Governance in the Chinese Stock Market'. *Corporate Governance: An International Review*, 17(4), 257–75.
Zhou, Z.H. (1988) 'Chinese Accounting Systems and Practices'. *Accounting Organizations and Society*, 13(2), 207–24.

25

Accounting Regulation and IFRS in Islamic Countries

Salim Aissat, Lotfi Boulkeroua, Mike Lucas and Carien van Mourik[1]

1. Introduction

Finance and investment in accordance with Islamic Shariah Law have been on the rise worldwide. In addition to wealthy Muslim individuals in oil rich countries in the Middle East, the wealthy and middle class in countries with large Muslim populations such as Indonesia, India, Nigeria, Pakistan and Turkey are seeking Shariah-compliant securities in which to invest. Muslims represent about 22 per cent of the world population (July 2012 estimates in the CIA World Factbook) and therefore a large potential market even if currently many of them live in poverty in developing countries (See the GDP per capita column in Table 25.1). To keep matters in perspective, one must keep in mind that the vast majority of financial transactions in Islamic countries are conventional rather than Shariah-compliant transactions.

In the 1980s conventional Western banks helped Islamic banks place funds in commerce and trade-related activities through intermediation (Iqbal and Mirakhor, 2011: 16). Soon they opened Islamic Windows in the UK and other Western countries to serve the immigrant Muslim population. Since the 2007/8 financial crisis, there has been an increase in non-Muslims opening savings accounts with Islamic banks in the UK because they are perceived as operating on less risky and more ethical principles (*The Times*, 8 September 2012).

The IASB and FASB put the topic of Islamic finance and financial reporting on the agenda for the IASB/FASB meeting in the week beginning 13 June 2011 and appeared to have a special interest in accounting for leases, one of the fastest growing products in Islamic finance. The Asian-Oceanian Standard-Setters Group (AOSSG)'s Working Group on Financial Reporting Issues Relating to Islamic Finance had issued a paper on 30 June 2010 which was appended to IASB Agenda Paper 2D and FASB Memo 168. The paper set out two contrasting views held in the Islamic world regarding accounting for Islamic financial transactions, one that IFRS can be applied to Islamic financial transactions although extra disclosure may be required, and the other that a separate set of Islamic accounting standards is required (AOSSG, 2010a: ES2).

These contrasting views bring us to the issue that Islamic countries are very diverse in almost every aspect and therefore also in their stance towards the adoption of IFRS. Section 2 of this chapter seeks to identify the status of IFRS adoption in the member countries of the

Organization for Islamic Cooperation (OIC) and a few other countries, describes the main Islamic accounting regulatory bodies and discusses reasons why Islamic countries might or might not wish to adopt IFRS. Section 3 then outlines how conventional and Islamic financial and other transactions might be different in nature, and how the IASB Conceptual Framework fits with Islamic principles. Section 4 summarizes and concludes.

2. Adoption of IFRS and accounting regulation in Islamic countries

2.1 The adoption of IFRS in OIC countries

This section provides a picture of IFRS adoption in Islamic countries as per the summer of 2012. One problem is how to define Islamic countries. Formerly known as the Organization of the Islamic Conference (OIC), the OIC was established in 1969 and currently has 57 member countries (from 25 founding members) spread over four continents. The main mission of the OIC is to act as a collective voice of the Muslim world and ensure the safety and protection of the interests of the Muslim world in the spirit of promoting international peace (OIC website). The OIC list of members excludes countries with considerable Muslim populations such as India, China, and Ethiopia, but it includes countries with small populations where Muslims comprise less than 10 per cent of the total population such as Gabon (1 per cent) and Guyana (7.2 per cent).

Another problem is to classify countries according to their approach to IFRS adoption and accounting regulation. The IAS Plus website presents a table on 'Use of IFRS by jurisdiction' which uses the following six categories:

1. IFRSs not permitted;
2. IFRSs permitted;
3. IFRSs required for some;
4. IFRSs required for all;
5. Audit report states compliance with IFRS (sometimes notes are added here); and
6. Use of IFRS for unlisted companies.

Category 6 is sometimes also used as additional explanation to the other categories. One could question whether these categories are suitable for our purpose here. Furthermore, it is not clear from the IAS Plus website to what date the information is correct.

This chapter is intended to present an overview of how Islamic countries (and some non-Islamic countries) have approached the questions of whether or not to adopt IFRS and whether or not there is a need to account for Shariah-compliant transactions in ways different from conventional financial accounting standards. For this purpose, a detailed study into each country is unnecessary and the use of the OIC list and the IAS Plus table will still provide an idea about different approaches taken by the different countries to these two questions.

Table 25.1 shows the 57 OIC countries as per the list on the OIC website, their population numbers, GDP per capita, the status of IFRS adoption, whether or not the audit report states that the financial statements have been prepared in accordance with IFRS as issued by the IASB, and the Muslim population as a percentage of the total population. Table 25.2 shows the same information for the OIC observer countries, such as Bosnia-Herzegovina and the Central African Republic, but also for India, China and a few other countries.

Table 25.1 IFRS adoption in OIC member countries

Country	*Population in 2011**	*GDP per capita in 2011 (Current US$)**	*Audit report states compliance with IFRS***	*Use of IFRS***	*Note***	*Muslim population percentage*	*Muslim population*
Albania	3,215,988	4,030		IFRSs not permitted	No stock exchange	70%	2,251,192
Algeria	35,980,193	5,244		IFRSs not permitted	No stock exchange	99%	35,620,391
Benin	9,099,922	802		IFRSs not permitted		24.40%	2,220,381
Burkina Faso	16,967,845	600		IFRSs not permitted		60.50%	10,265,546
Cote D'Ivoire	20,152,894	1,195		IFRSs not permitted		38.60%	7,779,017
Indonesia	242,325,638	3,495		IFRSs not permitted		86.10%	208,642,374
Iran	74,798,599	(4,526 in 2009)		IFRSs not permitted		98%	73,302,627
Malaysia	28,859,154	9,656		IFRSs not permitted	Intends full convergence with IFRS	60.40%	17,430,929
Mali	15,839,538	669		IFRSs not permitted		90%	14,255,584
Mauritania	3,541,540	1,151		IFRSs not permitted	No stock exchange	100%	3,541,540
Niger	16,068,994	374		IFRSs not permitted		80%	12,855,195
Pakistan	176,745,364	1,194		IFRSs not permitted		95%	167,908,096

Senegal	12,767,556	1,119		IFRSs not permitted		94%	12,001,503
Syria	20,820,311	(2,893 in 2010)		IFRSs not permitted		90%	18,738,280
Togo	6,154,813	584		IFRSs not permitted		20%	1,230,963
Tunisia	10,673,800	4,297		IFRSs not permitted		98%	10,460,324
Turkmenistan	5,105,301	4,722		IFRSs not permitted		89%	4,543,718
Uzbekistan	29,341,200	1,546		IFRSs not permitted		88%	25,820,256
Brunei-Darussalam	405,938	(31,008 in 2010)		IFRSs permitted	No stock exchange	67%	271,978
Gambia	1,776,103	625		IFRSs permitted	No stock exchange	90%	1,598,493
Guyana	756,040	(2,994 in 2010)	Yes	IFRSs permitted	Companies may choose full IFRSs or IFRS for SMEs	7.20%	54,435
Maldives	320,081	6,405	Yes	IFRSs permitted		100%	320,081
Suriname	529,419	(8,292 in 2010)	Yes	IFRSs permitted		19.60%	103,766
Turkey	73,639,596	10,498	Yes	IFRSs permitted		99.80%	73,492,317
Uganda	34,509,205	487	Yes	IFRSs permitted		12.10%	4,175,614
Yemen	24,799,880	1,361		IFRSs permitted	No stock exchange	100%	24,799,880
Bahrain	1,323,535	(18,184 in 2010)	Yes	IFRSs required for all	Including unlisted companies	81.20%	1,074,710
Bangladesh	150,493,658	735		IFRSs required for all	Except IAS 29 and IFRS 9	89.50%	134,691,824

(Continued)

Country	*Population in 2011**	*GDP per capita in 2011 (Current US$)**	*Audit report states compliance with IFRS***	*Use of IFRS***	*Note***	*Muslim population percentage*	*Muslim population*
Egypt	82,536,770	2,781	Yes	IFRSs required for all		90%	74,283,093
Iraq	32,961,959	3,501	Yes	IFRSs required for all	Including unlisted banks	97%	31,973,100
Jordan	6,181,000	4,666	Yes	IFRSs required for all		92%	5,686,520
Kuwait	2,818,042	62,664	Yes	IFRSs required for all	Including unlisted companies	85%	2,395,336
Kyrgyzstan	5,507,000	1,075	Yes	IFRSs required for all	Including unlisted companies	75%	4,130,250
Nigeria	162,470,737	1,452	?	IFRSs required for all	From 2012. Audit report to be determined	50%	81,235,369
Oman	2,846,145	25,221	Yes	IFRSs required for all	Including unlisted companies	75%	2,134,609
Qatar	1,870,041	92,501	Yes	IFRSs required for all		77.50%	1,449,282
Sierra Leone	5,997,486	374	Yes	IFRSs required for all	IFRS for some, IFRS for SMEs for others	60%	3,598,492
Tajikistan	6,976,958	935	Yes	IFRSs required for all	Including unlisted companies	90%	6,279,262
Azerbaijan	9,168,000	6,916	Yes	IFRSs required for some	For banks (listed and unlisted) and large state-owned enterprises. For others, IFRSs permitted	93.40%	8,562,912

Kazakhstan	16,558,459	11,245	Yes	IFRSs required for some	For all banks, joint stock companies, and other significant public interest companies, including extractive industry companies and companies with Governmental ownership)	47%	7,782,476
Lebanon	4,259,405	9,904	Yes	IFRSs required for some	For financial institutions. Not permitted for others	59.70%	2,542,865
Libya	6,422,772	(9,957 in 2009)		IFRSs required for some	For banks and listed companies, but practice has yet to apply IFRSs	97%	6,230,089
Morocco	32,272,974	3,054	Yes	IFRSs required for some	For banks/financial institutions IFRSs. Other listed companies may choose IFRSs or Moroccan GAAP	99%	31,950,244
Mozambique	23,929,708	535	Yes	IFRSs required for some	For banks (from 2007), large unlisted (from 2010), and medium-sized unlisted (from 2011)	17.90%	4,283,418
Saudi Arabia	28,082,541	20,540	Yes	IFRSs required for some	Banks and insurance companies listed on the Saudi Stock Exchange must use IFRS. IFRS not permitted for others	100%	28,082,541
United Arab Emirates	7,890,924	45,653		IFRSs required for some	For listed companies and banks, for unlisted companies IFRSs are permitted	96%	7,575,287

(Continued)

Country	*Population in 2011**	*GDP per capita in 2011 (Current US$)**	*Audit report states compliance with IFRS***	*Use of IFRS***	*Note***	*Muslim population percentage*	*Muslim population*
Afghanistan	35,320,445	576		Unknown		99%	34,967,241
Cameroon	20,030,362	1,271		Unknown		20%	4,006,072
Chad	11,525,496	823		Unknown		53.10%	6,120,038
Comoros	753,943	809		Unknown		98%	738,864
Djibouti	905,564	(1,203 in 2009)		Unknown		94%	851,230
Gabon	1,534,262	11,114		Unknown		1%	15,343
Guinea	10,221,808	502		Unknown		85%	8,688,537
Guinea-Bissau	1,547,061	629		Unknown		50%	773,531
Palestine	Unknown	Unknown		Unknown			
Somalia	9,556,873	Unknown		Unknown		100%	9,556,873
Sudan	34,318,385	1,234		Unknown		100%	34,318,385

* *Source*: World Bank Website (Accessed on 6 September, 2012)
***Source*: IAS Plus Website (Accessed on 6 September, 2012)
*** *Source*: CIA World Factbook Website (Accessed on 6 September, 2012)

Table 25.2 IFRS adoption in OIC observer countries and other countries with substantial Muslim populations

Country	*Population in 2011**	*GDP per capita in 2011 (Current US$)**	*Audit report states compliance with IFRS***	*Use of IFRS***	*Note***	*Muslim population percentage*	*Muslim population*
Bosnia and Herzegovina (obs)	3,752,228	4,821	Yes	IFRSs required for all	Large and medium-sized listed companies	40%	1,500,891
Central African Republic (obs)	4,486,837	483		Unknown		15%	673,026
China	1,344,130,000	5,430		CAS required	China claims CAS are IFRS equivalent?	2%	26,882,600
India	1,241,491,960	1,489	Yes	IFRSs permitted	For consolidated results only. Not permitted for unlisted companies.	13.40%	166,359,923
Russia (obs)	141,930,000	13,089	Yes	IFRSs required for some	Transition to IFRS for consolidated financial statements in progress	12.50%	17,741,250
South Africa	50,586,757	8,070	Yes	IFRS required for all	IFRSs or IFRS for SMEs	1.50%	758,801
Thailand (obs)	69,518,555	4,972		IFRSs not permitted		4.60%	3,197,854
United Kingdom	62,641,000	38,818	No. 'As Adopted by EU'	IFRSs required for all	IFRSs permitted in both consolidated and separate company statements	2.70%	1,691,307

* *Source:* World Bank Website (Accessed on 6 September, 2012)
***Source*: IAS Plus Website (Accessed on 6 September, 2012)
*** *Source:* CIA World Factbook Website (Accessed on 6 September, 2012)
(obs) = OIC observer

Of the 57 OIC countries,

- 18 do not permit the use of IFRSs;
- eight permit the use of IFRSs (including three that do not have a stock exchange);
- seven (Azerbaijan, Kazakhstan, Lebanon, Libya, Morocco, Mozambique and Saudi Arabia) require the use of IFRS for some listed companies, mainly for banks and other financial institutions (listed and unlisted);
- Dubai and Abu Dhabi in the UAE require IFRSs for listed companies and financial institutions, and permit IFRSs for others;
- 12 have made IFRS required for all listed (including six for unlisted) companies. These include Bahrain, Bangladesh, Egypt, Iraq, Jordan, Kuwait, Kyrgyzstan, Oman, Qatar, Sierra Leone and Tajikistan. In addition, Nigeria will do so from 2012 but what the audit report will say is yet to be decided; and
- For 11 of the OIC countries, the IAS Plus website shows the IFRS adoption status as unknown.

Table 25.2 shows countries that are not OIC members. Bosnia-Herzegovina, Russia and Thailand are observers of the OIC. Although not an OIC member, India is the country which has, after Indonesia and Pakistan, the largest number of Muslims among its population. Although in percentage terms the Muslim population is a small minority (2 per cent), there are more Muslims in China than, for example, in Yemen where the population is 100 per cent Muslim. South Africa is in the list because, although it has a small Muslim population, it has adopted a separate set of Islamic accounting standards which apply to Islamic business entities. The UK has been very active in facilitating the creation of Shariah-compliant financial products for Islamic Financial Institutions (IFIs) at home and abroad, but has not adopted separate Islamic accounting standards for IFIs.

Before looking in more detail at financial accounting and reporting regulation in some of the countries in the different groups identified above, the following section will briefly describe some of the existing non-national Islamic institutions that play a role in Islamic finance and accounting.

2.2 Non-national Islamic finance and accounting institutions

The Accounting and Auditing Organisation for Islamic Financial Institutions (AAOIFI)

With 200 member financial institutions, the AAOIFI was established in 1990 and is based in Bahrain. The AAOIFI issues Financial Accounting Standards (FAS) specifically tailored to IFIs and Shariah-compliant transactions. The AAOIFI also aims to develop accounting and auditing thought relevant to IFIs (AAOIFI website).

Since its inception, the AAOIFI has developed and issued over 50 standards on Shariah-compliant accounting, auditing and governance. It is widely regarded as a reference point for and a champion of Islamic accounting and financial reporting. A number of OIC countries have adopted the AAOIFI FAS as the main financial reporting framework to be used by IFIs. Other OIC countries have either adapted or partly based some of their accounting standards on the AAOIFI FAS. Very few non-OIC countries refer to the AAOIFI FAS in the preparation of their accounting standards. Many of the FAS issued by the AAOIFI do not appear to conflict with IFRS but this is only in those cases where just additional disclosures are required. Other instances that require different recognition and measurement principles may prove to be at odds with IFRS.

The Islamic Financial Services Board (IFSB)

The IFSB is based in Malaysia. It was officially inaugurated in late 2002 and started operations in early 2003. As of March 2012, the 187 members of the IFSB included 53 regulatory and supervisory authorities as well as eight international intergovernmental organizations including the International Monetary Fund, the World Bank, the Bank for International Settlements, the Islamic Development Bank and the Asian Development Bank. Also among the IFSB members are 126 market players, professional firms and industry associations operating in 43 jurisdictions (IFSB website).

The IFSB was created to develop common supervisory standards for Islamic financial institutions by providing guidance on the effective supervision and regulation of these institutions and encouraging cooperation amongst member countries in developing the Islamic financial services industry. The IFSB also serves as an international standard setting body of regulatory and supervisory agencies that have a vested interest in ensuring the soundness and stability of the Islamic financial services industry (IFSB website). The mission of IFSB is to develop and promote a prudent and transparent Islamic financial services industry through introducing new, or adapting existing international standards consistent with Shariah principles, and recommend them for adoption. The IFSB's aim is to develop global supervisory standards for Islamic financial institutions and harmonise these standards across countries (IFSB website). The IFSB has so far developed and published, in English and Arabic, 13 Standards (IFSB-1 to IFSB-13) as well as Guidance and Technical Notes geared towards the specific needs and requirements of the Islamic financial services industry.

The Asian-Oceanian Standard-Setters Group (AOSSG)

The formation of the Asian-Oceanian Standard-Setters Group (AOSSG) dates back to 2009. The AOSSG comprises national accounting standard-setters from Asia and Oceania (including the Pacific Rim). The main purpose of the Group is to act as a discussion forum regarding the main issue of IFRS adoption in its member countries and to contribute to the development of a high-quality set of global accounting standards (AOSSG, 2010b). The AOSSG has an active 'Islamic Finance Working Group' that specializes in all financial reporting issues relating to Islamic finance. The aim of the Working Group is to provide input and feedback to the International Accounting Standards Board (IASB) regarding the adequacy and appropriateness of IFRS applicability to Shariah-compliant transactions and IFIs.

The lead member of the AOSSG Islamic Finance Working Group is the Malaysian Accounting Standards Board (MASB). The MASB was established in 1997 and embarked on an 'Islamic financial reporting' project with the initial objective of developing and issuing AAOIFI-like accounting standards. Since then, however, it is worth noting that the MASB's objective and position have evolved away from that initial goal. Based on various arguments, the MASB now takes the position that the IFRS do not conflict with Shariah and hence can be adopted to report Shariah-compliant transactions. Other active members of the AOSSG include Indonesia, represented through the Indonesian Institute of Accountants (IAI); Pakistan, Institute of Chartered Accountants of Pakistan (ICAP); and Saudi Arabia, the Saudi Organization for Certified Public Accountants (SOCPA).

2.3 Approaches to IFRS and Islamic accounting standards

There is a wide spectrum of views on how accounting for Islamic transactions and Islamic business entities ought to be performed. At the one extreme, there are those who think that IFRSs are adequate and can be applied to Shariah-compliant transactions. At the other extreme, there are those who argue that a completely separate set of Islamic accounting standards is required. In between, there are two alternative views. One holds that the existing IFRS framework is largely adequate and can be applied to the Islamic transactions, though additional disclosures either in the notes or on the face of the financial statements may be required. The other considers the IFRS framework as applicable to many if not most Islamic transactions but recognizes that there are some areas which are not adequately covered by IFRS. This will therefore require specific supplements and further guidelines to address these gaps. The latter view opens also the debate about the compliance of the financial reports with IFRS if such departures from it were to be applied.

2.3.1 IFRS framework adequate for Islamic accounting disclosure

On the face of it, the group of OIC countries that requires IFRS for all listed (and in some cases unlisted) companies seems to have concluded that the IFRS framework is adequate for financial disclosure from an Islamic perspective. This is not necessarily true. For example, Bahrain, Jordan and Qatar apply AAOIFI Financial Accounting Standards to financial reporting for Islamic Financial Institutions.

2.3.2 Explanatory supplements, notes and additional disclosures

The overall standpoint of the AOSSG Working Group is that the existing IFRS framework is largely adequate for the purposes of financial reporting of Islamic financial transactions but in some instances, areas of divergent opinion or treatment 'may be resolved by further guidance or clarification to the IFRS in question' (AOSSG, 2010a: Par. 35). Essentially, IFRS does not prohibit business entities from making additional voluntary disclosures within their financial statements. Additional disclosures of issues not covered by IFRS can be made subject to two key conditions:

- they must not be misleading; and
- they do not conflict with the IFRS principles.

The latter raises the issue that the proposed Islamic reporting principle may be conflicting with the principles on which IFRS are based.

Malaysia

The Malaysian Accounting Standards Board (MASB) was the lead member of the above mentioned Working Group and is an important representative of this position. More precisely, the MASB in its *Statement of Principles (SOP i-1)* (MASB, 2009) concluded that:

- IFRS principles do not conflict with Shariah;
- financial reporting is a recording function that would neither sanctify nor nullify the Shariah validity of a transaction;
- the primary difference from conventional financial reporting is the extent of information provided to users.

The MASB then made the final recommendation that 'IFRS shall apply to Islamic financial transactions in the absence of any Shariah prohibition to doing so' (ibid.). On the face of it, these conclusions by the MASB may give the impression that convergence with IFRS is all but a formality.

The MASB has approved its own national accounting standards, which are based on IFRS. According to the MASB, the convergence to IFRS was completed in January 2012. These converged standards must also be applied to IFIs and used to report on Islamic transactions unless there is a strong case of an explicit Shariah prohibition which, according to the MASB, is very rare in Malaysia. Nevertheless, the MASB issues additional 'pronouncements' to provide supplementary guidance on the appropriate application of these standards to Islamic transactions specifically. Thus, rather than adopting separate Islamic accounting standards, the MASB provides 'Technical Releases' to explain and provide specific guidance on how best to report on Islamic transactions. Further guidance also comes from the Malaysian Central Bank. The MASB makes it clear that the purpose of these pronouncements is to complement and supplement the approved accounting standards, and in no way shall they override the national accounting standards. The MASB *Statement* (ibid.) concludes that financial reporting is a recording function that would neither sanctify nor nullify the Shariah validity of a transaction; and that the primary difference from conventional financial reporting is the extent of information provided to users.

2.3.3 Possible departures, modifications and exemptions from IFRS

In some countries and jurisdictions, such as Indonesia and Saudi Arabia, certain requirements of IFRS may be deemed to be in direct conflict with Shariah-based disclosure. The question then is whether an exemption for that requirement may be made without significantly compromising convergence with IFRS. The IASB/AOSSG Working Group states in its 2010 draft paper that 'even standards-setters which have pledged convergence with IFRS may allow or mandate departures and exemptions from one or more requirements of IFRS' (IASB/AOSSG, 2010: 34).

Indonesia

In Indonesia, according to the Indonesian Institute of Accountants (IAI), convergence to IFRS was completed in January 2012. However, for IFIs, separate national accounting standards exist which are partly informed by AAOIFI FAS. The IAI said that they would be retaining their own Islamic accounting standards beside IFRS. The IAI argues that additional Shariah-related disclosures in the form of notes and supplements to the financial statements are not sufficient. In order to achieve full compliance with Shariah, these disclosures 'must be reflected on the face of the financial statements' (IASB/AOSSG, 2010: 74). The key argument behind this view is that Shariah-compliant accounting disclosure for Islamic transactions and business entities does not only serve to provide information for decision making, but it also provides vital information about the level of compliance with the Shariah principles.

The Financial Accounting Standards Board (DSAK), which was established by the IAI, is responsible for setting Indonesian financial accounting standards or Pernyataan Standar Akuntansi Keuangan (PSAK). Within the organisational structure of the IAI, there is a Shariah Accounting Standards Board (DSAS) which is the accounting standards setting body for Shariah-compliant business entities. The IAI has issued a 'Framework for Preparation and Presentation of Shariah Financial Statements' and eight Shariah accounting standards: 'PSAK 10' *Presentation of Shariah Financial Statements*; 'PSAK 102' *Accounting for Murabaha*; 'PSAK 103' *Accounting for Salam*; 'PSAK 104' *Accounting for Istisna*; 'PSAK 105' *Accounting for Mudarabah*; 'PSAK 106' *Accounting for Musharakah*; 'PSAK 107' *Accounting for Ijarah*; and 'PSAK 108' *Shariah Insurance Transactions*' (IASB/AOSSG, 2010).

Saudi Arabia

There are no separate financial reporting requirements or accounting standards for Islamic business entities in Saudi Arabia. Up to very recently, all sectors reported under national accounting standards issued by the Saudi Organization for Certified Public Accountants (SOCPA) that also catered for IFIs and other Islamic transactions.

Since 2012, financial institutions have been reporting under IFRS and plans are also under way to converge financial reporting standards for all other sectors with IFRSs in the next five years through a phased programme. As part of the IFRS convergence plans, and in a recent survey by the AOSSG Working Group, SOCPA stated that 'SOCPA plans to issue local standards after making necessary changes which may relate to local laws, Shariah requirements etc.' This represents a unique approach in comparison to other national standard setters. In its latest official publication, and under the heading of 'accounting and auditing for Shariah compliant transactions', SOCPA asserts that,

> given the leading role of Saudi Arabia within the Islamic world, there will be an influential role for SOCPA in the provision of accounting and auditing standards and guidelines for Shariah-compliant transactions in areas that are not covered by the international accounting standards (IFRS) (SOCPA *Accountants Magazine,* April 2012: 34).

Interestingly, besides Indonesia and Pakistan, few OIC countries have issued their own Islamic accounting standards. Other OIC countries seem to adopt AAOIFI FAS as the main financial reporting framework to be used by Islamic business entities. These include Bahrain, Dubai (UAE), Jordan, Lebanon, Qatar, Sudan and Syria.

In the case of Dubai (UAE), the Dubai Financial Services Authority (DFSA) in its rulebook on Islamic finance, states that Islamic Financial Institutions 'must prepare and maintain all financial accounts and statements in accordance with the accounting standards of the AAOIFI' (DFSA, 2012a: 12). DFSA goes further by requiring that businesses operating an Islamic Window, 'must prepare and maintain all financial accounts and statements in accordance with the IFRS, as supplemented by AAOIFI FAS 18,[2] in respect of its Islamic Financial Business' (ibid.). Recently however, DFSA stated that it is currently considering whether it should change its rulebook either to require the use of IFRS for Islamic financial business or to permit them as an alternative to the AAOIFI standards.

It is clear that going forward, individual standard setters taking this position will need to strike the right balance between plans for convergence with IFRS principles on the one hand, and the Shariah specific reporting requirements on the other. The extent of 'compromise' in the form of departures, modification and exemptions, required from all parties involved is still an open question. Future developments will shed further light on this pressing issue which will determine levels of convergence.

2.3.4 Separate Islamic accounting standards are needed

The use of IFRSs is not allowed in 18 of the 57 OIC countries. There can be many different reasons not to adopt IFRSs or converge with IFRS. One reason could be that the national regulators take the position that separate Islamic accounting standards are needed. An example here is the Institute of Chartered Accountants of Pakistan (ICAP).

Pakistan

ICAP claims that financial reporting in Pakistan has already converged with IFRS but separate Islamic accounting standards are needed for IFIs. These standards are adapted from the AAOIFI FAS. ICAP has so far produced just two Islamic Financial Accounting Standards (IFAS), 'IFAS

1 Murabaha' and 'IFAS 2 Ijarah' (IASB/AOSSG, 2010). In spite of claiming full convergence with IFRS, ICAP said that they would be retaining their Islamic accounting standards for the foreseeable future (AOSSG Survey, 2011).

The contentious points regarding 'fair value', 'time value of money' and 'substance over form' are just some examples used by the ICAP to highlight areas of incompatibility between Shariah-compliant disclosure and the basic principles underpinning IFRS. ICAP claims that 'we cannot have a set of documents to ensure Shariah compliance and do whatever we were doing in conventional finance' (IASB/AOSSG, 2010: 75).

2.3.5 Non-OIC countries and the IASB

Two representative approaches in non-Islamic countries are those by South Africa and the UK. South Africa has already fully converged with IFRS but separate accounting standards, based on the AAOIFI FAS, apply to IFIs. The South African Institute of Chartered Accountants plans to maintain these separate standards but they admit that some of the requirements under these standards may need to be reviewed in due course (AOSSG survey, 2011).

In the UK, IFRS (as adopted by the EU) applies to listed companies. Legislation requires all listed companies to prepare their financial statements in accordance with IFRS. No specific financial reporting standards or requirements are in place for IFIs. The regulator essentially believes that the UK-based Islamic financial entities should be able to meet their reporting obligations principally under IFRS.

The IASB is open to the idea that standards for Islamic financial transactions may be necessary and has expressed the intention to put this issue on the agenda (IAS website).

2.4 Other reasons for Islamic countries to adopt or refuse IFRS

Most contributors to the literature inquiring into the reasons for the adoption of IFRSs by developing countries and Islamic countries seek to prove that economic dependency is the main explanatory factor. For example, if Algeria's main trading partner is France, it makes sense to use the same financial reporting standards as France. This argument is not limited to developing and Islamic countries. In the case of the EU, economic interdependency was the main reason to start harmonizing its accounting standards and, when this failed, to adopt IFRS.

Although the purpose of their study is to find reasons for the dominance of western accounting, and particularly IFRS, in developing countries, Al Tarawneh and Lucas (2012) discuss five possible explanations that may also apply to the case of Islamic countries. First, it may be simply that many accountants in Islamic countries (particularly those who received their university and professional education in the west) cannot conceive of any alternative to conventional accounting. Haniffa and Hudaib (2010a) touched upon this issue in the editorial for the launch of the inaugural issue of the *Journal of Islamic Accounting and Business Research* indicating this was part of the rationale for creating the new journal.

A second possibility is that where leading Islamic countries adopt IFRSs others will simply follow. The existence of uncertainty and ambiguity encourages imitation. See also DiMaggio and Powell (1983) who introduce the concept of 'institutional isomorphism' proposed by advocates of New Institutional Sociology (NIS) into management accounting research. Forrester (1996) has discussed how this occurs in the field of financial accounting. For example, European countries have had a tradition of looking at what the neighbours are doing and adopting their solutions for one's own use. Also, the IASB Conceptual Framework has been strongly influenced by the FASB Conceptual Framework.

A third possible reason is that it can be very expensive for a small country, particularly a developing country with limited resources, to develop its own accounting standards. When a set of internationally recognized, high-quality standards already exists it may be more cost-effective (at least in the short term) to adopt the existing standards (Allingham, 2002). This of course works not only with IFRSs but also with other standards. For example, smaller Islamic countries, which, unlike Indonesia and Pakistan, who developed their own Islamic accounting standards, adopt the AAOIFI's standards for Islamic Financial Institutions rather than develop their own.

Fourth, it is possible that using an internationally recognized set of high-quality accounting standards, such as IFRS, will help attract foreign investment and create a level playing field for companies wanting to raise capital on international capital markets. Higher quality accounting and disclosure standards may help reduce investor risk and thereby lower the cost of capital for companies in the country concerned (Leuz and Verrecchia, 2000). Developing countries are often perceived as posing higher risk to investors due to a variety of national differences in economic structures, policies, socio-political institutions, geography, and currencies. Similarly, since Islamic finance and banking is a relatively new phenomenon, with strict religious rules, investors may be more cautious of the additional risks involved. Hence, adopting an established accounting system and accounting standards will help gain investors' confidence to invest in the country.

Finally, Al Tarawneh and Lucas (2012) describe how, in 1999, the World Bank and the IMF instigated the mutual 'Reports of the Observance of Standards and Codes' initiative. It covers 12 areas and associated standards that need to be adopted by countries receiving aid, including the adoption of IFRS and the International Federation of Accountants' International 'Standards on Auditing'. In other words, the provision of assistance and aid by the World Bank and the IMF to the less developed nations relies on the willingness of these countries to undertake various social, cultural, economic and political changes. There is a parallel here with some issues discussed in Ahsan Habib's chapter on accounting regulation in emerging markets and newly industrialising countries and Rachel Baskerville's chapter on the influence of the World Bank and the IMF.

Reasons to refuse IFRS could be related to issues of sovereignty and independence, but also simply because the principles on which IFRSs are based do not agree with the dominant social or religious values in a jurisdiction. Islamic societies might prefer to choose an accounting system that suits the ideology and values of Muslims, to assist them in meeting their religious obligations (Hameed, 2001). Accounting derives its usefulness from its ability to reflect the social, cultural and economic aspects of the organisations on which it reports. Thus, transferring accounting doctrine and standards that reflect the cultural values of developed, capitalist nations onto some developing nations and societies which are governed by specific religious principles, has been criticised by various scholars (e.g. Briston, 1978, 1990; Hove, 1986; Samuels and Oliga, 1982; and Wallace, 1990).

3. How does IFRS fit with Islamic principles?

The previous section discussed motivations for governments and accounting regulators in Islamic countries to adopt or reject IFRS. The reasons for adopting IFRS were varied and primarily pragmatic or political in nature. One important reason for rejecting IFRS is that IFRS is based on concepts and principles that are, in some essential ways, almost diametrically opposed to the Islamic principles that govern every aspect of social and economic life (*muamalat*) under the Shariah Law.

This section looks into the differences between the main principles in the Shariah underlying Islamic financial and other commercial transactions and the requirements of Islamic financial reporting and the assumptions underlying conventional finance and financial reporting.

3.1 Islamic principles

3.1.1 Holistic view of society

In secular states, religious obligations are not normally incorporated into the legal system or regulatory requirements because they are often seen as matters of individual freedom and conscience. This is not to say of course that the law is not influenced by cultural and religious values in secular societies. Nevertheless, in Islam, in principle, there is no separation of state and religion. According to Iqbal and Mirakhor (2011: 1): 'Islam propounds the guiding principles, and prescribes a set of rules, for all aspects of human life, including the economic aspect.' These rules have been designed to 'establish a just and moral order through human agency. . . . What gives the behaviour of a believer its orientation, meaning and effectiveness is acting with the knowledge that justice invokes Allah's *(swt)* pleasure; and injustice, His displeasure' (Iqbal and Mirakhor, 2011: 5). 'Islam does not recognise the separation between temporal and spiritual affairs, and considers commerce as a matter of morality and is subject to the precepts of the Shariah' (Karim, 2001: 172).

3.1.2 Principles of Shariah and the Islamic concept of justice

As pointed out by Kuran (2004) and Kamla (2009: 923), much of the literature is primarily concerned with only two aspects of Shariah Law: the prohibition of *riba* (interest, which includes fixed rates of return determined *ex ante*) and the payment of *zakat*. *Zakat* is a form of worship for Muslims and is one the five pillars of Islam.[3] Giving *zakat* is a religious obligation for every Muslim who satisfies certain requirements. *Zakat* is a tax imposed on the rich amongst Muslims by a divine decree, to help the poor and needy and to allow the state to manage the affairs of its citizens and spread the word of God. Payment of *zakat* becomes only mandatory on Muslims whose wealth and earnings are sufficiently large to afford doing so.[4]

The principles of the Shariah include:

- the promotion of sharing of both risks and rewards;
- banning risk shifting;
- prohibiting excessive speculative behaviour;
- prohibiting the use of interest (*riba*);
- promoting a financial system with a strong link between individual assets and the return on capital used to finance them;
- discouraging the privatization of gains and the socialization of losses; and
- forbidding *gharar* (ambiguity of information), *maysir* (uncertainty or excessive risk), *haram* (not allowed by Islam) activities and upholding contractual obligations and the disclosure of information as a sacred duty (Iqbal and Mirakhor, 2011: 10-11).

Although most business activity is permitted by Shariah (*halal*), some business activity is not permitted (*haram*), for example the production of liquor and pornography.

Narrowing focus in the literature on the technical aspects of *riba* and *zakat* can be misleading and unfortunate for the following reasons. First, a narrow focus on the technical aspects of Islamic financial contracts obscures the fact that Islamic principles are based on a holistic and spiritual approach to knowledge, society and life. This sits uncomfortably with the main assumptions underpinning the IASB Conceptual Framework, which it shares with free market ideology and financial economics. These assumptions include methodological individualism (society is no more than the outcome of aggregate individual decisions and actions), materialism (the primary driving force for the actions of individuals consists of material needs and wants) and a utilitarian approach to ethics where the goal justifies the means (See also Chapter 2).

Second, a narrow focus blurs the line between Shariah-based and Shariah-compliant Islamic finance (Haniffa and Hudaib, 2010b: 89). The former is the type that was developed from about the 1940s to the 1970s as a consequence of decolonization (Haniffa and Hudaib, 2010b: 86–7; Tripp, 2006: Chapters 1–3). The goal was and is to create, apply and maintain means of mobilizing resources to finance private business enterprise as well as public and private investment in economic development, infrastructure, education and other social goods based on the principles in the Shariah in order to contribute to the common good.

The latter is the type that developed in the last quarter of the twentieth century, when the argument for Islamic economics and Islamic finance shifted away from the Islamic ethic of social justice to an argument from pragmatism (Tripp, 2006: 114). Conventional financial products which had been invented for the very purpose of financial engineering, that is, to provide means for risk shifting, off-balance sheet financing, balance sheet manipulation, earnings management, leveraging, tax avoidance, tax evasion, and regulatory arbitrage came to be increasingly mimicked by Shariah-compliant alternatives.

This is particularly unfortunate because it enhances the perception of Islamic finance to be competing on the same ground as the secular finance of financial capitalism. As such, it will be judged by the same criteria of success, which puts pressure on the Islamic ethos in different interpretations of the Shariah (Tripp, 2006: 117). As we will see below, this tension between the Islamic principles of the Shariah and the desire/need to function and compete in a global financial capitalist system is also visible in different Islamic perspectives on accounting concepts.

3.1.3 The role of capital markets

'Capital markets facilitate long-term financing for businesses and entrepreneurs by attracting savings from a large pool of investors' (Iqbal and Mirakhor, 2011: 173). Conventional capital markets consist of primary and secondary markets for both equity and long-term debt. Primary capital markets are seen as the means for an efficient allocation of capital to business enterprises that deliver the highest financial returns. Secondary capital markets facilitate the trading of existing securities and play a vital role in providing liquidity, low transaction costs, and information on risk and return through the market price of the securities. The price of a company's security in the secondary market is important in the determination of that company's cost of raising new capital in the primary markets.

For the reasons explained above, debt securities are out of the question for those who want to invest in Shariah-compliant securities. Investing in stocks or shares is in accordance with the principle of sharing of risks and rewards. However, investment in some business activity classified as *haram* is not permitted or limited to certain thresholds.[5] Some Islamic equity funds follow a particular procedure. They will first screen out shares of companies involved in business considered unlawful under Shariah. The Dow Jones Shariah Board excludes business activities such as distilling, gambling, pornography, alcohol and pork-related products, various forms of insurance, consumer finance and conventional banks and financial services (Iqbal and Mirakhor, 2011: 176–7). They will then apply a filtration process, which involves judgement as to the level of tolerance of a company's debt or income from debt products.

3.1.4 Public limited corporations

Limited liability is seen by some as conflicting with Islamic principles in different forms of contract. '*Shirka* is a contract in which participants contribute capital and/or services to a venture with a view to making a profit' (AOSSG, 2010a: Par. 57). Should one regard a limited liability company as a *musharaq mulk* (partnership based on rights to a specific real asset) or as a *musharaq aqd* (partnership based on ownership of the value of unspecified assets), or is a limited liability company perhaps both or neither? Furthermore, negotiability, tradability and transferability of shares and stocks in primary and secondary markets may also be problematic; even more problematic is the trading of corporate debt. Finally, margin trading, speculative trading and short selling are not compatible with Shariah (Iqbal and Mirakhor, 2011: 181–3).

3.2 Islamic principles in financial accounting and reporting

The IASB presents its accounting standards and accounting concepts as technical not ethical rules. See also Karim (2001: 173). In contrast, in Islam all actions in the public domain have a moral dimension. This is particularly clear in the objective of financial reporting.

3.2.1 The objective of accounting and financial reporting

The IASB Conceptual Framework (IASB, 2010: OB2–OB4) interprets decision-usefulness of financial reporting information as enabling the assessment of the amount, certainty and timing of future cash flows to the business (and ultimately to the investors). Implicit in the asset-liability approach to income determination adopted by the IASB, is the proprietary perspective on the firm which holds that it is owned and controlled by the common shareholders. Hence performance is measured as the increase in net assets.

On the Islamic view, one important purpose of financial accounting is to calculate income and wealth for the purpose of determining profit for the period and *zakat* owed over wealth and income (Iqbal and Mirakhor, 2011: 42). The objective of external reporting is to provide accountability to society as a whole by assessing whether the entity is operating within the bounds of the Shariah. Decision-usefulness can be interpreted as enabling the sharing of risks and rewards of productive enterprise in accordance with the Shariah.

3.2.2 Performance measurement and income determination

On the IASB and FASB view of performance measurement, it is financial performance that counts. Comprehensive income is the increase in net assets arising from transactions as well as from realized and unrealized market price increases. In other words, under IFRS, most of the time, recognition of income is based on the realization concept, but in some cases it is based on changes in the market price.

In spite of the fact that performance measurement and income determination concepts are closely related to the view of the functions of capital markets and corporations in society, definitions of performance measurement and income are largely neglected in discussions on financial reporting from an Islamic perspective. For example, the Malaysian Accounting Standards Board (MASB) in its *Statement of Principles i*-1 (SOP *i*-1) outlines that there are some who claim that 'financial reporting from an Islamic perspective should be concerned with formulating alternative recognition and measurement principles for Shariah-compliant financial transactions' (MASB, 2009: A5). The MASB does not share this view because it 'believes that the primary difference between financial reporting from an Islamic perspective and its conventional counterpart is not that of recognition and measurement, but the extent of information displayed' (ibid.).

Neither viewpoint is concerned with the concept of performance measurement or income per se. The former appears to be based on the concern that reflecting economic substance over legal form in the financial statements is against the Islamic principle that forbids *gharar* (ambiguity of information, particularly in contracts but also in disclosure). The latter viewpoint is concerned with disclosing enough information to enable accountability with respect to financial transactions being Shariah-compliant. So far, different approaches to the determination of income are only touched upon when it comes to measurement within the context of determining *zakat.*

For example, in its 'Assessment of *Framework for the Preparation and Presentation of Financial Statements* from an Islamic Perspective' (MASB, 2009: Appendix B, B80), the Malaysian Accounting Standards Board mentions that some think that remeasurement at current cost provides a more equitable basis for calculating *zakat* on business. However, '(t)here appears to be no prominent discussion as to whether those increases or decreases arising from remeasurement to current cost should be included in the income statement or taken to equity as capital maintenance adjustments or revaluation reserves' (MASB, 2009: Appendix B, B81). On the other hand, the Accounting and Auditing Association for Islamic Financial Institutions (AAIOFI)'s *Exposure Draft for Financial Reporting by Islamic Financial Institutions* proposed that 'gains may also result from holding assets while their value changes during the period covered by the income statement' (AAIOFI, 2009: Par. 6.6) and 'losses may also result from holding assets while their value changes during the period covered by the income statement' (AAIOFI, 2009: Par. 6.7).

3.2.3 Capital maintenance

The increases or decreases in equity that arise as a result of the revaluation or restatement of assets and liabilities meet the IASB Conceptual Framework's definition of both gains and losses, which it treats as no different in nature from income (IASB, 2010: Pars 4.29–4.32) and expenses (ibid.: Pars 4.33–4.35) and may include both realized and unrealized gains and losses. The recognition of income and expenses is tied to the definition of assets and liabilities and pertains to those 'items that can be measured reliably and have a sufficient degree of certainty' (IASB, 2010: Par. 4.48).

While these increases or decreases meet the definition of income and expenses, they are not included in the income statement under certain concepts of capital maintenance. Instead these items are included in equity as capital maintenance adjustments or revaluation reserves (IASB, 2010: Par. 4.36).

The IASB CF holds that choice of capital maintenance concept must be based on financial statement user needs (IASB, 2010: Par. 4.58). It is important to keep in mind that this chapter of the IASB CF is still the old 1989 Framework because this part has not yet been updated.

At the time, the idea was harmonization not unification of accountings standards, and different measurement, performance, income and capital maintenance concepts had to be accommodated in the one Framework.

As we saw above, the MASB did not think that capital maintenance had been properly discussed by scholars with an interest in financial reporting from an Islamic perspective (MASB, 2009: Appendix B, B80). However, AAIOFI, which is specifically catering to the needs of Islamic Financial Institutions, advocates recognizing unrealized gains as income without a corresponding revaluation reserve or capital maintenance adjustment (AAIOFI, 2009: Pars 6.6, 6.7).

3.2.4 Disclosure

On the mainstream and IASB view of disclosure, the information is material if it can make a difference to an investor's decisions (IASB, 2010: OB). The extent, the level of aggregation and disaggregation, and the quality of disclosure are limited by the perceived costs and benefits of production, auditing and disclosure of information.

To enable Muslim investors to assess an entity's performance, disclosure must include information on:

- what the company produces and/or trades (must be *halal* not *haram*);
- the ways in which operations, production and trade are financed and carried out (there must be no discrepancy between the intention behind, and the legal form and economic substance of contracts,[6] and in principle, no debt financing); and
- the economic and social value the corporation adds to society, and how this value is distributed over those who have a direct stake in the joint stock corporation as well as the members of society at large.

3.2.5 Specific accounting issues related to financial transaction contracts

Islamic financial transactions may be different from conventional financial transactions owing to the prohibition of interest, excessive ambiguity, and risk shifting. 'Since many, if not most, modern Islamic financial transactions comprise a multitude of contracts and arrangements, they are in legal form very different from many of the transactions with which standard setters are accustomed' (AOSSG, 2010a: Par. 13). The literature on accounting and financial reporting from an Islamic perspective includes, on the one hand, the view that IFRS can be used for Islamic financial transactions, and on the other, that a separate set of Islamic accounting standards would be required (AOSSG, 2010a: Par. 14). The AOSSG Working Group (ibid.: Par. 15) attributes these different views to differences in opinion on the concepts of 'the time value of money' and 'economic substance over legal form'.

With respect to the time value of money, Islamic scholars agree that it exists, but it can only be determined on an *ex post* basis (as the reward for sharing risk) because determining it *ex ante* amounts to the calculation of interest (Iqbal and Mirakhor, 2011: 63). Scholars disagree on whether recognizing transaction fees or recognizing the entire sale proceeds before they have been earned amounts to recognizing a financing effect that is equivalent to *riba* (AOSSG, 2010a: Par. 37–56). The concept of 'economic substance over legal form' appears to contradict the interpretation of the Shariah that the legal form and the economic substance of a transaction must be the same. For example, according to the AOSSG Working Group (ibid.: Par. 18) the Institute of Chartered Accountants of Pakistan (ICAP)'s interpretation recognizes neither the time value of money, nor substance over form. AAIOFI does not recognize the time value of money but is ambiguous about 'substance over form' (AOSSG, 2010a: Pars 22–3).

Owing to the above mentioned disagreements over interpretations with respect to the concepts of the time value of money and economic substance over legal form, controversies arise in accounting for profit sharing contracts (*shirkah*), Islamic mutual insurance contracts (*takaful*), leasing and hire contracts (*ijirah*), and contracts relating to bonds and special purpose entities (*sukuk*).

4. Conclusion

In Section 2, the review of IFRS adoption in the 57 OIC countries shows that 18 countries do not permit IFRSs. Also, 12 countries opted to require IFRS for all listed companies; eight require IFRS for some, and eight countries permit the use of IFRS. The review identified at least four different approaches ranging from accepting IFRS as suitable for Islamic transactions to insistence on the need for separate Islamic accounting standards and two positions in between. Some national accounting standard setters believe that having separate accounting standards specifically for Islamic entities would be incompatible with the IFRS convergence while others believe that compatibility would still be maintained. Furthermore, Section 2 discussed six alternative explanations for why Islamic countries might choose to adopt IFRSs and showed that the economic explanation holds as much for Islamic countries as for other countries.

Section 3 discussed the differences between Islamic principles aimed at business activity that promotes social justice and the assumptions of financial economics aimed at allowing the market mechanism to allocate and distribute resources efficiently. In addition, Section 3 showed some of the implications that these differences have for the definition of the objective of financial reporting, performance measurement, capital maintenance and disclosure of information and how these affect specific accounting requirements for finance transactions. As the objectives of Islamic accounting and conventional accounting are fundamentally different, performance measurement, capital maintenance and disclosure requirements are likely to be different as well. More research is needed to determine to what extent IFRS can fulfil these requirements or where alternative standards must be developed.

Notes

1 Carien gratefully acknowledges the excellent research assistance from Maximilien Genard-Walton.
2 AAOIFI FAS 18 sets out the accounting rules of disclosure for conventional financial institutions that offer Islamic financial services (Islamic Windows).
3 The pillars of Islam are: the Islamic creed (*Shahada*), Prayers (*Salah*), *Zakat*, Fasting during Ramadhan (*Sawm*), and Pilgrimage to Mecca (*Hajj*).
4 Rules on the value and quality of each type of wealth and income exist which also set a minimum value for each below which their owner is not liable to pay *zakat* (this threshold is called *nissab*).
5 This is also a subject of disagreement between different Shariah jurists.
6 Economic substance is not superior to legal form; they are equal in Shariah.

Bibliography

Books and journals

AAIOFI (2009) 'Exposure Draft Conceptual Framework for Financial Reporting by Islamic Financial Institutions'. Accounting and Auditing Organisation for Islamic Financial Institutions.

Al Tarawneh, G. and Lucas, M. (2012) 'Understanding the Dominance of Western Accounting and Neglect of Islamic Accounting in Islamic Countries' *Journal of Islamic Accounting and Business Research*, 3 (2): 99–120.

Allingham, M. (2002) '*Choice Theory: A Very Short Introduction*', New York: Oxford University Press.

AOSSG (2010a) 'Financial Reporting Issues Relating to Islamic Finance', Asian-Oceanian Standard Setters Group, Working Group on Financial Issues Relating to Islamic Finance, Research Paper, 15 September.

AOSSG (2010b) 'Financial Reporting Issues Relating to Islamic Finance', Appendix to IASB Agenda Paper 2D / FASB Memo 168.Asian-Oceanian Standard Setters Group, Working Group on Financial Reporting Issues Relating to Islamic Finance.

AOSSG (2011) *AOSSG Survey: Accounting for Islamic Transactions and Entities.* Asian-Oceanian Standard Setters Group, Working Group an Islamic Finance December 2011. www.aossg.org.docs/Publications/AOSSG_Survey_Report_2011FINAL_CLEAN_29_12_2011.pdf.

Briston, R. (1978) 'The Evolution of Accounting in Developing Countries', *International Journal of Accounting*, 16: 105–20.

Briston, R. (1990) 'Accounting in Developing Countries: Indonesia and The Solomon Islands as Case Studies for Regional Co-operation', *Research in Third World Accounting*, 1: 195–216.

DFSA (2012a) 'Dubai Financial Services Authority Rulebook: Islamic Finance Rules Module', December, Chapter 4, available at http://dfsa.complinet.com/en/display/display_main.html?rbid=1547&element_id=13871 (accessed 28 March 2013).

DFSA (2012b) 'Dubai Financial Services Authority Rulebook: General Module', December, available at http://dfsa.complinet.com/en/display/display_main.html?rbid=1547&element_id=1843 (accessed 28 March 2013).

Di Maggio, P.J. and Powell, W.W. (1983) 'The Iron Cage Revisited: Institutional Isomorphism and Collective Rationality in Organizational Fields', *American Sociological Review*, 48: 147–60.

Hameed, S. (2001) 'Islamic Accounting: Accounting for the New Millenium?', Paper presented at the *Asia Pacific Conference*, Kota Bahru, Kelantan.

Haniffa, R. and Hudaib, M. (2010a) 'The Two Ws of Islamic Accounting Research', *Journal of Islamic Accounting and Business Research*, 1 (1): 5–9.

Haniffa, R. and Hudaib, M. (2010b) 'Islamic Finance: From Sacred Intentions to Secular Goals?' *Journal of Islamic Accounting and Business Research*, 1 (2): 85–91.

Hove, M. (1986) 'The Anglo-American Influence on International Accounting Standards: The Case of the Disclosure Standards of the International Accounting Standards Committee', *Research in Third World Accounting*, 1: 55–66.

IASB (2010) *The Conceptual Framework for Financial Reporting.* London: International Accounting Standards Board.

IASB/AOSSG (2010) 'Asian–Oceanian Standard Setters Group (AOSSG) Working Group on Financial Reporting Issues Relating to Islamic Finance', *Financial Reporting Issues relating to Islamic Finance*, Appendix to IASB Agenda Paper 2D / FASB Memo 168.

Iqbal, Z. and Mirakhor, A. (2011) *An Introduction to Islamic Finance: Theory and Practice*, 2nd edn, Singapore: John Wiley & Sons.

Kamla, R. (2009) 'Critical Insights into Contemporary Islamic Accounting', *Critical Perspectives on Accounting*, 20: 921–32.

Karim (2001) 'International Accounting Harmonization, Banking Regulation and Islamic Banks', *International Journal of Accounting*, 36: 168–93.

Kuran, T. (2004) *Islam and Mammon: The Economic Predicaments of Islamism.* Princeton, NJ: Princeton University Press.

Leuz, C. and Verrecchia, R.E. (2000) 'The Economic Consequences of Increased Disclosure', *Journal of Accounting Research*, 38 (3): 91–124.

MASB (2009) *Statement of Principles i-1: Financial Reporting from an Islamic Perspective.* Kuala Lumpur: Malaysian Accounting Standards Board.

Samuels, J.M. and Oliga, J.C. (1982) 'Accounting Standards in Developing Countries', *International Journal of Accounting*, 18 (1): 69–88.

SOCPA Accountants Magazine, April 2012. Saudi Organization for Certified Public Accountants.

Tripp, C. (2006) *Islam and the Moral Economy: The Challenge of Capitalism.* Cambridge: Cambridge University Press.

Wallace, R.S.O. (1990) 'Accounting in Developing Countries: A Review of the Literature', *Research in Third World Accounting*, 1: 3–34.

Websites

AAIOFI (Accounting and Auditing Organisation for Islamic Financial Institutions)
www.aaoifi.com/aaoifi/ (accessed 5 September 2012).
CIA World Factbook
www.cia.gov/library/publications/the-world-factbook/geos/xx.html (accessed 6 September 2012)
IAS Plus website
www.iasplus.com/en/resources/resource64 (accessed 9 September 2012).
OIC website (Organisation of Islamic Cooperation)
www.oic-oci.org/member_states.asp (accessed 6 September 2012).
World Bank website
data.worldbank.org/indicator/NY.GDP.PCAP.CD (accessed 6 September 2012)

26

Accounting Tools for Environmental Management and Communication[1]

Charles H. Cho and Marie-Andrée Caron

1. Introduction

Environmental accounting is full of models that may emanate from conceptualizations that are sometimes widely opposed, as the 'outside-in' models and 'inside-out' models (Richard, 2012; Burritt and Schaltegger, 2010). The former are often associated with environmental communication, while the latter involve the integration of the environment into the managers' decision-making process. What is problematic beyond these distinctions is the motivation of the organizations to commit to such an approach, anticipating the impact of disclosure of their actions on stakeholders' expectations, on regulation and on the benefits they can derive from (Gray and Laughlin, 2012). Models of environmental accounting (communication and management) can thus be distinguished by the commitment opportunities they offer to businesses.

Nonetheless, one common and fundamental definition of (social and) environmental accounting was coined about twenty-five years ago by Gray *et al.* (1987, p. ix):

> the process of communicating the social and environmental effects of organizations' economic actions to particular interest groups *within society* and to society at large. As such, it involves extending the *accountability* or organizations (particularly companies) beyond the traditional role of providing a financial account to the owners of capital, in particular shareholders. Such an extension is predicated upon the assumption that companies do have wider responsibilities than simply making money for their shareholders [emphases added].

A similar concept can be applied as well to the environmental management accounting area, which includes a more internal view of managerial tools for decision-making processes. In some sense, environmental accounting challenges traditional mainstream financial reporting for giving a narrow view of the interaction between society and organizations, which can potentially restrain the subject of accounting. The idea is provide a broader view of accounting by focusing also on non-economic and non-financial events and stakeholders to ultimately help increase the social *accountability* of businesses.

More specifically, environmental communication is defined in relatively broad terms. For example, for Berthelot *et al.* (2003) it consists of 'the set of information items related to a company's past, current and future environmental management activities and performance' (ibid., p. 2). Therefore, environmental disclosure encompasses not only financial information associated with the physical environment, but also includes non-financial information disclosed to organizational stakeholders. Examples of environmental disclosure include (Patten, 2002; Cho *et al.*, 2006):

- statements or discussion of the company's environmental policy or concern for the environment;
- discussion of the company's pollution control facilities or processes;
- discussion of specific (non-hazardous waste-related) environmental regulations or requirements;
- statement or discussion of the company being in compliance with environmental regulations;
- disclosure of current or past years' capital expenditures for pollution control or abatement;
- disclosure of projected future capital expenditures for pollution control or abatement;
- disclosure of current or past years' operating costs for pollution control or abatement; and
- disclosure of projected future operating costs for pollution control or abatement.

Such disclosure is important for several reasons. First, a number of accounting standards and guidelines in terms of environmental communication or disclosure (reporting) have been issued by different regulatory bodies such as the American Institute of Certified Public Accountants (AICPA), the Securities and Exchange Commission (SEC), the Canadian Institute of Chartered Accountants (CICA) and the Association of Chartered Certified Accountants (ACCA) in the UK, but also by multi-party organizations such as the Global Reporting Initiative (GRI) and private international regulation organizations such as ISO 26000. Organizations are also under the jurisdiction of and subject to several pieces of legislation and regulation that aim at improving and protecting the environment – for example, the Nouvelles régulations économiques (NRE) in France, the Plan général de contabilidad (PCG) in France, the SEC Regulation S-K in the US or the Operating and Financial Review (OFR) requirement in the UK. Moreover, several studies suggest that the requirements and expectations from organizational stakeholders in terms of environmental disclosure have increased (Berthelot *et al.*, 2003; Cormier *et al.*, 2004) as this type of information is used more frequently in their decision-making process.[2] Finally, other studies[3] have revealed that the extent of environmental disclosure was, in general, directly associated with the environmental performance of organizations, but also with the regulatory context and media pressures.

However, in spite of these developments and findings, organizations communicate very little and provide insufficient and inadequate disclosures to their stakeholders at large for the ultimate objective to increase their social accountability. Based on this observation, we identify three broad orientations underlying the formal accounting tools and we examine in which ways managers, professional certified/chartered accountants and legislators would be able to make this communication more systematic, more prevalent and more accurate.

We will first look at the different drivers of communicating environmental information, also known as 'environmental disclosure'. We will then get into the different rationales, positions and tools for environmental management and communication tools, which are grouped in three positions:

- complying with laws and regulations;
- improving competitiveness; and
- reducing the negative impacts on the environment.

Finally, we will discuss the challenges and present some suggestions to the three stakeholder groups: managers, accountants and legislators.[4]

2. Drivers of environmental communication

Despite the existence of accounting standards, guidelines and even regulations in terms of environmental communication or disclosure, organizations often ignore or circumvent these frameworks, and do not disclose enough or adequately the information (Cho and Patten, 2008; Delbard, 2008; Chauvey, *et al.*, 2012; Larrinaga *et al.*, 2002). The information disclosed varies widely in terms of quantity and quality, primarily due to the voluntary nature of some of the disclosure frameworks but also to organizations' various motivations to disclose this type of information. Buhr (2007) suggests the following motives:

- moral or ethical considerations (sense of duty);
- quest for competitive advantage;
- desire to contribute to the development of voluntary disclosure frameworks (e.g. global reporting initiative);
- seeking to exert some influence on regulation;
- peer and industry pressure;
- organizational performance;
- image management (public relations management, participation in reporting awards);
- social pressures; investors' anticipated reaction; and
- current regulations in place.

Among these, image management in response to social pressures is often mentioned. As such, following negative environmental impacts (e.g. an oil spill), Patten (1992) documented a significant increase in the quantity and content of environmental information disclosed, not only from the affected organization but also from the industry to which the organization belongs in order to create an industry-wide effect. Therefore, disclosure of environmental information can be perceived as a legitimating or greenwashing tool, allowing organizations to obtain, maintain or repair an organization's reputation (Ashforth and Gibbs, 1990; O'Donovan, 2002). In fact, results from a recent study (Cho *et al.*, 2012b) take this reasoning further by showing a significant *negative* association between environmental performance and both membership in the Dow Jones Sustainability Index (DJSI) and reputation scores – the argument being that worse performing firms provide more extensive levels of disclosure and there is *positive* relation between environmental disclosure and both environmental reputation measures and DJSI membership. Hence, voluntary environmental disclosure appears to mediate the effect of poor environmental performance on environmental reputation, and membership in the DJSI (thus environmental reputation) appears to be driven more by what firms say than what they do.

Other studies suggest that some organizations produce this type of disclosure to alter the norms, values and beliefs of their stakeholders (Dowling and Pfeffer, 1975; Lindbolm, 1993), in other words as strategies to 'manage impressions' (Cho *et al.*, 2010; Neu *et al.*, 1998). Finally, some researchers documented that environmental information disclosed in sustainability reports primarily exhibits the 'business case' for sustainability as the organization is more concerned about the sustainability of its (business) performance by gaining competitive advantage (Caron and Turcotte, 2009).

Despite the availability of resources, which are sometimes granted, such superficiality of organizational environmental communication leads us to consider another approach to this issue. While it is important to communicate the efforts and achievements in terms of the environment, the primary goal remains the concrete improvement of performance. As such, the organization must undertake and carry out long-term investments in this area. These investments are commonly referred to as environmental capital expenditures, which are capital expenditures explicitly devoted to pollution control, prevention and abatement (SEC, 2008). Such investments can represent the result of the organization's position with respect to environmental issues (i.e. its desired results or intrinsic motivations).[5] More specifically, they can be seen as the result of environmental management decisions owing to their relevance for regulatory (Johnston, 2005; SEC, 2008), strategic (Buysse and Verbeke, 2003) and financial (Johnston and Rock, 2005; Johnston *et al.,* 2008) purposes. We noted earlier that these could be many, but only a few studies have examined the adequacy of how management tools and communication systems are used as well as the motivation of organizations' environmental management and communication. The range of environmental management and communication tools suggest that the organization has numerous choices. However, these tools in fact underlie different positions with respect to the environment and do not provide the same opportunities and constraints in terms of communication and management. As they are often divided between two broad categories of environmental accounting (outside-in and inside-out), we address them here from their potential in terms of commitment to the organization in order to clearly highlight their utilization and activation context.

3. Rationales, positions and tools for environmental management and communication

In the absence of norms or standards, organizations have considerable flexibility when it comes to management and environmental communication. They are able:

- to merely comply with laws and regulations;
- to aim at improving their competitiveness; or
- to attempt to reduce the negative impacts of their activities on the environment; and
- in all three cases, to be accountable for their actions.

These three forms of commitment emanate from recently developed typologies related to the position of organizations towards social and environmental responsibility (Acquier, 2008; Caron and Charbonneau, 2008).[6] Some environmental management and communication tools allow organizations to achieve these three forms of commitment, as shown in Table 26.1.

Before committing on the deployment of one or more of these tools, an organization must establish beforehand what type of engagement it wants to make in terms of management and communication in order to avoid undertaking a 'technical' process that could be too ambitious (in terms of cost, time, resources); that is, one that would not match management's will or that could be inconsistent with its traditional management practices. For example, an organization should not engage in a very complex evaluation of its intangible assets if managers merely want to stick to compliance. Instead, it should further the control of the three 'e's' (effectiveness, efficiency, and economy) to integrate it into an eco-control system if managers wish to adopt a step for a voluntary reduction of its negative impacts on the environment without knowing beforehand the effect on its competitiveness. In other words, there are adequate communication and management tools at each level of commitment toward the environment.

Table 26.1 Positions of organizations towards environmental management and communication

Positions of organizations	*Management and communication tools*
Complying with laws and regulations	Allocation of environmental costs. Hierarchical cost analysis. Activity-based costing
Improving competitiveness	Profitability analysis of investment projects. Assessment of intangible assets. Control of the three "e" (effectiveness, efficiency and economy)
Reducing the negative impacts on the environment	Life cycle analysis. Full environmental cost accounting. Environmental performance indicators. Eco-control. Performance in terms of sustainable development

3.1 Comply with laws and regulations

For the organization, compliance with the law is a position that usually does not require any fundamental changes in its management systems. This is essentially about complying with specific regulations[7] (conforming to social rights, product safety, etc.), including regulations on environmental communication and disclosure as discussed above. For relatively common cases of low or non-compliance with certain types of regulation, Bebbington *et al.* (2012) suggest that this phenomenon could potentially be due to a lack of normativity – the degree to which actors see rules as binding. Their argument is centred on the idea that formal regulation on its own would not be enough to create a norm and normativity can also change over time.[8]

Nonetheless, the organization's exemplarity in complying allows for some preventive measures against media crises and a deteriorating image, even if this does not constitute a source of strategic differentiation (Acquier, 2008). The adjustments made by managers appear necessary and legitimate, and tools are available to achieve them and measure their impact on the organization.

The disclosure of hidden costs as management and communication tools can help managers with the adjustments to make, given the applicable regulations and stakeholders' expectations (see Figure 26.1 for examples of internal and external environmental costs). Among the five 'cost analysis' tools suggested by the Society of Management Accountants of Canada (SCMC, 1999a), some are about complying with regulations while two of them are focused on reducing the negative effects on the environment. The distinction between these two levels of management and communication is based on the emphasis put on external costs also known as 'social costs' (full cost accounting, FCA). Life cycle analysis and full environmental cost accounting aim for a comprehensive identification of both internal and external costs. We will return to this issue later.

The allocation of environmental costs involves two steps: the identification of hidden costs associated with internal environmental costs and the allocation of these costs (often referred to as overhead) to affected products and activities and managers in charge. This tool leads managers to review the profitability of 'polluting' products, but also to empower their subordinates to get them to review the activities of the organization in order to prevent these costs (IFAC, 1998). When the allocation of environmental costs is linked to the compensation system (or other financial incentives), we are talking about eco-control, which is often used as a mechanism to reduce the negative effects on the environment as we shall see further. The hierarchical cost analysis of and activity-based costing are simply techniques to allocate more accurately environmental costs (e.g. by identifying cost drivers) and temporal costs (level 0: usual costs; level

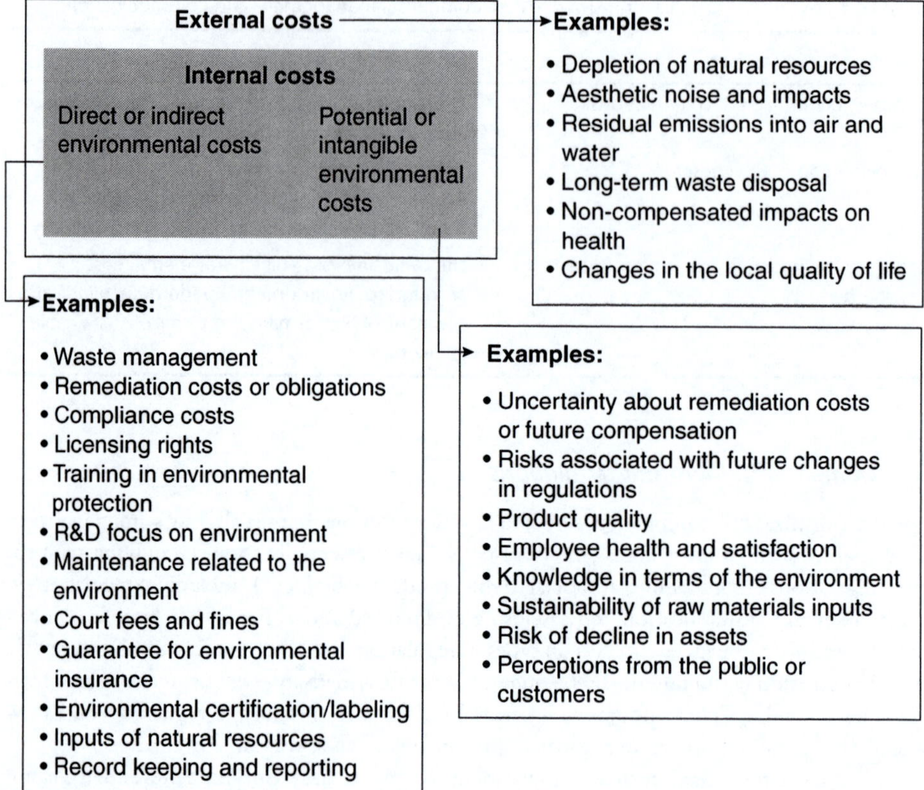

Figure 26.1 External effects considered as "external costs" and internal environmental costs

Source: SCMC (1999c)

1: hidden costs; level 2: environmental liabilities; level 3: less tangible costs), depending on the political and regulatory environment of the organization.

If compliance with regulations is essential to clean up an organization's production activities, or even just to survive, the other two positions with regards to environmental management and communication prominently feature the unfinished nature of this form of commitment for the planet, but also for the organization itself, considering the potential to improve competitiveness, which is contained in environmental management and communication. Richard (2012) calls this type of environmental accounting 'outside-in' in the sense that it is not about the preservation of natural capital, but for the protection of the organization's financial capital under the restriction of legal or contractual environmental rules and regulations.

3.2 Improve competitiveness

The issue of sustainable development is an area of environmental and social innovations, but also managerial and political (Acquier, 2008). The organization may decide to transform these innovations into opportunities to achieve competitive advantage (Porter and Reinhart, 2007; Porter and van der Linde, 1995). The win-win, or integrative logic makes it possible to believe in satisfying jointly the needs of the organization and those of the earth (as well as intra-generational and inter-generational needs). In other words, this logic is based on the idea of a possible reconciliation between economic (financial) objectives and social and environmental objectives. It contrasts with the win-lose logic that brings out the necessity to give up satisfying some of today's needs for those of future generations (Hoffman *et al.*, 1999). The latter focuses on the tensions (conflicts, contradictions) between the economic and financial objectives of the organization and its environmental and social needs, as we will discuss in the next section on the efforts to reduce the negative impacts on the environment.

Making the environment a way to improve the competitiveness of an organization involves the ability to evaluate the profitability of 'green' investments or environmental benefits related to covered costs. Decisions to be made in order to improve the competitiveness are, for example, related to:

- the acquisition or the disposal of ecological facilities;
- the measures to take in order to adopt management and control systems that provide access to markets (such as suppliers of organizations that require them);
- the steps to obtain some concessions from public services or implantation authorizations from national or regional authorities (telecommunications, mining industries, etc.) (Quairel, 2008);
- the design of new products to conquer a new market (organic food, recycled paper, pollution control equipment, renewable energy market, etc.); and
- the reengineering of the organization's production systems from a waste management perspective (e.g. energy efficiency, materials management, inventory management, etc.) to eliminate wasted resources, wasted time, duplication of efforts, poor planning of production and inventory systems, malfunctioning of equipment, etc. (Girardi, 1995). Some researchers have also shown that a company could orient itself towards revenues or costs (Journeault *et al.*, 2012).

If innovation is at the heart of these initiatives, the extent of their financial benefits is based on the analysis of 'environmental' data (physical and operational) often difficult to translate into financial terms. To achieve this, accounting organizations in collaboration with political bodies and academics, have proposed a number of models. The one from Girardi (1995) is particularly comprehensive:

- help in setting objectives for reducing waste;
- link these objectives to strategies;
- link these objectives and performance measurement systems (e.g. assessment of business unit profitability);
- link these objectives with investment decisions;
- link these objectives to the budget;
- estimate pollution prevention program and current and future regulation costs;
- estimate sales program and pollution credit trading/exchange costs; and
- design a system of accountability composed of both financial and non-financial indicators.

This model aims for the integration of waste management into the organization's central accounting information system, from the following four steps:

- calculation and disclosure of hidden costs (transparency);
- allocation of costs to corresponding products, activities and managers (accountability);

- identification of indirect costs related to waste (measuring the effect on the efficiency of labour, productivity, overhead expenses investment expenditures, etc.); and
- integration of the waste management into all stages of the product life cycle.

Improving the competitiveness of an organization deployed in the spirit of a win-win logic increases the likelihood of managers adopting the concept of the environment from a successful adaptation based their own criteria, which are often economic (Caron and Turcotte, 2009). However, as the activities under this type of management and communication are not intended for all environmental practices within the organization (they are often ad hoc, limited and targeted), they may serve to cover irresponsible practices and make the mobilized tools counterproductive (Milne and Gray, 2007). In this spirit, the tools associated with the efforts to reduce the negative environmental effects appear to be more credible and to vehicle the emergence of a regulation that is both realistic and fair, including the development of voluntary organizational performance in terms of environmental matters. However, as computing profit is not always possible, this commitment may well be unrealistic. Also, it may appear extremely simplistic in relation to the actual concerns of workers, who adopt responsible practices without always bearing in mind the increase in profit. A third position is thus to consider.

3.3 Reduce the negative impacts on the environment

Among the environmental management and communication tools that are able to manage and communicate activities aiming at reducing the negative impacts on the environment, we find full environmental cost accounting, life cycle analysis and performance indicators, as well as eco-control, as a broader and more inclusive system but that is often outside the organization's accounting system (Burritt *et al.*, 2002; Schaltegger and Sturm, 1998). These tools are working to conceive some layouts that are able to reduce the negative impacts of organizational activities on the environment. Improving the competitiveness of the organization cannot constitute a motivation here since the profitability horizon of such layouts is often very long, if not impossible to assess or inconclusive (Magness, 2006). They rather draw their justification from the win-lose logic, in which there is an emphasis on the need give up the satisfaction of certain current needs for those of future generations.

If the environmental cost accounting (also known as quantitative financial and social costs, full cost accounting and full cost reporting system) wants an overhaul of traditional accounting practices to allocate internal and external costs – monetary and non-monetary – to products, Herbohn (2005) updated the requirements for implementation of such a tool. These requirements are: understand the societal aspects beyond the technical aspects, involving stakeholders in determining adverse effects to prioritize and extend the assessment of environmental costs to the entire product life cycle of the organization.

With the adoption of life cycle analysis, the organization is not only to comply with government regulations; it also seeks to mitigate the adverse impact of its activities on the environment through a comprehensive assessment of all the effects of its activities and its 'upstream' and 'downstream'[9] products (SCMC, 1999a) in order to detect or create opportunities for improvement.

Finally, environmental performance indicators constitute the most comprehensive form of assessment of organizational environmental performance. Different approaches share the definition of these indicators, which are carried by four main organizations: the International Organization for Standardization (ISO 14000) in the United States, the Eco-Management and Audit Scheme (EMAS) in Europe, the Global Reporting Initiative (GRI) and the Organization for

Economic Cooperation and Development (OECD: key environmental indicators) in France. While the GRI indicators cover the three dimensions of sustainable development and those of ISO standards focus on the management components of the organization (management, operation, context), others are more centred around material flows of the organization (use of materials, energy consumption, output of non-products, releases of pollutants). The latest ISO 26000, described as 'non-standard standard' (Capron *et al.,* 2010), meanwhile focuses more on concrete actions 'agreed' upon with stakeholders than on indicators and results. Janicot (2007) groups these indicators into two categories: 'outcome' indicators and 'process' indicators. Stakeholders are more interested in outcome indicators while process indicators are designed to evaluate the efforts made by management to improve environmental performance at the organizational level.[10] The objective of process indicators is to assess whether a coherent environmental management is in place and well controlled, but it is an internal coherence that is primarily built in an operational vision of management. The contents of key outcome indicators touch upon performance measurement in terms of materials consumption, resources, energy and services (into the organization), products, services, waste and emissions (out of the organization), as well as physical facilities and logistics (operations of the organization).

To date, eco-control is the most complete control model of these indicators. It allows measurement and control of sustainable development practices from the link between three major control mechanisms, which are sustainable development performance indicators, financial incentives (compensation plans) and sustainable development strategy (Henri and Journeault, 2010). The purpose is to improve organizational performance based on outcome indicators, in addition to process indicators. The link with strategy motivates players who are eco-evaluated to innovate in order to discover new operating ways to minimize the adverse effects of organizational activities on the environment and optimize the positive effects. Eco-control is thus a select tool to bring managers to interact at the border of a more efficient organization. Invitations from multiparty organizations to participate in the development of sustainable development indicators (consultation meetings with the GRI or ISO 26000) and exchange forums between practitioners and researchers (Caron *et al.,* 2010) constitute some great opportunities.

Tools to reduce negative effects show that this commitment has two options – a process 'organized' by using economic valuation models or an approach that can be described as 'political' which relies much more on stakeholders. These environmental accounting tools are classified as 'inside-outside' (Richard, 2012), aiming at preserving the natural capital; however, proponents of the first approach emphasize *weak sustainability*, while those adhering to the second tend to defend *strong sustainability.*[11]

If the variety of these tools allows the organization to progressively engage environmental measurement and communication, some issues will need to be solved along the way.

4. Issues and limitations of environmental management and communication

The following issues may constitute some limitations for the usefulness of environmental management and communication tools presented in this article:

- The heterogeneity of these tools' components (e.g., physical units and monetary units, products and processes, but also externalities) presents significant assessment issues.
- In addition to presenting assessment issues, externalities are not subject to generally accepted values.

- The very definition of environmental costs is problematic because several definitions exist based on the interests of stakeholders and it is sometimes difficult to distinguish the current operating costs.[12]
- Managing change may become necessary and require the presence of stakeholders who are internally influential but still tied to external respondents.
- The multidisciplinary nature of the environment requires the leaders to collaborate with experts in natural sciences, sociology, law, engineering, environmental economics, etc.
- It is sometimes difficult, or even impossible, to associate environmental disclosure with actual environmental performance when it is measured based on standards that do not meet stakeholders' expectations.
- A paradigm shift – sometimes difficult to carry out – is required to evaluate investment projects according to environmental performance indicators, particularly to take into account the recovery period, which is generally longer for this type of project.

5. Suggestions on environmental management and communication

We have seen that environmental measurement and communication involve a number of issues that can constitute some important limitations if they are not resolved in time.We show here how some of the stakeholders involved with environmental issues – that is, managers, accountants and legislators – can help make environmental control and disclosure more systematic, more frequent and accurate.

5.1 Suggestions for managers

A good knowledge – but also an opinion and awareness of the three organizational positions discussed above – should contribute to an imminent improvement in the environmental management and communication of an organization. For managers, the implications remain at a macro level: give high priority to environmental issues and objectives by allocating adequate resources, follow a strategic plan predicting progressive commitment (compliance with laws and regulations, improving competitiveness and reducing the negative impacts on the environment), and provide complete, reliable, relevant and transparent environmental disclosures to increase the accountability of their organization. Managers will undoubtedly have to make decisions that could be conflicting with the purely economic objectives of the organization. In this context they will be called upon to demonstrate a spirit of sacrifice and deploy a long-term vision.

Leaving the environmental manager to solve alone the inherent problems associated with the implementation of environmental management and communication tools bears the risk to compromise the depth and viability of the efforts that are made (Parker, 2000b). Also, if we involve all key stakeholders of the organization, we will avoid bringing too drastic or too conservative answers to these crucial questions answers. Cross-participation by key stakeholders in the divergent logics around the development of management and disclosure tools will foster the emergence of realistic regulations that are built on the basis of entrenched practices in the management practices of organizations, even if they are innovative.

5.2 Suggestions for accountants

Several studies have emphasized the importance of the contribution from the accounting profession in the debate surrounding the environment (Bebbington and Gray, 2001; Parker,

2000a). However, these conceptual collaborations found little support in practice from professional certified/chartered accountants of the three Canadian professional accounting designations (Chartered Accountants, Certified General Accountants or Certified Management Accountants). Researchers[13] provided various explanations, using illustrative case scenarios, for this lack of commitment by practitioners: they occupy a passive (reactive) position, waiting for an explicit request from senior management or another part of the organization; they prefer to wait for stricter regulations that specify the requirements in terms of information; although they are interested in environmental issues, they do not see how to integrate these issues to their current responsibilities; or, they are opposed to an active contribution in environmental matters.

So far, professional literature has limited itself to illustrate the potential contribution of the professional certified/chartered accountant to environmental issues based on some lists of specific activities (see Table 26.2 for examples of these activities).

However, the vagueness, ambiguity and, in many cases, innovative feature of environmental management and communication highlights the importance of accountants' concrete experience to acquire the necessary skills (Caron *et al.*, 2006). The accounting profession, as well as the business community, needs to set up favourable conditions to enable professional certified/chartered accountants to participate in such experiments. More specifically, the accounting profession needs to provide its members adequate training in environmental matters and make sure they have an interest to acquire and apply such training.

5.3 Suggestions for legislators

It is in the interest of legislators to develop mechanisms (or, where appropriate, to improve them) that are able to monitor the various activities of organizations to ensure that regulations are enforced and, if necessary, impose sanctions against them.

The case of the Government Accountability Office (GAO) and the Securities and Exchange Commission (SEC) in the United States examined by Cho and Patten (2008) is an example of a quasi-failure due to the lack of compliance with and enforcement of environmental communication standards/regulations. This study firstly suggests that organizations that are subject

Table 26.2 Steps for integration of waste management into the organization's central accounting information system

Step	*Accounting tools and methods*
Step 1. Identification and disclosure (transparence) of costs associated to waste COSTS	Identification of costs associated to waste. Mapping or audit of waste costs
Step 2. Conception of an attribution structure (accountability) and of an assessment of managers' performance PEOPLE	Allocation of waste costs to cost centres
Step 3. Improvement of efficiency associated with waste PROCESS	Matrix of costs associated to waste. Waste ratio analysis. Activity-based costing
Step 4. Integration of waste reduction to all steps of product life cycle PRODUCTS	Life cycle cost analysis

Source: Adapted from Girardi (1995, p. 21).

to SEC rules on the disclosure of environmental information do not comply or comply very little with the disclosure regulations issued by the SEC, and that, although requested by federal legislators, a large governmental agency such as the GAO has not been able to determine the extent of the information gap caused by the non-compliance with disclosure standards despite conducting studies requiring significant resources. This example illustrates well the risks of a deficient legislation and shows what must be avoided at all costs. But it also highlights the very important role of the legislator in the 'efficient' deployment of a 'growing' pressure on organizations. In other words, passing laws and implementing regulations is a start but relying on a potential increase of normativity (see Bebbington *et al.*, 2012) to hope for compliance will certainly not be sufficient. As such, the most important aspect of the regulatory environment remains the strict enforcement of the regulations that are in place, including the application of sanctions and consequences for non- or low compliance.

5. Conclusion

If environmental management and communication are subject to regulations that are sometimes shy and often difficult to enforce, several management and disclosure tools are nonetheless available. These tools emanate from an extensive and more accessible literature for over thirty years, which is the result of close collaboration between professional organizations, including accountants, political bodies and the academic and scientific community. The diversity of these tools is a response to the wide variety of motivations that may lead an organization to get interested in environmental issues.

As such, some tools allow the organization to comply with laws and regulations, others to evaluate the improvement of its competitiveness, while others lead to the reduction of the negative impacts of its activities on the environment. Therefore, managers, accountants and legislators must above all ask themselves about the form of commitment to foster the environment according to the socio-political context of organizations, the availability of required resources and their experience in this area. In return, the appropriation and deployment of one of these three types of tools in management and communication practices of an organization can lead to a restatement or reformulation of its commitment. This commitment can change from a rather 'imposed' form (complying with laws and regulations) to a 'free' form, or as a starting point, be more 'interested' (improving competitiveness) or more 'altruistic' (reducing the negative impacts of activities on the environment).

The reflection presented in this article suggests the following question for future research: in which way(s) communication participates, or on the contrary harms the quality of environmental management? After more than forty years of more or less successful history, the main challenge of environmental accounting is now to link the *outside-in* with the *inside-out* (Burritt and Schaltegger, 2010) or the relevance for the stakeholder with the coherence within the organization (Janicot, 2007) in order to increase and deepen the commitment of the company. In turn, this commitment will encourage the development of accounting regulation in sustainable development.

Notes

1 This chapter is a translated adaptation and extension from Marie-Andrée Caron and Charles H. Cho "Positions des organisations face à la gestion et à la communication environnementales", *Revue Gestion* 34 (1), Spring, 59–67, and was reproduced, adapted, extended and translated with the authorization from *Gestion, Revue Internationale de Gestion*.

2 See Neu *et al.* (1998), Milne and Patten (2002), Cho *et al.* (2009).
3 See Cho and Patten (2007), Cho *et al.* (2012a), Deegan (2002), O'Donovan (2002), Patten (1992, 2002).
4 While we acknowledge that it is not very common to include managers and accountants as part of stakeholders, we do so here given their potential active involvement and implications in environmental management and communications issues.
5 It is important to note that some studies have shown environmental capital expenditures being disclosed to create an appearance of environmental care and legitimize past poor environmental performance rather than signalling improved future environmental performance (e.g. Cho *et al.*, 2012a, 2012b; Patten, 2002) and that even environmental governance mechanisms at the board level seem to be of more symbolic nature (vs. substantive) in terms of environmental action without a real impact on environmental investment decisions (Rodrigue *et al.*, 2012).
6 Acquier (2008) opposes the concept of free vs. compulsory figures, while Caron and Charbonneau (2008) show that commitment can be part of familiarity (routine), plan (objectives and accurate results) or justification (in line with public expectations).
7 For example, it relates to damages to the environment caused by acid rain resulting from the use of fossil fuels, health problems due to noise pollution near airports and highways, and ozone depletion due to aerosols containing chlorofluorides (CFC) (SCMC, 1999a).
8 More specifically, they argue that normativity 'starts with emergence of norms, characterized by the innovation of norm entrepreneurs, followed by diffusion leading to a 'tipping point' after which the norm cascades to reach a point at the end of the life cycle where norms are internalised and acquire a taken-for-granted quality' (Bebbington *et al.*, 2012: 79).
9 This technique involves the identification of energy and materials consumed (inputs), but also the releases into the environment (outputs), their quantification, the assessment of their impact in terms of environmental health, of human health and resource depletion, 'from cradle to cradle'.
10 The ISO 14000 standard defines environmental performance as measurable outcomes of the environmental management system, in connection with the organization's control of its environmental aspects on the basis of its environmental policy, its objectives and environmental targets (the objectives come from the company, internally).
11 The weak design of sustainable development provides a substitutability of financial, natural and social capital while the strong design prohibits the recognition of such substitution. For more details, see Herath (2005).
12 This example, taken from IFAC (1998: para. 31), is illustrative: 'For example, an investment may be made for operational reasons which has a positive impact on environmental performance. Is this investment to be defined as an *environmental* expenditure?'[added emphasis].
13 See Kuasirikun (2005), Wilmshurst and Frost (2001), Deegan *et al.* (1995).

Bibliography

Acquier, A. (2008) 'Développement durable et management stratégique: Piloter un processus de transformation de la valeur'. Paper presented at the 3rd conference of the Réseau International de Recherche sur les Organisations et le Développement Durable (RIODD).

Ashforth, B.E. and Gibbs, B.W. (1990) 'The Double-edge of Legitimization'. *Organisation Science*, 1(2), 177–94.

Bebbington, J. and Gray, R. (2001) 'An Account of Sustainability: Failure, Success and a Reconceptualisation'. *Critical Perspectives on Accounting*, 12(5), 557–605.

Bebbington, J., Kirk, E.A. and Larrinaga, C. (2012) 'The Production of Normativity: A Comparison of Reporting Regimes in Spain and the UK'. *Accounting, Organisations and Society*, 37(2), 78–94.

Berthelot, S., Cormier, D. and Magnan, M. (2003) 'Environmental Disclosure Research: Review and Synthesis'. *Journal of Accounting Literature*, 22, 1–44.

Buhr, N. (2007) 'Histories and Rationales for Sustainability Reporting.' In J. Unerman, J. Bebbington, and B. O'Dwyer (eds) *Sustainability Accounting and Accountability*, London: Routledge, pp. 57–69.

Burritt, R.L. and Schaltegger, S. (2010) 'Sustainability Accounting and Reporting: Fad or Trend?'. *Accounting, Auditing and Accountability Journal*, 23(7), 829–46.

Burritt, R.L., Hahn, T. and Schaltegger, S. (2002) 'Towards a Comprehensive Framework for Environmental Management Accounting: Links Between Actors and Environmental Management Accounting Tools'. *Australian Accounting Review*, 12(2), 39–50.

Buysse, K. and Verbeke, A. (2003) 'Proactive Environmental Strategies: A Stakeholder Management Perspective'. *Strategic Management Journal*, 24(5), 453–70.

Capron, M., Quairel-Lanoizelée, F. and Turcotte, M.F. (2010) *ISO 26000: Une norme 'hors norme'? Vers une conceptualisation mondiale de la responsabilité sociétale*, Paris: Economica.

Caron, M.A. and Charbonneau, M. (2008) 'Pour une traduction multiple de la responsabilité: engagement et action au pluriel'. In C. Eberhard (ed.) *Traduire nos responsabilités planétaires: Recomposer nos paysages juridiques'*, Brussels: Bruylant, 429–45.

Caron, M.A. and Turcotte, M.F. (2009) 'Path Dependence and Path Creation: Framing the Extra-financial Information Market for a Sustainable Trajectory'. *Accounting, Auditing and Accountability Journal*, 22(2), 272–97.

Caron, M.A., Fortin, A. and NasrEddine, M. (2006) 'Les comptables et la RSE: Une question de connaissances ou de compétences?'. *Revue Internationale de Gestion*, (31)2, 92–100.

Caron, M.A., Lapointe, A. and Gendron, C. (2010) 'Sustainability Reporting: An Incomplete Dialogue between the Firm and its Stakeholders'. In S.P. Osborne and A. Ball (eds) *Social Audit, Social Accounting, and Accountability for the Public Good*, Studies in Public Management Series, London: Routledge.

Chauvey, J.-N., Giordano-Spring, S., Cho, C.H. and Patten, D.M (2012) 'The Normativity and Legitimacy of CSR Disclosure: Evidence from France'. Working paper, Hong Kong Baptist University, available at http://ied-wbef.hkbu.edu.hk/forms/conferenceProg20121130.pdf.

Cho, C.H. (2009) 'Legitimation Strategies Used In Response To Environmental Disaster: A French Case Study of Total S.A.'s *Erika* and AZF Incidents'. *European Accounting Review*, 18(1), 33–62.

Cho, C.H. and Patten, D.M. (2007) 'The Role of Environmental Disclosures as Tools of Legitimacy: A Research Note'. *Accounting, Organisations and Society*, 32(7/8), 639–47.

Cho, C.H. and Patten, D.M. (2008) 'Did the GAO Get It Right? Another Look at Corporate Environmental Disclosure'. *Social and Environmental Accountability Journal*, 28(1), 21–32.

Cho, C.H., Patten, D.M. and Roberts, R.W. (2006) 'Corporate Political Strategy: An Examination of the Relation between Political Expenditures, Environmental Performance, and Environmental Disclosure'. *Journal of Business Ethics*, 67(2), 139–54.

Cho, C.H., Phillips, J., Hageman, A. and Patten, D.M. (2009) 'Media Richness, User Trust, and Perceptions of Corporate Social Responsibility: An Experimental Investigation of Visual Website Disclosure'. *Accounting, Auditing & Accountability Journal*, 22(6), 933–52.

Cho, C.H., Roberts, R.W. and Patten, D.M. (2010) 'The Language of US Corporate Environmental Disclosure'. *Accounting, Organisations and Society*, 35(4), 431–43.

Cho, C.H., Freedman, M. and Patten, D.M. (2012a) 'Corporate Disclosure of Environmental Capital Expenditures: A Test of Alternative Theories'. *Accounting, Auditing and Accountability Journal*, 25(3), 486–507.

Cho, C.H., Guidry, R.P., Hageman, A.M. and Patten, D.M. (2012b) 'Do Actions Speak Louder than Words? An Empirical Investigation of Corporate Environmental Reputation'. *Accounting, Organisations and Society*, 37(1), 14–25.

Cormier, D., Gordon, I. and Magnan, M. (2004) 'Corporate Environmental Reporting: Contrasting Management's Values with Reality'. *Journal of Business Ethics*, 49(2), 143–65.

Deegan, C. (2002) 'The Legitimizing Effect of Social and Environmental Disclosures: A Theoretical Foundation'. *Accounting, Auditing and Accountability Journal*, 15(3), 282–311.

Deegan, C., Geddes, S. and Staunton, J. (1995) 'A Survey of Australian Accountants' Attitudes and Environmental Reporting'. *Accounting Forum*, 19(2/3), 143–63.

Delbard, O. (2008) 'CSR Legislation in France and the European Regulatory Paradox: An Analysis of EU CSR Policy and Sustainability Reporting Practice'. *Corporate Governance*, 8(4), 397–405.

Dowling, J. and Pfeffer, J. (1975) 'Organisational Legitimacy: Social Values and Organisational Behavior'. *Pacific Sociological Review*, 18, 122–36.

Girardi, G. (1995) *Accounting for Waste as a Business Management Tool: A Best Practice Guideline*. Monash Centre for Environmental Management, Melbourne: Monash University.

Gray, R. and Laughlin, R. (2012) '"It Was 20 Years Ago Today: Sgt Pepper", *Accounting, Auditing & Accountability Journal*, Green Accounting and the Blue Meanies'. *Accounting, Auditing & Accountability Journal*, 25(2), 228–55.

Gray, R., Owen, D. and Maunders, K. (1987) *Corporate Social Reporting*. Englewood Cliffs, NJ: Prentice-Hall.

Henri, J.-F. and Journeault, M. (2010) 'Eco-control: The Influence of Management Control Systems on Environmental and Economic Performance'. *Accounting, Organisations and Society*, 35(1), 63–80.

Herath, G. (2005) 'Development and Environmental Sustainability Accounting: The Challenge to the Economics and Accounting Profession'. *International Journal of Social Economics*, 32(12), 1035–50.

Herbohn, K. (2005) 'A Full Cost Environmental Accounting Experiment'. *Accounting, Organisations and Society*, 30(6), 519–36.

Hoffman, A.J., Gillespie, J.J, Moore, D.A., Wade-Benzoni, K.A., Thompson, L.L. and Bazerman, M.H. (1999) 'A Mixed-motive Perspective on the Economics versus Environment Debate'. *The American Behavioral Scientist*, 42(8), 1254–76.

IFAC (1998) *Environmental Management in Organisations: The Role of Management Accounting*. International Federation of Accountants, Financial and Management Accounting Committee (FMAC), Study 6, March.

Janicot, L. (2007) 'Les systèmes d'indicateurs de performance environnementale entre communication et contrôle'. *Comptabilité, contrôle et audit*, 1(13), 47–67.

Johnston, D. (2005) 'An Investigation of Regulatory and Voluntary Environmental Capital Expenditures'. *Journal of Accounting and Public Policy*, 24(3), 175–206.

Johnston, D. and Rock, S. (2005) 'Earnings Management to Minimize Superfund Clean-up and Transaction Costs'. *Contemporary Accounting Research*, 22(3), 617–42.

Johnston, D.M., Sefcik, S.E. and Soderstrom, N.S. (2008) 'The Value Relevance of Greenhouse Gas Emissions Allowances: An Exploratory Study in the Related United States SO2 Market', *European Accounting Review*, 17(4), 747–64.

Journeault, M., De Rongé, Y. and Henri, J.F. (2012) 'Eco-control and Competitive Environmental Motivations'. Working paper presented at the 4th World Business Ethics Forum held at Hong Kong Baptist University in December 2012.

Kuasirikun, N. (2005) 'Attitudes to the Development and Implementation of Social and Environmental Accounting in Thailand'. *Critical Perspectives on Accounting*, 16(8), 1035–57.

Larrinaga, C., Carrasco, F., Correa, C., Llena, F. and Moneva, J.M. (2002) 'Accountability and Accounting Regulation: The Case of the Spanish Disclosure Standard'. *European Accounting Review*, 11(4), 723–40.

Lindbolm, C.K. (1993) 'The Implications of Organisational Legitimacy for Corporate Social Performance and Disclosure'. Paper presented at the Critical Perspectives on Accounting Conference, New York.

Magness, V. (2006) 'Strategic Posture, Financial Performance and Environmental Disclosure: An Empirical Test of Legitimacy Theory'. *Accounting, Auditing and Accountability Journal*, 19(4), 540–63.

Milne, M.J. and Gray, R.H. (2007) 'Future Prospects for Corporate Sustainability Reporting'. In J. Unerman, J. Bebbington, and B. O'Dwyer (eds) *Sustainability Accounting and Accountability*, London: Routledge, pp. 184–207.

Milne, M. and Patten, D.M. (2002) 'Securing Organizational Legitimacy: An Experimental Decision Case Examining the Impact of Environmental Disclosures'. *Accounting, Auditing & Accountability Journal*, 15: 372–405.

Neu, D., Warsame, H. and Pedwell, K. (1998) 'Managing Public Impressions: Environmental Disclosures in Annual Reports'. *Accounting, Organisations and Society*, 23(3), 265–82.

O'Donovan, G. (2002) 'Environmental Disclosures in the Annual Report: Extending the Applicability and Predictive Power of Legitimacy Theory'. *Accounting, Auditing and Accountability Journal*, 15(3), 344–71.

Parker, L. (2000a) 'Green Strategy Costing: Early Days'. *Australian Accounting Review*, 10(1), 46–55.

Parker, L. (2000b) 'Environmental Costing: A Path to Implementation'. *Australian Accounting Review*, 10(3), 43–51.

Patten, D.M. (1992) 'Intra-industry Environmental Disclosures in Response to the Alaskan Oil Spill: A Note on Legitimacy Theory'. *Accounting, Organisations and Society*, 17(5), 471–75.

Patten, D.M. (2002) 'The Relation between Environmental Performance and Environmental Disclosure: A Research Note', *Accounting, Organisations and Society*, 27(8), 763–73.

Porter, M.E. and Reinhart, F.L. (2007) 'A Strategic Approach to Climate'. *Harvard Business Review*, October, 23–26.

Porter, M.E. and van der Linde, C. (1995) 'Toward a New Conception of the Environment–Competitiveness Relationship'. *The Journal of Economic Perspectives*, 9(4), 97–118.

Quairel, F. (2008) 'La RSE est-elle soluble dans la concurrence? Proposition d'un nouveau cadre pour analyser la RSE en situation concurrentielle'. Paper presented at the 3rd conference of the Réseau International de Recherche sur les Organisations et le Développement Durable (RIODD).

Richard, J. (2012) *Comptabilité et développement durable*, Paris: Economica.

Rodrigue, M., Magnan, M. and Cho, C.H. (2012). 'Is Environmental Governance Substantive or Symbolic? An Empirical Investigation'. *Journal of Business Ethics*, 6 May, DOI 10.1007/s10551-012-1331-5, available at http://link.springer.com/article/10.1007/s10551-012-1331-5.

Schaltegger, S. and Sturm, A. (1998) *Eco-efficiency by Eco-controlling: On the Implementation of EMAS and ISO14001*, Zurich:Vdf.

SEC (2008) 'Electronic Code of Federal Regulation'. Available at www.gpoaccess.gov/ecfr.

SCMC (1999a) *Outils et techniques de comptabilité environnementale appliqués aux décisions de gestion*, Mississauga, Ontario: La Société des comptables en management du Canada.

SCMC (1999b) *Mise en œuvre de la stratégie environnementale de l'entreprise*, Mississauga, Ontario: La Société des comptables en management du Canada.

SCMC (1999c) *La comptabilité de développement durable: point de vue de l'entreprise*, Mississauga, Ontario: La Société des comptables en management du Canada.

Wilmhurst, T. D. and Frost, G.R. (2001) 'The Role of Accounting and the Accountant in the Environmental Management System'. *Business Strategy and the Environment*, 10(3), 135–47.

Index